THE ANCIENT EGYPTIAN
NETHERWORLD BOOKS

WRITINGS FROM THE ANCIENT WORLD

SBL PRESS

THE ANCIENT EGYPTIAN
NETHERWORLD BOOKS

John Coleman Darnell and Colleen Manassa Darnell

SBL PRESS

Atlanta

Library of Congress Cataloging-in-Publication Data

Names: Darnell, John Coleman, translator. | Manassa Darnell, Colleen, translator.
Title: The ancient Egyptian Netherworld Books / by John Coleman Darnell and Colleen Manassa Darnell.
Description: Atlanta : SBL Press, 2018. | Series: Writings from the ancient world ; Number 39.
Identifiers: LCCN 2017021415 (print) | LCCN 2017053013 (ebook) | ISBN 9780884140450 (ebook) | ISBN 9781628371277 (pbk. : alk. paper) | ISBN 9780884142768 (hardcover : alk. paper)
Subjects: LCSH: Religious literature, Egyptian—Translations into English. | Future life. | Egypt—Religion—History—Sources.
Classification: LCC BL2430 (ebook) | LCC BL2430 .A53 2017 (print) | DDC 299/.3123—dc23
LC record available at https://lccn.loc.gov/2017021415

Printed on acid-free paper.

For Erik Hornung

CONTENTS

Series Editor's Foreword

Writings from the Ancient World is designed to provide up-to-date, readable English translations of writings recovered from the ancient Near East.

The series is intended to serve the interests of general readers, students, and educators who wish to explore the ancient Near Eastern roots of Western civilization or to compare these earliest written expressions of human thought and activity with writings from other parts of the world. It should also be useful to scholars in the humanities or social sciences who need clear, reliable translations of ancient Near Eastern materials for comparative purposes. Specialists in particular areas of the ancient Near East who need access to texts in the scripts and languages of other areas will also find these translations helpful. Given the wide range of materials translated in the series, different volumes will appeal to different interests. However, these translations make available to all readers of English the world's earliest traditions as well as valuable sources of information on daily life, history, religion, and the like in the preclassical world.

The translators of the various volumes in this series are specialists in the particular languages and have based their work on the original sources and the most recent research. In their translations they attempt to convey as much as possible of the original texts in fluent, current English. In the introductions, notes, glossaries, maps, and chronological tables, they aim to provide the essential information for an appreciation of these ancient documents.

Covering the period from the invention of writing (by 3000 BCE) down to the conquests of Alexander the Great (ca. 330 BCE), the ancient Near East comprised northeast Africa and southwest Asia. The cultures represented within these limits include especially Egyptian, Sumerian, Babylonian, Assyrian, Hittite, Ugaritic, Aramean, Phoenician, and Israelite. It is hoped that Writings from the Ancient World will eventually produce translations of most of the many different genres attested in these cultures: letters (official and private), myths, diplomatic documents,

hymns, law collections, monumental inscriptions, tales, and administra-
tive records, to mention but a few.

The Society of Biblical Literature provided significant funding for
the Writings from the Ancient World series. In addition, authors have
benefited from working in research collections in their respective institutions and beyond. Were it not for such support, the arduous tasks of
preparation, translation, editing, and publication could not have been
accomplished or even undertaken. It is the hope of all who have worked
on these texts or supported this work that Writings from the Ancient
World will open up new horizons and deepen the humanity of all who
read these volumes.

Theodore J. Lewis
The Johns Hopkins University

PREFACE

The authors would like to offer their sincere appreciation to Theodore J. Lewis for the honor of being invited to write the present work in the series Writings from the Ancient World. The translations have their genesis in two earlier works by the authors: John Coleman Darnell, *The Enigmatic Netherworld Books of the Solar-Osirian Unity, Cryptographic Compositions from the Tombs of Tutankhamun, Ramesses VI, and Ramesses IX* (Fribourg: Universitätsverlag; Göttingen: Vandenhoeck & Ruprecht, 2004); and Colleen Manassa, *The Late Egyptian Underworld: Sarcophagi and Related Texts from the Nectanebid Period*, 2 vols., ÄAT 72 (Wiesbaden: Harrassowitz, 2007). We are grateful to Anthony Spalinger for taking on the role of editor for this project, during which he offered a number of helpful references and comments.

The plates and figures accompanying the present work derive from a variety of sources, including line drawings by the authors. In addition to a number of plates reproduced by permission of Princeton University Press and the Institut Français d'Archéologie Orientale, additional images are reproduced from drawings in the Natacha Rambova Archive at Yale University, donated by Edward L. Ochsenschlager in memory of Donald P. Hansen; for assistance in the transfer of this significant collection, we would like to thank Christine Lilyquist. We are especially grateful to Joshua Roberson for allowing us to reproduce his drawings of the Books of the Creation of the Solar Disk in the tombs of Ramesses VII and Ramesses IX. Alberto Urcia provided invaluable technical support during the preparation of the figures and plates, including the plans of the tombs in the Valley of the Kings.

Although we have restricted the number and scope of the footnotes and references in the present volume so as "not to multiply words" (following in the footsteps of Thutmose III), a perusal of the bibliography and of our earlier volumes referenced above will reveal the past and present scholars whose works have contributed in many ways to this translation volume. Given the ubiquity of the key terms throughout the body of the text (e.g., Re appears 1,401 times, Osiris 742 times, solar disk 308 times, and Horus 241 times), we have also omitted indices from this volume. Readers wishing to locate a particular scene or gather additional information about a deity, topic, or scholar are encouraged to consult the list of figures, concordance, and glossary or search the electronic version of this volume.

We would like to thank Theodor Abt and Erik Hornung for stimulating discussions over the years about the Netherworld Books and funerary imagery in general. We have both been personally inspired by the magisterial scholarship of Erik Hornung, without whose publications on the Netherworld Books our current project would not have been possible. To him we dedicate this book. The inclusion of hundreds of figures with the translations was essential to maintain the relationship between text and image in the Netherworld Books—for making this goal possible and assisting with multiple aspects of the editing and production process, we would also like to thank SBL Press, particularly Nicole Tilford and Bob Buller.

List of Figures

Introduction

Book of Adoring Re in the West

Book of the Hidden Chamber

Book of Gates

Book of Caverns

Books of the Creation of the Solar Disk

Books of the Solar-Osirian Unity

LIST OF PLATES

Book of the Hidden Chamber

Book of Gates

Book of Caverns

Books of the Creation of the Solar Disk

Books of the Solar-Osirian Unity

CHRONOLOGICAL TABLE

This table is based on I. Shaw 2000; all dates are BCE unless otherwise noted and approximate prior to 664 BCE.

Predynastic Period	ca. 5300–3000
Early Dynastic Period	ca. 3000–2686
Old Kingdom	2686–2160
First Intermediate Period	2160–2055
Middle Kingdom	2055–1650
Second Intermediate Period	1650–1550
New Kingdom	1550–1069
Eighteenth Dynasty	
Ahmose	1550–1525
Amenhotep I	1525–1504
Thutmose I	1504–1492
Thutmose II	1492–1479
Thutmose III	1479–1425
Hatshepsut	1473–1458
Amenhotep II	1427–1400
Thutmose IV	1400–1390
Amenhotep III	1390–1352
Amenhotep IV/Akhenaton	1352–1336
Neferneferuaten	1338–1336
Tutankhamun	1336–1327
Aye	1327–1323
Horemheb	1323–1295
Nineteenth Dynasty	
Ramesses I	1295–1294
Seti I	1294–1279
Ramesses II	1279–1213
Merneptah	1213–1203

Amenmesse	1203–1200(?)
Seti II	1200–1194
Siptah	1194–1188
Tawosret	1188–1186
Twentieth Dynasty	
Sethnakht	1186–1184
Ramesses III	1184–1153
Ramesses IV	1153–1147
Ramesses V	1147–1143
Ramesses VI	1143–1136
Ramesses VII	1136–1129
Ramesses VIII	1129–1126
Ramesses IX	1126–1108
Ramesses X	1108–1099
Ramesses XI	1099–1069
Third Intermediate Period	1069–664
Twenty-First Dynasty	1069–945
Twenty-Second Dynasty	945–715
Twenty-Third Dynasty	818–715
Twenty-Fourth Dynasty	727–715
Twenty-Fifth Dynasty	747–656
Late Period	664–332
Twenty-Sixth Dynasty	664–525
Twenty-Seventh Dynasty	525–404
Twenty-Eighth Dynasty	404–399
Twenty-Ninth Dynasty	399–380
Thirtieth Dynasty	380–343
Second Persian Period	343–332
Ptolemaic Period	332–30
Roman Period	30 BCE–395 CE
Byzantine Period	395–641 CE

Abbreviations

ÄA	Ägyptologische Abhandlungen
ÄAT	Ägypten und Altes Testament
ADAIK	Abhandlungen des Deutschen Archäologischen Instituts Abteilung Kairo
AegLeo	Aegyptiaca Leodiensia
AH	Aegyptiaca Helvetica
AIPhSup	Annuaire de l'Institut de Philologie et d'Histoire Orientales et Slaves Supplément
AnOr	Analecta Orientalia
Aof	*Altorientalische Forschungen*
AR	*Archiv für Religionsgeschichte*
ASAE	*Annales du service des antiquités de l'Egypte*
ASE	Archaeological Survey of Egypt
AV	Archäologische Veröffentlichungen
BAeg	Bibliotheca Aegyptiaca
BARIS	BAR International Series
BES	Brown Egyptological Studies
BiÉtud	Bibliothèque d'étude
BIE	*Bulletin de l'Institut d'Égypte*
BiOr	*Bibliotheca Orientalis*
BIFAO	*Bulletin de l'Insitut français d'archéologie orientale*
BIFAOSup	Bulletin de l'Insitut français d'archéologie orientale Supplement
BM	British Museum
BMSAES	*British Museum Studies in Ancient Egypt and Sudan*
BMusHongr	*Bulletin du Musée Hongrois des Beaux-Arts*
CdÉ	*Chronique d'Égypte*
CENIM	Cahiers Égypte Nilotique et Méditerranéenne
CGAE	Catalogue général des antiquités égyptiennes du Musée du Caire

CRAI	*Comptes rendus de l'Académie des Inscriptions et Belles-Lettres*
CSÉG	Cahiers de la Société d'Égyptologie, Geneva
CT	De Buck, Adriaan. *The Egyptian Coffin Texts.* 7 vols. Chicago: University of Chicago Press, 1935–1961.
DE	*Discussions in Egyptology*
EAO	*Égypte, Afrique et Orient*
EES	Egypt Exploration Society
EgRel	*Egyptian Religion*
ENiM	*Égypte Nilotique et Méditerranéenne*
ErJb	*Eranos-Jahrbuch*
ERTR	Egyptian Religious Texts and Representations
FIFAO	Fouilles de l'Institut français d'archéologie orientale du Caire
GöMisz	*Göttinger Miszellen*
GOF	Göttinger Orientforschungen
HÄB	Hildesheimer ägyptologische Beiträge
HdO	Handbuch der Orientalistik
JAEI	*Journal of Ancient Egyptian Interconnections*
JARCE	*Journal of the American Research Center in Egypt*
JE	Journal d'Entrée du Musée
JEA	*Journal of Egyptian Archaeology*
JEOL	*Jaarbericht van het Vooraziatisch-Egyptisch (Genootschap) Ex oriente lux*
JNES	*Journal of Near Eastern Studies*
JSSEA	*Journal of the Society of the Study of Egyptian Antiquities*
KSG	Königtum, Staat und Gesellschaft früher Hochkulturen
KV	Kings' Valley
LGG	Leitz, Christian, ed. *Lexikon der ägyptischen Götter und Götterbezeichnungen.* 7 vols. Leuven: Peeters, 2002–2003.
LingAeg-StudMon	Lingua Aegyptia, Studia Monographic
MÄSt	Münchner ägyptologische Studien
MÄU	Münchener ägyptologische Untersuchungen
MDAIK	*Mitteilungen des Deutschen Archäologischen Instituts, Abteilung Kairo*
MEOL	Mededelingen en verhandelingen van het Voor-Aziatisch-Egyptisch Genootschap Ex Oriente Lux

MIFAO	Mémoires publiés par les membres de l'Institut Français d'Archéologie Orientale du Caire
MMAEE	Metropolitan Museum of Art, Egyptian Expedition (New York)
MRÉ	Monographies Reine Élisabeth
NAWGPH	Nachrichten (von) der Akademie der Wissenschaften in Göttingen, Philologisch-Historische Klasse
OBO	Orbis Biblicus et Orientalis
OINE	Oriental Institute Nubian Expedition
OIP	Oriental Institute Publications
OLA	Orientalia Lovaniensia Analecta
OLP	*Orientalia Lovaniensia Periodica*
OLZ	*Orientalistische Literaturzeitung*
OrMonsp	Orientalia Monspeliensia
P.	papyrus
PAe	Probleme der Ägyptologie
PM	Porter, Bertha, and Rosalind Moss. *Topographical Bibliography of Ancient Egyptian Hieroglyphic Texts.* 7 vols. Oxford: Griffith Institute, 1995.
RCIN	Royal Collections Trust identification number
REg	*Revue d'egyptologie*
RHR	*Revue de l'Histoire des Religions*
SAGA	Studien zur Archäologie und Geschichte Altägyptens
SAK	*Studien zur altägyptischen Kultur*
SAKB	Studien zur altägyptischen Kultur. Beihefte
SAOC	Studies in Ancient Oriental Civilization
SAT	Studien zum Altägyptischen Totenbuch
SBAWPH	Sitzungsberichte der Bayerischen Akademie der Wissenschaften, Philosophisch-Historische Abteilung, 1947.
SPHKHAW	Schriften der Philosophisch-Historischen Klasse der Heidelberger Akademie der Wissenschaften
SSEA	Society of the Study of Egyptian Antiquities
StAeg	*Studia Aegyptiaca*
StAegSm	Studia Aegyptiaca Series maior
TT	Theban Tomb
TUAT	*Texte aus der Umwelt des Alten Testaments.* Edited by Otto Kaiser. 18 parts in 3 vols. Gütersloh: Mohn, 1982–1997. New series edited by Bernd Janowski and Gernot Wilhelm. Gütersloh: Gütersloher Verlagshaus, 2004–.

UAH	Untersuchungen zur altägyptischen Hymnik
VA	*Varia Aegyptiaca*
WAW	Writings from the Ancient World
WO	*Die Welt des Orients*
WÄS	Erman, Adolf, and Hermann Grapow, eds. *Wörterbuch des aegyptischen Sprache.* 7 vols. Leipzig: Hinrichs; Berlin: Akademie, 1926–1931. Repr., 1963.
WSA	Wahrnehmungen und Spuren Altägyptens
YEgS	Yale Egyptological Studies
ZÄS	*Zeitschrift für ägyptische Sprache und Altertumskunde*

EXPLANATION OF SIGNS

[ ]	missing or damaged text that can be partly or fully restored
[...]	missing or damaged text for which no restoration is proposed
⌐ ¬	damaged or partially damaged text that can be confidently restored
< >	omissions in the original text
( )	explanatory additions not part of original text
(?)	words or phrases with uncertain translation
italics	used to mark words for which a translation is not proposed (or to retain part of the ancient Egyptian term, e.g., *ba*-soul)
SMALL CAPS	designations of modern text divisions and headings

1
INTRODUCTION

Even before the dawn of pharaonic civilization, with the visual aspects thereof coming increasingly into focus in the art and iconography of the fourth millennium BCE, the ancient Egyptians speculated about the progress and transformations of the sun during the hours of the night. Already in late Predynastic rock inscriptions appear the earliest depictions of dual cosmic barks and representations of the towing of the vessels of the sun into the Netherworld.[1] The earliest surviving corpus of religious literature from ancient Egypt, the Pyramid Texts, contains a diverse array of texts, some of which describe certain elements and aspects the topography of the Netherworld (Allen 2005). Nevertheless, the Pyramid Texts emphasize the successful crossing of liminal boundaries, and the deceased ruler's assumption of a variety of roles and even physical forms of power, without developing any detailed depiction of a temporally connected solar journey through a topographically specific Netherworld. The geography of the nocturnal solar journey in the Pyramid Texts may assume the form of the corpse of Osiris (Barta 1985–1986; Barta 1990b), paralleling the personification of Netherworld space achieving clear depiction in Division 5 of the Book of Caverns and foreshadowing imagery developed in the Books of the Solar-Osirian Unity. Although the physical spaces and temporal divisions of the Netherworld are not easily imagined on the basis of the Pyramid Texts, the corpus itself interacts with the inner architecture of the pyramids in which the texts are carved, with segments of the Pyramid Texts concerning serpents appearing near doorways (Osing 1986), a harbinger of the rearing serpents at the portals of the Netherworld so well and prominently depicted and described in the Book of Gates.

---

1. Darnell 2009, 92; for solar imagery in Predynastic rock art, see also Huyge 2002, 200–201.

First with the Middle Kingdom Coffin Texts, in many ways presaging the major themes of the New Kingdom Netherworld Books (Bickel 1998), illustrated editions of funerary texts appear (Hermsen 1991; Backes 2005; Backes 2014, 78–84). The topographical aspects of the Coffin Texts focus on detailed plans of the Book of the Two Ways (Spells 1029–1130 long, 513, 577; 1131–1185 short) and the Field of Offerings (Spell 464). This concretization of speculation about the nature of the Netherworld—the earliest elements of the Coffin Texts proper appear during the late Old Kingdom[2]—appears to be a slightly belated result of the shift in emphasis in religious texts from the recording of ritual activity to statements of religious knowledge, a transition that begins to appear in private monuments about the reign of Teti, essentially corresponding to the appearance of the Pyramid Texts under Unas (Hays 2012). During the Middle Kingdom, Netherworldly imagery is not confined to coffins, but also appears on a corpus of "magical knives," several of which provide prototypes for imagery in the New Kingdom Netherworld Books (Roberson 2009; Liptay 2011).

The New Kingdom witnesses the flowering of a tradition of illustrated treatises describing the sun's journey through the Netherworld. First attested in examples spanning the Eighteenth through Twentieth Dynasties, although possibly of slightly earlier date (see below), the group of texts known as the "Netherworld Books" comprises six discrete compositions. Known primarily through their appearance in the New Kingdom royal tombs within the Valley of the Kings, the Netherworld Books have an important afterlife of their own in Third Intermediate period papyri (Piankoff and Rambova 1957; Niwiński 1989a) and royal tombs (Roulin 1998b) and enjoy an even later and perhaps more scholarly significant renaissance on sarcophagi of the Nectanebid and early Ptolemaic periods (Manassa 2007a). The Netherworld Books are distinguished from other corpora of ancient Egyptian religious compositions in their thorough and extensive integration of text and image; most of the compositions translated in the present work are annotations to illustrations, often elaborate, of the solar journey through the different regions of the Netherworld.

The present edition offers translations of six treatises from the tombs of the rulers of the New Kingdom that can be classified as the Netherworld Books: Book of Adoring Re in the West, Book of the Hidden Chamber,

---

2. See Jéquier 1935, pl. 14, Spell 216; pl. 11, Spell 397; and pls. 12–13, Spells 148 and 312; Valloggia 1986.

Book of Gates, Book of Caverns, Books of the Creation of the Solar Disk, and Books of the Solar-Osirian Unity. The terminology used here follows the ancient titles where possible and defaults to standard conventions when no ancient title is preserved. Thus, the text commonly referred to as the Book of Amduat is here called the Book of the Hidden Chamber, since the latter is clearly preserved as the ancient title of the composition; similarly, the text commonly called the Litany of Re is here termed, as in the ancient title, the Book of Adoring Re in the West. On the other hand, the treatise here termed the Books of the Creation of the Solar Disk, following the initial study by Alexandre Piankoff, preserves no ancient title for the composition, which is also called the Books of the Earth in modern Egyptological publications (Roberson 2012). We have used Books of the Solar Osirian-Unity as a descriptive title to cover the three enigmatic treatises with complementary content, although the example on the Second Shrine of Tutankhamun is termed a "(Book of) What Is in the Netherworld."

Early modern visitors to the Valley of the Kings, before the time of Jean-François Champollion—although they could not comprehend the content of the inscriptions—recognized to some extent the significance of the compositions. Claude Sicard in 1721 refers to each of the visible tombs in the Valley of the Kings as "a jewel of painting, a complete book of Egyptian theology" (Hornung 1990b, 2).[3] Richard Pococke (1743, 98) describes in somewhat greater detail the specific elements of the Netherworld Books, here most likely specifically evoking the Book of Adoring Re in the West: "The galleries within have hieroglyphics cut on each side … lower, figures are cut out representing mummies." The abundance of material seems to have been so daunting to these early visitors that no copies of major elements of the tombs appear before the time of the Napoleonic expedition. On May 26, 1829, Champollion composed a lengthy description of the decoration within the tombs in the Valley of the Kings, characterizing the chief visual features of the Netherworld Books, somewhat precociously discussing the possible theological significance of the scenes and images; in those passages, he enumerates the forms of Re in the Book of Adoring Re in the West and vividly expounds upon the elaborate portals in the Book of Gates (Champollion 2009, 206–7). By the end of the nineteenth century, Gaston Maspero, Eugène Lefébure, Édouard Naville,

---

3. Hornung (1990b, 1–6) describes the modern history of the tomb of Ramesses IV with references to early modern visitors.

and Gustave Jéquier had published copies—albeit imperfect—of the Book of the Hidden Chamber, the Book of Gates, and the Book of Adoring Re in the West.[4] First with the work of Piankoff, in the middle of the twentieth century, the Netherworld Books became more widely accessible through reliable editions with accurate translations. Publication of parallel texts, translations, and commentary for the Book of the Hidden Chamber and the Book of Gates, as well as additional translations of New Kingdom Netherworld Books and insightful commentary, are the work of Erik Hornung (1999, 2002). More recent editions of individual Netherworldly compositions are listed in the beginning of each of the following chapters.

Main Themes of the Netherworld Books

The New Kingdom Netherworld Books describe the solar progress through the twelve hours of the night: the sinking into the western horizon, the topography of the different areas, the deities that populate those dark and fitfully illumined regions, the solar combat with the chaos serpent Apep, the punishment of enemies and the damned, and finally, the triumphant appearance of the solar deity in the eastern horizon. Theological themes that predominate within the Netherworld Books include the union of Re and Osiris, the union of *ba*-soul and corpse, (re-)creation through light and speech, and the eternal cycle of cosmic battle and solar victory. While each book presents the topography, gods, and events within the Netherworld in a different fashion, together the compositions represent a unity of theological speculation about the journey of the solar god each night (Barta 1990a).

The solar deity is the focus of all six compositions, although his form—or multitude of forms—differs from book to book. In the Book of the Hidden Chamber and the Book of Gates, a ram-headed male figure (Wiebach-Kopeke 2000), called "Flesh" or "Flesh of Re" respectively, is the chief icon of the solar deity. The locomotive vessel of Re's journey through the Netherworld is the solar bark, whose origins reach back into Predynastic Egypt. The form and crew of the bark can differ between different compositions as well as within a single book (Barta 1990a, 63–65). In the Book of the Hidden Chamber, the solar bark of Hour 1 of the night appears with the "solar mat" attested more frequently for the day bark

---

4. Extensive bibliographic notes appear in Hornung 1999.

than for the night bark (Goebs 1998; Müller-Roth 2008, 53–58). While the ram-headed solar god stands within a shrine in the first six hours of the night, the protective Encircling Serpent replaces the shrine in the last six hours of the night; in Hours 4–5 of the night, the entire boat is replaced by a massive serpent that is hauled along the desert landscape of those regions of the night. Whereas the solar bark within the Book of the Hidden Chamber possesses an extensive crew of deities (Hornung 1963a, 19–23), the Book of Gates limits the crew to two deities—Magic and Divine Perception—and envelopes the ram-headed solar deity within a shrine itself surrounded by the Encircling Serpent (Hornung 1980, 54–56). The concluding scene of the Book of Gates contains a more elaborately populated solar bark, with the solar deity in the form of a large scarab (Minas-Nerpel 2006, 199–200).

The form of the solar deity, as well as his means of propulsion, differ significantly in the Book of Caverns, the Books of the Creation of the Solar Disk, and the Books of the Solar-Osirian Unity. The solar bark can be present within these compositions,[5] and the Books of the Solar-Osirian Unity in the tombs of Ramesses VI and Ramesses IX place particular emphasis on the ophidian form of the bark. While the ram-headed solar deity can also appear within these books, the chief icon of the solar deity becomes the disk itself, seemingly self-propelled throughout the Netherworld (Hornung 1999, 26–27).[6] The red-colored disk, appearing in different sizes relative to other figures, hovers over most scenes in the Book of Caverns, a visual representation of the speeches Re delivers to many of the Netherworldly denizens within the various divisions of the night. The solar disk is similarly present in many scenes of the Books of the Creation of the Solar Disk, simply accompanying other images or more actively engaged, with winged scarabs, or even the head of Hathor, emerging from the disk.

---

5. In the concluding scene of the Book of Caverns (Scene 77, p. 452), only half of the bark is visible, as if it is literally emerging from the primordial waters; similarly, in one of the Aker-based scenes of the Books of the Creation of the Solar Disk (Tomb of Ramesses VI, Section B, Register 4, Scene 38 [p. 497]), the day and the night bark each appear to either side of a pair of arms lifting a solar disk; the entire scene "represents one of the most detailed images of solar revivification through emersion in chaos known from ancient Egypt" (Roberson 2012, 152).

6. The transition from ram-headed solar divinity to the disk form as the predominant solar icon mirrors the development of the new solar theology (beginning already in the reign of Amunhotep III), which abandons the elaborate iconographic constellation of the solar journey (Assmann 1995, 67–70).

The solar deity communicates with the deceased through light and speech, which can be interchangeable in the Netherworld Books.[7] The means of illumination are alternatively characterized as the eyes, disk, or even the bark of the solar deity. As the light penetrates the corpses of the Netherworld Dwellers, they awaken and breathe; light as breath finds a particularly direct evocation in the lion-headed deities who literally breathe light on the Second Shrine of Tutankhamun (pp. 546–48).

One of the central themes of the Netherworld Books is the union of Re and Osiris, the most significant single event within the nightly journey of the sun.[8] This coming together of solar and chthonic elements, tomorrow and yesterday, can even be seen as the central mystery of Egyptian religion, as concisely expressed in P. Salt 825: "As for anyone who will reveal it, he will die a violent death, because it is the greatest mystery—it is Re and it is Osiris" (Derchain 1965, 19*, XVIII, ll. 1–2). The energy released within the crucible of this union refuels the solar god, enabling him to complete his journey through the night, rising in triumph in the eastern horizon each morning.

The Netherworld Books describe and portray the process of solar regeneration that occurs each night within the time-space continuum of the Netherworldly realm (Wiebach-Koepke 2007; Bónannó 2015). The sun enters as an aged deity—literally described as "Flesh" within the Book of the Hidden Chamber—and rises from the eastern horizon as the newborn solar child. The rejuvenation of the solar deity occurs through the union of *ba*-soul and corpse, one aspect of the unification of Re and Osiris; the corpse itself can be termed the mystery (*sštꜣw*)[9] and the union of the soul with that mystery creates what the Book of the Adoring Re in the West

---

7. The solar deity speaks by means of light—see Piankoff 1958, 153; among the many possible examples, note the straightforward statement in the Book of Caverns, Division 3, Registers 2–3, Scene 32: "Re speaks to them by means of his light" (p. 373). For the linking of breath and light, compare Derchain 1962, 261; in P. Harris Magical a baboon has fiery lips and flaming words (Borghouts 1978, 89, no. 132; te Velde 1988, 131); breath, speech, and fire all find numerous interrelationships in the Netherworld Books—Darnell 2004, 100–1, 103, 109–10, 113–14, 248, 364–65 (and n. 389).

8. Among the many possible references, see the studies of Derchain 1965, 35–37, 155–56; Hornung 1976, 53–54, 60; Niwiński 1987–1988; Willems 1988, 151–54; Zandee 1992, 250–53; Darnell 2004; Spalinger 2009; Stadler 2010.

9. Darnell 2004, 289–93, 384–85. This equation finds particularly strong expression in the Book of Gates, Hour 6, Register 2, Scene 38 (p. 289; see also Assmann 1969, 84–86; Hornung 1980, 164–65); compare also the Book of Gates, Hour 8, Register 2,

terms the "United One."[10] The unification with Osiris enables the revivification of the solar body, and in the final hour or division of the night, Re transforms into a scarab beetle or an anthropomorphic baby; intimations of this transformation appear throughout the night (e.g., the solar beetle-crowned corpse in Hour 6 of the Book of the Hidden Chamber). External forces can also work upon the rejuvenation of the solar god, such as the progress from tail to mouth through the serpent Life of the Gods in Hour 12 of the Book of the Hidden Chamber (Barta 1990a, 56–58). Other rejuvenating processes include contact with the primordial waters of Nun, from whose arms the solar deity can rise in the concluding scenes of the Netherworld Books (Hornung 1981b; Roberson 2012, 149–50).

Egyptian funerary religion concerns itself with the preservation of the eternal soul of the deceased, and the Netherworld Books provide the cosmic template for an individual's spiritual survival through eternal transformation. Mummification was employed to transform the corruptible corpse into a permanent receptacle for the soul; embalming halted the process of decomposition, although the inevitable presence of putrefaction was reconciled in the Netherworld Books (and other compositions) as a positive feature (Dobbin-Bennett 2014), associated with the Inundation waters flowing from the corpse of Osiris (Assmann 2003; Winkler 2006). Rotting deities abound in the Netherworld Books, from manifestations of the solar god himself, to deities whose putrefaction is so pungent that the solar deity does not draw near to them.[11] The ultimate fate of the deceased is not to remain as a mummy, but rather to be freed of the constricting bandages.[12]

Scene 50: "Make ovations, O foremost ones of the Netherworld, for Re, who is in his mystery" (p. 300).

10. As Hornung (1996, 96) explains, this unification is not a syncretism, but a "daily reenacted union."

11. For a manifestation of the solar god, see, for instance, the "Rotting One" in Address 60 in the Book of Adoring Re in the West (p. 97). For a pungent deity, see, for instance, the Book of Gates, Hour 10, Scene 62 (p. 311 and n. 143).

12. For this concept in Egyptian religion, see Hornung 1983b; 2002, 35–36. Examples from the Netherworld Books include the Book of the Hidden Chamber, Hour 2, Concluding Text (p. 156): "May your mummy wrappings open. May your legs stretch out, so that you might travel upon them. May your strides be wide." The theme is particularly prominent in the Book of Gates, including Hour 6, Register 3, Scene 40; Hour 8, Register 2, Scene 52; and Hour 8, Register 3, Scene 53. The loosening of wrappings also appears in the dedicatory inscription of Seti I for his father Ramesses

The resurrection of the solar body is possible only through the unification with the *ba*-soul, a concept central in the Netherworld Books. The *ba*-
soul—conceptualized as a bird with a human head—is a mobile element,
and as the *ba*-soul flies up to heaven, the corpse remains in the earth.[13]
The union of solar *ba*-soul and Osirian corpse fuels the solar cycle, and
Re resting upon his mysteries—the corpse of Osiris—is the ultimate goal
of the solar journey through the Netherworld.[14] The other elements of the
soul, including the shade,[15] *akh*-spirit, and *ka*-spirit receive less of a focus
within the corpus of Netherworld Books. Passages within the Netherworld Books emphasize that each spiritual aspect of the deceased requires

---

II; Seti says of his father (Kitchen 1976, 113, ll. 14–5, l. x+19 of the stela): "He is as a
god. When he travels the Netherworld, the Sun shines for him in the dark place, that
he might uncover his face and doff his dust, the North wind whistling before him."
The rushing North wind blows in the face of the deceased king, loosening the dust and
wrappings of the grave from about his face; compare also Pyramid Texts Spell 662 and
Book of Going Forth By Day ch. 68.

13. The complexities of the *ba*-soul for the individual deceased is beyond the
scope of the present study; for studies of the differentiation between the *ba*-soul,
ka-spirit, and *akh*-spirit, see *inter alia* Loprieno 2003; Assmann 2005, 87–112. The
dual fate of *ba*-soul and corpse is expressed frequently in Egyptian funerary literature
(Zandee 1992, 188–91; Assmann 2005, 91–94) and can appear in hymns to Amun
(Klotz 2012a, 60); compare among the many possible passages from the Netherworld
Books, the Book of Adoring Re in the West, Litany 9 (p. 125): "My *ba*-soul belongs
to the sky, that I might rest therein. My corpse belongs to the earth amidst the gods";
Book of Gates, Hour 6, Register 2, Scene 38 (p. 289): "Your *ba*-soul be to heaven, O
Foremost of the Horizon—it is your shadow that passes through the Mysterious Place.
Your corpse be to the earth, O One Who is in Heaven, while we give Re to it. You are
separated from it, O Re"; the Book of Gates, Hour 9, Register 1, Scene 56 (p. 306): "The
earth be to your corpse, the sky to your *ba*-soul, so that you may be content, O Re, with
what you have brought about."

14. For the Osirian corpse as "mystery," see above (p. 6); the Book of Gates, Hour
9, Register 2, Scene 57 clearly states that the purpose of the solar journey is for Re to
rest upon his corpse/mysteries: "Hail, we are opening for you the Mysterious Place, we
are preparing for you the ways of Igeret, so that you may go to rest, O Re, upon your
mysteries" (p. 306).

15. The shade of the solar deity is mentioned in the Book of Gates, Hour 10, Register 2, Scene 65: "The god is coming to his corpse, the god having been hauled to his
shade" (p. 312). The annotation to the Book of the Hidden Chamber, Hour 3, Register
1 refers to the shades of the Netherworldly gods: "They exist in this fashion in the
Netherworld, in the flesh of their own bodies, their *ba*-souls speaking over them, their
shades going to rest upon them, after this great god calls to them" (p. 157).

its own proper fate: alighting to shades, provisioning for *akh*-spirits, and purification to *ka*-spirits.[16] Provisioning of the dead is a constant concern throughout the Netherworld Books; in addition to liquid offerings and foodstuffs, the deceased also receive clothing and arable land.[17] Interesting exceptions to the proper fate of the deceased as mummified and provisioned corpses are the groups of Netherworld Dwellers who are drowned in the waters of Nun in Hour 10 of the Book of the Hidden Chamber and Hour 9 of the Book of Gates, beings who have undergone an "apotheosis by drowning," present in other contexts within Egyptian funerary literature.[18]

The damned are denied the life-giving solar rays,[19] condemned to utter darkness, bodily destruction, and an inverted existence. The punishment of the damned is a powerful motif within the Netherworld Books, which contain a myriad of painful—and often creative—ways of expressing divine retribution (Hornung 1968): the damned are bound to pillories, decapitated, and their respective parts burned in cauldrons, to name but

---

16. Compare the Book of the Hidden Chamber, Hour 6, Register 3, Scene 66: "What they do in the Netherworld is conduct *ba*-souls and help shades alight, and make provisions for the *akh*-spirits, namely water" (p. 193) and the Book of Gates, Hour 7, Register 1, Scene 42: "They who have thurified <to> their deities, and made purification to their *ka*-spirits; who have not turned aside an *akh*-spirit from his breathing, or a dead one from his libation. They are content with their victuals, with the result that their deities and their *ka*-spirits appeal to them, their arms to them when they enter to their cakes at the portal She Who Feeds Her Gods" (pp. 292–93). For the interrelationship of *ba*-soul, *ka*-spirit, and *akh*-spirit, see also the Book of Gates, Hour 8, Register 3, Scene 53 (p. 302).

17. The annotations to several of the groups of deities within Hour 8 of the Book of the Hidden Chamber begin: "They exist upon their clothing as the mysteries of Horus" (see p. 205). Clothing is also emphasized in Hour 8 of the Book of the Hidden Chamber, Register 3, Scenes 91 and 92 (p. 211). Among the many possible passages on land, compare the Concluding Text to Hour 1 of the Book of the Hidden Chamber: "May your cultivated land belong to you from your fields" (p. 146); and the Introductory Text to Hour 3 of the same composition: "He grants to them land-plots at this field" (p. 157).

18. Hornung 1980, 217–19; Delia 1992, 186–87 n. 39 (with references to earlier literature); Roulin 1996b, 129–30, 280–81; Volokhine 2000, 83–84.

19. Compare the Book of Caverns, Division 6, Register 3, Scene 73: "This great god inflicts punishment on them, when he passes by them, with the result that they persist in darkness, without seeing the light" (p. 446).

a few means of eternal punishment.[20] Certain Netherworldly deities are
assigned to punish the damned with cruel implements and destructive
intent. All of these punishments result in pain, although the Egyptian texts
do not dwell on wailing and the gnashing of teeth; instead, the damned
are ultimately condemned to nonexistence: inverted and deconstructed,
their souls cannot rest upon their bodies and thus enjoy no posthumous
continuation of life.[21] The damned are the enemies of the solar god, those
people who sinned in life and spoke against Re. Although individual judgment, such as that depicted in chapter 125 of the Book of Going Forth By
Day (Book of the Dead), does not appear within the Netherworld Books,
the Judgment Hall of Osiris (Book of Gates, Scene 33) and juridical processes that result in the punishment of the damned are prominent within
the compositions. No specific sins are mentioned, nor are particular trans-
gressions tied to individualized punishments (Hornung 1994a, 140–41),
but the damned are "those who belong to evil" and "who have summoned
evil for the one who is in the egg, who have hurled charges and who have
murmured against He of the Horizon."[22] One of the few specifications of
the actions of the damned that rendered them enemies of the solar god is
in an annotation showing Horus presiding over the punishment of "those
who smote his father Osiris."[23] The "Place of Destruction" figures prominently in the Netherworld Books, and as Hornung (2002, 43) has noted,
this is the true "hell" of the afterlife.

While the damned must be punished during the course of the nightly
journey, only one being embodies the inimical forces and destructive processes that threaten the physical attainment of solar renewal: the chaos
serpent Apep. One of the chief themes within the Netherworld Books is

---

20. Book of Gates, Hour 7, Register 2, Scene 45 (pp. 294–95); Books of the Creation
of the Solar Disk, Tomb of Ramesses VI, Section A, Register 1, Scene 4 (pp. 468–69).

21. Hornung 1994a, 145: "But the goal of all of these punishments is to inflict not
suffering itself, but rather complete elimination.... The damned are thus frequently
designated as 'eliminated' or 'non-being' and 'negated.' They are not, and they should
not be: extinguishing their existence is the 'second' or 'repeated death,' frequently
mentioned with fear in the Book of the Dead and its forerunners; it is then that even
the Ba-soul and the shade perish."

22. Book of Gates, Hour 2, Register 1, Scene 6 (p. 261); Book of Gates, Hour 2,
Register 3, Scene 8 (pp. 263–64).

23. Book of the Hidden Chamber, Hour 11, Register 3, Scene 120 (pp. 232–33);
enemies of Osiris are similarly mentioned in the Book of Gates, Hour 9, Register 2,
Scene 60 (pp. 308–9).

the combat against the giant serpent Apep whose defeat and destruction appear textually and/or pictorially in all of the compositions that form a part of the corpus.[24] As stated in the Book of Adoring Re in the West, the defeat of Apep is the defeat of evil itself: "My victory is the victory of Re, when he inflicts punishment on Apep, when he smites his evil in the West" (Litany 3, p. 105). Geographically, the defeat of Apep can appear in the middle of the night as well as at sunrise;[25] thus the solar god's combat against the serpent is an ongoing process throughout the nightly journey rather than a single event. In Hour 7 of the Book of the Hidden Chamber, Isis and the Elder Magician[26] enchant Apep with their spells, while a goddess, She Who Makes Throats Breathe, lassoes the creature, and other deities stab knives deep into his flesh (Régen 2015). Apep threatens the solar bark again in Hour 12 of the night, and goddesses in the first register of that hour are specifically said to punish "Apep in the sky" as he attacks Re in the eastern horizon (see p. 235).[27]

In the Book of Gates, the chaos serpent repeatedly threatens the progress of the solar bark. Hour 3, Scene 13 depicts the god Atum overseeing the destruction of the chaos serpent, and in Scene 14 the annotation claims: "As the earth opens to Re, so the earth seals to Apep" (p. 269). In Hour 6 of the Book of Gates, Scenes 34 and 35, Apep, who is called "Swallower," is destroyed both by guardian deities and by the very heads that emerge from his coils. These heads emerge literally to eat the chaos serpent, who is described as a mutilated ophidian demon: "One without his eyes is this snake, one without his nose, one without his ears. From his roar

---

24. Barta 1990a, 66–67; Hornung 1990a, 103–14; Borghouts 2007, 25–30. For the earlier history of Apep, see Morenz 2004 and references therein (particularly to the inscriptions of Ankhtyfy at Moalla). Ptolemaic texts give Apep a length of 120 cubits (Borghouts 2007, 9 n. 4).

25. Apep is similarly told to "leave the edge in the east of the sky" in the Book of Going Forth By Day (Book of the Dead) ch. 39 (Borghouts 2007, 13; see also 26–27 and 35–37 for the combat against Apep occurring at the end of the solar god's nightly journey). The combat against Apep continues during the hours of the day, as represented in the Book of the Day (Müller-Roth 2008, 471–81).

26. The Elder Magician (ḥkꜣ smsw) is not a hypostasis of Seth (Hornung 1963b, 131), but rather Heka as the eldest son of the creator deity (te Velde 1969–1970; Ritner 1993, 18–20).

27. Hour 12, Register 3, Scene 129 similarly labels oar-wielding deities as "It is they who repel Apep from the eastern part of the sky after the birth of the god" (see p. 240).

he breathes, from his own cry he lives" (p. 287). In Hour 10, Scene 66 of
the Book of Gates, thirteen throw-net wielding deities are "sailing before
Re and enchanting Apep for him," and the annotation further records their
actual magical incantation against the serpent: "Hail, rebel—away, Apep,
one to whom his evil is given. May your face be destroyed, O Apep—make
a way to the slaughtering place. Knives be against you, you having already
been cut; the Old Ones be against you, you having already been destroyed.
Those with spears lay into you, as we enchant you with what is in our
hand(s). Hail, the destroyed one is driven back, the Fettered Serpent is
annihilated" (p. 313) In the following Scene 67, Apep is again destroyed so
that the solar bark can sail past successfully, but instead of magical means,
direct physical weapons—spears—are used against the serpent. The theme
continues in Scene 69, where both Apep and his confederates are bound
and destroyed, so that the solar bark may sail by. Apep must be annihilated
again in the final hour of the night, in order to ensure the successful rising
of the sun in the eastern horizon (Scene 89).

The serpent Apep appears rarely within the Book of Caverns. In Division 5 of the Book of Caverns, Scene 50, rearing serpents cross the body of
the giant goddess called the Mysterious One. Labeled "One of the Navel"
and "One of the Umbilical Cord," the serpents appear to be noxious forces
controlled by the goddess, near whose hand is the annotation: "As Re comes
to rest in the western horizon in order to take care of those who are in
the earth, so he shines in the eastern mountain in order to drive out that
Wenty-Apep, evil of eye" (p. 402). Apep appears again in Division 6, Scene
73, where decapitated figures are labeled "enemies" as well as "Apep," linking
the punishment of the chaos serpent with the destruction of the damned.

In the Books of the Creation of the Solar Disk, Apep appears again
clearly as an enemy of the solar deity. For example, in the tomb of
Ramesses VI, two ram-headed deities "stretch out" Apep, his head pierced
by a knife;[28] one of the ram-headed gods is said to destroy the serpent's *ba*-
soul, mirroring the destruction of the components of the damned (souls,
shades, heads, heart, etc.) that appears frequently in the Netherworld
Books. In another scene from the tomb of Ramesses VI, the scarab Khepri
emerges from the "coils" of Apep,[29] suggesting that the chaos serpent, like

28. Section A, Register 4, Scene 15 (pp. 478–79; see Roberson 2012, 286–88
[Scene 76]).
29. Section A2, Register 1a, Scene 18 (see below, p. 481; Roberson 2012, 178–79
[Scene 18]).

the waters of Nun, can provide a regenerative force for the solar god. A similar concept may lie behind the serpents "Evil of Face"—an epithet of Apep—who appear on the Second Shrine of Tutankhamun (pp. 550–51), representing a vital element in a scene of solar regeneration, recalling the renewing power of the serpent Life of the Gods in Hour 12 of the Book of the Hidden Chamber. The danger of Apep resurfaces in the Enigmatic Wall in the tomb of Ramesses IX, where the solar bark is visibly run aground atop the back of the serpent (pl. 52).

Among the Netherworld Books corpus, several basic features thus emerge concerning the god Apep. In the Book of the Hidden Chamber, Apep is often called "Nehaher," literally "Terrible of Face," and in the Enigmatic Wall in the tomb of Ramesses IX, serpents Terrible of Face, confederates of Apep, are slaughtered with arrows. Yet Terrible of Face can also serve a protective function, as a serpent whose encirclement is not threatening but helps "pull together" and protect the corpse of the solar deity.[30] Such a positive function is not assigned to the serpent called Apep, who is both blind and deaf, yet whose roar reverberates through the Netherworld. In Hour 7 of the Book of the Hidden Chamber, the voice of Apep leads the crew of the solar god in their combat against the serpent, and in the Book of Gates, Apep's roar is a notable feature of the otherwise blind and deaf god.[31] The region of Apep can be called his "sandbank," recalling the threat that the solar bark will run aground and the solar eye be swallowed by the evil serpent.

One of the chief protections of the solar god against Apep is another serpent: Mehen, the Encircling Serpent.[32] The Encircling Serpent appears as a protective serpent surrounding the solar deity as early as the Book of the Two Ways (Willems 1996, 302–3), and the serpent can also embody the

---

30. Book of Caverns, Division 3, Registers 2–3, Scene 32: "Terrible of Face who is in the cavern pulls together your corpse" (p. 375). Note also the passage in Great Litany 15: "O Osiris! Great god, whose corpse is hidden, you with whom is Terrible of Face, he causing that he guard the corpse of the One Hidden of Name" (p. 428). For an overview of the roles of the god Terrible of Face (Nehaher) in Egyptian religious texts, see El-Sayed 1981; Manassa 2007a, 323–24.

31. Apep's roar is addressed in Borghouts 2007, 32–33; for Apep's lack of sensory organs, compare the Book of Gates passage quoted above (Hour 6, Register 1, Scene 35).

32. For the Encircling Serpent's multiple roles within the Netherworld Books and ancient Egyptian funerary literature see Ritner 1984, 219–20; Piccione 1990; Klotz 2006, 32–34; Manassa 2007a, 301–2.

actual fiery roads that lead to and emanate from the solar deity as he passes through the Netherworld (Hermsen 1991, 201–3). The Encircling Serpent as a representation of the space through which and routes along which the solar god travels probably explains the dual uroboroi on the Second Shrine of Tutankhamun, both of which appear to be Mehen serpents (p. 541). Encircling the head and the feet of the giant Re-Osiris, these serpents represent the upper and lower Netherworld (Darnell 2004, 380–81).

Chthonic deities appear frequently in the Netherworld Books. Tatenen as god of the primeval earth, Geb as a personification of the Netherworldly realm, and Nun as the primordial waters all play significant roles within the texts and scenes of the various compositions, in which those deities can appear in parallel environments.[33] In the Book of the Creation of the Solar Disk in the tomb of Ramesses VI, the corpses of Tatenen and Nun can stand side-by-side at the rebirth of the solar deity from his own corpse and appear together as deities elevating the solar bark at sunrise and sunset.[34] Tatenen can also represent the entirety of the Netherworldly realm, as in the Book of Gates, where the divine name Tatenen replaces the term Duat, "Netherworld."[35] An additional chthonic deity who plays a significant role in the Netherworld Books is the double sphinx/lion Aker, who appears first within the Book of the Hidden Chamber and later in the Book of Caverns and the Books of the Creation of the Solar Disk.[36] Like Tatenen, Aker can embody the Netherworld itself, and the two lions/sphinxes may serve to represent the twin hills of the horizon. Aker as earth god also guards the unification of Re and Osiris in the deepest parts of the Netherworld; in Hour 5, Register 3 of the Book of the Hidden Chamber, the sphinx Aker surrounds the egg of Sokar, while in Division 3 of the Book of Caverns, Aker appears above the corpse of Osiris[37] and in the introductory text to the division, Re says "I shall enter the cavern betwixt

---

33. Schlögl 1980, 93–96; Barta 1990a, 55–56.

34. At the rebirth of the solar deity: Section B, Register 3, Scene 35 (pp. 494–95); see Roberson 2012, 197–98, Scene 24. At sunrise and sunset: Section B, Register 4, Scene 40 (p. 498); see the commentary in Roberson 2012, 145–54.

35. Hour 8, Register 2, Scene 51 (pp. 300–301): "Your provisions be to you in Tatenen; the West be to your sanctified corpse"; and Hour 9, Register 1, Scene 55 (p. 305): "Foremost of the Westerners praises you, those who are in Tatenen rejoice for you." See also Schlögl 1980, 31.

36. Roberson 2009, 429–33; 2012, 133–54, passim. General discussions of the deity include de la Roque 1931; Ogdon 1986.

37. Surrounded by Terrible of Face as protective serpent, see above, p. 30.

the Aker, that I might illumine the great mystery that is beneath him" (p. 367). The "mystery" beneath Aker appears clearly in the Book of Caverns and the Books of the Creation of the Solar Disk as Osiris, the corpse of the solar god, called in the latter composition "The great god who is in his cavern; [the corpse] in which is Re."[38] The chthonic deities within the Netherworld Books serve as the space in which the solar god is resurrected, and their hypostases assist the god in his journey.

ROYAL TOMBS OF THE NEW KINGDOM

The descriptions and depictions of space-time landscapes through which the sun journeys in the New Kingdom Netherworld Books occupied more modest architectural spaces. Although the details of the development of the royal tombs of the New Kingdom are complex and beyond the scope and purpose of the present publication, as the walls of those tombs are the media through which most of the surviving New Kingdom versions of the Netherworld Books have come down to us, some presentation of the basic trends and major phases of the architectural development and epigraphic embellishment of those tombs provides useful background information for the following translations. The New Kingdom royal tomb as we know it developed during the reigns of Hatshepsut and Thutmose III, as a representation of the course of the night sun's journey through the realms described in the Netherworld Books of the New Kingdom; the treatises embellished a physical monument that architecturally reflected spaces depicted and described in those compositions.[39]

Although the royal burials of the Second Intermediate period appear to have focused on the hill of Dra Abu en-Naga, at the northern edge of the major necropoleis of Western Thebes (Polz 2007), the tombs of the last rulers of the Seventeenth Dynasty and the first pharaohs of the Eigh-

---

38. Tomb of Ramesses VI, Section B, Register 1, Scene 27 (p. 487); see Roberson 2012, 135–39, Scene 2.

39. The following overview is intended to summarize the architectural contexts of the Netherworld Books; plans of all of the tombs are available in the *Atlas of the Valley of the Kings* (http://www.thebanmappingproject.com/). For overviews of the Valley of the Kings and the architecture of royal tombs, see *inter alia* Romer 1981; Hornung 1990a; Reeves and Wilkinson 1996; Weeks 2000; Wilkinson and Weeks 2016; in the context of Netherworld Book decoration, see the convenient overview with references in Roberson 2012, 23–24.

teenth Dynasty remain unidentified (Dodson 2016, 66–68). The tomb of Ahmose may be at Abydos, although the presence of his mummy in the Deir el-Bahari cachette is suggestive of a burial at Thebes. The tomb of Amenhotep I has been sought on and near Dra Abu en-Naga, including the narrow wadi called Khawi el-'Alamat, curving up and south into the Dra Abu en-Naga spur, although the major early New Kingdom tomb in that narrow defile is more probably the burial place of Ahmose's great royal wife Ahmose Nefertari. In his tomb inscriptions, the official Ineni describes the construction of the original tomb of Thutmose I; like that of Amenhotep I, this burial has thus far eluded positive identification.

Hatshepsut is the first ruler known to have prepared a burial site in the Valley of the Kings, at the head of one of the prongs of the southern branch of the great Wadyein, which emerges from the cliffs just north of Dra Abu en-Naga. The unusual reign of Thutmose I's daughter, Hatshepsut, sees the construction of KV 20. Hatshepsut appears to have fulfilled the proper sepulchral responsibilities of the legitimate ruler she claimed to be through the exhumation of Thutmose I from his as yet unidentified original burial and the transference of his body to her own tomb, unless the tomb of Hatshepsut began as the burial of Thutmose I. The mummy of Thutmose I did not rest long with Hatshepsut; upon her death, Thutmose III fulfilled for his part the duty required for his own legitimate rule and removed Thutmose I to a separate burial in the Valley of the Kings (KV 38), a smaller and simplified version of the tomb Thutmose III had prepared for himself in the Valley.[40]

The Valley of the Kings spreads out amongst the multiple branching heads of the larger valley in the shadow of the Qurn, the pointed hill south of Deir el-Bahari and overlooking Deir el-Medina. Although that hill and its environs—at least some element of which appears textually as *tꜣ dhn.t*, "the peak, the brow"—came to be associated with the serpent goddess of the Theban necropoleis, Meretseger, "she who loves silence" (Yoyotte 2003), the wadis of the valley at the base of the hill do not appear to have possessed any great religious significance prior to the reign of Hatshepsut. The oft-expressed view of the peak as a "natural pyramid" is a comparison of modern date, one for which no ancient evidence may be adduced. The Valley of the Kings is, however, separated by a

---

40. For an alternate identification of KV 38 with the original tomb of Thutmose I as described by Ineni, see Roehrig 2005, 185–87; 2006, 246–47.

relatively narrow spur of the Theban western hills from an old cult site of the goddess Hathor. The orientation of tombs within the Theban landscape appears to follow basic rules, but the internal orientation of the tombs remained the more significant feature of the sepulchers' architectonic scheme (Wilkinson 1994).

Hatshepsut's tomb curves and descends in corkscrew-like fashion into the head of the fork of the valley that is essentially behind her mortuary temple at Deir el-Bahari. Her innovative tomb in the Valley of the Kings appears to be related to her equally innovative elaboration on the basic design of the platform temple of Monthuhotep II at Deir el-Bahri (Polz 2008). Hatshepsut developed a temple that created a ritual environment for the goddess Hathor and the cult of the queen.[41] As ultimately a hemispeos, partly within and partly outside the mountain, Hatshepsut's temple represents an architectural expression of images of the cow of the goddess Hathor literally emerging from the western hills—the temple is in the old bay of the goddess and represents the goddess herself (Darnell 2013, 77–78). The upper terrace of the structure bears the temple proper, itself an elaborated copy of the Middle Kingdom temple of Amun at Karnak—true to its name *ḥft.t-ḥr-nb=s*, Khefethernebes, "she who is opposite her lord," the Deir el-Bahari temple provides a mirror of Karnak to which Amun may journey in the major and initial portion of the Beautiful Festival of the Valley (M. Gabolde 1998b). The temple was also a terrace nestled in the western hills, recalling the very Puntite *ḥty.w*-terraces of the southeast to which Hatshepsut sent the expedition she immortalized on the walls of the temple—the temple combines the features, imagery, and locations of the eastern and western horizons, a massive, architectural recapitulation and assurance of the continued *perpetuum mobile* of the solar cycle.

In her introduction of a descending and curving burial in what would thereafter be the mortuary Valley of the Kings for the rulers of the New Kingdom, Hatshepsut appears also to have attempted the architectural representation of a procession into the bowels of the

---

41. Architectural innovation in general under Hatshepsut is discussed in a number of the contributions in Galan, Bryan, and Dorman 2014, particularly chs. 1, 2, 4, 6, 7, 9, 18, and 19.

mountain and the interior of the Netherworld. The tomb of Hatshepsut is located in the western face of the same escarpment as her temple at Deir el-Bahri, thereby linking the nascent Valley of the Kings to the earlier cult of Hathor and the Beautiful Festival of the Valley. As later developments of the New Kingdom royal tomb and the religious texts and accompanying images in those tombs reveal, the sepulchers in the Valley of the Kings were representations of the first half of the nocturnal journey of the deceased king and the dead sun toward rejuvenation in the bowels of the Netherworld.

Development of Tomb Architecture

Phase 1—Origins: Hatshepsut through Amenhotep II

Although the architecture of the New Kingdom royal tombs changes over time, revealing seven major periods of development, the basic features of descending passages ending in an upper hall and terminal burial chamber appear already during the reigns of Hatshepsut and Thutmose III. The early forms of the royal tomb reveal the development of a definite angle change, the long and curving form of the tomb under Hatshepsut becoming somewhat more angular with Thutmose III. The tomb of Hatshepsut (KV 20; fig. 1.1) reveals two curving angle changes, the first within the initial two passages and first descending corridor, the other in the long, curving passageway leading to the first, upper chamber near the end of the

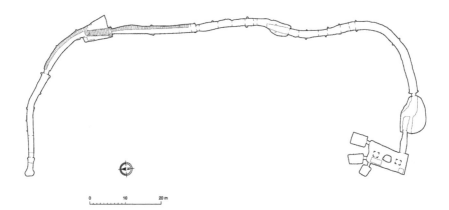

Fig. 1.1. Plan of the Tomb of Hatshepsut (KV 20). Figs. 1.1–7 by Alberto Urcia (after http://www.thebanmappingproject.com).

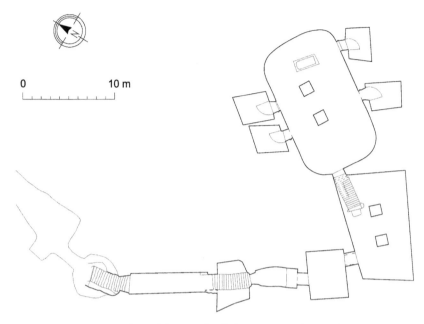

Fig. 1.2. Plan of the Tomb of Thutmose III (KV 34)

tomb. Although Hatshepsut's tomb has five irregular corridors, the second and fourth end in roughly shaped chambers, through the central axes of which are more steeply descending ramps; at the end of the fifth corridor is a chamber, from which a descending passage leads to the roughly rectangular burial chamber with three subsidiary rooms. The essentially three-segmented upper portion of the tomb, with upper room and lower burial chamber at the end of the tomb, is a pattern that all of the completed tombs in the Valley of the Kings will follow.

The more complex and tripartite upper portion of the tomb of Hatshepsut is simplified in the tomb of Thutmose III (KV 34) to a sloping corridor, descending corridor with stairs, and following, sloping corridor (fig 1.2). This pattern persists, with a few aberrations, through the reign of Merneptah, after whose reign the stairs in the second corridor cease to appear. Thutmose III dispensed with the extreme curve of the tomb under Hatshepsut, substituting a single, right angle change in direction between the well shaft—introduced under Thutmose III—and the upper chamber, now with two pillars as well. The room before the upper chamber, the well shaft in many tombs, is present in all except for those of Tutankhamun (KV 62), Ramesses I (KV 16), and Ramesses VII (KV 1). The descent to

the burial chamber in the tomb of Thutmose III opens off the left side of
the rear wall of the upper hall, to the left of the axis of the two pillars—this
offset descent from the upper, pillared hall remained a feature through the
tomb of Seti I (with the exceptions of the tombs of Aye and Ramesses I).
The two-pillared burial chamber of Thutmose III is oval, with four subsidiary rooms. The oval form of the room, similar to the shape of a cartouche,
recalls the appearance of the egg of Sokar in Hour 5 of the Book of the
Hidden Chamber.

The son of Thutmose III, Amenhotep II, regularized his father's tomb
design, introducing right angles to the corridors and chambers, increas-
ing the number of pillars in the burial chamber to six, and introducing
a change in floor level to the burial chamber. The tomb of Amenhotep II
(KV 35) separated the well shaft and upper, pillared chamber from the
burial chamber (again with four subsidiary rooms) by a short corridor.

Phase 2—Return of the Double Angle Change: Thutmose IV through
Amenhotep III

The tomb of Thutmose IV (KV 43; fig. 1.3) retained most of the features
present under Amenhotep II and introduced two corridors following the
stairs descending from the upper, pillared chamber, as well as a small antechamber before the burial chamber, features present in most subsequent
royal tombs in the Valley of the Kings; of the completed burials, only the
tomb of Ramesses XI has a single corridor between the upper hall and
the burial chamber. Thutmose IV retained the level change within the
burial chamber, a short flight of stairs leading to the lower level of the sarcophagus. More significantly, Thutmose IV reintroduced the double angle
change present in Hatshepsut's original tomb design. The burial chamber
is at a right angle, the door thereto opening not off the back wall of the
antechamber opposite the door from the corridor, but opening rather off
the wall to the left of the entrance to the room. The resulting design is a
counterclockwise double change of angle, essentially an angular mirror
image of the basic plan of the tomb of Hatshepsut.

Just as Thutmose IV modestly altered the plan of the tomb of Amenhotep II, with the more noticeable reintroduction of the second angle
change, between the final approach corridor and the burial chamber, so
the tomb of Amenhotep III (KV 22) essentially elaborated modestly on
the plan of the tomb of Thutmose IV, with the exception of a more marked
alteration of angle. The tomb of Amenhotep III retained a second angle

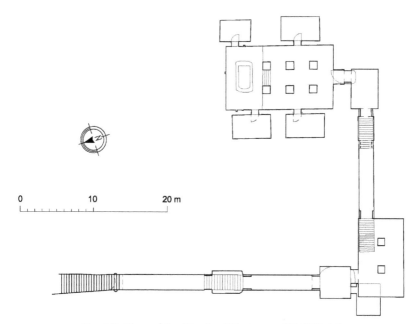

Fig. 1.3. Plan of the Tomb of Thutmose IV (KV 43)

change, except that the end of the tomb—the burial chamber—leads farther into the mountain. The subsidiary rooms of the burial chamber are
more complex, three being relatively simple, with two rooms being larger,
each with a central pillar and its own subsidiary room. Both Thutmose IV
and Amenhotep III retain the well shaft in front of the upper, pillared hall.
Finally, Amenhotep III more dramatically broke with his predecessors in
abandoning what had been and would continue to be the main concentra-
tion of royal tombs in the East Valley, locating his tomb in the West Valley.

Phase 3—Eclecticism of Extenuating Circumstances: Amenhotep IV/
Akhenaton through Aye

With the removal of the royal court to the new city of Akhetaton during
the reign of Amenhotep IV, who soon after his accession styled himself
Akhenaton, the Valley of the Kings was abandoned for a time. The burial
of the king at Akhetaton is atypical in comparison with what came before
and later in the Valley of the Kings, notably in the addition of a side corridor accessing an unfinished, secondary axis roughly parallel to the main
corridor of the tomb, and the presence of a suite of two rooms leading off

to the right just before a steeply descending stairway leading down to the twin-pillared burial chamber. Nevertheless, the overall form of the tomb—descending stairway, corridor, descending stairway, antechamber, and pillared burial chamber—retains some of the general features of other New Kingdom royal tombs, albeit without the use of any of the Netherworld Books within the decorative scheme of the tomb walls (Martin 1974; Gabolde 1998a, 105–46).

The return of the court to Thebes appears to have led to the reburial of Akhenaton, in a chaotic and anonymous manner, in a small tomb in the Valley of the Kings (KV 55), as insignificant in terms of the development of the Theban royal tomb as the king's sepulcher at Akhetaton (Gabolde 1998a, 227–76). The tomb of Tutankhamun (KV 62) in the East Valley, though small and lacking internal stairs and pillars of any kind, nevertheless has the two major chambers and angle change that are hallmark features of the earlier royal tombs in the Valley of the Kings. The tomb of Aye (KV 23) is straight, regular, and short, probably more the result of the brief time the apparently somewhat aged ruler had on the throne than evidence of any architectural innovation. Perhaps in an attempt to link his reign with that of the last "pre-Amarna" ruler, Amenhotep III, Aye located his own tomb in the West Valley. All of the Phase 3 burials dispense with the well shaft.

Phase 4—Introduction of the Offset Axis: Horemhab through Seti I

From the reign of Horemhab through the end of the New Kingdom, the royal tomb is relatively straight. The upper, pillared hall rotates ninety degrees clockwise, its long sides now oriented with the axis of the entrance corridors. The descending passage leading out of the upper hall continues to exit that chamber at the left end of the short wall farthest from the entrance, with the result that the burial chamber continues to lead farther into the mountain, following the orientation it had in the tomb of Amenhotep III. Horemhab reintroduces the well shaft in front of the upper chamber.

As with the tomb of Aye, so the tomb of Ramesses I (KV 16) is short and simple, the result of the brief reign of the king. The tomb of Seti I (KV 17; fig. 1.4) represents an elaboration of the plan of the tomb of Horemhab (KV 57), introducing a subsidiary, two-pillared room to the upper pillared chamber, and a four pillared room behind the burial chamber. The tomb of Seti I, while the last in the Valley of the Kings to have the offset descent from the upper pillared room to the burial chamber, is the first

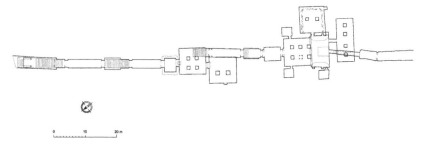

Fig. 1.4. Plan of the Tomb of Seti I (KV 17)

in the series with four pillars, which will be the norm in completed royal burials—excepting that of Tawosret—through the tomb of Ramesses XI (KV 4). The tomb of Seti I uniquely has a roughly cut descending stairway leading down and back from the burial chamber, ending in the underlying Esna shale. For the first time, the entire burial is decorated in relief. The royal sarcophagus, in earlier New Kingdom tombs having a chest-like appearance, is now anthropomorphic and fully decorated, as is the tomb itself. The ceiling of the sarcophagus chamber is curved, a suitable place for cosmographic compositions such as the Book of the Day and the Book of the Night—just as an image of the goddess Nut, carved in relief on the underside of the sarcophagus, overspreads the mummy of the king within, so the carved figure of the king atop the sarcophagus lies beneath the vault of the upper and lower skies.

Phase 5—Archaizing Innovation: Ramesses II

The tomb of Ramesses II (KV 7) represents a return to the form of the royal tomb last seen in the burial of Amenhotep III, the axis angling to the right (fig. 1.5). Just as Amenhotep III experimented with a more overt living deification, so Ramesses II represents a high-point of pharaoh as living deity and an even more remarkably long-lived and successful period of self-worship and reconfirmation of divinity in the ruler's multiple jubilee celebrations (Habachi 1969; Bickel 2002). The deification in Nubia of Amenhotep III's chief wife Tiye, and the corresponding deification there of Ramesses II's first chief wife Nefertari, on apparently even grander scale (Xekelaki and El-Khodary 2011, 563–65), is further evidence of a similar pharaonic religious and ritual policy for the two reigns, a similarity finding architectural expression in Ramesses II's return to the mortuary architectural style of Amenhotep III and the latter's predecessors.

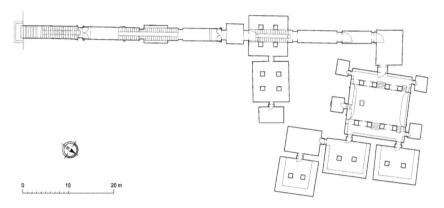

Fig. 1.5. Plan of the Tomb of Ramesses II (KV 7)

Ramesses II increases the number of pillars in the burial chamber to eight, a feature that will appear in a few subsequent royal tombs in the Valley of the Kings. Ramesses II dispenses with the offset descent from the upper, pillared chamber, the passage now descending between the pillars; this feature will be common in the later royal tombs in the Valley of the Kings.

Phase 6—Straight and Shallow Descent: Merneptah through Ramesses III

The tomb of Merneptah (KV 8; fig. 1.6) returns to the basic pattern of the tomb of Seti I but retains the straight descent from the upper, pillared hall introduced under Ramesses II. Merneptah also retains the eight pillars in the burial chamber, another innovation of Ramesses II. The tomb of Merneptah was cut into the mountain at a less steep angle of descent, a feature that the remaining royal tombs in the Valley of the Kings will continue—the tomb of Seti II (KV 15) is almost horizontal. The well shaft becomes less frequent, although it does appear in the tombs of Merneptah and Ramesses III. An unusual angle change in the forward portion of the tomb of Ramesses III (KV 11), begun for Sethnakht, is the result of an unfortunate collision of his tomb with that of Amenmesse (KV 10). The tomb of Tawosret (KV 14), subsequently enlarged for Sethnakht, lacks pillars in what is otherwise the upper, pillared hall and has the peculiarity of two burial chambers, the tomb having been enlarged. Both the medial and terminal burial chambers of the Tawosret/Sethnakht tomb have eight pillars.

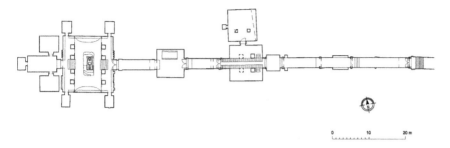

Fig. 1.6. Plan of the Tomb of Merneptah (KV 8)

Phase 7—Fewer Segments but Wider Passages: Ramesses IV through
Ramesses XI

The final phase of development of the New Kingdom royal tomb begins
with the burial of Ramesses IV (KV 2). The tomb is shorter, with a corresponding reduction in the number of corridors and the virtual disap-
pearance of subsidiary chambers. The corridors are wider, however, and
the ceilings thereof higher, giving a greater sense of space within the tomb;
from a width of ca. 1.7–2 meters under Thutmose III and his immediate
successors, the corridors widen to ca. 2.5–2.7 meters from Amenhotep III
through Ramesses III, attaining under Ramesses IV the ca. 3.2–3.3 meters
they will retain through Ramesses XI (compare the Tomb of Ramesses IX
[KV 6], fig. 1.7).

The tombs of Ramesses IV and Ramesses VII dispense with pillars
(the tomb of Ramesses X is unfinished). The tomb of Ramesses VI (KV 9;
begun by Ramesses V) is slightly longer, and may represent a slight return
to an earlier form. The tomb of Ramesses XI (KV 4) offers a final innovation, introducing a deep shaft—probably a version of the earlier well

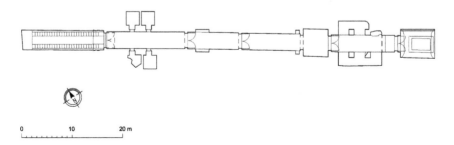

Fig. 1.7. Plan of the Tomb of Ramesses IX (KV 6)

shaft—into the center of the sarcophagus chamber. Even in its senility, the architectural tradition of the New Kingdom royal tomb was yet able to present a final innovation.

Development of Tomb Decoration and Use of Netherworld Books

Phase 1—Thutmose I through Amenhotep III

Although other scenes and texts appear, the mural decoration of the first royal tombs of the Eighteenth Dynasty is dominated by the Book of the Hidden Chamber, the first to appear of the two Netherworld Books with twelve major divisions corresponding to the hours of the night, each in three horizontal registers, through the middle of which travels the ram-headed form of the night sun in his bark (the other being the Book of Gates, first appearing during Phase 2).[42] Limestone blocks associated with the funerary equipment of Thutmose I appear to belong to the king's burial in the tomb of Hatshepsut, or perhaps to an original burial of the king (Mauric-Barbério 2001). The blocks bear the earliest evidence for any of the treatises we term the Netherworld Books of the New Kingdom—portions of the Book of the Hidden Chamber painted in ink—and would have served to provide a proper surface in a tomb cut into rock unsuitable for decoration.

In the tomb of Thutmose III, the Book of the Hidden Chamber appears in full in the burial chamber, with a "catalog" of the text also present in the upper, pillared hall. Prior to the placement of the text on a small corpus of Nectanebid/early Ptolemaic period sarcophagi, only the burial chamber of the tomb of Thutmose III, and that of his vizier Useramun, reveal a conscientious attempt to lay out the hours of the Book of the Hidden Chamber according to the instructions within the text (see pp. 131–32). The Book of the Hidden Chamber appears in the burial chambers of the royal tombs until the Amarna Period, with the exception of the tomb of Thutmose IV, in which the burial chamber is left undecorated.

The forms of Re from the Book of Adoring Re in the West appear on two columns in the burial chamber of the tomb of Thutmose III, although

---

42. The following summary relies on overviews of tomb decoration available in p. 15 n. 39 above as well as Abitz 1974, 51–80. The list of texts in Roberson 2016 is useful for individual sections of each composition.

the treatise itself was written on a shroud from the burial.[43] The appearance of the text of the treatise on the shroud and the illustrations of the solar forms on the pillar reveal an interrelationship of mummy, text, and burial architecture of a sort appearing already during the Old and Middle Kingdoms.[44] A virtually inextricable association of ritual, burial, and funerary accoutrements and religious treatise flows through the productive life of ancient Egyptian funerary literature, reflecting the primacy of ritual over mythology in Egypt.[45]

Phase 2—Tutankhamun through Ramesses I

The royal tomb prepared for Akhenaton at his sprawling new capitol of Akhetaton reveals some scenes similar to those appearing in New Kingdom nonroyal burials, including images of mourning, and others that represent visual realizations of nature worshipping the Aton, depictions of the concepts present in the Hymn to the Aton. Such "non-Netherworldly" scenes occur also in the tombs of Tutankhamun (a funeral procession and the Opening of the Mouth ritual) and Aye (the tomb owner fowling). Many of the religious texts in Tutankhamun's tomb are on the shrines that surrounded the royal sarcophagus, objects attested in the contents of the Theban reburial of Akhenaton (KV 55), and present in royal burials at least as late as the reign of Ramesses IV, as the Turin plan of that ruler's tomb reveals. The shrines of Tutankhamun are embellished with scenes and texts that include excerpts from the Book of Going Forth By Day (Book of

---

43. Compare the Book of Going Forth By Day (Book of the Dead), texts of that tradition appearing first on coffins (of both Middle Kingdom rectangular tradition [Geisen 2004; Quirke 2005] and Theban royal *rishi* tradition [Miniaci 2011, 149–53]), then on shrouds (Piankoff 1964a; Ronsecco 1996; note also the foreshadowing in the burial of Nubkheperre Antef V [Miniaci 2011, 152 n. 1061]), and normally on papyrus during the Thutmoside Period.

44. For the Pyramid Texts, see Allen 1994. In the Middle Kingdom, certain texts relate to specific areas of the coffin (see Nut texts on the lid, the Book of the Two Ways on the floor, etc. [Willems 1988, 1996]). The coffin becomes simultaneously a representation of the solar boat and the funerary barge, texts and physical ritual equating the funeral voyage and entombment of the deceased with the regenerative journey of the sun. Numerous references to integration and proper functioning of the body appear within the Coffin Texts, reflecting the proximity of the texts to the mummy (Nyord 2009).

45. Assmann 1977b; 2001a, 83–147; Lorand 2009, 59–61; Hays 2012.

the Dead), selections from the Book of the Hidden Chamber, the earliest version of the cosmographic text known as the Book of the Heavenly Cow, and the first of the surviving manifestations of the cryptographic Books of the Solar-Osirian Unity.

With the tomb of Horemhab, the mural decoration of the royal tomb, hitherto painted only, was planned to be both carved and painted, although much of the decoration was unfinished at the time of the burial. The tomb of Horemhab also contains—in the burial chamber—the earliest surviving (yet incomplete) copy of the Book of Gates, the second and last to appear of the treatises with twelve divisions focusing on the ram-headed solar deity in the bark. Both Horemhab and Ramesses I ignored the Book of the Hidden Chamber in favor of the Book of Gates.

Phase 3—Seti I through Ramesses III

The tomb of Seti I marks the beginning of a period of thorough decoration of the royal tomb and the development of standardized positions for various scenes and texts throughout the tomb. At the beginning and end of the third period appear the Netherworld Books that eschew the registers and twelve divisions of the Book of the Hidden Chamber and the Book of Gates, rather emphasizing the solar presence through multiple appearances of the solar disk, although the ram-headed form of the sun is still present—the Books of the Creation of the Solar Disk and the Book of Caverns. The latter appears in the Osireion (Cenotaph of Seti I) at Abydos (completed by Merneptah), not occurring in the Valley of the Kings until the next period; the Books of the Creation of the Solar Disk appear in incomplete forms beginning with Merneptah and Tawosret, with a substantial excerpt in the burial chamber of the tomb of Ramesses III.

The tomb of Seti I sets the basic template for the locations of the Netherworld Books and associated material through the tomb of Ramesses III, with the exception of the tombs of Seti II, Amenmesse, and Siptah, which are anomalous in the areas beyond the well shaft. The Book of Adoring Re in the West appears as the text filling the walls of the first and second corridors of the tomb, positions it occupies in most of the remaining tombs in the Valley of the Kings. The Book of the Hidden Chamber moves from the burial chamber to the third corridor, scenes of deities appear in the well shaft, the first half of the Book of Gates appears on the walls of the upper, pillared hall, along with the newly appearing and succinct treatise of the Resurrection of Osiris (except in the tombs of Amenmesse, Siptah, and

Tawosret/Sethnakht) (Roberson 2013). In the tomb of Seti I a complete version of the Book of Gates is present in the burial chamber, although not on the walls thereof, but as part of the decoration of the king's anthropoid sarcophagus. With the tomb of Seti I begins the tradition of showing the texts and scenes of the Opening of the Mouth Ceremony (first appearing in greatly syncopated form in the tomb of Tutankhamun) in the fourth and fifth corridors, a tradition continuing—with the exceptions of the tombs of Seti II, Amenmesse, and Siptah—through the tomb of Ramesses IV. In most of the royal tombs of the third period of decoration, the Book of Gates appears in the burial chamber, which also has an astronomical ceiling through the tomb of Tawosret/Sethnakht (again with the exception of the tombs of Seti II, Amenmesse, and Siptah).

Phase 4—Ramesses IV through Ramesses XI

With the tomb of Ramesses IV, the regular placement of scenes and treatises is abandoned; the same tomb also contains the only copy of the Blueprint of the Course of the Stars (Book of Nut) in the Valley of the Kings, and only the second surviving version after the initial appearance of that composition in the Osireion (Cenotaph of Seti I) at Abydos. The Book of Caverns appears for the first time in the Valley of the Kings in the tomb of Ramesses IV, occurring in some form in all of the major royal tombs of the fourth period. The tombs of Ramesses VI and Ramesses IX contain versions of the cryptographic Books of the Solar-Osirian Unity. The tomb of Ramesses VI also provides the only copy of the Book of the Day, as well as two versions of the Book of the Night, which first appeared in the Osireion at Abydos, with subsequent versions in the tombs of Merneptah and Ramesses IV. The longest and perhaps complete version of the Books of the Creation of the Solar Disk—snippets of which already appear as early as Merneptah—fills much of the wall surfaces in the burial chamber of the tomb of Ramesses VI, with other substantial sequences from the treatise known from the tombs of Ramesses VII and Ramesses IX. The tomb of Ramesses XI reveals only the most preliminary phases of decoration—scenes of the ruler and deities—in the first corridor.

Entrance Façade

From the reign of Ramesses II the entrance to the royal tomb has a decorated façade, with representations of the solar cycle on the exterior of the lintel (Lüscher 2000, 35–48). From the reign of Merneptah, this visible and decorated exterior to the tomb entrance appears more elevated, the entrance no longer descending from the Valley floor, but opening into the slope of the hillside. In the earliest form, the lintel has in its center an image of the sun of the upper sky, painted yellow, yet bearing within it the images of the solar deity in forms both diurnal—the scarab—and nocturnal—the ram-headed anthropomorphic figure. As befits the union of Re and Osiris, on which elements of the Netherworld Books focus so much attention, to either side of the central solar disk are the goddesses Isis and Nephthys, at once mourning the deceased deity of yesterday and representing the hills between which the newborn sun of tomorrow will rise.[46] With some variations, this decorative scheme continues through the reign of Ramesses VI.

On the façade of the tomb of Ramesses VII, the figure of the king appears to each side, alongside the goddesses; a royal figure takes up position to each side of the disk on the façades of the remaining royal tombs of the New Kingdom, through the reign of Ramesses XI. On the entrance to the tomb of Ramesses IX, the solar disk is within the womb of Nut, whose upper body appears above the disk, her head shown en face, her arms down to either side of the disk/belly of the goddess.[47]

Text and Architecture—The Book of the Hidden Chamber and Tomb Architecture

The corridors and descending passages of the royal tomb bear a visible similarity to the corridors and descending passages of the path called *rꜣ-stꜣw*, "Place of Hauling," in Hours 4–5 of the Book of the Hidden Chamber. The road leads to the realm of Imhet, the lowest region of the Netherworld, the land of Sokar (Hornung 1981a). The distribution of the hours of the Book of the Hidden Chamber in the royal tombs of the Valley of the Kings reveals at least some of the ways in which the royal tomb mirrors the events in that composition (Brunner 1980; Richter 2008). The Osireion at Abydos, decorated like the royal tombs with Netherworld Books, displays

----

46. Clère 1958, 30 n. 1, 31 fig. 1; Assmann 1995, 45; compare the scene of the sun rising on the arms of the goddesses at the beginning of the Second Shrine of Tutankhamun (fig. 7.2).

47. For an alternate interpretation of this scene, see Dorman 1999.

a similar architechtonic association of subterranean space with the Netherworld itself.[48]

Both the final chamber and the central portion of New Kingdom royal burials reveal connections with the bowels of the Netherworld as they appear in the Book of the Hidden Chamber. In the finished tombs of the Eighteenth Dynasty, that composition is associated with the burial chamber. In the tomb of Thutmose III—and in the tomb prepared for the final burial of Thutmose I in the Valley of the Kings—the burial chamber is cartouche shaped; the sarcophagi of the early Eighteenth Dynasty, and beginning again with Ramesses I, were also cartouche-shaped. This cartouche shape mimics the appearance of the egg of Sokar and the chamber of Sokar in Hour 5 of the Book of the Hidden Chamber. In post-Amarna royal tombs, from Seti I through Ramesses III, Hours 4–5 of the Book of the Hidden Chamber are associated with the third corridor. The architecture of the tomb to that point provides a three-dimensional version of the thrice-angled route appearing in Hour 4 of the Book of the Hidden Chamber (Brunner 1980, 82–83). The well shaft that follows the third corridor similarly provides an architectural rendering of the realm of Imhet, the descent to the chamber of Sokar that appears in Hour 5.

The New Kingdom royal tomb appears to represent the *r3-stзw*, "Place of Hauling," within the Land of Sokar, with the entire tomb depicting the route of the nocturnal solar cycle—the Land of Sokar at the end of the third corridor—and the realm at the end of the first half of the Place of Hauling in which the sun rejuvenates—the sarcophagus room, the lowest area of the tomb, as the cartouche-shaped chamber of Sokar in Imhet. An emphasis on the middle of the night—the time of the greatest cosmic danger, with the bark running aground on the sandy spine of the chaos serpent Apep, and the resurrection of Sokar in the bowels of Imhet in the depths of the Netherworld—and the end of the night—the time of the flaming rebirth of the solar child and the final, fiery destruction of the damned—appears elsewhere in the royal tombs, and in the so-called Mythological Papyri of the Third Intermediate period. An early expression of this concept of syncopation within the Netherworld Books is the abutting of Hours 5 and 12 of the Book of the Hidden Chamber, according to the internal instructions for laying out the hours within the burial chamber (see fig. 3.1).

---

48. See pp. 33–34, noting especially the identification of the space as the Mysterious Place (Shetayt) in a graffito.

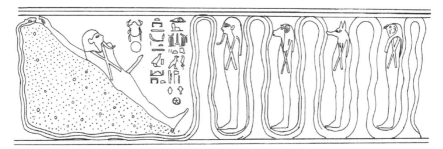

Fig. 1.8. Excerpt from the Papyrus of Heruben B
(after Piankoff and Rambova 1957, pl. 2)

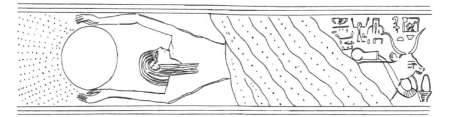

Fig. 1.9. Excerpt from the Papyrus of Nespautiutawy
(after Piankoff and Rambova 1957, pl. 3)

A syncopated representation of the Netherworld, linking the time of
the cosmic standstill atop the coils of Apep with the end of the Netherworld, appears in the tomb of Ramesses IX. There, in the third corridor,
a version of the Books of the Solar-Osirian Unity depicts the solar bark
aground on the back of Apep, the solar eye shooting fiery arrows at the
enemies of Re; the scene faces and is to some extent balanced by the large
figure of the unified Re-Osiris, reclining on—essentially becoming—the
root of the eastern horizon (see pp. 570–71). Similarly, other concluding scenes within the Netherworld Books can be composed specifically
to encompass the complete and ever-repeating cycle of the solar journey
(Hornung 1981b).

Several funerary papyri of the post-Ramesside period have similar
images linking the middle of the night and the regeneration in the chamber of Sokar with the end of the night and the rebirth of the sun in the
morning. So on P. Heruben B (fig. 1.8) appears a shortening of the final
hours of the night and a linking of the eastern horizon and destruction
of the damned. The fire-breathing serpent "Fiery One," who punishes the
damned in the third register of Hour 9 of the Book of Gates, bearing the

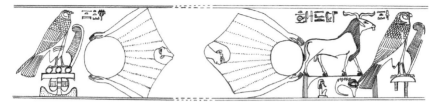

Fig. 1.10. Excerpt from the Papyrus of Khonsumes A
(after Piankoff and Rambova 1957, pl. 16)

sons of Horus within its coils, transforms in its forepart and head into the
protective Leaping-serpent of the eastern horizon, supporting within the
angle of its body and head the reclining Re-Osiris on the eastern horizon. On P. Nespautiutawy (fig. 1.9), images of the eastern and western
horizons emerge from either side of the same schematic representation of
the desert mountains; a similar representation, with east and west clearly
labeled, occurs on P. Khonsumes A (fig. 1.10). On P. Djedkhonsiuefankh
I (Piankoff and Rambova 1957, pl. 19), the middle and end of the night
come together in a scene of the morning sun rising in the serpent bark
of Hours 4–5 of the Book of the Hidden Chamber.[49] On P. Bekenmut
(Piankoff and Rambova 1957, pl. 20), images of Hour 4 of the Book of the
Hidden Chamber (sloping passage and the heads and stars of Imhet) lead
toward and abut a scene of the rising sun.

NETHERWORLD BOOKS IN TEMPLE SETTINGS

The Osireion at Abydos, commonly known as the Cenotaph of Seti I, preserves the largest variety of Netherworld Books outside of a funerary context. While the basic construction and initial decoration of the subterranean monument was completed by the end of the reign of Seti I, the relief
decoration was carried out during the reign of Merneptah (Brand 2000,
176–78). The architectural form of the monument, which appears to have
been entirely subterranean, mimics that of a New Kingdom royal tomb,
with its long sloping corridor and bent axis resembling the tomb of Amenhotep II (KV 35),[50] and perhaps provided inspiration for the form of the
tomb of Ramesses II (KV 7; Roberson 2012, 29) and later, that of Taharqa

---

49. A similar serpent bark appears in the Books of the Solar-Osirian Unity in the
tomb of Ramesses VI.

50. On this identification, see Frankfort 1933a, 26–27.

(Gozzoli 2010, 189–90 and n. 36). Rather than a royal tomb, however, the Osireion is a burial place for Osiris himself (Frankfort 1933a, 26–31). In the entrance passage of the Osireion—the area bearing copies of the Book of Gates and the Book of Caverns—a probably Twenty-First Dynasty visitor referred to the monument as the Shetayt, "Mysterious Place," of the Netherworld, apparently applying to the underground monument the terminology of the treatises on its walls (Gunn 1933, 88 [no. 3]; Frankfort 1933b, pls. 88 and 91).[51] The Netherworldly space of the Osireion provides the means of solar renewal, and the temple setting of that same space enables the king to participate within that rejuvenating cycle (von Lieven 2007a, 178).

While a complete analysis of the decorative scheme of the Osireion is outside the scope of the present work, the following sketches the basic elements of texts and scenes from the corpus of Netherworld Books.[52] The sloping entrance corridor of the Osireion is decorated with the Book of Gates on the west wall and the Book of Caverns on the east wall. After the change in axis, the Osireion opens to a transverse hall with the Book of the Night and then a large hall with monumental square pillars, in the middle of which is a sarcophagus. The emplacement for the sarcophagus is an island surrounded by a channel, intentionally filled with ground-water, by its very nature an intrusion into the ordered world of elements ultimately connected to the waters of Nun (Gessler-Löhr 1983, 430–37). The decoration in this pillared hall includes extracts from the Book of Adoring Re in the West. Behind (east of) the pillared hall is a transverse chamber, which has been identified as the model of a giant sarcophagus for the unified Re-Osiris (Roberson 2012, 30–31). This model sarcophagus is decorated with the Blueprint of the Course of the Stars (Book of Nut) and Book of the Night on the ceiling, while the walls contained excerpts from the Books of the Creation of the Solar Disk, now heavily damaged (Roberson 2007; 2012, 303–7).

A nearby temple at Abydos—constructed during the reign of Ramesses II—provides another piece within the larger puzzle posed by the Netherworld Books within the Osireion. An abbreviated copy of the Great Litany from the Book of Adoring Re in the West appears in a chapel adjoining the portico of the temple of Ramesses II (Mariette 1880, pls. 14–17; Hor-

---

51. For a discussion of similar architectural features and their interrelationships with texts and decoration, as a form of active mythic scenery, see Schmidt 1995.

52. A more in-depth analysis of the decoration appears in von Lieven 2007a.

nung 1976, 13). A similar juxtaposition of Netherworld Books in a temple setting appears within the temple complex of Karnak in ancient Thebes. Located outside the southern portion of the first pylon of the temple, the Chapel of Hakoris—or more properly, a bark-shrine—contains the expected depictions of the bark of Amun; on the east wall, however, is an unexpected element of decoration: named figures from the Great Litany of the Book of Adoring Re in the West (Traunecker, Le Saout, and Masson 1981, 55–61). Just as the Great Litany figures of the temple of Ramesses II appear to relate to the Osireion, the Chapel of Hakoris creates an architectural ensemble with the so-called Edifice of Taharqa, next to the sacred lake of Karnak Temple, which contains not only the Great Litany, but additional Netherworldly texts and scenes.[53]

Across the Nile on the west bank of ancient Thebes, the solar chapel in the temple of Ramesses III at Medinet Habu further reveals the nonmortuary nature of much we are content to call mortuary or Netherworldly (Voß 1996). The surviving scenes and texts in that room form an elaboration on the text known as "The King as Solar Priest," which appears within that very chamber (see below). A text in large hieroglyphs along the bottom of the west and south walls of the room details the responsibilities of the king as supreme solar priest, and provides the key for the content of the room (Epigraphic Survey 1963, pls. 422–23):

> Live the good god, intelligent like Re, insightful like the One in Hermopolis (Thoth), brilliant son who has come forth from Atum, defender of Horakhty, who overthrows the enemy[54] by means of the effective spells of his pronouncement, [who causes] that the bark (of the sun) travels in joy, the King of Upper and Lower Egypt, the lord of the Two Lands, Usermaatre-Meramun, the son of Re, the lord of glorious appearances, Ramesses, ruler of Heliopolis …

The King as Solar Priest text within the chapel provides an elaboration of the succinct statement in the bandeau text, and all of the divisions of the King as Solar Priest (discussed in more detail below) find visual and textual expression in the solar chapel at Medinet Habu.

---

53. Parker, Leclant, and Goyon 1979; Assmann 1983b; Roulin 1996b, 16; Cooney 2000, 19–26.

54. Here clearly Apep, depicted in the determinative of the word as a magically killed serpent.

Alongside solar hymns in the chapel are portions of the Book of the Day and the Book of the Night.[55] Through hymns and textual excerpts the solar chapel at Medinet Habu fulfills the claim of the opening section of the King as Solar Priest—the king adores the sun at sunrise, is aware of the hidden working of this ascension to the sky, and sees what is behind the seemingly simple image of the solar orb appearing to rise into the firmament. In the Medinet Habu solar chapel, the king is said to be powerful and efficacious for the sun through what he knows, and indeed the citation from the Book of the Day is an excerpt from a text of $r\underline{h}w$-knowledge (Assmann 1970, 56–57).

On the east face of the architrave crossing the solar chapel from north to south, the king can actually mimic and become an actor with the baboons who are the souls of the east (Epigraphic Survey 1963, pl. 421C; te Velde 1988). On the architrave, to each side of the solar bark, the king kneels in the company of four baboons, worshipping the sun. A separate text within the chapel—an augmentation to the King as Solar Priest also known from Deir el-Bahari, Luxor, the Edifice of Taharqa at Karnak, and the coffin of the Twenty-Fifth Dynasty ruler Aspalta—describes the rejoicing baboons praising Re-Horakhty as he rises in the eastern horizon, and the text concludes with how the benefits of this praise—in which the king clearly joins—should redound upon the ruler.[56] Text and scene interrelate between different areas of the solar chapel; even on the architrave itself, text and scene are inextricable—the word $dw\cancel{3}$, "to praise," is written as a small version of the larger adoring figure of the king.

FUNCTION OF THE NETHERWORLD BOOKS

The Netherworld Books have been characterized both as scientific and philosophical treatises (Werning 2011b, 1–5) and as compositions of psychoanalytic significance (Abt and Hornung 2003; Schweizer 2010). Interpretations of the texts as "instructional" literature have been subject to debate (Hornung 1979a). Statements within the texts themselves, including offering formulae in the Book of Gates and explicit references in the Book of Adoring Re in the West, attest to a ritual, if not even initiatory,

---

55. Müller-Roth 2008, 140–54. So also the first hour of the Book of the Night in Epigraphic Survey 1963, pl. 422, ll. 16–33; note also pl. 420 §B l. 2.

56. The text describing the worship of the baboons is Epigraphic Survey 1963, pl. 430. For the text with commentary see Assmann 1995, 24–25.

function.[57] The existence of cryptographic texts that require prior knowledge of textual content for proper understanding suggests at the minimum that the intended audience underwent some training in their use and memorization. The existence of Netherworld Books within temple contexts suggests that the Hidden Chamber may have existed in a nonfunerary context, perhaps as part of a Heliopolitan temple (Manassa 2007a, 472–75).

As chief solar priest, the Egyptian ruler is responsible for "bringing about Maat and destroying evil" (see below, p. 38). In the Netherworld, the king merges with the solar deity himself, partaking of the solar journey through the twelve hours of the night (Barta 1985). The Netherworld Books encode royal knowledge of the solar cycle, providing the ruler with the names, events, and places that he must traverse in order to attain cyclical rebirth. Just as earlier and contemporaneous funerary literature—the Pyramid Texts, Coffin Texts, and Book of Going Forth By Day—preserve the rituals and spells necessary to attain the status of an *akh*-spirit, so too do the Netherworld Books transfigure the deceased king.

Rather than containing specific spells or recitations, the Netherworld Books record the contents of the very cosmic events in which the king desires to participate, including the pronouncements of the solar deity himself. The title of the Book of the Hidden Chamber incorporates nine statements beginning with the verb $r\underline{h}$, "to know," implying that to know the Netherworldly beings and the solar deity's interactions with them is to be one of the blessed dead, to rise with the sun each day in glorious transfiguration. The Book of Adoring Re in the West, particularly with its hourly division on Late period sarcophagi, may have served as a liturgical composition complementing the cosmographic descriptions of the other Netherworld Books (Manassa 2007a, 473–74).

The Netherworld Books encapsulate the Egyptian ruler's esoteric knowledge of the solar cycle, and a text known as "The King as Solar Priest" provides a summary of that knowledge, shedding additional light on the function of the Netherworld Books corpus.[58] Of particular importance is

---

57. Wente 1982; Willems 1996, 279–84; DuQuesne 2002a; von Lieven 2002; Wiebach-Koepke 2007, 118–25.

58. Assmann 1970; Parkinson (1991, 38; 2002, 62) has suggested a Middle Kingdom date for the treatise. The treatise is known from the solar chapel of Hatshepsut at Deir el-Bahari, a copy from the reign of Amenhotep III with perturbated line order in Luxor Temple, the solar chapel of Ramesses III in his mortuary temple at Medinet

the first half of the text, describing the sun of the day and emphasizing the importance of the king's knowledge:

§1The king N praises Re in the early morning, at the time of his coming forth—when he opens his *nḥp*,[59] when he flies to the sky as Khepri; when he enters into the mouth, when he comes forth from the thighs, in his eastern celestial birth. §2As his father Osiris raises him up, so the arms of Heh and Hehet receive him, so that he might go to rest in the night bark.

§3The king N knows this mysterious language that the eastern *ba*-souls speak, they singing chatter for Re,[60] that he might rise and that he might appear in glory in the horizon; they opening for him the bolts in the portals of the western horizon, that he might navigate upon the celestial ways. §4He knows their emerging and their forms, and their locales that are in the divine land. He knows the place(s) in which they are stationed, after Re takes up the head of the roads. §5He knows that word which the two crews say, while they haul the bark of He of the Horizon. He knows the birth form of Re and his manifestation which is within the flood.[61] He knows that mysterious portal through which the great deity proceeds.

He knows those who are in the day bark, and the great image which is in the night bark. He knows your towrope in the horizon, your navigations[62] which are in Nut. §6Re has set king N upon the earth for the living forever and ever, judging men and pacifying the gods; bringing about Maat and destroying evil. He gives offerings to the deities and funereal offerings to the blessed dead.

The name of king N is in heaven like Re; he lives in joy like Re-Hora-khty. §7Through seeing him the patricians rejoice, the people performing jubilation for him, in his visible form of the child—(it is) the going forth of Re as Khepri.

Habu, and the Edifice of Taharqa on the northwest of the sacred lake at Karnak; nonroyal contexts include the Saite Period tombs of Padiamenope (TT 33) and Pasherientiasu at Saqqara (Betrò 1985); for the whole with comments see Assmann 1995, 17–30.

59. Possibly to be translated "opening the potter's wheel" (see Manassa 2007a, 177–80).

60. The "mysterious language of the baboons" is discussed in te Velde 1988; see also Manassa 2007a, 86–88.

61. For birth form and manifestation at the time of the solar birth, see the references in Darnell 2004, 345–46.

62. For references to the term *ḥp.wt* as ritual navigation, see Darnell 2008, 93, 104–5.

Knowledge, *rḫw*, is the focus of the text. The almost evenly bipartite text is iconographic, emphasizing the cyclical, hieroglyphic, mechanical working of the cosmos, stressing the community of worshippers and events in the personal sphere of the solar deity—the eastern souls (baboons), the words and actions of those intimately associated with the solar bark, the music at sunrise, the opening of the gates of the sky. The treatise also deals with the cosmographic nature of the eastern souls—their emergence across the liminal regions between the transcendental and imminent worlds (*bsi*) and manifestation (the *ḫprw.w* are baboons), as well as their home and position in the context of the solar journey.

The king of Egypt participates in the functioning of the cosmos, applying his knowledge and the accumulated power of the cults of Egypt, into the ever-repeated Armageddon between Egypt and order and the forces of chaos. In order to do this, the ruler must not merely know this text, but the texts to which it refers. With the repetition of "he knows" at the beginning of the divisions of the middle portion of the diurnal half of the treatise, the text echoes the repetitive sections of a litany. Like a litany, these lines describing what the king knows are allusive, recalling the genres and specific texts he must have at his command; like litanies, the King as Solar Priest is a précis of New Kingdom solar literature and iconography.

In the description of the rising sun, the first portion of the King as Solar Priest evokes the cosmographic texts, including the Blueprint of the Course of the Stars (Book of Nut) and the Book of the Day and the Book of the Night, in which the solar bark travels across the body of the sky goddess Nut. The second section of the King as Solar Priest describes how the arms of Osiris raise the solar deity ultimately into the bark of the day, alongside a reference to the arms of male and female embodiments of infinity ("millions")—Heh and Hehet. Cosmic arms appear in a number of scenes within the Netherworld Books, being particularly prevalent in the Book of Caverns and the Books of the Creation of the Solar Disk. A link between arms, Osiris, and the day bark in this passage strongly recalls the concluding scene to the Book of Gates, in which the god Nun lifts up the solar bark to meet the arms of Nut, herself supported by an image of the curled form of Osiris, embodying the Netherworld. In describing the mysterious language of the chattering, baboon-shaped eastern souls, and the manifestation and places of the eastern souls, the treatise makes reference to the cosmic cult-topographic portion of the Book of the Day. The knowledge of the stations, architectural environments, and even words of the Netherworldly denizens and the solar voyagers would encompass that very information as it appears within the corpus of the Netherworld Books of the New Kingdom. The King as Solar Priest treatise claims that the king knows what the introduction to the Book of the Hidden Chamber presents as the knowledge that treatise imparts.[63] The importance of knowledge of the solar environment during the perambulations of the sun, and what must and must not be said, finds confirmation in the third register of Hour 8 of the Book of Gates (Scene 53), in which the solar deity, as "One Hidden of Mysteries," addresses a group of twelve mummiform akh-spirits, each lifting its head from a prone position on a funerary bier: "One Hidden of Mysteries says to them: 'Hail, O akh-spirits! Hail, O Netherworld Dwellers. Opening be to your faces. Clearing be to your darkness. Effectiveness be to your ba-souls, potency be to your shadows;[64] knowledge be to your mouths; honor be to your hearts'" (see p. 302 below; Hornung 1979b, 288–89).

Although the Netherworld Books of the New Kingdom are predominately attested in royal contexts, their applicability is not limited to the pharaoh (Wente 1982; Baines 1990, 12–13). Already during the reign of Thutmose III, the tomb of the vizier Useramun (TT 61) contained a copy of the Book of the Hidden Chamber and the Book of Adoring Re in the West (Hornung 1994b). Papyri with versions of the last four hours of the Book of the Hidden Chamber and elements from the Book of Adoring Re in the West were owned by high priests of Amun and their families during the Third Intermediate Period (see pp. 55–56). The nonroyal use of Netherworld Books continues sporadically through the Saite Period, as in the tomb of Padiamenope (TT 33), which contains nearly complete copies of several Netherworld Books (Piankoff 1947b; Régen 2006, 2014; Traunecker 2014). A small corpus of Nectanebid through early Ptolemaic sarcophagi demonstrates that the textual and visual tradition of the Netherworld Books continues among both royal (e.g., Nectanebo II) and nonroyal individuals until that time (Manassa 2007a, 2007b). Although no complete copy of one of the compositions among the corpus of Netherworld Books is preserved from the Greco-Roman period, isolated scenes on coffins indicate that knowledge of the compositions persisted.[65]

---

63. See the comparison and discussion in Assmann 1995, 25–26.

64. Note the ba-soul and shade "als belebende Mächte," well attested in the Coffin Texts and the Netherworld Books (George 1970, 92–100).

65. Beinlich-Seeber 1998; note also the Ptolemaic papyrus of Nesmin, containing a nearly complete copy of the Book of the Hidden Chamber (p. 131 and n. 7).

The Netherworld Books appear to belong to a tradition of Egyptian funerary literature as compilations of what one must ritually do and recite.[66] The instructions within the introduction to the Book of Adoring Re in the West describe such a process: "One recites this book, while these images are executed in divisions upon the ground, in the deep of the night" (see p. 75). With the Book of Going Forth By Day, the textual process of transference of funerary ritual from the living to the dead—in evidence within the Netherworld Books—is essentially complete, with the "he" and "she" of earlier texts becoming the "I" of the funerary text as magical device in the mind and mouth of the dead (Servajean 2003). The interconnection of knowledge and ritual within the Netherworld Books, significant for both the living and the dead, suggests that in some instances, the cryptographic annotations may—as apparently in the Book of the Day and the Book of the Night—signal solar-esoteric significance of a passage (see below).

TOPOGRAPHY OF THE NETHERWORLD BOOKS: CONCEPTIONS OF SPACE AND TIME

Duat (*Dwꜣ.t*), here translated as "Netherworld," is a multivalent term, referring to a place beyond the horizon, a liminal area alternately in the earth or in the sky (Allen 1988, 5–6), but predominately a chthonic realm. In the Blueprint of the Course of the Stars, the entire Duat is "any place free of the sky and free of the earth" (von Lieven 2007c, 384). The Duat is simultaneously the chthonic body of Osiris and the celestial body of Nut, in both cases a place of gestation (Beaux 1994); the Duat could thus be equated with the physical space of the tomb (Allen 1989, 25; Hays 2009, 195–96). In secular texts, the term Duat can designate the inner chambers of the tomb (Capart, Gardiner, van der Walle 1936, 178), an apt equation of Netherworldly topography and terrestrial architecture, as the religious treatises that covered the walls were intended to enact just such a transformation.

As early as the Old Kingdom, a tomb can be designated a "Netherworld," Duat, an extension of the association of the royal necropolis and the horizon (Roberson 2012, 18). The New Kingdom royal tomb serves as a model of the Netherworldly sphere, each element designed to harness the power of solar resurrection—from the light-filled corridors of Shu, to the

---

66. In the Book of the Hidden Chamber, in some cases the verb *iri*, "to act," is substituted for the verb *rḫ*, "to know," when describing the efficacy of the composition (Wente 1982, 164–66).

well shaft symbolically accessing the limitless power of Nun (Abitz 1974; Roberson 2012, 18–19), to the sarcophagus chamber, with its microcosm of the Netherworld and the process of solar regeneration, the sarcophagus itself.[67] The Netherworld Books transform a chamber within the tomb into the "Hidden Chamber"—the very template mentioned throughout the Book of the Hidden Chamber. The dialectical relationship between text and architecture within the royal tombs extends to every surface, with the ceiling often being included to create a cyclical decorative scheme within a particular room.[68]

The "Netherworld" of the ancient Egyptian universe possessed dual properties as a defined extent of space and length of time (Hegenbarth-Reichardt 2006; Bónannó 2015). In the Book of the Hidden Chamber and the Book of Gates, the Netherworld is divided into twelve units, which can be measured as a unit of distance as well as a unit of time; for example, the first unit—hour—of the Book of the Hidden Chamber is 120 *iteru* in length, while the second and third units are each 309 *iteru* (see pp. 138, 140, 147, 157),[69] and like each of the twelve units within the book, each one also represents an hour of time. This hour of time is measured from the perspective of the earthly sphere, for that same unit of time can be conceived of as a "lifetime" for the Netherworld denizens. Thus, the Netherworld consists of units of space-time through which the sun god must travel. Several scenes within the Netherworld Books describe the destruction and accompanying re-creation of time.[70] The interaction of space and time in the Netherworld Books ultimately leads to the re-creation of the cosmos each night. As the sun descends into the depth of the Nun-waters and visits his Osirian corpse, time itself is renewed, enabling the resurrection of the dead king

---

67. Such architectural symbolism is not confined to royal tomb architecture, as demonstrated by the chamber resembling a giant sarcophagus within the Osireion at Abydos (Frankfort 1933a, 26–27; Roberson 2012, 28–32).

68. Discussions of royal tomb architecture abound; see, e.g., Barta 1984; Abitz 1989, 1990, 1992; Roberson 2012, 15–59; Wilkinson and Weeks 2016. For these same principles applied to sarcophagi, see Manassa 2007a, 443–44; Roberson 2012, 59–63.

69. For the measurements within the Book of the Hidden Chamber within the context of attempts to measure the Netherworld in other funerary literature, see Quirke 2003.

70. Among the many possible examples, compare the Book of Gates, Scene 20 (p. 274), Scene 36 (p. 288), Scene 49 (p. 299); in the Books of the Creation of the Solar Disk, note the scene in the Tomb of Ramesses IX, Right Wall, Register 2, Scene 18 (pp. 515–16).

and indeed all blessed dead. The geography of the Netherworld finds its most detailed expressions within the Book of the Hidden Chamber[71] and the Book of Gates, which clearly divide the Netherworldly topography into different zones (Barta 1990a, 47–50). In the Book of the Hidden Chamber, Hours 1–3 are a watery space with irrigated fields, while Hours 4–5 are desert regions inhabited by ophidian creatures and dominated by sloping corridors (Hour 4) and a pyramidal mound (Hour 5). Hours 4–5 are designated the realm of Rosetau, the "Place of Hauling," the sloping passageways of Hour 4 more specifically termed the "Mysterious paths of the Place of Hauling, sacred roads of Imhet" (Manassa 2007a, 427–28). A pyramid-shaped feature defines Hour 5, demonstrating an unusual interaction of registers within that hour and its accompanying geography (Backes 2014, 85–86). An oval-shaped "cavern of Sokar" appears in the lowest register of Hour 5 as the site of the stormy sound of re-creation.

The water on which the sun bark sails reemerges in the final seven hours of the night in the Book of the Hidden Chamber. By Hour 6, natural features give way to man-made topography, with the upper register of that hour depicting shrines of Heliopolis (including Kheraha), which contain the parts of the solar corpse. Heliopolitan toponyms, such as the Benben sanctuary and the Temple of the Benben also appear within the Book of Adoring Re in the West and prominently in Hour 6 of the Book of Gates (see pp. 101, 289–90); even outside of the Netherworld Books, the city of Heliopolis could be identified as the burial place of the solar corpse.[72]

Hour 7 of the Book of the Hidden Chamber is situated within the "grotto of Osiris," and the sandbank of the monstrous serpent Apep dominates the landscape, threatening the passage of the solar bark. Hour 8 is divided into ten separate caverns, each closed off by a door; the architectural setting of Hour 8 facilitates the reverberation of a variety of noises within each of the caverns, which ultimately represent re-creative sounds

---

71. Robinson 2003 provides an overview of topographic elements in the Book of the Hidden Chamber and its relationship to the clockwise motion of the hours in the tomb of Thutmose III; his equations with earthly geological formations are to be regarded with caution (compare the equation of Wernes with paleo-lakes in Schneider 2010, an equally tenuous proposition). Additional analyses of the topographical features of the Book of the Hidden Chamber appears in Hegenbarth-Reichardt 2006, 163–81; Maruéjol 2007, 350–53; Stadler 2014.

72. Kitchen 1979, 597, ll. 7–8: "Heliopolis, which hides his body, the *ba*-temple is his Netherworld of Egypt." For additional parallel texts, see Manassa 2007a, 424–27.

like that in the lowest register of Hour 5 (Manassa 2008). Hours 9–10 are watery realms, and the chaotic waters of Nun intrude into the lowest register of Hour 10, in which float the drowned yet blessed dead.

The punishment of enemies becomes one of the chief themes of Hour 11 of the Book of the Hidden Chamber, and an appropriate landscape of fiery pits appears in the lowest register. A serpent again dominates the final hour of the night in the Book of the Hidden Chamber, a gigantic creature through which the sun god must sail from tail to mouth in a physical representation of rejuvenation. The eastern horizon appears in the form of the head and arms of the god Shu at the rounded end of the Underworld; the entire Netherworldly space is an enormous oval, like the ovoid chamber of Sokar in the lowest register of Hour 5 of the night. This same oval shape provides the impetus for the form of the sarcophagus chamber in the tomb of Thutmose III (see above).

In the Book of Gates, "Hour 1" of the night is actually the entrance portal to the Netherworld (Barguet 1975, 30–31), dominated by the hill of the horizon, guardian deities, and the head and neck of the solar god. In Hour 1, some deities and one half of the mountain of the western horizon appear upside down in relation to the rest of the scene. Entry into the Netherworld may be envisaged as an inverted emergence into a mirror cosmos, with the blessed dead enjoying a reorientation to their new environment, and the damned remaining upside-down (Darnell 2004, 426–48). This corresponds to the concept of creation from de(con)struction that finds such emphasis in the Book of Caverns—the "atomizing" of the self results in a recreation of the blessed dead but leaves the several portions of the dismembered damned to cook in the fires of the Netherworldly deities.

Beyond the portal that forms the entirety of Hour 1 of the Book of Gates, each subsequent hour is introduced by an elaborate doorway, indicating that man-made architectural features delimit the natural space-time divisions of the Netherworld. Not all hours are rich in landmarks; Hour 2 consists almost entirely of groups of deities lacking a specific geographical affiliation, aside from their placement near the doorway of the hour of the night. One of the few consistent topographical themes of the Netherworld Books does appear within Hour 2 of the Book of Gates, as it does throughout the Book of Caverns: the punishment of the damned is executed in the lowest register of the hour, in the bowels of each division of the night.

The Lake of Fire in Hour 3 of the Book of Gates (Scene 10) has an interesting dual nature: it provides refreshing water for the blessed dead,[73] but a blasting flame against the damned. According to the annotation: "This waterway is filled with ears of barley, the water of this waterway being fire. When they see its water and they smell the stench which is in it, the birds fly away" (p. 266). The stench—decomposition—indicates that the dual nature of the water ultimately evokes the dual workings of deconstruction, both the regeneration of the blessed dead and the destruction of the damned. A lake in the lower register of Hour 5 of the Book of the Hidden Chamber is experienced in similarly divergent fashion, depending on one's status in the Netherworld.

Lakes appear again in the upper register of Hour 4 of the Book of Gates—the "Lake of Life," guarded by jackal-headed deities, and the "Lake of Uraei," guarded by rearing cobras. While the Lake of Life predictably dispenses life-giving provisions, the uraei at their lake blast flames against Re's enemies. Yet another lake in the middle register of Hour 4, with an unusual, dual triangular, ramp-like shape, is the setting for the rebirth of the hours from a multi-coiled serpent.

Hour 5 of the Book of Gates is filled with cultivated land, also referred to as the "Field of Reeds," a stark contrast to the sandy region in Hour 5 of the Book of the Hidden Chamber. Scene 24 of the Book of Gates further emphasizes the role of man—or here *akh*-spirits—in shaping the Netherworldly landscape; a row of twelve male figures carry a measuring rope with which to establish the field boundaries for the deceased. The lower register of Hour 5 is unique in incorporating foreigners into the chthonic realm, although the annotation to Scene 30 does not suggest that foreign toponyms are included within the Netherworld, only the inhabitants of the different realms of the Egyptian cosmos. Following Hour 5 is an interior space, the Judgment Hall of Osiris.

Hour 6 of the Book of Gates shares with Hour 6 of the Book of the Hidden Chamber an emphasis on Heliopolitan toponyms. In Scene 38, gods called "Those Hidden of Arm, who carry the mystery" guide the solar deity to the "Temple of the Benben," a Heliopolitan edifice, which is also mentioned prominently in Scene 39. The "mystery" that the gods carry in Scene 38 is the solar corpse, whose constituent parts appear in burial enclosures in the upper register of Hour 6 of the Book of the Hidden Chamber. Just as enemies of the sun god burn within the Temple of the Benben in

---

73. A collection of references to the Lake of Fire in Middle Kingdom through Third Intermediate period sources can be found in Abbas 2010, 29–34.

Scene 38, the lower register of Hour 6 expands upon the punishment of the damned with a "flaming pit" guarded by a fire-spitting uraeus.

Hour 7 places the destruction of the enemies in the middle register, in a scene immediately in front of the solar bark. The lowest register is instead reserved for the depiction of grain-producing fields, resuming the theme of fertile land present in Hour 5. While Hour 8 is devoid of specific topographic features, Hour 9 of the Book of Gates provides another interesting toponym: the "Island of Fire." While the annotation to Scenes 55 and 56 indicate that the Island of Fire is a Netherworldly location deep within the chthonic realm, earlier mortuary literature situated the island in a liminal area between this world and the next, at times even identifying the Island of Fire with the tomb chapel (Willems 2001, 292) or the land of the living.[74] The Island of Fire is juxtaposed with the waters of chaos, the Nun-waters, in the middle register; those waters hold drowned individuals, who, like in Hour 10 of the Book of the Hidden Chamber, are members of the blessed dead.

In the final three hours of the Book of Gates, Re approaches the eastern horizon of heaven as he repeatedly battles the chaos serpent Apep. The concluding scene summarizes the entire solar journey and its anthropomorphized topography—as Nun lifts up the solar bark, the solar scarab and disk are received by Nut, who herself is supported by an image of Osiris, literally bent back upon himself, "encircling" the Netherworld. The entire scene is placed on a watery backdrop, a theme resumed in the final scene of the Book of Caverns.

The Book of Caverns, Books of the Creation of the Solar Disk, and Books of the Solar-Osirian Unity, lacking the divisions into twelve discrete space-time units, present a less unified perspective on the topography of the Netherworld. While the Book of Caverns does not preserve an ancient title, it is an appropriate name, since the "cavern," Egyptian *qrr.t*, predominates as a topographical feature. Division 1 of the six divisions within the Book of Caverns describes this portion of the Netherworldly realm as "first cavern of the West," with the land of the setting sun interchange-

---

74. Eyre 2002, 81–82 (quote from p. 81): "The Island of Fire is envisaged in the mortuary literature as a place of passage at the edge of the cosmos, where the vision of fire is both dangerous but also positive. It is a seat of primordial creation, where the sun-god emerged from the waters of chaos." In Coffin Text Spell 75 (CT 1.365b–366a), the *ba*-soul of the deceased is sexually active with the "people who are in the Island of Fire." Willems (1996, 311–12) interprets these people as the living upon earth.

able with the Duat, the Netherworld. Annotations throughout the Book of Caverns reference toponyms present in the other compositions, but their exact locations or positions relative to one another are lacking; for example, in Scene 3, the sun god addresses three guardian serpents whose purview includes the "Mysterious Place," the "Place of Destruction," and the "Place of Hauling." The lower registers of the Netherworldly caverns are identified particularly closely with the Ḥtmy.t, "Place of Destruction," in which the damned are not simply annihilated, but deconstructed (see pp. 344–45). Division 2 of the Book of Caverns is literally "the second cavern of the first," a reference to the duality of the Netherworld itself. The cavern within Division 3, the middle of the night, is described in reference to the Aker, the double sphinx that guards the corpse of Osiris; the embodiment of the Netherworldly landscape as Aker in the deepest region of the Netherworld in the Book of Caverns provides one of the few intersections with the topography of the Book of the Hidden Chamber, which locates the chthonic sphinx in Hour 5.

The second half of the Book of Caverns, the final three divisions, continues to emphasize general toponyms, especially the Netherworld and the West. In contrast, the solar deity is the "One of the Horizon," whose disk is born within the Earth, the Netherworld. In Division 5, two divine entities—Mysterious One and Hidden One—fill the height of all three registers. The goddess Shetayt, "Mysterious One" is specifically said to stand in the Lower Netherworld, while her head reaches into the Upper Netherworld (Scene 50); she thus embodies the entire Netherworld, like the reclining Re-Osiris in the Enigmatic Wall of the tomb of Ramesses IX, who similarly is a giant deity that fills the entire space of the eastern horizon. In Litanies 7–8 of the Book of Caverns, the sun god traverses the Mysterious One, indicating that she embodies the chthonic realm, like Tatenen or Aker (see above). In Litanies 17–18, the text refers to the grotto of the corpse of Osiris and the grotto of Nephthys, and the latter becomes the site of the solar head and corpse. As the sun god sails through the final portion of the Netherworld to emerge triumphantly, the annotation to the concluding scene describes the great god entering the "eastern mountain."

The annotations within the Books of the Creation of the Solar Disk preserve a pattern similar to the Book of Caverns in their approach to toponyms. In the tomb of Ramesses VI, Section A (Scene 2), the goddess Mysterious One appears again as the embodiment of the Netherworld, as in the Book of Caverns, Division 5, Scene 50—her feet are in the Lower Netherworld, while her head is in the Upper Netherworld. In Scene 5 of the same section (p. 470), ram-headed gods are said to guard the "mysterious and hidden sky that is in the Netherworld," an unusual reference to a celestial vault within the Netherworld. As in several of the Netherworld Books, the lowest registers of the nightly journey in the Books of the Creation of the Solar Disk emphasize the punishment of the damned in the realm called the "Place of Punishment" (Ramesses VI, Section A, Scene 18). In Section B of the composition within the tomb of Ramesses VI, the double-lion Aker is again placed in the bowels of the Netherworld (Register 4, Scene 40), suggesting that the horizontal distribution of the registers in the Books of the Creation of the Solar Disk preserve some of the geographical distinctiveness of the other books.

All three templates of the Books of the Solar-Osirian Unity share a syncopation of the Netherworldly space (pp. 523–24). On the Second Shrine of Tutankhamun, the head and neck of Re signal the entrance to the Netherworld, paralleling Hour 1 of the Book of Gates, which is itself the gateway to the entire Netherworldly sphere. The Tutankhamun shrine identifies the top register of deities with the "Upper Region," while the lowest register is the "Place of Destruction"; the giant deity who fills the entire height of Side One thus serves as a male counterpart to the goddess Mysterious One as described in the Book of Caverns and Books of the Creation of the Solar Disk. Side Two mentions the Mysterious Place but does not specify its location. The ceiling of Corridor G in the tomb of Ramesses VI situates most of the figures within the Place of Destruction or the Mysterious Place and includes a reference to Imhet, a toponym otherwise found only in Hours 4–5 of the Book of the Hidden Chamber (p. 31). The final attestation of the Books of the Solar-Osirian Unity is the Enigmatic Wall in the tomb of Ramesses IX, which locates the Place of Destruction in the lowest register, and again, incorporates a giant deity who fills all of the space between that depth of the Netherworld and the Upper Region.

<h2 align="center">DATING THE NETHERWORLD BOOKS</h2>

A list of the first attestations of each of the Netherworld Books reveals a basic division into "early" and "late" books, the "early" books having twelve divisions and depictions of the solar bark, and the later books featuring the solar disk traveling through different regions of the Underworld. The first extant copies of the "early" books—the Book of the Hidden Chamber and the Book of Gates—date to the Eighteenth Dynasty, while the Books of the Creation of the Solar Disk and the Book of Caverns are first fully attested during the Ramesside Period. The earliest extant copy of the Book of Adoring Re in the West appears on the shroud of Thutmose III, with the illustrations of the forms of Re present on a pillar in the burial chamber of that ruler's tomb. The existence of the textual component of one of the Netherworld Books on a movable element from the burial equipment is cautionary for assuming that the earliest surviving appearance of a Netherworld book is necessarily the earliest occurrence of said text. At least some of the Netherworld Books may have existed earlier on funerary equipment that is no longer extant.

The "late" books first appear in the immediate post-Amarna Period, with enigmatic texts from the Books of the Solar-Osirian Unity, including a scene later known from the Books of the Creation of the Solar Disk, decorating the two long sides of the Second Shrine of Tutankhamun. Although the first occurrences of the entirety of the "late" books, the Book of Caverns and the Books of the Creation of the Solar Disk, are Nineteenth and Twentieth Dynasty royal tombs, those scenes on the Second Shrine of Tutankhamun strongly suggest that parts of both compositions—or some common templates of sources for the various compositions—may date to the late Eighteenth Dynasty (Darnell 2004, 468). The initial complete attestation of the Book of Caverns is in the entrance corridor of the Osireion at Abydos, decorated during the reign of Merneptah (Werning 2011b, 15–17); the tomb of Ramesses VI preserves the most comprehensive version of the Books of the Creation of the Solar Disk, although the earliest attestation of a reasonably large portion of a version of the composition is the Osireion at Abydos. In all of these examples, however, one cannot necessarily conclude that the first appearance of any book corresponds to its date of composition.

The dating of the Netherworld Books involves multiple fields of research, ranging from the question of the origin of the surviving versions of the compositions, to the grammar of the treatises, to the history and development of the imagery (both visual and textual) evoked within the individual compositions. In at least two cases—the Books of the Creation of the Solar Disk and the Books of the Solar-Osirian Unity—the textual history is complicated by the existence of compilations and incorporation of extracts from other books. The Books of the Creation of the Solar Disk only survive in an extensive fashion in the tomb of Ramesses VI, and the lack of comparative material makes it impossible to judge how complete that text is; the close relationship between the Books of the Creation of the Solar Disk and the Book of Caverns is suggested by the incorporation of scenes from both within the same registers in the tomb of Ramesses IX (Roberson 2012, 44).

Grammar, paleography, and content of the Netherworld Books all point towards a Second Intermediate period or early New Kingdom date for the "early" Netherworld Books, with the "late" books possibly dating, as with their first attestations, to the immediate post-Amarna period. While the presence of linguistic features suggestive of an archaic, even Old Kingdom date, have been noted within the corpus,[75] a proper analysis of those features in context suggests a date no earlier than the Second Intermediate period or early New Kingdom (Werning 2013). The sum of linguistic evidence indicates that none of the surviving Netherworld Books were composed in their extant forms earlier than the Middle Kingdom (Jansen-Winkeln 2004), although the possibility of the contributions and influences of earlier sources on the various elements of the corpus remains an open question. Independent confirmation of any pre-New Kingdom existence of the Netherworld Books is sparse, although the story of the Shipwrecked Sailor may provide an early allusion to the seventy-five forms of Re appearing in the Book of Adoring Re in the West, or at least a prototype thereof (Baines 1990b). Funerary architectural forms of the Middle Kingdom may provide early templates for the topography of some of the Netherworld Books (Gestermann 1999; Rössler-Köhler 1999; Wegner 2009).

Cryptography in the Netherworld Books

Beginning modestly during the Old Kingdom and continuing through the Greco-Roman period, the ancient Egyptian script made use of alternative signs and atypical values for more commonly used signs.[76] Texts employing these nonstandard, and therefore initially uncommon and seemingly obfuscating signs and sign values, are termed "enigmatic" or "cryptographic" (Brunner 1973). From Old Kingdom and First Intermediate period forays, with slightly longer and more complex snippets of Middle Kingdom date, cryptography becomes significant during the New Kingdom, occurring in royal titularies, in inscriptions from pri-

---

75. Quack 1997, 2000; see also Klotz 2011, 490.

76. Recent overviews of Egyptian cryptography in the Netherworld Books and the basic principles of enigmatic writing include Darnell 2004, 1–34; von Lieven 2007c, 27–34; Werning 2008; Klotz 2012b; Roberson 2012, 93–99; 2013, 3–8; Espinel 2014.

vate tombs, in private graffiti, and throughout the Netherworld Books preserved in the royal tombs. For the most part only partially cryptographic, select annotations in the Book of the Hidden Chamber, Book of Gates, Book of Caverns, and Books of the Creation of the Solar Disk are accompanied by transcriptions in normal hieroglyphic orthography; the cryptographic passages in the Books of the Solar-Osirian Unity are not so transcribed. Aside from the bulk of the cryptographic annotations in the Solar-Osirian texts, only the text of the Judgement Hall of Osiris in the Book of Gates (Scene 33), portions of Hours 4–5 of the Book of the Hidden Chamber, and scattered passages in the Book of Caverns are in full cryptographic orthographies.

During the Late period and throughout the Ptolemaic and Roman eras, reaching a complicated height in the texts of the temple of Esna, a number of signs and sign values occurring earlier only in cryptographic compositions became common in standard hieroglyphic texts. Champollion's original decipherment of Egyptian having been based primarily on a study of Ptolemaic hieroglyphic texts, with their "normalized" late cryptography, early Egyptologists not surprisingly, but nevertheless somewhat precociously, began to approach the earlier cryptographic texts. Such work did not have great issue, however, and cryptography languished somewhat until the mid-twentieth century, and the works of Étienne Drioton (1953a) and H. W. Fairman (1943, 1945). The best controls of a translation of a cryptographic text are the data of any accompanying iconography, and the search for texts that parallel both the content and concepts of the cryptographic passage.

Drioton's work postulates a system of acrophony, whereby a sign can have the value of the first radical of any word with which that sign is associated. Creating a near limitless potential number of phonetic values for each hieroglyphic sign, Drioton's "system" lacks a logical means to identify the most likely value of a particular cryptographic sign, and his resulting translations are normally divorced from both the context and the associated iconography of an enigmatic text.[77] More recent scholarship that continues to employ Drioton's acrophonic principles suffers from similar

---

77. As noted already by Fairman 1943; 1945; the one sign that appears frequently in the enigmatic Netherworld Books for which Fairman may allow an acrophonically derived sign value, the spewing mouth, has now been explained phonetically (Darnell 2004, 42–45).

shortcomings.[78] Instead, visual and phonetic substitutions[79] provide a systematic method for deciphering enigmatic texts; the translations of cryptographic compositions in the Netherworld Books that have employed these basic principles have resulted in annotations that correspond both to the adjacent imagery as well as to parallel texts within the Netherworld Book corpus. In each of the following principles of Egyptian enigmatic writing, the cryptic orthography of a word does not always correspond to that of the word in *Normalschrift*—determinatives are uncommon,[80] and ideograms are common; the normal reading order of signs may be altered for effect—"perturbation."

One of the most common principles of enigmatic sign derivation within the Netherworld Books is substitution. In substitutional cryptography, the normal appearance of a sign can be altered, such as by choosing an uncommon sign that represents the same object as a more normal sign; a common example is the use of the mouth viewed from the side (▷) in place of the standard hieroglyph of the mouth seen from the front (⬡). Substitutions of kind or class are frequently employed—one bird sign (usually a *s3*-goose [🦆] or abbreviated hieratic-style bird [🐦]) can be used for any other bird sign, or a plant sign (usually a reed leaf [𓏭] or three-pronged plant [🌿]) can replace another plant sign (fig. 1.11; see p. 538 for a translation of the text). The principle of *pars pro toto* also applies in substitutional cryptography; for example, the pupil (○) may replace the hieroglyph representing the entire eye (⬯), thereby adopting the ideographic and phonetic values of the eye hieroglyph. Some *pars pro toto* derivations are less obvious, with the part in question depicting a derivation from the original hieroglyph, one of the most frequently attested examples being the animal skin (🦴) with the value *k*, deriving, via consonantal principle (see below), from the complete bull (🐂), *k3*. Purposeful confusions of hieratic orthographies of otherwise unrelated signs can appear as a form of substitutional cryptography; for example, plural strokes (| |) can

---

78. Compare the presentations of Morenz 2005; 2008, arguing in favor of acrophony, with the persuasive critique in Klotz 2102b.

79. Termed "direct representation" and the "consonantal principle" in Fairman's seminal works (1945, 62–67; 1943, 287–305).

80. Exceptions to the common lack of determinatives in enigmatic inscriptions are some sections of the Books of the Creation of the Solar Disk (Roberson 2012, 94) and the texts on the ceilings of Corridor G in the Tomb of Ramesses VI (see Darnell 2004, 169–70).

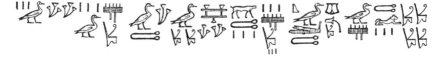

Fig. 1.11. Enigmatic annotation from the Second Shrine of Tutankhamun
(Side 1, Scene 3) (Piankoff and Rambova 1955, fig. 41,
reproduced by permission of Princeton University Press)

acquire the value *p* based on the use of three vertical strokes to write the
hieratic form of the stool/mat (□).

An additional and frequently attested source of enigmatic sign value
derivation at work in the Netherworld Books is the "consonantal principle," whereby weak sounds are omitted from the sign value, leaving
only the strong radicals as the phonetic values of new uniliterals—hence
"alphabetic," or abgadic—value for the sign (Fairman 1945, 62–64). Alphabetic cryptography (or more properly abgad cryptography), such as that
employed throughout the Books of the Solar-Osirian Unity, consists primarily of uniliteral signs, and other signs cryptographically acquiring a
uniliteral phonetic value. Enigmatic sign values can employ a combination
of both substitutional and consonantal principles; for example, the three-
pronged plant (𓇒), whose normal hieroglyphic value is *ḥn*, can substitute
for the *ḥꜣ*-plant (𓆷), which by consonantal principle becomes a uniliteral *ḥ*
(*ḥꜣ* > *ḥ*). Closely related to the consonantal principle are other sign values
derived from phonetic shifts and the interchangeability of certain conso-
nants, such as *ḏ* > *d*, *ṯ* > *t*, and *z* > *s*.

Less common within the Netherworld Books are ornamental and thematic cryptography. In ornamental cryptography, the decorative aspect
of hieroglyphic inscriptions could be expanded, royal epithets and lauds
of gods being written as friezes of divinities and geniuses, carrying various objects; here words literally march across the stones before the reader
(Drioton 1936). This form of cryptography appears primarily in monumental temple contexts, although examples do appear in the New Kingdom royal tombs. Thematic cryptography uses figures and objects of a
cryptic inscription to create two, perhaps differing, levels of meaning—
one pictorial, one textual. Enigmatic orthographies may at times allow for
two readings of a word, one when viewed as a cryptogram, another when
seen as *Normalschrift*, and an enigmatic orthography may even depict the
underlying concept behind the word so written. When an ideogram is
involved, such an orthography may cross into thematic cryptography.

The ancient Egyptians did not consider cryptography to be other than an extension of the normal system of sign value derivations in their scripts, and no term for "cryptography" exists in Egyptian.[81] The particular association of cryptography with the solar arcana and the Solar-Osirian unity during the New Kingdom does appear, however, to serve as a graphic evocation of the Solar-Osirian "mystery" (*štꜣw*) itself. Cryptography possessed a particularly solar significance in ancient Egypt, focusing as it does in the Netherworld Books on the regeneration of the sun and the liminal regions of the cosmos (Darnell 2004, 471–82). Cryptographic texts are not uniformly distributed throughout the Netherworld Books, but become densest at moments of cosmic danger, contact with the chaotic Nun waters, or the unification of Re and Osiris. Enigmatic annotations, accompanied by *Normalschrift* translations, in Hours 4–5 of the Book of the Hidden Chamber are thus associated with the land of Rosetau, where the solar bark must be hauled over the sandy landscape, and the descent into the chamber of Sokar signals the sun's renewal in the Nun waters. The Book of Gates employs cryptography in two scenes: portions of Hour 1, which may describe the decomposition and reconstruction of the eye of Horus (Manassa 2007a, 21–29); and the entirety of texts within the Judgment Hall of Osiris (Scene 33), the moment when the fate of the cosmos hangs in the balance.[82] Within the Book of Caverns and the Books of the Solar-Osirian Unity, cryptography expresses the mystery of the union of Re and Osiris, labeling the giant goddess Mysterious One, the counterpart of the corpse of Osiris (Book of Caverns, Division 5, Scene 50) and the combined Re-Osiris in various manifestations (Books of the Solar-Osirian Unity). Cryptographic texts within the Netherworld Books thus mirror the mystery of the Solar-Osirian Unity itself, and while challenging, these texts were intended properly to reveal their secrets to the initiated reader, who should not reveal such hard-won and cosmically significant knowledge; this underlying duality of enigmatic writing as vehicle of knowledge and barrier to understanding is described in a cryptographic passage in

---

81. The term *itnw* (*WÄS* 1:146.1–3; Redford 1986, 85 n. 42) describes difficult passages in texts and does not refer to "mysterious writings. For a suggested reading of a cryptographic group as the term "cryptogram," see Werning 2008, 133–34.

82. The two scenes may also share an emphasis on the *udjat*-eyes, whose constituent parts may have been weighed within the empty scale pans in the Judgement Hall (Manassa 2006, 137–41).

the cosmographic Book of the Day, following a passage concerning the liminal geography of the souls of the eastern horizon:[83]

I know them in hieroglyphs;
they are four statements of knowledge
within which you have entered (i.e., to which you are initiated);
do not speak (this) so that just anyone can hear!

POST–NEW KINGDOM OCCURRENCES OF THE NETHERWORLD BOOKS

With the end of the Ramesside period, and the removal of the royal necropolis from Thebes, both the architecture developed in the tombs in the Valley of the Kings and the resulting template for architectonic interrelationships of texts and tomb elements disappear. Although excerpts from the Book of the Hidden Chamber and the Books of the Creation of the Solar Disk appear in royal tombs of the Twenty-First and Twenty-Second Dynasties at Tanis (surveyed in Lull 2002; Taylor 2010a, 223–26), a more diverse sampling of excerpts from the Netherworld Books appears in the tomb decoration, painted coffins, and funerary papyri of non-royal funerary assemblages during the first millennium BCE.

This Late period "afterlife" of the New Kingdom Netherworld Books— like that of the Pyramid Texts, Coffin Texts, and Book of Going Forth By Day from the Twenty-Sixth Dynasty through the Greco-Roman Period (Smith 2009, 16–17)—represents a reproductive tradition (Assmann 1995, 4–11). The post-New Kingdom occurrences of the Netherworld Books are not slavish copies, but rather embody a continuing process of editing and augmenting the religious treatises of the past.[84] The Late period practice of intertextual commentary reveals an ancient Egyptian understanding of the texts here termed the Netherworld Books as a discrete genre, supporting as well the separation of these texts from the cosmographic treatises,

---

83. Piankoff 1942b, 86; Darnell 2004, 473–75. The hieroglyphic copy in Müller-Roth 2008, 128 (and commentary on p. 132–33) misidentifies the final bird sign in l. 33 and presents an imperfect restoration of the text; traces visible within the tomb and in Piankoff and Rambova 1954, pl. 151 support the reading of Piankoff 1942b, 86 with the exception of that final bird hieroglyph, which does indeed have a ḫꜣ-sign in its beak rather than a fish (Darnell 2004, 464–75).

84. Manassa 2007a, 437–78; for the Book of Caverns in particular, see Werning 2017.

which only rarely participate in the Late period commentary tradition on sarcophagi.

During the Third Intermediate period, texts variously termed "Amduat Papyri," "Litany Papyri," "Aker Papyri," and "Mythological Papyri" incorporate portions of the earlier Netherworld Books.[85] The "Amduat Papyri" are appropriately designated, as they bear the title *mdꜣ.t imy-dwꜣ.t*, "Book of What Is in the Netherworld (Amduat)"; their decoration consists of the last four hours of the Book of the Hidden Chamber or segments thereof. The Litany Papyri contain figures from the Book of Adoring Re in the West, the "Litany of Re," and can incorporate forms of the solar deity peculiar to the papyri, unattested in New Kingdom versions of the composition. The Aker Papyri, of which only a few examples are known, derive the majority of their decoration from the Books of the Creation of the Solar Disk, particularly that part of the composition that Piankoff termed the "Book of Aker," dominated by a large depiction of the horizon-deity Aker (Roberson 2012, 295–99). The known Aker Papyri can also incorporate texts and scenes from other Netherworld Books, including elements of the Book of the Hidden Chamber and the Book of Gates. The Mythological Papyri (compare figs. 1.8–10), having the most expansive range of sources, draw from a large number of compositions, including not only all of the major Netherworld Books appearing in the present volume (Manassa 2007a, 438–39), but also scenes attested only in the papyri and on contemporaneous coffins (Niwiński 2000).

The principle by which various components of the Netherworld Books were chosen during the Third Intermediate period differs from that utilized during the Late period, the transition between the two periods representing a shift from the employment of portions of texts to allude to the whole to an interchangeability of parts. The overriding compositional principle operating within Third Intermediate period survivals of the Netherworld Books is that of *pars pro toto*—an hour, scene, or deity from a Netherworld Book may substitute for the entirety of the composition from which it derives, and the final hours of the night (Hours 9–12) in the Book of the Hidden Chamber are sufficient to represent the totality of the solar journey. While the juxtaposition of various elements may appear to be at times capricious, the decorative scheme is often theologi-

---

85. Important publications of these corpora include Piankoff and Rambova 1957; Sadek 1985; Niwiński 1989a; for additional references to Amudat papyri, see p. 130 and n. 4.

cally complex, frequently stressing the concept of the unification of Re and Osiris (Niwiński 1987–1988). The decoration within sets of papyri and coffins can intentionally complement one another as well, indicating that the principle of *pars pro toto* extended across media (Niwinński 1989a, 219–28; 1989b), linking both the earlier texts and the elements of funerary equipment on which they appeared.

Between the Twenty-Second Dynasty and the Thirtieth Dynasty, the principle of "interchangeability of parts" began to guide the decoration of funerary monuments, particularly those containing texts and scenes from the Netherworld Books. In this new form of theological expression, entire segments of various treatises are integrated and associated in order to convey an understanding of the underlying significance of the different elements (Manassa 2007a, 441–45). These hybrid compositions also represent an attempt to fashion a type of scholarly commentary in which the juxtaposed portions of different Netherworld Books supplement and explain elements of those earlier compositions, a process that appears to have begun already during the Twenty-Sixth Dynasty.[86] That an ancient editor could both attempt and carry out such redacting reveals that the complexities of the Netherworld Books represent an ultimately flexible and cohesive corpus of interrelated iconographic and conceptual segments. The primarily Nectanebid period sarcophagi that represent the bulk of the surviving examples of the practice of "interchangeability of parts"—one such text termed *sš n ꜥ.t imnt.t*, "writings of the Hidden Chamber" (Manassa 2007a, 283–85)—provide the best evidence that the ancient Egyptians indeed recognized the Netherworld Books as they appear in the present volume as a compositional unity.

A Note on the Translations

The following chapters present brief introductions to each of the compositions, followed by a translation and notes that predominately address the theological issues of the texts. The notes are intended to augment, rather than replace, the annotated editions of other authors mentioned in the introduction of each chapter. While some notes refer to specific linguistic

---

86. As suggested by the decoration within the tomb of Padiamenope (TT 33) (see p. 40), as well as the use of the Book of the Hidden Chamber and Books of the Creation of the Solar Disk alongside portals from the Book of Gates in the tomb of Mutirdis (TT 410) (Assmann 1977a; Roberson 2012, 49–51).

forms, such as distinctive use of particles or grammatical constructions frequent in the Netherworld Books (such as the *sw sḏm=f*), a detailed grammatical analysis of the compositions remains outside the scope of the present work.[87] Names for units of the text as well as descriptions of scenes and individual deities are written in small caps and a smaller font, respectively, to distinguish them clearly from translations of the ancient Egyptian labels and annotations. Dividing the text into easily referenced units is challenging—scene divisions follow earlier editions where possible. The concordance of texts at the end of the present volume lists the page numbers of the hieroglyphic edition most conveniently consulted for each translated passage.

As a translation volume, an attempt was made to render nearly every ancient Egyptian word into a modern equivalent, although certain concepts (i.e., *ba*-soul, *akh*-spirit) are either translated as a hyphenated phrase or placed in italics. Names of common Egyptian deities (i.e., Osiris, Geb, Tatenen, Maat) are left untranslated, while the myriad of specialized names of Netherworldly beings are translated with each word of the name capitalized to distinguish names from epithets; such a distinction is mostly unmarked within the original hieroglyphic texts and thus can be arbitrary when not directly naming a depicted being. Many terms within the Netherworld Books have a range of meanings, so a single ancient Egyptian word may be translated with different English words depending on the context. Narrative annotations within the compositions are presented in continuous paragraphs, while litanies are set off as verses.[88]

Among the chief difficulties of translating the Netherworld Books are how to incorporate the subtle variants between different exemplars of the texts and what criteria to employ when choosing which of the versions to use as the base translation. Listing every variant among half a dozen or more New Kingdom attestations as well as incorporating the diverse post-New Kingdom material would make for an overly lengthy and cumbersome format. We have chosen to note the most significant variations but omit orthographic differences that do not affect the reading of the passage. The different attestations of the Books of the Creation of the Solar Disk

---

87. For the linguistic features of various books, see Baumann 1998; Zeidler 1999b (Book of Gates); Darnell 2004 (Books of the Solar-Osirian Unity); Werning 2011b (Book of Caverns); Roberson 2012 (Books of the Creation of the Solar Disk).

88. For a different approach, utilizing the theories of Gerhard Fecht, see Hornung 2002.

and the Books of the Solar-Osirian Unity do not overlap like the variants of the other four compositions and thus necessitated a different approach. In chapters 6 and 7, each exemplar receives its own section, with cross-references to parallel texts in the different versions of the Books of the Creation of the Solar Disk. Royal insertions specific to a particular tomb are omitted in the translations of the Book of Adoring Re in the West, the Book of the Hidden Chamber, the Book of Gates, and the Book of Caverns, but they are included in the individual templates of the Books of the Creation of the Solar Disk and Books of the Solar-Osirian Unity.

The order of the compositions follows an overall chronological format, with the Book of Adoring Re in the West and the Book of the Hidden Chamber attested earlier in the Eighteenth Dynasty than the Book of Gates, and the Book of Caverns and Books of the Creation of the Solar Disk appearing in Ramesside contexts (for more on the dating of the original composition of these texts, see above, pp. 48–50). The Book of Adoring Re in the West is a formally distinct composition but provides the "liturgical" component to the other books and is assigned the first chapter. The heterogeneous dates as well as contents of the enigmatic Books of the Solar-Osirian Unity suggested their placement within the last chapter.

The six books in the present work form a unified corpus. The intertextual allusions among the different Netherworld Books—even the formally distinct Book of Adoring Re in the West—emphasize the relationships within the corpus (Manassa 2007a, 9–10). Nevertheless, the other major treatises that appear commonly within the New Kingdom royal tombs have more a celestial than Netherworldly focus. The Book of the Day and the Book of the Night, although depicting the two halves of the solar journey, are predominately lists of names and descriptions of interrelationships of cosmic elements and their terrestrial counterparts, dominated by the literally overarching depictions of the body of the celestial goddess Nut in her diurnal and nocturnal manifestations.[89] Two scenes from Hours 7–8 of the Book of the Night are incorporated into the decoration of one type of Late period sarcophagus, situated at either end of a register containing figures from the Book of Adoring Re in the West, a doorway from the Book of Gates, and Hour 7 of the Book of the Hidden Cham-

---

89. The main editions of the Book of the Day are Piankoff 1942a and Müller-Roth 2008; the Book of the Night is published in Piankoff 1942a, Roulin 1996a, 1996b; on these compositions, see also Hornung 1999, 178–79. English translations of both texts appear in Piankoff and Rambova 1954.

ber, thereby interacting with the more Netherworldly treatises.[90] However, the Book of the Day and the Book of the Night are celestial, even astronomical, books of the nether*sky* rather than chthonic books of the nether*world*.[91] For this reason, these treatises are not included here. The Blueprint of the Course of the Stars, also known as the Book of Nut,[92] and the Book of the Heavenly Cow (Hornung 1991) are also omitted from the present volume, since they belong to a genre of cosmographic texts, which, while closely related to the Netherworld Books, possess celestial foci—the lives of the stars and the body of the sky goddess. The Spell of the Twelve Caverns,[93] also known as the Book of Quererets, exists on the boundary between the Netherworld Books and the Book of Going Forth By Day and is not included in the present volume. An illustrated text, the Spell of the Twelve Caverns is divided, like the Book of the Hidden Chamber and the Book of Gates, into twelve Netherworldly spaces each called a *qrr.t*, "cavern," a term which also appears frequently in the Book of Caverns; the composition appears in a papyrus from the Valley of the Kings (KV 35) as well as in the Osireion and is otherwise attested in private copies of the Book of Going Forth By Day (ch. 168). While the Spell of the Twelve Caverns possesses a format similar to two of the Netherworld Books and describes chthonic beings, it is omitted here due to the paucity of annotations. Other compositions incorporated within royal tombs, including the Book of the Going Forth By Day and the Opening of the Mouth Ritual (Fischer-Elfert 1998; Assmann 2001b, 408–31), do not fall under the scope of Netherworld Books.

---

90. Manassa 2007a, 138–43, 146–48; these two scenes share an emphasis on the enthroned Osiris and a possible functional equivalence in tomb decoration to the "Awakening of Osiris" scene (on the latter, see now Roberson 2013).

91. Compare the division in Hornung 1999 of the "Books of the Netherworld" and "Books of the Sky." The authors hope to present a collected translation of these Cosmographic Books in a companion volume. For the relationships among the two corpora, see also von Lieven 2007c, 20–26.

92. von Lieven 2007b, 2007c; Klotz 2011; for the name of the composition, see Klotz 2011, 491 n. 59.

93. Piankoff and Jacquet-Gordon 1974 (under the title Book of Quererets); Hornung 1999, 54–55; Méndez Rodríguez 2015; Roberson 2016, 324–25. A synoptic edition by Méndez Rodrígeuz is forthcoming.

2
BOOK OF ADORING RE IN THE WEST

INTRODUCTION

A composition first described by the explorer Pococke (see above, p. 3), Naville (1875) published the initial Egyptological edition of the text. Piankoff's (1964a) publication included both monumental and papyrus sources, while the chief modern edition for the former with commentary is now Hornung (1975, 1976);[1] additional translations of the text include Silvia Wiebach-Koepke (2003a) and Hanna Jenni (2011). Post–New Kingdom texts appear in the editions of Richard Parker, Jean Leclant, and Jean-Claude Goyon (1979), Jenni (1986), and Colleen Manassa (2007a, 2007b).[2]

The text of the Book of Adoring Re in the West first appears on the shroud of Thutmose III, dedicated by his son Amenhotep II, and the text and figures from the Great Litany are present within both the tombs of Thutmose III and his vizier Useramun (Hornung 1976, 9–11). All subsequent Eighteenth Dynasty tombs omit the Book of Adoring Re in the West in the decoration of tomb walls, and even in the tomb of Tutankhamun, whose funerary equipment was discovered nearly intact, the text is absent. Beginning with the tomb of Seti I in the Valley of the Kings, the book comes to be the standard decoration for the first two descending corridors—designated in ancient Egyptian as the first and second "God's Passage of the Path of Shu" (Weeks 2016, 104). The tomb of Seti I also marks the appearance of the introductory scene (see below). The reign of Ramesses II sees the only New Kingdom appearance of the Book of Ador-

---

1. For an additional overview of the composition and bibliography, see Hornung 1999, 136–47 and 179–81.
2. Schenkel (1978; 1980) and Werning (2007, 1937–39) have studied the stemma of the Book of Adoring the Re in the West.

ing Re in the West in a nonfunerary context in a temple at Abydos (see p. 34). The tomb of Ramesses VI is unusual in its exclusion of the Book of Adoring Re in the West from the decoration of its walls; excerpts from the composition appear for the last time in the Valley of the Kings in the tombs of Ramesses IX and Ramesses X (Hornung 1976, 19–20; Lüscher 2000).

The Book of Adoring Re in the West opens with a title that emphasizes its focus on the "United One," the unified Re-Osiris, whose adoration and accompanying images aid the living as well as the deceased. The title also dictates its recitation before the accompanying illustrations, and enumerates the efficacy of the composition—the defeat of Re's enemies as well as worldly and Netherworldly benefits for the practitioner. From the reign of Seti I, an introductory scene is also present (fig. 2.1): the ram-headed anthropomorphic solar deity—sun of night—and the scarab—sun of day—appear centrally within a large disk, sending out ophidian (above) and crocodilian (below) emissaries of solar power toward the edges of the cosmos, those outer regions appearing symbolically as horned animal heads with flames.[3] The following "Great Litany" is clearly divided into seventy-five addresses to the solar deity, each beginning with the refrain "Praise to you, Re, high and mighty," followed by a short list of epithets, and concluding with an association between the solar divine image and its

---

3. For this tableau and its significance, see Hornung 1976, 28–30; Darnell 2004, 273–74; Manassa 2007a, 454. In the Late period version of the scene on the sarcophagus of Tadipakem (CGAE 29316), the protective crocodile is "the crocodile who protects the western portal of the Netherworld," while the serpent is "the serpent of roasting flame who protects the portal of the West in the Netherworld." Parallels to protective serpents and crocodiles appear in the Book of the Creation of the Solar Disk, Tomb of Ramesses VI, Section A, Register 1, Scene 2 (p. 466; Roberson 2012, Scene 56) and Section B2, Scene 45 (p. 501; Roberson 2012, Scene 28). Similarly, in the dropped portion of the Corridor G ceiling in the tomb of Ramesses VI, a crocodile head and serpent emerge from solar disks in a scene of the punishment of enemies (p. 562; Piankoff and Rambova 1954, pl. 182). The pairing of protective crocodiles and serpents finds parallels in earlier contexts as well. In the threat against violators of the burial in the Sixth Dynasty tomb of Meni the text states—"The crocodile is against him in the water, and the serpent is against him on land, the one will do anything against this (tomb)" (Sethe 1932, 23, 12–14; see Morschauser 1991, 157; Assmann 2001c, 97). For the Old Kingdom appearance of the pair in curses, see Nordh 1996, 60–61 (she also notes on p. 60 the appearance of the snake and crocodile as the forms a vengeful mayor Sarenput I of Aswan will assume when he goes after any who might steal from the provisions of his statue cult).

own corpse. Each address of the Great Litany has a corresponding illustration of the specific manifestation of the corpse of the "Unified One," the Solar-Osirian deity.[4] In the tomb of Thutmose III, the depictions are placed on the pillars of the sarcophagus hall (plates 1, 2), separated from the text of the litanies that were written on a shroud; in Ramesside tombs, the individual litanies are each written in a vertical column above the accompanying figure. Already in the tombs of Thutmose III and Useramun, and continuing throughout the Nineteenth and Twentieth Dynasties, the figures from the Great Litany are divided into two sequences. In the first two corridors of royal tombs from the reign of Seti I, Addresses 1–51 are organized as follows: the figures corresponding to the odd-numbered litanies appear on the left-hand wall and the even-numbered litanies on the right-hand wall. A break in the sequence occurs with Address 52 following Address 51 on the left wall and Address 53 and 54 appearing on the right wall; the alternation of figures continues for the remaining addresses, with odd numbered addresses now on the right wall and even numbered ones on the left wall.

The seventy-five addresses in the Great Litany encompass the most significant aspects of the "United One," Re and Osiris, whose temporary union results in a divine being called *Djeba-demedj*,[5] who is hailed in the first address of the Great Litany, and who appears throughout the later litanies of the composition. The following summary highlights some of the most prominent features of the list of Netherworldly solar manifestations, but each individual litany summons forth a host of theological concepts, three of which are examined in detail below (pp. 70–74). The Ennead of Heliopolis forms the focus of Addresses 11–19, with the addition of Khepri and the substitution of Horus for Seth; the solar corpse can be equated with both the expected gods (e.g., Atum, Shu, Geb) as well as goddesses (e.g., Tefnut, Nut, Isis, Nephthys), the latter phenomenon fitting well with the feminine gender of the word corpse (*ḥꜣ.t*) in ancient Egyptian. Address 2 praises Khepri, the scarab-form of the solar god and embodiment of the sun's transformative powers; he is one of the most significant solar manifestations within the composition, appearing

---

4. For the discrepancies between the number of addresses (seventy-five), the number of names for Re's manifestations (seventy-six), and the number of depictions of those manifestations (seventy-four), see Barta 1986, 83–86.

5. *Djeba-demedj* is a description of the unified Re-Osiris, although the term's exact translation remains uncertain (Manassa 2007a, 430–35).

several times in the Great Litany as well as in the later litanies (Minas-
Nerpel 2006, 235–46). The Great Litany incorporates cosmic phenomena
and toponyms, such as Nun (Address 20), He of the Cavern (Address 28),
He of the Netherworld (Address 41), and the female West (Address 27).
Several forms refer to the manifestations of the solar eye or *ba*-soul, and
the punishing aspect of the Netherworldly sun is personified by an enemy
at the pillory (Address 8), a mummy with ropes in place of his head, the
"Binder" (Address 64), and a mummy crowned with a cauldron as place of
destruction of the damned (Address 65). Animal forms abound, including a mullet-fish, ram, bull, oryx, baboon, and felines, the final example
appearing prominently as a large seated tomcat in addition to a cat-headed
mummiform figure. The mummified corpse of the sun appears in its rotting form—"Putrefaction" (Address 22) and "Rotting One" (Address 60)—
as well as the more expected epithets, such as "Hidden of Corpse" (Address
39) and "United of Limbs" (Address 43). The duality of the Netherworldly
sun appears in his names of "Bright One" (Address 42) and "Illuminer"
(Address 50) juxtaposed with "Darkened One" (Address 9), "Dark of Face"
(Address 62), and "Lord of Darkness" (Address 75).

Following the Great Litany, the remainder of the text can be organized into nine separate litanies (Hornung 1976, 25), which contain their
own sub-units (Abitz 1995, 56–62), such as the divinization of the elements of the body ("Gliedervergottung") in Litany 7 (pp. 117–18). Litany
1 addresses the solar deity as a cavern dweller, a Netherworldly being, who
is simultaneously *gšy*, "the migratory one," whose *ba*-soul travels through
the worldly and otherworldly halves of the cosmos. The ritualist who
speaks Litany 1 claims that he knows the names, manifestations, corpses,
and mysterious visible forms of the solar deity—the same emphasis on
knowledge that appears so prominently in the King as Solar Priest and
the title of the Book of the Hidden Chamber (see pp. 35–39). Through the
king's knowledge of divine forms, he becomes one with the solar deity in
all of his manifestations, and Litany 1 concludes with "I am exactly like
one among them."[6] The brief Litany 2 requests that the forms of the solar
deity "make a path" for the deceased, an emphasis on straightening the
tortuous paths of the Netherworld (see p. 93). The introductory portion

---

6. Such statements accord well with the fact that within a temple at Abydos,
Ramesses II includes his own father, grandfather, and even Eighteenth Dynasty predecessors along with the figures of the Great Litany (Mariette 1880, 20; Hornung
1976, 13).

of Litany 3 resumes this theme, requesting guidance along the paths of the Netherworld and its various components. Throughout Litany 3, the ritualist who speaks proclaims his complete identity with both Re and the unified Re-Osiris (always addressed as *Djeba-demedj*)—the *ba*-soul, corpse, effective spells, travels, and crossings of the deceased king are identical to those of the solar god. Re even speaks directly of this equation, exclaiming at one point: "One exactly like me, my very own twin!" After the ritualist then greets the gods of the West, he exhorts them to aid the unified Re-Osiris in the destruction of his enemies; in the next portion of the litany, the strength and victory of Re are also those of the deceased king, who is similarly justified against his enemies. Litany 3 concludes with Re felling Apep, and the juxtaposition of Osiris (and the Osiris king) triumphing over his enemies at the time of cosmic victory over Apep finds a parallel in Hour 7 of the Book of the Hidden Chamber.

Litany 4 begins with jubilation for the victorious Osiris, who as a red-colored, aggressive *ba*-soul destroys his enemies, again as Re defeats Apep. The unified Re-Osiris, *Djeba-demedj*, like the deceased himself, is justified—the same cosmic judgement that is depicted in Scene 33 of the Book of Gates. The second half of the litany emphasizes illumination and the transformational potential of sunlight in the Netherworld; the deceased requests that he be given his two divine eyes (simultaneously those of Re himself), so that they might guide him through the Netherworld. The litany concludes a phrase referring to Re's ability to ensure that his "manifestation manifests," deploying the sun's own ability to adopt a multitude of forms in his combat with Apep; thus, Litanies 3–4 conclude with the same motif of solar triumph over the chaos serpent.

Re as "He of the Horizon" forms the focus of the beginning of Litany 5; the *ba*-soul of this specifically liminal form of the solar god "comes forth" from a variety of Netherwordly locations, the epithets of the *ba*-soul mimicking their topographical dominance. The deceased king then addresses the "terrible fear" of the Netherworldly realm, the knife-wielding demons who threaten to destroy the *ba*-soul, resulting in the dreaded second—and permanent—death. Again, the text emphasizes that here it is not ritual performance that saves the soul, but rather *knowledge* of the Netherworldly mysteries, known by only a select few; the Book of Adoring Re in the West, like the King as Solar Priest, proclaims the efficacy of the knowledge that is encoded in the corpus of texts translated in the present volume as the Netherworld Books. The remainder of Litany 5 affirms the deceased's worthiness and knowledge, alluding to deities and concepts present in the other Netherworld Books, including the Book of Gates and the Books of the Creation of the Solar Disk.

The refrain "O Re, come to me, rightly traveling" begins Litany 6, punctuating statements that associate the deceased with beneficial activities within the Netherworld. The litany then proclaims that Re has given birth to the deceased king, all three forms of the tripartite solar god—Re, Atum, and Khepri—participating in the physical delivery of the new-born and resurrected corpse. The deceased is again protected from punishment in the afterlife and identifies himself with other divine manifestations, such as Divine Utterance (Hu) and Divine Perception (Sia). The following statement is then heard in the Mysterious Place: "It is Re who rests in Osiris—and vice versa!" This Solar-Osirian credo also accompanies an illustration that is not part of the Book of Adoring the Re in the West, but which appears within the tomb of Nefertari and two Deir el-Medina tombs (TT 290 and 335): a ram-headed mummy crowned with a solar disk.[7] Much of the rest of Litany 6 consists of speeches delivered by the deities of the Netherworld that yet again equate the beauty and power of the deceased with *Djeba-demedj* and reaffirm the deceased's knowledge of the "mysterious inductions."[8] A conversation then ensues between the deceased and the Pelican Goddess, who guides the king and opens the Netherworld for his *ba*-soul. The conclusion of Litany 6 repeats the theme of the Solar-Osirian Unity and the deceased king's identification with that powerful syncretistic combination of deities in the Netherworld.

Litany 7 begins with the ascension of the deceased to various mysterious locales within the Netherworld, which then introduces the lengthy subunit of the litany that equates each body part of the deceased with a divinity or divine manifestation (DuQuesne 2002b; Nyord 2009, 510–23); as the deceased bluntly states at the conclusion of the list: "I am entirely a god. There is no limb of mine that is free from a god." The focus of Litany 7 then shifts to Osiris, Foremost of the Westerners, and his transfiguration through the wailing and weeping of mourners. The deceased, previously identified with Osiris, then claims to be Horus, his son; such seeming contradictory statements accord well with an almost riddling-like statement

---

7. The discussion of Assmann 1969, 101–5 remains useful; for other references to the Solar-Osirian Unity, see p. 6 n. 8.

8. See p. 114 n. 113 below for the verb involved; on "mysticism" in the Netherworld Books, see the references collected in pp. 36–37 and n. 57.

in the Book of Gates, Scene 8: "I am the son who came forth from his father; I am the father who came forth from his son."

Litany 8 emphasizes properly traveling through the Netherworld, reaffirming the identifications that have been made throughout the previous litanies. Some new theological concepts also occur in this litany, such as the "mysterious *benu*-bird," an avian manifestation of the unified Re-Osiris (see p. 123 n. 140). The deceased then addresses the personified West in her many epithets, again claiming knowledge of her nature and the names of those who are in her following, a reference to the names so dutifully recorded in the Book of the Hidden Chamber and the other Netherworld Books. Litany 9 and the conclusion of the Book of Adoring Re in the West begins with another address to the personified goddess West and then stresses the deceased's adoration of her. The speech of the deceased concludes after he identifies himself for a final time with several powerful deities—Re, Geb, Horakhty, Atum, and Khepri. The colophon of the text mimics the title, describing a ritualist who will recite the book "being pure at the hour of the middle of the night," thus gaining access to the hidden deity—a fact truly attested.

Much of the concluding portion of the Book of Adoring Re in the West—from part of Litany 7 through to its end—is adopted in private contexts as chapter 180 of the Book of Going Forth By Day.[9] The repetition of the royal cartouche within the Book of Adoring Re in the West reinforces one of the chief themes of the book: the direct identification of the king and the solar deity (Hornung 1976, 22–23); an enumeration of the cartouches reveals several units of twelve (Abitz 1995, 68–72), evocative of the hourly division of the figures of the Great Litany attested in Late period copies of the book.

In addition to the Third Intermediate period papyri, which contain images of the solar deity from the Great Litany as well as additional, innovative forms (see p. 56), the Book of Adoring Re in the West appears as a significant component of the decorative scheme of a corpus of Late period monuments, including temples, tombs, and anthropoid and trapezoidal sarcophagi.[10] The most commonly utilized portions of the Book

9. Hornung 1998, 380–85; Lapp 2002. For a royal example of Book of the Dead ch. 180, the lid of the inner sarcophagus of Seti I, see Hornung 1986. Parts of Book of the Dead ch. 127 are also an adaptation of the Book of Adoring Re in the West (Hornung 1999, 140–42).

10. For temples, see pp. 34–35 above. For tombs, see Aba (TT 36) (Kuhlmann and

of Adoring Re in the West in the post-New Kingdom era are the figures and addresses of the Great Litany; in addition to the statement "You are indeed the corpse of" followed by the name of that particular figure, the Late period copies of the Great Litany also equate each figure with the corpse of the Osiris N. On two types of Late period sarcophagi, as well as in the tomb of Padiamenemope (TT 33), the litanies of the Great Litany are distributed according to an hourly structure, suggesting a liturgical use of the text throughout the night, which is in keeping with the introduction of the book: "One recites this book …" The sarcophagus of Tjaihorpata (CGAE 29306), which includes figures from the Great Litany as well as other excerpts from the book, preserves an otherwise unique annotation to the forms of the solar god (Manassa 2007b, pls. 210–11):

> Names of the gods, who receive Re in the Netherworld. May they receive the Osiris N with their own arms! May his manifestations be like those within his bark! May they open for Osiris N the doors of Igeret, so that he might travel over their caverns, so that he might enter the portals of the West, he having trodden the secret roads, he having passed by the gods, he having traversed the beautiful road of the Place of Hauling. May he enter into the West with Re in his bark, so that he might adore the cavern-dwellers of the Netherworld, so that he might rise with him in the eastern horizon like the lord of cyclical eternity.

The Late period text asserts the importance of adoration of the figures of the solar god for the eternal existence of the deceased; the manifestations of Re literally open the doors of the Netherworld when the deceased calls them by their names. The juxtaposition of figures from the Great Litany with portals is also reminiscent of another type of Late period sarcophagi (type II) that places figures from the Great Litany before *sbḫ.t*-gateways from the Book of Gates, which front an hour of the Book of the Hidden Chamber (see Manassa 2007a, 71–78). In a few cases, the figure from the Great Litany chosen to appear before a certain hour of the Book of the Hidden Chamber shares themes with texts and scenes in that hour; for example, Hour 5 of the Book of the Hidden Chamber is associated with

---

Schenkel 1983, 253–56 and pls. 146–47, 150); Montuemhat (TT 34) (Piankoff 1964a, pl. 2). Blocks from an anonymous Heliopolitan tomb reused in the Nilometer on the island of Roda also contain excerpts from the Book of Adoring Re in the West (see p. 130 n. 6). For anthropoid sarcophagi, see sarcophagus JE 60597 (Manassa 2007a, 456). For trapezoidal sarcophagi, see Manassa 2007a.

Address 48 of the Great Litany, both of which emphasize the straightening of paths in the Netherworld (Manassa 2007a, 105–6).

Litany and Praise

In Egyptian religion a human can participate in the worship of the solar stages, the full knowledge of which is a royal prerogative. Apparently, eternal cycle and innovative praise were not always considered to be compatible, and in litanies the worshiper, even the cultically powerful king, seeks to worship through the words, deeds, and interactions of the worshiped deities. The worshiper assumes the role of other deities praising the divine object of human adoration. So in a hymn in the temple of Ramesses III at Medinet Habu Temple (Epigraphic Survey 1963, pl. 422A):

> Hail to you with what your eye says to you,
> > which opens up for you the Way of Eternity.
> Hail to you with what your solar disk says to you,
> > when it causes to come up to you those that are in fear of you.
> Hail to you with what the night-bark says to you,
> > when it sails there in a favorable wind …

This sort of praise does not mean that personal innovation is unacceptable in Egyptian religion, however, but rather points to the fact that much of formally recorded Egyptian religious expression is of a didactic nature, often in the form of a litany. The worshiper expresses these seemingly formulaic statements as though his or her personal belief. These praises in which the worshiper is subsumed by some aspect of the worshiped or by some intermediary and worshipful divine figure or element—such as the eye, disk, and night-bark—are in the nature of a credo, allowing the worshiper to profess what should be common beliefs. The similarity of the first two passages in the Medinet Habu hymn to Address 57 in the Great Litany in the Book of Adoring Re in the West (see below) indicates that the Medinet Habu text is not a prayer or an example of personal worship as such, but rather an instance of the ability of the individual in Egyptian worship to insert himself or herself into more formal worship by transforming litany into personal praise.

The Book of Adoring Re in the West is an excellent example of a series of adorations of a deity, each of which is at first demonstrably short and at times seemingly obscure. Upon scrutiny, however, the adorations may be seen to contain allusions to texts and iconography that explain the brief statements. Each of the litany sections is an encapsulation of lengthier texts and graphic representations, the litanies being to some extent catalogues of the information the reader or hearer should have at his or her intellectual disposal in order to understand the religious concepts they express. Viewed in such a manner, the Book of Adoring Re in the West is a textual rosary of New Kingdom solar devotion.

Address 57: The Speaking Solar Eye

Some of the litanies in the Book of Adoring Re in the West provide images that invite considerable textual and iconographic comparisons, the pithy statements and seemingly enigmatic combinations serving as succinct allusions to complex theological associations, such as Address 57 of the Great Litany:

> Praise to you, Re, high and mighty!
> Whom his eye saves, whose effective eye speaks,
>   when the corpses lament.
> You are indeed the corpse of One Whose Effective Eye Speaks.

Each statement in Address 57 alludes to a multiplicity of texts and images. The eye of Re, the sun, saves the dead—so on the New Kingdom stele London BM 1224, l. 7, the owner of the monument prays: "May you set your iris-and-pupil (*dfd*) as my protection" (Jansen-Winkeln 1990, 217, ln. 7). The protective iris-and-pupil is the goddess of the eye of the sun as the *udjat*-amulet, and at least a few examples link the amulet of the eye with a goddess who protects the dead in the netherworld. The passage from the stele BM 1224 is perhaps an allusion to the wearing of such an amulet. According to Coffin Texts Spell 60 (CT 1.250a–e; Darnell 1997, 41):

> Bastet, the daughter of Atum, the first daughter of the All Lord,
> she is your protection till dawn,
>   until you descend into the necropolis;
> the eye of Horus is she who sheds light for you.
> Into the necropolis does she come with you.

The protective eye-goddess slakes her wrath on enemies of the sun and of the associated blessed dead. The hymn of the early Eleventh Dynasty Theban ruler Antef II refers to the protection of the solar eye as an angry power directed at the enemies of the sun: "protection surrounds me as the (angry) red glow of your eye" (Clère and Vandier 1948, 9–10, ln. 6). In a Netherworldly context, the image of the protective eye may allude to the eastern end of the Netherworld, the place of the *ḏfḏy.w*, "those relating to the iris-and-pupil," the blessed dead whose heads leave their corpses to mingle with the face of the sun (Barguet 1976, 36). The concept of the eye that lights the way in the Netherworld may also find pictorial expression, as in the image of an *udjat*-eye with arms, holding a flaming torch, in the tomb of Pashed at Deir el-Medina (Zivie 1979, pl. 18).[11]

The protective action of the solar eye, and the interplay of eye and corpse in Address 57, recall a number of textual and pictorial references to the solar eye encountering, hovering over, shining upon, and joining with the solar corpse. The mummiform figure of the Osiride king on the Enigmatic Wall in the tomb of Ramesses IX wears on its breast the image of a solar disk in which appears a scarab emerging from the disk, a miniature mirroring of the large scarab emerging from the solar disk above the reclining deity (see pp. 569–71). This depiction of the sun at night shining on the breast of the deceased king finds textual expression in a line from the text on the lid of the outermost sarcophagus of Merneptah: "His image passes over your breast" (Assmann 1972, 62 n. 22). In the tomb of Paheri at Elkab, this shining on the breast appears in a passage describing the daily east to west journey of the blessed dead, and the torch-eye protects their necropolitan slumber until Re awakens them at the eastern horizon (Tylor and Griffith 1894, pl. 9, ll. 17–18):

> You going outside each morning, and returning each evening,
>> a torch being lit for you in the night,
>> until the sunlight rises upon your breast.

In both this passage and in the decoration of the Enigmatic Wall in the tomb of Ramesses IX, the shining on the breast occurs in the eastern horizon. The single litany that is Address 57 from the Book of Adoring Re in the West makes allusion to the entire constellation of images of the saving eye, illuminating (i.e., speaking) in the Netherworld.

---

11. On the eye as disk, torch, and goddess, see Assmann 1969, 143, text note a.

Address 56: The Great Cat

Other of the litanies evoke an established image of the solar deity, providing a verbal description of an icon the reader or reciter might well have in the mind's eye, if not in the more concrete form of an illustration, amulet, or sculpture. So in Address 56 of the Great Litany:

> Praise to you, Re, high and mighty!
> Great cat, protector of the gods.
> Judge, chief of the council, foremost of the sacred cavern.
> You are indeed the corpse of the Great Cat.

In this litany the solar deity appears first as a cat, evoking the destruction of chaos, then as a Netherworld deity, all summarized as "the corpse of the Great Cat"—chiastically arranged, the text describes the sun as cat and deceased deity, deceased deity and cat.

The great cat appears in chapter 17 of the Book of Going Forth By Day, the vignettes to which include the powerful image of a knife-wielding solar feline slicing into the ophidian manifestation of chaos (Corteggiani 1995). Texts and image further evoke the destruction of Apep at the base of the sacred *ished*-tree of Heliopolis. Already in Address 33 of the Great Litany, the sun is "Cat-Like One," a designation that appears in the Book of Gates (Scene 100; see below, p. 335), on the Second Shrine of Tutankhamun (Scenes 3 and 11; see below, pp. 538, 545), and in Division 4 of the Book of Caverns (Scene 47; see below, pp. 392–93), in the last as the name of a guardian of punishment from whom the damned may never escape. In the Theban context of a royal tomb, the subterranean context of the passage, and the reference there to the sacred cavern and the corpse of the Heliopolitan great cat, may allude to the later concept of a subterranean connection between Heliopolis and Thebes (Klotz 2012a, 181–82).

Re as "foremost of the sacred cavern" in Address 56 states that Re is Osiris, a state possible only in the form of the "the unified *ba*-soul," the form of Re and Osiris as a single deity that marks the cusp between night and day, yesterday and tomorrow, death and rejuvenation. The Osirian epithet itself, "foremost of the sacred cavern," references not only the preeminence of the dead god in the afterlife, but also his physically prominent location at the root of the eastern horizon, physically becoming both end of the Netherworld and the divine mantle atop which the visible hills of the east rest as a merely physical crust. So in the treatise on the Enigmatic

Wall in the Tomb of Ramesses IX, Osiris becomes the horizon, greeting the sun disk who rises through him.

In Address 73 in the Book of Adoring Re in the West, deities called "those of the forehall," appear:

> Praise to you, Re, high and mighty!
> Lord of power, who is within his Benben sanctuary.
> Chief of the gods of the forehall.
> You are indeed the corpse of Lord of Power.

The forehall is the place of the unification of Re and Osiris, and the deities in that area, "those of the forehall," are associated with the newly rejuvenated and rising sun. The reference to the Benben sanctuary of Heliopolis confirms the association with the area of the solar rebirth, and the nature of the Heliopolitan shrines, with the multitude of open courts, provides another excellent link for the use of the term "forehall" for the cusp of the Netherworld and the dawn (Klotz 2012a, 66 n. 158).[12] The forehall of the Netherworld is the horizon, the geography of the afterlife compared to the architecture of an Egyptian temple. The same equation of temple space and cosmic time is apparent in many Egyptian texts—so the first hour of the Book of the Hidden Chamber describes the solar entry into the West as "this god enters into the western portal of the horizon" (p. 138).

Address 69: The Netherworldly Baboon

Bridging the litanies of reasonably straightforward iconographic reference (such as Address 56), and those more subtly alluding to multiple texts and images, and requiring more contemplation on the part of the worshiper who would properly interpret and correctly understand the interrelationships of the elements of the litany (such as Address 57), are others such as Address 69, in which Re is a jubilating and at the same time Netherworldly baboon:

> Praise to you, Re, high and mighty!
> Jubilating baboon, he of Wetchnet.

---

12. For the Netherworld and Heliopolis, see Assmann 1969, 311 (n. 47), 241 (ll. 17–18), and 242 (n. i).

Khepri, correct of visible forms.
You are indeed the corpse of the Netherworldly Baboon.

Wetchnet, the place whence the solar baboon hales, is in the southeast-ern region of the ordered world. The baboon assumes a pose similar to the Egyptian *orans* stance of adoration and was for the ancient Egyptian a zoomorphic symbol of the adoration of the new born sun. The souls of the eastern horizon, who praise the sun and chatter for him to aid the rising sun, assume the forms of baboons. Baboons are a model of proper worship for the king and are even said to have taught the Egyptians how to worship the sun, such that the king himself "knows this mysterious lan-guage that the *ba*-souls speak, they singing chatter for Re, that he might rise and that he might appear in glory in the horizon" (p. 38). In Address 69, Re is identified with a worshiper—albeit a divine one—rejoicing at his own rebirth. In the Netherworld, Re and Osiris are mystically combined (Osiris is yesterday, Re is tomorrow); at times,[13] Osiris adores the rising Re—yesterday praises tomorrow. So in Address 69 of the Book of Adoring Re in the West, the newborn sun is the solar deity and at the same time the adoring Osirian element himself. What at first may seem a potentially theologically sound albeit overtly humorous statement to the uninitiated is actually a subtle reference in rich imagery to a profound mystery at the heart of the Egyptians' religious beliefs.

13. As in the Book of Caverns, Division 5, Scene 51 (pp. 403–4) and the clos-ing scene of the Books of the Solar-Osirian Unity in the Tomb of Ramesses IX (pp. 569–71).

Book of Adoring Re in the West

INTRODUCTORY SCENE (FROM THE TOMB OF SETI II,
AFTER HORNUNG 1976, 55)

Fig. 2.1. A solar disk containing a scarab beetle and ram-headed male figure—facing into the tomb—appears in the middle of a vertically oriented rectangular space; at the top and bottom a serpent and crocodile, respectively, are oriented diagonally toward an antelope head with a flame between its horns, the heads occupying the corner of the rectangle closest to the interior of the tomb.[14]

Beginning of the Book of Adoring Re in the West,
   adoring the United One in the West.
One recites this book,
   while these images are executed in divisions[15]
   upon the ground,
   in the deep of the night.
It means that Re triumphs over his enemies in the
   West.

---

14. See p. 62 and n. 3 above.

15. A term *ḥsb.w* appears in the stela of a high official, Antef (son of Miyt) from Thebes, who describes his knowledge of crafts and his ability to give instruction, including the expression *dd ḥsb.wt n imy-rꜣ ḥmww nb*, "who assigns the divisions to the chief artisans" (Clère and Vandier 1948, 46, ln. 2; see also Hannig 2006b, 1773). The term may well in this context refer to the work of an outline draftsman or the person who has arranged for some chief design, perhaps referencing initial measuring of the surface to be decorated or of a scale drawing of the decoration of the work to be executed (for "poetic" references to the use of a layout grid in Egyptian art, see Fischer-Elfert 1998, 16–26). In the context of the Book of Adoring Re in the West, the *ḥsb.wt* may refer to measured divisions allotted to individual addresses (for an alternate interpretation of *ḥsb.wt* as a form of pigment, see Clère 1979). The text of the Book of Adoring Re in the West appears to say that each address receives the same space as the others, regardless of the length of the text when copied. Unlike most other Egyptian compositions, the text does not follow continuously but apparently was intended to adhere to a layout similar to that in the tomb of Seti II, in which each address begins at the top of a vertical line, but with variable ending points.

It is effective for a man on earth;
it is effective for him after he moors.[16]

GREAT LITANY

ADDRESS 1 (PLATE 1, NO. 1)

Fig. 2.2. Mummiform male with white crown and divine beard

Praise to you, Re, high and mighty!
Lord of caverns, which are hidden of visible forms.[17]
Who rests in the mysteries,
    when he transforms into *Djeba-demedj*.
NAME: *Djeba-demedj*

ADDRESS 2 (PLATE 2, NO. 2)

Fig. 2.3. Mummiform figure with winged scarab for head

Praise to you, Re, high and mighty!
Khepri,[18] alighting of wings.
This one who rests in the Netherworld,
    when he transforms into the One Who Comes Forth
    from His Limbs.[19]
NAME: Khepri

---

16. "To moor" is an Egyptian euphemism for death (Zandee 1960, 53).

17. For places that "hide" mysteries and members, compare the passages cited in Darnell 2004, 290–91.

18. The god Khepri is one of the most significant deities within the Book of Adoring Re in the West, appearing in the Great Litany as well as the following litanies (textual references collected in Minas-Nerpel 2006, 235–46).

19. This is probably yet another reference to the wings as ꜥ.*wy*-arms/ꜥ.*t*-limbs (Darnell 2004, 237).

ADDRESS 3 (PLATE 1, NO. 3)

Fig. 2.4. Mummiform male with white crown and divine beard

Praise to you, Re, high and mighty!
Tatenen[20] who gives birth to the gods.
This one who protects those with him,
    when he transforms into the One Foremost of His Cavern.
NAME: One Foremost of His Cavern

ADDRESS 4 (PLATE 2, NO. 4)

Fig. 2.5. Sun disk containing a scarab[21]

Praise to you, Re, high and mighty!
Who causes the earth to see,[22] who illumines those of the West.
This one whose manifestations are his visible forms,[23]
    when he transforms into his Great Disk.[24]
NAME: Re, He of the Disk.

ADDRESS 5 (PLATE 1, NO. 5)

Fig. 2.6. Mummiform male with divine beard

Praise to you, Re, high and mighty!
Whose *ba*-soul speaks, who is content with his utterance.
This one who protects the *akh*-spirits, those of the West,
    so that they might breathe by means of him.
NAME: He Who Protects *Ba*-Souls

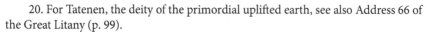

20. For Tatenen, the deity of the primordial uplifted earth, see also Address 66 of the Great Litany (p. 99).

21. In the tomb of Thutmose III, the scarab is black, while the disk is red.

22. For the verb *sm3(ꜣ)* in the Coffin Texts, see Hannig 2006b, 2205. Personified earth and sky may rejoice at the time of a divine appearance—compare earth and sky rejoicing at the time of the Opet Festival (Epigraphic Survey 1994, 14–15 and pl. 28).

23. For *irw.w*, "visible forms," see Assmann 1969, 390; Hornung 1967, 126–28; Ockinga 1984, 103–6.

24. A comparison of this address and the didactic names of the Aton appeared already in Piankoff 1964c, 208–9.

ADDRESS 6 (PLATE 2, NO. 6)

Fig. 2.7. Mummiform figure with ram head

Praise to you, Re, high and mighty!
Sole one, powerful of face, who unites with his corpse.
This one who calls to his gods,
    when[25] he passes over his mysterious cavern.
NAME: Powerful of Face

ADDRESS 7 (PLATE 1, NO. 7)

Fig. 2.8. Mummiform male with divine beard

Praise to you, Re, high and mighty!
Whose eye summons, whose head calls.
This one who gives breath among the *ba*-souls at their places,
    so that they might receive their breath.
NAME: He Who Gives Breath among the *Ba*-Souls

ADDRESS 8 (PLATE 2, NO. 8)

Fig. 2.9. Kneeling enemy figure bound to pillory[26]

Praise to you, Re, high and mighty!
Whose *ba*-soul arrives, who destroys his enemies.
This one who commands punishment among the dead.[27]
NAME: One of Punishment at the Pillory

---

25. For the subordinating particle *ṯf* in the Netherworld Books, see Roberson 2012, 117–19.

26. Beaux 1991, 46.

27. Late period sources can add the following text (Manassa 2007a, 170; 2007b, pl. 159): "Osiris N always praises Re. He assigns evil against the punished one. He destroys all of his enemies."

ADDRESS 9 (PLATE 1, NO. 9)

Fig. 2.10. Solar disk containing ram-head and smaller disk[28]

Praise to you, Re, high and mighty!
Darkened one who is in his cavern.
This one who commands his darkness in the cavern that hides
    those who are in it.
NAME: Darkened One

ADDRESS 10 (PLATE 2, NO. 10; PLATE 1, NO. 10)

Fig. 2.11. Mummiform figure with falcon head; Fig. 2.12. alternate figure: solar disk containing a ram-headed bird

Praise to you, Re, high and mighty!
Who illumines the corpses, one who is within the horizon.[29]
This one who enters into his cavern.
NAME: He Who Illumines the Corpses
ALTERNATE FIGURE: *Ba*-Soul of Re

ADDRESS 11 (PLATE 1, NO. 11)

Fig. 2.13. Mummiform male with divine beard

Praise to you, Re, high and mighty!
Who ascends to the cavern of the Hidden One.
You are indeed the corpse of Atum.
NAME: Atum

---

28. An additional figure that can appear with this address is a ram-headed *ba*-bird within a disk. For the coloration of the figures, see Hornung 1976, 102–3 n. 38.

29. The reading provided by Useramun, Thutmose III, and Ramesses III, while the other versions give the variant "who illumines the corpses of those of the horizon."

ADDRESS 12 (PLATE 2, NO. 12)

Fig. 2.14. Scarab pushing a solar disk

Praise to you, Re, high and mighty!
Who ascends to what Anubis has made mysterious.
You are indeed the corpse of Khepri.
NAME: Khepri

ADDRESS 13 (PLATE 1, NO. 13)

Fig. 2.15. Mummiform male with divine beard

Praise to you, Re, high and mighty!
Greater of lifetime than She Who Hides Her Images.[30]
You are indeed the corpse of Shu.
NAME: Shu

ADDRESS 14 (PLATE 2, NO. 14)

Fig. 2.16. Mummiform female

Praise to you, Re, high and mighty!
One who is starrier than the (other) bodies.
You are indeed the corpse of Tefnut.
NAME: Tefnut

---

30. The reference to a goddess with a multitude of forms as a counterpart to Re-Osiris who is here equated with Shu also finds parallels in the Book of Caverns, Division 5, Scene 50 (pp. 401–3) in which the goddess Mysterious One bears various zoomorphic and solar manifestations on her body and stands as a counterpart to the ithyphallic Osiris. The relationship of the goddess to Shu is that of the celestial goddess Nut bearing cosmic manifestations and supported by Shu as described in the Book of the Heavenly Cow (Hornung 1991, 12–14, 42, vv. 140–165).

ADDRESS 15 (PLATE 1, NO. 15)

Fig. 2.17. Mummiform male with divine beard

Praise to you, Re, high and mighty!
Who commands those of time at the (proper) time.
You are indeed the corpse of Geb.
NAME: Geb

ADDRESS 16 (PLATE 2, NO. 16)

Fig. 2.18. Mummiform female

Praise to you, Re, high and mighty!
Great of reckoning among those with him.
You are indeed the corpse of Nut.
NAME: Nut

ADDRESS 17 (PLATE 1, NO. 17)

Fig. 2.19. Mummiform female

Praise to you, Re, high and mighty!
Lord of upward motion[31] with regard to She Who is atop Him.[32]
You are indeed the corpse of Isis.
NAME: Isis

---

31. Compare Hornung 1976, 165 n. 53; Meeks 1998a, 1–2 (77.0010–77.0011).

32. This reference to an upward motion relative to a female manifestation atop the solar deity, here identified with Isis, probably alludes to the helical rising of Sothis, who is described as the goddess atop the head of Re (Darnell 1997, 46–47). The same concept is probably behind the head of Isis atop the pyramidal mound above the chamber of Sokar in Hour 5 of the Book of the Hidden Chamber (p. 180).

ADDRESS 18 (PLATE 2, NO. 18)

Fig. 2.20. Mummiform female

Praise to you, Re, high and mighty!
Shining of head for She Who is in front of Him.
You are indeed the corpse of Nephthys.
NAME: Nephthys

ADDRESS 19 (PLATE 1, NO. 19)

Fig. 2.21. Mummiform figure with falcon head

Praise to you, Re, high and mighty!
Whose limbs are complete, sole one united of semen.[33]
You are indeed the corpse of Horus.
NAME: Horus

ADDRESS 20 (PLATE 2, NO. 20)

Fig. 2.22. Mummiform figure with antelope horns standing over
a rectangle with vertical dotted lines, representing water[34]

Praise to you, Re, high and mighty!
Formed one[35] who shines in the flood.
You are indeed the corpse of Nun.[36]
NAME: Nun

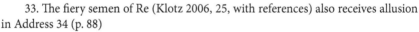

33. The fiery semen of Re (Klotz 2006, 25, with references) also receives allusion in Address 34 (p. 88)

34. In relief versions of this figure, the painted dotted lines are replaced with carved rippling water lines.

35. Taking *imy* as a derivative of *im* "form" (*WÄS* 1:78.1) with Hornung 1976, 105 note 58; one may also note the term *im* "clay" (*WÄS* 1:78.2), which in this context might reference the forming of Khepri atop the potter's wheel (Dorman 1999); for the watery associations of this image, see Manassa 2007a, 179–80.

36. The Nun waters relate closely to the Osirian aspect of the rejuvenating solar deity (see Darnell 2004, 391–97); Nun is also the recipient of the semen of the creator deity in later texts detailing the theology of the Ogdoad (Klotz 2006, 102–7; Klotz 2012a, 174–85).

ADDRESS 21 (PLATE 1, NO. 21)

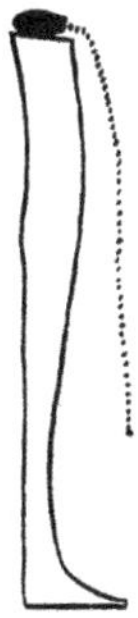

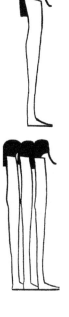

Fig. 2.23. Mummiform figure with a pouring pot in place of head[37]

Praise to you, Re, high and mighty!
Who protects Nun, who comes forth from those with him.
You are indeed the corpse of Weeper.[38]
NAME: Weeper

ADDRESS 22 (PLATE 2, NO. 22)

Fig. 2.24. Mummiform male with divine beard

Praise to you, Re, high and mighty!
He of the twin uraei, equipped with two feathers.
You are indeed the corpse of Putrefaction.[39]
NAME: Putrefaction

ADDRESS 23 (PLATE 1, NO. 23)

Fig. 2.25. Three mummiform males with divine beards

Praise to you, Re, high and mighty!
Who enters and goes forth, and vice versa.
Who belongs to his mysterious and hidden cavern.
You are indeed the corpse of the Mullet-fish.[40]
NAME: Mullet-Fish

---

37. An alternative figure is a mummiform male (without wig) and a stream of water descending from his forehead.

38. The tears of the solar deity produce humans, through a pun between *rmṯ* (people) and *rmy.t* (tears) (Hornung 1976, 106 n. 62; Klotz 2006, 143).

39. For the positive associations of putrefaction, see the study of Dobbin-Bennett 2014. The juxtaposition of Address 21 to "Weeper" with Address 22 to "Putrefaction" is particularly interesting in light of Coffin Texts Spell 755 (CT VIII 464g–465a): *iw rm.wt nṯr m ḥwꜣꜣ.t ꜥ.t im=i*, "The tears of the god are the putrefaction of the body part within me" (see Dobbin-Bennett 2014, 277 for commentary to this passage).

40. A surprisingly well-attested designation of the solar god; "ꜣdw," *LGG* 2:76.

ADDRESS 24 (PLATE 2, NO. 24)

Fig. 2.26. An *udjat*-eye in an oval sarcophagus

Praise to you, Re, high and mighty!
Ba-soul, to whom is offered his damaged eye.
You are indeed the corpse of the Divine Eye.
NAME: Divine Eye

_____

ADDRESS 24 (LATE PERIOD VARIANT) (AFTER MANASSA 2007A, PL. 156)

Fig. 2.27. An *udjat*-eye in an oval sarcophagus

Praise to you, Re, high and mighty!
Ba-soul who is in the *udjat*-eye.[41]
Who commands his light rays.
You are indeed the corpse of the Divine Eye.
NAME: Divine Eye

_____

ADDRESS 25 (PLATE 1, NO. 25)

Fig. 2.28. Male with bent knees and arms hanging down,
wearing a calf-length garment and divine beard

Praise to you, Re, high and mighty!
Standing of *ba*-soul, unique one who protects his creations.
You are indeed the corpse of He Who Belongs to the Engen-
    derer.[42]
NAME: He Who Belongs to the Engenderer

_____

41. For a deity in the eye, particularly Amun-Re, see Klotz 2006, 175–85.
42. *nltwty* is only attested in the Book of Adoring Re in the West ("*Nltwty*," *LGG* 4:388), but the Engenderer *wtt* is a common designation of the solar deity ("*Wtt*," *LGG* 2:597–98).

ADDRESS 26 (PLATE 2, NO. 26)

Fig. 2.29. Vertically oriented ram with its hooves raised in adoration[43]

Praise to you, Re, high and mighty!
Attached of head, begetting[44] of horns.
You are indeed the corpse of the Ram, great of manifestations.[45]
NAME: Great Ram

ADDRESS TO FOREMOST OF THE WEST[46] (AFTER MANASSA 2007B, PL. 156)

Fig. 2.30. Ram-headed mummy

Praise to you, Re, high and mighty!
The great *ba*-soul, who speaks to the gods.
You are indeed the corpse of Foremost of the West.
NAME: Foremost of the West

ADDRESS 27 (PLATE 1, NO. 27)

Fig. 2.31. Mummiform female

Praise to you, Re, high and mighty!
Who casts light, Shu in Igeret.
You are indeed the corpse of the West.
NAME: West

43. In the tomb of Thutmose III, the ram is facing to the left, its praising limbs up against the sarcophagus in which rests the *udjat*-eye in the sarcophagus (Address 24).

44. Reading ⸢ꜣ as a variant of ꜣꜥ, "to beget, to ejaculate" (Darnell 2004, 320 n. 203); for deities who come forth from the horns of another deity, see *WÄS* 1:297.16; the sun himself can emerge from the horns of the celestial cow (see p. 113 n. 111).

45. The litany evokes the engendering and transformational solar deity as the Mendesian ram (Klotz 2006, 98–99).

46. This address occurs between Address 26 and a variant of Address 30 in several Late period sources but is not attested in the New Kingdom (Manassa 2007a, 165–66).

ADDRESS 28 (PLATE 2, NO. 28)

Fig. 2.32. Mummiform male with divine beard

Praise to you, Re, high and mighty!
Perceptive of *ba*-soul in the West.
You are indeed the corpse of He of the Cavern.
NAME: He of the Cavern

ADDRESS 29 (PLATE 1, NO. 29)

Fig. 2.33. Mummiform male with lock of hair emerging from
his forehead

Praise to you, Re, high and mighty!
This one whose *ba*-soul wails, weeper.
You are indeed the corpse of Mourner.[47]
NAME: Mourner

ADDRESS 30 (PLATE 2, NO. 30)

Fig. 2.34. Mummiform male within a mound[48]

Praise to you, Re, high and mighty!
Inducting of arm, who acclaims his eye.
You are indeed the corpse of Hidden of Limbs.
NAME: Hidden of Limbs

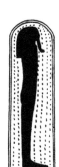

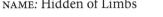

47. The address evokes the names and descriptions of the Book of Caverns, Division 2, Register 2, Scene 18 (pp. 358–59).
48. Some versions show the figure within a sarcophagus.

ADDRESS 30 (LATE PERIOD VARIANT) (AFTER MANASSA 2007B, PL. 156)

Fig. 2.35. Ram-headed mummy within oval sarcophagus

Praise to you, Re, high and mighty!
Who inducts your manifestation for the Netherworld Dwellers.
You are indeed the corpse of Hidden of Limbs.
NAME: Hidden of Limbs

ADDRESS 31 (PLATE 1, NO. 31)

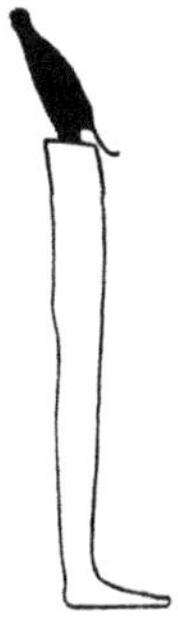

Fig. 2.36. Mummiform male with white crown and divine beard

Praise to you, Re, high and mighty!
Who shines[49] at the Mysterious Place.
You are indeed the corpse of Foremost of the West.
NAME: Foremost of the West

ADDRESS 32 (PLATE 2, NO. 32)

Fig. 2.37. Scarab-headed figure wearing floor-length garment

Praise to you, Re, high and mighty!
Plentiful of manifestations in the sacred chamber.
You are indeed the corpse of the Manifesting One.
NAME: Manifesting One

---

49. Meeks 1998a, 111; Wiebach-Koepke 2003a, 381 n. 3. Compare the use of *bꜣḥ.t*, "white of the eye," in the Heqanakht Letters (Allen 2002, 38, II 3); Pyramid Texts Utterance 43 similarly refers to the white and black portions of the eye: "Here are Horus's two eyes, black and white: take them to your countenance, that they may brighten your face." (translation of Allen 2005, 20 [Spell 31]; the authors would like to thank Anthony Spalinger for noting this passage).

ADDRESS 33 (PLATE 1, NO. 33)

Fig. 2.38. Mummiform figure with a feline head

Praise to you, Re, high and mighty!
Who gives his enemies over to their captivity.
You are indeed the corpse of the Cat-Like One.[50]
NAME: Cat-Like One

ADDRESS 34 (PLATE 2, NO. 34)

Fig. 2.39. Male wearing floor-length garment with erect phallus[51]

Praise to you, Re, high and mighty!
He of the rays in the Mysterious Place.
You are indeed the corpse of He Who Ejaculates.[52]
NAME: He Who Ejaculates

ADDRESS 35 (PLATE 1, NO. 35)

Fig. 2.40. Mummiform male with divine beard within sarcophagus

Praise to you, Re, high and mighty!
Enclosed of corpse, breathing of throat.
You are indeed the corpse of He of the Sarcophagus.
NAME: He of the Sarcophagus

---

50. See pp. 72–73.
51. In some versions, the figure is mummiform, but retains an erect phallus.
52. This litany expressly links light and semen, an equation depicted in the Books of the Solar-Osirian Unity, Tomb of Ramesses IX, Enigmatic Wall, Left Section, Register 3 (pp. 532–33, 566–67; see also Darnell 2004, 320–21).

ADDRESS 36 (PLATE 2, NO. 26)

Fig. 2.41. Mummiform figure with bull head

Praise to you, Re, high and mighty!
Who calls to the corpses who are among the Netherworld
    Dwellers,
so that they might breathe and their efflux[53] be destroyed.
You are indeed the corpse of Breather.
NAME: Breather

ADDRESS 37 (PLATE 1, NO. 37)

Fig. 2.42. Mummiform figure with boar head

Praise to you, Re, high and mighty!
Mysterious of face, whom the divine eye leads.[54]
You are indeed the corpse of Fate.
NAME: Fate[55]

ADDRESS 38 (PLATE 2, NO. 38)

Fig. 2.43. Mummiform male with divine beard

Praise to you, Re, high and mighty!
Lord of distinctions, who alights in the Netherworld.
You are indeed the corpse of Alighting of *Ba*-Soul.
NAME: Alighting of *Ba*-Soul

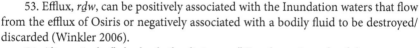

53. Efflux, *rḏw*, can be positively associated with the Inundation waters that flow from the efflux of Osiris or negatively associated with a bodily fluid to be destroyed/discarded (Winkler 2006).

54. Alternatively, "who leads the divine eye." For the active role of the eye, compare Address 57 and the commentary on pp. 70–71.

55. For alternate readings of the address to Shai and the associations of this form of Re with the god Seth, see Manassa 2007a, 154–55. Volokhine 2014, 223–25 similarly associates this boar of Re with the positive role of Seth against the serpent Apep.

ADDRESS 39 (PLATE 1, NO. 39)

Fig. 2.44. Mummiform male with divine beard

Praise to you, Re, high and mighty!
Who hides the corpse from those with him.
You are indeed the corpse of Hidden of Corpse.
NAME: Hidden of Corpse

ADDRESS 40 (PLATE 2, NO. 40)

Fig. 2.45. Mummiform male with divine beard and taper atop his head

Praise to you, Re, high and mighty!
More powerful than those in his following.
Who commands a blaze in the Place of Destruction.
You are indeed the corpse of the Blazing One.
NAME: Blazing One

ADDRESS 41 (PLATE 1, NO. 41)

Fig. 2.46. Mummiform figure with falcon head

Praise to you, Re, high and mighty!
Who commands destruction,[56]
who creates breath by means of his manifestations within
    the Netherworld.
You are indeed the corpse of He of the Netherworld.
NAME: He of the Netherworld

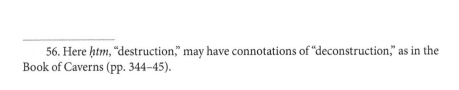

56. Here *ḥtm*, "destruction," may have connotations of "deconstruction," as in the Book of Caverns (pp. 344–45).

ADDRESS 42 (PLATE 2, NO. 42)

Fig. 2.47. Mummiform male with divine beard

Praise to you, Re, high and mighty!
Distinguished of head, foremost of the oval.[57]
Who brightens in the Mysterious Place.
You are indeed the corpse of the Bright One.
NAME: Bright One

ADDRESS 43 (PLATE 1, NO. 43)

Fig. 2.48. Mummiform figure with bundled object and two ties
in place of a head[58]

Praise to you, Re, high and mighty!
United of limbs, who distinguishes the one within the earth.
You are indeed the corpse of United of Limbs.
NAME: United of Limbs

ADDRESS 44 (PLATE 2, NO. 44)

Fig. 2.49. Mummiform male with divine beard

Praise to you, Re, high and mighty!
Who creates the mystery,[59] who engenders the corpse.
You are indeed the corpse of the Mystery.
NAME: Mystery

---

57. The oval could refer to the oval of Sokar in the Book of the Hidden Chamber, Hour 5, Register 3, Scene 56 (pp. 182–85), which itself can be a microcosm of the Netherworld (Wiebach-Koepke 2003a, 385 n. 1).

58. Some versions add eyes to the bundle; for a discussion of this depiction, see Hornung 1976, 111–12, n. 117.

59. The "mystery" is the corpse of Osiris (see Assmann 1969, 85; Darnell 2004, 384–85 n. 54).

ADDRESS 45 (PLATE 1, NO. 45)

Fig. 2.50. Mummiform figure with shrew head

Praise to you, Re, high and mighty!
For whom those within the Netherworld have been equipped,
    when he passes by the mysterious caverns.
You are indeed the corpse of the Equipped One of the Earth.
NAME: Equipped One of the Earth

ADDRESS 46 (PLATE 2, NO. 46)

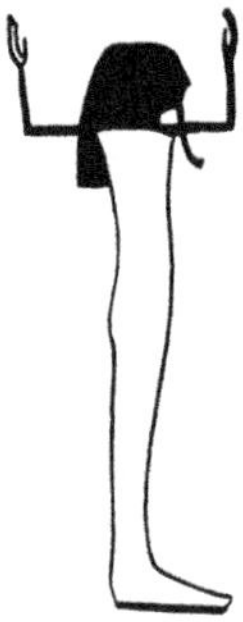

Fig. 2.51. Mummiform male with divine beard and two arms
raised to either side of head, palms facing inwards

Praise to you, Re, high and mighty!
Whose flesh rejoices, when he sees his corpse.
Strong of *ba*-soul, when he passes by the body.[60]
You are indeed the corpse of Rejoicer!
NAME: Rejoicer

ADDRESS 47 (PLATE 1, NO. 47)

Fig. 2.52. Mummiform male with divine beard

Praise to you, Re, high and mighty!
Distinguished one, dripping of *udjat*-eye.[61]
He of the *ba*-soul, for whom the effective eye becomes full.
You are indeed the corpse of the Distinguished One.
NAME: Distinguished One

---

60. The juxtaposition of *ba*-soul, corpse, and rejoicing mirrors the "greeting" of Re and Osiris during the unification of soul and corpse (see p. 146 n. 37, p. 571 n. 75).

61. Reading *nḏfḏf* as the term *nḏfḏf* (*WÄS* 2:368.13), appearing in Ptolemaic texts as *tf*(*tf*) (Žabkar 1988, 44–45; Wilson 1997, 1141); the eye of Horus "drips" already in the Pyramid Texts and in New Kingdom visitor's graffiti heaven "drips" with myrrh (Darnell 2013, 79–80 n. 563). The "drippings" from the eye most likely refer to the *iзd.t rnp.t*, "dew of the year."

ADDRESS 48 (PLATE 2, NO. 48)

Fig. 2.53. Mummiform male with divine beard

Praise to you, Re, high and mighty!
Who straightens[62] paths that are in the Netherworld.
Who opens roads in the Mysterious Place.
You are indeed the corpse of Straightener of Paths.
NAME: Straightener of Paths

ADDRESS 49 (PLATE 1, NO. 49)

Fig. 2.54. Mummiform male with divine beard

Praise to you, Re, high and mighty!
Traveling *ba*-soul, who passes by (with great) strides.
You are indeed the corpse of Traveler.
NAME: Traveler

ADDRESS 50 (PLATE 2, NO. 50)

Fig. 2.55. Scarab beetle pushing a solar disk

Praise to you, Re, high and mighty!
Who commands his stars,
    as he illumines the darkness in the caverns.
One mysterious of visible forms.
You are indeed the corpse of Illuminer.
NAME: Illuminer

---

62. For *mꜣꜥ wꜣ.wt*, "to straighten (make right) paths," see Manassa 2007a, 105–6 and parallels cited therein.

ADDRESS 51 (PLATE 1, NO. 51)

Fig. 2.56. Mummiform figure with ram head

Praise to you, Re, high and mighty!
Who makes caverns, who creates corpses
    by means of what he himself has commanded.
May you, Re, command for those who are and those who
    are not, namely the gods,
    the *akh*-spirits, and the dead.
You are indeed the corpse of He Who Creates Corpses.
NAME: He Who Creates Corpses

ADDRESS 52 (PLATE 1, NO. 52)

Fig. 2.57. Mummiform figure with bull head

Praise to you, Re, high and mighty!
Most mysterious one. Hidden one.
This power of whose head is like his image,
    as he gives passage to those who are in his following.
You are indeed the corpse of Hidden One.
NAME: Hidden One

ADDRESS 53 (PLATE 2, NO. 53)

Fig. 2.58. Mummiform figure with oryx head

Praise to you, Re, high and mighty!
Rising of horns, pillar of the West.
Dark of lock who is within the cauldron.[63]
You are indeed the corpse of Rising of Horns.
NAME: Rising of Horns

---

63. The oryx-headed manifestation of the solar deity is here associated with a cauldron, a common means of punishment in the Netherworld Books. The oryx can be a sacrificial creature or one capable of dispelling evil (Manassa 2006, 117–18), and as with the god Shai, a Sethian aspect who turns against chaos.

ADDRESS 54 (PLATE 2, NO. 54)

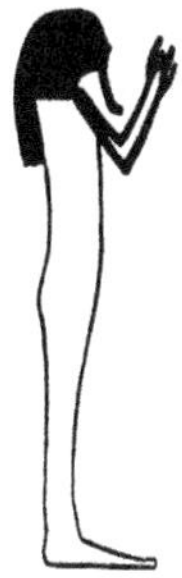

Fig. 2.59. Mummiform male with two arms raised in adoration

Praise to you, Re, high and mighty!
Distinguished of visible forms,
    as he crosses the Netherworld,
    as he causes that the *ba*-souls acclaim within their caverns.
You are indeed the corpse of Distinguished of Forms.
NAME: Distinguished of Forms

ADDRESS 55 (PLATE 1, NO. 55)

Fig. 2.60. Mummiform male with divine beard

Praise to you, Re, high and mighty!
Who joins with the beautiful West.
As soon as they see him, the Netherworld Dwellers rejoice.
You are indeed the corpse of the Pleased One.
NAME: Pleased One

ADDRESS 56 (PLATE 1, NO. 56)

Fig. 2.61. Seated tomcat

Praise to you, Re, high and mighty!
Great cat, protector of the gods.
Judge, chief of the council, foremost of the sacred cavern.
You are indeed the corpse of the Great Cat.[64]
NAME: Great Cat

---

64. For commentary to this litany, see pp. 72–73.

ADDRESS 57 (PLATE 1, NO. 57)

Fig. 2.62. Mummiform figure with ram head

Praise to you, Re, high and mighty!
Whom his eye saves, whose effective eye speaks,
    when the corpses lament.
You are indeed the corpse of the One Whose Effective
    Eye Speaks.[65]
NAME: One Whose Effective Eye Speaks

ADDRESS 58 (PLATE 2, NO. 58)

Fig. 2.63. Mummiform figure with falcon head

Praise to you, Re, high and mighty!
Whose *ba*-soul is far, whose corpse is hidden![66]
Who shines when he sees his mystery.[67]
You are indeed the corpse of the One Far of *Ba*-soul
NAME: One Far of *Ba*-Soul

ADDRESS 59 (PLATE 2, NO. 59)

Fig. 2.64. Mummiform figure with ram head

Praise to you, Re, high and mighty!
Ba-soul who drives off his enemies.
Who decrees flame among his punished ones.
You are indeed the corpse of One High of *Ba*-soul.
NAME: One High of *Ba*-Soul

---

65. For commentary to this litany, see pp. 70–71.
66. This statement is parallel to other references to a dual future for the elements of the deceased (Hornung 1976, 116, n. 161; p. 8 n. 13).
67. For Re shining on the corpse, as he rises on the breast of the Osirian form, see p. 71.

ADDRESS 60 (PLATE 1, NO. 60)

Fig. 2.65. Mummiform male with divine beard

Praise to you, Re, high and mighty!
Rotting one, who hides the putrefaction.[68]
Power of the *ba*-souls of the gods.
You are indeed the corpse of the Rotting One.
NAME: Rotting One

ADDRESS 61 (PLATE 2, NO. 61)

Fig. 2.66. Mummiform male with divine beard and a skull-cap

Praise to you, Re, high and mighty!
Great elder in the forecourt of the Netherworld.
Khepri who develops as[69] the Child.[70]
You are indeed the corpse of the Child.[71]
NAME: Child

ADDRESS 62 (PLATE 1, NO. 62)

Fig. 2.67. Mummiform figure with bread loaf in place of head

Praise to you, Re, high and mighty!
Great of travels, who renews movements.[72]
Ba-soul, bright of body, dark of face.
You are indeed the corpse of Dark of Face.
NAME: Dark of Face

68. Dobbin-Bennett 2014, 321–22.

69. Parallel to the idiom *ḫpr nḫnw*, "develop through childhood" (*WÄS* 3:262.1); Hornung 1976, 117 n. 170.

70. The term *sḏ.ty*, "child," here puns with the term *sḏ.t*, "flame," a reference to the youthful rising sun (see p. 567 n. 72).

71. Some Late period versions (Type II sarcophagi and the sarcophagus of Nectanebo II) add the line: "It is he who is the Child, the egg who emerged before him" (see further Manassa 2007a, 99–100).

72. Reading (with Hornung 1976, 117 n. 171) *nti* as *ntꜣ* (see also Hannig 2006a, 1366); this epithet refers to the sun god as the cosmic runner. See also Address 49.

ADDRESS 63 (PLATE 2, NO. 63)

Fig. 2.68. Mummiform male with divine beard and a skull-cap

Praise to you, Re, high and mighty!
Who greets his body, who judges the gods.[73]
The mysterious burning one within the earth.
Indeed, you are the corpse of the Burning One within the Earth.
NAME: Burning One within the Earth

ADDRESS 64 (PLATE 1, NO. 64)

Fig. 2.69. Mummiform figure with two ropes in place of a head

Praise to you, Re, high and mighty!
Lord of binding against his enemies.
Great unique one, chief of his monkeys.[74]
You are indeed the corpse of the Binder.
NAME: Binder

ADDRESS 65 (PLATE 2, NO. 65)

Fig. 2.70. Mummiform male with divine beard wearing a cauldron
on his head

Praise to you, Re, high and mighty!
Who decrees flame in his cauldrons.
This one who cuts off the heads of the destroyed ones.
Indeed, you are the corpse of He of the Cauldron.[75]
NAME: He of the Cauldron

---

73. Re greets Osiris in the eastern horizon, at the same time he judges the damned, related events to which Address 63 alludes (Manassa 2007a, 92).

74. The *gf.t*-monkey may appear in the Judgment Hall (Scene 33) in the Book of Gates (Hornung and Abt 2014, 188; alternate reading in Manassa 2006, 124–25; see also p. 284–85).

75. For decapitated enemies within cauldrons, compare the Book of Caverns, Division 5, Scenes 57–58 (pp. 408–9).

ADDRESS 66 (PLATE 1, NO. 66)

Fig. 2.71. Mummiform male wearing *atef*-crown

Praise to you, Re, high and mighty!
Engenderer, complete of birth forms.
Unique one, who raises the earth through his effective spells.
You are indeed the corpse of Tatenen.[76]
NAME: Tatenen

ADDRESS 67 (PLATE 2, NO. 67)

Fig. 2.72. Three mummies oriented vertically, rising out of an oval[77]

Praise to you, Re, high and mighty!
For whom the Waking Ones stand, while yet upon their biers,
     without seeing their mysteries.
Indeed, you are the corpse of the Waking Ones.
NAME: Waking Ones

ADDRESS 68 (PLATE 1, NO. 68)

Fig. 2.73. Mummiform figure with falcon head

Praise to you, Re, high and mighty!
Water clock[78] of the sky, star of the Netherworld.
Who conducts his mummies.
You are indeed the corpse of the Conductor.
NAME: Conductor

---

76. For Tatenen in the Book of Adoring Re in the West, see Schlögl 1980, 26–30.

77. The oval can also be depicted as a disk; for the position of these mummies—prone but with heads uplifted—see the commentary to the Book of Gates, Hour 8, Register 3, Scene 53 (p. 302). For the apparently animal (jackal?) headed figures in the Thutmose III version (as in fig. 2.72), compare the rare appearance of a jackal-headed form of the otherwise anthropomorphic cosmic deity Tekem (see Darnell 2004: 229–30).

78. Manassa 2007a, 81.

ADDRESS 69 (PLATE 2, NO. 69)

Fig. 2.74. Mummiform figure with baboon head

Praise to you, Re, high and mighty!
Jubilating baboon, he of Wetchnet.
Khepri, correct of visible forms.
You are indeed the corpse of the Netherworldly Baboon.[79]
NAME: Netherworldly Baboon

ADDRESS 70 (PLATE 1, NO. 70)

Fig. 2.75. Mummiform male with divine beard

Praise to you, Re, high and mighty!
Who renews the earth, who opens what is therein.
Whose *ba*-soul speaks, who nurses his limbs.
You are indeed the corpse of Renewer of the Earth.
NAME: Renewer of the Earth

ADDRESS 71 (PLATE 2, NO. 71)

Fig. 2.76. Mummiform figure with baboon head

Praise to you, Re, high and mighty!
Nehi[80] who burns the enemies.
Fiery one, flaming of tongue!
You are indeed the corpse of Nehi.
NAME: Nehi

79. For commentary to this passage, see pp. 73–74.

80. Nehi appears as an epithet of Ptah-Tatenen (Schlögl 1980, 73–74), and this form of the solar deity is also linked to the guinea fowl. By its cry the guinea fowl is an animal whose vocalization accompanies and thereby magically assists the rising of the sun (Beaux 2004, 28–31; for animals assisting the rising sun, compare te Velde 1988); by play on the phonetic similarity between the term for the guinea fowl and the word for cyclical eternity, the cry of the *nḥ*-guinea fowl may evoke *nḥḥ*-eternity (Beaux 2004, 28–29 and 31–35). Nehi appears again in Litany 7 (p. 116) and in the Book of Caverns, Division 2, Register 4, Scene 23 (p. 365).

ADDRESS 72 (PLATE 1, NO. 72)[81]

Fig. 2.77. Mummiform figure with falcon head

Praise to you, Re, high and mighty!
Traveler, transiting of luminosity.
Who creates darkness in the following of his light.
You are indeed the corpse of Traveler.
NAME: Traveler

ADDRESS 73 (PLATE 2, NO. 73)

Fig. 2.78. Mummiform male with divine beard

Praise to you, Re, high and mighty!
Lord of power, who is within his Benben sanctuary.[82]
Chief of the gods of the forehall.
You are indeed the corpse of Lord of Power.
NAME: Lord of Power

ADDRESS 74 (PLATE 1, NO. 74)

Fig. 2.79. Mummiform male with divine beard

Praise to you, Re, high and mighty!
Obelisk point, he of the Benben sanctuary.
The great god who binds time.
Indeed, you are the corpse of the Obelisk Point.
NAME: Obelisk Point

---

81. Addresses 68 and 72 both reference the same mummiform falcon-headed figure, since both names—"Conductor" (Address 68) and "Traveler" (Address 72)—are clearly written above the hieracocephalic mummy; among the possible examples, compare the tombs of Thutmose III (Hornung 1975, 57) and Seti I (Hornung and Burton 1991, 94).

82. The Temple of the Benben also appears within the Book of Gates, Hour 6, Register 2, Scene 38 (p. 289); for commentary to this passage, see p. 43.

ADDRESS 75 (PLATE 2, NO. 75)

Fig. 2.80. Mummiform figure with ram head

Praise to you, Re, high and mighty!
Lord of darkness, who speaks by means of the mystery,
Ba-soul, who calls to those who are in their caverns.
You are indeed the corpse of the Lord of Darkness.
NAME: Lord of Darkness

LITANY 1

O, Re, he of the cavern!
O, Re, who calls to the cavern dwellers!
O, Re, who is within his cavern!

Praise be to you, Re, migratory one[83] (four times)!
Praise belongs to your *ba*-soul, migratory one.
The cavern dwellers give praise to his *ba*-soul,
    and adore your corpses that are with you.
Praise be to you, great one, migratory one (four times)!
Praise be to you, *ba*-soul, migratory one, in your seventy-four manifestations,
    who manifest in your seventy-four caverns.

I know it in their names.[84]
I know all of their manifestations.
I know that which is in their corpses and all their mysterious visible forms.
I summon them in their names.
I call them in their manifestations—
    that they open for me the Netherworld,
    that they throw open the mysterious gates for this *ba*-soul of his,
        exactly like your *ba*-soul.

---

83. For this epithet of the solar deity, see Manassa 2007a, 83–83.

84. The first-person pronoun is used in the versions of Useramun and Thutmose III; all other versions employ predominantly the royal name and third-person pronouns. Even when not fully preserved, the first-person translation is maintained throughout the following litanies, since the third-person pronouns appear to be a secondary development (Werning 2007, 1938–39).

May you greet them, may you greet me.
My corpse breathes, exactly like you,
    because I am a unique one among these that are in your following,
    those foremost of their caverns who speak in their grotto,
    those who grow strong in your protection.
They breathe when you call to them.
I am exactly like one among them, who speaks in the mysterious cavern.

LITANY 2

Hail, make for me a path!
I pass by in the following of the *ba*-soul of Re.
Hail, make for me a path, this one of Khepri!

Hail, make for me a path!
I know the natures of the Westerners.
Hail, make for me a path among you.

Praise belongs to the *ba*-soul of the migratory one (four times!).
O, Re who is in the West, who is placed in the earth and who casts light
    among the Netherworld Dwellers.
O, Re who is in his disk!

LITANY 3

May you guide me along the hidden paths, which the *ba*-souls of the West-
    erners traverse.
May you guide me along the paths, mysterious of necessities.
May you guide me along the paths of the West,
    so that I might cross the caverns of She Who Is in Igeret.
May you guide me along the paths of the West,
    so that I might adore these (gods) in the Hidden Chamber.
May you guide me along the paths of the West,
    so that you might raise me up to the cavern of Nun.

Hail, Re, I am Nun!
Hail, Re, I am you and vice versa.
Hail, Re, your *ba*-soul is my *ba*-soul; your journeys are my journeys in the
    Netherworld.
Hail, Re, as I go to rest in the Netherworld, so do I cross the beautiful West.

As you are, so am I.
Your effective spells are my effective spells.
I adore the Westerners, exalt their *ba*-souls.
Your travels are my travels.
Your crossings are my crossings.
I am a great god, Foremost of the Netherworld,
     O, he of the solar disk, great of light.
Praise be to the *ba*-soul of the migratory one (four times)!

Hail to you, this one, *Djeba-demedj*.[85]
May your *ba*-soul be strong, may your corpse breathe.
I cross your mysterious cavern; I traverse the mystery that is with you.
I call to you exactly like the *ba*-soul of Re.
You call to me exactly like the *ba*-soul of Re.
My *ba*-soul is your *ba*-soul. My corpse is your corpse.
I pass by in the following of the *ba*-soul of Re to the place mysterious of
     caverns,
          while I praise by means of my effective spells,
          and I praise by means of your effective spells,
          O one exactly like me, my very own twin!

Re says to me: "One exactly like me, my very own twin!"
Djeba-demedj says to me, "O, may you guide me,
     one foremost of his cavern (four times)!"
Say this spell for every god, namely these (gods) drawn in their forms
     upon the two side walls[86] that are in the Netherworld.
Two portions exist for them as divine offerings.
"You are a *ba*-soul who exists as the twin of Re, the heir of *Djeba-demedj*."
One recites this book in the course of every day when Re rests in the
     West—truly attested!

Greetings to you, those of the cavern, gods who are in the West.

---

85. For this form of the unified Re-Osiris, see Address 1 of the Great Litany (p. 63
n. 5); this subunit of Litany 3—the address to *Djeba-demedj* (ending with "One recites
this book in the course of every day when Re rests in the West—truly attested!")—is
placed on the ceiling of the tombs of Seti I through Ramesses III (Abitz 1995, 67).

86. *pd.wy* can also refer to the heavens, suggesting a relationship between parts of
the tomb and celestial elements (Manassa 2007a, 391–92); that these are in the Netherworld is consistent with the royal tomb being a model of the solar journey into the
realm of nocturnal rejuvenation.

May you be effective.
May your *ba*-souls be strong.
May you destroy the enemies of Re.
May you cause *Djeba-demedj* to breathe.
May you illumine,
    so that your darkness is dispelled.
May you call to the One Who Is within His Disk,
      so that the One Who Is within His Disk calls to you.
May you pass by (just as) Re passes by.
May you see the sanctity of Osiris.
May you live just as he lives.
May you guide me along your paths.
May my *ba*-soul pass over your mysteries.
I am one among you.

My strength is the strength of Re (and vice versa),
    when he reaches[87] the sandbank of traversing.
My victory is the victory of Re,
    when he inflicts punishment on Apep,
    when he smites his evil in the West.
I inflict punishment on my enemies exactly like Re;
I smite their evil in the West exactly like Re.
My strength in the earth is exactly[88] the strength of the *ba*-soul of He of
    the Horizon.
My victory in the earth is exactly the victory of the *ba*-soul of He of the
    Netherworld.
You are justified against your enemies, great god within the horizon (four
    times)!
You are justified against your enemies, O you Osiris, United One (four
    times)!
I am justified against my enemies in the sky, in the earth,
    in the council of every god and every goddess,
    in the council of Osiris Foremost of the Westerners,
      because I am Re, I am the great one who is in the sky.
I speak before the Westerner.
I am justified in the great council.

---

87. A *sḏmt=f* used adverbially (Baumann 1998, 267).
88. For the particle *ỉs* see Oréal 2011, 106–11.

I am pure, and that which is in me is pure.
I am the ruler of the two banks.
I am justified against my enemies (four times)!

Re is powerful as Foremost of the Netherworld.
Re is powerful as Foremost of the Netherworld.
When he crosses, the Netherworld is in rejoicing,
    he having felled Apep.

LITANY 4

Jubilation belongs to you, One Who Is within the Horizon, Osiris, Ruler
    of the West.
Jubilation belongs to you, aggressive *ba*-soul.
You are indeed the one who destroys his enemies.
Jubilation belongs to the red one, red *ba*-soul who opens the West.[89]
You give your arm to Osiris,
    as the beautiful West receives you,
        as its gods jubilate for you.
Osiris gives his arm to you,
    as Foremost of the Westerners receives you.

How shining is the *ba*-soul of Re in the Netherworld!
How luminous is the corpse of *Djeba-demedj*!

Re is justified in the Netherworld,
    he having felled Apep.
Djeba-demedj is justified.
Just as he praises the *ba*-soul of He of the Horizon, so the *ba*-soul of He of
    the Horizon praises him.
I am justified against my enemies in the great council of Tjeba.[90]

O mysterious one!
One who opens the Netherworld and the Mysterious Place,
    who uncovers the darkness and dispels the cloudiness.

---

89. Red is the color of sunrise, and the "aggressive" connotations of the color red
(Goebs 2008, 297–99, passim) fit well within the context of this litany.
    90. For this deity, related to the solar god, see Hornung 1976, 129 n. 306; "*Tbi*,"
LGG 7:381.

Lightning flashes,[91] the Netherworld Dwellers go to rest.
The *ba*-soul of Re sees his corpse,
> when he makes manifestations in (the cavern) mysterious of condition,
> when he casts light into the darkness, which hides the corpses of the naked ones.[92]

He opens the mysterious caverns, and gives eyes to the gods,
> with the result that they see and their *ba*-souls are strong.

Hail, Re, may you give to me my eyes!
May you give to me my two divine eyes,
> so that they might lead me.[93]

Hail, Re, may you give my heart to me,
> so that I might inherit the earth,
> so that I might cross its banks exactly like Re.

What you have done for yourself is that which you have commanded—
> that the manifestation manifest[94] therein.

LITANY 5

You have commanded for me, as for He of the Horizon,
As I extol your *ba*-soul, so I adore you.
You have commanded for me, as for He of the Horizon,
> O Effective One, Shining One, who comes forth from the Place of Shining (the East).[95]

---

91. Spell 148 (CT II 209d) uses the same phrase, *qȝ sšd*, as opening to the spell "making transformation into a falcon" and describing the events of the divine epiphany coinciding with the pregnancy of Isis (Hornung 1976, 130 n. 310; Kurth 1984; contra Hannig 1990).

92. The "naked ones" are mummies whose wrappings have been removed as an expression of resurrection in the Netherworld (Hornung 1983b; see also Book of Gates, Hour 6, Register 3, Scene 40 [pp. 290–91]). Covering effects of light are described as clothing and depicted as billowing waves of light in the Books of the Solar-Osirian Unity on the Second Shrine of Tutankhamun (p. 526 and n. 5).

93. The eyes of the solar deity, as divine barks, can literally lead the solar bark through the navigable waters of the Netherworld (Hegenbarth 2002).

94. The manifesting of manifestations occurs at the time of the encounter with Apep in the Book of Gates, Hour 5, Register 2, Scene 27 (p. 280).

95. All of the following passages that begin with "you have commanded for me" utilize a pun on the epithet of the *ba*-soul and the place from which he comes forth.

You have commanded for me, as for He of the Horizon,
    O strong *ba*-soul who comes forth from the Strong Place.
You have commanded for me, as for He of the Horizon,
       O mysterious *ba*-soul who comes forth from the Place of Mystery.
You have commanded for me, as for He of the Horizon,
    O destroying *ba*-soul who comes forth from the Place of Destruction.
You have commanded for me, as for He of the Horizon,
    O *ba*-soul who opens, who comes forth from the open court.
You have commanded for me, as for He of the Horizon,
    O *ba*-soul who joins, who comes forth from the Place of Joining.
You have commanded for me, as for He of the Horizon,
    O hidden *ba*-soul who comes forth from the Hidden Place.

May you save me from a terrible fear,
    O one who transforms the Netherworld Dwellers into *ba*-souls.
They shall not perform their usual performance[96] against me before the
    knife-wielders.
I shall not fall into their cauldrons.
Their fire-pits shall not be laid against me.
My *ba*-soul is there—it ascends to heaven;
my *ba*-soul is here—it enters into the Netherworld,
    because I know the mysteries that are in the Netherworld
    and those who guide the mysteries of Osiris,
       which even those in his following do not know
       because of the mysteriousness of the Hidden Chamber.[97]

Hail to you—I know your mysteries,
    with the result that you make me justified.
Hail to you—I am one who knows your manifestations, great god, mysteri-
    ous one.
May you save me from your demons, those sharp of knives, the bloody
    ones, those who cut out hearts, those who seize for the ovens.
They shall not perform their actions against me.

---

96. The term here, *n.t-ꜥ*, as repetitive performance, occurs in parallel to the *tp-rd*, "prescription," as elements of a ritual (Darnell 1995, 49–50 and 53 n. g; Wilson 1997, 555; Klotz 2006, 17).

97. For the select few who know the mysteries of the solar cycle, compare the concluding title of the Book of the Hidden Chamber: "Select guide, mysterious writings of the Netherworld, which is not known by any people, except for a select few" (p. 248).

They shall not place me in their ovens because I am Re (and vice versa).
My *ba*-soul is one who is in his disk.
My corpse is (that of) Foremost of the Westerners.
Just as they justify me, so do I justify them.
I am justified,
     with the result that I occupy my *ba*-soul, just like you occupy the West.

The *ba*-soul of Re appears in glory by means of his manifestations,
     while his corpse is content with his (mourning) cries.[98]
The god enters into his light,
     with the result that the Netherworld lights up by means of the rays
     of its creator.
The *ba*-souls stand atop their corpses, while they praise atop their mounds.[99]
The Ennead counsels, with the result that the doorways,
     mysterious of visible forms, are renewed.[100]
Made straight are the paths for the *ba*-soul of Re;
open are the banks for the Remote *Ba*-Soul.[101]
His solar disk traveling around,
     while his *ba*-soul travels rightly.[102]
He calls the corpse of Aqed,[103]
     as he places the star gods in their tracks,

---

98. Compare Address 57 for the connection between the solar epiphany and the lamentations of the dead. For the beneficial effects of mourning and shouting for the solar deity, compare Darnell 2004, 183–85 and 366–68.

99. This line perfectly describes a scene within the Books of the Creation of the Solar Disk (Manassa 2007a, 42–43; below p. 521).

100. Possibly an allusion to the Enneads within the *sbḫ.t*-doorways in the Book of Gates; see p. 264.

101. See Address 58, p. 96.

102. Compare the address to the "rightly traveling" one in Litany 6 (pp. 110–11) and Litany 8 (p. 121).

103. Attested only in the Book of Adoring Re in the West ("*ꜣqd*," *LGG* 1:82). Note Hornung 1976, 133 n. 356; Hannig, 2006a, 45—the crocodile determinatives there, especially in the name of a Netherworldly being in CT 4.127d, suggests the usage here, with star determinative, perhaps at once allusive both to the crocodilian aspects of certain elements of the northern constellations, in proximity to the Osirian Orion (Neugebauer and Parker 1969, 183–89 and 193–94) and the crocodiles such as (Pen)-Wenty of the Books of the Creation of the Solar Disk who assist in the destruction and resurrection of the sun (pp. 501, 506; see also the introductory scene to the Book of Adoring Re in the West—pp. 62, 75).

so that they might lead He of the Pillar[104] and his hours.
The two sisters unite with him;
they appear in glory atop him in his visible appearance of Appearing *Ba*-
   Soul.

O, Re, may you lead me in your following.
I am the respected one, whose places are mysterious,
      who knows the affairs of the *akh*-spirits,
            because of the greatness of my power over my enemies.
I am strong by means of my two eyes.
O traveler, my travels are your travels.
O Re, my crossings are your crossings.
O Re, you are justified against my enemies,
      and I am justified against your enemies in the great council.
Re rises from the Netherworld,
      while the bull is pleased in Kenset.[105]
O Re, as soon as you occupy your corpse, you are strong in your mysteries.

LITANY 6

O Re, come to me, rightly traveling![106]
Djeba-demedj, praise!
O Re, come to me, rightly traveling!
      Youthful is your *ba*-soul, (re-)born is your corpse!

---

104. An epithet of Osiris as lunar deity ("*iwn*," *LGG* 1:193–94). Compare also Address 53 in the Great Litany (p. 94): "Rising of horns, pillar of the West."

105. Compare the sound heard in the fourth cavern of Hour 8, Register 1, Scene 83, of the Book of the Hidden Chamber (p. 206): "A sound of something is heard in this cavern like the sound of the bull of bulls being pleased (*nim*)"; a passage in the Book of Gates, Hour 3, Register 2, Scene 11 provides another parallel: "The earth quakes, the earth quakes; as the *ba*-soul grows strong so the double bull bellows in pleasure (*nim*)." For the rich allusions of the pleasurable sound of the bull, see Manassa 2008, 121–22 with 122 n. 63 collecting references to the toponym Kenset; for divine names with the toponym Kenset, note also "*Knst*," *LGG* 7:291.

106. Alternatively, this could be an epithet of the solar god as "Leitender" (Hornung 1976, 81 and 135, n. 372); the versions in the tombs of Ramesses II and Merneptah confuse this for *mꜣꜥ-ḫrw*, "justified." For the verb *mꜣꜥ*, compare Address 48 in the Great Litany (p. 93). Note also the passage in Litany 5 above "his (Re's) solar disk traveling around, while his *ba*-soul travels rightly" (p. 109) and the address in Litany 8 to the "rightly traveling" one.

O Re, come to me, rightly traveling!
  May you guide me to the sacred places!
O Re, come to me, rightly traveling!
  May you guide me on the beautiful paths!
O Re, come to me, rightly traveling!
  May you guide me on the paths of Nut!
O Re, come to me, rightly traveling!
  May you guide me along the roads of heaven!
O Re, come to me, rightly traveling!
  I am greeting the corpse of Osiris.
O Re, come to me, rightly traveling,
  while I place One Weary of Heart atop his dais,[107]
    in the place, which no one knows.
O Re, come to me, rightly traveling,
  with the result that my body speaks as Osiris.
O Re, come to me, rightly traveling!
  I am beholding that which is within the chest.[108]
O Re, come to me, rightly traveling!
  The rays of your sun disk are upon my perfection.
O Re, come to me, rightly traveling!
  I begin a perfect journey.
O Re, come to me, rightly traveling!
  I am adoring your *ba*-soul in the horizon.
O Re, come to me, rightly traveling!
  May you commend me as One within His Earth.
O Re, come to me, rightly traveling!
  I am the unique one who is in your Ennead.

107. The term *mk.t* is determined with a stairway, suggesting that this is not the term *mk(ꜣ).t*, appearing elsewhere in the Netherworld Books as "bier," but rather related to the term "socle, podium" (Hannig 2003, 573). For Osiris atop a dais, compare the Judgment Hall in the Book of Gates (Scene 33), pp. 284–86.

108. The sacred chest containing the Solar-Osirian corpse appears multiple times within the Netherworld Books—the Book of the Hidden Chamber, Hour 6, Register 1, Scene 61 (p. 189); Book of Caverns, Division 2, Register 3, Scene 21 (pp. 361–62); the Books of the Creation of the Solar Disk in the Tomb of Ramesses VI, Section A, Register 1, Scene 4 (pp. 468–69); and Books of the Solar-Osirian Unity, Second Shrine of Tutankhamun, Side 1, Register 3, Scene 9 (p. 543).

You, Re, give birth to me;

you create me in your very likeness, O He of the Horizon.

My births are the births of Re in the West (and vice versa).

My births in heaven are the births of the *ba*-soul of Re in heaven (and vice versa).

My lives are the lives of the *ba*-soul of Re (and vice versa).

The breathing of my corpse is the breathing of the corpse of Re (and vice versa).

Re is pregnant with me;

Atum gives birth to me.

I am the child of Khepri.

Nut nurses me;

she suckles me exactly like the *ba*-soul of Re who is within her.

O Re who is in the West, starry of forms, Foremost of the Netherworld.

May you save me from your messengers, those who seize *ba*-souls and corpses, those who rush, those who hurry, those within your places of punishment.[109]

They will not seize me;

they will not grasp me.

Their strides will not hurry against me;

they will not put me in their places of punishment.

Their ropes will not coil around me.

They will not place me upon their offering tables.

I will not sink into the land of the destroyed ones.

I will not be punished in the West.

As He of the Horizon goes, go I.

As Re travels, travel I,

　　making jubilation for those within the earth,

　　adoring those mysterious of corpse.

They lead my *ba*-soul; they speak to me.

"Divine Utterance" they say to me,

　　because I am the *ba*-soul of Divine Utterance.

---

109. Parallel to the Book of the Heavenly Cow (Hornung 1991, 6, ll. 61–63): "Then Re said: 'Pray summon to me messengers, these who rush and those who hurry, whose running is as swift as the shadow of a corpse.'" For the role of messengers in the Netherworld Books, see Darnell 2004, 329–33, 412–13 (note particularly Epigraphic Survey 1934, pl. 173 for the frenetic atmosphere of a temple slaughter house).

Divine Perception is as one within my protection,
  he who causes the *heden*-plant[110] to grow,
    so that I might not be ignorant.

The voice of rejoicing is in the Mysterious Place: "It is Re who rests in
  Osiris—and vice versa!"

Hail to you, those weary of heart!
You shall make praise to Re—Re praises you.
Re shall go forth from the Great Flood;[111]
the United One shall go to rest in the Great Water.
I shall go forth from the Great Flood like Re,
  so that he (Re) may rest in the Great Water exactly like the United
  One.
My name is his name within the Great Flood.
My restings are his restings within the Great Water.

"How beautiful are you!"
  So say the Netherworld Dwellers concerning me.
"How powerful are you!"
So say the Westerners concerning me.

"Your beauty is that of the one of Kenset;
your power is that of *Djeba-demedj*!"[112]
  So say the Westerners about me,
    as they rejoice when seeing me.

"Hail equipped *akh*-spirit who comes forth from Tatenen,
  one provided with manifestations,
  one great of visible forms,
  lord of *ba*-soul and shade,
  for whom destruction does not exist,
  who lives as we live,
  who knows our primordial visible forms,

---

110. For the identification of this plant, see Goyon 1984; Meeks 1998a, 232; Meeks 1998c, 181 (no. 79.1848); for *hdn* as a member of the plant family *Apiaceae*, see Hannig 2006a, 1581, suggesting "Hasenohr, Bupleurum."

111. For the image of Re atop the horns of Mehetweret (the Great Flood) and other heavenly cows, see Klotz 2006, 103–5; Verhoeven 2007.

112. Note that this evokes the end of Litany 5, with the bull in Kenset, and Re uniting with his corpse (p. 110).

who knows the mysterious inductions[113] that are within the Netherworld.
You are one who enters the mysterious sanctities!"[114]
So say the gods to me,
as they rejoice when seeing me.

"Pass by, one whose *ba*-soul travels rightly, excellent *akh*-spirit.
You are indeed this unique one among us!"
So say the gods to me,
as they rejoice when they see me.

"Appear in glory, Re! Shine, two *akh*-eyes!"
The Pelican Goddess[115] comes forth, she who calls.
She calls to the door-keepers, those who guard their gates,
those who consume *ba*-souls, those who swallow the shades of the
dead who pass by them, whom they reckon to the Place of Destruction:
"O door-keepers! Guardians of their gates, those who consume *ba*-souls,
those who swallow the shades of the dead
who pass by them, whom they reckon to the Place of Destruction.
Lead rightly this *ba*-soul of the excellent *akh*-spirit,
great of sanctity in the places of Igeret.
O He of the *Ba*-soul just like Re!
Praised one just like Osiris!"
So says the Pelican Goddess who calls to me.

O Pelican Goddess—lead me rightly!
O Pelican Goddess! She guides me.
O Pelican Goddess—open for me the Netherworld.

---

113. The verb *bsi* refers to crossing a liminal boundary (Kruchten 1989, 147–202; Jasnow and Zauzich 2005, 29; Manassa 2007a, 127–28); on *bsi* and sunrise, see Malaise 1990, 691–92. Compare also the name of the Book of Gates, Doorway 1, "She Who Is Mysterious of Inductions."

114. "Enter" here may both provide the concluding element to the "coming forth" at the beginning of the section, and parallel occurrences of *rḫ*, "to know," as ʿ*q* can also have the sense of "to understand."

115. For this goddess, see "*Ḥnt*," *LGG* 5:158, citing among others Otto 1951, suggesting that the pelican as goddess who cares for the dead represents an Egyptian origin of imagery of the pelican in the *Physiologus* (see Ritner 1989, 114 citing speculation on another Egyptian contribution to the *Physiologus*); for doubts concerning the equation of Pelican Goddess and Nut, see Billing 2002, 22–23.

I give victuals to He of the Netherworld.

I establish the *nemes*-headdress for its owner, the one foremost of the
Hidden Chamber.

Hail to you!

I pass by you, Pelican Goddess,
     so that you might guide me along the paths.

Just when you call to me do I exult in your summons.

Just as you see my *ba*-soul, so do you jubilate—Pelican Goddess, she who
calls."

The gates that are in the Netherworld open;

wide open are the earth and its caverns.

Indeed, the scepter of Re is that which is in my hand;
     the staff is that which is in my grasp.

My scepter smites my enemies.

My staff destroys the punished ones.

My victuals are the victuals of He of the Horizon.

My thrones are the thrones of Re.

"You are indeed Horakhty.

How renewed is this *ba*-soul of the excellent *akh*-spirit!

How powerful is that which is in his two hands!"
     So say the two great and mighty gods to me,
          as they jubilate over me,
          as they praise that which is in my hands,
          as they give to me their protection,
               as they commend to me their lives.

I have appeared in glory as the *ba*-soul of He of the Horizon,
     the successor of Re who is in the sky.

As they issue to me commands, so they lead me into their council,
     that I might open the gate of the sky and of the earth just like my father
     Re.

The *ba*-soul shines forth in the warmth of the offerings, which rest over
     the spine of Osiris,
     with the result that I cause that the one mysterious of places be at rest,
          he having appeared in glory as the lord of luminosity,
               the successor of Re and He of the Horizon.[116]

---

116. Apparently the reciter of the hymn appears as a successor of Re, noting that

I am Re—and vice versa!
It is I who am the *ba*-soul of Osiris,
    when he (Re) rests in him (Osiris).[117]
I cross over those of the portal,
    with the result that they praise when they see me,
        when I pass by.
Then they become beautiful for me exactly like (for) Re within the horizon.

Those who praise Re and those who adore He of the Horizon—
Praise the *ba*-soul of Re, and adore the Netherworldly *ba*-soul.
When One within His Solar Disk calls to you,
    your *ba*-souls ascend to the one who created you.

LITANY 7

Indeed, you have caused that I ascend to this stairway to which you have
    drawn near,
    to which are summoned, the gods in the following of Re and Osiris.
Indeed, you have caused that I ascend to that mysterious and hidden
    shrine of Osiris-Nehi,[118]
    lord of years, whose protection the two female companions are.
Indeed, you have caused that I ascend to the chamber, hidden of mysteries,
    in which Osiris exists.
Indeed, you have caused that I ascend to the monument that is in the West,
    the mysterious shrine of He Who is Foremost of His (Offering)-Legs.[119]

---

he himself will put the Netherworldly power—Osiris—to rest, that one himself having
already appeared as solar replacement of Re. The passage appears to emphasize the
eternal cycle of *nḥḥ*-time with the continuous succession of linear *ḏ.t*-time. This finds
clear expression in the following text, in which the reciter is both Re and Osiris at the
time of the union of the two.

117. Compare the illustration of the union of Re and Osiris in the tomb of Queen
Nefertari and two tombs from Deir el-Medina (TT 290 and TT 335); the tomb of
Irinefer (TT 290) states specifically: "It is Re who sets in Osiris, and Osiris who sets
in Re, daily." On this key aspect of the Solar-Osirian Unity, see Derchain 1965, 35–37,
155–56; Assmann 1969, 101–5; Willems 1988, 151–54; Zandee 1992, 250–53; Darnell
2004, 414–15.

118. On the deity Nehi, see the commentary to Address 71 above (p. 100).

119. This name also appears in no. 717 of the Book of the Hidden Chamber (Hour
10, Register 1, Scene 104, p. 221) and the Book of Gates, Hour 3, Register 2, Scene 12
(p. 268); for a complete list of attestations, see "*Ḫnty-mnwt.f*," *LGG* 5:815–16.

Indeed, you have caused that I ascend,
　　while you open your shoulders for me[120] and bend for me your arms.[121]
May you reveal for me what you hide by means of this my visible appearance,
　　great of mystery, whom the *akh*-spirits and the dead do not know, except for him, (namely) Re, He of the Horizon—Osiris, ruler of the West.

I am one of you.
I have appeared in glory as a vulture;[122]
　　my face as a falcon;
　　my brow as Re;
　　my two eyes are the two female companions;
　　my nose is the Netherworldly Horus;
　　my mouth is the ruler of the West;
　　my throat is Nun;
　　my arms are the Embracer;
　　my fingers are the Seizers;
　　my breast is Khepri;
　　my heart is Horus-Sunen;
　　my liver is She Who Lives;
　　my spleen is the Beaky One;
　　my lungs are He of the Throat;
　　my stomach(?) is the Opener;
　　my viscera are those Mysterious of Affairs;
　　my back is One Weary of Heart;
　　my spine is He of the Pedestal;
　　my sides are Horus and Thoth,
　　my buttocks are the Great Flood,
　　my phallus is Tatenen,
　　the tip of my phallus is She Who Is Sacred in Kheraha,

---

120. The sentence employs a subordinate use of the *sw sḏm=f* construction, for which see Roberson 2010; Roberson 2012, 105–7. In Hour 8, Register 3, Scene 53 of the Book of Gates, the Netherworld itself performs the action of "opening the shoulder" so that the sun disk might enter the Netherworld (p. 303): "May Igeret open to you her shoulder, that you might enter the sanctity of Osiris."

121. The guardians of the portals of the Book of Gates are also said to "bend the arm" for Re; for one of many examples, compare the text to the second gate (p. 264).

122. For the divinization of body parts, see above, p. 66.

my testicles are the two hidden ones,
my thighs are the two goddesses,
my calves are the two luminous goddesses,
my feet are He Who Crosses the Mysteries,
my toes are uraei.[123]

My limbs are gods.
I am entirely a god.
There is no limb of mine that is free from a god.
Just as I enter as a god,
so do I go forth as a god,
    the gods having manifested as my limbs.
I am one who manifests the visible appearance of the lord of the *akh*-spirits.
My limbs guide me.
My flesh leads me rightly along the paths.
Those who manifest from me protect me.
They grow content with what they bore.
It is I who bore them.
It is I who engendered them.
It is I who created them.
My births are those of Re in the West,
He giving birth to me,
    and giving birth to my forms.

O Re—open the earth for my *ba*-soul.
Behold, it is I who know that which is in the Netherworld.
I am a great one, lord of life, Osiris, Ruler of the West.
I am Osiris, my effectiveness is that of Osiris.
My strength is (that of) Osiris.
My honor is (that of) Osiris.
My command is (that of) Foremost of the Westerners.
My *djam*-scepter is (that of) Orion.
I am a great one, chief of the *akh*-spirits, complete and unique,
    who knows what is made mysterious from him,
    great of sanctifications in the forehall of the Netherworld.

---

123. Note that the goddesses and, by extension, uraei associated with the legs and feet find elaboration in the Book of the Solar-Osirian Unity in the Tomb of Ramesses VI (pp. 561–63).

The *ba*-soul of the migratory one rejoices in the Netherworld,
    when he reckons his body in the West.
He speaks to what manifests from him,
    namely, Osiris, Foremost of the Westerners.

How equipped is your face, One within the Netherworld!
How at peace are those who are with you!
How equipped even is your face, One within the Netherworld!
The mourners pull their hair for you,[124]
    they flail their arms for you,
    they cry out for you,
    they wail for you,
    they weep for you.
It is when they wail that your *ba*-soul jubilates,
      with the result that your corpse becomes transfigured.
How equipped is your face, One within the Netherworld,
    he of the dais,
    chief of his scepter,
    king of the Netherworld,
    ruler of Igeret,
    prince,
    great of the white crown,
    great god,
    hidden of place,
    lord of judgments,
    chief of the council.
How equipped is your face, One within the Netherworld!
Your son, Horus, goes to rest within you,
That you issue your commands for me,
    is with the result that you cause him to appear in glory as the pillar[125]
    of the Netherworld,
      (as) the great star,
        who brings his affairs (to fruition),
        who knows the Netherworld and crosses what is in it,

---

124. Hair also plays a role in the mourning goddesses in the Book of Gates, Hour 12, Register 3, Scene 98 (for references to the *nwn*-gesture, see p. 334 and n. 200).

125. For the pillar as Osiris and other references in the Book of Adoring the Re in the West, see p. 110 and n. 104.

son of Re who comes forth from Atum.
O, Osiris, I am your son.
That you issue your commands to me,
> is with the result that you cause me to appear in glory as the pillar of heaven,
>> (as) the great star,
>>> who brings his affairs (to fruition),
>>> who knows the Netherworld and crosses that which is in it,
>>> son of Re who comes forth as Atum.

I go to rest in the Netherworld.
I have power over the deep of the night.[126]
I enter into it.
I go forth from it.
The arms of Tatenen receive me and they raise me up.[127]
Those of the offerings give me their arms.
Those who know how to speak properly guide me.
Praise belongs to you, you of the offerings.
Your praise belongs to me, ones of the offerings,
> so that you might jubilate over me like Re,
> so that you might jubilate over me like Osiris.
That I establish for you your offerings
> is with the result that I cause that you have power over your victuals according to what my father, Re, has commanded.
I am his representative;[128]
I am his heir on earth.
You of the offerings—make for me a path—
> because[129] I am entering into the Netherworld,
> and opening the beautiful West,

---

126. The deep of the night (*wšꜣw*) is the time mentioned in the title of the Book of Adoring Re in the West (see p. 75) and is also the name of Hour 8 of the night in the Book of the Hidden Chamber (pp. 140, 204).

127. In the Netherworld Books, the arms of various deities, including Tatenen, Atum (p. 136 n. 16), and Nun, can lift up and receive the solar deity, an image depicted with Nun raising up the solar bark in the concluding scene of the Book of Gates (p. 336). For Tatenen specifically, see Schlögl 1980, 34–36.

128. For the term *mḥtyw*, see Hannig 2006a, 1119.

129. This sentence is introduced with *mtn*—for this particle following an imperative, see Oréal 2011, 320–24.

that I may establish the crown of Osiris for him,
and make Geb satisfied with his heir.
I am establishing the *was*-scepter for Orion,
while I give the *nemes*-headdress to One Hidden of Name.
Look at me, you of the offerings!—because I am receiving my transfigurations,
I having appeared in glory as He Who Is upon His Mysteries.
May you save me from those of the mooring-posts,
those who bind to their pillars.
They shall not bind me to their mooring-posts.
They shall not assign me to the places of punishment.
I am this one, the heir of Osiris,
I causing that he receive the *nemes*-headdress in the Netherworld.

May the *ba*-soul of Re be high in the West.
May his corpse be strong in its images.
May the *ba*-souls jubilate as they breathe.
May worship come into being in the caverns of the Netherworld for the
ba-soul of Re,
the one in the Netherworld,
Djeba-demedj who rests in his sarcophagi.

LITANY 8

Hail, rightly traveling one!
Hail, rightly traveling *ba*-soul of Re!
Hail, rightly traveling one!
Hail, rightly traveling *ba*-soul like the United One!
Hail, I am one who transforms into Re—and vice versa!
Hail, United One[130] who transforms into Re—and vice versa!

I am one among you.[131]
I am one whom you bore;
I am one whom you nursed;
I am one whom you transfigured.

---

130. Thutmose III writes "*ba*-soul of the United One" (Hornung 1975, 239).

131. The plural "you" is not otherwise specified but should refer to the seventy-five forms of the solar god in the Great Litany.

Hail, I speak, while my body is among you.[132]
Hail to you, one who transforms into Re!
Hail, I am the one who protects you.

Look at me![133]
I have appeared in glory as one who goes forth from your limbs,[134]
      having transformed into this one who adores his father,
      who transfigures the exalted,[135] who exalts his mother.
Look at me!—Jubilate for me!—for[136] I am high in my visible forms,[137]
      I having manifested as one provided with his manifestations.

May you open the paths for my *ba*-soul.
May you stand for me atop your biers.
May you cause that I rest upon my body.
May you open wide my place amidst the earth.
May you open for me your shrines.
May you throw open for me their door-bolts.

O, Re, lead me!
O *Djeba-demedj*, guide me!
He is indeed the one who guides *ba*-souls.
He is indeed the one who leads the gods.
I am his gatekeeper, who hauls the haulers.[138]

---

132. Note the dual nature of the Netherworldly solar deity—the speaking solar aspect while the Osirian corpse is among the gods of the Netherworld. The speech of the solar deity to the denizens of the Netherworld appears throughout the Books of the Creation of the Solar Disk, the Book of Caverns, and the Books of the Solar-Osirian Unity; for a discussion of the interchange of light and speech and a collection of relevant passages, see Darnell 2004, 108–17.

133. The imperative is to a plural entity, and the second person pronoun throughout this and the next set of addresses ("May you open …") is plural.

134. Emergence from the limbs of the solar manifestations is reminiscent of Horus emerging from the body of Osiris in the Books of the Creation of the Solar Disk (Tomb of Ramesses VI, Section A, Register 2, Scene 8): "He of Behdet comes forth from the corpse of his father, acclaiming this one who bore him." See further p. 472 and Roberson 2012, 172–73.

135. The verb *swꜣs*, "to exalt, glorify," appears frequently in the Netherworld Books—for a discussion of earlier translations of the term and its relationship to the term *sꜣḫ*, see Werning 2011a, 484–86.

136. For *mk* following the imperative, see p. 120 n. 129.

137. The term *qꜣi*, "to be high," is similarly used in each address of the Great Litany.

138. Only the version of Thutmose III has the phrase *stꜣ stꜣy.w*, while all other

I am a unique one who guards his doorways,
    who assigns the gods to their places.
I am one who is at his positions in the Netherworld.
I am a land-plot owner belonging to those of the land-plots.[139]
I am one who is in the boundaries of the Netherworld.
I am one provided with offerings in Igeret.
I am making my setting in the West among the *ba*-souls that are among
    its gods.

I am the representative of Re.
I am the mysterious *benu*-bird.[140]
I am the one who enters when he sets in the Netherworld,
    who goes forth when he sets in Nut.
I am the lord of the thrones in heaven,
    who crosses the nethersky in the following of Re.
I go to rest in the sky, in the fields of Re.
My victuals are in the horizon, in the Fields of Reeds.
Exactly like Re do I cross the earth, one who judges like Thoth.

As I shall travel according to the wish of my heart,
    so shall I run according to my strides in this dignity of mine of one
    mysterious of affairs,

---

versions appear to contain a direct address to the *sṯ3y.w*, "haulers." The deceased has identified himself with the "gatekeeper" (*iry-sbḫ.t*), which may be an allusion to the *sbḫ.t*-doorway in the Book of Gates, then the "haulers" would be the four "Netherworld Dwellers" who haul the solar bark through each of the hours (compare p. 262).

139. Ownership of land-plots forms a significant theme in the Book of the Hidden Chamber, Hour 2 (p. 147); again, like with the "gatekeeper," the Book of Adoring Re in the West alludes to texts and iconography in the other Netherworld Books.

140. The *benu*-bird is a divine bird associated with Re as well as Osiris (see inter alia van den Broek 1972; Labrique 2013. In the Book of Going Forth By Day, ch. 17, the deceased claims "I am that *benu*-bird who is in Heliopolis, the one who reckons all which exists," followed by the gloss "Who is it? It is Osiris" (Naville 1886, 39–40 [version Aa]). In this short passage, the solar phoenix is simultaneously a manifestation of Osiris, and it is that dual nature of the bird that makes the identification of the deceased with the "mysterious *benu*-bird" so appropriate to the Solar-Osirian Unity emphasized throughout the Book of Adoring Re in the West. Compare also Book of Caverns, Division 2, Register 2, Scene 19 (p. 360): "O *Benu*-bird, *ba*-soul of the Netherworldly ones—the one who clothes the visible form of Osiris," and in Scene 46, which identifies as the *benu*-bird as the "*ba*-soul of Osiris" (p. 392).

one who transforms into the two gods.[141]
I am one who transforms into the two gods.
It is the one who bore Re who bore me.
Just as I wish, so do I act, my condition is as a transfigured one.
That which I hate I can never do.

I am chief of the victuals of the gods, who gives offerings to the *akh*-spirits.
I am one who takes up his scepter as the one who causes that I come.
I am powerful of heart who smites his enemies.

O gods, O *akh*-spirits, those who are before Re, those who are in the fol-
    lowing of his *ba*-soul—may you lead me like Re;
may you haul me in your haulings.
Indeed they are those who guide Re, the haulers who are within heaven.
I am the *ba*-soul of Re (and vice versa).
I am the one distant of praise, the one who manifests manifestations.

O West! O West!
O Beautiful One! O Beautiful One!
O Strong One! O Strong One!
O Powerful One! O Powerful One!
O Hidden One! O Hidden One!
O Concealed One! O Concealed One!
O Mysterious One! O Mysterious One!
I know you; I know the one who guides you;
I know the names of those who are in (your) following.

O West, who hides my body!
Beautiful One, Beautiful One, who hides my corpse!
O Peaceful One, I am at peace with that which is in you.
O Strong One, I am strong by means of your strength.
O, I am powerful by means of your power.
O Hidden One, open for me your shoulder!
O Concealed One, conceal my rot![142]
O Mysterious One, equip for me your arm!

---

141. As Hornung (1976, 151 n. 571) observes, the "two gods" refers to Re and
Osiris, although Book of the Dead ch. 180 can use determinatives of Horus and Seth
(Lapp 2002, 51). The reading of Seth and Horus is also reminiscent of the "two faced"
god in the Book of the Hidden Chamber and the Book of Gates (pp. 149, 310).

142. For hiding putrefaction, see p. 97 above.

LITANY 9

Hail to you sacred West[143] of Osiris, She Who is Mysterious of Affairs,
    great of sanctity, mysterious and hidden one.
Hail to you, adoration to you![144]
I am extolling the great one within you.[145]
Hail to you!
I am adoring you, so that your mysterious door-leaves might open to me.
Hail to you!
I am adoring you and your mysterious caverns,
        because[146] my place is in the sky like Re,
    and my thrones are in the earth like Geb,[147]
    that I might sit upon the stairway of Geb, upon the thrones of Hora-
    khty.
My *ba*-soul belongs to the sky,
    that I might rest therein.
My corpse belongs to the earth amidst the gods.[148]
That I travel as Re, my fields being (those of) Atum,
    is so that I might manifest as Khepri.[149]
Truly, truly, shall I live by means of that upon which I have lived.

As for the one who recites this book,

---

143. The following addresses are made to *Imn.t*, the feminine personification of
the West (on this goddess, see Refai 1996 and pp. 5–6 on the goddess in the Netherworld Books, omitting examples from the Book of Adoring Re in the West).

144. "You" here is feminine, continuing to address the personification of the West.

145. The "great one" is a reference to Osiris; for the size of the "giant deity" in the
Netherworld and the unified Re-Osiris, see Darnell 2004, 374–424.

146. For this use of the particle *ist/ist*, compare Oréal 2011, 226–29.

147. The earth god Geb is also the focus of Address 15 in the Great Litany, part of
the section in which Re manifests as the different members of the Ennead.

148. The dual fate of the *ba*-soul and corpse find expression in numerous Egyptian funerary texts (see p. 8 n. 13).

149. Here the text expresses that Re travels through the Netherworld to be reborn
as the scarab Khepri, as depicted throughout the concluding scenes of the Netherworld
Books (Hornung 1981b); compare among the many possible parallels the scarab who
emerges from the eastern horizon through the arms of Shu in Hour 12 of the Book of
the Hidden Chamber (p. 238–39); the scarab in the solar bark lifted up by Nun in the
concluding scene of the Book of Gates (p. 336); the ram-headed scarab transforming
into the solar child in the concluding scene of the Book of Caverns (p. 445).

while being pure at the hour of the middle of the night[150] shall he
recite it,
Re having set in the West.
It is the One Who Is (in) the West who joins Re[151] in the West,
though he is hidden from us[152]—truly attested!

---

150. *wšꜣw* appears as the time when one recites the book in the title of the Book
of the Hidden Chamber (see p. 75).

151. Reading *nty* (*m*) *Ꞌmn.t* as a separate noun phrase—"the One Who is in the
West"—rather than *nty Ꞌmn.t*, an otherwise inexplicable modification of *Ꞌmn.t*, "West"
(compare *nty Ꞌmn.t* for *nty.w* (*m*) *Ꞌmn.t*, "those who are (in) the West" [Piankoff and
Rambova 1957, pl. 20] and a Greco-Roman name *Pꜣ nty m Ꞌmn.t* ["*Pꜣ-nty-m-imn.t*,"
LGG 3:11]). Alternatively, if the pouring vessel were assumed missing from the determinative, one might interpret *ꜥb Rꜥ m Ꞌmn.t* as "Re becomes pure in the West" (compare Re becoming pure in the arms of his father Osiris in the Blueprint of the Course
of the Stars [von Lieven 2007c, 135–36]).

152. The "hiddenness" of the god is a feature of the New Kingdom solar deity
(for a series of names and epithets that relate to the concept, see *LGG* 1:339–57; see
also the discussions of Assmann 1969, 50–51 (the god hiding within his disk); 1995,
70–72, chapter 5.

3
BOOK OF THE HIDDEN CHAMBER

INTRODUCTION

Third Intermediate period papyri that contain scenes from the last four hours of the Book of the Hidden Chamber can bear the title *t₃ mḏₐ.t imy-dwₐ.t*, "The Book of What Is in the Netherworld," hence the modern designation of the composition as the Book of Amduat (Piankoff 1964b; Niwiński 1989a, 162). The ancient title to the oldest surviving exemplars of the composition designates the text as the *šš n ʿ.t imn.t*, "Book of the Hidden Chamber" (Schott 1990, 333–34), and that original title is utilized here. The first modern translation, albeit partial, for the Book of the Hidden Chamber was published by Gaston Maspero (1888, 1893); Jéquier (1894) used Third Intermediate period papyri to publish an edition of the "short" version of the Book of the Hidden Chamber. Budge produced type-set hieroglyphic editions of both versions in 1925, but the most significant editions were those of Piankoff and Rambova (1954) and Hornung (1963a), until a complete critical edition of the New Kingdom texts were made available by Hornung (1987b, 1992, 1994b). Translations of the New Kingdom texts include Hornung (1963b, 2002), Barré (2003), Wiebach-Koepke (2003a), Warburton (2007), Carrier (2009), with Third Intermediate period papyri treated in Sadek (1985) and Late period copies translated by Manassa (2007a); the most complete commentary remains Hornung (1963b).

The Book of the Hidden Chamber exists in three separate ancient recensions. Each of these three versions is divided into the twelve hours of the night: the "long" text includes elaborate illustrations divided into three registers[1] and lengthy annotations; the "short" text contains summaries of

---

1. The registers in the Book of the Hidden Chamber, like that of the Book of Caverns, are to be read top to bottom (Barta 1987).

the names and events of each hour; and the "catalog" includes depictions of every deity within each hour, but only their names as text.[2] The lengthy title to the "long" version of the Book of the Hidden Chamber emphasizes knowledge of the inhabitants of the Netherworld and their environs. The title of the "short" Book of the Hidden Chamber specifically refers to the text as *šḥwy n šfdw pn*, "summary of this writing"; this abbreviated version appears at the conclusion of the "long" text, and both can be present within the same tomb. The "catalog" is attested only once, in the upper pillared hall of the tomb of Thutmose III (KV 34) (Abitz 1995, 32–43; Roehrig 2006, 241–42). Since the present edition provides complete translations of the "short" and "long" texts and all of the names of the "catalog" are included within the latter, the "catalog" is not presented separately.

Royal New Kingdom copies of the Book of the Hidden Chamber begin with blocks belonging to a burial of Thutmose I and conclude with the tomb of Ramesses IX; among these sources are seventeen separate tombs, with additional partial copies appearing on the Third Shrine of Tutankhamun and the sarcophagi of Merneptah and Ramesses III (Hornung 1987b, X–XVI; Abitz 1995, 4–23). The earliest example of the Book of the Hidden Chamber appears as painted depictions on blocks deriving primarily from tomb KV 20, with two small fragments from KV 38 (Mauric-Barbério 2001); while the former was the final resting place of Hatshepsut, the original owner of the latter—who may be Thutmose I—remains disputed (see p. 16 and n. 40), but analysis of the blocks suggests that the first exemplar of the Book of the Hidden Chamber should be dated to the reign of the female pharaoh Hatshepsut (Mauric-Barbério 2001, 334). The tomb of Thutmose III is unique including all three recensions of the Book of the Hidden Chamber: the "catalog" in the upper pillared hall, the "long" text on the walls of the sarcophagus chamber, and the "short" text on the pillars within the sarcophagus chamber. The tombs of Amunhotep II and Amunhotep III also utilized all twelve hours from the "long" and "short" versions of the Book of the Hidden Chamber, but placed the hours sequentially around their sarcophagus chambers, ignoring the directions within the text itself, which had been followed within the tomb of Thutmose III (see below). Important among the early attestations of the Book of the Hidden

2. The main edition of the text remains Bucher 1932, pls. 14–22; the texts from the "catalog" are included in Hornung's synoptic edition (1987b, 1992, 1994c), with source note in 1:xi. For the relationship between the forms in the catalog and lists of "demons," see Manassa 2013.

Chamber is the one attestation from a nonroyal burial, the copy in the tomb of Useramun (TT 61), a vizier who served both Hatshepsut and Thutmose III. The burial chamber of Useramun's tomb contains both the "long" and "short" versions and, like the tomb of Thutmose III, also includes the Book of Adoring Re in the West; study of the Useramun version suggests a direct relationship with the royal template of Thutmose III (Hornung 1994b).

After the reign of Akhenaten, the prominence of the Book of the Hidden Chamber within royal tomb decoration diminishes. Tutankhamun and Aye incorporate only excerpts from Hour 1 into the decorative scheme of their sarcophagus chambers, reserving the other walls for unusual depictions, such as the Opening of the Mouth performed by Aye (in the tomb of Tutankhamun) and Aye hunting in the marshes (in Aye's own tomb); the Third Shrine that surrounded the sarcophagus of Tutankhamun incorporates incomplete versions of Hours 2 and 6, as well as the concluding text of Hour 1. The sarcophagus chambers in the tombs of Horemhab and Ramesses I replace the Book of the Hidden Chamber with the Book of Gates (p. 28). The absence of surviving tomb equipment from most royal tombs leaves unclear whether the Book of the Hidden Chamber was present—as in the tomb of Tutankhamun—on shrines rather than the tomb walls.

The tomb of Seti I breaks with earlier decorative schemes by distributing the hours of the Book of the Hidden Chamber throughout the rooms and corridors of the tomb (Barta 1974). The tomb of Seti I also introduces the placement of Hours 4–5 in the third corridor of the tomb, a feature that is present in all subsequent Nineteenth Dynasty tombs (with the exception of the tomb of Tawosret/Sethnakht) and the tomb of Ramesses III. The sarcophagi of Merneptah and Ramesses III also incorporate excerpts from the Book of the Hidden Chamber. From the reign of Ramesses IV onwards, most Twentieth Dynasty royal tombs either employ short excerpts from the Book of the Hidden Chamber or omit the composition entirely; the tomb of Ramesses VI is a notable exception, the fourth and fifth corridors preserving a nearly complete example of the Book of the Hidden Chamber, omitting only Hour 12. The tomb of Ramesses IX resumes the practice of placing the Book of the Hidden Chamber in the third corridor but chooses Hours 2–3, rather than Hours 4–5 that previously occupied that position.

The presence of the phrase *gm wš*, "found missing" (the Egyptian expression corresponding to Latin *lacuna*), as well as the presentation of the text within the tomb of Thutmose III, point toward papyrus copies of the Book of the Hidden Chamber, although no New Kingdom fragments thereof have yet been identified.[3] Third Intermediate period Amduat papyri contribute greatly to the number of copies available of Hours 9–12 of the Book of the Hidden Chamber,[4] and analysis of the papyri from the Cairo Museum suggests that the *Vorlage* of those later papyri is the copy of the text appearing in the tomb of Amunhotep III.[5] In some cases, the annotations on the Amduat papyri preserve the retrograde text appearing in New Kingdom royal tombs. In many examples, the retrograde text of the New Kingdom template was copied incorrectly, producing a perturbated text (Sadek 1985, 305–11; Mauric-Barbério 2003, 186). Additional Third Intermediate period copies of the Book of the Hidden Chamber include fragments from the cenotaph of Iuput (Vernus 1975).

The Book of the Hidden Chamber is the most frequently occurring composition among the corpus of Late period Netherworld Books.[6] While

---

3. On the phrase *gm wš*, see Altenmüller 1967–1968. Missing passages should be distinguished from intentional empty spaces in the text, which serve a multitude of functions, including the facilitation of the spacing of the text and as a symbolic representation of the enemy as nothingness (Rössler-Köhler 1984–1985; Hornung 1994a). The phrase *gm wš* is omitted from Late period copies of the Book of the Hidden Chamber, and various solutions are utilized to create a coherent text (Manassa 2007a, 447).

On textual transmission of the *Book of the Hidden Chamber*, see Jürgens 1999; von Lieven 2007c, 210–14; Werning 2007, 1935–37.

4. The main sources remain Sadek 1985 and Niwiński 1989a; for additional papyri, see Hornung 1999, 171–72 (to which many additional sources might be added including Binder 2006; Liptay 2006a, 2006b; Bommas 2015; Taylor 2016).

5. Sadek 1985, 295–96; see Bommas 2015, 56 for the complexities of textual transmission and his discussion on pp. 50–51 on the accessibility of New Kingdom tombs to Third Intermediate period scribes.

6. An examination of Twenty-Sixth through Thirtieth Dynasty tombs with the Book of the Hidden Chamber remains incomplete (for the state of research, see Régen 2006). The importance of the tomb of Padiamenope (TT 33) was signaled already in Piankoff 1955, although much of the tomb remains unpublished, and an ongoing expedition of the IFAO is in the process of completing the publication of the tomb (bibliography and updates available at http://www.ifao.egnet.net/archeologie/tt33). Within the Theban Necropolis, the tomb of Mutirdis (TT 410) includes portions of Hour 12 (Assmann 1977a, 75–77). Two Twenty-Sixth Dynasty Heliopolitan tombs contain images from the Book of the Hidden Chamber: Panehsi (el-Sawi and Gomaa 1993, 41–43, 74–76) and blocks from an anonymous tomb, reused in the Nilometer on the island of Roda (Drioton 1953b, 291–92; for these blocks, which also include portions of the Book of Adoring Re in the West, the Book of Caverns, and the Book of the Night, see also Roulin 1996b, 21 and Werning 2011b, 45).

many alterations to the New Kingdom texts represent Late period scribal rationalizations for difficult orthographies or obscure passages, some important variants do occur in the Late period copies, such as the addition of a text called the "Amduat Cosmogony" in Hour 8 of the Book of the Hidden Chamber. As with some New Kingdom royal copies of the Netherworld Books, a small corpus of Late period sarcophagi incorporate personalized insertions into the Book of the Hidden Chamber (Jenni 1986, 34–35; Manassa 2007a, 447–48); on one sarcophagus template (Type II), which does not include complete annotations to the hours of the Book of the Hidden Chamber, such personalizations often summarize important theological principles within the annotations, a type of *pars pro toto* approach to the textual material. A final distinction between the New Kingdom and Late period editions of the Book of the Hidden Chamber is the lack of cryptographic writings in the later sources; earlier cryptographic writings are either correctly transcribed in the Late period sources or cryptographic signs are read with *Normalschrift* vales. A small corpus of Ptolemaic wooden coffins includes excerpts from the Book of the Hidden Chamber (Hornung 1999, 30–31; Manassa 2007a, 353), and a remarkable Ptolemaic papyrus belonging to the priest Nesmin contains complete versions of the first eight hours of the composition.[7]

The Book of the Hidden Chamber is unique for its inclusion of directions within the text for the placement of particular hours on specific walls of the "Hidden Chamber" (Schott 1958, 327–28, 334; Abitz 1995, 43–46). Those internal locational instructions indicate that Hours 1–4 should occupy the west wall, with Hours 5–6 on the south wall, Hours 7–8 on the north wall, and the concluding Hours 9–12 on the east wall (fig. 3.1). Reading the treatise south to north on the west wall, then east to west on the south wall, west to east on the north wall, and north to south on

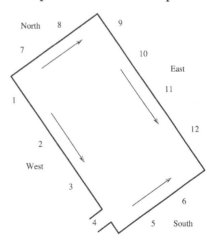

    7. Acquired by the future King Edward VII in 1862, now in the Royal Collections Trust (RCIN 1145266). See Gordon 2013, 59–62.

the east wall takes the reader ultimately from an entry into the netherworld in the southwest corner of the burial chamber to the rising of the rejuvenated solar deity in the southeast corner of the same room (Abt and Hornung 2003, 18–19). Despite the preservation of these directional indications within the Book of the Hidden Chamber, only three versions of the text follow the instructions within the text: the copy of the treatise in the copy in the sarcophagus of Thutmose III, the sarcophagus chamber of the tomb of Useramun, and one template of Late period sarcophagi (Manassa 2007a, 77–78); interestingly, the sarcophagi present the hours of the Book of the Hidden Chamber correctly according to the instructions preserved in the New Kingdom attestations, even though the Late period copies routinely omit the instructions. The placement of the hours of the Book of the Hidden Chamber creates a circular motion about the "Hidden Chamber" (Maruéjol 2007, 349–50), mimicking and thereby enhancing the cyclical regeneration of the solar god, one of the main themes of the composition (Barta 1969–1970; Hegenbarth-Reichardt 2006, 257–60).

In the pre-Amarna period, the annotations and labels within the Book of the Hidden Chamber were written in cursive hieroglyphs and the figures themselves were rendered in a cursive, abbreviated fashion, in red and black ink, creating what appears to be a papyrus unrolled on the walls of the tomb.[8] In post-Amarna tombs, the texts and scenes are formally carved with polychrome images expected for stone wall decoration. Each hour has a standard layout: an introductory text setting forth the main events of the hour as well as the name of the hour and its portal; three registers of texts and scenes, including labels to individual deities; and a lengthy concluding text for Hours 1, 2, and 3. The texts are typically written in a retrograde fashion (Mauric-Barbério 2003, 176–77). The format of several hours possess unique properties, such as the individual rectangles containing deities in Hour 1, the slanting roadways of Hour 4, or the caverns separated by portals in Hour 8. All hours share a common focal feature: the presence of a solar bark in Register 2 (middle).

In the Book of the Hidden Chamber, the crew of the solar bark is consistent across the hours, with a few variations. From the prow to the stern, the typical crew consists of: Opener of Paths (Wepwawet), Divine Percep-

---

8. An oft-observed visual parallel. See further Quirke 2003, 178; Robinson 2003, 52.

tion (Sia), Mistress of the Bark,[9] Flesh,[10] Horus Who Praises, Bull of Maat, Wakeful One,[11] Divine Utterance (Hu), and Director of the Bark. In Hours 4–5 of the night, the bark transforms into a giant serpent that carries the divine crew. In these two hours, the solar serpent-bark is hauled by towers, a feature also present in Hours 8 and 12.[12] During the last six hours of the night, the ram-headed solar deity, Flesh, is surrounded by the Encircling Serpent (Mehen). While the deceased pharaoh does not appear within the solar bark,[13] in the tomb of Useramun, the deceased individual controls the rudder of the ship (Hornung 1994b). In several Late period sarcophagi copies of the Book of the Hidden Chamber, the deceased faces the solar deity, in a kneeling pose with his arms raised in adoration of the ram-headed god (Manassa 2007a, 468).

The Book of the Hidden Chamber begins with a lengthy title qualifying its contents as the positions of various Netherworldly deities and the

---

9. With her cow-horns and solar disk, this goddess is a hypostasis of Hathor (Hornung 1963b, 20–21).

10. On the ram-headed solar figure in the Book of the Hidden Chamber, see Wiebach-Koepke 2000.

11. Nehes could be a hypostasis of the god Seth (Hornung 1963b, 22); Seth appears in the title of Hour 1 (p. 138) and the *mzt-Nhs*, "Staff of Nehes" in the lower register of Hour 10 (no. 753) has the head of Seth (p. 225). While Nehes as the animal of Seth appears in negative contexts ("*Nhs*," LGG 4:269), Seth can aid the solar god in his combat against Apep in Egyptian texts and iconography (Broze 1996, 119–20; Petschel and von Falck, 2004, 21–22; Klotz 2006, 90–95; Régen 2015, 249 n. 11). However, in the solar chapel of Medinet Habu, an image of the solar bark with its crew contains an image of Seth, labelled as such, at the prow; behind the shrine containing the ram-headed solar god stands a deity "Bull of Maat," followed by Nehes (Epigraphic Survey 1963, pl. 421), probably the same Nehes as appears in the crew of the bark in the Book of the Hidden Chamber; note that the solar bark with a crew approximating that in the Book of the Hidden Chamber, including the god Nehes, also appears in the decoration of Luxor Temple carved during the reign of Amunhotep III (Brunner 1977, pl. 66). The appearance of Seth and a separate Nehes in the same bark suggests that Nehes as an anthropomorphic deity in the solar bark represents a hypostasis of solar wakefulness. For other deities with the name Nehes related to the root *nhs* "wakeful" see Meeks 1998a, 196 (Nehes in solar bark as "wakeful one") and "*Nhs*," LGG 4:267–68; compare also the hauler named "Wakeful One" in the concluding scene of the Book of Caverns (pp. 452–53).

12. In the Book of Gates, four Netherworldly gods tow the solar bark in every hour, with the exception of the first.

13. The king does appear within one of the barks in the Tomb of Ramesses IX, Hour 2, Register 2 (Abitz 1992, 170).

geographic extent of the Netherworld, whose beginning and end is the western horizon.[14] The remainder of the title consists of nine statements of knowledge about the Netherworld and its denizens, an emphasis the Book of the Hidden Chamber shares with the text known as the King as Solar Priest (see pp. 37–39).

It is in Hour 1 that Re transforms into "Flesh," the ram-headed *ba*-soul of the Netherworldly sun who travels in a bark—or serpent-bark—through the twelve hours. As the sun god sails through Hour 1, he is acclaimed by groups of deities, such as the hour goddesses who embody the complete journey through the Netherworld. Similarly, in the second half of the middle register Osiris adores a scarab beetle, presaging the emergence of the scarab beetle from the eastern horizon at the conclusion of Hour 12. All of the deities within this hour are placed within their own rectangular spaces, reminiscent of the layout of the "catalog," and reflecting the rule of Maat, who herself appears twice in Hour 1. Specific measurements are given for the fields that comprise Hours 1 and 2 of the night, a region called Wernes.[15]

The watery landscape of Wernes continues in Hour 2, and one of the chief themes of the hour is Re's distribution of land-plots to the Netherworldly beings. The deities of Hour 2 aid Re through their cries, only one of many instances of the importance of sound within the Netherworld. The text to Register 2 is fragmentary in all copies, but Register 3 describes deities linked with the division of time who both provide for the blessed dead and punish Re's enemies, a dichotomy present throughout the remaining hours of the night. A lengthy concluding text summarizes the themes of the hour: the provisioning of deities and the defeat of all who oppose the sun god.

Hour 3 is organized similarly to Hour 2, with an introductory text, annotations to each register, and a concluding text. This hour emphasizes the destruction of the *ba*-souls of the damned, thus allowing the *ba*-soul of Re to travel to the sky while his corpse remains in the Netherworld; the *ba*-soul and corpse of Osiris are said to have the same twin fates in the concluding text of the hour. The Netherworldly floodwaters within Hour

---

14. While seemingly contradictory, the passage in the title of the Book of the Hidden Chamber can serve as a textual description of the figure of Osiris curled back over himself in the concluding scene of the Book of Gates (p. 336).

15. For Wernes, see most recently Schneider 2010 (without accepting his terrestrial identification of the area).

3 embody the regenerative powers of the annual inundation, and deities who carry the solar pupil in the upper register may allude to Hathoric theology and to the goddess of the eye of the sun (Manassa 2007a, 251–52).

The landscape of the Netherworld changes dramatically in Hours 4 and 5, the land of Rosetau, "the Place of Hauling." The irrigated fields of the first three hours give way to a sandy terrain filled with ophidian deities; the bark of the sun god itself transforms into a giant serpent that must be hauled over the desiccated surface. Hour 4 is punctuated by sloping passages sealed with doors, architectural forms that provided the template for the corridors of New Kingdom royal tombs (see p. 31). A variety of deities, many of whom are legged serpents, confined to their places within the Netherworld, hear the voice of Re, although they cannot see the light of the sun.

A further unifying feature of Hours 4 and 5 is the presence of cryptographic annotations that appear alongside noncryptographic texts. The use of cryptography mirrors the secretive nature of the land of Sokar described in the introductory text of the hour: "mysterious cavern of Sokar, who is upon his sand. Unseen and unperceived is this mysterious image of the earth that carries the flesh of this god." By descending into the cavern of Sokar—a large oval serpent's egg—the solar deity contacts the chaotic and rejuvenating waters of Nun. The sound of re-creation is like the "roar of heaven when it storms," a signal of the enormous potential energy contained within the Nun waters.

In Hour 6, the solar bark resumes its canonical shape and no longer requires haulers. Among the foci of this hour are the constituent elements of the solar corpse in Register 1 and the corpse of Khepri guarded by a multi-headed serpent in Register 2 (Manassa 2007a, 238–39). Symbols of royal power and crowned mummiform figures embody Re's rule over the Netherworld and the assimilation of the deceased pharaoh to the solar god.

Hour 7 juxtaposes the destruction of Re's ultimate enemy, Apep, with the ordering of time. The Encircling Serpent (Mehen) replaces the shrine that surrounds "Flesh" within the bark, a feature present in all remaining hours. In the upper register, a cat-headed demon dispatches headless figures before an enthroned Osiris, mimicking the destruction of Apep in the central register. The evil serpent is defeated by physical means—binding and slicing—as well as through magical spells spoken by Isis and the Elder Magician (see p. 196). The defeat of Apep allows time itself to proceed, and Horus orders the hours in Register 3.

Hour 8 is divided into ten separate caverns, each of which is associated with a sound. In Register 2 are the four crown-wearing rams, manifestations of the creator deity Tatenen. The sounds of Hour 8 also allude to the act of creation and its result, forming a unifying theme for the hour. In some Late period sources, a hymn to Tatenen, the "Amduat Cosmogony," augments Hour 8 and further emphasizes the link between that hour and solar creation.[16] The other theme of Hour 8 is the provisioning of clothing, atop which the deities in this hour sit.

The final four hours of the Book of the Hidden Chamber are those most commonly occurring on Third Intermediate Amduat papyri, representing *pars pro toto* the entirety of the solar journey through the Netherworld. Hour 9 continues the previous hour's emphasis on clothing, with twelve gods and twelve uraei seated atop cloth signs in Registers 1 and 3 respectively. The twelve gods holding oars in Register 2 are members of the crew of the solar deity, whose actions assist Re with his triumphant exit from the Netherworld into the eastern horizon of the sky.

Hour 10 includes tableaux that summarize the entirety of the solar journey, such as a scarab-beetle holding aloft an oval at the beginning of Register 1. Deities associated with the eye of Horus in Register 1—the gods who "make whole the effective eye"—include the goddess Sakhmet. In Register 2 is a group of gods holding spears and bows who punish the enemies of Re "at the gateway of the horizon." Register 3 is filled with depictions of the drowned in Nun, to whom the sun god decrees a blessed afterlife, free from constriction and putrefaction.[17]

At Hour 11, the sun god makes his final preparations before entering the last hour of the night. Deities in Register 1 are mysterious beings who set in place the image of the solar god and to whom Re commands breath and offerings. Dominating Register 2 is a group of twelve gods who hold aloft the Encircling Serpent (Mehen), who is set on his course to the eastern horizon. Register 3 illustrates the fiery punishment of the enemies of

---

16. "The Osiris N has received the solar regalia, so that he might rise as Horakhty. He is Tatenen, the bull of bulls, great of sexual pleasure, who created the Ogdoad in the palms of his hands. He has repeated births as Atum. He is Re who has become Ptah. The arms of Atum surround you and receive him as the secret image of the Netherworld." The sarcophagus of Nectanebo II provides a variant: "The arms of Atum receive him as the secret, Netherworldly image of Tatenen." For an analysis of this text, see Manassa 2007a, 157–61.

17. For the concept of "apotheosis by drowning," see p. 9 and n. 18.

Re: five fire pits contain constituent parts of the enemies, each guarded by a knife-wielding goddess.

With the victory over Apep in Hour 7 of the night and the destruction of enemies in Hour 11, the sun god can proceed triumphantly to the final hour of the night. Register 1 and 3 are filled with deities praising the solar deity; additional deities in these registers provide further protections against the depredations of Apep as Re rises in the eastern horizon. In the middle register, the solar bark sails through a giant serpent, Life of the Gods, beginning at the tail and ending at the mouth; this retrograde action reverses time itself, rejuvenating the solar god and facilitating his transformation into the solar beetle who emerges from the arms of Shu at the far edge of the Netherworld.[18] The curved terminus also contains a reclining mummy, the corpse that must remain below while the *ba*-soul flies off to heaven.

The translations of the "long" and "short" editions of the Book of the Hidden Chamber in this volume do not follow a single version of the text but rely primarily on the texts within the tombs of Thutmose III and Ramesses VI. The insertions describing the actions of the king (Abitz 1995, 23–25) are not included here.

"Long" Book of the Hidden Chamber

TITLE

Book of the Hidden Chamber,[19]
> the positions of the *ba*-souls, the gods, the shades, the *akh*-spirits, and visible forms.

The beginning is the horn of the West, namely, the gate of the western horizon;
> the end is the utter darkness, the gate of the western horizon.

To know the *ba*-souls of the Netherworld Dwellers;
to know their visible forms;
to know their effective spells for Re;

---

18. For regeneration within a serpent in the Netherworld Books, see Barta 1990a, 56–58.

19. The ꜥ.t imn.t is also mentioned in the annotations to the gateways in the Book of Gates (Hornung 1980, 43–44; compare among the many examples, Doorway 1, p. 259). For the Netherworldly significance of an ꜥ.t-chamber, see Jasnow and Zauzich 2005, 36–37.

to know the mysterious *ba*-souls;
to know what is in the hour and their gods;
to know how he calls them;
to know the gates and the paths by which the great god passes;
to know the courses of the hours and their gods;
to know the honored and the damned.

HOUR 1

INTRODUCTORY TEXT

When this god enters into the western portal[20] of the horizon, Seth assumes his station at the bank. It is 120 *iteru* in this portal, before the bark reaches the Netherworld Dwellers. Thereafter he passes by Wernes.[21]

REGISTER 1 (PLATE 3)

3.2. Scene 1. Nine kneeling baboons arranged in three columns and three rows

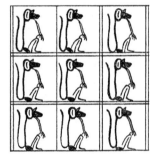

Names of the gods within the Netherworld who open for the great *ba*-soul

1 (BABOON): Baboon
2 (BABOON): Jubilating One
3 (BABOON): *Djehdjeh*[22]
4 (BABOON): Heart of the Earth
5 (BABOON): Favorite of the Earth
6 (BABOON): Praising One
7 (BABOON): Opener of the Earth
8 (BABOON): *Ba*-Soul of the Earth
9 (BABOON): He whom Re Sees

---

20. For the theological significance of the ʿ*rry.t*-portal, see Konrad 2006, 219–24.
21. For the toponym Wernes, see above, p. 134.
22. "*Ḏḥḏḥ*," *LGG* 7:650–51. Deities bearing the name appear as protectors, and the name can appear in a verbal form as an action the deity performs against enemies (Wilson 1997, 1246, renders the verbal form as "to kill").

3.3. Scene 2. Twelve standing goddesses arranged in four columns and three rows

Names of the goddesses who praise the One within the Earth

10 (GODDESS): She of the Throat
11 (GODDESS): Youthful One
12 (GODDESS): Mistress of Life
13 (GODDESS): She Praised of Her *Ba*-Soul
14 (GODDESS): She High of Her *Akh*-Spirit
15 (GODDESS): She Who Has Power over Her Enemies
16 (GODDESS): Great Hidden One
17 (GODDESS): She of Awe
18 (GODDESS): She of the Bindings[23]
19 (GODDESS): High of Arm
20 (GODDESS): Mistress of Protection
21 (GODDESS): Deaf One

3.4. Scene 3. Nine kneeling gods, arms raised in adoration; gods in the first column are crocodile-headed, second column jackal-headed, and third column human-headed

Names of the gods who adore Re

22 (CROCODILE-HEADED GOD): He Who Traverses the Netherworld
23 (CROCODILE-HEADED GOD): He Who Cries Out
24 (CROCODILE-HEADED GOD): Powerful of Face
25 (JACKAL-HEADED GOD): Lord of the Sacred Land
26 (JACKAL-HEADED GOD): Divider of the Two Lands
27 (JACKAL-HEADED GOD): Divider of the Two Powers
28 (GOD): Illumining of Arm
29 (GOD): Seeing of Arm
30 (GOD): Praising of Arm

23. Reading with Hornung 1976, 12, (*i*)*r*(*y.t*)-*ntt*; for *ntt* in divine names, see "*Ntt*," *LGG* 4:576–77.

3.5. Scene 4. The twelve hour goddesses are arranged in four columns and three rows

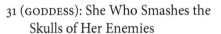

Names of the goddesses who guide the great god

31 (GODDESS): She Who Smashes the
    Skulls of Her Enemies
32 (GODDESS): Wise One Who Protects Her Lord
33 (GODDESS): She Who Cuts *Ba*-Souls
34 (GODDESS): Great One Who Is in the Netherworld
35 (GODDESS): She Who Is in Her Bark
36 (GODDESS): She of the Harbor
37 (GODDESS): She Who Opposes the Associates of Seth
38 (GODDESS): She of the Deep of the Night
39 (GODDESS): She Who Protects Her Lord
40 (GODDESS): Raging One
41 (GODDESS): Starry One
42 (GODDESS): She Who Sees the Perfection of Her Lord

REGISTER 2 (PLATE 3)

ANNOTATION TO THE ENTIRE REGISTER

It is the two Maat-goddesses who haul this god in the night-bark while sailing in the portal of this locale—it is 120 *iteru*. Afterwards, he traverses water to Wernes, which is 300 *iteru* in its length.[24] [He] distributing [fields] to them,[25] namely, the gods who are in his following.

The Floodwater of Re is the name of this field. Keeper of the Flame is the name of its protector. At this field this god begins to proclaim the caring for[26] those who are in the Netherworld.

---

24. For translating the pw clause as a virtual relative, although more likely "parenthetic" in Egyptian, see Wente 1967, 13 (n. e to pl. 9).

25. Reading ḥnb[=f ꜣḥ.wt] r=sn (noting the phrase gm wš after ḥnb and comparing the passage to the sentence in the Short Version: "This great god will grant to him cultivated land at their places in the field of Wernes."); a variant reading may be ḥnb[=f ꜣḥ.wt] r=s n ....

26. The phrase ir.t sḥr.w, "to care for" has the sense of controlling destinies (Derchain 1972, 37 n. 14).

3.6. Scene 5. The solar bark sails with the ram-headed solar deity within a shrine. The crew of the bark consists of two gods at the prow followed by a goddess crowned with horns and the solar disk. Behind the shrine are a falcon-headed deity and three additional gods.[27]

43 (GOD): Opener of Paths
44 (GOD): Divine Perception
45 (GODDESS WITH HORNS AND DISK): Mistress of the Bark
46 (RAM-HEADED GOD): Flesh
47 (FALCON-HEADED GOD): Horus Who Praises
48 (GOD): Bull of Maat
49 (GOD): Wakeful One
50 (GOD): Divine Utterance
51 (GOD): Director of the Bark

3.7. Scene 6. Twelve figures before the solar bark

52 (GODDESS WITH MAAT-FEATHER): Maat
53 (GODDESS WITH MAAT-FEATHER): Maat
54 (GOD HOLDING A KNIFE): Punisher
55 (MUMMIFORM FIGURE WEARING WHITE CROWN): Foremost of the West
56 (LIONESS-HEADED GODDESS): Sakhmet
57 (RAM-HEADED GOD): Great Illuminator
58 (HUMAN-HEADED STELA): Command of Re

27. For the crew of the bark, see p. 132–33 above.

59 (HUMAN-HEADED STELA): Command of Atum
60 (HUMAN-HEADED STELA): Command of Khepri
61 (HUMAN-HEADED STELA): Command of Osiris
62 (SERPENT STANDING ON TAIL): Starry One[28]
63 (GOD HOLDING MAGICAL WAND[29]): He Who Traverses the Hours

CONTINUATION OF ANNOTATION

Portal through which the great god passes by them as a ram. After he passes this portal, he transforms,[30] without the dead ascending after him, they halting at this portal. He commands to these gods who are in this portal. This is done in the hidden part of the Netherworld according to this image, sacred and hidden because of the small number of those who know it.[31]

3.8. Scene 7. A bark containing a large scarab and two praising deities (who face in towards the scarab) sails on a rectangle of water.

64 (PRAISING GOD): Osiris
65 (SCARAB): Khepri
66 (PRAISING GOD): Osiris

28. Alternatively, "One of the Hour."
29. Koenig 1994, 87.
30. For an alternate reading of the text involving assumed scribal errors, see Wiebach-Koepke 2000; 2003a, 8–9.
31. For this statement of knowledge and similar statements throughout the Book of the Hidden Chamber, see Wiebach-Koepke 2007, 98–109.

3.9. Scene 8. Three serpents, one atop the other, are followed by thirteen additional figures, including various deities and a horned staff.

67 (SERPENT): Pure of Mouth
68 (SERPENT): One Who Slices
69 (SERPENT): Sharp One
70 (GOD HOLDING SERPENT STAFF): He of the Field
71 (GOD HOLDING SERPENT STAFF): He of the Vegetables
72 (GOD HOLDING SERPENT STAFF): He of the Pyramid[32]
73 (FALCON-HEADED HOLDING SERPENT STAFF): He of the Bark
74 (FALCON-HEADED HOLDING SERPENT STAFF): He of the Staff
75 (FALCON-HEADED HOLDING SERPENT STAFF): One Who Is Well
76 (GOD HOLDING TWO CROOKS): He of the Land-Plots
77 (GODDESS WEARING WHITE CROWN): Neith
78 (GODDESS WEARING RED CROWN): She Goat
79 (GODDESS): Nephthys
80 (HORNED STAFF WITH MUMMIFORM FIGURE AND TWO SERPENTS):
     Divider of the Floodwaters
81 (LARGE *HEQA*-SCEPTER): Staff
82 (GOD FACING LEFT): Sealer of the Earth

REGISTER 3 (PLATE 3)

3.10. Scene 9. Nine kneeling baboons arranged in three columns and three rows

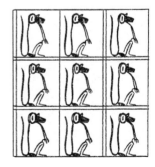

Names of those who make music for Re, when he enters the Netherworld

83 (BABOON): Jubilating One
84 (BABOON): One Who Cries(?)
85 (BABOON): Flaming One

---

32. Alternatively, "He of the (pyramid-shaped) Bread" (Hornung 1963b, 26).

86 (BABOON): He Who Praises with His Flame
87 (BABOON): Dancer
88 (BABOON): He Who Adores[33]
89 (BABOON): One within the Shrine
90 (BABOON): Foremost of His Land
91 (BABOON): He of the Phallus

3.11. Scene 10. Twelve uraeus-serpents
arranged in four columns and three rows

Names of the goddesses who illumine
the darkness in the Netherworld

92 (URAEUS): She of the Flame
93 (URAEUS): She Who Burns
94 (URAEUS): Cobra
95 (URAEUS): Painful of Flame
96 (URAEUS): She Who Cuts
97 (URAEUS): She Who Brightens
98 (URAEUS): She Who Protects the Lands
99 (URAEUS): She Who Decapitates the Enemies
100 (URAEUS): Beautiful of Forms
101 (URAEUS): She of the Fire
102 (URAEUS): Pacified One
103 (URAEUS): […]

3.12. Scene 11. Nine standing deities, arms
raised in adoration arranged in three columns
and three rows

Names of the gods who adore the Lord of
the Ennead

104 (PRAISING GOD): He of the Netherworld
105 (PRAISING GOD): He Who Praises Re

---

33. Only attested in Late period versions (Hornung 1963b, 29).

106 (PRAISING GOD): Praiser[34]
107 (PRAISING GOD): One Justified of Bank
108 (PRAISING GOD): He Who Roars
109 (PRAISING GOD): Bull of Visible Forms
110 (PRAISING GOD): Bull of the Netherworld
111 (PRAISING GOD): Provided of Heart
112 (PRAISING GOD): Guardian(?)[35]

3.13. Scene 12. Twelve standing goddesses
arranged in four columns and three rows

Names of the goddesses who give ovation to Re when he passes by Wernes

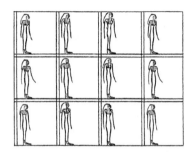

113 (GODDESS): She of the Locale
114 (GODDESS): She of the West
115 (GODDESS): Isis
116 (GODDESS): Nephthys
117 (GODDESS): Her Two Faces
118 (GODDESS): Tefnut[36]
119 (GODDESS): She of the Floodwaters
120 (GODDESS): Equipped of Mouth
121 (GODDESS): She of the East
122 (GODDESS): She Who Sees Her God
123 (GODDESS): She Who Pertains to Her God
124 (GODDESS): She Who Praises

CONCLUDING TEXT

Halting by the majesty of this god after he goes to rest at this portal. Issuing commands to these who are within it: "Open for me your gates. Swing
open for me your portals. Light up for me, those whom I made. Guide me,

---

34. Translation based on Late period copies, since New Kingdom versions all preserve an incomplete writing.
35. The name appears to be incomplete in the New Kingdom versions (Hornung
1963b, 31).
36. Only attested in Late period versions (Hornung 1963b, 32).

those who came about from my flesh. To my corpse have I commended you. Just as I have created you for my *ba*-soul, so have I fashioned you for my *akh*-spirit. That I have come here is to greet myself[37] and give breath to my limbs, so that they (the limbs) might arise for him (Osiris). I always destroy those who act against it and always give breath as the One Secret of Visible Forms[38] <to> Osiris, Foremost of the Westerners. Open for me your arms, O baboons! Swing open for me your portals, O baboons! O goddesses who came about from my *ba*-soul! O my gods, who have manifested <from my corpse>—it is for Khepri that you have manifested, O those who are foremost of the Netherworld! May you stop at Wernes. May you moor at the hidden bank. May you act for the Netherworld Dwellers at the portal which belongs to you as your place. May your cultivated land belong to you from your fields."

The gods of this portal (speak) to Re, when they extol the great god: "Just as the West, hidden of visible forms, is opened for you, so are the two door-leaves of the great locale thrown open for you. Illumine for yourself the darkness and thereby cause the Place of Destruction to breathe, so that you might ascend in your name of Re to the place Osiris, Foremost of the Westerners, is. Jubilation be to Re at the entrance of the earth. Ovation be to you, who causes *akh*-spirits to breathe, when you enter the door of Wernes. As *benty*-baboons do we open for you the two door-leaves; as *hetut*-baboons do we swing open for you the two door-leaves.

As your extollers extol you, so your *akh*-uraei illumine for you the darkness. As your gods adore you, O Re, so the hours among whom you are guide you. That your two daughters haul you by means of your power,[39] is so that you may occupy the stelae that are upon the fields of the land.

---

37. "Greeting"—especially Re's greeting of Osiris—is an important activity in Egyptian religious literature, especially the Netherworld Books (Assmann 1969, 132–33; Darnell 2004, 346–47; compare already CT 7.329b, the solar *sḥtp ḥr* of Osiris). Among the many possible examples in the Netherworld Books, compare the Book of Adoring Re in the West, Address 63 (p. 98) and Litany 6 (p. 111) and the Book of Caverns, Division 1, Register 1, Scene 3 (p. 347) and Division 3, Introductory Text (p. 367).

38. A possible translation of the name *Sfg-irw* (see Wiebach-Koepeke 2003a, 15 n. 5; "*Sfg-irw*," *LGG* 6:305: "Der mit verborgener (?) Gestalt").

39. Reading here under the influence of the Ramesses VI version. Alternate readings based on the Late period variants—"among you" or "being those among whom you are"—are possible (see Manassa 2007a, 209); also possible is: "in your visible forms" (Wiebach-Koepke 2003b, 16 n. 9 with references to earlier literature).

May you take away the night; may you bring the day. You are this god who traverses the hours, as you occupy the bark of Khepri. You have taken possession of the produce of He of the Land-plot among the lake. May Neith be pacified for you, so that you might open the floodwaters. May the Sealer of the Earth uncover for you his shoulder. May the goddesses of Wernes adore you; the praising goddesses worship you. May you triumph over your enemies! May you assign punishments among the sinful!"

Commanding by the majesty of this god after reaching this portal: "Aggressiveness be to your portal. Firmness be to your door-leaves. Sealing be to your bolts. O those who come before me at my passings and before me at my crossings—remain in your places, stand at your banks."

When this great god passes by them, they mourn when he travels past them in the field of Wernes.

This is done according to this image[40] in the hidden part of the Netherworld. As for the one who knows these images, (he is) the likeness of the great god himself. It is effective for him on earth very greatly like their secret written images.

It is 120 *iteru* of going in this portal. The hour who guides (in)[41] this portal is She Who Smashes the Skulls of the Enemies of Re. It is the name of the first hour of the night.

HOUR 2

INTRODUCTORY TEXT

Resting in Wernes by this god. Making the navigation of the field-dwellers in the floodwater of Re. 309 *iteru* is the length of this field; 120 is its width, while this great god makes land-plots for the gods at this locale. The name of the hour of the night that guides this god is Wise One Who Protects Her Lord. The name of the gate of this locale is Swallower of All.[42]

---

40. Translated here as "image," the term *sšmw* is commonly used in the Book of the Hidden Chamber to denote a "potential epiphany" that differentiates it from other terms for cultic image or transformation (Eschweiler 1994, 191–96).

41. The ancient Egyptian term *sšm.t ʿrr.t tn* could also be translated "who governs this portal."

42. For the notion of the Netherworld as a "black hole" that devours all who enter, see Hornung 1994a.

When this great god apportions cultivated land to the gods of the Netherworld, he cares for them at this field. Come to know the Netherworld Dwellers! As for the one who knows their names, he exists before them, and the great god apportions to him cultivated land at their places in the field of Wernes; he takes his place at the standing place of the *ba*-soul(s). Just as he passes by after this great god, so he enters the earth, he opening the Netherworld, he parting the locks of the Hairlock-Wearers. In the following of Maat of the Land-plots does he pass by the Donkey-Swallower. He always eats bread at the bark of the earth; the prow-rope of the *Tebiu*-bark[43] is given to him. These images of the *ba*-souls of the Netherworld Dwellers are made in writing according to this template in this Hidden Chamber of the Netherworld, the beginning of the West.[44] One offers to them on earth. It is effective for a man on earth—truly attested millions of times.

REGISTER 1 (PLATE 4)

ANNOTATION TO THE ENTIRE REGISTER

They exist in this fashion;[45] they adore this great god after he reaches them. It is their voice that guides him to them; it is their cries that follow him after he issues commands to them. It is these gods who lift up the words of those on earth; it is they who lift up the *ba*-soul to their sleep. What they do is create the messengers of the deep of the night and act (against)[46] the enemies at their hours. It is they who guard the day and bring the night, so that this great god might emerge from the utter darkness, in order to rest at the portal of the eastern horizon of the sky. They cry out for this god and mourn for him after he passes by them. The one who knows them is one who goes forth by day, and he is taken in the night to the grove of the great locale.

---

43. Hornung 1963c, 45 n. 19.

44. The tomb of Thutmose III writes "The beginning of the book to the West."

45. The verb *wnn*, which appears frequently in this construction within the Netherworld Books, is a nominal form emphasizing "in this fashion" (compare Baumann 1998, 31–33).

46. For *iri*, "to do" as "to treat violently," see Darnell 2006, 39 and n. 191 (and references therein).

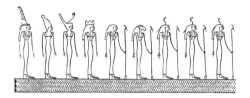

3.14. Scene 13. Nine goddesses with various attributes

125 (GODDESS CROWNED WITH MAAT-FEATHER): Maat Who Is atop the Valley

126 (GODDESS WITH WHITE CROWN): She of the White Crown Who Is atop the Valley

127 (GODDESS WITH RED CROWN): She of the Red Crown Who Is atop the Valley

128 (GODDESS CROWNED WITH KHASET-DESERT SIGN): Beautiful West

129 (GODDESS HOLDING ANKH-SIGN AND WAS-SCEPTER): Swallower of All

130 (LIONESS-HEADED GODDESS HOLDING ANKH-SIGN AND WAS-SCEPTER): Sakhmet of the Was-Scepter

131 (GODDESS HOLDING ANKH-SIGN AND WAS-SCEPTER WITH SERPENT ON HER HEAD): Chief of the Netherworld Dwellers

132 (GODDESS HOLDING ANKH-SIGN AND WAS-SCEPTER WITH SERPENT ON HER HEAD): She Who Swallows the Dead

133 (GODDESS HOLDING ANKH-SIGN AND WAS-SCEPTER WITH SERPENT ON HER HEAD): She Who Gives Birth to Herself

3.15. Scene 14. Ten deities and divine objects of various forms

134 (KNEELING LIONESS-HEADED GODDESS): She Whom the Akh-Spirits Fear

135 (HUMAN-HEADED STELA): Command of Osiris

136 (LARGE SERPENT-SHAPED STAFF): Staff of Osiris

137 (LARGE STAFF): Staff of Osiris

138 (GOD WITH SETH-HEAD AND FALCON-HEAD): He of the Two Faces[47]

139 (SEATED BABOON): Baboon

47. For this deity compare "His Two Faces" in Book of Gates, Hour 10, Register

140 (SEATED BABOON): Benty-Baboon

141 (GOD HOLDING KNIFE WITH ARM RAISED TO SMITE): One Who Prostrates and Cuts off Shades

142 (FALCON-HEADED GOD CROWNED WITH SERPENT): Horus of the Netherworld

143 (GOD HOLDING *SEKHEM*-SCEPTER): One Who has Power over His Enemies

---

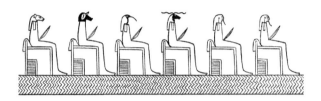

3.16. Scene 15. Six deities seated on thrones

144 (LION-HEADED GOD HOLDING KNIFE): He of the Cauldron Who Slices *Ba*-Souls

145 (BABOON-HEADED GOD HOLDING KNIFE): Flesh Who Is upon His Throne

146 (IBIS-HEADED GOD HOLDING KNIFE): Thoth Who Is upon His Throne

147 (RAM-HEADED GOD HOLDING KNIFE): Khnum of the Council-Chamber

148 (GOD HOLDING KNIFE): Geb of the Council-Chamber

149 (GODDESS HOLDING KNIFE): Isis Who Inquires

REGISTER 2 (PLATE 4)

In all attested New Kingdom versions, the annotation to Register 2 is fragmentary.[48] Complete versions do not appear to have been available to Late period scribes either, and interesting solutions are found to the "problem" on Thirtieth Dynasty/early Ptolemaic period sarcophagi. The sarcophagus of Nectanebo II (BM EA 10) writes only a single sentence: "They exist in this fashion, as he travels in the barks within the earth. Osiris King, lord of the two lands, Senedjem-ib-re, whom Hathor chose, son of Re, lord of diadems, effective at the place of Maat, Nectanebo (II), beloved of Hathor, justified, <travels> in the barks within the earth." Full writings of words (i.e., triplicates of determinatives rather than plural

---

1, Scene 61 (p. 310); the same deity appears in the Book of Gates, Hour 11, Register 2, Scene 78 (p. 322).

48. For the partial reconstruction of the text, primarily followed here, see Hegenbarth 2002, 174–75.

strokes) and the abundant epithets of the king help fill the space of the apparently incoherent New Kingdom text. The sarcophagus of Weresh-nefer (MMAEE 14.7.1) reproduces the New Kingdom text, leaving gaps between words so as to fill the same space as the complete annotations to Registers 1 and 3; finally, the sarcophagus of Tjaihorpata (CGAE 29306) omits the annotations of Register 2 of Hours 2 and 3 entirely.

ANNOTATION TO THE ENTIRE REGISTER

\<This> great \<god sails(?) by this locale(?) in> this \<fash>ion. He is rowed in the barks that are within the earth. Th\<ose who are> in \<Wer>nes come, as he makes a course to this field. \<He> issues commands to them \<and calls to them from> his bark, when he moors. The course … these barks perambulate greatly in Wernes, bearing Osiris. Then they mourn \<in(?) …> their barks. This great god and the Grain-god command \<to> them from their barks(?), so that they have power over the fields. The one who knows (it) is one who descends as a great one to the necropolis \<in(?) his(?)> bark.

3.17. Scene 16. The solar bark sails with its typical crew (see Scene 5) with the addition of two uraei at the prow.

LABEL TO BARK: Bark of Re

150 (URAEUS): Isis
151 (URAEUS): Nephthys
152 (GOD): Opener of Paths
153 (GOD): Divine Perception
154 (GODDESS WITH HORNS AND DISK): Mistress of the Bark
155 (RAM-HEADED GOD): Flesh
156 (FALCON-HEADED GOD): Horus Who Praises
157 (GOD): Bull of Maat
158 (GOD): Wakeful One

159 (GOD): Divine Utterance
160 (GOD): Protector of the Bark[49]

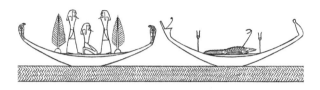

3.18. Scene 17. Two barks sail to the right. First, a bark whose prow and stern are shaped like cobras contains three deities—two gods and a goddess—as well as two large sheaves of grain. Second, a bark whose prow is a white crown and stern is a red crown contains a crocodile flanked by two *sekhem*-scepters.

LABEL TO BARK: Bark that Travels the Floodwaters

161 (GOD WITH NO ARMS): Grain-god
162 (KNEELING GOD): *BLANK*
163 (GOD WITH NO ARMS): Staff of Cereal

LABEL TO BARK: Bark that the Gods Steer

164 (CROCODILE): One Who Guides Those Who Are in It

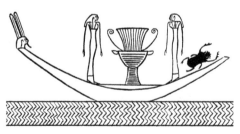

3.19. Scene 18. A bark whose stern is shaped like a head with a divine beard wearing two tall feathers contains a large Hathor-head (human face with cow-ears and sistrum-like crown) flanked by two goddesses.[50] A scarab rests in the prow of the bark.

---

49. This deity does not appear in the version in the tomb of Thutmose III, as depicted in fig. 3.17.

50. For the theology of the barks in Scenes 18 and 19, see Hegenbarth 2002.

LABEL TO BARK: One Who Carries Wernes

165–167: Gods Who Are within It

3.20. Scene 19. A bark whose stern ends with the head of a deity contains three images: a kneeling deity who places his arms upon a large Maat-feather and a stand with crescent and disk.

LABEL TO BARK: Ship of the Netherworld Dwellers

168 (KNEELING GOD): He of Khepri
169 (STAND WITH CRESCENT AND DISK): One Who Carries Maat

REGISTER 3 (PLATE 4)

ANNOTATION TO THE ENTIRE REGISTER

They exist in this fashion. As they praise this great god with their season-signs, so they praise him with the year-signs that are in their hands. This great god issues commands to them, with the result that they call to him. It is from the voice of this great god that they live;[51] it is when he calls to them that their throats breathe, commanding to them their duties, presenting to them their plants that are in their fields. It is they who nourish the gods who are in the following of Re, with the green plants that are in the fields of Wernes. It is they who grant water to the effective spirits, as this great god commands. It is they who stoke the consuming flame in order to burn the enemies of Re. It is they who place the hearts upon the

---

51. Breath through light appears often in the Books of the Creation of the Solar Disk (Roberson 2012, 324 n. 135) and is part of the interchange of light, breath, and speech common in the Netherworld Books (Darnell 2004, 113–14).

fire. Then they cry out, and they mourn when this great god passes by them. He Who Is in the Flame is the guardian of this field. The one who knows it is an equipped spirit whom they protect.

3.21. Scene 20. Four deities, legs out-stretched as if running, with rear arms bent. The first three hold season-signs, while the fourth figure carries a knife.

170 (RUNNING GOD HOLDING SEASON-SIGN): Divider of Time
171 (RUNNING GOD HOLDING SEASON-SIGN): Keeper of Time
172 (RUNNING GOD HOLDING SEASON-SIGN): He Who Carries
173 (RUNNING GOD HOLDING KNIFE): Arm that Carries

3.22. Scene 21. Six deities: the first three hold year-signs, while the next three hold stars.

174 (GOD HOLDING YEAR-SIGN): He of the Year
175 (GOD HOLDING YEAR-SIGN): He of the Grain-sheaf
176 (GOD HOLDING YEAR-SIGN): He Who Requests
177 (GOD HOLDING STAR): Bright One
178 (GOD HOLDING STAR): Great Youth
179 (GOD HOLDING STAR): Great Great Bright One

3.23. Scene 22. Three deities with various attributes

180 (GOD WITH TWO HEADS, GRASPING HIS HANDS
    TOGETHER AT HIS CHEST): His Two Faces and
    His Two Arms
181 (GOD HOLDING TWO LONG PAPYRUS STAFFS
    TOPPED BY STARS): He of the *Akh*-Spirit
182 (MUMMIFORM GOD WITH WHITE CROWN): Osiris-Wennefer

3.24. Scene 23. Three gods seated on thrones; the first two hold stars in their laps, the third holds a knife.

183 (JACKAL-HEADED GOD) Lord of the
   Sacred Land
184 (GODDESS): Slurper[52]
185 (BULL-HEADED GOD): Donkey-Swallower

3.25. Scene 24. Seven deities facing right and an eighth facing left. The first god (186) holds a knife, the next three sheaves of grain (187–189). The following three gods wear sheaves of grain on their heads. The left-facing deity has no attributes.

186 (GOD WITH KNIFE): He Who Pertains to the Divine Throne
187 (GOD WITH GRAIN-SHEAF IN HAND): Grain
188 (GOD WITH GRAIN-SHEAF IN HAND): Scepter
189 (GOD WITH GRAIN-SHEAF IN HAND): Illuminated of Arm
190 (GOD WITH GRAIN-SHEAF ON HEAD): He of the Head
191 (GOD WITH GRAIN-SHEAF ON HEAD): Grain-god
192 (GOD WITH GRAIN-SHEAF ON HEAD): Protection
193 (GOD): He of the Double Flame

CONCLUDING TEXT

Words spoken by the Netherworldly deities, when this great god enters into the (door) Swallower of All, as he traverses the Floodwater of Re up to the (region of) Wernes: "O may the great *ba*-soul appear in glory, the Netherworld having received to herself the Flesh that belongs to the sky, so that you may live, O Flesh, in the earth which has been sanctified for you. Come, Re, may you <act> in your name of Living One, Khepri, who is foremost of the Netherworld. May you cross the field, She Who Pro-

---

52. "ꜣḥb," *LGG* 1:60: "Der Einschlürfer."

tects. May you bind the *Hiw*-snake, and may you smite Terrible of Face! Jubilation is in the sky and ovation is in the earth, for the one who opens his corpse! Illumine, great illuminator! Shine, one upon the head of Re! Dispel the darkness in the Hidden Chamber, in your name of the one who drives out the one mysterious of arm! Illumine the utter darkness, so that Flesh might live and he might be renewed in his own presence. Welcome, Re in the West! Your bark belongs to proper navigation; your crew, which is in the earth, leads you, their arms hidden, so they might destroy for you Apep at the hour of She Who Protects Her Lord.

Praise, one who goes to his *ba*-soul, who rushes on, being equipped, who returns to his corpse, who opens the turquoise region,[53] who throws open the door-leaves of the land! Mysterious are your goings <before> Osiris! Your protection is the protection of Osiris. You are justified against your enemies, as one who rests, as one who rests for the West, as one who manifests, as one who manifests for the East.

Commanding by the majesty of this great god to the Netherworld Dwellers, these foremost of Wernes: "Open your mysterious portals! Behold (my) flesh, that your darkness be uncovered. Water be to you at Wernes, so that bread might come to you from the plants therein. Breath be to you, and you shall not be destroyed. Desiccation be to your corpse, because evil is the stench of your putrefaction. May your mummy wrappings open.[54] May your legs stretch out, so that you might travel upon them. May your strides be wide. To you belong your *ba*-souls; they shall never be far from you. May your visible forms live, so that they may speak your efficacious spells. May your swords be sharp, so that you might conquer the enemies of Osiris. May your seasons endure and your years be stable. Manifest your manifestations at your hours. May you occupy your fields. Emmer be to you as bread, and grain be to you as justification. May you navigate my barks. May you return to the image that enlivens the field anew! You are the field-dwellers of Wernes. May my *ba*-soul that is among you live. You are those who fight for my flesh—protect me from Apep. As you are enlivened for my *ba*-soul, so do you breathe for my corpse. May you remain in your sacred place. One commands to you that you exist

---

53. For the association of the turquoise region and the eastern horizon, see Assmann 1969, 127; Aufrère 1991, 496–503, 506–7; Zandee 1992, 361–64; Billing 2002, 207–10.

54. For releasing the deceased from the constricting mummy-wrappings, see pp. 290–91.

within it. I return the day to my followers in the Netherworld; I go by the night, so that I might dispel the darkness. O, behold, I am following the effective eye; I travel behind the left-eye. O Netherworld Dwellers, protect yourselves! O, I have taken care of you."

During the navigation of his bark which is in the earth this god calls to them. It is when he passes them in order to rest in the field of the Grain-god, in the following of Osiris, that they mourn. This is done according to this image in the hidden part of the chamber of the Netherworld. The one who knows this speech is one who draws near to the Netherworld Dwell-ers. It is effective for a man on earth—truly attested.

This hour is Wise One Who Protects Her Lord.

HOUR 3

INTRODUCTORY TEXT

Resting in the fields of the grain-gods by the majesty of this great god and pursuing the navigation in the floodwaters of Osiris. There are 309 *iteru* in the length of this field. This great god issues commands to the *akh*-spirits who are in the following of Osiris at this locale. The name of the hour of the night that leads this great god is She Who Cuts *Ba*-Souls. The name of the gate of this locale is One Who Seizes.

This great god cares for the gods who are in the following of Osiris, and he grants to them land-plots at this field. Come to know the secret *ba*-souls! As for the one who knows their names, he always ascends to the place in which Osiris is, with the result that water is given to him at this his field. The Floodwaters of the Sole Lord (called) Creator of Victuals is the name of this field. These images of the mysterious *ba*-souls are made according to this template which is in writing in the hidden part of the Netherworld. The beginning of the writings is to the West. It is effective for a man on earth and in the necropolis—truly attested.

REGISTER 1 (PLATE 5)

ANNOTATION TO THE ENTIRE REGISTER

They exist in this fashion in the Netherworld, in the flesh of their own bodies, their *ba*-souls speaking over them, their shades going to rest upon them, after this great god calls to them. They always speak to him, praise him, and mourn after he has passed by them. What they do in the West is to pulverize the rebel, to cause Nun to develop, to stride forth in the inundation waters. When the storm-wind goes forth from the earth beneath them, they cry out and they grind the rebel. The one who knows them is one who passes over them. He cannot perish at their roar. He cannot descend into their fire-pits.

3.26. Scene 25. Six deities with various attributes. First are a baboon seated atop a sandy oval and a mummiform baboon seated within a shrine. Two striding gods, one jackal-headed (194) and the other crocodile-headed (195), each carry a *was*-scepter and *ankh*-sign. The final two (198–199) hold divine pupils in their hands.

194 (SEATED BABOON): He Who Is upon His Sand

195 (MUMMIFORM SEATED BABOON IN SHRINE): He of the Divine Sarcophagus(?)

196 (JACKAL-HEADED GOD): Anubis

197 (CROCODILE-HEADED GOD): Jubilating of Voice

198 (GOD HOLDING PUPILS): He Who Brings

199 (GODDESS HOLDING PUPILS): She Who Brings

3.27. Scene 26. Nine deities and divine objects and animals with various attributes

200 (RAM WITH KNIFE NEAR HOOF): He Who Slays His Enemies

201 (MUMMIFORM FIGURE, ARMS OUTSTRETCHED): Standing Bow

202 (JACKAL ON SHRINE): Anubis of the *Was*-Scepter

203 (SEATED FIGURE HOLDING A PUPIL): He Who Brings the Eye and Pacifies the God

204 (A *WADJ*-SCEPTER WITH MAGIC KNIFE ATOP): Great of Magic

205 (GOD): Noble of Heart

206 (GOD): Potent One

207 (GOD): Youthful One of the Nobles

208 (GOD): He Who Seizes in the Night

3.28. Scene 27. Four mummiform gods with various
attributes atop their heads

209 (MUMMIFORM GOD): Covered One

210 (MUMMIFORM GOD WITH SERPENT ON HIS
   HEAD): Thief

211 (MUMMIFORM GOD WITH SHORT HORNS): Bull
   of Visible Forms

212 (MUMMIFORM GOD WITH LONG HORNS): That *Ba*-Soul

3.29. Scene 28. Four goddesses are followed by a falcon on a standard and three
deities, holding *was*-scepters and *ankh*-signs.

213 (GODDESS): Weeper

214 (GODDESS): She Who Grieves(?)[55]

215 (GODDESS): Mourner

216 (GODDESS): She Who Laments

217 (FALCON ON STANDARD): Falcon

218 (GOD): Horus of the Terrace

219 (GOD): Perfect One of the Gods

220 (GOD): He Who Fills Maat

---

55. "*Mꜣtyt*," *LGG* 3:238–39: "Die Klagefrau (?)" (based on the context of the other
goddesses).

REGISTER 2 (PLATE 5)

ANNOTATION TO THE ENTIRE REGISTER

This great god traverses the Floodwaters of the Lord of All that Create Sustenance. <He exists in> this fashion, as he travels in the barks which are in the earth, as he carries out the navigation of Osiris at this locale. This great god rests a lifetime in this locale. He issues commands to Osiris together with those who are in his following. It is these secret barks which guide him in this field. It is the navigation of this great god in this field during the hour She Who Cuts Ba-Souls. It is after traversing this locale that these barks go around the bank of One Who Seizes. The one who knows it is one who belongs to the places, his rations up with Re.

3.30. Scene 29. The solar bark sails with its typical crew in the version in the tomb of Useramun (compare Scene 5); all other versions of the scene, including the tomb of Thutmose III, omit either the solar god or part of his crew.[56]

221 (GOD): Opener of Paths
222 (GOD): Divine Perception
223 (GODDESS WITH DISK AND HORNS): Mistress of the Bark
224 (RAM-HEADED GOD): Flesh
225 (FALCON-HEADED GOD): Horus Who Praises
226 (GOD): Bull of Maat
227(GOD): Wakeful One
228 (GOD): Divine Utterance
229 (GOD): Director of the Bark

---

56. Hornung 1963b, 68.

3.31. Scene 30. A bark whose prow ends in the head of a lioness carries a crew of six deities with various attributes.[57]

LABEL TO BARK: Pakhet[58]

230 (GOD WITH STEERING OAR): He of the Rudder
231 (MUMMIFORM GOD): One within the Earth
232 (GOD WEARING KNEE-LENGTH GARMENT AND RAM-HORNS): He of Awe
233 (GOD HOLDING *WAS*-SCEPTER): Lord of the *Was*-Scepter
234 (SERPENT STANDING ON HIS TAIL): One Who Shoots Fire with His Eye
235 (GOD WITH STEERING OAR): *BLANK*

3.32. Scene 31. A bark whose prow and stern end in baboon heads contains a crew of six deities with various attributes.

LABEL TO BARK: Baboon Bark

236 (GOD WITH STEERING OAR): One Who Cuts with His Face
237 (GOD WITH KNEES BENT): Renewed One[59]
238 (MUMMIFORM FIGURE): *BLANK*

57. In the tomb of Thutmose III, the stern of the boat is not drawn (as in fig. 3.31).
58. Referring to a lioness goddess (Hornung 1963b, 68–69).
59. "*Mꜣwt,*" *LGG* 3:235; in the tomb of Thutmose III, the head of the deity is not drawn (as in fig. 3.32).

239 (GOD HOLDING *ANKH*-SIGN): *BLANK*
240 (SERPENT STANDING ON TAIL): One Who Shoots Fire with His Face
241 (GOD WITH STEERING OAR): One Who Rows without Weariness

3.33. Scene 32. A bark with papyrus-bundles as both prow and stern carries six entities. An oarsman at the stern is preceded by a falcon-headed god standing atop a serpent. Next, two mummiform falcon-headed goddesses face in towards one another. At the prow is another oarsman followed by a serpent standing on its tail.

LABEL TO BARK: Equipped Bark

242 (GOD WITH STEERING OAR): Fiery of Face
243 (FALCON HEADED GOD HOLDING *ANKH*-SIGN AND *WAS*-SCEPTER): One Who Awaits Horus
(SERPENT ON WHICH 243 STANDS): Follower of Horus.
244 (MUMMIFORM FALCON-HEADED GODDESS): Female Falcon
245 (MUMMIFORM FALCON-HEADED GODDESS): Female Falcon
246 (SERPENT STANDING ON ITS TAIL): Burning of Face
247 (GOD WITH STEERING OAR): *BLANK*

3.34. Scene 33. Four gods stand facing the procession of barks; their hands are clasped before their chests.

248 (GOD): Lord of the Floodwaters
249 (GOD): One Who Moors to the Land
250 (GOD): One Who Makes the Boundaries
251 (GOD): One Who Sees the Boundaries

REGISTER 3 (PLATE 5)

ANNOTATION TO THE ENTIRE REGISTER

They exist in this fashion, they adoring the great god. This great god continually issues commands to them, with the result that they live when he calls to them. He commends to them their water, and they receive their heads from the breath atop his mouth. What they do in the West is make a roasting and slaughter of the *ba*-souls, suffocating the shades, delivering those who are not, those without being, to their Place of Destruction. They cast fire. They cause the enemies to burn up by means of that which is at the tips of their swords. As they cry out so they mourn, after this great god has passed over them.

Kheteri[60] is the name of the guardian of this field. The one who knows it is an *akh*-spirit with power over his legs.

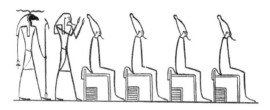

3.35. Scene 34. A ram-headed god holding an *ankh*-sign and *was*-scepter is followed by a deity with his arms raised in adoration. Four mummiform deities wearing white crowns are seated on thrones.

252 (RAM-HEADED GOD): Khnum
253 (GOD): Protector of the Earth
254 (SEATED MUMMIFORM GOD): Osiris Lord of the West
255 (SEATED MUMMIFORM GOD): Osiris Foremost of the West
256 (SEATED MUMMIFORM GOD): Osiris of the Place
257 (SEATED MUMMIFORM GOD): Osiris Who Seizes Millions

---

60. Of uncertain translation, as this is the sole attestation of the name; "*Ḫtrỉ*," *LGG* 5:972. Perhaps compare deity number 733, "Gorey-Headed One," reading *khw*, "He who protects," as the first element of the name; "He Who Protects the Gorey-One" would be appropriate to a deity overseeing deities who act as punishers of the damned.

3.36. Scene 35. Five stork (variant: ibis)-headed deities brandish knives. In front, two pairs of deities: a goddess and a deity holding a knife before him with both hands, followed by another goddess and god, without attributes.

258 (STORK-HEADED GOD): Piercing of Face
259 (STORK-HEADED GOD): Their Flood
260 (STORK-HEADED GOD): Destroyer
261 (STORK-HEADED GOD): Screamer
262 (STORK-HEADED GOD): One Who Cries Out
263 (GODDESS): Birthplace
264 (GOD HOLDING KNIFE): Guardian Who Slaughters
265 (GODDESS): She Who Is atop Her Flame
266 (GOD): He of the West

3.37. Scene 36. Four mummiform deities wearing red crowns are seated on thrones. Next are two figures, knees flexed, looking back over their shoulders (271–272); they each grasp a *was*-scepter with both hands. They are followed by three bending figures (273–275), appearing to crawl on their hands and knees. At the far right of the scene, two deities look to the left: a goddess offering two pupils and a god holding an *ankh*-sign and *was*-scepter.

267 (SEATED MUMMIFORM GOD): Osiris Bull of the West
268 (SEATED MUMMIFORM GOD): Osiris Chief of His Staircase
269 (SEATED MUMMIFORM GOD): Osiris King of Lower Egypt
270 (SEATED MUMMIFORM GOD): Osiris Powerful One of the Gods
271 (GOD WITH FLEXED KNEES): Orion
272 (GOD WITH FLEXED KNEES): He Who Awaits

273 (CRAWLING GOD): Stooped One
274 (CRAWLING GOD): One Who Pays Homage
275 (CRAWLING GOD): Secret of Goings
276 (GODDESS HOLDING PUPILS): She of the Eastern Mountain
277 (GOD): *Kheteri*[61]

CONCLUDING TEXT

Words spoken by the mysterious gods before this great god when he enters (the portal) Seizer, as he navigates the floodwaters of the Sole Lord, (called) Creator of Victuals: "Come to us, one whose flesh is navigated, who is guided to his own limbs, interpreter of the Netherworld,[62] possessor of breath, whose limbs speak, and who creates his own life. May your *ba*-soul appear in glory. May your power be strong. May your two Maat's guide you on the paths of darkness. The sky belongs to your *ba*-soul, as the earth belongs to your corpse.[63] May the Unique One stand up for you, she who is alone at the tow-rope, when the jackals bring you to moor. May the arms of the Westerners receive you in your sacred visible forms of the ancient one.

How beautiful it is that the Westerners see, and how peaceful is it that the Netherworld Dwellers hear Re, when he sets in the West and illumines the arms in the chamber She Who is Dark of Images.

Come to us, Re of the Horizon, Khepri, swimmer[64] of the gods! May you navigate the banks of the Netherworld. May you traverse your hidden fields. May you make your manifestations in that earth of yours. The great locale jubilates for you, that place at which you have halted.

---

61. Divine name with uncertain translation (see p. 163); Wiebach-Koepke 2003a, 45 suggests "Ichneumon."

62. The term ⁽w refers to a speaker of a foreign language (Bell 1976) and can be used in extended ways to refer to someone who makes sense of a topic on the basis of knowledge; compare the statement by a metallurgist with reference to his use of raw materials (Bell 1976, 63–65) and a physician describing the knowledge of his craft (Morenz 1997). The epithet of the deity here in the concluding text of Hour 3 precedes the high percentage of cryptographic texts in Hours 4–5 of the Book of the Hidden Chamber.

63. For parallels to this expression, see p. 8 n. 13.

64. The verb *nbi*, "to swim" is a pun on *nb*, "lord," a play on words also utilized in the Books of the Solar-Osirian Unity in the Tomb of Ramesses IX (Darnell 2004, 276–85; p. 531 n. 13, p. 565).

Give praise to Osiris, while he praises you with his body which is within the Netherworld. O Re, justified one! O Re who smites his enemies! You are justified, Re, against your enemies. The lord of the disk, shining of *ba*-soul, is the one who illumines the earth."

Issuing commands by the majesty of this great god to the mysterious *ba*-souls, who are in the following of Osiris: "O these whom I have made mysterious, whose *ba*-souls I have hidden—ascend to me and to Osiris in his following, in order to greet him, in order to pass over his images, in order to destroy those who make bindings against him.

May Divine Utterance belong to you, O Osiris! May Divine Perception belong to you, Foremost of the Westerners! O *akh*-spirits of Osiris who are in the entourage of Foremost of the Westerners! Stability be to your visible forms, transfiguration be to your manifestations. The breath of air be to your noses. Sight be to your faces and hearing to your ears. Uncovering be to your wrappings. Loosening be to your bandages. May offerings be to you upon earth, and water in the divine bank. May cultivated land of your field belong to you.

Your *ba*-souls will never be felled. Your corpses shall not go upside down.[65] Opening be to your gates. Light be to your caverns. Uprightness be to you at your places.

That I have come here is to see my corpses, after having reckoned my images within the Netherworld. O rowers of Tatenen—row me![66] Those extended of arm—may they carry out my navigation.

Your *ba*-soul be to heaven, Osiris! Your corpse be to the earth, Foremost of Igeret! Your gods be in your following! Your *akh*-spirits be before you, your forms which are in you having already manifested. Meanwhile, effectiveness be to your *akh*-spirit, Osiris; and effectiveness be to your *akh*-spirits, O *akh*-spirits who are in the following of Osiris!

I am ascending to the earth, daytime in my wake. That I go by night, is in order to pacify my *ba*-soul. Your visible forms be to the day—but for the night-time have I fashioned your *akh*-spirits. I have fashioned your *ba*-souls for myself to be in my following. Thus have you been created! You shall not fall into the Place of Destruction."

This great god moors near them. Then they call to his bark, after he has commanded to them. (This) is done accordingly in the hidden part of

---

65. For the dangers associated with inversion in the Netherworld, see Darnell 2004, 426–48.

66. For an alternate translation, see Wiebach-Koepke 2003a, 48–49 (esp. 48, n. 5).

the Netherworld. The one who knows this is an effective *ba*-soul, having power over his two feet, without entering into the Place of Destruction. He goes forth in visible form in the day and inhales breath at his hour.

The hour who guides at this field is She Who Cuts *Ba*-Souls.

HOUR 4

INTRODUCTORY TEXT

Going to rest by means of hauling by the majesty of this god in the mysterious cavern of the West, Sacred of Visible Forms. Caring for those who are within it by means of his voice, without his seeing them. Living of Manifestations is the name of this cavern. The name of the gate of this cavern is One Who Hides the Hauling. The name of the hour of the night who guides this great god is Great in Her Power. Whoever knows this image is one who eats food intended for the mouths of the living in the temple of Atum.

It is the mysterious paths of the Place of Hauling, the sacred roads of Imhet, the hidden gates within the land of Sokar who is upon his sand. (This) is done according to this image that is in writing in the hidden part of the Netherworld, upon the western side of the Hidden Chamber. The one who knows it is one who travels rightly, who goes along the roads of the Place of Hauling, and sees the image in Imhet.

TEXTS WITHIN THE DESCENDING PATH THAT ZIG-ZAGS ACROSS HOUR 4

The one belonging to the Place of Hauling. The mysterious paths of the Place of Hauling. The Divine Gateway. He does not pass by them; it is his voice that they hear.

The path of accessing the corpse of Sokar who is upon his sand. It is a mysterious image, unseen and unperceived.

The mysterious path upon which Anubis enters in order to hide the corpse of Osiris.[67]

The mysterious path of the entrance of Imhet.

67. Anubis appears often as one who hides the Osirian corpse within the Netherworld Books. Compare the Book of Adoring Re in the West, Address 12 (p. 80) and several passages within the Book of Caverns (pp. 370, 392, 396).

REGISTER 1 (PLATE 6)

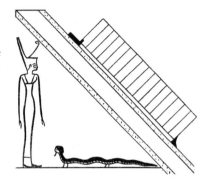

3.38. Scene 37. A goddess wearing a red crown faces a serpent with four legs and a human head with divine beard; the scene is tucked beneath the first descending portion of the path of the Place of Hauling.

LABEL TO SANDY PATH: The path that is on the way to the Place of Hauling. This gate.

278 (GODDESS WITH RED CROWN): She exists at the rising.

279 (HUMAN-HEADED SERPENT): Human-Headed One who guards the road. He exists as the guardian of the road, without being able to go to any other place daily.

LABEL TO DOOR: Sharp One Who Buries[68]

3.39. Scene 38. Three serpents, one atop the other, face right; in front of the serpents is a coiled cobra with an *ankh*-sign. Behind stands a deity holding two pupils followed by a three-headed serpent with legs and wings, an *ankh*-sign before its front-most mouth.

280–282 (SERPENTS): Those who are upon their bellies. They exist in this fashion, without going to any other place daily.

283 (COBRA): Selket. She exists in this fashion, her position is the Place of Hauling, the beginning of this road.

284 (GOD HOLDING TWO PUPILS IN OUTSTRETCHED HANDS): One Who Separates the Two Gods. He is in this fashion as the image of Horus himself, discerning the image in the sacred path.

---

68. Or "One Who Cuts off the Landing."

285 (MULTIHEADED SERPENT): Great God. He exists in this fashion in the Netherworld at the entrance of this sacred road of the Place of Hauling. By the wind of his two wings does he live, both his corpse and heads.

3.40. Scene 39. A Seth-headed deity holding *ankh*-sign and *was*-scepter faces right towards a dual-headed serpent. Next, a crocodile-headed deity (288) looks left, back over his shoulder, holding a serpent (who emerges from the earth) in his left hand and a coiled object in his right. A falcon headed god (289) holding a *was*-scepter faces left. Finally, two goddesses—one wearing a red crown, the other a white crown—stand looking right.

286 (SETH-HEADED GOD): One Who Separates the Netherworld. He exists in this fashion as the image that Horus made, separating the two gods upon this path.

287 (TWO-HEADED SERPENT): Nehebkau.[69] He exists in this fashion at his place of the sacred road, of the path of the Place of Hauling, without his ever going to any other place daily. He lives from the breath of his utterance.

LABEL TO 288–291: They exist in this fashion as images that Horus made. It is they who guard One Who Leaps Up,[70] the protector of the earth,[71] who show the way toward the mysteries in this sacred path.

288 (CROCODILE-HEADED GOD): Praising of Head
289 (FALCON-HEADED GOD): He Whom the Netherworld Vaunts
290 (GODDESS WEARING WHITE CROWN): Southerner
291 (GODDESS WEARING A RED CROWN): Northerner

---

69. "*Nḥb-kзw*," *LGG* 4:273–76 and literature there.

70. For *nhp* as a leaping action that occurs at the restoration of order and defeat of Apep, see Darnell 2004, 120–21, 297–99.

71. Or, "when the earth quakes."

REGISTER 2 (PLATE 6)

3.41. Scene 40. The solar bark sails through the hour—the standard bark has transformed into a large serpent whose prow and stern end with snake heads. The typical crew of the solar bark is present. Before the bark are four gods (300–303) hauling a rope connected to the prow of the serpent vessel.

NAME OF THE SOLAR BARK: One Who Cleaves the Road

292 (GOD): Opener of Paths
293 (GOD): Divine Perception
294 (GODDESS WITH HORNS AND DISK): Mistress of the Bark
295 (RAM-HEADED GOD WITHIN SHRINE): Flesh
296 (FALCON-HEADED GOD): Horus Who Praises
297 (GOD): Bull of Maat
298 (GOD): Wakeful One
299 (GOD): Divine Utterance
300 (GOD): Mysterious One
301(GOD): He of the Tow-Rope
302(GOD): Chief of the Cord
303 (GOD): He Who Stretches the Rope

This great god sails over them in this fashion. It is the flame upon the mouth of his bark that guides him on the mysterious paths, without him seeing their image. He calls to them in their vicinity; it is his voice which they hear.

LABEL TO DOOR: One Who Sharpens the Sickles of the Earth[72]

---

72. The tomb of Thutmose III adds the comment: "way of the entering of the corpse of Sokar" (Hornung 1963b). For sickle-wielding deities in the Book of Gates, see pp. 261, 296–97.

3.42. Scene 41. Eight deities and divine objects with various attributes. Left to right, a mummiform deity wearing a white crown (304), a large crook, and a small tableau: an ibis-headed god facing right holds up his arms to support the *udjat*-eye (306), while a falcon-headed god facing left also supports the eye. A striding deity with white crown is followed by a figure whose head has been replaced by two ropes (310); the rightmost figure is a deity without attribute (311).

304 (MUMMIFORM GOD WITH WHITE CROWN): He of the Counterweight

305 (LARGE CROOK): *Meset*-stave of Osiris

306 (*UDJAT*-EYE): One of Sokar

307 (IBIS-HEADED GOD HOLDING ALOFT THE *UDJAT*-EYE): He Who Raises Up

308 (FALCON-HEADED GOD HOLDING ALOFT THE *UDJAT*-EYE): He Who Extends the Arm

309 (GOD WITH WHITE CROWN): Distinguished of Forehead[73]

310 (GOD WITH TWO ROPES EMERGING FROM NECK): Chief of His Sarcophagus

311 (GOD): Flourishing of Face

TEXT OVER THE GODS TO THE RIGHT OF THE SLOPING SANDWAY: They exist in this fashion as images of their bodies that Horus has hidden upon this sacred path of the One Hidden of Mysteries. As protectors of the sacred path of accessing the hidden part of the Netherworld do they exist. It is they who protect Anubis in his image belonging to the paths upon which he has passed in the sacred land.

---

73. For names compounded with *s̠tni*, "to distinguish," see Darnell 2004, 139.

3.43. Scene 42. A god holding a magic knife with both hands faces right. Following him are four deities, facing left—three gods followed by a goddess, all of whom hold *ankh*-signs in their outstretched arms.

312 (GOD HOLDING MAGIC KNIFE): He Who Pacifies
313 (GOD): One Who Guides the Living One
314 (GOD): Onuris
315 (GOD): One Who Commands
316 (GODDESS): Mistress of Life

REGISTER 3 (PLATE 6)

3.44. Scene 43. A papyrus bark—with human-headed prow and stern—contains a large serpent with an *ankh*-sign before his mouth.

317 (LARGE SERPENT): *Nau*-serpent who illumines.[74] He exists in this fashion in his bark, namely the one who guards Imhet. He stands at this mysterious path of Imhet. From the voice that the human heads of his bark speak does he live.

---

74. The *Nau*-serpent also appears in Hour 12, Register 2, Scene 126 (p. 238).

3.45. Scene 44. Five deities of various attributes: two goddesses, a baboon-headed mummiform figure seated on a throne, a lioness-headed goddess, and a seated goddess with horns (but lacking a throne).

LABEL TO 318–322: They exist in this fashion as images that Horus has made, standing in the earth at this mysterious path of Imhet, namely, their primordial access into the earth.

318 (GODDESS): She of the Road
319 (GODDESS): She of the Bird-Claw
320 (BABOON-HEADED MUMMIFORM FIGURE): Ape
321 (LIONESS-HEADED GODDESS): She of the Gullet
322 (GODDESS WITH HORNS): Attached of Horns

3.46. Scene 45. Two large serpents face to the right; the first serpent has an *ankh*-sign in front of his mouth, while the second serpent has a human head coming forth from her tail.

323 (SERPENT): One Who Is Hidden. He exists in this fashion as protector of this mysterious path of Imhet, without being able to go forth to any other place each day. On the words of the gods who belong to this path does he live.

324 (SERPENT): Praised One. She exists in this fashion as the guardian of this path. She praises with her two faces to the great image which is within it.

LABEL TO THE ROAD: Floodwaters of the Corpses

3.47. Scene 46. A complex scene dominated by the depiction of fourteen heads, disks, and stars, arranged in two rows. Below is a three-headed serpent. To the right is a deity with arm raised up as if to smite, although his hands are empty. A goddess wearing a maat-feather appears at the far right of the scene, next to a door-leaf. Above the scene is a winged sun disk.

325 (THREE-HEADED SERPENT): He Who Trembles. It is this[75] mysterious image of Imhet. Light is in it daily until the birth of Khepri, who comes forth from the three heads of He Who Trembles. Then Khepri removes himself.

326 (WINGED SUN DISK): Khepri. In his visible forms of the god variegated of plumage does he truly rest.

327 (GOD WITH ARM RAISED): One within Heaven

328 (GODDESS CROWNED WITH MAAT-FEATHER): Maat

LABEL TO THE DOOR: Cleaver of Eternity

HOUR 5

INTRODUCTORY TEXT

It is the hauling of this great god upon the proper paths of the Netherworld in the upper half of the mysterious cavern of Sokar, who is upon his sand. Unseen and unperceived is this mysterious image of the earth that carries the flesh of this god. Those amongst whom this god is, they hear the voice of Re, when he calls in the vicinity of this god.

The name of the gate of this locale is Positions of the Gods. The name of the cavern of this god is West. The name of the hour of the night that guides this great god is She Who Guides within Her Bark.

Mysterious paths of the West, gates of entering the hidden place, the sacred place of the land of Sokar, limbs, flesh and body being the first

---

75. For this Old Egyptianism (N pi), see Edel 1955, 87 (§193).

manifestation. Knowing the *ba*-souls within the Netherworld, their visible forms that belong to that which is within the hours, in their mysterious names, unknowable, unseen, and unperceived, in the image of Horus himself.

This is done according to this image that is in writing in the hidden part of the Netherworld on the southern side of the Hidden Chamber. The one who knows this is one who is satisfied of *ba*-soul; it is with Sokar's offering that he becomes satisfied. She of Destruction will never slice his corpse. One offers to them upon the earth.

REGISTER 1 (PLATE 7)

3.48. Scene 47. A goddess, with both of her arms raised in front of her, wears a feather. She faces nine divine standards (*nṯr*-signs); the first wears a white crown, the last a red crown.

Words spoken by this great god: "O, West, give your arms! Beautiful is the great road within the earth, the path of the tombs, the resting place of my gods. May you breathe, O you ennead of gods,[76] who came about from my flesh entirely. Manifesting be to your forms; endurance be to your chattels. When you greet me do I protect you. You are the ones whom I have commanded to be sanctified, while greeting me in the western land."

OVER THE NINE DIVINE STANDARDS: It is the chattel[77] of these gods in the Netherworld. They are in this fashion.

329 (GODDESS): She Who Protects(?) the Earth

330 (DIVINE STANDARD WEARING WHITE CROWN): Southern Divine Standard of Khepri

---

76. Here and throughout this annotation also to be read literally as "*nṯr*-signs."

77. For *ḥnw.w* as, "chattels," see "Sachen, Hausrat u.ä.," *WÄS* 3:107.11; Sauneron 1958, 275(a).

331 (DIVINE STANDARD): Divine Standard of Shu
332 (DIVINE STANDARD): Divine Standard of Tefnut
333 (DIVINE STANDARD): Divine Standard of Geb
334 (DIVINE STANDARD): Divine Standard of Nut
335 (DIVINE STANDARD): Divine Standard of Osiris
336 (DIVINE STANDARD): Divine Standard of Isis
337 (DIVINE STANDARD): Divine Standard of Nephthys
338 (DIVINE STANDARD WEARING RED CROWN): Northern Divine Standard
    of Horus of the Netherworld

3.49. Scene 48. Five striding deities with various attributes

Words spoken by this great god: "Stand at your water, guard your banks, and cause the flooding of the drowned who are in Nun, and land them to the banks. The deluge be to your water, that they not go dry; elevation be to your banks, that they not become barren. May you bend your arms, O Water-crosser, until I pass by you in peace."

    They exist as guardians of the water of the drowned in the Netherworld; what they do is navigate the bark.

339 (GOD): Gaurdian of the Water of the Drowned
340 (GOD): Protector of the Banks
341 (FALCON-HEADED GOD): Living of Heart
342 (CROCODILE-HEADED GOD): Primeval One of the Nethersky
343 (JACKAL-HEADED GOD): Anubis of the Chest

3.50. Scene 49. A large mound—called a "chest"—is
topped by a hieroglyph for "night." To either side of
the chest birds are perched; these birds are Isis and
Nephthys. A scarab (who grasps a rope from the
middle register) emerges from the bottom of the
chest.

Words spoken by this great god: "Protect your
chest.[78] Elevation be to your voice. Straightness be
to your throats. Hiddenness be to this, the image
that you protect. Opening be to your wings. Do your duty, until I pass by
you in peace."

344 (*GRḤ*-HIEROGLYPH): Night
345 (BIRD): Isis
346 (BIRD): Nephthys

3.51. Scene 50. A double-headed snake faces left, towards the chest labeled "Night."

Words spoken by the majesty of this great god: "O sacred snake, sanctify
for me your two members.[79] Open for me your coils! O sacred snake, sanctify for me your two limbs! Open for me your coils and your two faces in
the earth! You will not shoot me; you will not attack those who are in my
following, until I pass by you in peace."

From the voice of Re does he live daily, without ever going forth to any
other place in the Netherworld. At the chest of Khepri does he exist.

347 (DOUBLE-HEADED SERPENT): *BLANK*

---

78. On the "chest" of Osiris, see p. 111 n. 108, p. 468, p. 543 n. 36.
79. The term ʿ here may refer to the bifurcated neck of the serpent, since he does
not appear to have any visible limbs.

3.52. Scene 51. Eight gods with various attributes stride towards the right. At the far right is a goddess, facing left, holding a dead enemy.

Words spoken by this great god: "O slaughterers, who guard the slaughtering places, who are engaged in[80] the chastisement of the dead. Manifestation be to your speech! Light be to your magic! Skill be to your *ba*-souls! Thriving be to your power! Squelch the enemies, destroy the dead, and slice up the shades of those to be destroyed and those to be punished in your cauldrons. It is you who greet Osiris and hear commands before Wennefer. Sharpness be to your knives, chastisement to your slaughtering places, and binding be to your fetters! Your two hands be upon the representation among which you are, until I pass by you in peace."

It is they who persist in vanquishing the dead in the Netherworld. What they do is burn up the corpses of the dead with the flames of their mouths in the course of every day.

348 (GOD): He Who Pacifies the Gods

349 (SHREW-HEADED GOD): He Whom the Westerners Fear

350 (BULL-HEADED GOD WITH SHORT HORNS): Staff

351 (BULL-HEADED GOD WITH LONG HORNS): Swallower

352 (GOD WITH SHADOW SIGN BEHIND HIS HEAD): Horned One

353 (GOD CROWNED WITH MAAT-FEATHER): He Who Brings Maat

354 (GOD LOOKING BACKWARD HOLDING TWO COILED ROPES): Reversed of Face Who Lassos

355 (RAM-HEADED GOD): That *Ba*-Soul to whom the Dead Belong

356 (GODDESS WITH IMAGE OF A PRONE FIGURE): She Who Destroys, chief of the slicing of the dead

OVER THE GODDESS (356): The one who knows her is one who will cross over her in peace. She lives on the blood of the dead, consisting of the provisions that these gods give.

---

80. An early use of *ꜥḥꜥ.n=f* followed by a stative (compare Kruchten 1982, 34, 36, 82 n. 83; Broze 1991, 65–77).

Register 2 (plate 7)

3.53. Scene 52. The solar bark is transformed into a serpent vessel with prow and stern ending in snake heads. The typical crew populates the bark, and the vessel is hauled by seven deities.

By means of the hauling does the great god travel upon this cavern in his bark which is in the land (named) Living of *Ba*-Souls. So say the Netherworld Dwellers to this great god: "Welcome, lord of life! Welcome, one who occupies the West! Welcome, opener of the earth! Welcome, revealer of the earth! Welcome, one within the sky! Welcome, one who occupies the nethersky! Welcome, vindicated one, lord of the ennead!

Welcome! May the earth open (its) arms for you. May the Beautiful Land straighten its paths for you. Your voice, O Re, be to Osiris, your call, O Re, be to the land of Sokar, so that Horus upon his sand, may live. Come to Khepri, O Re! Come, O Re, to Khepri! The tow-rope that we have brought is the tow-rope which we shall raise up to Khepri, that he might give his hand to Re, that he might straighten[81] the mysterious paths for Re-Horakhty. May the sky be at peace, for Re belongs to the good West."

LABEL TO THE BARK: Living of *Ba*-Souls

357 (GOD): Opener of Paths
358 (GOD): Divine Perception
359 (GODDESS WEARING DISK AND HORNS): Mistress of the Bark
360 (RAM-HEADED GOD IN SHRINE): Flesh
361 (FALCON-HEADED GOD): Horus Who Praises
362 (GOD): Bull of Maat
363 (GOD): Wakeful One

---

81. For the verb *mꜣꜥ* in this context, see p. 93 (Address 48 of the Great Litany in the Book of Adoring Re in the West).

364 (GOD): Divine Utterance
365 (GOD): Director of the Bark

OVER THE HAULERS: Netherworld Dwellers. What they do is haul this god over the cavern of Sokar.

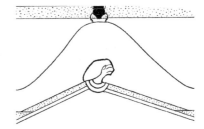

3.54. Scene 53. The head of a goddess (Isis) crowns a pyramid-shaped mound that juts into the middle of Register 2. The tow-rope of the solar bark curves over the mound, reaching its apex in the forelegs of the scarab that emerges from the chest in Scene 49.

So says this great god who is atop this cavern: "May you announce[82] this your image, Sokar, hidden of mysteries. My call be to you, so that you might be an *akh*-spirit. My words be to you, so that you might praise by means of them.[83] Isis be to your image. The great god be to your corpse. He is the one who shall guard it."

When this god halts at the head of this goddess, he issues commands in the land of Sokar daily. It is Khepri within his chest who conducts the tow-rope during the hauling over this cavern, so that he might occupy the paths of the Netherworld.

AT THE HEAD OF ISIS (374): Flesh of Isis who is upon the sand of the land of Sokar.

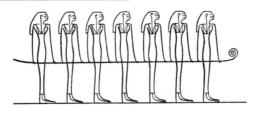

3.55. Scene 54. Seven goddesses haul the end of the tow-rope of the solar bark.

82. The verb *sy* appears to be a writing of "jem. melden einem Höheren," *WÄS* 4:34.1–5.

83. The solar deity is here providing the "script" of solar praise; compare a series of passages from the solar chapel in the temple of Ramesses III at Medinet Habu (see p. 69).

Traveling by means of hauling by this great god; reception by these god-desses. So say these goddesses to this great god: "Re comes to the Nether-world in peace. May the path of Re in his bark, which is within the earth, in its bodily form, he who annihilates his enemies, be rightly guided. To you belongs the West, O Re, that you might rest within it. May you ascend to the sky as a great *ba*-soul, chief of the powers of the horizon. It is your hauling which effects your hauling. That you are vindicated is with your enemies having been beaten down."

The goddesses who haul Re in the Netherworld over this cavern. What they do is haul this great god, so that he might occupy his bark within Nun in the Netherworld.

375–381: *BLANK*

3.56. Scene 55. Four deities holding various staffs, followed by a goddess

Words spoken by this great god: "Receive to yourselves your staffs, raise up[84] your *djam*-scepters. Lean upon your *ames*-scepters. May you stand up for your *ba*-souls, but may you sit for your offerings. You are the ones to whom victuals and foodstuffs belong, O possessors of provisions in the West. Isis gives you the West, so that it might be at peace with you. Stand for me in your visible forms, until I pass by you in peace."

They exist in this fashion. They are the council who make firm the victuals in this cavern.

382 (GOD HOLDING STRAIGHT STAFF): Chief of the Visible Forms
383 (GOD HOLDING *WAS*-SCEPTER): He Who Brings Offerings
384 (FALCON-HEADED GOD HOLDING *HEQA*-SCEPTER): Horus of the *Heqa*-scepter

---

84. Reading *wꜣ* as *twꜣ*; for a similar group of staff–wielding deities, see Book of the Hidden Chamber, Hour 9, Scene 100 (p. 218).

385 (GOD HOLDING LARGE PALM BRANCH): Issuer of Commands
386 (GODDESS): Isis, Goddess of the West[85]

REGISTER 3 (PLATE 7)

LABEL TO THE ROADS: The mysterious path of Imhet, upon which this god is hauled. It contains the abomination of Nehes.[86] Gateway of the West.

The mysterious path of the land of Sokar, upon which Isis enters in order to be in the following of her brother. It exists full of the flames of the fire at the mouth of Isis. The gods, *akh*-spirits, and dead cannot pass over it.

The mysterious path of the land of Sokar. It is the Westerners who haul this god, without gods, *akh*-spirits, or the dead passing over it. It exists full of the flames of the fire at the mouth of (the serpent of) Roasting Flame.[87]

LABEL TO THE RIGHT DOOR: He who does not go around his image

3.57 (top), 3.58 (middle), 3.59 (bottom). Scene 56. A complex scene (see thumbnail below) centered on a large oval flanked by an Aker sphinx. The oval contains a falcon-headed god lifting the wings of a serpent with three heads and whose tail ends in a human head. To the left of the oval are four human heads with tapers atop them, followed by a serpent with baboon head above the snake head (facing right, toward the Aker). To the right is another serpent (facing right, away from the Aker) and four seated deities, each holding at their knees a different form of regalia: white crown, red crown, ram-head, and double *šw.ty*-feathers. At the far right of the scene is a serpent standing on his tail, with a star before him.

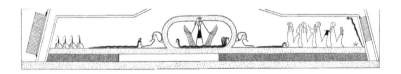

---

85. For the reading of 'Is.t-'Imnt.t here see Refai 1996, 29 and n. 276.

86. This Nehes may refer to the "Wakeful One" or Seth. See p. 133 n. 11.

87. For the dual nature of this serpent within the Netherworld Books, see Manassa 2007a, 129–30 (including the discussion of the serpent Roasting Flame in a variant Late period scene of the introduction of the Book of Adoring Re in the West [see also p. 62 n. 3]); on Wamemti note also Borghouts 2007, 24.

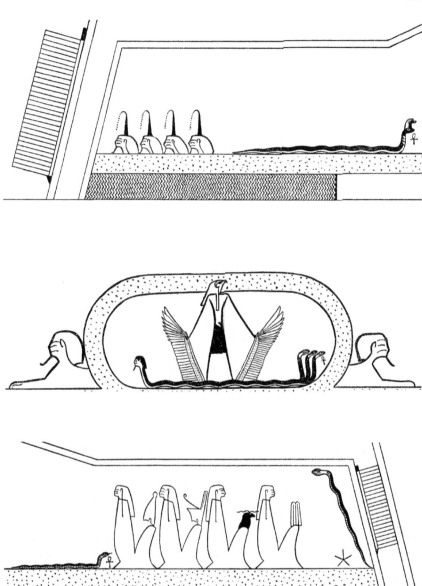

LABEL TO THE HEADS WITH FLAMES: They exist in the following of this god. What they do is to burn up the footsteps of his enemies. Heads of the burning tapers.

391 (SERPENT WITH BABOON HEAD): Sacred of Head.[88] From the voices of the gods that are on earth does he live. He enters and goes forth, causing to ascend the provisions of the living to this great god daily, unseen.

LABEL TO EACH OF THE AKER-LIONS: Flesh. From the voice of the great god does he live. What he does is guard his image.

LABEL TO THE OVAL OF SOKAR: This image exists in this fashion in the utter darkness. That this oval pertaining to this god is bright is by means of the two eyes of the heads of the great god. It is within the coils of the great god that his feet shine, while he guards his image. The sound of something is heard in this oval when this god passes by them, like the roar of heaven when it storms.[89]

393 (FALCON-HEADED GOD WITHIN OVAL): Flesh of Sokar who is upon his sand

IN THE SAND WAYS (2x): Aker who guards the mysterious flesh. Land of Sokar.

394 (WINGED SERPENT WITHIN OVAL): By means of the breath of his utterance does he live daily. What he does is guard his image. The great god who opens the wings of He Dappled of Plumage.

395 (SERPENT RIGHT OF THE OVAL): (Serpent of the) Roasting Flame. By means of the flame that is atop his mouth does he live. What he does is guard the oval, without going to any other place in the Netherworld.

396–399 (GODS WITH REGALIA): The gods who bear the mysterious image of Sokar who is upon his sand. Their images being what has come from their own bodies. They exist in the following of this great god, unseen and unperceived.

400 (SERPENT STANDING ON TAIL): Living god. He comes and goes, traveling that he might open the (door named) One Who Cuts.

---

88. For the serpent ḏsr-tp, see Goebs 2008, 243.
89. For re-creation in the Netherworld as a noisy affair, see Manassa 2008, 132.

LABEL TO THE FIRE-SEA BENEATH THE OVAL OF SOKAR: Floodwater of the mourning ones, the gods who are in Imhet. The bark cannot pass over them. The Netherworld Dwellers cannot have power over their water which is in this god's necropolis.[90] It as fire that their water exists against those who are therein (the damned).

HOUR 6

INTRODUCTORY TEXT

Resting by the majesty of this great god in the deep waters, Lady[91] of the Netherworld Dwellers. This great god gives commands that these gods within it have power over their divine offerings at this locale. That he sails in this <locale> is being equipped in his bark. He commands to them their cultivated land to be their offerings, giving to them water from their flood-waters, in passage of the Netherworld daily.

The name of the gate of this locale is Sharp of Blades. The name of the hour of night that guides this great god is Harbor Granting (Proper) Offerings.

The mysterious path of the West through which this great god sails in his bark, in order to care for the Netherworld Dwellers, pronounced of their names, known in their bodies, engraved in their visible forms, their hours mysterious of affairs, without this mysterious image of the Netherworld being known by any people.

This image is made in writing according to the template in the hidden part of the Netherworld on the southern side of the Hidden Chamber. The one who knows it is a possessor of victuals in the Netherworld, he being satisfied with the divine offerings of those who are in the following of Osiris. One offers to him, while his relations are in the earth.

---

90. The phrase is ḥr.t-nṯr pn, which refers not to "*this* necropolis," but rather to the "necropolitan area of *this* god."

91. Alternatively, the term nb.t could refer to a topographical feature related to water (Vercoutter 1947, 154–56).

REGISTER 1 (PLATE 8)

3.60. Scene 57. Nine gods with various attributes are in a seated posture, but without a throne beneath them.

Words spoken by the majesty of this great god to the gods who are in this field: "O Seated Ones who are in the Netherworld! O those of the offerings who pertain to their baskets—may your offerings be offered to you; your offering fields be to you, so that you might be content with them daily.

You are those who are content with the provisions, possessors of arms, straight of feet, high of your visible forms. Greatness be to your manifestations. As you grow strong, so you grow powerful, and vice versa! Strength be to you in your necks;[92] power be to you by means of your scepters,[93] so that you might protect Osiris from the binders and the robbers against him."

What they do in the Netherworld is to give offerings to the Netherworldly gods. Their offerings manifest immediately as victuals at the tip of the tongue of the great god.

401 (GOD CROWNED WITH A LOAF OF BREAD AND JAR OF BEER): One Who Rests Foremost of the Netherworld

402 (GODDESS WEARING RED CROWN): Isis of Imhet

403 (GOD): Osiris, Beloved of the Gods

404 (FALCON-HEADED GOD): Horus, Foremost of His Cultivated Land

405 (BABOON-HEADED GOD): Baboon Who Pertains to His Cultivated Land

406 (GOD WEARING WHITE CROWN): Renewed of Heart, Foremost of His Cultivated Land

407 (GODDESS): She of the Land-Plot

408 (GODDESS): Provided One

409 (GODDESS): She Who Pacifies the Gods

---

92. Creating a pun between strength (wsr) and necks (wsr.w).

93. Creating a pun between power (sḫm) and scepters (sḫm.w).

3.61. Scene 58. Nine *heqa*-scepters appear in three groups of three. The first group wears white crowns, the second wears red crowns, and the third group uraei. At the base of each scepter is a knife.

Issuing commands by the majesty of this great god regarding the scepters of the kings of Upper and Lower Egypt in the Netherworld: "O may you be renewed! Raise up the white crown. Carry the red crown among the common people. May your Netherwordly fields, through which your offerings manifest, be to you daily. Rectitude be to your scepters be to your scepters. Life be to your *ba*-souls. Breathing be to your throats. You are those who manifested on earth, those who give praise at the casting out of my enemy." It is upon their *heqa*-scepters, whose pommels are provided with blades, that their *ba*-souls stand in the Netherworld, the Robber not being aware of them.

410 (*ḤQꜣ*-SCEPTER WEARING WHITE CROWN): Staff
411 (*ḤQꜣ*-SCEPTER WEARING WHITE CROWN): Pestilence of the Earth
412 (*ḤQꜣ*-SCEPTER WEARING WHITE CROWN): *Heqa*-scepter of the Netherworld
413 (*ḤQꜣ*-SCEPTER WEARING RED CROWN): Justice of the Gods
414 (*ḤQꜣ*-SCEPTER WEARING RED CROWN): One who Unites the Netherworld Dwellers
415 (*ḤQꜣ*-SCEPTER WEARING RED CROWN): Floodwater of Tatenen
416 (*ḤQꜣ*-SCEPTER WEARING URAEUS): One Who Protects the Gods
417 (*ḤQꜣ*-SCEPTER WEARING URAEUS): One Who Pertains to the Head of the Gods
418 (*ḤQꜣ*-SCEPTER WEARING URAEUS): One Who Pertains to the Fields of the Netherworld Dwellers

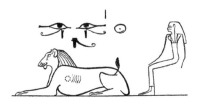

3.62. Scene 59. A recumbent lion faces to the left with two *udjat*-eyes above. To the right is a goddess seated, but with no throne beneath her.

It is the divine eye of Re—it exists above Lord[94] of Roaring in the Netherworld. Lord of Roaring is pleased, when Re rests upon his divine eye. The image of Isis-Tayt[95] exists in the vicinity of this divine eye.

419 (*UDJAT-EYES*): Icon of Re
420 (RECUMBENT LION): Lord of Roaring
421 (GODDESS): Isis-Tayt

3.63. Scene 60. Two deities, who are guardians of the following burial chests, stand facing to the right. The first, male deity is naked, while the second is a goddess holding a crook and flail.

Words spoken by the majesty of this great god: "O Bright One, guard your image! O She Whom the Gods Respect, you who are respected by means of your scepters—hiddenness be to your images, light be to their darkness, breath be to his limbs, the flesh which you guard. I am passing over you in peace."

422 (NAKED GOD): Bright One
423 (GODDESS HOLDING CROOK AND FLAIL): She Whom the Gods Respect

---

94. "Bull" here as parallel to *nb*, "lord/possessor of." For this figure and his relationship to Osiris, see Westendorf 2003, 471–72; on the theology of the lion in this passage, see Manassa 2007a, 229–30.

95. Here Isis is syncretized with Tayt, the goddess of weaving.

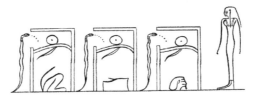

3.64. Scene 61. Three burial chests dominate this scene; each chest is topped by a solar disk and contains an object, a part of the solar corpse: the first has hind-quarters, the second a wing, and the third a disk.[96] Each chest is guarded by a serpent standing on its tail, and a goddess, looking left, appears at the far right of the scene.

The words that this god speaks in the vicinity of this mysterious image of the Netherworld: "May the darkness in the earth become bright. Rejoicing be to the flesh. That the head speaks is having already joined together his flesh."

It is the mysterious image of the Netherworld. As guardians do those upon their bellies exist. Re illumines their darkness and the head speaks, after She Who Adores the God calls to him.

424 (SERPENT): He Who Shoots with His Eye

425 (FIRST BURIAL CHEST): Burial Enclosure, One Who Praises Seth

426 (SERPENT): He Who Shoots with His Tongue

427 (SECOND BURIAL CHEST): Burial Enclosure, Haulings of Kheraha

428 (SERPENT): High of Flame

429 (THIRD BURIAL CHEST): Burial Enclosure, Unifier of Horus

430 (GODDESS): She Who Adores, who pertains to the beginning of the enclosures

96. For an alternate identification of these body parts, see Gestermann 1999, 102–4, with a critique in Westendorf 2004.

REGISTER 2 (PLATE 8)

3.65. Scene 62. The solar bark again sails on a rectangle of water. The bark and its crew takes on the same form as it had in Hours 1–3 (see Scene 5).

This great god sails in this locale upon the water, as he sets a course in this field in the vicinity of the corpse of Osiris. That this great god issues commands to the gods who are in the field is when he moors at these mysterious burials that contain the images of Osiris. This great god calls out atop these mysterious burial enclosures. It is the voice that is heard. Then this great god passes by, after he calls out.

LABEL TO THE SOLAR BARK: Bark of Re

431 (GOD): Opener of Paths
432 (GOD): Divine Perception
433 (GODDESS WEARING DISK AND HORNS): Mistress of the Bark
434 (RAM-HEADED GOD): Flesh
435 (FALCON-HEADED GOD): Horus Who Praises
436 (GOD): Bull of Maat
437 (GOD): Wakeful One
438 (GOD): Divine Utterance
439 (GOD): Director of the Bark

3.66. Scene 63. A baboon-headed god, seated on a throne, holds an ibis and faces to the right. A goddess, facing to the right, holds two pupils behind her back.

So says the majesty of this god who establishes fields for these gods <in> this locale in the Netherworld. Re says to this god: "Endurance be to your visible forms, and endurance be to your effective spells! The Hidden One leads you to your field by means of the mystery, which she has hidden. O Hidden One, hiddenness be to your arms because of their nakedness!"

440 (ENTHRONED BABOON-HEADED GOD): Thoth, who is before the Lady of the Netherworld Dwellers
441 (GODDESS HOLDING TWO PUPILS): She Who Hides Their Visible Forms

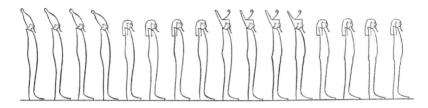

3.67. Scene 64. The kings of Upper and Lower Egypt are represented as sixteen mummiform figures standing in groups of four. The first four, the kings of Upper Egypt, wear white crowns, and the third group, the kings of Lower Egypt, wears red crowns; the second and fourth groups, those provided with their offerings and the *akh*-spirits, respectively, have bare heads.

This god commands the giving of divine offerings to the Netherworld Dwellers. He halts at them, so that they might see him and have power over their fields, with the result that their victuals manifest with them, by means of what this great god commands to them. Deep Waters, Well of the Netherworld Dwellers is the name of this field. It is the path of the bark of Re.

Words spoken by the majesty of this god to the kings of Upper Egypt, those who are provided with offerings, the kings of Lower Egypt, and to the *akh*-spirits who are in this locale: "Your kingship be to you, kings of Upper Egypt. Receive your white crowns upon your heads. May you be content, ones provided with offerings. Your red crowns be to you, kings of Lower Egypt. Your efficacious spells be to you, *akh*-spirits. Your divine offerings be to you, so that you might become satisfied, that you might have power, that you become *ba*-soul-like, that you become honored. May you be kings (in) your locales; may you occupy your cultivated land; may you unite with the mystery in your lower Egyptian crowns. Be efficacious by means of your efficacious spells. You are those content with the offerings, which the speech of the gods has given to them. It is you who greet me on earth and who punish Apep."

The kings of Upper Egypt, those who are provided with offerings, kings of Lower Egypt, and the *akh*-spirits who are in the earth. They exist in this fashion, standing at their caverns. They hear the voice of this god, daily.

442–445 (MUMMIES WEARING THE WHITE CROWN): King of Upper Egypt
446–449 (MUMMIES LABELED COLLECTIVELY): Those Provided with Offerings
450–453 (MUMMIES WEARING THE RED CROWN): King of Lower Egypt
454–457 (MUMMIES LABELED COLLECTIVELY): *Akh*-spirits

3.68. Scene 65. A supine deity crowned with a scarab beetle is surrounded by a four-headed serpent. The deity's legs are spread as if striding and his right arm is placed before his face.

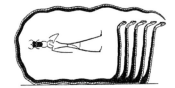

It is the corpse of Khepri in his own flesh,
He of Many Faces as protector. He exists in this fashion—his tail in his mouth.[97] What he does is stretch himself out underneath this image. Then there comes to him the entire West, without him going to any other place in the Netherworld. It is the voice of Re from which the images come.

458 (MULTIPLE-HEADED SERPENT): He of Many Faces
459 (SUPINE FIGURE WITH SCARAB BEETLE): Flesh

REGISTER 3 (PLATE 8)

3.69. Scene 66. A seated crocodile-headed god, lacking a throne, is followed by a standing crocodile-headed goddess. Next are two triplets of male deities without attributes and four seated goddesses (although without thrones).

---

97. While the tail of the serpent in this scene is near the mouth of the serpent, the depiction is not that of a true uroboros as described in the annotation; compare the two uroboroi in the Books of the Solar-Osirian Unity, Second Shrine of Tutankhamun, Side 1, Scene 6 (p. 541), where the tails do literally touch the mouths of the serpents.

Words spoken by the majesty of this great god to these gods: "O gods, foremost of the Netherworld, who are in the following of the Lady of the Netherworld Dwellers! O those who stand and those who sit for Nun, those who are in their fields.

You are the gods whose heads light up and whose corpses stand upright. You are these goddesses who turn away in the following of Khepri, at the place that bears his corpse in the Netherworld. Life be to your faces and breath to your hearts. Illumination be to your darkness. Power over waters be to you; enjoyment of your offerings be to you. Emergence be to your *ba*-souls, so they might pass by in my following. My *ba*-soul is with me, so that I might rest upon my corpse. I cross over you in peace."

They hear the voice of Re daily, and they breathe by means of his voice. What they do in the Netherworld is conduct *ba*-souls and help shades alight and make provisions for the *akh*-spirits, namely, water.

460 (CROCODILE-HEADED GOD): Crocodile
461 (CROCODILE-HEADED GODDESS): One within Great Nun
462 (GOD): Ihy
463 (GOD): Roaring One(?)
464 (GOD): He Who Protects His Father
465 (GOD): Living of Face
466 (GOD): Speaking of Face
467 (GOD): Protector
468 (GODDESS): She of the Fetters
469 (GODDESS): She of the Reversal
470 (GODDESS): She Who Drives Back
471 (GODDESS): She Who Collects(?)

3.70. Scene 67. A large serpent with its head slightly raised and an *ankh*-sign before its mouth faces right. From the serpent's back emerge the heads of the four sons of Horus.[98]

98. The children of Horus are similarly associated with a punishing serpent in the Book of Gates, Hour 9, Register 2, Scene 60 (pp. 308–9).

The one who cannot see him, namely, this great god. These images which are in his coils breathe, when they hear the voice of this great god daily. What he does in the Netherworld is digest shades and swallow the enemies who are felled in the Netherworld.

472 (SERPENT): Swallower of the Dead
472A (HEAD): Imsety
472B (HEAD): Hapi
472C (HEAD): Duamutef
472D (HEAD): Qebehsenuef

3.71. Scene 68. Four gods are seated (with no thrones beneath them); based on their names, these gods suffer from various maladies. Both of their arms are out in front of their bodies, palms downwards.

Words spoken by the majesty of this great god to these gods: "Stand up and do not retreat; stretch out and do not be weary. Manifestation be to your *ba*-souls; rest be to your shades; stretching out be to your legs; straightening out be to your knees. May you rest in your flesh. May your mummy bindings not be bound."

From the voice of this great god do they live daily. What they do is witness the coming of He of the Horizon.

473 (SEATED GOD): Confined One
474 (SEATED GOD): Pained of Leg
475 (SEATED GOD): Legless One
476 (SEATED GOD): Weary One

3.72. Scene 69. Nine serpent staffs spit fire; at the pommel of each staff is a knife. A deity facing left appears at the far right of the scene.

Words spoken by the majesty of this great god to the staffs of the male gods, foremost of this locale: "O staffs of the great ennead, images of the visible forms of his gods. Burning be to your faces; sharpness be to your swords, so you might burn the enemies of Khepri and cut up their shades. You are the guardians of the mysterious limbs, whose places Nun made. You are those within the water of Tatenen, manifested ones, who protect Khepri."

By means of the voice of Re do they breathe daily. What they do in the Netherworld is to roast the dead and give the *ba*-souls over to the Place of Destruction.

477 (SERPENT STAFF): Tatenen
478 (SERPENT STAFF): Atum
479 (SERPENT STAFF): Khepri
480 (SERPENT STAFF): Shu
481 (SERPENT STAFF): Geb
482 (SERPENT STAFF): Osiris
483 (SERPENT STAFF): Horus
484 (SERPENT STAFF): He of the Horns
485 (SERPENT STAFF): He of the Offerings
486 (GOD): Nun

HOUR 7

INTRODUCTORY TEXT

Resting by the majesty of this great god in the grotto of Osiris. Issuing commands by the majesty of this great god in this grotto to the gods who are in it. This god takes on another visible form at this grotto, so that he might deflect the path from Apep, by means of the magic of Isis and the Elder Magician.[99]

The name of the gate of this locale over which this god passes is Gateway of Osiris. The name of this locale is Mysterious Grotto. The name of the hour of the night that leads this great god is Repeller of the *Hiu*-Snake Who Smites Terrible of Face.

The mysterious path of the West over which this great god passes in his sacred bark. Just as he passes over this path, without water or its haulings, so does he sail by means of the magic of Isis and the Elder Magician and by means of the effective spells which are in the mouth of this god himself. Making the slaughter of Apep in the Netherworld at this cavern, it means his place in the sky.

This is done according to the template on the northern side of the Hidden Chamber of the Netherworld. It is effective in the sky, in the earth, and on earth. The one who knows it is (one of) the greatest *ba*-soul(s) before Re.

REGISTER 1 (PLATE 9)

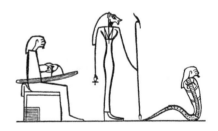

3.73. Scene 70. An enthroned deity holds a falcon head attached to an oblong-shaped object that crosses the body of the deity. A lioness-headed goddess holds a *was*-scepter and *ankh*-sign. She is followed by a human-headed uraeus.

Words spoken by this great god: "O Dignified One, give me your hand. It is from your loins that Horus emerged. O She Who Praises, give to me your voice; straightness be to your throat! O Living One, open your coils! That I have come, is so that I might illumine One Foremost of the Darkness, and so that I might make a place of repose for the one within the Encircling Serpent."[100]

488 (ENTHRONED GOD WITH FALCON HEAD): Dignified One
489 (LIONESS-HEADED GODDESS): She Who Praises
490 (HUMAN-HEADED URAEUS): Living One

---

99. For this deity, see p. 11 and n. 26.
100. Further details about the Encircling Serpent appear on p. 13 and n. 32.

3.74. Scene 71. Osiris, wearing two *šw.ty* feathers, appears enthroned, holding a *was*-scepter in one hand and an *ankh*-sign in the other. A serpent arches over the figure of Osiris. Before Osiris are three kneeling, decapitated enemies presided over by a deity with cat ears who holds a rope and a knife.

So says this great god to Osiris who is within the Encircling Serpent: "O you, Osiris foremost of the Netherworld, lord of life, ruler of the West! Life be to you, that you fully live. The *ba*-soul be to you, that you be fully *ba*-soul-like within the earth. Exaltation in excess of (that of) those of your following be to you. Cast down your enemies beneath your feet! Exert power over those who act against you! The flame of Living of Visible Forms be against them, so that he might consume them. Sharp of Face is against them and cuts them, so that he might roast them as a roasting for him. I reckon you, Osiris, daily. I always pass by you in peace."

490 (OSIRIS FIGURE): Flesh
491 (ENCIRCLING SERPENT): Living of Visible Forms
492–494 (DECAPITATED KNEELING FIGURES): Enemies of Osiris
495 (CAT-EARED GOD): Sharp of Face

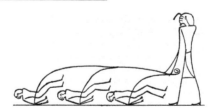

3.75. Scene 72. Three supine enemies have hands bound behind their backs, with heads turned and looking down toward the ground. The enemies' bindings are connected to ropes in the hand of a deity with prominent hair-lock.

So says the majesty of this god: "O you who make bindings against Osiris, crooked ones against the one foremost of the Netherworld. Binding be to your arms; tightening be to your bonds; destruction be to your *ba*-souls; restraining be to your shades, that the Punisher might punish you with his punishing knife. You cannot escape his ropes[101] forever."

OVER THE BOUND ENEMIES: Those who make bindings against Osiris

496–498 (ENEMIES): Bound Ones
499 (GOD WITH HAIR-LOCK): Punisher

3.76. Scene 73. Three *ba*-birds wear double crowns. A male deity, Atum, rides atop a serpent, holding a *was*-scepter and *ankh*-sign.

So says this great god: "O living *ba*-souls, upon whom the mysteries live, to whose heads the manifestations belong, as what manifests through me, those who are in the following of the flesh of Atum. Act as the protection of his body within the Netherworld. Life be to your *ba*-soul, Atum, that the Assembler who is within the earth might make you firm, so that he might cast his flame among the crooked ones who are against you."

500 (*BA*-BIRD): Praiser
501 (*BA*-BIRD): He of the Manifestation
502 (*BA*-BIRD): *Ba*-Soul of Tatenen
503 (GOD SEATED ON SERPENT): Flesh of Atum
504 (SERPENT): Assembler

---

101. The unusual word for "ropes," *sꜣw.wt*, creates a pun with the term *sꜣw*, "guardianship."

REGISTER 2 (PLATE 9)

3.77. Scene 74. The solar bark sails with most of its typical crew, but with the addition of a goddess (505, Isis), who stretches her arms out over the prow, and the Elder Magician. Beginning with Hour 7, the ram-headed solar god, Flesh, is surrounded by the Encircling Serpent rather than a shrine.

That this great god sails in this locale on the path of the cavern of Osiris, past those laid low[102] by means of the magic of Isis and the Elder Magician, is in order to deflect the path from Terrible of Face. These spells of Isis and the Elder Magician are performed for the repelling of Apep from Re,[103] in the West, in the hidden part of the Netherworld.

This is done on earth likewise. The one who does it is one within the bark of Re in the sky and in the earth. It is only the select who can know this image, without the knowledge of which Terrible of Face may not be repelled.

505 (GODDESS): Isis
506 (GOD): Divine Perception
507 (GOD): Elder Magician
508 (ENCIRCLING SERPENT): Encircling Serpent
509 (RAM-HEADED GOD): Flesh
510 (FALCON-HEADED GOD): Horus Who Praises
511 (GOD): Bull of Maat
512 (GOD): Wakeful One
513 (GOD): Divine Utterance
514 (GOD): Protector of the Bark

---

102. *WÄS* 4:362.11: "von erschlagenen Feinden, die rücklings daliegen"; "those laid low" refer to the enemies of Osiris depicted in the upper register, Scene 72.

103. The version in the tomb of Seti I and the sarcophagus of Tjaihorpata (CGAE 29306) write "he being sealed up" rather than "from Re."

3.78. Scene 75. A giant serpent faces the solar bark. From his back protrude multiple knives, and he is lassoed by a goddess at his head and a god at his tail. Four goddesses, each holding a knife, stand behind the serpent.

The sandbank of Terrible of Face in the Netherworld; it is 440 cubits in its length, and he fills it with his coils. His slaughter is made against him, without this great god passing by him. He deflects the path from him at the grotto of Osiris. In the image of the Encircling Serpent does this great god sail in this locale.

LABEL TO APEP: In this fashion does he exist at his sandbank in the Netherworld. Bringer of Water is the name of this sandbank; (it is) 440 cubits in its length and 440 cubits in its width. It is his voice that leads the gods against him. He always moves when this great god passes by this locale. Then Flesh swallows his eye[104] in the earth so that he might pass by him. Then She Who Makes Throats Breathe throws the lasso[105] on (his) head, while Chief of His Knives places the punishing knife into his legs, after Isis and the Elder Magician seize his power by means of their magical spells.

One who knows it on earth is one whose water Terrible of Face will not drink.

515 (SERPENT): Apep
516 (GODDESS WITH LASSO): She Who Makes Throats Breathe
517 (GOD WITH LASSO): Chief of His Knives

LABEL TO THE PUNISHING GODDESSES: It is these goddesses who punish Apep in the Netherworld, who repel the actions of the enemies of Re. They exist in this fashion bearing their knives, so that they might punish Apep in the Netherworld daily.

---

104. An alternate reading "disk" is also possible.

105. The term *sph*, "lasso," is misplaced after the phrase "The Elder Magician places" in all versions, except for Useramun (see Hornung 1963b, 133 n. 7).

518 (GODDESS HOLDING KNIFE): She Who Unites
519 (GODDESS HOLDING KNIFE): She Who Cuts
520 (GODDESS HOLDING KNIFE): She Who Punishes
521 (GODDESS HOLDING KNIFE): She Who Destroys

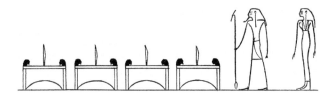

3.79. Scene 76. Four rectangular chests each are topped by two human heads look-ing in toward each other; a knife rises from the center of each chest. To the right is a god holding a *was*-scepter, and a goddess, each facing left.

It is the mysterious visible forms of the Netherworld, the chests of the mys-terious heads. They exist at the end of this sandbank, with the heads and the images that are in them coming forth, when they hear the enchant-ment of Terrible of Face. Then they swallow their images, after this great god passes by this locale.

Lord of the *Was*-Scepter and the One Equipped with a Heart exist as the guardians of this mysterious image. The *ba*-soul of the one who knows it does not succumb to the force of their swords.

522 (CHEST): The one that bears the image of Atum
523 (CHEST): The one that bears the image of Khepri
523 (CHEST): The one that bears the image of Re
524 (CHEST): The one that bears the image of Osiris
525 (GOD HOLDING *WAS*-SCEPTER): Lord of the *Was*-Scepter
526 (GODDESS): One Equipped with a Heart

REGISTER 3 (PLATE 9)

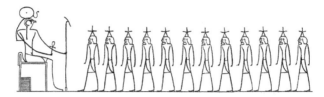

3.80. Scene 77. A falcon-headed god crowned with a solar disk and holding a *was*-scepter and *ankh*-sign is seated on a throne, facing right. Facing him are twelve striding male deities, facing left, each crowned with a star.

This image: Horus upon His Stairs. This image exists in this fashion. What he does in the Netherworld is cause the stars to rise and set the positions of the hours in the Netherworld. So says the majesty of the Netherworldly Horus to the gods of the stars: "Order be to your flesh and manifestation to your visible forms, so that you might rest in your stars. Take up your positions for this Re of the horizon who is within the Netherworld daily, you being in his following, while your stars are before him, so that I might pass by the beautiful West in peace. You are the standing ones who are in the earth. You belong to me, and your stars belong to the one within the sky—then, indeed, the Lord of the Horizon shall go to rest."

528 (FALCON-HEADED GOD): Horus upon His Stairs
529 (GOD CROWNED WITH STAR): Great of Provisions
530 (GOD CROWNED WITH STAR): Lord of Provisions
531 (GOD CROWNED WITH STAR): Lord of Provisions in the Earth
532 (GOD CROWNED WITH STAR): Netherworldly One
533 (GOD CROWNED WITH STAR): Herdsman of the Stars
534 (GOD CROWNED WITH STAR): Herdsman of the *Akh*-Spirits
535 (GOD CROWNED WITH STAR): Distinguished of Arm
536 (GOD CROWNED WITH STAR): Sacred of Arm
537 (GOD CROWNED WITH STAR): Powerful of Arm
538 (GOD CROWNED WITH STAR): He Who Cuts with His Tongue
539 (GOD CROWNED WITH STAR): He Who Cuts with His Eye
540 (GOD CROWNED WITH STAR): He Who Smites Heads

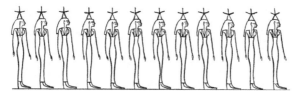

3.81. Scene 78. Twelve goddesses standing, facing right, are crowned with stars.

So says the majesty of the Netherworldly Horus to the hour goddesses who are within this locale: "O, hours who have manifested! O, stellar hours! O, hours who protect Re, who fight on behalf of the one who is within the horizon! Receive to yourselves your visible forms; support for yourselves your images; lift up for yourselves your heads, that you may lead this Re, who is within the horizon, to the beautiful West in peace."

So say these gods and goddesses who lead this great god along the mysterious path of this locale.

541 (GODDESS CROWNED WITH A STAR): She Who Praises
542 (GODDESS CROWNED WITH A STAR): Mistress of the Earth
543 (GODDESS CROWNED WITH A STAR): Mistress of Mistresses
544 (GODDESS CROWNED WITH A STAR): She of the Netherworld
545 (GODDESS CROWNED WITH A STAR): She of the West
546 (GODDESS CROWNED WITH A STAR): She Who Is Atop the *Ka*-Spirits
547 (GODDESS CROWNED WITH A STAR): She Who Brings
548 (GODDESS CROWNED WITH A STAR): She of the Color
549 (GODDESS CROWNED WITH A STAR): She of Weaving (Tayt)
550 (GODDESS CROWNED WITH A STAR): She Who Makes Luminosity
551 (GODDESS CROWNED WITH A STAR): She Who Does What Is Done
552 (GODDESS CROWNED WITH A STAR): She Who Releases Sin

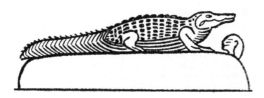

3.82. Scene 79. A crocodile perches on a sandbank with a human head, the head of Osiris, before him. The labels mention an "eye of Osiris" that is not otherwise depicted.

He exists in this fashion upon the sandbank. It is he who guards the images of this locale. When he hears the voice of the crew of the bark of Re, the eye emerges from his vertebra. Then the head that is within his bank emerges. Then he swallows his image after this great god passes by him. The one who knows it is one whose *ba*-soul the crocodile will not swallow.

553 (CROCODILE): The Crocodile in the Netherworld
554: Eye of Osiris
555 (HUMAN HEAD): Head of Osiris

HOUR 8

INTRODUCTORY TEXT

Resting by the majesty of this great god at the cavern of the mysterious gods who are upon their sand, issuing commands to them from his bark. It is his gods who haul him in this locale in the sacred visible form of the Encircling Serpent. The name of the gate of this locale is One Who Stands without Wearying. The name of this locale is Bank[106] of Its Gods. The name of the hour of the night who guides this great god is Mistress of the Deep of the Night.

The mysterious cavern of the West through which the great god passes in his bark, by means of the hauling of his gods who are in the Netherworld. This is done according to this image on the northern side of the Hidden Chamber of the Netherworld. The one who knows it in their names is the possessor of clothing on earth, without being repelled from the mysterious gates, being provided with a great tomb—truly attested!

---

106. Although the term *ḏbꜣ.t* often means "sarcophagus" in the Netherworld Books (and can be translated as such here; see Hornung 1963b, 142, n. 6), the determinative here, as well as its replacement by the term *ỉdb*, "bank" in Late period copies, suggests that *ḏbꜣ.t* in the name of the locale also refers to a "bank" or "earthen mound" (Manassa 2007a, 253).

REGISTER 1 (PLATE 10)

3.83. Scene 80. The First Cavern is framed by two doors and contains three deities seated on cloth signs, consisting of the first three gods of the Heliopolitan ennead.

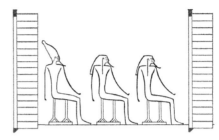

They exist upon their clothing as the mysteries of Horus, the heir of Osiris. This great god calls to their *ba*-souls after he enters into this locale of the gods who are upon their sand. A sound of something is heard in this cavern like a swarm of honey-bees.[107] It is their *ba*-souls who call to Re. Mysterious is the name of this cavern.

LABEL TO THE FIRST DOOR: Knife, Lord of Sacred Items

556 (GOD WEARING WHITE CROWN): Image of Atum
557 (GOD): Image of Khepri
558 (GOD): Image of Shu

3.84. Scene 81. The second cavern contains a goddess and two male deities seated on cloth signs; these three deities are also members of the Heliopolitan ennead.

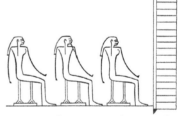

They exist in this fashion upon their clothing, remaining upon their sand, as mysteries that Horus has made. This god calls to their *ba*-souls in their vicinity. A sound of something is heard in this cavern like the sound of striking cymbals. It is their *ba*-souls who call to Re. Netherworld is the name of this cavern.

LABEL TO THE SECOND DOOR: Knife, Standing Place of Tatenen

559 (GODDESS): Image of Tefnut
560 (GOD): Image of Geb
561 (GOD): Image of Nut

---

107. The sounds heard in each of the caverns weave a rich theological tapestry of the rebirth of the sun (Manassa 2008).

3.85. Scene 82. The third cavern contains a male deity, female deity, and a falcon-headed deity seated on cloth signs; this triad completes the ennead.

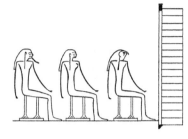

They exist upon their clothing, remaining upon their sand as mysteries that Horus has made. This god calls to their *ba*-souls in their vicinity. A sound of something is heard in this cavern like people when they mourn. It is their *ba*-souls who call to Re. Tomb of the Gods is the name of this cavern.

LABEL TO THE THIRD DOOR: Knife that Extinguishes[108] *Ba*-Souls

562 (GOD): Image of Osiris
563 (GODDESS): Image of Isis
564 (FALCON-HEADED GOD): Image of Horus

3.86. Scene 83. The fourth cavern contains three animal-headed deities seated on cloth signs.

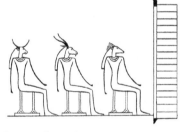

They exist upon their clothing, remaining upon their sand as mysteries that Horus has made. This god calls to their *ba*-souls in their vicinity. A sound of something is heard in this cavern like the sound of the bull of bulls being pleased.[109] It is their *ba*-souls who call to Re. Mourning is the name of this cavern.

LABEL TO THE FOURTH DOOR: Girdle of the Gods

565 (BULL-HEADED GOD): Image of the Bull of the West
566 (GOAT-HEADED GOD): Image of the Noble One of the Gods
567 (RAT-HEADED GOD): Image of the Crying One of the Gods

---

108. Wiebach-Koepke 2003a, 127 n. 2.
109. For the verb *nim* and its parallels in the Netherworld Books, see the commentary of the Book of Adoring Re in the West (p. 110 n. 105).

3.87. Scene 84. The fifth cavern contains another three animal-headed deities seated on cloth signs.

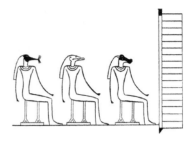

They exist in this fashion upon their clothing, remaining upon their sand as mysteries that Horus has made. This god calls to their *ba*-souls in their vicinity. A sound of something is heard in this cavern like the sound of a demand, great in its raging. It is their *ba*-souls who call to Re. Mistress of Wind is the name of this cavern.

LABEL TO THE FIFTH DOOR: Knife that Unites the Darkness

568 (ICHNEUMON-HEADED DEITY): Image of the Ichneumon
569 (CATFISH-HEADED DEITY): Image of the Catfish
570 (HIPPOPOTAMUS-HEADED DEITY): Image of the Keeper of His Stalk

LABEL TO THE SIXTH DOOR: Knife of the Shades of the Netherworld Dwellers

REGISTER 2 (PLATE 10)

3.88. Scene 85. The solar bark, with the ram-headed sun god surrounded by an encircling serpent, is hauled by a group of deities (Scene 86). The crew of the bark is the typical complement of deities.

This god sails in this locale by means of the hauling of the Netherworld Dwellers, in his mysterious image of the Encircling Serpent. This god calls to the vicinity of each cavern of this locale on behalf of the Netherworld Dwellers who are in it. It is the voices thereof that this god hears after he calls to them. Their images of their own bodies remain over their corpses that are under their sand. Their portals open at the voice of this god daily. Then they are concealed after he passes by them.

571 (GOD): Opener of Paths
572 (GOD): Divine Perception
573 (GODDESS WITH DISK AND HORNS): Mistress of the Bark
574 (ENCIRCLING SERPENT): Encircling Serpent
575 (RAM-HEADED GOD): Flesh
576 (FALCON-HEADED GOD): Horus Who Praises
577 (GOD): Bull of Maat
578 (GOD): Wakeful One
579 (GOD): Divine Utterance
580 (GOD): Director of the Bark

3.89. Scene 86. Eight gods haul the solar bark.

What they do in the Netherworld is to haul Re to the paths of this locale. After they haul to this portal, they halt. They say to this god, when they haul him: "Come to your images, O our god, (and to) your crew,[110] those foremost of the West, so that you might occupy your visible forms in the great locale. Then, indeed, the cavern dwellers exalt (you), when you illuminate the darkness of those who are upon their sand. Come, so that you might rest, Re, hauled one, lord of hauling!"

LABEL TO THE HAULERS: Netherworldly gods who haul Re in Bank of Its Gods

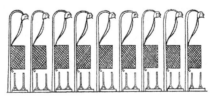

3.90. Scene 87. Nine *sšm*-signs have human heads depending from their tops. Below the *sšm*-signs are small cloth-signs.

---

110. Alternatively, an *isw*-object, referring to the *sšm*-signs (Hornung 1963b, 146 and n. 3), which does appear in the label to Scene 87.

They exist in this fashion on the paths upon which this god is hauled, their clothing before them, as images of the god himself. It is when this great god calls to them, that what is within them lives, and the heads emerge from their images. This god calls them by their names. What they do is put the enemies of Re to the knife in the vicinity of this locale, to which they pertain. Then they swallow their heads and their knives, after this great god passes by them.

LABEL: The *isyw*-signs of Re who are in this locale. The mysterious images of Tatenen, from whom Horus hid the gods.

589 (SŠM-SIGN WITH HUMAN HEAD): He Who Occupies the Earth
590 (SŠM-SIGN WITH HUMAN HEAD): Hidden One
591 (SŠM-SIGN WITH HUMAN HEAD): Mysterious of *Ba*-Souls
592 (SŠM-SIGN WITH HUMAN HEAD): He Who Causes *Ba*-Souls to Alight
593 (SŠM-SIGN WITH HUMAN HEAD): Lord of All
594 (SŠM-SIGN WITH HUMAN HEAD): Offering Vase
595 (SŠM-SIGN WITH HUMAN HEAD): He of the Road
596 (SŠM-SIGN WITH HUMAN HEAD): One of Correctness
597 (SŠM-SIGN WITH HUMAN HEAD): He Who Obeys

3.91. Scene 88. Four rams stride to the right; the first ram wears a solar disk, the second a white crown, the third a red crown, and the fourth *šw.ty*-feathers. A small hieroglyph for cloth appears between the forelegs of each ram.

They exist in this fashion in the Netherworld, their clothing being before them, as images of the god himself. This god calls to them when he reaches them. They call to this great god in their voices of mysterious rams, so that this god takes pleasure in their voices. Now after he passes by them, then the darkness conceals them. As soon as they receive the solar crowns, the *ba*-soul of Tatenen goes to rest in the earth.

LABEL: Mysterious images of Tatenen, first manifestations, ram-forms in the earth, from whom Horus hid the gods.

598 (RAM WEARING SOLAR DISK): Image of Tateten, first manifestation
599 (RAM WEARING WHITE CROWN): Image of Tatenen, second manifestation
600 (RAM WEARING RED CROWN): Image of Tatenen, third manifestation
601 (RAM WEARING ŠW.TY-FEATHERS): Image of Tatenen, fourth manifestation

---

REGISTER 3 (PLATE 10)

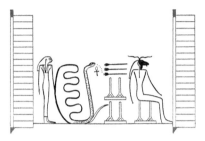

3.92. Scene 89. The sixth cavern contains several figures: a standing goddess, serpent with multiple coils behind him, four cloth signs topped by three arrows, and a ram-headed god seated atop cloth-signs.

They exist in this fashion upon their clothing, as mysteries of Horus, heir of Osiris. This great god calls to their *ba*-souls when he enters this locale of the gods who are upon their sand. This god calls to them on both sides of the earth. The sound of something is heard in this cavern like the cry of a tom-cat. It is their *ba*-souls who call to Re. She Who Pacifies Her Lord is the name of this cavern.

LABEL TO THE SEVENTH DOOR: Knife that Supports the Earth

602 (GODDESS): Young Girl
603 (SERPENT): Encircling Serpent of the Earth
604 (ARROWS): Arrow of Re
605 (RAM-HEADED GOD): Lord of the *Rekhyt*-people

3.93. Scene 90. The seventh cavern has three figures: a goddess, a male deity, and a crocodile-headed god, all seated on cloth-signs.

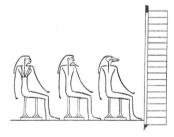

They exist in this fashion upon their clothing, remaining upon their sand, as mysteries that Horus has made. This god calls to their *ba*-souls in their vicinity on both sides of them. The sound of something is heard in this cavern like the roar of the living. It is their *ba*-souls who call to Re. She Who Destroys the Ignorant is the name of this cavern.

LABEL TO THE EIGHTH DOOR: Knife that Repels Its Enemies

606 (GODDESS): Locale
607 (GOD): Earth
608 (CROCODILE-HEADED GOD): Splendid of Face

———

3.94. Scene 91. The eighth cavern contains four standing female mummiform figures with small cloth-signs before them.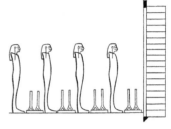

They exist in this fashion with their clothing before them, remaining upon their sand, as mysteries that Horus, heir of Osiris, has made. This god calls to their *ba*-souls on both sides of them. The sound of something is heard in this cavern like banks falling into Nun. It is their *ba*-souls who call to Re. Concealed of Her Images is the name of this cavern.

LABEL TO THE NINTH DOOR: Knife, Powerful of Visible Forms

609 (FEMALE MUMMY): Clothed One
610 (FEMALE MUMMY): Dark One
611 (FEMALE MUMMY): She of the Sarcophagus
612 (FEMALE MUMMY): She Who Is United

3.95. Scene 92. The ninth cavern contains four standing male mummiform figures with small cloth-signs before them.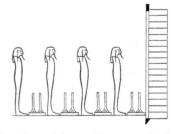

They exist in this fashion, with their clothing before them, remaining upon their sand, as mysteries that Horus has made. This god calls to their *ba*-souls on both sides of them. The sound of something is heard in this cavern like the screech of a divine falcon. It is their *ba*-souls who call to Re. Far of Its *Ba*-Souls is the name of this cavern.

LABEL TO THE TENTH DOOR: Knife, Sharp of Flame

613 (MUMMY): Darkness
614 (MUMMY): Slaughterer(?)
615 (MUMMY): Strong of *Akh*-Spirit
616 (MUMMY): One Who Hacks the Earth

3.96. Scene 93. The tenth cavern has four uraei atop cloth signs.

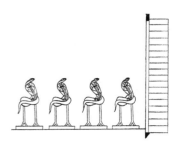

They exist in this fashion upon their clothing, remaining upon their sand. This god calls to their *ba*-souls in their vicinity. Then they illumine their darkness with what is upon their mouths, without going forth from their caverns. The sound of something is heard in this cavern like the cry of an entire marsh, when they call to Re. Great of Taper is the name of this cavern.

LABEL TO THE ELEVENTH DOOR: Knife, Effective of *Akh*-Spirits

617 (URAEUS): Uraeus
618 (URAEUS): She of the Windings
619 (URAEUS): Flame
620 (URAEUS): Sharp of Moment

LABEL TO THE TWELFTH DOOR: Knife that Burns the Dead within It

---

HOUR 9

INTRODUCTORY TEXT

Resting by the majesty of this great god in this cavern, as he issues commands from his bark to the gods who are in it, with the result that the crew of the bark of this god goes to rest at this locale. The name of the gate of this locale into which this great god enters, when he occupies the floodwaters that are in this locale is Guardian of the Deluge. The name of this locale is Inducting of Visible Forms, Living of Manifestations. The name of the hour of the night who guides this great god is Starry One Who Protects Her Lord.

The mysterious cavern of the West at which the great god and his crew rest in the Netherworld. This is done in their names according to this image that is in writing on the eastern side of the Hidden Chamber of the Netherworld. The one who knows their names upon earth and who knows their thrones in the West is one who occupies his throne in the Netherworld; one who stands among the lords of provisions; one who is justified within the council of Re,[111] who reckons the balances. It is effective for him on earth.

REGISTER 1 (PLATE 11)

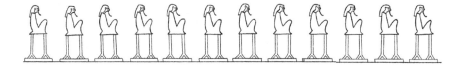

3.97. Scene 94. Twelve mummiform figures are seated on cloth signs.

They exist in this fashion in the Netherworld, established upon their clothing as linen-covered ones, being an image that Horus made. Re says to them: "Covering be to you, by means of your raiments. May you be sanctified with your clothing. Just as he hides his father in the Netherworld, which hides the gods, so did Horus cover you there. Uncovering be to your heads, gods. Opening be to your faces. May you carry out your duties for Osiris. May you exalt the lord of the West. May you vindicate him against his enemies daily."

It is this council of gods who investigate on behalf of Osiris daily. What they do in the Netherworld is fell the enemies of Osiris.

621 (SEATED MUMMY): One who Repels[112] the Earth
622 (SEATED MUMMY): Covered One
623 (SEATED MUMMY): Linen-covered One
624 (SEATED MUMMY): He of the Raiment
625 (SEATED MUMMY): He of the Clothing
626 (SEATED MUMMY): He of the Basket

---

111. For an alternate reading "Gerichtshof am Tage des 'Berechnens der Differenz,'" see Wiebach-Koepke 2003a, 141.

112. Compare Roulin 1996b, 146.

627 (SEATED MUMMY): He of the Place of the Gods
628 (SEATED MUMMY): He of the Place of the Ennead
629 (SEATED MUMMY): He who Destroys *Akh*-Spirits
630 (SEATED MUMMY): Lord of the Patricians
631 (SEATED MUMMY): He Who Unites
632 (SEATED MUMMY): Hidden of Arm

3.98. Scene 95. Twelve standing goddesses face to the right.

They exist in this fashion in their Netherworldly bodies, as images that Horus made. This god calls to them when he reaches them. When they hear his voice, they breathe. What they do in the Netherworld is raise up Osiris and cause the mysterious *ba*-soul to alight by means of their words. It is they who lift up life and dominion as the glorious appearances of the Netherworldly One, when he protects the Netherworld each day. It is these goddesses who follow after Osiris when he enters into the Netherworld.

633 (GODDESS): She Who Goes Forth
634 (GODDESS): Demon of the *Akh*-Spirits
635 (GODDESS): Mistress of Slaughter
636 (GODDESS): Mistress of Awe
637 (GODDESS): Great of Pestilence
638 (GODDESS): Mistress of Trembling
639 (GODDESS): She Who Governs Her Locale
640 (GODDESS): Mistress of Towns
641 (GODDESS): She Who Sanctifies the West
642 (GODDESS): Great of Luminosity
643 (GODDESS): Powerful of Words
644 (GODDESS): Musician of Re

REGISTER 2 (PLATE 11)

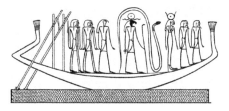

3.99. Scene 96. The solar bark sails with the same crew present in Hour 8.

That this great god goes to rest is alongside his rowers at this locale. His crew occupies his bark, alongside his mysterious image of the Encircling Serpent. This great god issues commands to the gods who are in this locale.

645 (GOD): Opener of Paths
646 (GOD): Divine Perception
647 (GODDESS WITH DISK AND HORNS): Mistress of the Bark
648 (ENCIRCLING SERPENT): Encircling Serpent
649 (RAM-HEADED GOD): Flesh
650 (FALCON-HEADED GOD): Horus Who Praises
651 (GOD): Bull of Maat
652 (GOD): Wakeful One
653 (GOD): Divine Utterance
654 (GOD): Director of the Bark

3.100. Scene 97. Twelve gods holding oars stride to the right.

These gods are the crew of the bark of Re, these who row the One within the Horizon, so that he might rest in the eastern portal of the sky. What they do in the Netherworld is row Re at this locale daily. That they take up positions is at the flood waters of the bark within this locale. It is they who row with their oars for the *akh*-spirits who are in this locale, those who praise the Lord of the Disk. It is they who cause the *ba*-soul to appear within his visible form, by means of their mysterious speech, daily.

655 (GOD HOLDING OAR): Rower
656 (GOD HOLDING OAR): He Who Does Not Weary
657 (GOD HOLDING OAR): He Who Does Not Tire
658 (GOD HOLDING OAR): He Who Does Not Retreat
659 (GOD HOLDING OAR): He Who Does Not Retire
660 (GOD HOLDING OAR): He Who Does Not Go Back(?)
661 (GOD HOLDING OAR): Rower in His Hour
662 (GOD HOLDING OAR): He of the Oar of His Land
663 (GOD HOLDING OAR): He Who Occupies the Bark
664 (GOD HOLDING OAR): God of Gods
665 (GOD HOLDING OAR): He Who Traverses the Netherworld
666 (GOD HOLDING OAR): He of the Boat

3.101. Scene 98. Three mummiform animals rest atop baskets.
The first is a human-headed mummiform falcon wearing twin feathers; the second is a ram mummy,
while the third is a cow mummy
wearing a disk between its horns.
A standing male mummy appears to the right.

They exist in this fashion in this locale. It is they who dispense offerings to
the gods who are in the Netherworld, when Re commends bread and beer
to them. It is in the following of this great god that the gods pass toward
the eastern horizon of the sky, after the Netherworld Dwellers go to rest.

667 (HUMAN-HEADED FALCON MUMMY): One Who Offers(?), foremost of
   the Netherworld
668 (RAM MUMMY): One of Necessities, foremost of the Netherworld
669 (COW MUMMY): Lord of Victuals, foremost of the Netherworld
670 (MALE MUMMY): Divine Offerings

REGISTER 3 (PLATE 11)

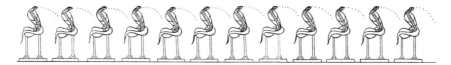

3.102. Scene 99. Twelve uraei are coiled atop cloth signs.

The names of the uraei who shoot flames for Osiris, foremost of the Netherworld, by means of the fire that is in their mouths. It is after this great god passes by them that they swallow their fire. They exist in this fashion in the Netherworld, firmly established upon their clothing, in their own flesh. It is they who illuminate the darkness of the room that contains Osiris. It is the flame upon their mouths that effects slaughter in the Netherworld. It is they who repel every serpent that is within the earth, whose visible form the Netherworldly One does not recognize. It is from the blood of those whom they behead that they live daily. The *akh*-spirits and the dead cannot pass by them, because their visible forms have become mysterious. The one who knows it is one who sees their visible forms and is not one who passes through their flame.

671 (URAEUS): Painful of Flame
672 (URAEUS): Burning One
673 (URAEUS): Fiery One
674 (URAEUS): She Who Protects the Netherworld
675 (URAEUS): She Who Drives Away Rage
676 (URAEUS): Illuminated of Star
677 (URAEUS): Living of Face
678 (URAEUS): Distinguished of Form
679 (URAEUS): Beautiful of Forms
680 (URAEUS): Great of Visible Forms
681 (URAEUS): Mistress of Embers
682 (URAEUS): Mistress of the Blazing Fire

3.103. Scene 100. Nine standing deities hold *djam*-scepters (or in some versions sheaves of grain), followed by a mummiform god.

They are the field gods of this locale, lords of life who carry *djam*-scepters. They exist in this fashion, standing holding their life (signs), and leaning on their *djam*-scepters. This great god calls to them. It is they who understand the words of the gods who are in the Netherworld at this locale. It is they who cause all trees and all plants of this locale to grow.[113] Horus, Chief of the Lakes of the Gods, is the guardian of the image of this field.

683 (GOD): He of the Field
684 (GOD): He Who Is in His Field
685 (GOD): He of the (Plant) Bud
686 (GOD): He of the *Djam*-scepter
687 (GOD): Lord of the *Iaat*-scepter
688 (GOD): *Heqa*-scepter of His Gods
689 (GOD): Wise of Visible Forms
690 (GOD): Sanctified of Visible Forms
691 (GOD): He Who Stands at the Field
692 (MUMMY): Horus, Chief of the Lakes of the Gods

HOUR 10

INTRODUCTORY TEXT

Resting by the majesty of this great god in this cavern, while he issues commands to the gods who are in it. The name of the gate of this locale into which this great god enters is Great of Manifestations, Engendered of Visible Forms. The name of this locale is Deep of Water, High of Banks. The name of the hour of the night that leads this great god on the mysterious paths of this locale is Raging One Who Beheads the Crooked-hearted One.

113. On this passage, see Aufrère 2001, 163–68.

The mysterious cavern of the West, in which Khepri rests in the presence of Re, in which gods, *akh*-spirits, and the dead cry out over the mysterious image of Igeret. This is done according to this image that is in writing on the eastern side of the Hidden Chamber of the Netherworld. The one who knows it in their names is one who crosses the Netherworld to its end, without being repelled from the hall before Re.

REGISTER 1 (PLATE 12)

3.104. Scene 101. A standing god holding a *was*-scepter and *ankh*-sign faces a scarab beetle lifting an oval.

They exist in this fashion in the Netherworld as visible forms that Khepri bore. He is lifting his oval at this locale, in order to go forth afterwards to the eastern horizon of the sky.

693 (GOD): Wise of Visible Forms
694 (SCARAB BEETLE): Living Khepri

3.105. Scene 102. In the center of the scene are two entwined, vertically oriented serpents with a solar disk between their heads. Two seated goddesses, wearing a white crown and red crown respectively, appear to either side of the entwined serpents. Two addition goddesses flank a central *ntr*-sign crowned with a solar disk.

These gods exist in this fashion. The left eye emerges from the double snake. The right eye emerges from She Who is Expunged (of sins) (?), with the result that the *ba*-souls cry out for them in the earth, and the *akh*-spirits expunge for them sins in the Netherworld,[114] while leading the

---

114. In the Book of Gates, Hour 4, Register 1, Scene 15, the term *sdfs-try.t* is also used (see p. 271).

Mystery that is in it. Then they swallow their visible forms, after this great god passes over them.

695 (GODDESS WEARING RED CROWN): Red Crown
696 (ENTWINED SERPENT): Double Snake
697 (GODDESS WEARING WHITE CROWN): White Crown
698 (GODDESS): She Who Binds
699 (*NTR*-STAFF): *BLANK*
700 (GODDESS): One Who Cries Out (to) the Gods

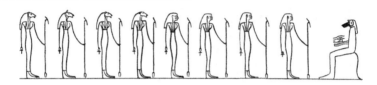

3.106. Scene 103. Eight goddesses, four lion-headed and four human-headed, stand holding *was*-scepters. They face a seated baboon holding a solar eye.

The goddesses who inspect the eye of Horus for him in the Netherworld. Re says to them: "Power be to your visible forms, powerful ones. May you inspect the eye of Horus for him; may you establish the eye of Horus for him; may you pacify Horus by means of his image. May you exalt Horus by means of his eye, you having established for him his *tepyt*-eye, which is within the arms of Flesh Who Carries His Eye.[115] It is you who greet Horus, manifest ones who manifest manifestations."

What they do in the Netherworld is greet the eye of Horus for him and cause the effective eye to be whole daily.

701 (LIONESS-HEADED GODDESS): Sakhmet
702 (LIONESS-HEADED GODDESS): Lion's Tail
703 (LIONESS-HEADED GODDESS): Girlish One
704 (LIONESS-HEADED GODDESS): She of the *Was*-Scepter
705 (GODDESS): Purifier of Her Gods
706 (GODDESS): She Whom Tatenen Made
707 (GODDESS): She Who Stands
708 (GODDESS): Powerful of Arm

---

115. The sarcophagus of Tjahorpata interprets the cryptographic name as "Heir of the Eye." For commentary see Manassa 2007a, 345–46.

709 (BABOON-HEADED GOD HOLDING AN *UDJAT*-EYE): Flesh Who Carries His Eye

3.107. Scene 104. Four deities with various attributes face to the right, each holding a *was*-scepter and *ankh*-sign. In front of them are four standing mummiform figures wearing white crowns and also holding *was*-scepters.

They exist in this fashion as images that Horus has made. This great god calls to them in their names, so that they might rest, so that they might breathe the breath that is in the mouth of this great god. Their *ba*-souls pass by afterwards to the horizon. It is they who uncover the corpses, tearing off the wrappings of the enemies, commanding their punishment in the Netherworld.

710 (TWO ROPES IN PLACE OF HEAD): Double-armed[116]
711 (JACKAL-HEADED GOD): Lord of Entrance
712 (FALCON-HEADED GOD): He Who Hides the Visible Forms
713 (GOD): Chief of the Mysteries
714 (MUMMY WEARING WHITE CROWN): Great Image
715 (MUMMY WEARING WHITE CROWN): Great Hidden One
716 (MUMMY WEARING WHITE CROWN): Foremost of His Place
717 (MUMMY WEARING WHITE CROWN): Foremost of His (Offering)-Legs[117]

116. This figure may be related to *intty* in Address 64 of the Great Litany of the Book of Adoring Re in the West (see p. 98).
117. "*Ḥnty-mnwt.f*," *LGG* 5:815; Hornung 1980, 90. Compare the Book of Gates, Hour 3, Register 2, Scene 12 (p. 268).

REGISTER 2 (PLATE 12)

3.108. Scene 105. The crew of the solar bark is unchanged from the last two hours.

This great god sails in this locale in this fashion in his bark, while his crew of gods transports him. The gods who are in this locale go to rest in the water, where their oars are located. They breathe by means of the sound of the splashing of this divine crew.

718 (GOD): Opener of Paths
719 (GOD): Divine Perception
720 (GODDESS WITH DISK AND HORNS): Mistress of the Bark
721 (ENCIRCLING SERPENT): Encircling Serpent
722 (RAM-HEADED GOD): Flesh
723 (FALCON-HEADED GOD): Horus Who Praises
724 (GOD): Bull of Maat
725 (GOD): Wakeful One
726 (GOD): Divine Utterance
727 (GOD): Director of the Bark

3.109. Scene 106. Two goddesses—the one on the left wearing a red crown, the one on the right a white crown—face inward toward a double-headed serpent with four legs whose body forms a U-shape. In the middle of the U-shaped serpent perches a falcon. The serpent's right head wears a white crown, his left head a red crown.

They exist in this fashion as supporters of (the serpent) Linked of Faces. He is the ba-soul of Sokar, foremost of the Netherworld. That this entire image passes by is in the following of this great god towards the horizon. Then he enters with him into the earth daily.

728 (GODDESS WEARING RED CROWN): She of the Bow
729 (FALCON): Foremost of the Sky
730 (DOUBLE-HEADED SERPENT): Linked of Faces
731 (GODDESS WITH WHITE CROWN): She Who Is on the (Other) Side

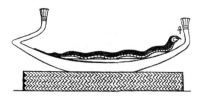

3.110. Scene 107. A divine bark, with papyrus-bundle prow and stern contains a single large falcon-headed serpent with *ankh*-sign slightly above his head.

He exists in this fashion in his bark. That he takes up position is at the utter darkness at this portal of the eastern horizon. Then he occupies his place daily. He is the Rearing One[118] of the Netherworld, sacred *ba*-soul of Foremost of the Westerners.

732 (SERPENT WITH FALCON-HEAD): Living One of the Earth

3.111. Scene 108. Twelve gods serve as the armed crew of Re. The first four, solar disk-headed deities carry arrows; the second group, fully anthropomorphic, carry spears; the third group, also fully anthropomorphic, carry bows.

They exist in this fashion holding their arrows, their spears, and their bows in front of this great god, going forth before him to the eastern horizon of the sky. This great god says to them: "Swiftness be to your arrows; sharpness be to your spears; spanning be to your bows, so that you may punish for me my enemies who are in the darkness at the gateway of the horizon.

---

118. The ʿḥʿw serpent is a frequently occurring apotropaic creature (Wilson 1997, 174ff.).

You belong to me, in my following, when I occupy the nethersky, when my flesh becomes strong in the day-bark."

It is they who repel the rebels belonging to Terrible of Face in the utter darkness, so that this great god shall pass by the eastern portal of the horizon and so that they shall pass by this god afterwards.

733 (DISK-HEADED GOD HOLDING ARROW): Gorey-Headed One
734 (DISK-HEADED GOD HOLDING ARROW): He of the Arrow
735 (DISK-HEADED GOD HOLDING ARROW): Binder
736 (DISK-HEADED GOD HOLDING ARROW): Slinger
737 (GOD HOLDING HARPOON): Shooter
738 (GOD HOLDING HARPOON): Thrower
739 (GOD HOLDING HARPOON): He Who Repels
740 (GOD HOLDING HARPOON): He Who Punishes
741 (GOD HOLDING BOW): He of the *Pedjet*-Bow
742 (GOD HOLDING BOW): He of the *Shemeret*-Bow
743 (GOD HOLDING BOW): He of the Knot
744 (GOD HOLDING BOW): Appearing of Arm

REGISTER 3 (PLATE 12)

3.112. Scene 109. The scene is dominated by a large body of water in which float the drowned. A total of twelve drowned individuals are depicted in various positions, including supine and prone within the water. To the left, a falcon-headed god leaning on a staff and crowned with a solar disk presides over the scene.

Words spoken by Horus to the drowned, the capsized, the overturned ones, those within Nun, namely, the Netherworld Dwellers: "O drowned ones, who are dark in Nun, whose arms are in the vicinity of their faces. O ones capsized of face in the Netherworld, whose vertebrae belong to the floodwaters. O those who swim through Nun as those overturned of face, they being in the following of their *ba*-souls. Breath be to your *ba*-souls, so that they do not lack; stroking be to your arms, so that they are not turned back. May you travel Nun rightly by means of your feet, so that your knees are not repelled. May you go forth into the floodwaters. May you descend into the flowing water. May you be immersed in the Great Flood. May you moor at the banks. Your limbs shall not rot. Your flesh shall not putrefy. Power be to you in your water. May you breathe that which I have commanded for you. You are those who are within Nun, the drowned who are in his following. May life belong to your *ba*-souls."

745 (FALCON-HEADED GOD): Horus
746 (DROWNED FIGURES): Drowned Ones within the Netherworld
747 (DROWNED FIGURES): Capsized Ones within the Netherworld
748 (DROWNED FIGURES): Overturned Ones within the Netherworld

3.113. Scene 110. Four goddesses crowned with uraei stand, facing right. A *ḥqꜣ*-scepter crowned with a Seth head is the final image of Hour 10.

They exist in this fashion, their living images as their heads. It is they who illumine the road for Re in the utter darkness, when he goes forth from the eastern portal. The staff of Nehes[119] passes before him.

749 (GODDESS CROWNED WITH URAEUS): Destroyer
750 (GODDESS CROWNED WITH URAEUS): Glowing One
751 (GODDESS CROWNED WITH URAEUS): She Who Stings
752 (GODDESS CROWNED WITH URAEUS): Uraeus
753 (STAFF WITH HEAD OF SETH): Staff of Nehes

HOUR 11

INTRODUCTORY TEXT

Resting by the majesty of this great god in this cavern, while he issues commands to the gods who are in it. The name of the gate of this locale by which this god enters is Alighting Place of the Netherworld Dwellers. The name of this locale is Entrance of the Cavern that Reckons Corpses.

---

119. Here Nehes appears as a hypostasis of Seth; for Nehes as the "Wakeful One" in the solar bark, see p. 133 n. 11.

The name of the hour of the night that leads this great god is Starry One, Mistress of the Bark Who Repels the Rebels from His Emergence.

The mysterious cavern of the Netherworld through which this great god passes in order to go forth from the eastern mountain of the sky. Eternity swallows its images in the presence of the Seeing One who is in this locale, with the result that it presents them at the birth of Khepri in the earth. This is done according to the template like this image that is in writing on the eastern side of the Hidden Chamber of the Netherworld. The one who knows it is one who will have as his portion an equipped *akh*-spirit in the sky and on earth—truly attested!

REGISTER 1 (PLATE 13)

3.114. Scene 111. A double-headed god wearing white and red crowns with a solar disk between the two heads

He exists in this fashion, taking his position for Re, without moving from his place in the Netherworld.

754 (DOUBLE HEADED GOD): Equipped of Face, lord of
    eternity

1.115. Scene 112. A deity crowned with solar disk holds out the wings of a serpent with two sets of legs. Large *udjat*-eyes appear to either side of the scene.

He exists in this fashion. When this god calls to him, the image of Atum comes forth from his back. Then he swallows his images afterwards. He lives from the shades of the dead, and his corpse (also lives from) the heads.

755 (GOD WITH SOLAR DISK): Atum
756 (WINGED SERPENT): He Who Perceives

3.116. Scene 113. A diagonally oriented snake, facing left, carries a goddess on its back. Interspersed around the figures are nine stars.

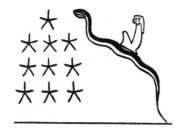

Her own body. She exists atop (the snake) He Who Takes the Hours.[120] What she does is live (by means of) the commands of Re daily, swallowing her image at this locale. She is the eleventh hour, the first in the following of the god.

757 (GODDESS): Eternity
758 (SERPENT): He Who Takes the Hours

3.117. Scene 114. Twelve gods with various attributes stride to the right. The first deity has two human heads; the second a ram-head, the third has his arms raised in adoration. The next five gods have no arms depicted: the fourth deity has two serpents emerging from his neck in lieu of a head, while the next four deities have no attributes. The last four male deities are without attribute.

They exist in this fashion. This great god calls to them by name: "Come forth to me, O hidden ones! Light up for me, O those mysterious of arms. Life be to your *ba*-souls, so that they might alight upon your shades. You are the ones mysterious[121] of hiddenness, who set the image at its sacred place. Your breath is upon my mouth so that your noses might breathe therefrom. The offerings that are on my bark be to you, so that your *ba*-souls might live therefrom. Water be to you from the high point of Nun, at which water is given to the Netherworld Dwellers. Hail, may your visible forms be proper! Your *ba*-souls be in the following of my manifestations."

---

120. An alternate reading is "He Who Rescues the Hours" (see Manassa 2007a, 354).

121. For the reading *štꜣw*, see Manassa 2007a, 355–56.

What they do in the Netherworld is to cause the mysteries of this great god to approach the Hidden Chamber daily. It is before this great god that they shall go forth to heaven.

759 (DOUBLE-HEADED GOD): He of the Head
760 (RAM-HEADED GOD): Khnum-Renyt
761 (GOD WITH ARMS RAISED IN ADORATION): Protector of the Earth
762 (DOUBLE SNAKE-HEADED GOD): He Whose Arms Are in Him
763 (GOD WITH HIDDEN ARMS): Messenger(?) of the Two Lands
764 (GOD WITH HIDDEN ARMS): Beloved of His Two Arms
765 (GOD WITH HIDDEN ARMS): Hidden of His Two Arms
766 (GOD WITH HIDDEN ARMS): Haunch of Flesh[122]
767 (GOD): One Who Praises Horus
768 (GOD): True One
769 (GOD): *Mesekhtiu*-Constellation
770 (GOD): Retiring of Arm

3.118. Scene 115. Four goddesses ride on double-headed serpents. Each goddess has one arm placed before her face, while her other arm hangs behind her.

They exist in this fashion, their thighs being in the earth, their legs being in the utter darkness. This great god calls to them in their own bodies. Then they mourn, without leaving their places. Their *ba*-souls live from the voice of the image which comes forth from their legs daily. The counter-wind and uproar of the wind, which manifests in the Netherworld, come forth from the faces of these goddesses.[123]

771 (GODDESS ON SERPENT): Mistress of Life
772 (GODDESS ON SERPENT): Mistress of *Akh*-Spirits

---

122. "*sw.t*," *WÄS* 4:60.2–3; Hannig 2006b, 2131.
123. For these goddesses as hypostases of Nut, see Westendorf 2003. For a good storm wind in the Netherworld, see Schott 1964, 29, n. 6 (§23).

773 (GODDESS ON SERPENT): She Who Protects the Two Banks
774 (GODDESS ON SERPENT): She Who Guards the Gods

REGISTER 2 (PLATE 13)

3.119. Scene 116. The solar bark sails with its usual crew; a new addition to the bark is the presence of a female solar disk[124] on the prow.

The great god sails in this locale in this fashion, while the divine crew transports him to the eastern horizon of the sky. She Who Shines at the Head of the Bark leads this great god towards the roads of darkness by means of what is in her, which illumines those within the earth.

775 (GOD): Opener of Paths
776 (GOD): Divine Perception
777 (GODDESS WITH DISK AND HORNS): Mistress of the Bark
778 (ENCIRCLING SERPENT): Encircling Serpent
779 (RAM-HEADED GOD): Flesh
780 (FALCON-HEADED GOD): Horus Who Praises
781 (GOD): Bull of Maat
782 (GOD): Wakeful One
783 (GOD): Divine Utterance
784 (GOD): Director of the Bark
785 (SOLAR DISK): She Who Shines (in) the Netherworld

124. See p. 362 n. 39.

3.120. Scene 117. Twelve gods carry a serpent atop their heads. Each god bears two coils of the serpent and has his hands before him, supporting the serpent's body as it stretches across the spaces between the bearers.

They exist in this fashion in front of this great god. As they carry the Encircling Serpent of the earth upon their heads at this locale, so do they pass in the following of Re to the eastern horizon of the sky. This god calls to them by their names, and commands to them their duties.

Re says to them: "Watch over your images and lift up your heads. Firmness be to your arms and steadfastness to your legs. Propriety be to your movements, wideness be to your strides. May you be content with your offerings at the portal of the eastern horizon of the sky."

What they do is set the Encircling Serpent on his course at the portal of the eastern horizon. Then they occupy their thrones after this great god passes through the darkness and occupies the horizon.

786 (GOD CARRYING SERPENT): He Who Lifts
787 (GOD CARRYING SERPENT): He Who Carries
788 (GOD CARRYING SERPENT): He Who Loads
789 (GOD CARRYING SERPENT): He Who Grasps
790 (GOD CARRYING SERPENT): He Who Receives
791 (GOD CARRYING SERPENT): Firm of Arm
792 (GOD CARRYING SERPENT): He Who Seizes
793 (GOD CARRYING SERPENT): Pleasant One(?)
794 (GOD CARRYING SERPENT): He Who Takes
795 (GOD CARRYING SERPENT): He Who Embraces
796 (GOD CARRYING SERPENT): He Who Leads the Image
797 (GOD CARRYING SERPENT): He of the Encircling Serpent

3.121. Scene 118. Two serpents, facing right, carry crowns on their backs. The first has a red crown with a small human head coming out from the flat portion of the crown. The second serpent has a white crown with two small human heads emerging from the bulbous top of the crown.

They are the mysterious images of Horus. They exist at the second gate of the utter darkness, the sacred road of Sais.[125] This god calls to them, then their mysterious heads come forth. Then they swallow their image afterwards.

798 (SERPENT WITH RED CROWN ON BACK): Image of Isis
799 (SERPENT WITH WHITE CROWN ON BACK): Image of Nephthys

3.122. Scene 119. Four standing goddesses face right; the first two wear red crowns, while the second two wear white crowns. All four are hypostases of the goddess Neith.

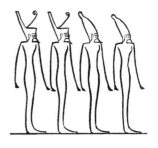

They exist in this fashion at this gate as images that Horus made. This god calls to them by name, with the result that they breathe when hearing his voice. It is they who protect the sacred gate of Sais, unknowable, imperceptible, invisible.

800 (GODDESS WEARING RED CROWN): Male Neith
801 (GODDESS WEARING RED CROWN): Neith of the Red Crown
802 (GODDESS WEARING WHITE CROWN): Neith of the White Crown
803 (GODDESS WEARING WHITE CROWN): Neith-Osiris

125. For the correlation of worldly and Netherworldly geography with the city of Sais, see Manassa 2007a, 428–29.

REGISTER 3 (PLATE 13)

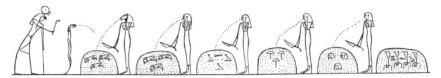

3.123. Scene 120. This scene is a depiction of the punishment of the damned. On the far left, a falcon-headed god crowned with a solar disk leans on a staff and holds out a serpent-headed stick. A serpent standing on its tail appears before him. Next are six fire-pits containing depictions of enemies or parts thereof, from left to right: three prone enemies, another three prone enemies, three *ba*-souls, three shades, three heads, and four inverted enemies. Between each fire pit is a goddess brandishing a knife.

Commanding by the majesty of this god the slaughtering of those who smote his father Osiris, (namely), the corpses of the enemies, the flesh of the dead, those who are inverted, those who are hindered from movement, the dead, and the destroyed.

(Horus says): "It was after my father was struck down in the wake of his weariness that I came forth from him.[126] Punishment be to your corpses with the punishing knives.[127] Destruction be to your *ba*-souls. Trampling be to your shades. Severing be to your heads. You shall not exist. You shall go upside down. You shall not rise up, for you have fallen into your fire-pits. You shall not move, you shall not travel. The consuming fire of (the serpent) She Who Burns Millions is against you. The scorching flame of She Who Is upon Her Cauldron is against you. The shooting flame of She Who Is upon Her Fire Pit is against you. The blaze in the mouth of She Who Is upon Her Slaughtering Block is against you. The knife of She Who Is upon Her Swords is among you, making your massacre, carrying out your slaughter. Never shall you see the living on earth forever."

They exist in this fashion in the Netherworld. Their ruin is commanded by the majesty of the Netherworldly Horus daily.

---

126. The resurrection of Horus from the rotting body of Osiris is an important theme within Egyptian funerary literature, particularly the Netherworld Books—compare commentary to Books of the Creation of the Solar Disk, Tomb of Ramesses VI, Section A, Register 2, Scene 8, in which Horus emerges from the body of his father Osiris (pp. 472–73). Compare also the statement in the Book of Gates, Hour 2, Register 3, Scene 8 (p. 264).

127. Compare goddess no. 811, "She Who Punishes," who brandishes a knife.

804 (FALCON-HEADED GOD): Horus
805 (SERPENT STANDING ON TAIL): She Who Burns Millions

LABEL TO THE FIRE-PITS: Fire-Pit

806 (ENEMY FIGURES): Enemy
807 (GODDESS HOLDING KNIFE): She Who Is Chief of Her Cauldron
808 (ENEMY FIGURES): Flesh (of the enemies)
809 (GODDESS HOLDING KNIFE): She Who Is Chief of Her Fire-Pit
810 (BA-SOULS): Ba-Souls (of the enemies)
811 (GODDESS HOLDING KNIFE): She Who Punishes
812 (SHADES): BLANK
813 (GODDESS HOLDING KNIFE): She Who Is Chief of Her Slaughtering Block
814 (HEADS): Heads (of the enemies)
815 (GODDESS HOLDING KNIFE): She Who Is Chief of Her Swords

LABEL TO THE FIRE-PIT: Valley of the Inverted Ones

816 (INVERTED ENEMIES): Inverted Ones

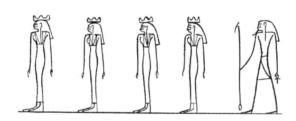

3.124. Scene 121. Four goddesses crowned with *khaset*-signs face left. Also facing left, at the far end of the register, is a male deity holding a *was*-scepter and *ankh*-sign.

They exist in this fashion. It is they who make execrations[128] among the enemies of Osiris in the Netherworld. The chief of his cauldrons is the

---

128. For the identification of *tms.w* as "execration rituals" see Ritner 1993, 169–70. The term also appears in the Book of Gates, Hour 12, Register 3, Scene 97, where four goddesses are those "who bring about the years for those who belong to execration in the Netherworld" (p. 333).

guardian of this cavern. They live from the voices of the enemies, consisting of the cries of the *ba*-souls and shades. It is to their fire pits that they are assigned.

817 (GODDESSES CROWNED WITH *KHASET*-SIGN): She Who Cooks
818 (GODDESSES CROWNED WITH *KHASET*-SIGN): She Who Blazes
819 (GODDESSES CROWNED WITH *KHASET*-SIGN): She Who Is upon Her Sand
820 (GODDESSES CROWNED WITH *KHASET*-SIGN): She of Destruction
821 (GOD): Chief of His Cauldrons

HOUR 12

INTRODUCTORY TEXT

Resting by the majesty of this great god in this cavern of the end of the utter darkness. It is at this cavern that this great god is born in his manifestation of Khepri. Nun and Nunet, Heh and Hehet exist at this cavern at the birth of this great god, when he comes forth from the Netherworld, when he rests in the day-bark, when he appears in glory from the thighs of Nut. The name of the gate of this locale is Distinguishing the Gods. The name of this locale is Manifesting of Darkness and Appearing of Births. The name of the hour of the night, at which this great god manifests, is She Who Sees the Perfection of Re.

The mysterious cavern of the Netherworld at which this great god is born, when he comes forth from Nun, when he rests in the belly of Nut. This is done according to this image that is in writing on the eastern side of the Hidden Chamber of the Netherworld. It is effective for one who knows it on earth, in the sky, and in the earth.

REGISTER 1 (PLATE 14)

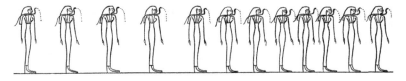

3.125. Scene 122. Twelve standing goddesses have spitting cobras crossing their shoulders.

They exist in this fashion in their own bodies. From their arms do these uraei come forth, when this great god reaches this locale. They exist in the following of this god. It is the flames at the tips of the tongues of their uraei that repel Apep from Re at the eastern portal of the horizon. They cross heaven in his following in their places of the day-bark. These god(desse)s turn themselves back after this great god traverses the mysterious sand-bank of the sky. Then they rest on their thrones.

It is they who please the hearts of the gods of the West with Re-Horakhty. What they do in the earth is causing those who are in the dark-ness to be loosed, by means of the tapers of their uraei, when they come, leading Re, having punished for him Apep in the sky.

822 (GODDESS WITH COBRA): Perfect of Glorious Forms
823 (GODDESS WITH COBRA): She Who Makes the Path for Re
824 (GODDESS WITH COBRA): Mistress of the Powers of the Earth
825 (GODDESS WITH COBRA): Chief of the Cobras
826 (GODDESS WITH COBRA): She Who Commends the Two Banks of the Sky
827 (GODDESS WITH COBRA): She Who Rejoices in Her Two Lands
828 (GODDESS WITH COBRA): High in Her Visible Forms
829 (GODDESS WITH COBRA): Powerful of Her *Akh*-Spirits
830 (GODDESS WITH COBRA): She Who Rejoices (for) Re in His Visible Forms
831 (GODDESS WITH COBRA): She Who Sees the Corpse when He Stands in His Bark
832 (GODDESS WITH COBRA): She Who Comes Forth from the Forehead of Re
833 (GODDESS WITH COBRA): Mistress of Uraei in the Bark of Millions

3.126. Scene 123. Twelve gods stride forward, their arms raised in adoration.

They exist in this fashion, adoring this great god in the early morning, when he rests in the eastern portal of the sky.

They say to Re: "Born is the one who is born! Manifested is the one who is manifest! Venerated one of the earth, *ba*-soul, lord of heaven! The sky be to your *ba*-soul, so that it might rest within it. The earth be to your corpse, lord of veneration. May you seize the horizon, so that you might occupy your shrine and the two goddesses celebrate you in their bodies. Jubilation be to you, O *ba*-soul who is in heaven! May your two daughters receive you in your visible forms."[129]

What they do in the Netherworld is adore this great god. They take up position at this locale, and reckon for the turquoise gods.[130] It is after Re rests in the sky that the turquoise gods give praise to Re, with the result that he appears in glory in the eyes of the sun-folk. Then these gods go to rest in their cavern.

834 (ADORING GOD): Lord of Life
835 (ADORING GOD): He Who Jubilates
836 (ADORING GOD): Lord of Worship
837 (ADORING GOD): Lord of Adorations
838 (ADORING GOD): Pleasant of Heart
839 (ADORING GOD): He Who Rejoices in Re
840 (ADORING GOD): Honored of Heart
841 (ADORING GOD): Youth
842 (ADORING GOD): He Who Extols the Left Eye
843 (ADORING GOD): He Who Renews(?) the Heads of the Gods
844 (ADORING GOD): He Who Ties on the Heads of the Gods
845 (ADORING GOD): He Who Praises Khepri

REGISTER 2 (PLATE 14)

3.127. Scene 124. The solar bark is hauled forward, containing the same crew it has had since Hour 7. The only difference is the addition of a scarab, horizontally oriented, at the prow.

---

129. Compare the role of Isis and Nephthys as the horizon through which the sun god travels (p. 30 and n. 46).

130. For the theological significance of turquoise, see p. 156 n. 53.

This great god sails in this fashion in this locale in the vertebrae of this mysterious image of Life of the Gods. It is his gods who haul him. Just as he enters into his tail, so does he emerge from his mouth, having been born in his manifestation of Khepri, the gods who are in his bark likewise. That he goes to rest upon the mysterious image of Shu, who separates the sky from the land, is at the utter darkness. It is his arms which seal the Netherworld. Then this god rests in the eastern horizon of the sky, so that Shu might receive him, namely his manifestation at the eastern bank.

846 (GOD): Opener of Paths
847 (GOD): Divine Perception
848 (GODDESS WITH DISK AND HORNS): Mistress of the Bark
849 (ENCIRCLING SERPENT): Encircling Serpent
850 (RAM-HEADED GOD): Flesh
851 (FALCON-HEADED GOD): Horus Who Praises
852 (GOD): Bull of Maat
853 (GOD): Wakeful One
854 (GOD): Divine Utterance
855 (GOD): Director of the Bark
856 (scarab beetle): Khepri

3.128. Scene 125. Twelve hauling gods stand atop a giant serpent. Each god looks back toward the solar bark.

They exist in this fashion, hauling this great god in the vertebrae of Life of the Gods, being the venerated ones of Re who are behind him and before him. That they are born in the earth daily is after the birth of the great god in the eastern part of the sky. They enter the mysterious image of Life of the Gods as venerated ones, so that they might emerge as youthful ones of Re, daily. Their abomination is shouting on earth and pronouncing the name of the great god. They exist in their own bodies. It is into the sky that <they> follow this great god.

857 (HAULING GOD): Great One

858 (HAULING GOD): Elder
859 (HAULING GOD): Old One
860 (HAULING GOD): Wise One
861 (HAULING GOD): He Who Strikes His Life
862 (HAULING GOD): He Who Passes His Years
863 (HAULING GOD): Powerful of Time
864 (HAULING GOD): Venerated One
865 (HAULING GOD): Lord of Veneration
866 (HAULING GOD): Greying One
867 (HAULING GOD): One of the Grey (Hair)
868 (HAULING GOD): Living One

3.128. Scene 126. The giant serpent through which the solar bark sails (same as scene 125).

This mysterious image of Life of the Gods exists at his Netherworldly loca-tion, without going to any (other) place daily. This great god speaks to him in his name of *Nau*-serpent, so that he might aid the birth of the god.[131] To him belong 1,300 sacred cubits of the god in length. He lives on the shouts of the venerated ones who are among his vertebrae, who come forth from his mouth daily.

869 (GIANT SERPENT): *Ka*-Spirit of the One Who Causes the Gods to Live

---

3.129. Scene 127. Thirteen standing goddesses also haul the solar bark and look back over their shoulders. Above the last three is a giant scarab beetle, which appears to enter the horizon, which is depicted as the rounded end of Hour 12. Within the horizon is a human head and two arms with a sun disk below the head.

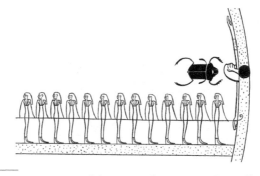

---

131. For the *Nau*-serpent and the eastern horizon, see Darnell 2004, 322–23.

They exist in this fashion. It is they who take up the tow-rope of the bark of Re, when he emerges from the vertebrae of Life of the Gods. It is they who haul this great god in the sky and who lead him to the paths of heaven. It is they who manifest in heaven by means of wind, calm, storm, and rain. What they command as living ones is what the great bark does in the sky.

870 (HAULING GODDESS): Hauler
871 (HAULING GODDESS): She Who Sees the Perfection of Re
872 (HAULING GODDESS): She Who Sees Khepri
873 (HAULING GODDESS): She Who Sees the Corpse of Her God
874 (HAULING GODDESS): Mistress of Youthfulness
875 (HAULING GODDESS): Mistress of Eternity
876 (HAULING GODDESS): She of Everlastingness
877 (HAULING GODDESS): Living of Shoulder
878 (HAULING GODDESS): She Who Speaks atop the Bark
879 (HAULING GODDESS): She Who Rejoices in Her Horizon
880 (HAULING GODDESS): She Who Rests in Her Horizon
881 (HAULING GODDESS): She Who Brings Her God
882 (HAULING GODDESS): She Who Sanctifies the East
883 (SCARAB BEETLE): Khepri
884 (HUMAN HEAD AND ARMS): Image of Shu

REGISTER 3 (PLATE 14)

3.130. Scene 128. Two male-female pairs of the Ogdoad appear as two striding gods holding *was*-scepters and *ankh*-signs, along with two standing goddesses holding the same objects.

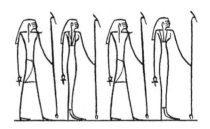

They exist in this fashion in their own bodies, when they go to rest before Re in the sky. It is they who receive this great god in his emergence from them in the eastern portion of the sky daily. They exist at their portal of the horizon, their Netherworldly forms at this cavern.

885 (GOD): Nun
886 (GODDESS): Nunet
887 (GOD): Heh
888 (GODDESS): Hehet

3.131. Scene 129. Eight gods holding oars are arranged in two groups of four with a serpent standing on its tail between them. All of the oarsmen are fully anthropomorphic male deities, with the exception of 891 and 892, who have a crocodile head and a double bird-head respectively.

They exist in this fashion, carrying their oars. It is they who repel Apep from the eastern part of the sky after the birth of the god. What they do is perform the elevation of the great disk in the eastern horizon of the sky daily. It is He Whose Eye Flames who cooks the enemies of Re in the early morning. As these gods cross heaven in the following of this great god, daily, so do they receive their visible forms at this cavern.

889 (GOD WITH OAR): Clothed One
890 (GOD WITH OAR): High of Awe
891 (CROCODILE-HEADED GOD WITH OAR): Jubilating(?) One
892 (DOUBLE BIRD-HEADED GOD WITH OAR): He Who Prays
893 (SERPENT): He Whose Eye Flames
894 (GOD WITH OAR): Fiery of *Akh*-Spirits
895 (GOD WITH OAR): Foremost of His Cavern(?)
896 (GOD WITH OAR): Powerful of Heart
897 (GOD WITH OAR): He of the Netherworld

3.132. Scene 130. Ten gods stride forward with their arms raised in adoration.

They exist in this fashion all around the image of Osiris, foremost of the utter darkness. Commands that this god says to them after this great god passes over it: "Live, live, one foremost of his darkness! Live, Great One, foremost of his darkness, lord of life, ruler of the west, Osiris, Foremost of the Westerners. Give life, give life, Foremost of the Netherworld! The breath of Re be to your nose, the inhalation of Khepri is before you, so that you may live and be alive. Hail Osiris, lord of life!"

They are the gods who are in the following of Osiris, who manifested in his presence at the first occasion. They exist around this mysterious image at this cavern. As they live on the things on which he lives, so they breathe by means of the word of this god, by means of their own adoration.

898 (ADORING GOD): Boasting of *Akh*-Spirit
899 (ADORING GOD): Mighty of Mouth
900 (ADORING GOD): He Who Unites
901 (ADORING GOD): He Who Embraces
902 (ADORING GOD): He Who Carries
903 (ADORING GOD): Musician
904 (ADORING GOD): Shining of Arm
905 (ADORING GOD): Effective of Mouth
906 (ADORING GOD): *Itjep*[132]
907 (ADORING GOD): One with the God

3.133. Scene 131. A large mummy reclines at the rounded end of Hour 12.

He exists in this fashion as the image that Horus hid in the utter darkness. It is this mysterious image that supports Shu beneath Nut. From this image does the great flood come forth in the earth.[133]

908 (RECLINING MUMMY): Image of Flesh

---

132. Name of uncertain translation, since this is the sole attestation of the deity ("*Itp*," *LGG* 1:639).

133. The "great flood" is here conceived as the putrefaction of the corpse of Osiris (see p. 89 n. 53).

"Short" Book of the Hidden Chamber

TITLE

Summary of this writing. The beginning is the horn of the West; the end is the utter darkness.

HOUR 1

This god enters into the earth at the portal of the western horizon. It is 120 *iteru* of sailing in this portal, before he reaches the Netherworld Dwellers. The Floodwater of Re is the name of the first field of the Netherworld. He grants cultivated land to them, namely, the gods who are in his following. He begins to issue commands and to care for the Netherworld Dwellers at this field.

This is done according to this image in the hidden part of the Netherworld. As for the one who knows these images, (he is) the likeness of the great god himself; it is effective for him on earth—truly attested; it is very effective for him in the Netherworld.

She Who Smashes the Skulls of the Enemies of Re is the name of the first hour of the night who guides this great god in this portal.

HOUR 2

Resting afterwards by this great god in Wernes. There are 309 *iteru* in the length of this field; 120 *iteru* in width. The *Ba*-Souls of the Netherworld Dwellers is the name of the gods who are in this field. As for the one who knows their names, he will exist near them. This great god will grant to him cultivated land at their places in the field of Wernes, as he takes his place before the Standing One. Just as he passes by after this great god, so he enters the earth, he opening the Netherworld, he parting the locks of the Hairlock-Wearers. In the following of Maat of the Land-Plots does he pass by the Donkey-Swallower. He always eats bread at the bark of the earth; the prow-rope of the *Tebiu*-bark is given to him.

These (images) of the *ba*-souls of the Netherworld Dwellers are made in writing in their template, in the hidden part of the Netherworld. The beginning of the book is at the West. One offers to them on earth in their names. It is effective for a man on earth—truly attested millions of times. The one who knows these words that the Netherworld Dwellers speak to this god and the words this god speaks to them is one who ascends before the Netherworld Dwellers. It is effective for a man on earth—truly attested a million times.

The name of the hour of the night that guides this god in this field is Wise One Who Protects Her Lord.

HOUR 3

Resting afterwards by the majesty of this great god in the field of the grain-gods and pursuing the navigation by this god in the floodwaters of Osiris. There are 309 *iteru* in the length of this field, 120 in its width. This great god issues commands to those in the following of Osiris at this locale; he grants to them cultivated land at this field. Mysterious *Ba*-Souls is the name of the gods who are in this field.

As for the one who knows their names on earth, he is always one who ascends to the place in which Osiris is; one gives to him water at this, his field. The Floodwaters of the Sole Lord (called) Creator of Victuals is the name of this field.

These mysterious images of the mysterious *ba*-souls are made in this template that is in writing in the hidden part of the Netherworld. The beginning of the writing is to the West. It is effective for a man on earth and in the necropolis, truly attested. The one who knows them is one who passes over them. He cannot perish at their roar; he cannot fall into their fire pits. The one who knows it is one who belongs to the proper place, his offering loaves before <him> with Re. The one who knows it is an effective *ba*-soul, with power over his legs, one who does not descend into the Place of Destruction. He always goes forth in visible forms, as he breathes air at his hour.

The name of this hour that guides this god in this field is She Who Cuts *Ba*-Souls.

HOUR 4

Resting afterwards by means of hauling by the majesty of this god in the mysterious cavern of the West, caring for those who are within it by means of his voice, without his seeing them. The name of this cavern is Living of Manifestations. The name of the gate of this cavern is One Who Hides the Hauling.

The one who knows this image of the mysterious paths of the Place of Hauling, the sacred roads of Imhet, the hidden gates that are in the land of Sokar, who is upon his sand, is one who eats bread intended for the mouths of the living in the temple of Atum. The one who knows it is one who travels the paths rightly, who goes along the roads of the Place of Hauling, who sees the images in Imhet.

The name of the hour of the night which guides this great god is Great in Her Power.

HOUR 5

It is the hauling of this great god upon the proper paths of the Netherworld in the upper half of the mysterious cavern of Sokar, who is upon his sand. Unseen and unperceived is this mysterious image of the earth that carries the flesh of this god. Those among whom this god is, they hear the voice of Re, when he calls in the vicinity of this god.

The name of the gate of this locale is Positions of the Gods. The name of the cavern of this god is West. Mysterious paths of the West, gates of entering the Hidden Chamber, the sacred place of the land of Sokar, limbs, flesh, and body being in (its) foremost manifestations.

The name of the gods who are in this cavern are *Ba*-Souls within the Netherworld, their visible forms which are within their hours, their mysterious manifestations, unknowable, unseen, unperceived, this image of Horus himself.

This is done according to this image that is in writing in the hidden part of the Netherworld on the southern side of the Hidden Chamber. The one who know is it one who is satisfied of *ba*-soul; it is with Sokar's offerings that he becomes content. She of Destruction will never slice his corpse. He will cross over her in peace. One offers to these gods on earth.

The name of the hour of the night who guides this great god in this cavern is She Who Guides from within Her Bark.

HOUR 6

Resting by the majesty of this great god in the Deep Waters, Lady of the Netherworld Dwellers, so that he might issue commands to these gods who are within it. He commands that they have power over their offerings at this locale. That he sails in this <locale> is being equipped in the great bark, he commanding to them cultivated land to be their offerings, he giving to them water of their floodwaters, in passage of the Netherworld daily.

The name of the gate of this locale is Sharp of Blades. The mysterious path of the West through which this great god sails in his bark, in order to care for the Netherworld Dwellers, united[134] in their names, known in their bodies, engraved in their visible forms, their hours mysterious of affairs, without this mysterious Netherworldly form being known by any people.

This image is made in writing according to this template in the hidden part of the Netherworld on the southern side of the Hidden Chamber. The one who knows it is a possessor of victuals in the Netherworld, he being satisfied with the offerings of the gods who are in the following of Osiris. One offers to him, while his relations are in the earth.

Issuing commands by this god to give divine offerings to the Netherworldly gods. He tarries by them, so they might see him, with the result that they have power over their fields. Their victuals come into existence, when this great god commands to them. Deep Waters, Lady of the Netherworld Dwellers is the name of this field; it is the path of the bark of Re. The name of the hour of night that guides this great god in this field is Harbor Granting (Proper) Offerings.

HOUR 7

Resting by the Majesty of this great god in the grotto of Osiris. Issuing commands by the majesty of this great god at this grotto to these gods who are in it. This god takes on another visible form at this grotto, so that he might deflect the path from Apep, by means of the magic of Isis and the Elder Magician. The name of the gate of this locale over which this god passes is Gateway of Osiris. The name of this locale is Mysterious Grotto.

The mysterious path of the West over which this great god passes in his sacred bark. Just as he passes over this path, without water or its hauling, does he sail by means of the magic of Isis and the Elder Magician and by means of the effective spells which are in the mouth of this god himself. Making the slaughter of Apep in the Netherworld at this cavern, it means his place in the sky.

This is done according to this template in writing on the northern side of the Hidden Chamber in the Netherworld. It is effective for the one

---

134. The "Long" version of the Book of the Hidden Chamber uses the more logical phrase "pronounced of their names" (p. 185).

for whom it is done in the sky and in the earth. The one who knows it is (one of) the greatest *ba*-soul(s) before Re. One performs this magic of Isis and the Elder Magician. What they do is the repelling of Apep from Re in the West.

This is done in the hidden part of the Netherworld; this is done on earth likewise. One who knows it is one who resides in the bark of Re in the sky and in the earth. Few are those who know this image—whoever does not know it cannot repel Terrible of Face. As for the sandbank of Terrible of Face, it is 460 cubits in length, and he fills it with his coils. One performs his injury, without which this god cannot pass over him, so that he might deflect the path from him at the grotto of Osiris.

That this god sails in this locale is in the image of the Encircling Serpent. The one who knows it on earth is one whose water Terrible of Face cannot drink, one whose *ba*-soul will not perish at the injury of the gods who are in this cavern. The one who knows it is one whose *ba*-soul the crocodile will not swallow. The name of the hour of the night who guides this great god in this cavern is Repeller of the *Hiu*-Snake Who Smites Terrible of Face.

HOUR 8

Resting by the majesty of this great god at the cavern of the mysterious gods who are upon their sand. He issues commands to them from his bark. It is his gods who haul him in the sacred embrace of the Encircling Serpent. The name of the gate of this locale is One Who Stands without Wearying. The name of this locale is Bank of Its Gods. The mysterious cavern of the West through which the great god passes in his bark, by means of hauling of his gods who are in the Netherworld.

This is done according to this image in writing on the northern side of the Hidden Chamber in the Netherworld. The one who knows it in their names is <the possessor of> clothing on the earth, without being repelled from the mysterious gates, being provided with a great tomb—truly attested! The name of the hour of the night who guides this great god is Mistress of the Deep of the Night.

HOUR 9

Resting by the majesty of this great god in this cavern, as he issues commands from his bark to the gods who are in it, with the result that the crew of the bark of this great god goes to rest at this locale. The name of the gate of this locale over which this great god passes, when he occupies the floodwaters that are in this locale is Guardian of the Deluge. The name of this locale is Inducting of Visible Forms.

The mysterious cavern of the West at which the great god and his crew rests in the Netherworld. This is done in their names according to this image that is in writing on the eastern side of the Hidden Chamber of the Netherworld.

The one who knows their names upon earth and who knows their thrones in the West is one who occupies his throne in the Netherworld; one who stands among the lords of provisions; one who is justified within the council of Re, who reckons the balances. It is effective for the one who knows it on earth.

The name of this hour of the night who guides this great god in this cavern is Starry One Who Protects Her Lord.

HOUR 10

Resting by the majesty of this great god in this cavern, while he issues commands to the gods who are in it. The name of the gate of this locale over which this great god passes is Great of Manifestations, Engendered of Visible Forms. The name of this locale is Deep of Water, High of Banks.

The mysterious cavern of the West, in which Khepri rests in the presence of Re, in which gods, *akh*-spirits, and the dead cry out over the mysterious image of Igeret. This is done according to this image that is in writing on the eastern side of the Hidden Chamber of the Netherworld.

The one who knows it in their names is one who crosses the Netherworld to its end, without being repelled from the council before Re. The name of the hour of the night that leads this great god on the mysterious path of this locale is Raging One Who Beheads the Crooked-Hearted Ones.

HOUR 11

Resting by the majesty of this great god in this cavern, while he issues commands to the gods who are in it. The name of the gate of this locale through which this god passes is Alighting Place of the Netherworld Dwellers. The name of this locale is Entrance of the Cavern that Reckons Corpses. The mysterious cavern of the Netherworld through which this great god passes in order to go forth from the eastern mountain of the sky. Eternity swallows its images in the presence of the Seeing One who is in this locale, with the result that it presents them at the birth of Khepri in the earth.

This is done in this template according to this image that is in writing on the eastern side of the Hidden Chamber of the Netherworld. The one who knows it is one who will have as his portion an equipped *akh*-spirit in the sky and on earth—truly attested!

The name of the hour of the night that guides this great god is Starry One, Mistress of the Bark Who Repels the Rebels from His Emergence.

HOUR 12

Resting by the majesty of this great god in this cavern of the end of the utter darkness. It is at this cavern that this great god is born in his manifestation of Khepri. Nun and Nunet, Heh and Hehet manifest at this cavern at the birth of this great god, when he comes forth from the Netherworld, when he rests in the day-bark, when he appears in glory from the thighs of Nut.

The name of the gate of this locale is Distinguishing the Gods. The name of this locale is Manifesting of Darkness and Appearing of Births. The mysterious cavern of the Netherworld at which this great god is born, when he comes forth from Nun, when he rests in the belly of Nut.

This is done according to this image that is in writing on the eastern side of the Hidden Chamber of the Netherworld. It is effective for one who knows it on earth, in the sky, and in the earth.

CONCLUDING TITLE

Beginning of the light, end of the utter darkness. The travelings of Re in the West. The mysterious manner in which this god acts. Select guide, mysterious writings of the Netherworld, which is not known by any people, except for a select few.

This image is made according to this template in the hidden part of the Netherworld, without seeing, without perceiving. The one who knows these mysterious images is an equipped *akh*-spirit who goes forth and descends into the Netherworld, who communicates with the living—truly attested millions of times!

4
Book of Gates

INTRODUCTION

Following the publication of the version of the Book of Gates on the sarcophagus of Seti I by Joseph Bonomi and Samuel Sharpe (1864), an early study by Lefébure (1878, 1881) was the first influential study of the treatise. The initial presentation in hieroglyphic type is a series of articles by Charles Maystre and Alexandre Piankoff (1939, 1961); Piankoff and Rambova (1954) also published the texts within the tomb of Ramesses VI. Parallel texts of the New Kingdom versions appear in Hornung (1979b), now the standard edition. Translations of the Book of Gates include Jan Zandee (1969), Hornung (1980, 2002), Jürgen Zeidler (1999a, 1999b),[1] Carrier (2009), and Hornung and Abt (2014).

Over a dozen royal New Kingdom attestations of all or part of the Book of Gates survive, spanning the reigns of Horemhab through Ramesses VII.[2] In its first attestations, the tombs of Horemhab and Ramesses I, the Book of Gates replaces the Book of the Hidden Chamber as the chief decorative element of the sarcophagus chamber. In the tomb of Seti I (see fig. 1.4), the pillared halls between the sloping corridors serve as the architectural setting for the first half of the Book of Gates; the entire composition—with the hours placed in a continuous manner—decorates Seti I's anthropoid sarcophagus. Ramesses II similarly uses the Book of Gates in the pillared halls, while the tomb of his successor Merneptah has hours

---

1. Zeidler includes the stemma of the text; see also the brief note in Werning 2007, 1939.

2. Hornung 1979a, 10–21; Abitz 1995, 73–80; Zeidler 1999b, 85–97. In addition to the monuments listed in those sources, one may add the sarcophagus fragment with two figures from Scene 33 from the tomb of the sons of Ramesses II (KV 5)—published in Weeks 2006, 114.

from the composition in the upper pillared hall as well as the sarcophagus chamber. Merneptah also commissioned a complete copy of the Book of Gates within the Osireion, pairing the text with the Book of Caverns in the long entrance corridor. In the late Nineteenth and early Twentieth Dynasty, portions of the Book of Gates continued to be used in pillared halls, sarcophagus chambers, and on sarcophagi. The tomb of Ramesses VI includes all twelve hours of the Book of Gates, arranged in a continuous sequence on the left wall of the sloping corridors and well chamber, concluding in the pillared hall; following the model of the Osireion, the tomb of Ramesses VI includes a complete copy of the Book of Caverns on the corridors and walls opposite the Book of Gates. The tomb of Ramesses VII places the first two hours opposite a portion of the Book of Caverns and situates the Judgment Hall of Osiris (Scene 33) prominently in a room behind the sarcophagus chamber. While the tomb of Ramesses IX does not contain any full scenes from the Book of Gates, the entrances to the corridors of the tomb are decorated with carved door-leaves guarded by rearing serpents with annotations echoing the Book of Gates (Guilmant 1907, pls. 8–9, 25–26, 39–40, 63; Abitz 1990, 12–16). Portions of the Book of Gates are only attested in a single private New Kingdom tomb, that of Tjanefer (TT 158), a third priest of Amun during the reign of Ramesses III.[3] A version of the concluding scene of the Book of Gates appears in the Twentieth Dynasty papyrus of Anhai (British Museum EA 10472).[4]

Unlike the Book of the Hidden Chamber, the Book of Gates was not a commonly utilized treatise on Third Intermediate period papyri and coffins, although a few isolated scenes do appear, including Scene 60 (p. ###) and the Concluding Scene.[5] In the Theban Necropolis, the tombs of Padiamenope (TT 33; Régen 2014) and Mutirdis (TT 410; Assmann 1977a, 75) contain portions of the Book of Gates. Late period sarcophagi decorated with the Netherworld Books rarely employ the Book of Gates, with the exception of Hour 1 on Type I sarcophagi (for more on these sarcophagi and their decoration, see p. 308) and part of Hour 4 (Scene 21) on the sarcophagus of Tjaihorpata (CG 29306) (Manassa 2007a, 313–19). The Type II sarcophagi are important for employing a $sbḫ.t$-doorway from the

---

3. Seele 1959, pls. 31–38; Hornung 1980, 18; Abitz 1995, 80.

4. Budge 1899, pl. 8; for the date and additional bibliography, see Taylor 2010b, 71.

5. Papyrus of Khonsumes (Piankoff and Rambova 1957, no. 30); see also Hornung 1980, 21.

Book of Gates as an introductory element before hours of the Book of the Hidden Chamber and incorporating the Judgment Hall of Osiris (Scene 33 of the Book of Gates) into a position before Hour 5 of the Book of the Hidden Chamber.

Like the Book of the Hidden Chamber, the Book of Gates is divided into twelve hours, each partitioned into three horizontal registers. Parallelism in content between the two books includes the Heliopolitan burial of Re in Hour 6 of the night and the presence of the blessed dead as drowned individuals in either the Ninth (Book of Gates) or Tenth (Book of the Hidden Chamber) Hour of the night. One of the notable differences between the two compositions, and the feature that provides the modern name to the "Book of Gates," is the placement of elaborate *sbḫ.t*-doorways after Hours 2–12 of the composition; each doorway is complete with a door-leaf guarded by a serpent standing on his tail, two bands of *ḥkr*-friezes delimiting the larger architectural feature, and further protective deities: typically, two uraei, mummiform gods with aggressive names, and an ennead of mummiform figures. While the Book of the Hidden Chamber names each *sbꜣ*-portal of the night, the feminine names of the doorways in the Book of Gates reflect their nomenclature as *sbḫ.t*-doorways.[6] The elaborate depictions of doorways within the Netherworld also finds parallels in the Book of Going Forth by Day, particularly chapters 144–47, which substitute for the more royal-oriented Book of Gates in the burials of queens and other royal family members.[7]

Another aspect that differentiates the Book of the Hidden Chamber from the Book of Gates is the makeup of the crew of the solar bark; the much larger crew of the former is restricted to two figures in the Book of Gates: Sia "Divine Perception" and Heka "Magic." The ram-headed solar god in the Book of Gates is the "Flesh of Re," and like in the latter half of the Book of the Hidden Chamber, in each hour of the Book of Gates he is surrounded by the protective Encircling Serpent. In all but Hour 1 of the Book of Gates, the solar bark is hauled by four "Netherworld Dwellers."

Annotations and labels within the Book of Gates tend to refer to distinct groups of deities or the blessed dead rather than labeling each being individually as in the Book of the Hidden Chamber (Barta 1990a, 44–45). The Book of Gates lacks both a title[8] and instructions as to its proper

---

6. Barta 1990a, 48–49 provides a comparison of these names.

7. See the references collected in Manassa 2007a, 73 n. 32.

8. Contra Zeidler 1999a, 10–13; see further, p. 285 n. 83.

placement within a chamber or tomb. The annotations within the Book of Gates appear as continuous texts, written in a retrograde fashion (Mauric-Barbério 2003, 176–77) above the depictions of the Netherworldly deities. The Judgment Hall of Osiris (Scene 33)—between Hours 5 and 6—interrupts the division of the text into twelve hours; a Concluding Scene further augments the twelve hourly divisions. In several royal editions of the Book of Gates, depictions of the king can be inserted among the typical pictorial program of the composition (Abitz 1995, 81–85). Interaction between the imminent and transcendental realms appears within the Book of Gates as a series of offering formulae (Wente 1982; Wiebach-Koepke 2007, 110–14): the one who offers victuals to the various deities is provided with certain privileges in the Netherworld.

Hour 1 follows a slightly different pattern than the following eleven hours, as it represents the approach (ʿrry.t-portal) to the Netherworld and the mountains of the western horizon. Rather than the ram-headed solar deity who sails through the remaining hours, a scarab within the Encircling Serpent appears in Hour 1. The annotation to Hour 1 is obscure, describing the eye of the solar god, its creative acts, and how creation must be "removed," presumably from the chaotic forces of *isfet*.

Hour 2 begins the Netherworld proper and concludes with the first of the *sbḫ.t*-doorways that follow each hour. Two groups of the blessed dead fill Register 1; they are provided with offerings and are doers of Maat who adore Re and defeat Apep, presaging Re's combat with that evil serpent throughout the night. In Register 2, the annotation emphasizes the dual fates of the blessed and the damned: while the *akh*-spirits of the former take up their proper positions, the corpses of the latter are utterly destroyed. Atum appears at the far left of Register 3, presiding over twenty bound figures; Atum's speech focuses on the punishment of the damned, and includes a paradoxical statement of eternal recreation of the son through the father and vice versa, an early reference to the union of yesterday and tomorrow as Osiris and Re at the end of the Netherworld.[9]

Mummies and wrapped figures dominate Register 1 of Hour 3. The mummies are guarded by a fire-breathing serpent, and Re commands that light penetrate the gloom that surrounds them. The wrapped figures, whose heads are uncovered, exist at the banks of the Lake of Fire, which transforms into cool water for the blessed dead. In Register 2, the solar

---

9. See further, p. 6 and n. 8.

bark is hauled through the unusually-shaped Bark of the Earth, whose prow and stern are bull-heads that "bellow" as the earth quakes. Re then commands to the four mummiform figures at the end of Register 2, who are to be freed from their wrappings. Atum guards the serpent Apep in Register 3, continuing the punishment of Re's enemies within the lowest parts of the Netherworld. Apep's body is physically attacked and his evil acts thwarted by the enchantment of the "council that drives back Apep."

The tripartite soul—*ba*, *ka*, and *akh*—features prominently in the annotation to the first scene of Register 1 of Hour 4 (Scene 15); that same annotation praises Re as "cyclical eternity, lord of years, linear eternity, without extinguishing," and this theme of time appears prominently in Register 2. Two sacred lakes—the Lake of Life and Lake of the Uraei—fill out the remainder of Register 1, guarded by jackal-headed deities and uraei, respectively. Following the solar bark in Register 2 are nine mummies, each within their own pit; despite their mummified status, these bodies are trapped in a process of putrefaction, which paradoxically provides nourishment. The twelve hour-goddesses at the end of the register participate in the destruction and resurrection of time itself. The lowest register consists of two scenes: an enshrined Osiris and fire pits. The lengthy annotation to Osiris, Foremost of the Westerners, describes how Horus restores Osiris's fillet, glorifies him, and punishes his enemies. That punishment is vividly depicted in the next scene in which four gods guard tall fire pits to which Re has commended his enemies.

Two groups of the blessed dead appear in Register 1 of Hour 5; the first group, who are said to have had solar knowledge while alive, make ovation to Re, while the second group is tasked with measuring fields in the Netherworld. In front of the solar bark in Register 2 are six mummiform gods restraining a malicious serpent, a hypostasis of Apep. Another group of blessed dead, who "spoke Maat on earth," and a judging deity conclude the register. Horus presides over the four recognized human populations—Egyptians, Western Asiatics, Nubians, and Libyans—in the lowest register; both Egyptians and foreigners are addressed as the "cattle of Re," and an etiology is provided for the name of each race. The remaining deities of Register 3 reckon lifetimes and punish the damned.

The Judgment Hall of Osiris (Scene 33) follows Doorway 5, filling the space of all three registers, thus setting this scene apart as one of particular significance. The attestations of Scene 33 also highlight its significance within the composition. The Judgment Hall of Osiris forms the focus of the Book of Gates in its earliest appearance in the tomb of Horemhab

(Davis 2001, pls. 53–55), but the scene is replaced on most Nineteenth Dynasty royal tomb walls by an image of the king before the enthroned Osiris (Abitz 1984, 17–21); Ramesses III similarly positions the scene prominently at the end of his tomb, while other versions, such as the sarcophagus of Seti I and the tomb of Ramesses VI, place the scene within the continuously organized hours of the Book of Gates, without specific emphasis (Hornung 1980, 143–44). An entirely different textual tradition is offered by the presence of Scene 33 of the Book of Gates on a small corpus of Late period sarcophagi (Type II), where the scene appears after four addresses from the Book of Adoring Re in the West (Addresses 48, 50, 53, 54) and before Hour 5 of the Book of the Hidden Chamber (Manassa 2007a, 109). In all cases, the focus of the Judgment Hall scene is a stepped dais on which Osiris sits, with a set of empty scales placed atop a mummiform figure. This and additional figures, including a monkey striking a pig, a divine Ennead on the steps, a jackal-headed deity, and enemy figures beneath the dais, are labeled with cryptographic annotations. These texts render interpretation of the scene difficult, but the very presence of cryptography marks the scene as a depiction of a momentous event in the solar journey through the Netherworld (see pp. 50–55).

During Hour 6 of the Book of Gates, as in the same hour in the Book of the Hidden Chamber, the sun god unites with his corpse in a Heliopolitan setting. Protecting this critical event are deities who restrain a serpent, avatar of Apep, in Register 1. The long body of the serpent is mimicked in the entwined ropes that emerge from the neck of the mummiform Aqen, each coil embodying an hour. The luminous union of *ba*-soul and corpse in this hour triggers a literal re-creation of time. The solar body—the "mystery of the great god"—is not depicted within Hour 6, but cloaked deities carry its constituent elements in Register 2 (for the elements of the solar corpse, compare also Hour 6 of the Book of the Hidden Chamber). Mummies in Register 3 rest atop a benevolent serpent, as the solar presence resurrects them, loosening their wrappings and causing them to arise from their biers. Although not depicted, the annotation to the final scene in Register 3 describes the fiery punishment of enemies.

The blessed dead—those provided with offerings and those who performed Maat—fill Register 1 of Hour 7. Their fate contrasts with that of the damned in Register 2 who are bound to jackal-headed staffs, the *wsr*-posts of Geb; the punishment of enemies in Hour 7 of the Book of Gates mirrors the destruction of Apep in Hour 7 of the Book of the Hidden Chamber. Register 3 again concerns itself with the provisioning of offerings, represented by enormous ears of grain that are to be harvested by sickle-wielding gods.

Register 1 of Hour 8 reveals two sets of deities carrying long ropes. The first rope "gives birth to the mysteries" of the solar god, while the second rope regenerates time. Register 2 resumes the concept of judgment that appears so prominently in the Judgment Hall of Osiris (Scene 33); in the speech of the Netherworldly council, the destruction of enemies is paired with the provisioning of Re (and by extension the blessed dead themselves). In Register 3, mummies rise up from their biers, praising the sun god as he in turn shines upon them. A council of judges completes Register 3.

Hour 9 juxtaposes the Island of Fire in Register 1 with the waters of Nun in Register 2. The *ba*-souls in the Island of Fire enjoy their provisions while praising the solar deity and proclaiming the dual fates of his elements: the *ba*-soul to the sky and his corpse to the earth. Drowning individuals in Register 2 are not being punished—instead, Re grants breath to those immersed in the creative Nun-waters.[10] As in many hours in the Book of Gates, Register 3 of Hour 9 is reserved for the punishment of the damned; this time their destruction comes from the mouth of a fire-breathing serpent. Horus tells the bound enemies of Osiris that they shall not exist—the ultimate fate of evil.

A complex series of figures fills Register 1 of Hour 10, several of which relate to the juxtaposition of opposites: a double-faced god embodies the reconciliation of Horus and Seth, while gods of Upper and Lower Egypt pull at slanting staffs. Ophidian forms dominate the remainder of Register 1, along with deities holding magical throw nets. Additional deities with throw nets stand before the solar bark in Register 2; they assist with the destruction of Apep who appears at the end of the register. In Register 3, groups of deities haul a serpent-bark, and the annotation describes the manifestation of Re in the eastern horizon of heaven, presaging his triumphant rise to start the new day.

Apep and his minions are bound yet again in Register 1 of Hour 11. As Apep is punished, Re sails by the manifestations of the evil serpent. In addition to Selket who binds Apep, the four sons of Horus subdue the "children of weakness." The focal point of Register 2 is a giant image of the face of the solar god, surrounded by protective deities. Register 3 has

---

10. The concept of "apotheosis by drowning" is discussed on p. 9 and n. 18.

depictions of the circumpolar stars, those "who do not know perishing," and the hour goddesses who assist with the hauling of the solar god. The final scene of Hour 11 consists of seven different gods. The annotations to each of these deities demonstrate their diverse functions in relation to the rising of the sun, including the opening of portals and calling to and assigning the celestial retinue of the solar god. While the solar eye takes up a place within the solar bark, the final deity, He Who Is upon His Throne, remains in his place, guarding the door to the cavern.

The final hour of the night emphasizes the number four, evocative of the corners of the cosmos, as quartets of gods participate in the final triumphant exit of the sun god from the Netherworld. In Register 1, groups of gods in Scenes 84, 85, and 86 represent personifications of the solar deity as forms of Osiris, Atum, and Horus (Zeidler 1999a, 345). As Re sails in Register 2, he passes by yet another depiction of a fettered Apep, who receives painful punishments at the hands of a divine Ennead bearing scepters and knives. The deities in Register 3 assist Re in various ways, and like Osiris, their corpses remain in the Netherworld while their *ba*-souls ascend with Re. The scenes in Register 3 of Hour 12 share several significant parallels with the texts that accompany the "divine birth" scenes of Hatshepsut and Amunhotep III (Zeidler 1999a, 369).

The Book of Gates concludes with a representation of the entirety of the solar journey.[11] As Nun, half-emerged from the primeval waters, lifts up the solar bark, a scarab beetle within the bark pushes a solar disk into the awaiting arms of Nut. Supporting Nut is an image of Osiris, curled around himself, embodying the circuit of the Netherwordly journey. Pairs of arms lifting up and receiving the solar disk—either attached to deities as in the Book of Gates or depicted as disembodied arms in the Books of the Creation of the Solar Disk and the Second Shrine of Tutankhamun—are a common motif in concluding scenes within the Netherworld Books.[12] The Book of Gates, like all of the Netherworld Books, provides a unique template for understanding the proper positions of the chthonic deities and how Re must navigate the gloomy underworld, defeating again and again

---

11. For the Concluding Scene and parallels in Third Intermediate period papyri, see Hornung 1980, 289–92.

12. Hornung 1981b; compare also the scene with arms flaking a mummy crowned with solar disks that serves as the concluding scene on sarcophagus decoration (New Kingdom through Late period) with scenes taken from the Book of Gates and the Books of the Creation of the Solar Disk (see p. 522).

his nemesis Apep. The Concluding Scene dispenses with any depictions of opposition, serving as both summary and magical confirmation of the daily solar journey and his ever-triumphant reemergence from the eastern horizon each day.

BOOK OF GATES

HOUR 1[13]

REGISTER 1 (PLATE 15)

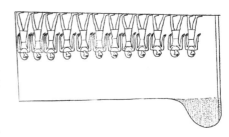

4.1. Scene 1. Twelve gods stride forward labeled "Gods of the Desert"; these gods are inverted in a desert mountain frame.

Those who came about from Re by means of his luminous eye, who came forth from his eye, to whom he commends the hidden place, from whom the people, gods, all mammals, all reptiles, which this great god created, are removed.[14] This god orders affairs for them, even after he ascends from the earth, which he created for his right eye.[15]

REGISTER 2 (PLATE 15)

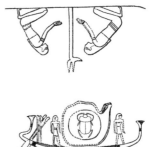

4.2. Scene 2. A solar bark contains a scarab within a multiple-coiled Encircling Serpent; the crew of the bark consists of two deities, "Divine Perception" and "Magic." Above the bark (and inverted with respect to the bark) is a jackal-headed staff with two kneeling deities, labeled "Netherworld" and "Desert."

---

13. The following scenes are all part of one larger tableau; for the entire image of Hour 1, see plate 15.

14. For the verb *stp* "to remove," see Manassa 2007a, 22–23.

15. The right eye is the solar disk (Zandee 1992, 41; Darnell 2004, 305–6); compare also the statement in the Hymn to the *Ba*'s of Amun from Hibis Temple: "O Amun, Ba inside his right-eye, within his solar-disk in heaven during the day" (translation of Klotz 2006, 55).

Re says to the desert: "Brighten, O desert—for you does that in which I am shine. Without the gods being able to remove your eye have people removed the filled (eye). Breath be to you, O you amongst whom I am. Light be to you, O ones of the forehall.[16] My luminous eye be to you, O you whose removing I have commanded, for whom everything is removed. From those upon the earth, those adorned with the fillet upon the desert, do I hide you."

These gods say: "As for this neck, it is the command of the great god, when he distinguishes his flesh. Come away to us, O one from whom we have come forth. Hail to the one in his disk, the great god, plentiful of manifestations." Their victuals are bread and beer.

Recitation:[17] it is Khepri who pacifies the *ba*-soul. The manifestations occupy the Great One.... He presents the head;[18] he offers the *udjat*-eye ... his every part. Khepri goes to rest within (them). Give the two siblings to him.[19] No sooner does the *ba*-soul go to rest than the *ba*-soul of Re shines. It is because the disk has gone to rest that the disk manifests.[20]

4.3. Scene 3. A ram-headed pole sits atop the mountain guarded by two gods, "Netherworld" and "Desert."

(TEXT A)[21] "Light be to you, on behalf of the One of the Forehall, so that he might rest among you. My luminous eye be to you, O you whose removal I have commanded, for whom everything is

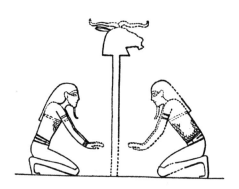

---

16. Reading the lotus flower as *ḥnt*—see Darnell 2004, 65–66 n. 137, and pp. 421–24 for the forehall.

17. Here begins an obscure and perturbated cryptographic text attested on the sarcophagus of Merneptah (Hornung 1979b, 6), a tentative translation of which is proposed here.

18. For the expression *dỉ=f tp*, see *WÄS* 5:268.6–8.

19. The "two siblings" may be a reference to Shu and Tefnut, although the translation of this passage remains speculative.

20. The cryptographic text here exploits visual cryptography to show the *perpetuum mobile* of the solar journey, for which see Derchain 1975–1976.

21. The following translation follows the reconstruction presented by Hornung 1980, 39–41; compare Zeidler 1999a, 16–19.

removed. It is from those who are upon the earth that I hide you, O fillet-adorned ones upon the desert."

These gods say: "As for this head, it is the command of the great god, who distinguishes his flesh."

(TEXT B) Those who are in the desert say to Re: "O one who hides us—come to us! O, Re, from whom we come forth. Hail to the one in his disk, the great god, plentiful of manifestations."

Their victuals are bread, their beer of *djeseret*-drink[22]; their libations are water.[23] The one who offers to the desert and gives victuals to those who are in it is one of these who are in it.

REGISTER 3 (PLATE 15)

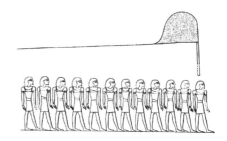

4.4. Scene 4. A desert mountain frames this scene and contains twelve gods labeled "Gods of the Western Desert." The annotation is identical to Hour 1, Register 1, Scene 1.

DOORWAY 1 (PLATE 16)

4.5. Doorway 1. Depicted as a single door leaf with a vertically oriented serpent, the first gate is the only doorway in the Book of Gates to be shown in an abbreviated fashion, because the entire Hour 1 is actually the doorway of the western horizon. The door is labeled "Watcher of the Desert."

He exists at this door so that he may open to Re. Divine Perception (says) to the Watcher of the Desert: "Open your gate to Re, swing open your door-leaf to He of the Horizon." The Hidden Chamber is in darkness, until the manifestations of this god manifest. Then this door seals after this god enters; those in their desert wail when they hear this door-leaf slam shut.

---

22. A fermented drink that appears to be a type of beer (Wilson 1997, 1248).

23. Water libations are ubiquitous in offering statements within the Book of Gates, mirroring their significance in Egyptian funerary practice and its abundance in ritual contexts; among the many possible studies, see Delia 1992; Bommas 2005.

HOUR 2

REGISTER 1 (PLATE 16)

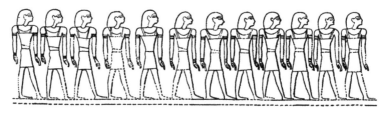

4.6. Scene 5. Twelve striding male figures are labeled "Those (Endowed with) Offerings, Who Adore Re."[24]

Those who praise Re upon the earth, and who enchant Apep, and who offer their offerings and thurify to their gods. They are behind their offering provisions, having use of their libations, receiving their victuals, making a meal from their offerings at the doorway Hidden of Name.[25]

Their victuals are at this doorway, and their offerings are with the one who is in it. Re says to them: "Yours are your offerings. You shall control your libations. Your *ba*-souls have not been removed, your victuals have not been destroyed. You are they who adore me at my time,[26] and who bind[27] Apep for me."

---

24. In addition to the annotation to Scene 5, the sarcophagus of Merneptah also adds a litany that associates the deceased king with the Netherworldly deities (Maystre and Piankoff 1939, 42–43; see also Hornung 1980, 47; Zeidler 1999a, 25).

25. Known primarily as an epithet of the god Amun, "Hidden of Name" can appear in conjunction with several other deities (*LGG* 1:343–47); for the significance of the epithet, see Assmann 1995, 137–39.

26. These times would be the morning, midday, and evening manifestation forms (Assmann 1969, 43–44, 333–39).

27. For the writing of the coil for *nwh*, see "*nwḥ*," *WÄS*, 2:223.14–15; the quail chick is a false substitution for the coil. For binding Apep in the Book of Gates, compare Hour 12, Register 2, Scene 89—the deities fly up in adoration to Re holding the bonds, a combination of concepts found here.

4.7. Scene 6. Twelve striding male figures are labeled "Those of Maat, who are in the Netherworld."

Those who spoke Maat on earth, who did not approach impropriety—to this doorway are they called. They shall live from Maat, their libations in their waterway.

Re says to them: "Maat be to you, that you may live. Your offerings be to you because of Maat. You shall control your libation—those (whose) water is as fire against those who belong to evil, and those who are assigned to the sickle-wielders."[28]

These deities say to Re: "Re shall endure because of his disk,[29] having control of the shrine and that in which it is. The Encircling Serpent[30] is for his protection. The torches of He of the Horizon shall release those who are in the doorway of the Mysterious Place."[31]

The one who gives victuals to them is one who occupies a place in their cavern.

---

28. This passage refers to those who have done evil on earth and are therefore assigned to be punished by sickle-wielding deities (Darnell 2004, 350–51). For sickles put to agricultural use within the Book of Gates, compare Hour 7, Register 3 of the Book of Gates (p. 296).

29. The disk appears prominently in Hour 1 of the Book of Gates and is the chief representation of the solar deity in the Book of Caverns and Books of the Creation of the Solar Disk (for the disk, see pp. 5–6).

30. For the role of the Encircling Serpent (Mehen), see pp. 13–14.

31. The "torches" relate to the solar uraei, whose illuminating qualities, release the blessed dead from the bounds of darkness (Hornung 1980, 51–52).

REGISTER 2 (PLATE 16)

4.8. Scene 7. In this hour, the solar bark takes on its canonical form in the Book of Gates: a ram-headed solar deity labeled "Flesh of Re" appearing within a shrine surrounded by a multi-coiled serpent called "Encircling Serpent." The crew of the bark consists of two male deities, "Divine Perception" and "Magic." In Hour 2, four male figures labeled "Netherworld Dwellers" haul the solar bark. Facing the haulers are fourteen deities, the first seven of which are labeled: "Grain," "The One without an Arm," "Ram," "Horus," "Understanding," "Khnum," and "Child."[32] The next six gods have hieroglyphs interspersed that write "Gods who are in the entering," while the fourteenth god, who holds a staff, is not labeled.

Navigating by this great god on the paths of the Netherworld; hauling this god by the Netherworldly gods, in order to distribute what is in the earth and care for those who are in it; to judge matters in the West, and to distinguish the great from the small[33] amongst the gods who are in the Netherworld; to assign the *akh*-spirits to their places and the dead to their judgment; in order to destroy the corpses of those to be punished and to restrain [the] *ba*[-souls of the damned[34]].

Re says: "O, look, I have tied on the fillet, having already exercised power over the shrine which is in the earth. Divine Perception and Magic join with me,[35] in order to take care of you and in order to bring about your functions for you.[36] You are satisfied with the Desert."[37]

---

32. The name *sḏ.ty* is also that of the sun god Re in the Book of Adoring Re in the West, Address 61 (p. 97, with references to parallels in other Netherworld Books).

33. For the complexities of this statement, see Zeidler 1999a, 35 n. 1; the translation follows Quack 2000, 544.

34. Hornung 1980, 60–61 n. 7 observes that the empty space following the phrase *ḥnr bꜣ* represents the damned themselves, through a representation of nothingness; see also Hornung 1994a (citing this passage on p. 133).

35. These two deities ride with the solar deity in his bark through most of the hours of the Book of Gates.

36. The text that follows is obscure and possibly perturbated. The following translation attempts to understand the text in the order in which it is written. An

His breath is the offerings of the one who is there.[38] He will not seal their mouth(s). The dead will not enter after you; divine provisions belong to you.

These gods say to Re: "Darkness is in the paths of the Netherworld—open the sealed gates, O opener of the earth, whom the gods have hauled, who created himself."

Their victuals are offering gifts; their beer is their libation. The one who gives victuals to them is one in Igeret, in the West.

REGISTER 3 (PLATE 16)

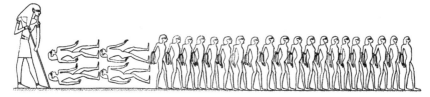

4.9. Scene 8. A god labeled "Atum," leaning on a staff, appears before four gods lying on their backs, "Weary Ones."[39] Twenty bound figures walk in front of these figures with hieroglyphs interspersed, writing "Desert Dwellers of the broad hall of Re, who cry out on earth for Re, those who have summoned evil for the one who is in the egg, who have hurled charges and who have murmured against He of the Horizon."

What Atum does for Re—making the gods effective, adoring the *ba*-soul, placing evil amongst his enemies.

---

alternative translation, reconstructing the text by rearranging the order of the signs, could read as follows (Hornung and Abt 2014, 42): "He does not cut breath from you, as well as the offerings which are in (this hour). The damned do not enter after you, to you belongs what is due to the deities." Compare also Zeidler 1999a, 37; Wiebach-Koepke 2003a, 225.

37. Desert is here a personified deity (see "*Smyt*," *LGG* 6:308; Darnell 2004, 52).

38. "The one who is there" referring to a deceased individual; in the Book of the Hidden Chamber, Hour 3, Register 3, the deities live through the calls of the solar god (Hornung 1987b, 302–3; p. 163 above). For the life-giving properties of breath, compare also p. 6 n. 7; as Assmann 2001a, 4, notes: "One of the meanings of the word hu is 'abundance, plenitude'; the concepts of plenitude and speech were closely connected."

39. For the potential cosmic significance of these figures, see Hornung 1980, 66–67.

(He says:) "As my father Re is justified against you, so am I justified against you. I am the son who came forth from his father; I am the father who came forth from his son. As you will be roped so will you be bound with stout ropes. With the result that your arms cannot open have I decreed against you that you should be bound. As Re grows effective against you, so does his *ba*-soul grow skilled against you; as my father grows powerful against you, so does his *ba*-soul grow strong against you. Your evil be to you, your slaughter be to you, your punishment be to you. To evil are you summoned; before Re who smites have you (already) been damned.[40] Your testimonies be to you, for they are evil; your utterances be to you, for they are bad. Before my father have you been damned. You are the ones who have done evil, who have committed slaughter in the great broad hall. Your corpses be to beheading; your *ba*-souls to not being—those who will not see Re in his visible forms, when he travels in the Mysterious Place. Hail Re, may you be strong, O Re! May your enemies be to the Place of Destruction!"

DOORWAY 2 (PLATE 17)

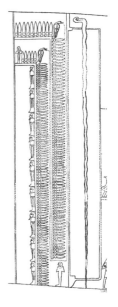

4.10. Doorway 2. The doorway following Hour 2 takes on its canonical form in the Book of Gates. A door-leaf with a vertically oriented serpent appears before two nested walls crowned with *ḫkr*-friezes along their edges and spitting uraei at their corners. The serpent bears the annotation: "Winding One. That he is at this door-leaf is so he might open to Re." Each uraeus is labeled "For Re she casts fire." A standing mummy appears below the first wall and atop the second wall; the upper mummiform figure is called "Swallower of the Dead, bending his arm for Re," while the lower is labeled "Drinker of Blood, bending his arm for Re." Inside the first wall are nine mummies standing end-to-end, named "Second Ennead." The doorway of this hour is named "Piercing of Embers."

Reaching this doorway by this great god; entering this doorway. The gods who are in it praise this great god.

---

40. Here a *sḏmnw/ny* form, discussed by Edel 1959, 30–37; Baumann 1998, 436–38; see also Stauder 2014, 195–98.

"As the doorway has been opened for He of the Horizon, so the door-leaf has been swung open for He Who is in the Sky. Hail, come away, O you traveler who traverses the West."

Divine Perception (says) to the Winding One: "Open your gate to Re, swing open your door-leaf to He of the Horizon."

He illumines the utter darkness, casting light into the Hidden Chamber. Then this door seals after this great god enters; those who are in the doorway wail, when they hear this door-leaf slam shut.

HOUR 3

REGISTER 1 (PLATE 17)

4.11. Scene 9. Twelve mummies, each within a vaulted shrine with two open door-leaves, stand beneath a large serpent. Hieroglyphs interspersed among the figures label them "Sanctified Gods Who Are in the Netherworld," and in the annotation the serpent is called "Flaming One." The label to the gods is also read as the first words of the annotation.

Sanctified Gods Who Are in the Netherworld, in their shrines, flesh of the god. Flaming One guards their shrines. Re says to them: "Opening be to your shrines, that my light may enter into your gloom. Mourning, with your shrines sealed over you did I find you. But (now) I give breath to your nostrils, and commend to you your effectiveness."

They say to Re: "Hail, Re, come to us, O great god, who does not know his perishing,[41] whom those who are in front of him and those in his following, the retinue, greet. How jubilant is Re, when he crosses the land, the great god, as he passes by the Mysterious Place."

---

41. A reference to the *ỉḫm.w-sk* "those who do not know perishing," the name of the circumpolar stars; on these astronomical beings, see below Book of Gates, Hour 11, Register 3, Scene 79 (pp. 322–23).

Their victuals consist of bread, their beer of *djeseret*-drink, their libations of water. The one who offers to them is one who lives on what they and the Flaming One live. Then their doors seal over them, after this god passes by. They wail when they hear them (the doors) slam shut over them.

4.12. Scene 10. Twelve wrapped human-headed figures appear atop the "Lake of Fire"; in between the divine images are large ears of barley. The wrapped human-headed figures are labeled "Gods Who Are at the Lake of Fire."

That lake exists in the Netherworld, surrounded with these gods. In linen coverings[42] do they exist, their heads being uncovered. This waterway is filled with ears of barley, the water of this waterway being fire.[43] When they see its water and they smell the stench which is in it, the birds fly away.

Re says to them: "Your requirements be to the gods, consisting of the wheat of your lake. Uncovering be to your heads; mystery be to your members; breath be to your noses. Your offerings be to you—barley; victuals of your lake be to you, its water be to you, without its heat against you, without its blasting flame being against your corpses."

They say to Re: "Come to us, O one who traverses in his bark, for whom his eye sets fire to the taper, that his luminous eye might then illuminate the Netherworld Dwellers. Hail, may you ascend, O one who is beneficial to us, O great god who casts fire by means of his eye."

Their victuals consist of barley bread, their beer of barley, their libation of water. The one who gives to them food is a possessor of a sickle(?)[44] in this lake.

42. The term for "linen coverings" is written differently in each version (Hornung 1980, 82 n. 3; perhaps this is the result of a confusion in a hieratic original; see Zeidler 1999a, 53). For the form in the tomb of Horemhab, ꜣw, note Hannig 2003, 260; Hannig 2006a, 484; Wilson 1997, 135–37.

43. For the dual nature of the Lake of Fire, see above, pp. 44–45.

44. Alternatively "ears (of grain)" (Zeidler 1999a, 57 n. 1).

REGISTER 2 (PLATE 17)

4.13 (left side), 4.14 (right side). Scene 11. The solar bark (see Scene 7) is hauled by two sets of four male figures, each labeled "Netherworld Dwellers." In the space between the two groups of haulers, the tow-rope enters the mouth of a long pole with bulls' heads on either end, which is called "Bark of the Earth." The pole rests on the shoulders of seven mummiform deities labeled "Those Who Carry." Atop the "Bark of the Earth" are two bulls, each facing outwards, and seven seated mummiform gods.

Hauling this great god by the Netherworldly gods. Then this great god reaches the Bark of the Earth, the boat of the gods.

Re says to them: "O gods bearing the Bark of the Earth, those who carry the boat of the Netherworld—uplifting be to your visible forms, light be to your boat, so that what is in it might become sanctified. The Bark of the Earth has turned back to me—it is the boat of the Netherworld that lifts up my visible forms. Behold me passing by the Mysterious Place in order to care for those who are therein."

The earth quakes; the earth quakes;[45] as the *ba*-soul grows strong so the double bull bellows in pleasure.[46] Into what he has created does the god go to rest.

These gods say to Re: "As Re grows strong, so his ram-form[47] becomes skilled, together with Earth.[48] May his gods grow strong for Re, he having

---

45. The movement of the earth as an indication of divine epiphany can be traced as far back as the Pyramid Texts, such as the introductory passage of the Cannibal Hymn (Eyre 2002, 76–78), which is also juxtaposed with the appearance of the king as a bull.

46. For the verb *nim* and its parallels in the Netherworld Books, see the commentary of the Book of Adoring Re in the West (p. 110 and n. 105); the sound of the bellow appears to precede a moment of creation, and in other Egyptian religious texts, a strong correlation exists between sound and creation (see Darnell 2013, 37–40).

47. In the tombs of Horemhab, Ramesses I, and Seti I sarcophagus, the *b₃* here is written specifically as a "ram form" rather than a "*b₃*-soul," a pun on the ram-headed solar deity.

48. This appears to be a masculine personification of the Netherworld (Hornung

gone to rest. May the boat of the Netherworld rejoice, may this bark praise."

They wail after Re passes by them. Their offerings are fresh plants. The one who offers to them their offerings is one who hears the voices of those who are (in the Netherworld).

4.15. Scene 12. Four standing mummiform figures with their arms crossed over their chests are
labeled "Wrapped Ones[49] of the Earth."

Hauling this great god by the Netherworld
Dwellers in the sanctified bark which is in the
earth. Issuing commands to the Wrapped Ones of the Earth, those hidden
of arm(s): "Your provisions be to you, O Wrapped Ones of the Earth. The
roar of Foremost of His (Offering) Leg[50]—uncover your heads, hide your
arms; breath be to your noses, loosening be to your bandages. May you
control your victuals, after you have gone to rest in what I have created."

Their victuals are bread; their beer is *djeseret*-drink; their libation is
water. The one who gives them their victuals is with those shining of clothing in the Netherworld.

REGISTER 3 (PLATE 17)

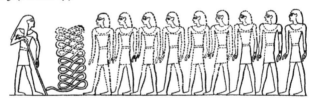

4.16. Scene 13. A god "Atum," leaning on a staff, faces a multicoiled serpent labeled
"Apep." Nine striding figures called "Council that Drives Back Apep" follow.

That which Atum has done for Re: glorifying the deity and overthrow-
ing the rebel. (Atum says): "As you have been overthrown, such that you

---

1980, 88), parallel to the feminine Mysterious One (Shetayt) who is herself placed
opposite the giant Osiris in Division 5 of the Book of Caverns (see p. 401).

    49. For the term *wtȝ.w*, see Zeidler 1999a, 65.

    50. This deity also appears as a mummy wearing a white crown in the Book of the
Hidden Chamber, Hour 10, Register 1, Scene 104, deity no. 717 (p. 221).

cannot stand, so have you been enchanted, such that you cannot find yourself. As my father becomes justified against you so do I become justified against you. As I repel you for Re so do I punish you for He of the Horizon."

So they say, the Ennead of Re, driving back Apep from Re: "As your head is severed, Apep, so are the coils cut up. You shall not go near the bark of Re, you shall not go down to the divine boat. The blasting flame of the Mysterious Place will go forth against you. We damn you to your destruction."

That they live is from the victuals of Re and the offerings of Foremost of the Westerners. The one who makes offerings to them upon the earth and who pours libations for them is a possessor of victuals before Re.

4.17. Scene 14. A god, "Atum," leaning on a staff, faces nine deities holding scepters labeled "Lords of Provisions."

Atum says to these gods: "O gods who bear life and dominion, who support themselves upon their *djam*-scepters, who repel the rebel from He of the Horizon, who commit slaughter to the flesh of Evil of Character."

So they say, these gods, as they enchant Apep: "As the earth opens to Re, so the earth seals to Apep. O Netherworld Dwellers of Foremost of the Westerners, those who are in the Mysterious Place—adore Re and cast out his enemies, O you who protect the Great One from the flesh of the Evil One. Hail, fall to Re, O enemy of Re."

They live from the victuals of Re, from the offerings of Foremost of the Westerners. The one who makes offerings to them upon the earth and who pours libation for them is one who is justified in the West, sanctified of shoulder in the hidden place. They wail for Re, they mourn for the great god, after he passes by them. No sooner does he cross over than darkness conceals them, as their cavern seals over them.

DOORWAY 3 (PLATE 18)

4.18. Doorway 3. The gate appears in its standard form (see p. 264), with the name "Mistress of Nourishment." The uraei are each labeled "For Re she casts fire." The upper mummiform deity is named "Earthquake,[51] bending his arms for Re"; the lower mummiform deity is called similarly "Trembling of the Earth, bending his arms for Re." The Ennead of mummies is labeled "Third Ennead, amongst whom is the great god." The serpent of the door-leaf is named "One with a Stinger."

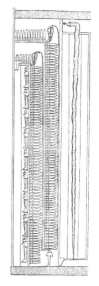

Arrival by this great god at this doorway, entering into this doorway. The gods who are in it extol this great god. "As you have opened the earth, so have you revealed the Netherworld. O One of the Sky, you uncover our gloom. Hail, Re, come away to us."

That he (One with a Stinger) exists at this door is that he might open to Re. Divine Perception speaks to One with a Stinger: "Open your gate to Re, swing open your door-leaf to He of the Horizon."

He illumines the utter darkness and casts light into the hidden chamber. Then this door seals after this great god enters. Those who are in this portal wail when they hear this door slam shut.

HOUR 4

REGISTER 1 (PLATE 18)

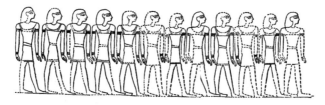

4.19. Scene 15. Twelve striding gods are labeled "Gods Who Have Passed On to Their *Ka*-Spirits."

---

51. The names of the two mummiform deities within Doorway 3 are reminiscent of the passage in Hour 3, Register 2, Scene 11: "the earth quakes, the earth quakes" (see p. 267).

Those who have passed on to their *ka*-spirits, being purified by means of absolution,[52] cut off in their lifetime, who conduct offerings to his place.

Re says to them: "Your provisions be to you, O gods, from your offerings. May you guide your *ka*-spirits to you, that you might be at peace. Your enemies have been destroyed, without being. Your *akh*-spirits shall be to their thrones, the *ba*-souls be to the seal."[53]

They say to Re: "Ovation be to you, O Re, He of the Horizon. Jubilation be to you, O skilled *ba*-soul in the earth. Jubilation be to you, cyclical eternity, lord of years, linear eternity, without extinguishing."

Their victuals are offerings; their libations are water. They wail when they hear their doors slam shut over them. The one who gives to them their victuals is one who hauls (the ship) She Who Grasps the *Ba*-souls.

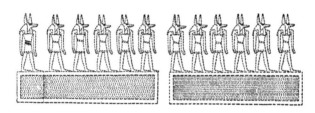

4.20. Scene 16. Twelve gods with jackal heads—"Jackals Who Are at the Lake of Life"—stand atop a lake called the "Lake of Life."

They are in the circumference of this lake. The *ba*-souls of the dead cannot ascend to it because what exists in it is sanctified.

Re says to them: "Your provisions be to you, O gods in this lake. In your lake shall you guard your lives. Your offerings consist of what the jackals who rest at the end of your lake guard."

---

52. Following Zeidler 1999a, 81; to the study of Morschauser 1988 cited by Zeilder, one can add Menu 1998.

53. The reference to a "seal" here is obscure. For a possible parallel to the seal, see Coffin Texts Spell 657 (CT 6.278q): "The scroll comes forth from the House of Re, the seal of the House of Thoth; I have recalled all the magic that was within me"; in this spell the papyrus scroll and a seal facilitate the deceased's access to magical power. The Book of Gates passage appears similarly to relate to elements of the deceased acquiring physical (throne) and conceptual (sealing/documents thereby sealed) power in the afterlife.

They say to Re: "May you be pure, Re, in your sacred lake, in which you purify the gods and to which the *ba*-souls of the dead do not ascend, which you yourself—O He of the Horizon—have commanded."

Their victuals are bread; their beer is *djeseret*-drink; their libation is wine. They wail when they hear their doors slam shut over them. The one who gives their victuals to them is a possessor of a lunar monument(?)[54] among them in the circumference of this lake.

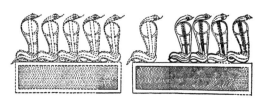

4.21. Scene 17. Ten uraei, called "Living Uraei," appear above a lake labeled "Lake of the Uraei."

They speak when Re reaches them. The *ba*-souls retreat and the shades are destroyed when the voices of the uraei are heard.

Re says to them: "Your provisions be to you, O uraei in that lake which you guard. Your flames are blasting flames in my enemies; your fire is in those who do evil against me. Hail to you, uraei!"

They say to Re: "Come away to us, one who traverses Tatenen. Come away to us, one who protects himself,[55] for you are the luminous one of the Netherworld, the great god in the Mysterious Place."

They wail after Re passes over them.

---

54. The reading of this passage is problematic. Wente 1982, 174 tentatively suggests "quota of water," while Hornung and Abt (2014, 109) have "a master of the rest of them." If the reading is compounded with *i'ḥ*, as the moon-sign suggests, this may relate to Osiris as a lunar deity (Smith 2006, 224–25). The word *ḏ3* here with determinatives of a stela or obelisk suggests some sort of monument or marker; this otherwise unattested *ḏ3*-monument/marker might relate to the attested *ḏ3*-measurement, which by the time of the New Kingdom appears to be 1/64 of an oipe (Pommerening 2005, 239–61), itself the missing portion of the eye of Horus, magically supplied by Thoth (which may play a role in the Judgment Hall of Osiris, Book of Gates Scene 33—Manassa 2006, 137–41).

55. The solar god who "protects" himself also "greets himself," like the giant unified Re-Osiris does in the root of the Eastern Horizon. See Darnell 2004, 346–47 (see also p. 6 n. 8).

REGISTER 2 (PLATE 18)

4.22. Scene 18. The solar bark (see Scene 7) is hauled by four male figures labeled "Netherworld Dwellers."

Hauling this great god by the Netherworld Dwellers, sailing in the Mysterious Place, taking care of those who are in it.

(Re says:) "May you haul me, O Netherworld Dwellers, whom I have beheld. It is I who made you. Stretch forth your arms and haul me with them. Retreat to the eastern part of the sky, to the places which lift up the one who made it, that mysterious mountain. This light be to those surrounded by deities, when they receive[56] me as I go forth from this, (namely) from the Mysterious Place. Haul me, while I take care of you, at the doorway She Who Covers the Netherworld Dwellers."

4.23. Scene 19. Nine mummies called "Gods Who Follow Osiris, Who Are in Their Pits," lie in separate compartments within a large structure with cavetto cornice.

Re says to them: "Look at me, O gods! Be quiet[57] for me, O ones who are in your pits. Raise yourselves, O gods. I order affairs for you, that you

---

56. Creating a pun on *šzp* "to receive" and *šzp* "to shine," coordinating with the word *špw* "light" in the earlier sentence.

57. Although Hornung 1980, 110 reads "gewalttätig sein" (so "*ỉd*," *WÄS*, 1:152.4), the verb *ỉdỉ* appears to be the same as that occurring in Coffin Texts Spell 75 (CT 1.332–33; Willems 1996, 476, n. x), meaning "to be quiet" (Hannig 2003, 240–41; 2006a, 451). The Coffin Text passage makes clear that *ỉdỉ* is parallel to *grḥ* "to be silent," occurring in a context in which the deceased will relate what he desires of his manifestations, and the deities are not to seek to know more. Meeks 1998b, 257 no. 78.0574

should be within your pits. It is you who protect the *ba*-souls, living on their putrefaction, breathing from their rot.[58] Raise yourselves to my disk, travel rightly to my dawning light. May your provisions belong to you in the Netherworld, from these which I have commanded for you."

Their victuals are flesh; their beer is *djeseret*-drink; their libation is water. They wail after they hear their doors slam shut over them.

4.24. Scene 20: This scene consists of two ramps, half of which consists of water, angling up towards a pit containing a multi-coiled serpent. Six goddesses stand on each ramp, these twelve figures being "Hour Goddesses Who Are in the Netherworld"; an additional short text associated with the goddesses is "They stand at their lake. They rightly guide Re upon their banks." The multi-coiled serpent bears a name and short text: "She Who Exorcises, who bears twelve serpents, who become destroyed before her, swallowed on the part of the Hour Goddesses."

Re says to them: "Hear, O Hour Goddesses, what has been called out to you: Spend for yourselves (the time) in which you are;[59] occupy for yourselves your doorway. Your fronts be to the darkness, your backs be to the light. Your station is (that of) She Who Exorcises, and you shall live from what comes forth from her. Your provisions are in the Netherworld, and you will swallow the offspring of She Who Exorcises, and destroy what comes forth from her. May you guide me—it is I who bore you; that I have acted is according to my greeting. May you go to rest, O my hours."

Their victuals are bread; their beer is *djeseret*-drink; their libation is water. The one who gives victuals to them is one who goes forth in front of the *akh*-spirits.

---

suggests that "*id*," *WÄS* 1:152.4 belongs with "*idj*," *WÄS* 1:152.5–6, "to be refreshed," which seems unlikely in both the Book of Gates and Coffin Text examples.

58. Compare the Book of Caverns, Division 3, Registers 2–3, Scene 32: "one through the breathing of whose stench of putrefaction those who are in the West live" (p. 375) For the life-giving properties of putrefaction, see Dobbin-Bennett 2014.

59. Commentary to this scene as the re-creation of time appears in chapter 1, pp. 42–43.

REGISTER 3 (PLATE 18)

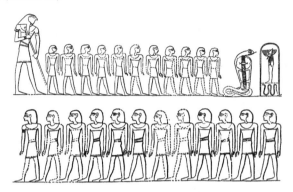

4.25 (left side), 4.26 (right side). Scene 21. Osiris, standing atop a serpent,[60] within a vaulted shrine[61] forms the focus of this scene; Osiris is labeled with his epithet "Foremost of the Westerners." Before Osiris is an uraeus called "Flaming One." Eleven deities stand before the shrine of Osiris labeled "Gods Who Appertain to the Fillet";[62] twelve gods behind the shrine are labeled "Gods Who are Behind the Shrine." At the far edge of the scene is a falcon-headed deity, "Horus," leaning on a staff.

That which Horus did for his father Osiris—glorying him, restoring to him the fillet.

(Horus says:) "As my heart travels south before my father, so my heart travels rightly, O my father. As I protect you from those who would act against you, so I glorify you by means of your possessions. Power be to

---

60. The anonymous serpent has been variously interpreted as a noxious manifestation of Seth (Niwiński 1989b, 312–14) or more likely as a protective serpent (based on parallels with Osiris in a shrine surrounded by guardian serpents in the Book of Caverns, Division 3, Register 1, Scene 29—see pp. 370–71).

61. Although interpreted as a *nb*-basket behind the head of Osiris in the Ramesses VI version, the painted image in the tomb of Ramses I (and later tombs) shows Osiris to be standing in a shrine with the background divided between a white upper portion and a red lower portion; the curved dividing line between the two colors corresponds to the base of the *nb*-basket in the Ramesses VI exemplar. The red coloration appears to represent a shroud, and such a depiction also appears in the tomb of Seti I (in a niche representation that is not part of one of the Netherworld Books)—Hornung and Burton 1991, 228 (fig. 164).

62. On the sarcophagus of Tjaihorpata (CGAE 29306), these gods are labeled: "Gods Who Pertain to Horus" (Manassa 2007b, pl. 224); the Horus falcon also appears to label the falcon-headed god at the end of the register.

you, Osiris; lifting up[63] be to you, Foremost of the Westerners, your provisions be to you, ruler of the Netherworld, high of visible forms in the Mysterious Place. The *akh*-spirits belong to fear of you, the dead to awe of you, restoration to your fillet. I am your son Horus. I reckon what is disloyal therein."[64]

These gods say <to> Foremost of the Westerners: "May you be high, one of the Netherworld; may you be strong, Foremost of the Westerners. Your son Horus restores your fillet, glorifies you, and punishes your enemies. Leaping be to you, and rejoicing be to your two arms,[65] Osiris, Foremost of the Westerners."

Foremost of the Westerners says: "Come to me, O my son Horus, protect me from those who would act against me, and commend them to the Chief of Destruction—he it is who guards the fire pits."

Horus says to these deities behind the shrine: "To me shall you be reckoned, gods who are in the following of Foremost of the Westerners. You shall stand still and not retreat; you shall become powerful. Come, so that from the bread of Divine Utterance and the beer of Maat will you be fed. From what my father lives will you live. Your provisions are in the Mysterious Place. Around the shrine, as Re commands, do you exist. Though it is he who provides for you, I call out to you."

Their victuals are bread; their beer is *djeseret*-drink; their libations are water. The one who gives them their victuals is one who belongs to the meals in the shrine.

4.27. Scene 22: Four deities, labeled "Those over Their Fire Pits," guard tall fire pits. A deity at the end of the register, holding an ankh-sign and was-scepter, is named "Chief of Destruction."

Horus says to these gods: "That you have taken hold of the enemies of my father, whom you have snatched up to your fire pits, is because of these pains which you have inflicted on the Great One[66]—whom one found,

---

63. For the term *bwꜣ*, see Wilson 1997, 314.
64. Hornung and Abt 2014, 129 translates "I repair the damage in it."
65. For an analysis of the verbs in this passage, see Darnell 2004, 297 n. 104.
66. An allusion to the murder of Osiris (Zeidler 1999a, 109 n. 3).

the one who bore me. Your provisions be to you in the Netherworld, that the fire pits and those of the flames be protected, as Re has commanded. Though it is he who provides for you, I call out to you. That this god exists is standing atop these fire pits."

DOORWAY 4 (PLATE 19)

4.28. Doorway 4. This doorway (see p. 264), called "One Who is Made," is associated with two jackal-headed (rather than human) mummiform figures. The upper jackal is called "Swallower,[67] bending his arms for Re," while the lower is labeled "He Who Draws Near,[68] bending his arms for Re." Each uraeus is labeled "For Re she casts fire." The nine mummies are called the "Fourth Ennead." The serpent in the door-leaf is named "Burning of Face."

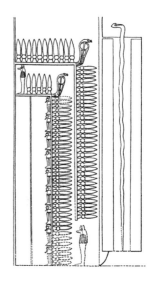

Arrival by this great god at this doorway, entering into this doorway. This great god is extolled by the gods who are in it. "As our door-leaves have been opened, so our door-ways have been swung open for Re-Horakhty. Hail Re, come away to us, O great god, lord of mysteries." As for Burning of Face—that he exists is at this door, so that he might open to Re.

Divine Perception speaks to Burning of Face: "Open your gate to Re, swing open your door-leaf to He of the Horizon."

He illumines the utter darkness and casts light into the Hidden Chamber. Then this door seals after this great god enters. Those who are in this portal wail when they hear this door slam shut.

---

67. Compare the jackal-headed figure in Scene 33 labeled (in cryptographic text): "Anubis, as he swallows his father" (p. 285).

68. For the name Tekemy see Darnell 2004, 661–63; see also p. 561 n. 57.

HOUR 5

REGISTER 1 (PLATE 19)

4.29. Scene 23. Twelve male figures, slightly bent at the waist with their arms before them, stride forward. They are named "Those Who Make Ovation, Who Are in the Netherworld."

They are making ovation for Re in the West, and elevating Horakhty—those who have come to know Re who are upon the earth,[69] those who have presented to him their offerings from their places while their *akh*-spirits were at the Sacred Place of the West.

They say to Re: "Welcome, Re, as you ascend to the Netherworld. Ovation be to you, as you enter the sanctity in the Encircling Serpent."

Re says to them: "Offerings be to you, O you of offerings. Even while I shine in the eastern part of the sky, and while I set in the columned sanctuary of my eye, I have become content with what you have done for me."

Their victuals are offerings of Re; their beer is his *djeseret*-drink; their libation is water. The one who offers to them upon the earth is one given praise before Re in the west.

4.30. Scene 24. Twelve male figures carrying a coiled rope are labeled "Those Who Carry the Measuring Rope in the Fields of the Netherworld."

O you who carry the measuring rope in the West, who assign cultivated land to the *akh*-spirits—receive the measuring rope, take up the prepara-

---

69. The text here implies that these worshippers are some sort of transcendental hypostases of "terrestrial" worshippers, so those not yet dead but who have entered the other world by means of *rḥw*-knowledge (for "mysticism" in the ancient Egyptian Netherworld Books, see pp. 36–37).

tion of the cultivated land for the Westerners. Their *akh*-spirits are at your places, the gods are at your seats. The *akh*-spirits of the divine one are content. The field of the *akh*-spirit is reckoned by means of what is in the measuring rope. You will be proper for those who exist, and you will not be proper for the nonexistent.

They say to Re: "The measuring rope will be proper in the West, so that Re may be content with the preparation. Your provisions be to you, O gods, your portions be to you, O *akh*-spirits, since Re is making your cultivated land, and commands to you the parcels in which you are. Hail, let He of the Horizon travel—behold, the gods are content with their provisions, the *akh*-spiritis are content with their portions."

Their victuals are in the Fields of Reeds, their offerings being what comes forth therefrom. The one who offers to them on earth is in this cultivated land of the Field of Reeds.

———

4.31. Scene 25. Four gods stride forward carrying *was*-scepters; they are labeled "Chiefs of the Measuring Rope in the West."

Re says to them: "Sanctification be to you, you who lay out the land-plots, chiefs of the measuring rope in the West. Establish the cultivated land which has been given to the gods and to the *akh*-spirits, they who belong to the preparation (of fields) in the Field of Reeds. It is they who give cultivated land and parcels to the gods and to the *akh*-spirits, those who are in the Netherworld."

Their victuals are in the Field of Reeds, their offerings consisting of what comes forth from it.

REGISTER 2 (PLATE 19)

4.32. Scene 26. The solar bark (see Scene 7) is hauled by four male figures labeled "Netherworld Dwellers."

Hauling this great god by the Netherworld Dwellers, sailing in the Mysterious Place.

(Re says): "May you haul for me, O Netherworld Dwellers; may you make ovation for me, O you foremost of the stars. Strength be to your ropes, that you may haul me with them; let your arms be strong. Running be to your strides; glorification be to your *ba*-souls; power be to your hearts, so that you may open the good path to the caverns, mysterious of contents."

4.33. Scene 27. Nine mummiform gods with their arms hidden carry a serpent with a coil between each figure. The deities are labeled "Those Who Carry the Slithering One."

They exist carrying this serpent, whom they seize when Re approaches them, in order that he may go to rest in Mistress of the Lifetime.[70] Without it being able to pass by it (the doorway) is this serpent restrained from it.

Re says to them: "Take hold of the Slithering One![71] Do not give him the path, so that I may pass by you. Mystery be to your arms, destruction be to what you guard. As you guard that my manifestations manifest,[72] so you bind that my glorifications come about."

---

70. This is the name of the Doorway 5 (see p. 284).
71. The term *nwd* as applied to a snake may be most appropriately rendered "to slither" (Darnell 2004, 265–66).
72. For this passage, see Darnell 2004, 238–39.

Their victuals are hearing the voice[73] of this god. The one who offers to them is one who hears the voice of Re in the Netherworld.

4.34. Scene 28. Twelve figures striding forward are named "The *Ba*-souls of the People Who Are in the Netherworld."

Those who spoke Maat upon the earth, those who respected the visible forms of the god.

Re says to them: "Strength be to your *ba*-souls, breath be to your nostrils, parcels be to you from the Field of Reeds. You belong to those of Maat. Your places be to you at the law-court, at which those amongst whom I am render judgment."

Their victuals are bread; their beer is *djeseret*-drink; their libation is water. The one who offers to them upon earth is among those who are content with their likenesses.[74]

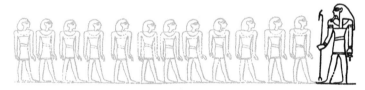

4.35. Scene 29: A deity holding a *was*-scepter faces the *ba*-souls in human form. He is labeled "He Who is in Charge of His Law Court."

Re says to this god: "Call out, He Who is in Charge of His Law Court, to the *ba*-souls of those of Maat. Let them go to rest in their seats at the law-court of those amongst whom I myself am."

---

73. For the role of the solar "voice" in the Book of Gates, see Zeidler 1999a, 127.

74. Reading *mIn.t* "likenesses" as in Hornung 1976, 123 (223); compare Hornung and Abt 2014, 166 as "daily rations."

REGISTER 3 (PLATE 19)

4.36, 4.37 (detail of foreigners). Scene 30. A falcon-headed god, Horus,
leans on a staff. In front
of him are four represen-
tatives each of the four
races of mankind: "People
(Egyptians)," "Asiatics,"
"Nubians," "Libyans."[75]

Horus says to these
cattle of Re: "O those in
the Netherworld, Egypt, and the foreign lands—glorification be to you,
O cattle of Re, O you who came about from the Great One, foremost of
heaven. Breath be to your noses, loosening to your bandages—you are the
tears of my luminous eye, in your name of people.[76] Great is the water of
transforming, so you say in your name of Asiatics. For them does Sakhmet
come into being—she is the protector of their *ba*-souls. You are these
against whom I have struck, so that I might become content with the millions who came forth from me, in your name of Nubians. For them does
Horus come into being—it is he who protects their *ba*-souls. As I have
sought my eye so have you come into being, in your name of Libyans. For
them does Sekhmet come into being—it is she who protects their *ba*-souls.

---

75. Some versions of this scene show each figure as an Egyptian male wearing
a white kilt, while others, such as the tomb of Seti I (fig. 4.37), incorporate detailed
depictions of the skin tone, dress, and hair of each foreign group. Figure 4.37 follows
Belzoni 1820, pls. 7–8.

76. Each of the names of the four races of mankind rely on puns, for example *rmy*
"tears" are identified as *rmṯ* "people." See further Jansen-Winkeln 1998.

4.38. Scene 31. Twelve deities carry a long serpent from whose body sprout solar disks crowned with *ḥꜥ*-signs, meaning "lifetime"; these deities are labeled "They Who Carry the Lifetime in the West."

It is they who establish the lifetime, who set up the days of the *ba*-souls who are in the West, who command to the Place of Destruction.

Re says to them: "O gods foremost of the Netherworld, who carry the chord[77] as hauler(s) of the lifetimes. Seize for yourselves the chord, and haul the lifetimes upon him for the *ba*-souls that are in the West. Command to the Place of Destruction, and destroy the *ba*-souls of my enemies, whom you have commanded to the Place of Destruction; they shall not see the Mysterious Place."

It is the council that destroys the enemies. Their victuals are justification. The one who offers to them upon the earth is one justified before them.

4.39. Scene 32. Eight[78] deities without attributes are labeled "Council which is in the Netherworld."

It is they who command destruction, and who write the lifetime(s) for the *ba*-souls, those foremost of the West.

"Your destruction be against my enemies, whom you have ascribed to the Place of Destruction. That I have come here is in order to reckon my corpse, and in order to inflict punishment on my enemies."

Their victuals are bread; their beer is *djeseret*-drink; their libation is water. The one who offers to them upon the earth—he is unable to enter into the Place of Destruction.

---

77. For the term *mty* "chord," see Meeks 1998b, no. 1907; *mty* seems to refer to the serpent as a chord and is probably related to the *mt* of "*mt*," *WÄS*, 2:167.9–14 (for the phrase *itḥ mt* of 167.14, see Tacke 2013, 28 n. d).

78. The number of deities can vary from six to nine (Hornung 1980, 140).

DOORWAY 5 (PLATE 20)

4.40. Doorway 5. The doorway (p. 264) at the end of Hour 5 is named "Mistress of the Lifetime." Each uraeus is labeled "For Re she casts fire," while the upper mummiform figure is called "Correct of Heart, bending his arms for Re" and the lower "Mysterious of Heart, bending his arms for Re." Unusually, twelve mummies appear inside the doorway, labeled "Gods and goddesses who are in this doorway."

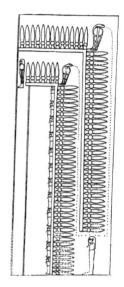

Arrival by this god at this doorway, entering into this doorway. This great god is extolled by the gods who are in it.

(The mummiform figures say): "Come to us, Foremost of the Horizon, great god who has opened the mysteries. As the sanctified doorways have been opened for you, so the mysterious doorleaves have been swung open for you."

JUDGMENT HALL OF OSIRIS (PLATE 20)

4.41. Scene 33. This scene is commonly called the "Judgment Hall of Osiris," since it indeed depicts Osiris presiding over a scale; cryptographic texts annotate the scene.[79] The entire scene is topped by a ḫkr-frieze and the bottom of the scene consists of a stepped platform on which all of the figures stand. To the left is Osiris, wearing a double crown and holding a ḥqꜣ-scepter and crook; in front of

79. The Late period versions contribute to our understanding of the cryptographic text (see Heerma van Voss 1998). The following translations primarily follow those presented in Manassa 2006. On the context of the scene within nonroyal depictions of the Judgment Hall, see Beinlich-Seeber 1976, 187–92. For cryptographic texts within the Netherworld Books in general, see chapter 1, pp. 50–55.

Osiris is a human figure bearing a scale, labeled "God Who Carries the Scale."[80] Above Osiris are four hartebeest heads labeled "Roaring Ones." Nine male figures, "Ennead among whom is Osiris, *akh*-spirits who are in the West," appear atop the steps to the right. In the upper right of the scene is a jackal-headed deity, "Anubis, as he swallows his father."[81] Hovering over the stairs is a boat that contains a monkey brandishing a stick behind a pig, the latter named "Swallower";[82] in front of the boat is another monkey with a stick. Below the steps is the label "Enemies of Osiris."

TITLE:[83] Those who clothe[84] the one who is in the Netherworld in order to protect He of the Dais.[85]

LABEL TO THE HARTEBEEST HEADS: They destroy the dead, namely, those who judge those who are reckoned.[86] It is they who distinguish themselves. It is those within the earth who assigned them to the Place of Destruction, whose heads come forth from the mystery, they appearing in their visible forms. [...] which are given to the effective spirits [...].

LABEL TO THE BOAT WITH MONKEYS: The words of those of Maat are distinguished, as he renders judgment, namely Thoth.

LABEL TO THE UPPER MONKEY: The god appears in glory, the eye atop(?) his head (?). The Netherworld Dwellers pertain to his guardianship. Distinguish yourself, Netherworld Dwellers, by means of your images.

LABEL TO THE LOWER MONKEY: The monkey. This god has appeared in glory, causing to be spat out that which was swallowed.

LABEL TO THE GOD OF THE SCALE: God who causes the apportioning of offerings and portions among the *akh*-spirits. Who carries the weights

---

80. Horemhab and Ramesses II add: "The plummet which unites the scale."

81. For an alternate reading of this epithet, see Gabolde 2006, 12–14.

82. For an analysis of the pig as "swallower" in the context of this scene, see Volokhine 2014, 118–26.

83. Zeidler 1999a, 11–13 reads this cryptographic as the title of the entire composition of the Book of Gates: "Das Buch von den Unterweltsbewohnern, die Osiris beistehen."

84. The "clothing" aspect of the deities within the gateway relate to a Netherworldly doorway known as "the one who clothes the Weary One (Osiris)" (Assmann 1989, 147–49).

85. Hornung 2014, 185 (following Hornung 1980, 146, based on Drioton 1944, 33) alternatively reads the title in a perturbated fashion as: "The Book of Protecting Osiris among those of the Netherworld."

86. "Those who are reckoned" are the damned.

on the scale, with the result that the evil-doers and the dead have ceased to exist. The one who judges, who protects the eye.

OVERALL LABEL TO SCENE: The standing place of Re, he having become beautiful in redness. Re becomes luminous, when he rests in the Netherworld, when he opens the utter darkness, with the result that he rejuvenates in life. The god is content with what he has commanded and shines from his disk.

LABEL BENEATH THE STAIRCASE: His enemies are beneath his two soles, while the gods and the *akh*-spirits are before him. He makes a reckoning among the Netherworld Dwellers.[87] He commands the enemies to the Place of Destruction. As for their *ba*-souls, he makes their slaughter.

HOUR 6

REGISTER 1 (PLATE 21)

4.42. Scene 34. Twelve gods wielding forked staffs labeled "Those Who Carry Forked Staves."

Re says to them: "Receive your forked staves, which you have seized in your hands. Hail, your <forked staves> are in Swallower, your bonds are in him, until the heads within him come forth and he retreats."

They say to Re: "Our forked staves, O Re, are in Swallower; our bonds in the evil serpent. O Re, see the heads are emerging from the coils of this retreating serpent.[88] It is the deities who are in the bark who repel Apep in Nut. To the Netherworld they journey. It is they who repel Apep from Re in the West, so that this deity may travel rightly."

---

87. The Late period sources replace this sentence with: "opposite the slaughtering blocks containing the enemies and the dead of the Netherworld."

88. As indicated by the annotation of the next scene, these heads swallow the evil serpent, Swallower, a hypostasis of Apep.

Their victuals are bread; their beer is *djeseret*-drink; their libation is water. The one who offers to them on earth is one who repels the rebel from Re in the West.

4.43. Scene 35. Twelve gods carry a serpent from which twelve human heads emerge. The deities are labeled "Those Who Carry Swallower, from whose coils the heads emerge."

Those who punished Evil of Face, as they fell the enemies of Re. It is they who seize the rebel, and who let the head of the ones who are in him come forth.

Re says to them: "Let the rebel turn away from you, let Apep get back from you, that the heads of those who are in him may come forth while he perishes. With the result that he is destroyed do I call to them. O heads—swallow for yourselves the one who swallowed you, and eat the one from whom you came forth."

With the result that they come forth does Re call out to them. They proceed to eat the coils until he passes by them, with the result that the heads enter into their coils afterwards.

One without his eyes is this snake, one without his nose, one without his ears. From his roar he breathes, from his own cry he lives.[89]

Their victuals are what is offered on earth before Re, when he comes forth from the Netherworld. The one who offers to them is one who takes up a position beneath the trees.[90]

---

89. For this description of Apep, see the commentary in chapter 1, pp. 11–12.

90. The *imꜣ* tree evokes Osiris (Zeidler 1999a, 165 n. 4), citing Baum 1988, 183–96 (note particularly her observation on p. 190 that the tree is associated with the provisioning of the dead) and Koemoth 1994, 261; compare also the description in Hour 8, Register 3, Scene 53: "May you take up position beneath the overarching tree" (see the commentary on p. 302).

4.44. Scene 36. Twelve deities—labeled "Those Who Carry the Double-coiled Rope, from which the hours come forth"—carry a coiled rope that emerges from neck of a mummiform figure, "Aqen."[91]

"Seize hold of the double-coiled rope,[92] which you have taken from the mouth of Aqen. Going forth be to your hours, that you might become transfigured by means of them. The resting of your hours will be your provisions."

That the double-coiled rope enters into the mouth of Aqen is so that a coiling may go forth, and an hour may come into being. No sooner does Re call than it occupies its seat. Then Aqen swallows the double-coiled rope.

They say to Re: "The double-coiled rope belongs to Aqen. The hours belong to the great god. May you become transfigured, O Re, through the light. May you occupy your corpse, the one hidden of matters."

Their victuals are bread; their beer is *djeseret*-drink; their libation is water. The one who offers to them upon the earth is one pertaining to a coil in the double-coiled rope.

_____

REGISTER 2 (PLATE 21)

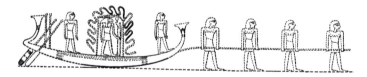

4.45. Scene 37. The solar bark (see Scene 7) is hauled by four male figures labeled "Netherworld Dwellers."

_____

91. The deity Aqen ("ꜥqn," *LGG* 2:237; Hornung 1980, 160) also appears as a ferryman in the Coffin Texts (Bidoli 1976, 29; on the context of the spell, see Willems 1996, 156–77).

92. Zeidler 1999a, 167 n. 2.

Hauling this great god by the Netherworld Dwellers.

They say to Re: "Hauling be to you, O great god, lord of the hours, who has taken care of the earth, from whose visible forms the gods and the *akh-*spirits live, when they see his manifestations."

Re says to them: "Effectiveness be to you, O haulers; sanctity be to you, O haulers. Convey me to the provisions of the Netherworld, haul me to the (place) enduring of plans, and take up position at that mysterious mountain of the horizon."

4.46. Scene 38. Twelve gods whose arms are hidden beneath their cloaks, labeled "Those Hidden of Arm, who carry the mystery."

They exist carrying the mystery of the great god, without those who are in the Netherworld seeing him. As soon as the dead see him, they burn in the Temple of the Benben,[93] at the place bearing the corpse of this god.

Re says to them: "Take to yourselves my images, embrace your mysteries, so that you may go to rest in the Temple of the Benben, at the place bearing my corpse. That which is in me is a mystery for that which is in you—mysterious be the Netherworld and covered be your arm."

They say to Re: "Your *ba*-soul be to heaven, O Foremost of the Horizon—it is your shadow that passes through the Mysterious Place. Your corpse be to the earth, O One Who is in Heaven, while we give Re to it. You are separated from it, O Re. May you breathe and occupy your corpse, which is in the Netherworld."

Their victuals are the entire offering with which the *ba*-souls are content. The one who offers to them upon the earth is one who glimpses light in the Netherworld.

93. The "Temple of the Benben" as a Heliopolitan solar edifice, which can be linked with the punishment of enemies in the eastern horizon (Klotz 2008, 73–76), is here associated with the destruction of the damned in the middle of the night. In the Book of Adoring Re in the West, the *benben*-sanctuary is the location of the solar deity in Addresses 73 and 74 of the Great Litany (p. 101). The Heliopolitan toponym Kheraha also appears in the Book of the Hidden Chamber, Hour 6 (p. 189).

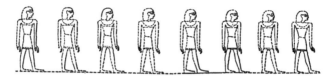

4.47. Scene 39. Eight gods are labeled "Gods of the Temple."

They exist outside the Temple of the Benben, seeing what Re sees, having access to his mysterious images, whom <Re> has reckoned. It is they who dispatch messengers.

<Re> says to them: "My victuals are your victuals; what I breathe is what you breathe. It is you amongst whom are my mysteries, and the one who exists as protection of my mysteries, which are in the Temple of the Benben. Hail to you; may your *ba*-souls live."

Their victuals are the victuals of He of the Horizon.

REGISTER 3 (PLATE 21)

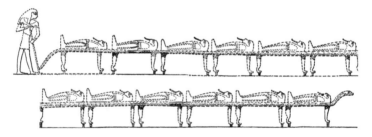

4.48, 4.49. Scene 40. A deity leaning on a staff is called "He of the Netherworld." In front of him is a long bier whose horizontal surface is a long serpent called "One Who Leaps Up";[94] resting on the bier are twelve mummies called "Those who are in the following of Osiris, the sleepers who are in the weariness of death."

He of the Netherworld says to them: "O gods who are foremost of the Netherworld, who are in the following of the Ruler of the West, who are stretched out on their sides, who lie upon their biers—raise up your flesh; tie up for yourselves your bones; gather together your members; assemble for yourselves your flesh. The sweet wind be to your noses, loosening be to your mummy wrappings, removal be to your head cloths.[95] Gleaming

94. On this name, see Book of the Hidden Chamber, Hour 4, Scene 39 (p. 169).
95. For loosening mummy wrappings in the Netherworld, see p. 7 and n. 12.

be to your divine eyes, with the result that you see the light thereby. Stand up from your tiredness, and receive to yourselves your cultivated land at the field of Mistress of Offerings. Cultivated land be to you of this field; its water be to you, that you might become content with me—(namely) the fields in the Mistress of Offerings."

Their libations are water. One Who Leaps Up guards their corpses; their *ba*-souls travel to the Field of Reeds, in order to exert control over their libations, the earth leaping up as they reckon their flesh.

Their victuals are bread; their beer is *djeseret*-drink; their libations are water. The one who offers to them upon the earth is a mummy who rests on his bier.

4.50. Scene 41. Two mummiform gods stand to either side of a circular pit of flames that contains a uraeus; one mummy is called "Fiery of Face," the other named "Flaming of Face." Twelve gods, bending slightly, appear behind the mummies and are labeled "The Gods Who are in the Flaming Pit of the Earth."

Just as they exist in the circumference of this flaming pit, so does a living uraeus serpent exist in this flaming pit. That the water of this flaming pit is fire, is without the deities of the earth and the *ba*-souls of the earth being able to descend to this flaming pit because of the flame of this uraeus. That this great god, foremost of the Netherworld, breathes is from the sacred water of this flaming pit.

Re says to them: "Hail, gods, guardians of the sacred flaming pit, which sends out water for the one foremost of Igeret. The water of the flaming pit belongs to Osiris, and your libation to the one foremost of the Netherworld. The fire of your blasting flame[96] is the licking fire against the *ba*-souls, when they ascend to transgress Osiris. The flaming pit shall neither languish nor rage. There is not another one, over the water of which the gods who guard it may exercise authority."

Their victuals are bread; their beer is *djeseret*-drink; their libation is water. The one who offers to them upon the earth is a sacred one in the West.

---

96. *nsr.t* and *nsby.t* as names of Hour 5 goddess appear in "*nsbj.t*," WÄS 2:334.17; and "*nsr.t*," WÄS 2:336.7; for *nsby.t* see also Wilson 1997, 545.

DOORWAY 6 (PLATE 21)

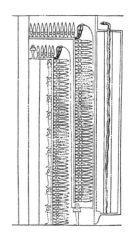

4.51. Doorway 6. Doorway 6 displays the standard iconography (p. 264) and is named "Handiwork of Her
Lord."[97] The upper mummiform figure is "Unifier,
bending his arms for Re" the lower one "Standing One,
bending his arms for Re." The uraei are each labeled
"For Re she casts fire." Nine mummies appear again
inside the doorway, labeled "The Sixth Ennead in <...>."
The serpent at the door-leaf is labeled "One Who Seizes
with His Eye. He is at this door-leaf, he opens for Re."

Arrival by this great god at this doorway, entering
into this doorway. This great god is extolled by the
gods who are in it. "Come to us, Foremost of the
Horizon, great god who has opened up the mysteries. As the sacred doorways have been opened for you, so the mysterious door-leaves have been
swung open for you."

Divine Perception speaks to One Who Seizes with His Eye: "Open
your gate to Re, swing open your door-leaf to He of the Horizon."

He illumines the utter darkness and casts light into the hidden chamber. Then this door seals after this great god enters. Those who are in this
portal wail when they hear this door slam shut.

HOUR 7

REGISTER 1 (PLATE 22)

4.52. Scene 42. Twelve male figures carry baskets on their heads; they are labeled
"Those Belonging to the Offerings, manifested of victuals."

They who have thurified <to> their deities, and made purification to their
ka-spirits; who have not turned aside an *akh*-spirit from his breathing, or

---

97. For the magical connotations of this name, see Zeidler 1999a, 189 n. 2.

a dead one[98] from his libation. They are content with their victuals, with the result that their deities and their *ka*-spirits appeal to them, their arms to them when they enter to their cakes at the portal She Who Feeds Her Gods.

Osiris says to them: "Your bread be to you, that which is in your mouths, O you belonging to the offerings, manifested of victuals. Have use of your legs, and may you become content with your hearts. The portion of your gods be to you, your cakes be to your *ka*-spirits."

Their victuals are bread; their beer is *djeseret*-drink; their libation is water. The one who offers to them upon the earth is a possessor of offerings in the West.

4.53. Scene 43. Twelve male figures with their hands raised and a Maat-feather crowning their heads; they are labeled "Those of Maat, Who Carry Maat."

Those who performed Maat, while yet upon the earth, who fought on behalf of their gods. They have been summoned to the resting place of the earth, to the mansion of the one who lives on Maat, with the result that their Maat is reckoned for them in the presence of the great god, the one who destroys evil.[99]

Osiris says to them: "Your Maat is proper.[100] May you become content with what you have done and with what has happened, O you who are in my following, O you who are in the forehall of the One Sacred of His *Ba*-soul. You shall live from what they have lived; you shall breathe from what they breathe. Have power over the libation of your lake. To you have

---

98. This is an unusual use of the term *mwt* "dead" in a positive sense of blessed dead, rather than the damned, to whom the term *mwt* frequently refers.

99. Translating *isf.t*, a complex concept in Egyptian theology that is the negative counterpart of Maat; for example, in the text King as Solar Priest, the pharaoh's duty is "bringing about Maat and destroying evil (*isf.t*)" (see p. 38).

100. This reading renders a restored *n* unnecessary (contra Zeidler 1999a, 197: "*Maat* soll euch gehören.").

I commended one who exists until his limit, bearing Maat, (one) against whom evil cannot approach."

Their victuals are Maat; their beer is wine; their libation is water. The one who offers to them upon the earth is one of Maat belonging to their lake.

REGISTER 2 (PLATE 22)

4.54. Scene 44. The solar bark (see Scene 7) is hauled by four male figures labeled "Netherworld Dwellers."

Hauling this great god by the Netherworldly gods.

They say, while they haul Re: "High is the disk, the one in front of the Encircling Serpent. May the head of the one who is in his shrine light up."

(Re speaks to them:) "Sight be to you, O you who are foremost of the Netherworld. Your eyes be to you, O gods—since Re has exerted power over Igeret. The great god has ordered affairs for you."

4.55. Scene 45. Two gods leaning on staffs, "Atum" and "Golden One of the Gods," appear to either side of seven jackal-headed staffs (wsr-posts). To each staff are bound two enemies, and a mummiform figure guards each group of enemies. Each staff has a slightly different annotation, the first referring to the enemies, the second to the mummiform guardian: first—"Enemies of Re" and "Grasper"; second—"Enemies of Atum" and "Masher"; third—"Enemies of Khepri" and "Violent One"; fourth—"Enemies of Shu," and "Frightful One"; fifth—"Enemies of Geb" and "Corrector"; sixth—"Enemies of Osiris" and "Thrasher"; and seventh—"Enemies of Horus" and "Awesome of Face."

Arrival by this great god at the *wsr*-posts of Geb,[101] to which the enemies are reckoned, after judgment in the West.

Divine Perception says to this god, when he reaches the *wsr*-posts of Geb: "Nod assent, O Re, great god, for you have reached the *wsr*-posts of Geb."

Atum says to the *wsr*-posts: "Guard the enemies, grasp those to be punished, O gods who follow after the *wsr*-posts, who are in the following of Geb, the heir—take hold of the enemies, guard those to be punished, with the result that they have not escaped under your arms, they not wriggling out from beneath your fingers. O enemies, your reckoning is beheading, like that which Re has commanded against you, when he laid out Igeret for his corpse, and created the Netherworld for his forms. As he commands you to your slaughter, so he reckons you because of that which you have done in the broad hall of Re, even while the gods are mourning the *udjat*-eye, and he is setting the Golden One of the Gods as your guard."

The enemies and the ones to be punished who are in the Netherworld are damned to the *wsr*-posts.

REGISTER 3 (PLATE 22)

4.56. Scene 46. A god leaning on a staff, "Lord of Joy,"[102] surveys twelve gods, each facing a large stalk of grain (almost tree-like in its proportions). The twelve gods are labeled "Those Who Make Sustenance from Lower Egyptian Grain in the Fields of the Netherworld."

They are making sustenance from grain, embracing Nepri-Hety.[103] Their grains in the earth are growing more effective than the effective eye of Re. As soon as he enters among them, it (the grain) goes forth.[104]

101. Miosi 1982; Beaux 1991, 48. Note commentary in Hornung 1980, 184–85.

102. On the compound ꜣw.t-ib and its solar connotations, see Epigraphic Survey 1994, 1 (n. *b* to pl. 3). For the connection of ꜣw.t-ib and the rejuvenation of the ruler, see Gabolde and Gabolde 1989, 174 n. 279, and the references cited therein.

103. "*Npr-ḥty*," *LGG* 4: 203–4.

104. Zeidler 1999a, 209 n. 5.

The Lord of Joy says to them: "Effectiveness be to your grain,[105] growth be to your barley—your offerings be to Re, your cakes be to Foremost of the Netherworld. Your victuals be to you, your offerings consisting of what is in your arms. The vegetables—this within which you are—be to Osiris, that he might become content therewith."

They say to Re: "May Nepri flourish, and may Osiris manifest, he at the sight of whom the Netherworld Dwellers breathe, and he at the smelling of whose scent the *akh*-spirits breathe. Luminosity be to you, Osiris; magnificence be to you, Nepri-Hety; skill be to you, Foremost of the Westerners, he who is in the fields of the Netherworld."

When they bind together their grain, they say to Re: "Piles of grain will flourish in the field of the Netherworld, when Re shines upon the limbs of Osiris.[106] When you rise, plants manifest, O great god, creator of the egg."[107]

Their victuals are grain; their beer is *djeseret*-drink; their libation is water. The one who offers to them upon the earth is a possessor of grain in the fields of the Netherworld.

4.57. Scene 47. Seven gods carrying sickles are named "Those Who Pertain to the Sickles."

That they bear sickles is so they might reap grain in their fields.[108]

---

105. The term *ꜣḫ* "effective" also has connotations of "luminosity"—for "luminous" plants, compare the theological significance of the onion (Graindorge 1992, 1999).

106. This passage evokes the artifacts known as "corn mummies" (Onstine 1998, 67); see further Centrone 2009.

107. The primordial egg from which creation comes forth (Rashed 2015 and references therein).

108. In the Book of Gates, Hour 2, Scene 6 the sickle-wielding deities are punishers of the damned (p. 261).

Re says to them: "Receive your sickles, and reap your grain, which you have cast in your peas.[109] Make Osiris content, the one foremost of the cavern Mysterious of Visible Forms. Hail to you, sickle-wielders."

Their victuals are bread; their beer is *djesert*-drink; their libation is water. The one who offers to them upon the earth is among the sickle-bearers in the fields of the Netherworld.

___

DOORWAY 7 (PLATE 23)

4.58. Doorway 7. Doorway 7 is like those of earlier hours (p. 264) and is called "Shining One." The upper mummiform figure is "Damaged Eye,[110] bending his arms for Re" the lower one "Blind One, bending his arms for Re." The uraei are each labeled "For Re she casts fire." Nine mummies appear again inside the doorway, labeled "The Seventh Ennead." The serpent at the door-leaf is labeled "Closed of Eye. He is at this door-leaf, he opens for Re."

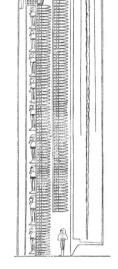

Arrival by this great god at this doorway, entering into this doorway. This great god is extolled by the gods who are in it. "Come to us, Foremost of the Horizon, great god who has opened up the mysteries. As the sacred doorways have been opened for you, so the mysterious door-leaves have been swung open for you."

Divine Perception speaks to Closed of Eye: "Open your gate to Re, swing open your door-leaf to He of the Horizon."

He illumines the utter darkness and casts light into the Hidden Chamber. Then this door seals after this great god enters. The *ba*-souls who are in this portal wail when they hear this door slam shut.

___

109. Identifying this as "*thwy*," WÄS, 5:323.1–4; while some have suggested "garlic" (Meeks 1998c, 327, no. 79.3430), a reading "peas" is more likely—Meeks 1998a, 420, no. 77.4846, has "pois," *pisum sativum*; so also Hannig 2006b, 2705, "peas." This passage appears to describe wheat mixed in among peas, perhaps alluding to planting peas in rotation with wheat in arid environments (Schillinger 2017). Zeidler 1999a, 215 emends the text to "Legt (sie) zu eurem Nutzen in eure Höhlen."

110. Meeks 1998a, 231, nos. 77.2528–9; the name also refers to the solar deity in the Book of Adoring Re in the West, Address 24 (p. 84; see also Hornung 1976, 106 n. 68).

HOUR 8

REGISTER 1 (PLATE 23)

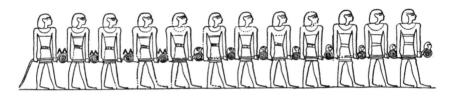

4.59. Scene 48. Twelve gods, who are called "Carriers of the Rope Which Gives Birth to the Mysteries," are holding a rope from which emerge three sets of four objects: human heads, falcon heads, and *dmd*-signs (meaning "to unite").

They exist bearing the rope which they carry. When Re appears in glory, the heads that are in the rope come forth. They draw Re toward their doorway, with the result that they turn back at the portal of Nun.[111] They make allotments for the Netherworld Dwellers when their foreheads come forth and the rope straightens.

<Re speaks to them:> "As the rope progresses, so my own mysteries grow bright, while the faces go forth from their coils. The forms which I have formed light up, while the heads which are in Osiris come forth. Open, O haulers! Straighten out the coils![112] May you haul for me, O carriers of the rope. May you turn back at the cavern of Nun."

Their victuals are bread; their beer is *djeseret*-drink; their libation is water. The one who offers to them upon the earth is one who knots the rope in the bark.[113]

---

111. Wiebach-Koepke 2003a, 299 n. 2.

112. Compare the noun *ʿnnw* "coils" attested in the Coffin Texts (Hannig 2006a, 507); see also the commentary to the *mʿnn* cord in Book of Gates, Hour 6, Register 1, Scene 36 (p. 288).

113. Knotting (and binding) is a significant element in Egyptian magical practice (Ritner 1993, 142–44).

4.60. Scene 49. A god without attributes faces twelve gods carrying a rope in the shape of a coiled serpent; they are labeled "Those Who Carry Swallower, who gives birth to the hours." A star hovers above each coil of the serpent.

They exist bearing Swallower,[114] whom they seize, as Re passes by.

Divine Perception says to these deities: "Speak out to Swallower, O you who are in the Netherworld. Behold, Re is reckoning his hours."

They say—these gods: "Open your coil, that your mysteries might come forth. The great god stands still, until he is provided with his hours." So says each one of these gods, then an hour comes forth from a coil, and occupies (its) seat.[115]

Re says to them: "Take to yourself Swallower; seize hold of the Coiled One. Bread be to you, that which is in your hours; water be to you, which comes forth from Igeret. May you have power over those whom you protect, the one of whom Ikeky[116] is the protector. Ikeky is the protector."[117]

Their victuals are bread; their beer is *djeseret*-drink; their libation is water. The one who offers to them upon earth is an *akh*-spirit of his hour.

---

114. Alternatively, this name may represent an *m*-preformative of the verb ꜥꜣ, "to beget, engender" (for the verb see *inter alia* the references in Bell 1976, 30–34; Darnell 2004, 320–21). Less likely is a relationship to the old *mꜥꜣ* "helm" ("*mꜥꜣwj*," *WÄS*, 2:46.8; Hannig 2006b, 1037).

115. On conceptions of time in the Netherworld Books, see chapter 1, pp. 41–43 above.

116. A god only attested here ("*ikky*," *LGG* 1:570; Zeidler 1999a, 227 n. 2); for a possibly related god Ika(?) in the Book of the Solar-Osirian Unity on the Second Shrine of Tutankhamun, see p. 540 and n. 35.

117. Alternatively, *zp snw* may be read as the final word of this phrase: "Ikeki is the guardian of him who is to be guarded" (Hornung and Abt 2014, 281).

REGISTER 2 (PLATE 23)

4.61. Scene 50. The solar bark (see Scene 7) is hauled by four male figures labeled "Netherworld Dwellers."

Hauling this great god by the gods of the Netherworld.

They say, while they haul Re: "Make ovations, O foremost ones of the Netherworld, for Re, who is in his mystery.[118] Behold, he judges your words and destroys for you your enemies. Behold, he commands for you offerings, and he presents to you your thrones. May you give to him worship in your visible forms (saying): 'You (Re) are this one who made your[119] visible forms.' May you give to him ovation in your manifestations (saying): 'You are this one who manifests your manifestations.' May you give praise to him, O Netherworld Dwellers."

4.62. Scene 51. Twelve male figures without attributes stride forward; they are called "Lords of Provisions in the West."

It is the council that is in the Netherworld that judges matters on behalf of He of the Horizon.[120]

Re says to them: "O council that is in the Netherworld, lords of provisions in the West! May you adjudicate for me by means of your judgments. May you decree evil against my enemies, according as I give to you my

118. Re is here within his own corpse, as in Hour 6, Register 2, Scene 38 (see the commentary above, p. 289).

119. This your is plural, possibly for "our."

120. Zeidler 1999a, 231 n. 1.

Maat.[121] Judge commensurate with your judgments; act for me like (you act for) the gods."

They say to Re: "You become justified, O Re, your enemies having been cast out. Your provisions are our provisions. You are this one from whom we have come forth, the one who created us in order to defend his *ba*-soul. Your provisions be to you in Tatenen; the West be to your sanctified corpse. Your provisions be to you in Nut, while your *ba*-soul rules heaven."

Their victuals are bread; their beer is *djeseret*-drink; their libation is water. The one who offers to them upon the earth is amongst the followers of the Lords of Provisions.

4.63. Scene 52. Four mummiform deities are called "Warlike of Face."[122]

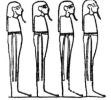

Re says to them: "Uncovering be to your head-cloths,[123] O Warlike of Face! Loosening be to your bandages![124] My light be to you, O gods!"

Their victuals are bread; their beer is *djeseret*-drink; their refreshment is water. The one who offers to them upon the earth is one who sees light in the Netherworld.

---

121. Baumann 1998, 265 entertains the possibility of *mi* + *sḏm.t=f*, following (but not there citing) Hornung 1980, 200 n. 4. The solar god refers to Maat as his own property—for the close relationship between the solar deity and Maat, see Assmann 2001c, 177–84, *passim*. The status of Maat as encompassing all offerings (Teeter 1997, 82) ties together the judgment of the enemies in Re's speech with the focus on provisions in the speech of the "Lords of Provisions in the West."

122. These beings also appear in the annotation to the Book of the Creation of the Solar Disk, Section B, Register 1, Scene 25 (see pp. 485–86; Roberson 2012, 204 n. 506, 244).

123. For the significance of *ꜥfn.t* "head cloth," see Assmann 1972, 64.

124. The ideal situation in the Netherworld is to be freed from one's mummy bandages—see the commentary and parallels in chapter 1, p. 7 and n. 12.

REGISTER 3 (PLATE 23)

4.64. Scene 53. A deity leaning on a staff is labeled "One Hidden of Mysteries." Twelve mummies (lying on their bellies, their heads raised) on biers have the annotation "*Akh*-spirits, potent ones, excellent *akh*-spirits."[125]

One Hidden of Mysteries says to them: "Hail, O *akh*-spirits! Hail, O Netherworld Dwellers! Opening be to your faces. Clearing be to your darkness. Effectiveness be to your *ba*-souls, potency be to your shadows;[126] knowledge be to your mouths; honor be to your hearts; rising be to your biers; breath be to your noses. May the odor of your unguents be sweet. Loosening be to your bandages, that you might go and come, and that you might have control over refreshment.[127] May you praise, O *ba*-souls. May you be skilled, so that you might take food, and that you might be content with offerings. May you pour for yourself cool water from the winding lakes in the Netherworld. May you take up position beneath the overarching tree,[128] which the *akh*-spirit of He of the Horizon lifts up.[129] May you light up by means of your clothing—may you shine by means of the effective eye of

---

125. For parallels to "awakening" figures in a prone posture and heads uplifted, see Roberson 2013, 11 n. 47; vertically oriented mummied in a similar pose appear in the Book of Adoring Re in the West, Address 67 (p. 99) and the Books of the Creation of the Solar Disk (Roberson 2012, 263–64).

126. Note the *ba*-soul and shade "als belebende Mächte," well attested in the Coffin Texts and the Netherworld Books (George 1970, 92–100).

127. For loosening bandages, see chapter 1, p. 7 and n. 12.

128. Baum 1988, 247–48 n. 84. The idea is probably that appearing in the well-known scene of the tree goddess dispensing water to the deceased and their *ba*-souls (Billing 2002). Such a thought is no doubt behind the ingenious use of the undulating ceiling as grape arbor in the Eighteenth Dynasty tomb of Sennefer (TT96).

129. The lifting by "He of the Horizon" (Akhty) refers to the concept of the flag, fan, and tree as providing evidence for the presence of the divine breath—see Darnell 2004, 414–15 (and n. 194 in particular). This passage illustrates the richness of imagery and the various senses to which a seemingly simple and at first glance obscure passage actually appeals. For the religious, and particularly royal, associations of the sacred trees of various nomes in the Graeco-Roman period, see Aufrère 1999.

Re. May Igeret open to you her shoulder,[130] that you might enter the sanctity of Osiris. Hail to you, O *akh*-spirits. Prone upon their beds do they exist upon their biers."

Their victuals are bread; their beer is *djeseret*-drink; their refreshment is water. The one who offers to them upon the earth is an effective *akh*-spirit who has power over (his) shade.

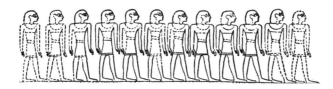

4.65. Scene 54. Twelve male figures are labeled "The Council of Judges."

It is they who judge at this portal, and who hear the matters of those who are there.

Re says to them: "Hail, O gods, council of judges, who judge the dead and protect the *ba*-souls. The Divine One is assigned to his throne.[131] Your Maat be to you, O gods."

They say to Re: "Hail, O He of the Horizon, great god, lord of the Ennead. We are performing the judgments of the dead, we are protecting the *akh*-spirits, so that they may manifest, and we are causing that the god rest upon his throne."

Their victuals are bread; their beer is *djeseret*-drink; their refreshment is water. The one who offers to them upon the earth is one who judges in (this) council.

---

130. The Book of Adoring Re in the West, Litany 7 similarly states "Indeed, you have caused that I ascend, while you open your shoulders for me and bend for me your arms" (pp. 116–17).

131. The "Divine One" is Osiris (Zeidler 1999a, 243 n. 4), who is enthroned in the Book of Gates, Scene 33, the "Judgment Hall of Osiris."

DOORWAY 8 (PLATE 23)

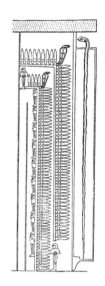

4.66. Doorway 8. Doorway 8 has the same template as the earlier hours (p. 264) and is called "Glowing One." The upper mummiform figure is "Pointed One, bending his arms for Re" the lower one "Embracer, bending his arms for Re." The uraei are each labeled "For Re she casts fire." Nine mummies appear again inside the doorway, labeled "The Eighth Ennead." The serpent at the door-leaf is labeled "Flaming of Face. He is at this door-leaf, he opens for Re."

Arrival by this great god at this doorway, entering into this doorway. This great god is extolled by the gods who are in it.

"Come to us, Foremost of the Horizon, great god who has opened up the mysteries. As the sacred doorways have been opened for you, so the mysterious door-leaves have been swung open for you."

Divine Perception speaks to Flaming of Face: "Open your gate to Re, swing open your door-leaf to He of the Horizon."

He illumines the utter darkness and casts light into the Hidden Chamber. Then this door seals after this great god enters. The *ba*-souls who are in this portal wail when they hear this door slam shut.

HOUR 9

REGISTER 1 (PLATE 24)

4.67. Scene 55. Twelve male figures (without attributes) are labeled "The Council that gives bread and offers vegetables to the *ba*-souls in the Island of Fire."

It is they who provide the *ba*-souls with vegetables in the Island of Fire.

Re says to them: "O council of gods, court[132] of the Island of Fire,[133] who set the *ba*-souls upon their vegetables. They shall have power over their bread. Offer your bread, usher in your vegetables for those with *ba*-souls, whom I have commanded to breathe in the Island of Fire."

They say to Re: "The bread has been offered and the vegetables given to those with *ba*-souls, whom you have commanded to breathe in the Island of Fire. Hail, behold the perfect path.[134] Foremost of the Westerners praises you, those who are in Tatenen[135] rejoice for you."

Their victuals are bread; their beer is *djesert*-drink; their libation is water. The one who offers to them upon the earth is an appointed one in the council.

4.68. Scene 56. Nine human-headed *ba*-souls have their arms raised in adoration towards a deity holding a *was*-scepter and *ankh*-sign. They are labeled "Those with *Ba*-souls Who are in the Island of Fire."

They are in the Island of Fire, receiving their bread, having power over this island, praising this great god.

Re says to them: "Eat your vegetables, enjoy your loaves. Fullness be to your bellies, strength to your hearts. Your vegetables be to the Island of Fire, to which island no one can ascend. May you praise me and honor me—I am the Great One, who founded the Netherworld."

132. Following Zeidler 1999a, 251.

133. For the "Island of Fire," see above, p. 46.

134. The *wꜣ.t nfr.t* is an accessible, open path (Zeidler 1999a, 253 n. 2), as opposed to a difficult or mysterious path (such as those seen in the Book of the Hidden Chamber, Hour 4). The concern with "straightness" in paths is present also in the Book of Adoring Re in the West—compare the Great Litany, Address 48: "Who straightens paths that are in the Netherworld. Who opens roads in the Mysterious Place. You are indeed the corpse of Straightener of Paths." Note also a statement in Litany 6 (p. 111): "May you guide me on the beautiful paths!"

135. For Tatenen as the entirety of the Netherworldly sphere, see Hour 8, Register 2, Scene 51 above.

They say to Re: "Hail to you, O one great of power. Acclamation to you, O one great of hauling. The Netherworld belongs to you according to your desire, (namely) that which you have hidden from those who are in their caverns. The sky belongs to you according to your desire, (namely) that which you have made mysterious from those who are near it. The earth be to your corpse, the sky to your *ba*-soul, so that you may be content, O Re, with what you have brought about."

Their victuals are bread; their vegetables are herbs; their libation is water. The one who offers to them upon the earth is a possessor of a *ba*-soul of this Island of Fire.

REGISTER 2 (PLATE 24)

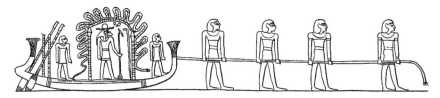

4.69. Scene 57. The solar bark (see Scene 7) is hauled by four male figures labeled "Netherworld Dwellers."

Hauling this great god by the Netherworldly gods.

They say, as they haul Re: "Ovation in the sky for the *ba*-soul of Re, reverence in the earth for his corpse—again through sky to his *ba*-soul, again through the earth to his corpse. Hail, we are opening for you the Mysterious Place, we are preparing for you the ways of Igeret, so that you may go to rest, O Re, upon your mysteries, with the result that the ones of the mysteries adore you in your visible forms. Hail, we are hauling you, O Re, we are guiding you, O Great One, foremost of the sky."

4.70. Scene 58. A god leaning on a staff labeled "One Who Is in Nun" stands before a lake. The lake contains four sets of three swimming figures: "Immersed Ones," "Shipwrecked Ones," "Swimming Ones," and "Stretched Out Ones."

Reaching the Immersed Ones, those who are in the water; navigating by them.

Those who are in Nun say to them: "O Immersed Ones, who are herein, the Swimming Ones who are in the flood—behold Re, who is passing in his bark, great of mystery. He orders affairs for the gods, he takes care of the *akh*-spirits. Hail, stand up, O weary ones—Re is ordering your affairs."

Re says to them: "Emergence be to your heads, O Immersed Ones; rowing be to your arms, O Shipwrecked Ones; hurrying be to your navigations, O Swimming Ones; air be to your nostrils, O Stretched Out Ones. May you have power over your water, may you become content with your libation. Your going be to Nun, your coming be to the flood; your *ba*-souls upon the earth become content with their breathing, without suffering destruction."

Their victuals are the offerings of the earth. The one who offers to them upon the earth is one who has power over his offerings on earth.

REGISTER 3 (PLATE 24)

4.71. Scene 59. A falcon-headed deity leaning on a staff is labeled "Horus." A series of bound enemies—three sets of four—have the annotation "Enemies of Osiris, who belong to the burning."

That which Horus has done for his father Osiris. These enemies are in this fashion, Horus commands their evil to them.

Horus says to them: "Binding be to your arms, O enemies of my father. Your arms be to your heads, O you overturned ones—from behind have you been bound, ones of evil, you have been beheaded and do not exist.

Your *ba*-soul has been destroyed, so that it might not live, because of this which you have done against my father Osiris—you are placing the mystery behind you,[136] and you are taking the image of the Mysterious One.[137] As my father Osiris is triumphing against you, so am I triumphing against you. It is you who reveal what is hidden, as the one who engendered me in the Netherworld goes to rest. Ho, you shall not be, O you who are not."

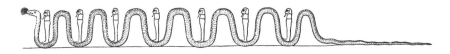

4.72. Scene 60. A multi-coiled serpent has seven mummies standing amongst its coils. The serpent, called "Flaming One," shoots fire against the bound enemies of Scene 59. The mummies within the coils are labeled "Gods upon the Flaming One."

Horus says <to> the Flaming One: "O Flaming One, great of fire, O you at the tip of whose mouth is my eye.[138] It is my offspring whom his (your) coils protect.[139] Open your mouth, separate your jaws, as you cast fire into the enemies of my father. May you scald their corpses, their *ba*-souls having already been boiled in that blasting flame on the tip of your mouth, and the fire which is in your belly. My children be against them, so that they might be destroyed; the *akh*-spirits who come forth from me be against them,[140] such that they do not exist."

---

136. Contra Zeidler 1999a, 267 n. 4.

137. The enemies of Osiris commit crimes against the solar corpse, the "mystery" and "image of the Mysterious One."

138. The solar eye is the flame at the mouth of the serpent; for commentary to the flaming, protective solar eye, see chapter 2, pp. 70–71.

139. Here Horus indicates that his children—the sons of Horus—are the deities who stand among the coils of the fire breathing serpent; a parallel for this scene appears in the Book of the Hidden Chamber, Hour 6, Register 3, where the heads of the four sons of Horus emerge from a serpent labeled "Swallower of the Dead." This scene is one of the only images from the Book of Gates that is frequently used in Third Intermediate period papyri and coffins (Taylor 2016, 146–47). Another possible derivation may be a distinct Third Intermediate period tableau on papyri and coffins (Niwiński 1989b, 309–14) that show (most often) animal-headed mummies among the coils of a serpent, who may be a nefarious being (and stuck with knives) or, based on the Book of Gates, Hour 9, Register 2, Scene 60, a protective serpent.

140. For the children of Horus as *akh*-spirits, see Hornung 1980, 222 n. 6a.

The flame which is in this serpent shall come forth, and these enemies are scalded, after Horus calls to him. The one who knows the enchantment of this serpent is one who cannot come near his flame. The one who offers to those upon this serpent is one whose *ba*-soul is not in the flame.

DOORWAY 9 (PLATE 24)

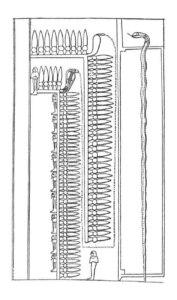

4.73. Doorway 9. Doorway 9 has the same template as the earlier hours (p. 264) and is called "Great of Awe." The upper mummiform figure is "One Who Surrounds the Earth, bending his arms for Re" the lower one "Carrier of the Earth, bending his arms for Re." The uraei are each labeled "For Re she casts fire." Nine mummies appear again inside the doorway, labeled "The Ninth Ennead." The serpent at the door-leaf is labeled "Opener of the Earth. He is at this door-leaf, he opens for Re."

Arrival by this great god at this doorway, entering into this doorway by this great god. This great god is extolled by the gods who are in it. "Come to us, Foremost of the Horizon, great god who has opened up the mysteries. As the sacred doorways have been opened for you, so the mysterious door-leaves have been swung open for you."

Divine Perception speaks to Opener of the Earth: "Open your gate to Re, swing open your door-leaf to He of the Horizon."

He illumines the utter darkness and casts light into the Hidden Chamber. Then this door seals after this great god enters. The *ba*-souls who are in this portal wail when they hear this door slam shut.

HOUR 10

REGISTER 1 (PLATE 25)

4.74. Scene 61. This scene has a complex series of figures that all center on a fal-con-headed sphinx wearing a white crown, named "Horus Who Is in the Bark." The sphinx has a human head wearing a white crown emerging from its rump; the head is labeled "Turning Back." A deity with two heads—a falcon head and Seth-animal head—stands on its back; he has the annotation "His Two Faces."[141] To either side of the sphinx are deities pulling a rope that is connected to a slanting staff with a human head. The staff to the left has a white crown and is pulled by deities with white crowns in place of their heads, called "Southern Gods"; facing these deities is a god also pulling on the rope who is named "Chief of the Prow Rope." To the right, the staff has a red crown and the deities have red crowns in place of their heads, a group labeled "Northern Gods." A god without attributes facing these deities is called "Chief of the Stern Rope."

They exist in this fashion, standing up for Re.

Re says to them (the southern gods): "Receive to yourselves your heads, O gods;[142] lay hold of your prow rope. Hail, manifestations of the

---

141. The two faces of Horus and Seth placed atop a single deity encapsulate in a single powerful icon the reconciliation of the two opposing forces; one should not assume, however, that Seth represents evil, since in the Netherworld Books, he can be instrumental in the combat against Apep (p. 133 n. 11). For the deity "His Two Faces," compare the "two-faced" god in the Book of the Hidden Chamber, Hour 2, Register 1, Scene 14, no. 138 (p. 149) and the god with the same appellation in the Book of Gates, Hour 11, Register 2, Scene 78; on this deity, see Hornung 1980, 228–29; Zeidler 1999a, 279 n. 2. For a possible "two-faced" evening star already in the Pyramid Texts see Goebs 2008, 285–86.

142. As noted in the description to the scene, the "southern gods" are depicted with white crowns in place of their heads, making it logical that they need to "receive" their heads; the Book of Gates, Hour 10, Register 1, Scene 61 is another example of headlessness outside of the realm of the damned, and the solar god can himself be headless (Darnell 2004, 110–15; Manassa 2007a, 40–41). Other headless deities within the Netherworld Books include mummies in the Book of Caverns, Division 6, Regis-ter 2, Scene 72 (p. 445) and the Second Shrine of Tutankhamun (p. 545).

gods! Hail, *akh*-spirits of the gods! May you become manifest, O gods. May you become luminous, O gods, because of my manifestations in the Mysterious Place, because of my luminosity in the places hidden of affairs."

(At the sphinx:) When this god stands up for Re, then His Two Faces enters into this god, after Re passes by him.

Re says to them (the northern gods): "Your heads be to you, O gods. O, receive to yourselves your red crowns, lay hold of your stern rope of the bark of the one who has manifest from me. You are indeed Horus, distinguished of face."

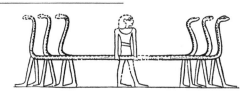

4.75. Scene 62. A serpent with six heads and six pairs of legs is held by a deity who stands in the center of the creature. The serpent is named "Traveler," while the standing deity is called "Opener."

He exists in this fashion. He traverses the Mysterious Place—at High of Piercing, (namely) the portal of the West, does he turn back. Those who are in it swallow their heads, when they smell the odor of Traveler.[143] Opener is the one who guards him.

4.76. Scene 63. A deity—"Trapper"—stands in the middle of the scene, grasping a serpent with eight pairs of legs and eight human-headed uraei emerging from

---

143. The emphasis upon the odor of the god—here the multiheaded serpent Traveler—is not unique to this scene; in the Book of the Creation of the Solar Disk, Tomb of Ramesses VI, Section A2, Register 1, Scene 21: the solar god does not travel into a particular cavern, "because of the putrefaction, stench, and rot of their *ba*-souls" (p. 483); and in Section B2, Scene 43, the annotation reads: "This great god calls to their *ba*-souls, without him seeing them, because of their stench and their rot" (p. 500).

the body; this serpent's name is "One with Human Head(s)." At the base of the scene is another double-headed serpent wearing a white crown on each head; this serpent is labeled "Marvel of the Earth."[144]

He exists in this fashion. When he stands up for Osiris, the *ba*-souls of those to be punished who are in the Netherworld are reckoned to him. He traverses the Mysterious Place—at She Who Is Sacred of *Ba*-souls, (namely,) the gate of the West, does he turn back. The One with Human Head(s) enters into Marvel of the Earth. Those who are in it swallow their heads, when they smell the odor of Marvel of the Earth. Trapper is the one who guards him.

4.77. Scene 64. Two gods hold nets above their heads; the deities are not provided with names.

It is the gods who enchant on behalf of Re-Horakhty in the West. Their magic is that which is at the top of the throw nets, and that which is in the throw nets, in their hands.[145]

REGISTER 2 (PLATE 25)

4.78. Scene 65. The solar bark (see Scene 7) is hauled by four male figures labeled "Netherworld Dwellers."

Hauling this great god by the Netherworldly gods.

They say when they haul Re: "The god is coming to his corpse, the god having been hauled to his shade. May you occupy your body, you having

---

144. Alternatively "Entfernende (in) der Erde" (Zeidler 1999a, 285).

145. Several versions add the text (Hornung 1979b, 342–43; Zeidler 1999a, 286): "May they set the king, lord of the Two Lands RN together with Re-Horakhty, lord of heaven, that he may fraternize with the one who is in heaven, and that he traverse the darkness in the West, that Osiris, lord of glorious appearances RN triumph against his enemies."

been hauled.[146] O one who is healthy in his mystery[147]—Re comes! May you occupy your body. May the chiefs of their throw nets protect you."

4.79. Scene 66. A series of fourteen deities each hold a throw net above their heads. The first three are called "Chiefs of Words"; the first, fourth, fifth, and sixth are human-headed, the second has a double serpent-head, and the third has a bird-head.[148] The next three human-headed figures are "Enchanters." Four monkeys follow, labeled "Protectors of Re." Finally, there are three goddesses also labeled "Protectors of Re."

They exist in this fashion, sailing before Re and enchanting Apep[149] for him. At the portal of He of the Horizon they retreat, while they pass before him toward the sky. On both sides do they manifest for him; it is they who cause him to appear in glory from Nut.

They say, as they enchant: "Hail, rebel—away, Apep, one to whom his evil is given.[150] May your face be destroyed, O Apep—make a way to the slaughtering place. Knives be against you, you having already been cut; the Old Ones be against you, you having already been destroyed. Those with spears lay into you, as we enchant you with what is in our hand(s). Hail, the destroyed one is driven back, the Fettered Serpent[151] is annihilated."

146. Rather than an unusual use of an Old Egyptian pronoun *kw* (*sṯꜣ=sn kw* as Zeidler 1999a, 289 reads; followed by Werning 2013, 241), the *k* is part of a *sḏm.n(y)* form (*sṯꜣ.n(y)=k*), which gives the proper passive sense; compare a passage in the Book of Caverns (Piankoff 1944, pl. XIV, ll. 3–4): *ntṯn stpw m stp=i stp.n(y)=tn m-ḫt stp=i* "You are the chosen ones of my choice; (only) after I was chosen were you chosen" (p. 357 below).

147. The "mystery" of the solar god is his corpse, most often personified in the Netherworld Books by the god Osiris (see pp. 6–7 for further discussion).

148. In the version on the sarcophagus of Seti I, all six figures have human heads.

149. For enchanting Apep, see the commentary in chapter 1 (pp. 10–13), noting especially the parallels in the Book of the Hidden Chamber, Hour 7.

150. Hornung 1980, 235 suggests "gebunden"; note also Hannig 2006a, 585 ("*s. wehren").

151. "*Ssy*," *LGG* 6:597–98 reads this name as "He belonging to the ashes(?)," citing examples that clearly relate to punishment by fire, a reading also proposed by Zeidler

4.80. Scene 67. Three gods holding a coiled rope and armed with spears are labeled "They of the Spears." A deity who is lying prone, with his torso lifted up, also holds onto the rope and is labeled "Old One." A multi-coiled serpent, the object of the deities' aggression, is labeled "Apep." Above Apep is a crocodile whose tail ends in a serpent, called "Crocodile(?)."[152]

They are in this fashion, carrying their spears. They protect the rope of the Old One, without them allowing this serpent to draw near to the bark of the great god. In the following of this god in heaven do they pass by. It is these gods who fight on behalf of this god in Nut.

REGISTER 3 (PLATE 25)

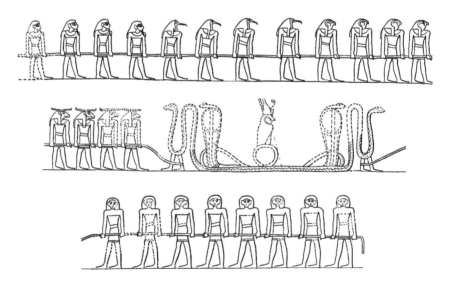

1999a, 293; rather than a general description of punishment (Hornung 1980, 236), *iss* in the Pyramid Texts (Hannig 2003, 219) and Coffin Texts (Hannig 2006a, 412) can specifically refer to capturing with a net in the Netherworld (Bidoli 1976 provides an analysis of the relevant Coffin Text spells).

    152. No compelling interpretation has been offered for the name of the crocodile *šsš* (Zeidler 1999a, 295; "*Šsš*," *LGG* 7:128).

4.81, 4.82, 4.83. Scene 68. The entire Register 3 of Hour 10 consists of one complex scene. The focus of the scene is a double-sided uraeus serpent inside another double serpent with two pairs of legs, the latter labeled "Khepry."[153] In the middle of these serpents is a falcon with double crown called "Netherworldly Horus." To the left are four sets of four gods pulling a rope connected to the serpents; from left to right, these deities are labeled "*Ba*-souls of the West" (human-headed); "Those in the Following of Thoth" (ibis-headed), "Those in the Following of Horus" (falcon-headed), and "Those in the Following of Re" (ram-headed). To the right of the serpents are two sets of four human figures, in Ramesses VI depicted with faces toward the viewer, labeled "Powerful Ones."[154]

They are in this fashion—in their hands is the tow rope which exists at the feet of (the serpent) Khepry. When he retreats at the portal of the horizon, they loosen this tow rope from this god at the horizon. It is they who haul him from Nut. As they live on the south winds, so they breathe from the north winds—namely, from that which comes forth from the mouth of Re.[155] The voice of (the serpent) Khepry circulates through[156] the Mysterious Place, when Re enters into the sky.

They say to Re: "The one who comes after his manifestations is coming. Re is coming after his manifestations. The one who comes forth after his manifestations is coming forth. Re is coming forth after his manifestations. To the sky, to the sky, O Great One.[157] Hail, we commend you upon your throne by means of the tow rope which is in our fingers—She Great of Visible Forms in the Mysterious Place."

He is in this fashion, the Netherworldly Horus coming forth from him, (namely) the head. It is from the coils that the manifestations come forth. Re calls to this god, and his two uraeus goddesses unite with him. Then Horus enters into (the serpent) Khepry when Re calls to him. In their hands is the tow rope, which exists at the feet of (the serpent) Khepry.

---

153. Minas-Nerpel 2006, 194–97.

154. Their front depiction may underline their power (Volokhine 2000, 79).

155. Wind in the Netherworld plays a prominent role in the description of goddesses in the final scene of the Book of the Hidden Chamber, Hour 11, Register 1, Scene 115 (pp. 228–29). For the winds, see also Kurth 1994.

156. The encircling motion of Khepry's cries possess a magical significance (for *pḥr* in magical texts, see Ritner 1993, 57–67).

157. As Hornung (1980, 243–44) notes, this address to Re appears to originate in an archaic source, sharing a strong parallel with Pyramid Text Spell 506 (§1101d): *r p.t zp znw r s.t wr.t mm nṯr.w* "To the sky, to the sky, to the great place among the gods!"

They say to Re: "May the ways of the Mysterious Place open to you, may the doors which are in the earth swing open to your *ba*-soul, so that he may occupy Nut. We are following you in the waterways of Kenset.[158] Hail, you are entering the East, may you sail from the thighs of your mother."

DOORWAY 10 (PLATE 25)

4.84. Doorway 10. Doorway 10 is like those of earlier hours (p. 264) and is called "Sanctified." The upper mummiform figure is "Screamer(?), bending his arms for Re" the lower one "One Who Uncovers, bending his arms for Re." The uraei are each labeled "For Re she casts fire." Rather than mummiform figures, the interior of the doorway has sixteen uraei. The serpent at the door-leaf is labeled "Fire-Shooter. He is at this door-leaf, he opens for Re."

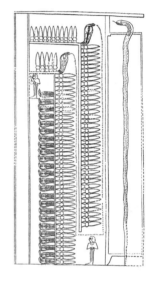

Arrival by this great god at this doorway, entering into this doorway by this great god. This great god is extolled by the gods who are in it. "Come to us, Foremost of the Horizon, great god who has opened up the mysteries. As the sacred doorways have been opened for you, so the mysterious door-leaves have been swung open for you."

Divine Perception speaks to Fire-Shooter: "Open your gate to Re, swing open your door-leaf to He of the Horizon."

He illumines the utter darkness and casts light into the Hidden Chamber. Then this door seals after this great god enters. The uraei who are in this doorway wail when they hear this door slam shut.

---

158. For the toponym Kenset, see the commentary to the Book of Adoring Re in the West, Litany 5 (p. 110).

HOUR 11

REGISTER 1 (PLATE 26)

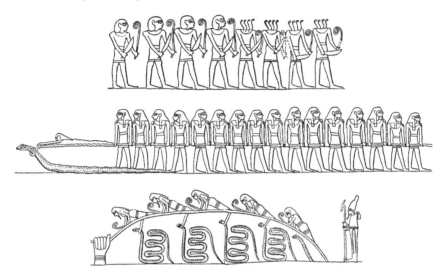

4.85, 4.86, 4.87. Scene 69. The scene takes up the entire register and consists of several distinct groups of deities. At the far left are two sets of four deities, each holding a coiled rope and a knife—the human-headed figures are called "They of the Fetters," while the next set have four serpents in place of a head and are called "Slaughterers." In front of them is a bound serpent, "Apep," with the short annotation "His voice circulates in the Netherworld." Atop the serpent is a prone goddess labeled "Selket." Four deities facing the serpent grasp the rope, "Those of the Chord," while twelve more deities facing away are labeled "Gods Who Cut Throats." A giant fist, "Hidden of Corpses," holds onto the same rope;[159] the rope then ascends over four coiled serpents. The first serpent is called "Roasting Flame," and the others bear the collective name "Children of Weakness." Geb and the four sons of Horus—"Imsety," "Hapy," "Duamutef," and "Qebehsenuef"—appear as prone figures atop the serpents. Finally, a figure of Osiris concludes the register and is named "Foremost of the Westerners."

They exist in this fashion. As they stand up for Re,[160] so he appears in glory, as he reaches them.

---

159. Sourdive 1984, 418; for fist-shaped images in the hands of baboons, see Hour 12, Register 2, Scene 90, below (p. 330).

160. For an alternative interpretation of ꜥḥꜥ n as "await," see Zeidler 1999a, 309 and n. 1.

They say to Re: "Appear in glory, O Re; be powerful, O He of the Horizon. Behold, we are felling Apep, the one who has been put in his bonds. You shall not approach, O Re, to your enemies, and your enemies shall not approach, O Re. May your sanctity be manifest, O One in the Encircling Serpent,[161] with the result that Apep is broken in his blood, he being punished while Re stands still at the hour of contentment."

Then this great god passes by, after his (Apep's) bonds have been tied.

This serpent exists in this fashion. It is Selket who appoints his bindings.[162] The bark of this great god pursues its course toward the vicinity of Apep. After his (Apep's) bindings have been tied, this great god sails.

They exist in this fashion, as they grasp the ropes of that evil serpent. They say to Re: "Sail, O Re; hurry, O He of the Horizon, for the sword is stuck in Terrible of Face—Apep is in his bindings."

They exist in this fashion, as guardian(s) of the Children of Weakness. By means of the punishing rope in the hand of Hidden of Corpses do they guard. At the portal of Foremost of the Westerners are the dead placed all around him.[163]

These deities say: "Darkness be to your face, O Roasting Flame (serpent); destruction be to you, O Children of Weakness, by means of the hand of the Hidden One, as it casts evil by means of that which binds the damned. Geb is watching your bindings,[164] the children of roping leave you entrapped—guard yourselves from the condemnation of Foremost of the Westerners."

They exist in this fashion, installing the ropings of the Children of Weakness. The bark of the great god pursues its course to this vicinity of Apep. After laying on your bindings, he travels.

161. The deity within the Encircling Serpent (Mehen) is the sun god, who is depicted in the middle register of every hour surrounded by the protective serpent.

162. For the role of scorpion goddesses in the destruction of Apep, see Borghouts 2007, 34.

163. The dead—a reference to the damned—are assembled around Apep and thus share his fate in the Netherworld (Zeidler 1999a, 313 n. 1).

164. Geb protects the solar deity against Apep, which is appropriate given the god's control over the earth and thus serpents (Beidier 1995, 187 and n. 14; Klotz 2006, 93). Note also the role of Geb against Apep in chapter 39 of the Book of Going Forth By Day (Borghouts 2007, 16).

REGISTER 2 (PLATE 26)

4.88. Scene 70. The solar bark (see Scene 7) is hauled by four male figures labeled "Netherworld Dwellers."

Hauling this great god by the Netherworldly gods.

They say, as they haul Re: "To the sky we haul, to the sky we haul; to Nut do we follow Re. May you grow powerful, O Re, by means of your face. May you grow great and may you go to rest, O Re, by means of your mysterious face.[165] May the face of Re open, may the eyes of He of the Horizon illumine,[166] that he might dispel darkness from the West, as he sets the dawn by means of that which illumines for him the darkness."

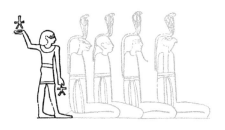

4.89. Scene 71. A deity holds a star aloft in his left hand, while another star appears below his right hand. He is named "One of the Hour."

As he stands up for Re, so he occupies the sky at One of the Hour, this god acting as the one who guides him. The hour performs its duties.

<hr>

165. Zeidler 1999a, 315 n. 1 reads *tp štꜣ* as "Mumienmaske"; since the solar face depicted in Hour 11, Register 2, Scene 73 shows no features suggesting that is to be identified as a piece of funerary equipment, the reading *ḥr štꜣ* in the Seti I sarcophagus version is given here.

166. For the reading *bꜣq*, see Zeidler 1999a, 315, n. 2.

4.90. Scene 72. The scene contains four kneeling deities, each with a cobra atop the head. The first, falcon-headed figure is "Horus"; next is a human-headed figure with wig "Breathing One"; third is a human-headed figure without wig called "Angry One";[167] finally, a lioness-headed figure is labeled "Sakhmet."

They exist in this fashion, those who are in the earth[168] being their guardians. As they stand up for Re, so they sit down with the great image beneath them. Then they pass after Re, bearing the mysterious image that is beneath them.

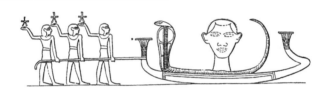

4.91. Scene 73. A bark contains a uraeus serpent and large face with the annotation "This is the face of the solar disk."[169] Three gods hold a rope attached to the bark and in their left hands hold aloft stars; they are named "Those of the Stars."

They exist in this fashion, praising by means of their stars, seizing hold of the prow rope of this bark, they having entered into Nut. This is the face of Re. He performs a navigation in the earth, while those who are in the Netherworld praise him.

---

167. "ꜥbš," LGG 2:90; the name also appears as a designation for a crocodile in the Book of the Hidden Chamber, Hour 7, Register 3, Scene 79. For an alternate reading "Überschwemmender," see Zeidler 1999a, 317.

168. The serpent determinative indicates that this epithet describes the uraei who rest atop the heads of the deities; the apotropaic function of these deities is further indicated by their appearance in other tombs (Hornung 1980, 254)

169. The itn "disk" is also one of the forms of Re in the Book of Adoring Re in the West, Address 4 (p. 77). For the frontally viewed face here, see also Volokhine 2000, 75–76.

4.92. Scene 74: A winged serpent is labeled "Guide."

For Re she stands up. It is she who guides this great god to the gate of the eastern horizon.

4.93. Scene 75. A deity holding a taper is called "Flaming One." The flame from the taper falls between the horns of a bull-headed staff crossed by a knife.[170]

To Re does he stand up. When he casts fire into the horns, the knife which is in the hand of the Fighter, who is in the retinue of this god, goes forth.

4.94. Scene 76. An upright serpent is flanked by two human heads and is called "Living One."

For Re she stands up, established of lifetime, inscribed with years by means of this uraeus. Near him she mounts to heaven.

---

170. The bull-headed staff "is a reference to the eastern corner of the cosmos (bull's head) as the place of fiery rebirth (flame) and final perdition (flame and knife)" (Darnell 2004, 165). The bull-headed staff recalls the four bull-heads with solar disk in the Books of the Solar-Osirian Unity within the Tomb of Ramesses VI, Corridor G Ceiling, Register 1, Scene 1 and Tomb of Ramesses VI, Corridor G Ceiling, Register 3, Scene 8 (pp. 553, 558).

4.95. Scene 77. Four goddesses stand with their arms raised in adoration; they are labeled "Those of Crying Out."

They say, as they call out to Re, as Re passes by: "Hail, come, child. Hail, come, one who fashioned the Netherworld. Come, O one whom heaven rears.[171] Hail, you are become manifest, O Re."

4.96. Scene 78. Two bows appear below two sets of three uraei—"That Encircling Serpent of the Uraei"—between which is a figure with both a falcon-head and Seth-head labeled "His Two Faces."[172]

That Encircling Serpent of the uraei traverses the Netherworld. The bows carry His Two Faces as his mystery. It is they who proclaim Re in the eastern horizon of the sky, they crossing heaven after him.

REGISTER 3 (PLATE 26)

4.97. Scene 79. Twelve gods carrying oars are named for the circumpolar stars, "The Gods Who Do Not Know Perishing."[173]

---

171. Interpreting *ꜣtw* as the verb *ꜣt* "to nurse" (Wiebach-Koepke 2003a, 343 n. 1), which appears in the Pyramid Texts (Hannig 2003, 21) and Ptolemaic sources (Wilson 1997, 26–27). This reading provides a nice parallel to addressing the solar god as "child" and is to be preferred over Zeidler 1999a, 323 "Instrukteur des Himmels" and Hornung 1980, 258 "der (du) den Himmel betrittst."

172. For this dual-natured deity, see 310 n. 141.

173. These gods personify the circumpolar stars—Leitz 1989, 62, 64; Krauss 1997, 86–130 argues that the definition can also include non-circumpolar stars in the northern portion of the sky.

They exist in this fashion. For Re they stand up, receiving their oars at this cavern of One of the Hour.[174] At the birth of Re from Nut do they manifest, their manifestations corresponding to the birth forms of Re, they coming forth from Nun near him.[175] It is they who row this great god after he goes to rest in the eastern horizon of the sky.

Re says to them: "Receive to yourselves your oars, occupy for yourselves your stars. Your manifestations are indeed my manifestations; your birth forms are indeed my birth forms. O my rowers, you shall not perish, O gods who do not know perishing."

4.98. Scene 80. Twelve goddesses grasp a long rope and are crowned with stars; they are labeled "Hour Goddesses Who Haul."

They exist in this fashion, receiving this towrope of the bark in order to haul Re from Nut. It is they who haul Re, who show the ways in Nut. It is these goddesses who guide this great god in the Netherworld.[176]

Re says to them: "As you receive the towrope, so you become content. May you haul my entourage into heaven, and guide me to your roads. My birth forms are indeed your birth forms; my manifestations are indeed your manifestations. Hail, may you establish the lifetime, and may you assign years according to what is in you."

---

174. "One of the Hour" is a reference to the god in Hour 11, Register 2, Scene 71. Gods who carry oars also appear in the Book of the Hidden Chamber, Hour 12, Register 3, Scene 97 (pp. 215–16), those deities being given the task of repelling Apep as the sun rises in the eastern horizon of the sky.

175. For the manifesting of stars near sunrise in Egyptian astronomical conceptions, see Quack 1999.

176. The hour goddesses as divine guides within the Netherworld is a frequent motif within the Book of the Hidden Chamber—among the many examples, compare the Hour 1, Register 1, Scene 4 description of the twelve personified hours as "Names of the goddesses who guide the great god" (p. 140); each hour of that book also concludes with the statement: "The hour who guides (in) this gateway …"

4.99. Scene 81. Seven gods with separate annotations: a crocodile-headed god labeled "One of the Neck"; a deity crowned with star named "Rustling One"; a bull-headed god named "Bull of the West"; another deity crowned with a star named "Nurse of the Stars"; a monkey on a standard named "One of the Nethersky"; an *udjat*-eye on a standard named "Divine Eye"; and a deity with *was*-scepter called "He Who is Upon His Throne."

This god (One of the Neck) is in this fashion. It is he who cries out so that the doorways of Re open, he passing near him.

This god (Rustling One) is in this fashion. It is he who cries out to the stars at the birth of this great god, he passing near him.

This god (Bull of the West) is in this fashion. It is he who calls the gods of the bark of Re, he passing near him.

This god (Nurse of the Stars) is in this fashion. It is he who assigns the stars to their towns, he passing near this great god.

When he (One of the Nethersky) praises Re, he makes ovation to He of the Horizon.

It (Divine Eye) is the eye of Re. This god is becoming content with her, when she takes up her seat in the bark.

As he (He Who Is Upon His Throne) opens, the doorman of this cavern, so he remains at his place, without passing near Re.

DOORWAY 11 (PLATE 27)

4.100. Doorway 11. Doorway 11 is similar to the other portals (p. 264), but rather than an ennead of mummies inside the inner doorway there are two *was*-scepters, wearing white crowns, facing one another. The doorway is called "She Who Is Mysterious of Inductions."[177] The upper mummiform figure is labeled "Sharp of Cut, bending his arms for Re," while the lower figure has the annotation "He Who Slices, bending his arms for Re." The uraei are each labeled "For Re she casts fire." The one *was*-scepter is named "Horus," the other "Osiris." The serpent at the door-leaf has the annotation "One Who Is in His Watery Efflux. He is at this door-leaf, he opens for Re."

---

177. For the term *bsi*, see p. 114 n. 113.

Arrival by this great god at this doorway. Entering into this doorway by this great god. This
great god is extolled by the gods who are in it.

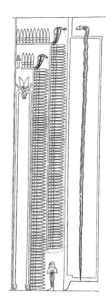

They (Horus and Osiris) say to Re: "In peace,
in peace, O Re; in peace, in peace, O One Plentiful of Manifestations. Your *ba*-soul be to heaven,
your corpse to the earth, you who has decreed to
yourself greatness on your own."

Divine Perception speaks to One Who Is in
His Watery Efflux: "Open your gate to Re, swing
open your door-leaf to He of the Horizon."

He illumines the utter darkness and casts
light into the Hidden Chamber. Then this door
seals after this great god enters. The gods who
are in this doorway wail when they hear this
door slam shut.

HOUR 12

REGISTER 1 (PLATE 27)

4.101. Scene 82. Four gods hold aloft a disk with their left hands; they are labeled
"Those Bearing the Luminous One."

They are in this fashion, bearing the disk of Re. It is they who join the
Netherworld to heaven, by means of this image which is in their hands,
who guard affairs at the doorway of Igeret, until Re goes to rest in the body
of Nut.

4.102. Scene 83. Four gods hold aloft a star with their left hands; they are labeled "Those Who Carry the Stars."

They are in this fashion, bearing the stars, as the arms of Nun receive Re.[178] By means of their stars do they praise. As they pass near him to heaven, so they go to rest in the body of Nut.[179]

4.103. Scene 84. Four gods hold was-scepters; they are named "Those Who Go Forth."

They exist in this fashion, their *djam*-scepters in their hands. It is they who establish the land-plots[180] for this god in heaven, when Re commends their thrones.

---

178. Nun's reception of the solar deity is depicted in the Concluding Scene (p. 336).

179. As Zeidler 1999a, 341 notes, this scene shows an intertextual relationship with the cosmographic books, especially the Blueprint of the Course of the Stars (Book of Nut). The motion of the stars, who follow the solar deity, is similarly explained in the Book of Nut: "It is from the Netherworld that the majesty of this god goes forth; it is from the Mesqet-region that these stars go forth behind him" (von Lieven 2007c, 55, 379 [§21]).

180. The distribution of land-plots forms a main theme in the Book of the Hidden Chamber, Hour 2 (p. 147); compare the passage from the introductory text of that hour: "This great god makes land-plots for the gods at this locale." Note also the granting of land-plots by the gods who measure the cultivated fields in the Book of Gates, Hour 5, Register 1, Scene 25 (p. 279).

4.104. Scene 85. Four ram-headed deities, holding *was*-scepters, are labeled "Ram," "Khnum," "*Pender*,"[181] and "One Who Rages(?)."

They exist in this fashion, their *djam*-scepters in their hands. It is they who supply the offerings of the gods who are in this sky, who assign the movement of the flood,[182] before Re arrives at Nun.

4.105. Scene 86. Four falcon-headed deities, holding was-scepters, are labeled "Horus," "Falcon," "Sopdu," "He Who Is in His Two Barks."[183]

They exist in this fashion, their *djam*-scepters in their hands. It is they who establish the shrine, and who stretch out the arm to the crew (of gods) who are (in) the two barks of the god, after the coming forth from the mouth of

181. "*Pndr*," *LGG* 3:39; Hornung (1980, 269) relates *pndr* and the following *dnd* (here tentatively translated as "One Who Rages") to the designations of the solar deity as *pndn* and *dnd(n)* that appear in Pyramid Texts Spell 222 (§§200b–c), for which Allen (2005, 39) proposes the following translation: "[he] has come [to you], his father: he has come to you, O Fertilizer; he has come to you, his father: he has come to you, O Rager."

182. Following Baumann 1998, 264, contra Zeidler 1999a, 343; Hornung (1980, 269) reads this as a *ni sḏmt=f* form "bevor die Flut hervorströmt." While the gemination of *ni sḏmt=f* form is unusual, Hornung's reading does find support in the description of the "great flood" in the final scene of the Book of the Hidden Chamber (Scene 131, p. 241): "From this image does the great flood come forth from the land."

183. The two barks refer to the *mʿnḏ.t* and *mskt.t*, the day and night bark of the sun, whose depiction prow-to-prow signals the transitions of dawn and sunset (Thomas 1956; Roberson 2013, 14–15, *passim*).

the Unified One.[184] As soon as they set the course in Nut, the hour comes about before (the hour) She Has Become Content.[185]

4.106. Scene 87. Eight goddesses are seated upon uraei and hold stars in their right hands. They are labeled "The Protecting Morning Stars."[186] A crocodile-headed god at the end of the register holds a *was*-scepter and serpent and is called "Splendid of Mouth."

They (the goddesses) exist in this fashion, their Encircling Serpents beneath them, their arms bearing stars, they coming forth on either side of this great god—four to the East, four to the West. It is they who call the eastern *ba*-souls. They praise this god, and they adore him after he has gone forth. As the Child[187] does he come forth in his manifestations. It is they who guide the rowing of the crew in the bark of this great god, they calling to this god and taking hold of their Encircling Serpents.

The one who passes by heaven after him (Splendid of Mouth) is in this fashion. His stride corresponds to their stride. As soon as they stand up for this god, this god turns himself back at this doorway. At the gate of the West he goes forth and stands up.

184. Alternatively, a location *Rꜣ-smꜣ* (Zeidler 1999a, 345).

185. "She who Becomes Content" is the first hour of the day, as mentioned in the Book of the Day and the Blueprint of the Course of the Stars (Book of Nut) (von Lieven 2007c, 139, §25).

186. The visibility of stars just before sunrise indicates a lack of the dangerous clouds that might obscure the sun. For an alternative reading for the names of these goddesses, see Zeidler 1999a, 347: "Die 'Anbetenden' und die 'Grüßenden.'"

187. The solar god as the child appears elsewhere in the Netherworld Books—compare the Book of Adoring Re in the West, Address 61 (p. 97, p. 567 n. 72).

REGISTER 2 (PLATE 27)

4.107. Scene 88. The solar bark (see Scene 7) is hauled by four male figures labeled "Netherworld Dwellers."

The Netherworldly gods say: "Go forth from the West; go to rest on the two banks of Nun; make transformations on the two arms of Nun[188]—this god has not (yet) entered heaven." By means of his manifestations which are in Nun shall he separate the Netherworld from heaven.[189] As for the separation of the Netherworld from Nut, it is the arms of Hidden of His Name.[190] In the utter darkness does he exist, they coming forth, Re being in the morning glow.

4.108. Scene 89. Nine gods (five human-headed and four jackal-headed)—"The Ennead that Punishes Apep"—brandish scepters and knives. The object of their aggression is a serpent, "Apep," who is tied to stakes labeled the "Children of Horus."

They exist in this fashion, their staves in their hands, they receiving their knives so that they might punish Apep. It is they who carry out his slaughter, who cause deep wounds at the sandbanks which are in heaven.[191] In

188. The Osirieon and tomb of Tauseret add the word *ḥtp* following Nun (Hornung 1979b, 387; Zeidler 1999a, 351 n. 2).

189. In Hour 12, Register 2, Scene 88, the solar deity separates heaven from the Netherworld, while in Hour 12, Register 1, Scene 82, the solar disks in the hands of the gods unite the two realms.

190. The arms of Osiris function similarly in the Blueprint of the Course of the Stars (Book of Nut) (von Lieven 2007c, 137–39).

191. Probable pun on sandbanks and neck vertebrae (Assmann 1969, 296 n. 59). The celestial location of the punishment of Apep parallels a statement in the Book of the Hidden Chamber, Hour 12, Register 1, Scene 122, which also mentions the "mysterious sandbank of the sky … having punished for him Apep in the sky" (p. 235).

the hands of the Children of Horus are the measuring ropes of this rebel. They fly up before this god, their bond(s) in their fingers, this god counting his members after the Hidden One opens his arms in order to prepare the way for Re.

This serpent (Apep) is in this fashion, the Children of Horus seizing hold of him, as they go to rest in Nut.

They (the Children of Horus) are in this fashion, weighing down his bonds. It means that his sandbanks exist in heaven, his poison descending in the West.[192]

4.109. Scene 90. Four apes, each holding a fist, are labeled "Baboons."[193]

They exist in this fashion. It is they who proclaim Re in the eastern horizon of the sky.[194] They proclaim this god who created them, by means of their hands, two upon the East and two upon the West, on both sides of this god. Just as they come forth after him, so his *ba*-soul becomes strong when he sees them. It is they who establish his solar disk.

---

192. Alternatively "the sphere of action (*ḥꜣ.w*) of his poison is in the West" (Borghouts 2007, 28).

193. For the symbolism of this scene, see Kurth 1988; Sourdive 1984, 419 (for fist-shaped amulets, see 449–53).

194. A parallel to this statement appears in the Solar Chapel of Medinet Habu (Epigraphic Survey 1963, pl. 420b): "Baboons who announce Re, when this great god is born at the hours in the Underworld. After he transforms do they appear for him. It is when he rises in the eastern horizon of heaven that they (again) are on both sides of this god …" Similarly, in the text King as Solar Priest, the baboons appear as the "eastern *ba*-souls" whose mysterious language the king knows (on this passage, see p. 38 and n. 60). Baboons acclaiming Re allude to Re himself as the Netherworldly baboon in the Book of Adoring Re in the West, Address 69 (see pp. 73–74); on baboons in the Netherworld Books, see also Manassa 2007a, 86–88.

4.110. Scene 91. This scene includes three deities: a goddess wearing a white crown, labeled "West"; a goddess wearing a red crown, named "She of Sais";[195] and a god holding a *was*-scepter and *ankh*-sign, labeled "He of the Doorway."

They exist in this fashion. It is at this doorway of the Netherworldly One, the one who opens the caverns and establishes the mysterious doorways, that they turn themselves back. Their *ba*-souls pass by in his following.

REGISTER 3 (PLATE 27)

4.111. Scene 92. Four deities wearing white crowns are labeled "Distinguished of Heads."

They exist in this fashion. It is they who establish the white crown for the gods who are in the following of Re. With their *ba*-souls having already passed by shall they remain in the Netherworld. At this doorway do they stand up.

4.112. Scene 93. Four gods are named "Those Who Mourn."

They exist in this fashion in this doorway, mourning Osiris when Re comes forth from the West, their *ba*-souls having passed by him. In the following of Osiris do they exist.

195. Sais also figures prominently within the Book of the Hidden Chamber, Hour 11; the middle register text describes Isis and Nephthys as serpents existing at the "sacred road of Sais," while the following depiction of four hypostases of Neith is labeled "It is they who protect the sacred gate of Sais" (p. 231).

4.113. Scene 94. Four deities wearing red crowns are labeled "Those Who Form."

They exist in this fashion. It is they who unite with Re, and who bring about his birth in the earth.[196] When their *ba*-souls enter after them, their corpses remain in their places.[197]

4.114. Scene 95. Four deities without attributes are called "Those Who Nurse."

They exist in this fashion. It is they who nurse Re,[198] and who aggrandize the names of his manifestations. Their *ba*-souls pass by after him, their corpses remaining in their places.

---

196. The fours gods labeled "Those Who Form" are hypostases of the god Khnum, who creates upon his potter's wheel; the formation of the solar god atop a potter's wheel is depicted explicitly in the concluding scene of the Book of the Night (Dorman 1999; Manassa 2007a, 177–80).

197. For the dual fates of the *ba*-soul and corpse, see the commentary to the Book of Adoring Re in the West (p. 8 n. 13).

198. The "nursing" relates to the child-form of the solar deity (Hornung 1980, 282–83); compare also the statement in the Book of Gates, Hour 12, Register 1, Scene 87 (p. 328): "As the Child does he come forth in his manifestations."

4.115. Scene 96. Four goddesses wearing white crowns are named "Distinguished Ones."

They exist in this fashion. It is they who cause Maat to mount up, and who establish her in the shrine of Re, when he goes to rest in Nut. Their *ba*-souls pass by in his following, while their corpses remain in their places.

4.116. Scene 97. Four goddesses wearing red crowns are labeled "Those Who Form."

They exist in this fashion. It is they who establish the lifetime and who bring about the years for those who belong to execration[199] in the Netherworld, and for those who live in the sky. In the following of this god do they exist.

199. For the term *ṯms* "execration" see above, p. 233, commentary to the Book of the Hidden Chamber, Hour 11, Register 3, Scene 121, which similarly describes four goddesses as "It is they who make execrations among the enemies of Osiris in the Netherworld" (p. 233).

4.117. Scene 98. Four goddesses are named "Those Who Mourn."

They exist in this fashion in this doorway, mourning by means of their hair[200] in front of this great god in the West. That they turn themselves back at this doorway is without entering into heaven.

4.118. Scene 99. Four gods leaning forward (in an attitude of old age) are named "The Old Ones."

They exist in this fashion. As they praise Re, so they adore him, glorifying him by means of their summons. They are the gods who are in the Netherworld,[201] doormen of the Mysterious Place, they remaining in their places.

---

200. The use of hair in mourning recalls the *nwn*-gesture, in which the mourner pulls at hair that is flipped in front of his/her face (Manassa 2007a, 30–32); in the Book of Adoring Re in the West, Litany 7, this gesture is described as transformative (p. 119): "The mourners pull their hair for you.... It is when they wail that your *ba*-soul jubilates, with the result that your corpse becomes transfigured." For male deities in this position and their mourning for Osiris, compare also the Book of Caverns, Division 2, Register 2, Scene 18 (pp. 358–59).

201. While seemingly obvious, this statement asserts that while the deities are at the cusp of this world and the next, they still belong to the class of Netherworldly beings (Zeidler 1999a, 371 n. 1)

4.119. Scene 100. A cat-headed deity holding a *was*-scepter and a serpent is appropriately named "The Cat-Like One."[202]

He is the door-keeper of the cavern. In his place will he remain.

DOORWAY (PLATE 28)

4.120. Doorway 12: Doorway 12 of the Book of Gates has two door-leaves with upright serpents; the doorway is named "Sacred of Power." The lower mummiform figure is labeled "One of the Morning Glow, bending his arm for Re"; the upper figure has the annotation "The One Who Flies Up, bending his arm for Re." The uraei are each labeled "For Re she casts fire." Inside the doorway are two human-headed staves named "Khepri" and "Atum"; they bear the additional annotation: "They stand atop them. They manifest upon their staves at this doorway, their heads standing at this doorway." The serpent at the first door-leaf has the annotation: "One of the Gate. He is at this door-leaf; he opens for Re." The serpent at the second door-leaf is named "Coiled One" and has the same text. To the 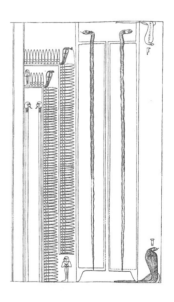 right of the door-leaves are two uraei named "Isis" and "Nephthys"; between them is the following text: "It is they who protect this mysterious doorway of the West. In the following of this god do they pass by."

Arrival by this great god at this doorway, entering into this doorway. This great god is extolled by the gods who are in it.

202. This feline manifestation of the solar deity is praised in the Book of Adoring Re in the West, Address 33 (p. 88); see also p. 72–73 for commentary on the solar god as the Great Cat.

Divine Perception (says) to One of the Gate: "Open your gate to Re, swing open your door-leaf to He of the Horizon."

He emerges from the Mysterious Place, and goes to rest in the belly of Nut. Then this door seals, and the *ba*-souls who are in the West wail, when this door slams shut.

Divine Perception (says) to the Coiled One: "Open your gate to Re, swing open your door-leaf to He of the Horizon. He emerges from the Mysterious Place, and goes to rest in the belly of Nut. Then this door seals, and the *ba*-souls who are in the West wail, when this door slams shut."

CONCLUDING SCENE (PLATE 28)

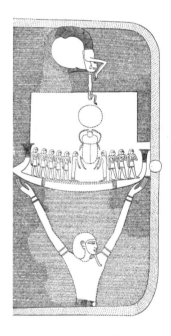

4.121. Concluding Scene. The final scene of the Book of Gates is complex. Beginning at the bottom of the scene, there is a large depiction of a male deity, labeled "Nun," who is only visible from the chest upwards; he lifts aloft a solar bark and a short annotation between his arms reads: "So that they might lift up this god, do these arms emerge from the water."[203] The solar bark contains ten deities. At the prow are three gods labeled "Door-(keepers)." They are followed by "Isis" and "Nephthys" whose arms support a large scarab pushing a solar disk. The remainder of the crew is: "Geb," "Shu," "Magic," "Divine Utterance," and "Divine Perception." Over the solar bark is the annotation: "This god rests in the day-bark. The gods who are within it." The solar disk pushed by the scarab is met by a goddess, who is inverted with respect to the rest of the scene; hieroglyphs label her as: "She is Nut, as she receives Re." Nut is supported by a representation of Osiris who is curled back around himself, his feet touching the back of his head; an annotation within the circle formed by Osiris's body reads: "It is Osiris, as he encircles the Netherworld."

---

203. For the symbolism of the uplifted arms, see Sourdive 1984, 410–14; compare pairs of arms uplifting the solar disk in the Books of the Creation of the Solar Disk (pp. 495, 498, 507) and Books of the Solar-Osirian Unity, the Second Shrine of Tutankhamun (pp. 551–52).

5
BOOK OF CAVERNS

INTRODUCTION

The sole synoptic hieroglyphic edition of the Book of Caverns remains Piankoff (1942a, 1944, 1945—collected in 1946; with index 1947a), with the versions of the tomb of Ramesses VI available in Piankoff and Rambova (1954) and the important Osireion copy in Henri Frankfort (1933). Translations include Piankoff and Rambova (1954), Hornung (2002), Carrier (2009), and Daniel Werning (2011b); the most complete analysis of transmission history and grammar is Werning (2011a).

The earliest attested copy of the Book of Caverns was placed in the entrance corridor of the Osireion (Cenotaph of Seti I), completed during the reign of Merneptah (Werning 2011b, 15–17). Within the Osireion, the Book of Caverns appears opposite the Book of Gates, creating an interesting juxtaposition of an "earlier" Netherworld book with twelve divisions and a "later" composition that deviates from the hourly template.[1] The tombs of Merneptah (KV 8), Tawosret/Sethnakht (KV 14), and Ramesses III (KV 11) incorporate a variant of the concluding scene of the Book of Caverns (Werning 2011b, 20–24); in the tomb of Tawosret/Sethnakht, the alternative concluding scene appears among scenes from the Books of the Creation of the Solar Disk (see p. 458 and n. 4). The wall decoration of the tombs in the Valley of the Kings does not utilize other portions of the Book of Caverns until the Twentieth Dynasty, although occurrences on moveable surfaces, such as shrines or shrouds (significant in the textual transmission of the Book of Adoring Re in the West and the Book of the

---

1. Similarly, the Thirtieth Dynasty sarcophagus of Tjaihorpata (CG 29306) juxtaposes Divisions 1–2 of the Book of Caverns with six hours from the Book of the Hidden Chamber (Manassa 2007a, 459).

Hidden Chamber), may have been present between the reigns of Merneptah and Ramesses IV.[2] The tomb of Ramesses IV situates Divisions 1–2 of
the Book of Caverns in the third corridor, a location previously reserved
for Hours 4–5 of the Book of the Hidden Chamber (pp. 28–29). The tomb
of Ramesses VI mimics the layout of the Osireion, opposing the Book of
Caverns and the Book of Gates in the first three corridors of the tomb,
with scenes continuing into the first pillared hall. The version of the Book
of Caverns within the tomb of Ramesses VI is notable for its frequent personalizations (Abitz 1995, 126–132).[3] The tomb of Ramesses VII, which
consists of a single corridor prior to the burial chamber, also juxtaposes
the Book of Gates with the Book of Caverns, but due to space constraints,
the decoration includes only the beginning scenes of each composition.
The tomb of Ramesses IX distributes the divisions of the Book of Caverns throughout the tomb, and in the sarcophagus chamber, scenes from
the Book of Caverns can appear fully integrated into registers containing
scenes and texts otherwise attested in the Books of the Creation of the
Solar Disk (see pp. 462–63).

Following the end of the New Kingdom, the Book of Caverns appears
rarely in nonroyal contexts. Diverging from the more common use of the
Book of Adoring Re in the West and the final four hours of the Book of
the Hidden Chamber, the Twenty-First Dynasty papyrus of Nedjmet (BM
10490) includes several scenes from the Book of Caverns interspersed
with hieratic texts from the Book of Going Forth by Day.[4] The Twenty-
Sixth Dynasty tomb of Padiamenope (TT 33) contains a complete copy
of the Book of Caverns, the well-preserved text often providing readings
otherwise not preserved in the New Kingdom exemplars.[5] Additional Late
period copies of the Book of Caverns include blocks from an anonymous
tomb from the Heliopolitan necropolis (later incorporated into the Nilometer on the island of Roda; see p. 130 n. 6) and lengthy excerpts on the

---

2. For details of the distribution of the Book of Caverns within New Kingdom
royal tombs, see Werning 2011b, 25–36.

3. The Twenty-Sixth Dynasty tomb of Padiamenope (TT 33) repeats many of the
personalizations found specifically within the tomb of Ramesses VI, indicating the
importance of that tomb within the reception history of the composition (Werning
forthcoming).

4. Werning 2011b, 36–39 (note also the individual scenes from two other Third
Intermediate period contexts that he discusses on pp. 39–41).

5. Publication of the tomb is in progress: see pp. 40, 130 n. 6; for the distribution
of the Book of Caverns within the tomb, see Werning 2011b, 42–45.

Thirtieth Dynasty sarcophagus of Tjaihorpata (CG 29306).[6] Divisions 1–2 of the Book of Caverns on the sarcophagus of Tjaihorpata diverge significantly from the New Kingdom copies of the text, omitting the depictions of the damned in the lowest registers and reproducing only a portion of the solar speeches, omitting repetitive sections (Manassa 2007a, 457–58). The images of the goddess Mysterious One appears on the floor of the sarcophagus (Division 5, Registers 1–3, Scene 50), while the lid contains portions of two litanies (Litanies 19 and 21) that have been heavily edited, even going so far as to make the speech of Re into a speech of the deceased himself, who then refers to Re in the third person.[7]

The Book of Caverns comprises six major divisions, in two major portions of discontinuous length, along with twenty-one litanies, in three sections (Werning 2011b, 5–8).[8] The first half of the treatise is introduced by two vertical bands, the first (to the left) occupied by a solar disk in the middle, the right by the standing figure of the ram-headed, anthropomorphic sun god of night.[9] Divisions 1–2 are divided into five horizontal registers; within Divisions 1–2 the images appear in essentially continuous lines, as in the Book of the Hidden Chamber and the Book of Gates, but without the accompanying annotations present in those compositions. In the Book of Caverns, the principle text of Divisions 1–2—solar monologues—are written in text blocks separate from the images.

The solar monologues of Divisions 1–2 of the Book of Caverns address each group of deities within the scenes, calling on them to perform certain actions (particularly gestures of respect for the sun god) and detailing to them the benefactions that Re will deliver in the Netherworld. The main themes of the Book of Caverns, and indeed of the Netherworld Books as a whole, are prominent within these speeches: the sun god illuminates

---

6. Manassa 2007a, 319–42, 377–86, and 404–9; Werning 2011b, 47–50; Werning forthcoming. Note also the presence of the goddess Mysterious One with short annotations on the sarcophagus of Padi-isis (Berlin 29), also of Thirtieth Dynasty date (Manassa 2007a, 404; 2007b, pls. 287–89; Werning 2011b, 46).

7. Manassa 2007a, 377; for the "creative reception" of the Book of Caverns on the sarcophagus, see also Werning forthcoming, section 7.2.

8. A narrative summary of the deities and events of the six divisions of the Book of Caverns also appears in Meeks and Favard-Meeks 1996, 151–63.

9. The orientation of the figures within the scenes all follow the template of the Osireion version; the images that accompany the scenes in the present translation, which are derived primarily from the Tomb of Ramesses VI, have been reoriented to correspond to that earliest template.

the Netherworld Dwellers, thereby caring for them, as he visits Osiris, his corpse. For example, in Scene 9 (p. 350), Re addresses Osiris, Foremost of the Westerners, directly and proclaims how he will "cause the *ba*-souls to occupy their corpses after I have occupied (my) corpse"—a perfect summary of how the actions of the solar god within the Netherworld provide the template for the resurrection of the deceased king in the royal tomb, or in rare cases and later periods, private individuals. The tone of the solar speeches changes dramatically in the lowest register of the Divisions 1–2 when Re addresses the damned and their guardians, specifying the range of punishments to be inflicted on the enemies of Osiris.

That Divisions 1–2 are introductory is clear from certain of the images they contain. Guardian serpents appear at the left end of Divisions 1–2, in the upper and lower registers of Division 1, and in the upper register of Division 2. The second half of Division 2, Register 3 sees four ram-headed posts with disks before them, and four jackal-headed posts with accompanying disks as well, multiple numbers of the same pair of posts that mark the entrance to the Netherworld in the Book of Gates (pp. 257–58). The text accompanying Division 2 indicates entrance into the realm of Aker, and this realm of Aker—appearing in the middle of Division 3—coincides with the three registers of image clusters and text blocks that betoken in the Book of Caverns the true, inner Netherworld. Although images of Osiris appear in all divisions of the composition, and although solar disks appear with the posts at the end of the middle register of Division 2, Division 3 marks the appearance of a multiplicity of solar disks that hover above various clusters of images, a feature ending in the far left—the beginning—of the concluding scene of the treatise.

Division 3 introduces the pattern that will continue through the remaining divisions of the composition. The Divisions 3–6 have essentially three horizontal registers, the images more discontinuous than in the Book of the Hidden Chamber and the Book of Gates, dividing rather into discreet and often complex groups, with at times lengthy texts intervening between the groups. The core image of Division 3 is the depiction of Aker in the middle register, with the corpse of Osiris, Ruler of the West, placed within a protective serpent[10] in the third and lowest register; rather than an immobile mummified figure, Osiris appears supine, yet striding, with an

---

10. The serpent literally "pulls together" the corpse and bears the unusual name "Terrible of Face," which is otherwise applied to inimical serpents (see p. 13).

erect phallus, ready to receive the life-giving light of the solar disk placed above him. As Re states in the introductory text to this division: "Behold, I am entering into the earth, from which I came forth, that I might go to rest upon my first birth form." The corpse becomes the birth-form, the child who enters the sun disk in the Concluding Scene of the Book of Caverns. In addition to solar monologues, Division 3 also introduces annotations to the scenes, descriptions of the deities and their actions like those present in the other Netherworld Books (with the exception of the Book of Adoring Re in the West). The solar disk that appears above most scenes, although notably absent from all depictions of enemies and the damned, signals not only the light of the sun, but also his speeches themselves, an association made explicit in the annotation to Scene 27: "This great god speaks to them, with the result that they behold the light of his disk."[11] The enemies in the lowest register, the Place of Destruction as well as the reconstruction of the corpse of Osiris (see below), incorporate male and female individuals "who have done what disturbs the one Foremost of the Netherworld," bringing down upon themselves abundant punishments— inversion, beheading, slaughtering, and destruction of their *ba*-souls.

Division 4 begins with three vertical bands: the left band occupied by a solar disk in the middle; the central band having a serpent rearing on its tail, head up and to the left; and the rightmost band having a standing, ram-headed, anthropomorphic deity facing right, arms raised in praise—these bands evoke those of Division 1 and introduce the second half of the composition. Division 4 has fewer scenes and texts than the other divisions, although the main themes continue to be present. In the first scene of the upper register, Scene 41, Isis and Nephthys lift up Osiris, of whose odd curved form Re says "you encircle the Netherworld with your arms"; this single scene represents a syncopation of the Concluding Scene of the Book of Gates, which similarly shows the actions of Isis and Nephthys (there lifting up a scarab) as essential to the solar journey through the Netherworld, depicted as a curled Osiris figure (see p. 336). One of the emphases of Division 4 is the resurrection of Osiris's corpse through the actions of Horus, who appears both as a falcon-headed deity and as Horus-Mekhentyenirty, whose animal form is an ichneumon. One of the punishments meted out to the damned in this division is that the Eye of Horus will not be near them.

---

11. For references and parallels in other Netherworld Books, see p. 6 and n. 7.

In Division 5 of the Book of Caverns, a large image of Osiris, nude and ithyphallic, stands opposite the large figure of the goddess Mysterious One (Shetayt); these twin figures dominate the division, stretching the height of all three registers, signaling their importance, like the Judgment Hall of Osiris (Scene 33) in the Book of Gates. At the beginning of the division, Scene 50, the goddess Mysterious One holds in one hand the small, ram-headed figure of the night sun, in the other a solar disk, while images of the solar cycle progress up one side of her and down the other; the presence of cryptographic annotations to her figure is a further indication of the significance of this particular image as well as her "mysterious" nature. The goddess, divine personification of the Netherworld, the Mysterious Place (Shetayt) as the place of the *štʒ*-mystery—the corpse of Osiris—is the counterpart of Osiris, himself a divine personification of the space through which the night sun travels (Scene 59). Already in the Pyramid Texts, Osiris could be a portion of the Netherworld, and within the Netherworld Books he can be the space of the Netherworld as womb of the newborn sun (see pp. 41–43). This latter concept of the Osirian space is in keeping with the Blueprint of the Course of the Stars (the Book of Nut), in which the Netherworld (Duat) itself is located within the body of Nut.[12] The three registers that appear between the Mysterious One and Osiris as well as behind Osiris emphasize again the corpse of Osiris, along with the corpse of Atum and the corpse of Khepri (Scene 52). Four manifestations of Horus make an appearance (Scene 54), and the head of Re appears as a ram-head, referencing Division 2. The punishment of enemies in this division involves large cauldrons that cook the corpses, souls, and constituent parts of the enemies.

The three registers of Division 6 consist of small vignettes, each of which is centered on a series of sarcophagi or mounds that conceal the corpse of Osiris and the solar deity. Scarab forms occur three times within this division, presaging the sun's triumphant rising from the eastern horizon, as Re proclaims in Scene 66: "Look at me, I having been born in the Netherworld, I having manifest in the manifestation of Khepri, I having become young in the beautiful West." Osiris-Orion appears in the upper register (Scene 67), triumphing over an enemy; the annotation to this figure emphasizes the stellar connection of Orion and the solar eye and

---

12. Zago 2018; Allen 1988, 3–7, 61; 1989, 21–25. For the association of Nut with different spaces, including the sarcophagus chamber, see Billing 2002.

eye of Horus. The headless figures in sarcophagi at the end of Register 2 (Scene 72) are not damned, but rather directly related to the solar eye, their heads having traveled away from the corpses to join the solar deity in his journeys. These deities are thus contrasted in the strongest possible terms with the decapitated corpses of the damned in the lowest register.

A final, concluding scene has three registers to the left, with two diagonal lines crossing from top and bottom, converging at the right end of the book—curved like the end of Hour 12 of the Book of the Hidden Chamber. This scene contains the only depiction of the solar bark within the Book of Caverns, only its prow visible, as if literally emerging from the Netherworldly depths. The bark contains three figures—the ram-headed solar god, a scarab, and a bird, whose name is Osiris[13]—and is hauled by a complement of twelve deities. Above and below the bark, deities arch over mysterious mounds, a final acknowledgment of the hidden corpse of the unified Re-Osiris, whose diverse forms populate the bark. Bodies of water and praising deities appear both above and below the final image—a ram-headed scarab followed by a child and the solar disk, which lacks an annotation, but can be read as a pithy statement of solar manifestation (p. 455).

The Book of Caverns differs from the Book of the Hidden Chamber and the Book of Gates in having several sequences of litanies. Most of these occur between the major divisions of the treatise: Litanies 1–3 appear between Divisions 3–4; Litanies 4–6 between the Divisions 4–5; Litanies 7–20 between Divisions 5–6; and finally, the last litany, the Litany 21, following Division 6. The litanies summarize the actions of Re, Osiris, and the various denizens of the netherworld and contain references to the various scenes of the divisions of the Book of Caverns, providing an overview and chorus-like commentary to the more episodic texts and vignettes that make up the various divisions of the composition.

Litanies 1–3 introduce the *dramatis personae* of the treatise, addressing Re and the denizens of the Netherworld. Litany 1 repeats the introductory passage "how beautiful is Re, when he passes by the darkness." Litany 2 repeats an introduction that links Re and the inhabitants of the Netherworld—"Jubilation belongs to you, Re, with the result that we draw in breath." Finally, Litany 3 devotes itself more exclusively to those inhabitants, with the introduction "possessors of provisions in the West."

---

13. Compare the Osiris *benu*-bird as the "*Ba*-soul of Osiris" in Division 4, Register 3, Scene 46 (p. 392).

The second group, Litanies 4–6, stresses the motion and exuberance of the traveling solar deity as he moves through the Netherworld, and his interactions thereby with the denizens of the Netherworld; the solar deity himself speaks these verses in Litanies 4–5. Litany 4 opens with the repeated line "My solar disk has penetrated the darkness," thereafter describing the effect this has on the sun's Osirian aspect and on other inhabitants of the nether regions. Litany 5 is similar, repeating the opening line "I am traveling by you, O Netherworld Dwellers," again describing interactions with the Netherworldly aspect of the sun and the other denizens as well. Litany 6, as though in response to the preceding two self-addressed litanies of the sun, contains the repeated address of the inhabitants of the Netherworld: "You are adored, O One of the Horizon," with following adjuncts.

The third and largest group of litanies, Litanies 7–20, contains insistent references to the onrushing sun as he races to greet Osiris and unite with this Netherworldly aspect of himself. Litanies 7–8 address various beings and then refer to the speed of the solar approach: "I am crossing through to take care of my corpse" in Litany 7; "I am crossing through to take care of Osiris" in Litany 8. Litany 9 addresses Tatenen; Litany 10 refers to the appearance of light in the West; and Litany 11 addresses Anubis. Litanies 12–14 address denizens of the Netherworld, both the blessed and finally the damned. Finally, Litanies 15–19 address Osiris and hypostases thereof and urge the rising of the resurrected deity, while Litany 20 offers a final, protective warding off of the enemies of Osiris.

The final, Litany 21, is longer than the others and addresses the *ba*-souls of various deities. These lines reference Atum, Khepri, Shu, Re, Osiris, Tatenen, Isis, et cetera, the constellation of deities we might expect to find in the clockwork-like descriptions of the deities inhabiting the complete cosmos. The implication is that after the union of Re and Osiris and the recreation of the morning, the completed cosmos is also renewed. The Ennead of deities has returned for the dawn of the next day.

One of the most prominent of the Netherworldly toponyms to appear in the Book of Caverns is *Ḥtmy.t*, *Hetemyt*, translated here as the Place of Destruction. The concept of destruction for the Egyptians, as we find it manifest in the Netherworld Books, is one of deconstruction rather than annihilation. The Place of Destruction is a realm in which the damned remain inverted (so the text to Division 3, Register 3, Scene 37). That absolute nonexistence is not the goal or result of consignment to the Place of Destruction is clear from passages that refer to those assigned to the realm being unable to escape the region once they are consigned to it (so the text to Division 4, Scene 39). According to the text of Division 4, Register 3, Scene 49, the enemies consigned to deconstruction will go upside-down— in other words, they shall have an inverted but continual existence. Their existence is also renewed, like the renewal of the sun. Even the damned who remain in the Place of Destruction have their eternal deconstruction as assured as the coming of the *ba*-soul of Re; a text following Litany 2 referring to the lords of the West states: "Just as they bring into existence the destroyed ones, so they summon the *ba*-soul of Re."

Ultimately, the deconstruction appears to refer to the falling apart of the decomposing body. The text to Division 4, Register 3, Scene 48 emphasizes through repetition various forms and derivatives of the term *ḥtm* and refers specifically to a deconstructed corpse, from the putrefaction of which the deconstructing entities come forth. In the texts to Division 5, Register 3, Scenes 57 and 63, arms of the Place of Destruction hold cauldrons in which the elements of the damned are cooked. The bodies of the damned are cut apart to achieve deconstruction, and the names of the deities along with the texts of Division 6, Register 3, Scene 73 make clear the association between cutting up with knives and deconstructing the multifaceted physical and psychic being in the Netherworld.

The deconstruction of the Book of Caverns is similar to the swallowing of the hours of the night that appears in the Book of the Hidden Chamber (p. 227) and the Book of Gates (pp. 274, 288). So in the Book of Caverns, Division 6, Register 3, Scene 76, upside-down beings descend into the ground line, down into which descends and ultimately up out of which ascends a great serpent, with a deity—Osiris as the accompanying text reveals—rising from the hidden middle of the ophidian body. The text to the scene refers to heads emerging from the Place of Destruction, like the heads that emerge from a serpent in Book of Gates, Hour 6, Register 1, Scene 35, closely related in Scene 36 to the emergence of the hours from a coiled rope. Indeed the swallowing of the hours can be a deconstruction, as the term *ḥtm* refers, in the Book of Gates, Hour 4, Register 2, Scene 20, to the hour goddesses swallowing down twelve serpents, who themselves appear to embody the concept of the decay of time (p. 274). In the concluding scene to the Book of Caverns, the figures hauling Re out of the eastern mountains say: "The Great One is in the Place of Destruction, his place is in the serpent bark." Although not so depicted in the scene, the text refers to the serpent bark, as we see in Hours 4–5 of the Book of the Hidden Chamber, and on the ceiling of Corridor G in the Tomb of Ramesses VI.

BOOK OF CAVERNS

DIVISION 1

INTRODUCTION (PLATE 29)

5.1. Scenes 1–2. A solar disk is placed behind a ram-headed solar deity, his arms stretched out, palms pointing down, facing a line of eleven bowing deities (they stand in Division 1, Register 3). Ten of the eleven deities are gods, while the second one in the row is a goddess.

"O gods who are in the Netherworld, the first cavern of the West, door-keepers of the districts of Igeret, Ennead of the Ruler of the West. I am Re within heaven. I am entering into the uniform darkness; I am opening the gates of the sky in the West. Behold, I enter into the Western Land. Receive me, give to me your arms. Behold, I know your place in the forepart of the Netherworld. Behold, I know your names, your grottos, and your mysteries.[14] I know your means of life, consisting of what the Netherworldly One commanded for you. That you live and that your throats breathe is when you hear the words of Osiris, after I have passed through the Netherworld.[15] I have occupied the roads of the West, so that you might go to rest, so that your *ba*-souls might grow strong, and so that you might grow powerful in the forepart of your cavern. At the same time, you have heard my words, after I called to you by your names." So says Re to the gods who are in the first cavern of the Netherworld.

---

14. The knowledge claimed by the solar deity mirrors the multiple uses of the verb *rḫ* "to know" in the title of the Book of the Hidden Chamber (see pp. 37–38, 137–38).

15. Note the emphasis on the speech of Osiris after Re's passage, presaging the later union of the two deities within the Netherworld.

REGISTER 1 (PLATE 29)

5.2. Scene 3. Three serpents with multiple coils appear, one atop the other.

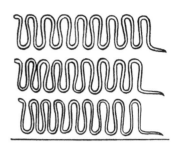

"O Horned One, foremost of his cavern, great of terror, first of the Netherworld. Bend your arm, bow your shoulder. Behold, I enter into the beautiful Western Land in order to care for Osiris and in order to greet those with him. I give his enemies over to their places of punishment, and I command to those in his following. I illuminate the darkness of the Mysterious Place in the beautiful West.

O Terrible of Face, foremost of his cavern, to whom is assigned those within the Netherworld and the *ba*-souls of the Place of Destruction. Bend your arm, bow your shoulder. Behold, I enter into the beautiful Western Land in order to care for Osiris and in order to greet those with him. I give his enemies over to their places of punishment, and I command to those in his following. I illuminate the darkness of the Mysterious Place.

O that Son of the Earth, who encircles the Place of Hauling for the Ruler of the Netherworld. Bend your arm, bow your shoulder. Behold, I enter into the beautiful Western Land in order to care for Osiris and in order to greet those with him. I give his enemies over to their places of punishment, and I command to those in his following. I illuminate the darkness of the Mysterious Place."

5.3. Scene 4. Nine uraeus-serpents

"O this Ennead of uraei, whose flames are at their mouths, who burn up the enemies of Osiris. Bend your arm, bow your shoulder. Behold, I enter into the beautiful Western Land in order to care for Osiris and in order to greet those with him. I give his enemies over to their places of punishment, and I command to those in his following. I illuminate the darkness of the Mysterious Place."

5.4. Scene 5. Nine bull-headed deities stand with both arms before their bodies, palms facing downwards.

"O Ennead of gods who are in the following of the Bull of the West. Bend your arm, bow your shoulder. Behold, I enter into the beautiful Western Land in order to care for Osiris and in order to greet those with him. I give his enemies over to their places of punishment, and I command to those in his following. I illuminate the darkness of the Mysterious Place."

ANNOTATION TO SCENES 3–5

"O gods, O gods within the mysterious places, those foremost of the Netherworld. Behold, I enter into the West, having entered its first cavern. I have spoken to those who are within it. What I said is what they have done. What I have commanded is that about which they should be at peace. May they bend their arms for me; may they bow to me their shoulders. Behold, I am passing by you, so that you may act."

REGISTER 2 (PLATE 29)

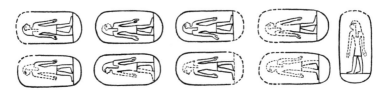

5.5. Scene 6. Nine gods lie within sarcophagi. The sarcophagi are arranged in two horizontal rows of four with a final, ninth sarcophagus oriented vertically. The eight figures within the horizontal sarcophagi are alternately prone and supine.

"O Ennead of gods who rest in their mysterious sarcophagi, possessors of hair-locks, great of resting places who rest in the uniform darkness."

5.6. Scene 7. Nine jackal-headed deities stand with both arms before their bodies, palms facing downwards.

"O Ennead of gods, great of silence in the West, who exist as guardians of *ba*-souls, possessors of necessities in the West, whose faces are in the form of hounds in order to lick up the rot and putrefaction."[16]

5.7. Scene 8. A god and goddess, each lift aloft a solar disk.

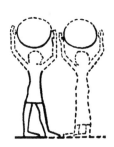

O this god, great of visible forms, in whose grasp is the secret[17] of Osiris, namely, the efflux[18] of Foremost of the Netherworld.

O this goddess, great of mysteries, over whom is the flesh of Osiris, to whom is entrusted the great image of the Ruler of the West.[19]

ANNOTATION TO SCENES 6–8

"O gods, bend for me your arms, bow for me your shoulders. Behold, I enter the West in order to care for Osiris, in order to greet those with him. I give his enemies over to their places of punishment, and I command to those in his following. I illuminate the darkness of the Mysterious Place. You are the manifestations who are at rest inside their sarcophagi, corpses, strong of *ba*-soul, who hear Osiris. O, behold, I enter among you. Indeed he is the one who breathes and who sees; indeed he is the one who breathes and rejoices over my visible form."

---

16. For the association of jackal deities and putrefaction, see Manassa 2007a, 324.

17. The reading *sštꜣ* is suggested by the copy of the text on the sarcophagus of Tjai-horpata (Manassa 2007a, 324–25); for the disk as the "mystery" compare the annotation in the Books of the Creation of the Solar Disk (Tomb of Ramesses VI, Section A2, Register 1, Scene 19) that labels a scene of a falcon head emerging from a disk: "These gods in this fashion, Atum acclaiming Re, as he calls to these among whom he is, with the result that they receive Horus of the Netherworld, as he emerges from his mystery that is in the Netherworld." For an alternate reading, compare Werning 2011a, 19 "Rund."

18. Manassa 2007a, 325, n. b.

19. The annotation, by describing an element in the grasp of the male deity and above the female deity, equates the mystery of Osiris with the flesh of Osiris (*sštꜣ* as corpse), the efflux of the same deity and his image. As is typical for many of the texts in the corpus, information is clearly conveyed through parallelism and interrelationship of text and image, although the annotations alone do not overtly relate the information in a didactic manner.

REGISTER 3 (PLATE 29)

5.8. Scene 9. Osiris, wearing a white crown and carrying a *was*-scepter, stands within a shrine surrounded by the Encircling Serpent. To the left are four vertically-oriented sarcophagi each containing a deity and serpent. On the right are four vertically-oriented sarcophagi with a goddess and serpent in each.

"O Osiris, Foremost of the Netherworld, I am Re. Extend to me your arm. I am the lord of the *ba*-soul, one who has power over the past,[20] fear of whom is among the Westerners. I care for the Netherworld Dwellers, with the result that I cause the *ba*-souls to occupy their corpses after I have occupied my corpse. The Netherworld Dwellers lead my divine *ba*-souls to the mysterious place of my images.

O Ennead of Osiris, who judge on behalf of He of the Netherworld, Osiris, Foremost of the West. O those who are in his following, namely, the one who rests in the shrine, with the great Son of the Earth as the one who protects him. His companions rest in their sarcophagi, while their corpses, mysterious of nature, and those (serpents) within the earth unite therein. O great gods, who extend to me your arms; Ennead in whom is Osiris, may you lead me along the Netherworldly roads to the mysterious cavern, so that I might call to those within the Mysterious Place, so that I might protect them, and so that I might care for them. I will illumine them, so that I might drive away their darkness, so that I might cause them to occupy their thrones. I greet those who are in your following and illuminate the darkness of the Mysterious Place. You are the great one, chief of the mysteries, foremost of the place."

---

20. Osiris's control over the past finds a clear parallel with the identification of Osiris as yesterday and Re as tomorrow featured prominently in the Book of Going Forth By Day, Chapter 17 (Griffiths 1992, 227–28)—a blending of time and deity to show equation, and the *perpetuum mobile* of the solar cycle. See also the graffito in the tomb of Ramesses IX (pp. 535–36).

REGISTER 4 (PLATE 29)

5.9. Scene 10. Nine goddesses stand atop shade signs; their arms are before their bodies, palms facing downwards.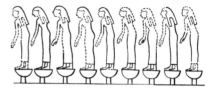

"O Ennead of goddesses, who stand respectfully for the desert dwellers, those who conduct the mysteries that are beneath them for the Great One, Foremost of the Westerners."

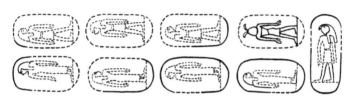

5.10. Scene 11. Nine gods and goddesses lie within sarcophagi, arranged in two rows of four horizontally oriented sarcophagi and a final, ninth vertically oriented sarcophagus. The first three sarcophagi of the first row contain gods, alternately supine and prone; the second row contains four goddesses, again alternately prone and supine. The fourth sarcophagus of the first row has a prone catfish-headed god, all black. The vertically oriented sarcophagus at the end contains a falcon-headed god.

"O gods and goddesses within sarcophagi, strong ones, those in the following (of Osiris), those foremost of the West."

5.11. Scene 12. Two gods stand over a circular feature containing four flesh-signs; next, two goddesses stand over another circular feature with images of a hair-lock and beard. An ichneumon-headed being stands to the right, facing the gods and goddesses.

"O great mysterious one, hidden of nature, who guards the secret image of Osiris, Lord of the West! O those who guard the mysterious images of Osiris, Lord of the Westerners!

O Isis! O Nephthys! O two great goddesses of the West, extend to me your arms, tie[21] together your protection over the great image that is in your hands![22]

O Vigorous One, mysterious of manifestations, foremost of the cavern of Osiris! You belong to the visible forms of the one foremost of the Netherworld, from whom you have manifested, after he assigned you as the one foremost of his cavern. You belong to his putrefying corpses."

ANNOTATION TO SCENES 10–12

"O gods, those who rejoice at my approach. Give to me your arms. Receive me. Lead me along the roads of the West. I will enliven your corpses that are within it, while I cause their *ba*-souls to rest upon them, so that they might breathe. I will illuminate their darkness, so that I might place peace in my cavern. I will greet you, O gods, Ennead among whom is Osiris. I shall place <your> enemies in their slaughtering places. I command to you, as I illuminate the darkness of the Mysterious Place. I am passing over you, while you lead my *ba*-soul."

REGISTER 5 (PLATE 29)

5.12. Scene 13. Three serpents with multiple coils appear, one atop the other.

"O Eldest One of the Earth, great of strength. Rumbling One, who rumbles those who are above him.

O Flaming One, great of fire, who gives his own blasting flame.

O Serpent Who is in the Lower Earth,[23] who does not behold the great god.

---

21. The act of "tying" can be an inherently apotropaic act (Ritner 1993, 142–44). For the use of magical practices within the Netherworld Books, compare the use of magical spells to "deflect the path from Apep" in the Book of the Hidden Chamber, Hour 7 (pp. 195–96) and the technical term "execration (rituals)" in the Book of the Hidden Chamber, Hour 11 and Book of Gates, Hour 12 (see p. 233 and n. 128).

22. The "great image" refers to the hair-lock and beard. For the significance of hair in the Netherworld Books, see Manassa 2007a, 329–30.

23. The sarcophagus of Tjaihorpata replaces this toponym with "Land of Silence" (Werning 2011a, 35 n. d).

O serpents, you serpents who are in the lowest regions of the Netherworld, beneath Osiris, guardians of the portals of the One Mysterious of
Nature, those who do not go forth from their cavern. Behold, I call your
names, without you seeing me. I am assigning you to the Place of Destruction, door guardians of She Who Is Great of Darkness. I cause that you
remain in your places like this. I have given commands to you, so that you
might carry out the guarding of the enemies of Osiris, those who do not
escape from your grasp forever. You are remaining in your places; you are
provisioned in your caverns in the Netherworld beneath Osiris in order to
carry out the guarding of his enemies. You are these Sons of the Earth, to
whom I have assigned the guarding of the [... enemies] among the rebels,
severing the necks of those to be decapitated, and removing the heads of
those to be destroyed. You are those who execute that which I have commanded to you—Sons of the Earth."

 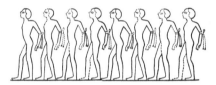

5.13 (left side), 5.14 (right side). Scene 14. Four groups of four enemies stand,
each with their arms bound beneath their backs. The first two sets of four are
decapitated.

"O [...] punishments, which I have inflicted among you. You are the ene-
mies of Osiris, who have done evil in the hidden earth. I consign you to the
Sons of the Earth, so that you will not escape from their guardianship! [...]
I place [...] them, I consign them to the Place of Destruction.

O Destroyed ones! O decapitated ones! Enemies of Osiris, severed of
head, without necks, without *ba*-souls, destroyed of corpse. Behold, I pass
over you, above you. I inflict your punishments. I consign you to non-
existence. You are these who bear evil, the ones foremost of the Place of
Destruction."

ANNOTATION TO SCENES 13–14

"O great serpents, Sons of the Earth, door-keepers of the Place of Destruction! Guard! Obstruct these enemies of Osiris. Behold, I am passing over

your caverns, so that I might rest in the Beautiful West, in order to create their slaughtering places against them, in order to destroy their *ba*-souls, in order to wipe away their shades, in order to cut off their corpses, in order to seize their *akh*-spirits. Your enemies are bound and fettered, O Ruler of the West. I enter the West and those who are within it, who rejoice at my approach."

DIVISION 2

REGISTER 1 (PLATE 30)

5.15. Scene 15. A serpent standing on his tail appears before four multicoiled serpents, one above the other.

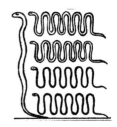

The second cavern of the first.[24] What this great god says when he reaches those who are within it: "O Serpent, foremost of his grotto, doorkeeper of those among whom he is, from whose guard there is no going forth. O you, whose head is in darkness, whose tail is in the mystery of the cavern in which he is, who makes his own place in the West, because his visible forms are more mysterious than those foremost of his grotto.

O One Dark of Head. I am passing your cavern, in order to see He Who Is Hidden of Name, in order to care for the West, in order to traverse the mysterious Netherworld. May you hide yourself from me, when I pass by. It is only when I hurry on that you show your head. You are this one, the serpent Dark of Head, having no egress from your cavern, the inhabitants of which do not come forth.

O Mysterious of Arms, hidden of legs,[25] this second serpent, namely, Dark of Head.

O Sand-Dweller, whose eyes are destructive, of whom the Netherworldly ones are afraid, when they behold him.

O Burning One, powerful of flame, who casts fire against those who ascend against him.

---

24. For the dual nature of the Netherworld, see Werning 2011a, 45 n. a. The parallelism between Divisions 1–2 of the Book of Caverns is further enhanced on the sarcophagus of Tjaihorpata (CG 29036), which includes only three serpents at the introduction of Division 2, mirroring the first scene of Division 1 (Manassa 2007b, pl. 239).

25. The Book of the Hidden Chamber contains numerous depictions of serpents with legs; for serpent "limbs," see Manassa 2007a, 333.

O serpents, O you serpents, doorkeepers of He Who Is Hidden of Name. Behold me reaching your grotto, traversing the mysteries of the Netherworld. My solar disk has entered into the Mysterious Place in order to illumine those foremost of their darkness, so I might care for those within their sarcophagi and assign the enemies to the Place of Destruction. O door-keepers of Osiris, serpents who are within the Mysterious Place. I traverse your grottos in order to see He Who Is Hidden of Name, in order to care for the West, in order to cross the mysterious Netherworld.

May you hide yourselves from me, so that I might pass over you. It is only when I hurry on that you show your heads. You are these door-keepers who do not go forth from their caverns, who do not go forth from those with them."

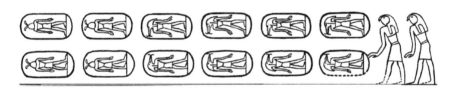

5.16. Scene 16. Twelve sarcophagi, all oriented horizontally, are arranged in two rows. The first two in each row contain catfish-headed deities; the remaining eight have shrew-headed deities. To the right, two hieracocephalic gods bow towards the sarcophagi, each with both arms before him, palms facing downwards.

"O you twelve gods, foremost of the Mysterious Place, within sarcophagi, lords of manifestations, chiefs of their *ba*-souls, who have power over their corpses!

O Catfish-Like Ones, lords of provisions, those who have transformed into Osiris!

O you who exist as Mekhentyenirty,[26] gods who transform into Horus,[27] lords of the provisions in the forepart of the Netherworld, powerful upon their corpses, equipped of *ba*-soul upon their bodies!

---

26. Mekhentyenirty can take the form of a shrew or an ichneumon; for the theological associations of these creatures, see Brunner-Traut 1965; Manassa 2007a, 330; Leitz 2009.

27. The catfish-headed deities are manifestations of Osiris, while the shrew-headed deities are manifestations of Horus (Manassa 2007a, 335).

O you in the following of Foremost of the Netherworld, fish,[28] great of provisions! O you great gods within their sarcophagi! Behold, I cry to you, with the result that your *ba*-souls might be powerful therein, you remaining in your grottos, and your corpses resting in their sarcophagi.[29] Behold, I illuminate you, with the result that your countenance belongs to me, and my countenance belongs to you.[30] I am the one whose *ba*-soul protects, whose body speaks, the great god being in the cavern of the Netherworld. I cross the mysteries of the earth, the West, with the result that I cause *ba*-souls to […], so that they might be powerful over their corpses, after I have spoken to them. O, behold, I speak to you, so that those within their sarcophagi might praise me.

O gods! O you gods within the Mysterious Place! I cross over your grotto, in order to see He Who Is Hidden of Name, in order to take care of the West, in order to traverse the mysterious Netherworld. May your *ba*-souls go forth. May your *ba*-souls be strong. May your corpses rest in their sarcophagi. Your *ba*-souls, whom I call, pass by in my following, as they guide me. You are those with Osiris, possessors of *ba*-souls, great of provisions, whose guardian is Horus, [He of the Nether]world(?) is their protection as one who allows their *ba*-souls to go forth.

May your passings by be with me, O One Foremost of the Netherworld. I enter into the earth, so that I might go forth from it. I reckon my first birth form."[31]

5.17. Scene 17. Seven goddesses within vertically-oriented sarcophagi appear in a single row. A deity stands to the right, slightly bowing forward with both arms before him, palms facing downwards.

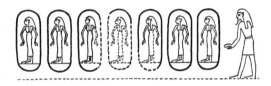

28. Werning 2011a, 51 n. e.

29. The two sentences "you remaining in your grottos, and your corpses resting in their sarcophagi" utilize a subject-stative construction, which could also be interpreted as a hortative stative: "May you remain … may your corpses rest …"

30. Compare the face of the solar deity depicted prominently in the Book of Gates, Hour 11, Scene 73 (p. 320).

31. This passage expresses the *perpetuum mobile* of the solar journey. Re sets into the earth to rest on the birth form of the eastern horizon; on the theological significance of this passage, see also Werning 2011a, 55 n. b.

"O She of the Netherworld, foremost of the Netherworld, she of the West, who protects her body.

O She Whose *Ba*-Soul Speaks, who inquires after her corpse, foremost of the mysterious Netherworld.

O Living *Ba*-Soul, powerful of shade, who protects those who are within the West.

O Cheerful-faced One,[32] great of mysteries, courageous within her cavern.

O Female Corpse, mistress of putrefaction, to whose putrefaction (one) does not approach.

O She Whose *Ba*-Soul Speaks, so that those within the Place of Destruction hear.

O She Who Cares for Those with Her, goddess perfect of *akh*-spells.

O He of the Corpse, he of rot, powerful of arm in the protection of the goddesses.

O seven goddesses, great of form within the Mysterious Place, powerful of *ba*-souls upon their corpses. O, behold, I have entered into the earth. I transform into one who opens the Netherworld. I myself have divided it on the first occasion, as I myself have established me. You are the chosen ones of my choice; (only) after I was chosen were you chosen.[33] Just as my *ba*-soul has lived, so have you lived. Just as it became strong in me, so have you become strong. I am the unique one who establishes your thrones, indeed, the one who cares for you.

Rejoice for me, O goddesses! Be strong for me, O those within their sarcophagi! May you speak to He Who Is Hidden of Name. May you exist as the protection of Osiris after I have passed over you. May you guide my *ba*-soul to my corpse. O you—I guide your *ba*-souls to the sarcophagi that bear your corpses. As I illumine you so do I dispel your darkness.

O you seven goddesses who are in the Mysterious Place. I cross over your grotto in order to see He Who Is Hidden of Name, in order to care for the West, in order to traverse the mysterious Netherworld. May your *ba*-souls go forth. May your *ba*-souls be strong, while your corpses rest in their sarcophagi. Your *ba*-souls, whom I summon, pass in my following, so that they might guide me. [You] are these goddesses, great of provisions

---

32. "Ḥnt-ḥr-ꜥꜣt-štꜣw," LGG 3:157–58.

33. For the emphatic *sḏm.ny* form in the Netherworld Books, see Baumann 1998, 436–38 (with a translation of this passage on p. 437).

in the West, who embrace the mysterious image in the places of He Who is Hidden of Name.

O He of the Corpse, lord of rot, who guards the corpses of the goddesses, great of provisions as those whom he guards, who give assistance to the *ba*-soul so that he might call out. Behold, I have entered into the earth, from which I have gone forth, that I might go to rest upon my first birth form."

REGISTER 2 (PLATE 30)

5.18. Scene 18. A shrew-headed deity faces nine mourning deities. Each deity bends forward slightly and pulls at a piece of his wig that is flipped over his face.

"O Horus, Mekhentyenirty, foremost of the grotto, who mourns the great god, power of the West, who protects those who are in his following.

O Mourner, great of hair-locks, who cries out in the West.[34]

O Weeper, powerful of screams, high of voice in the regions of Igeret.

O Sniveller, chief of the mourners, unique god, who mourns himself.

O One Who Makes the Arm Firm for Those Who Are in His Following, who bears the water that goes forth from their divine eyes.

O One Whose Voice Is Heard by the Weary-hearted,[35] with the result that he gathers together his limbs for himself.

O One Whose Arms Are before His Face, at whose call the Netherworldly gods come.

O One Who (Re)assembles Him with His Crying, who hears his own voice with the result that his *ba*-soul lives.

O One with a Wig, chief of his mourners, who gives forth his voice so that the *ba*-souls call to him.

34. Mourning for the solar deity assists with his transfiguration in the Netherworld—compare the Book of Adoring Re in the West: "The *ba*-soul of Re appears in glory by means of his manifestations, while his corpse is content with his (mourning) cries" (see p. 109).

35. The "Weary-hearted" deity is Osiris.

O Dark of Face, foremost of the sanctified region, at whose cries the *ba*-souls breathe.

O this Ennead of gods who mourn over Osiris, who cry over Foremost of the Netherworld. O, behold, I am passing over you. I am crossing over your grottos, so that I might call to you, with the result that you cry out for me. He of the Netherworld always becomes peaceful by means of your voice. Mourners, those foremost of the Netherworld, mysterious of face, who grasp the hair-locks—your voice be to me. I always call to you. I always become peaceful by means of your cries. I always illuminate you, O mourners, so that I might cause that you be pacified by means of your provisions. May you give to me jubilation, so that you might live. May you rejoice for me, so that you might become strong. May you cry out to Foremost of the Netherworld. May you call to He Who Is Hidden of Name. May you guide me, while I pass over you. Indeed, your *ba*-souls protect (me), with the result that I cause that you be powerful by means of my light, as I dispel for you the darkness that is upon you.

O this Ennead of gods who mourn, those foremost of the Netherworld, those who are in the Mysterious Place. I am crossing over your grottos in order to see He Who Is Hidden of Name, in order to care for the West, in order to traverse the mysterious Netherworld. May your *ba*-souls go forth. May your *ba*-souls, whom I summon, be strong. You are these who cry out and who call, those foremost of the Netherworld, who are in mourning in the West over Osiris, Foremost of the Netherworld, those who are great of mourning-hair, lords of provisions, chiefs of the hair-locks in the land of the West. I am entering into the earth, from which I have gone forth, that I might go to rest upon my first birth form."

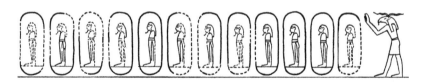

5.19. Scene 19. Twelve sarcophagi, oriented vertically, each contain a deity. At the far right of the scene, a ram-headed deity bends forward, arms before him, palms downward.

"O gods, Westerners, council of Foremost of the Netherworld, those of the sarcophagi, those strong of *ba*-soul, pacified ones, lords of provisions. Behold, I am entering into your cavern, so that I might give you assistance in your grottos, so that I might cause your *ba*-souls to rest upon you, and so that I might rejuvenate you upon your corpses. I am the one who enters his birth form, who is at peace with the rejuvenation of his flesh. I am Re who enters into the darkness. I always illuminate the Netherworld by means of my solar disk. O, may you remain, Westerners, in [your] places. [You are] these gods whose places I have commanded be mysterious. Come, O *ba*-souls of the Westerners. Your corpses are in your grottos; your mysteries are in your sarcophagi. I will pacify you by means of my light. I will give you breath so that you might breathe.

O Westerner who is in his grotto—
   the one who clothes the visible form of Osiris.
O Netherworldly One, foremost of the Netherworld—
   the one who clothes the visible form of Osiris.
O Lord of Hair-locks, loud of moans—
   the one who clothes the visible form of Osiris.
O Possessor of a Head within the Netherworld—
   the one who clothes the visible form of Osiris.
O Great of Broad-collar, possessor of a counterweight—
   the one who clothes the visible form of Osiris.
O Lord of the Serpents in the Hidden Chamber—
   the one who clothes the visible form of Osiris.
O Lord of flame, great of fire—
   the one who clothes the visible form of Osiris.
O *Benu*-bird,[36] *ba*-soul of the Netherworldly ones—
   the one who clothes the visible form of Osiris.
O Acclaiming One, who has raised his arm—
   the one who clothes the visible form of Osiris.
O Lord of Offerings, great of altar—
   the one who clothes the visible form of Osiris.
O One with a Head-cloth, great of clothing—
   the one who clothes the visible form of Osiris.
O One with a Fillet, great of ribbons—
   the one who clothes the visible form of Osiris.

O behold, you Westerners, may you be at peace with what I say to you. <I> protect you. [I discern] your need. I place He of Terror as your protec-

---

36. For the solar-Osirian imagery of the *benu*-bird, see p. 123 n. 140.

tion. Indeed, I am your protector, so that you might breathe, while I pass over you.

O you Ennead of gods, Westerners, those foremost of the Netherworld, those who clothe Osiris, whom the ruler of the West has transformed, council foremost of the West who [are in the Myster]ious Place. I cross over your grottos in order to see He Who Is Hidden of Name, in order to care for the West, in order to traverse the mysterious Netherworld. May your *ba*-souls go forth. May your *ba*-souls, whom I summon, be strong. You are these Netherworldly gods, Westerners, [lords] of provisions. I enter into the earth, from which I have gone forth, that I might go to rest upon my first birth form."

REGISTER 3 (PLATE 30)

5.20. Scene 20. A ram-headed god leaning on a staff faces five gods with arms raised in adoration.

"O gods, you gods, over whom I pass, whom I adore.[37] May you give to me your arms. May you rejoice at seeing my solar disk. O those within the earth, who give adoration. I am arriving at your grotto. Praise me. I am making you strong and your *ba*-souls pass by in my following."

5.21 (left side), 5.22 (right side). Scene 21. Two pairs of gods hold their arms in praise over a chest containing a solar disk. Four ram-heads with solar disks are followed by four jackal-headed staffs with shining solar disks.[38]

"O gods, you gods, may your arms be over the chest of Osiris, great of provisions, mysterious of manifestations, as the protection of whose mys-

---

37. For the term *nꜣš*, see Werning 2011a, 81 n. a.

38. The scene here omits the extra two deities that occurs to the left of the chest in the Tomb of Ramesses VI and adds the shining disks that appear in the Osireion and post-New Kingdom copies of this scene; for an examination of the textual history, see Werning forthcoming.

tery my heads, mysterious of nature, and my necks exist. [The goddess] es, hidden of visible forms and my effective eye, behind my solar disk, illuminate him. The divine eye of Foremost of the Netherworld and the *udjat*-eye of Atum are in the grotto of the chest of the mystery, which the Netherworld Dwellers see, so that they might breathe. You are these gods who protect the provisions of the Netherworld and the great mystery of the West.

> O One of the Female Sun,[39] who guards the mystery, who places his hand over the mysterious chest.
>
> O Secret of Heart, who guards the hidden things, who places his hand over the mysterious chest.
>
> O Dark-faced One, who guards the hidden one, who places his hand over the mysterious chest.
>
> O Covered One, who guards the corpse, who places his hand over the mysterious chest.

O you four gods—praise me. I enter into the earth, while I am adoring <you> whose arms are over the chest of Osiris.[40] Make yourselves fast upon your mysteries, this body of Foremost of the Netherworld. Behold, I am entering among you, your *ba*-souls, whom I summon, <pass by in my following>, while you remain in your grottos. My solar disk, my head, and my neck are [your] protectors. I am indeed your protector. May you breathe, even while I enter among you.

O you four gods, chiefs of the mysteries of Osiris who are in the Mysterious Place, those who exist as the protection of the anus(?)[41] of Osiris, so that the dead cannot behold their mysteries. I am crossing over your grottos in order to see He Who Is Hidden of Name, in order to care for the West, in order to traverse the mysterious Netherworld. May your *ba*-souls go forth. May you *ba*-souls, to whom I have called, be strong. You are these gods, mysterious ones, foremost of the Netherworld. I am entering into

---

39. For the female solar disk, see von Lieven 2001 (albeit assuming that all references thereto are references to Sothis); Darnell 2004, 219–23; Klotz 2012a, 204. The concept of the female disk appears already in Coffin Texts Spell 482 (CT 6.48–52), and perhaps already in the Pyramid Texts—see Troy 1986, 22. Compare also "She of the Disk" in the Books of the Creation of the Solar Disk (p. 468) and the "Female Disk" in the Books of the Solar-Osirian Unity (p. 559).

40. The sarcophagus of Tjaihorpata provides this reading, which fits well with the scene that accompanies this annotation (Manassa 2007a, 339); alternate readings appear in Werning 2011a, 85–86.

41. Werning 2011a, 87 n. b.

the earth, from which I have gone forth, that I might go to rest upon my first birth form."

REGISTER 4 (PLATE 30)

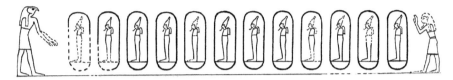

5.23. Scene 22. A falcon-headed deity stretches his arms out, palms downward in front of twelve vertically oriented sarcophagi. In each sarcophagus is a figure of Osiris, wearing a white crown, divine beard, and broad-collar with counterweight. At the end of the scene is a male figure with his arms raised in adoration.

O ⌜Horus⌝! Behold, I am passing over you. Give your arm to those who are in your cavern. Behold, I am entering into the earth who has given birth to me. The West gives her arm to me, so that her first cavern might be prepared for me. O, behold, I am calling to those who are with you and I am summoning those foremost of your cavern. [...] those foremost of your cavern that is in the West.

> O Osiris, Foremost of the Westerners, whose cavern his son Horus protects.
> O Osiris, ruler of the Netherworld, lord of the coffin,[42] great of sarcophagus.
> O Osiris, lord of Tatenen,[43] whose place is more mysterious than (those of) those who are in his following.
> O Osiris, lord of the West, whose travels are greater than (those of) those who are in his following.
> O Osiris, who destroys the enemies, lord of the dead, ruler of the akh-spirits.
> O Osiris, lord of the council, who judges the words of the Westerners.
> O Osiris, king of the West, who cares for the one foremost of Igeret.

---

42. Elsewhere ḏry.t refers to a sanctuary, constructed of wood (Wilson 1997, 1241–42).

43. Tatenen, literally "emerging land," is here synonymous with the Netherworld, a concept that appears frequently within the Book of Caverns (Schlögl 1980, 84–85).

O Osiris, lord of the white crown, who issues commands to his son
   Horus.

O Osiris, foremost of the Netherworld, lord of the cavern, ruler of the
   grotto.

O Osiris, who straightens paths, lord of the many mysterious roads.

O Osiris, lord of the Ennead, whose words destroy his enemies.

O Osiris, who repels his enemies, who destroys the *ba*-souls of those
   who rebel against him.

O you twelve gods who are in the following of Osiris, who have transformed into him. You are the Westerners, the council of the one who is
within the Netherworld, whom Horus summons, those distinguished of
visible form[44] as their [...]."

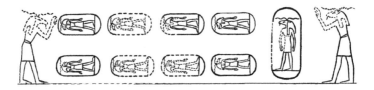

5.24. Scene 23. Two ram-headed gods stand, arms raised in adoration, to either
side of nine sarcophagi. The sarcophagi are arranged in two horizontal rows of
four with a ninth sarcophagus, vertically oriented, at the end. Each sarcophagus
contains a ram-headed figure. The figures in the top row are prone; those in the
bottom row are supine.

"O Divine Image in His Sarcophagus, lord of the two horns, great in
   his cavern.

O Corpse-like One, powerful of *akh*-spirit [... the dead], their darkness [...].

O Retreating One, plentiful of names [...].

O One Who Hides the Corpses of the Gods, mysterious of stench.

---

44. The concept of "distinguished" can relate to crowns, and the beings in the sarcophagi here are indeed crowned (see Darnell 2004, 139–40, noting several parallels
within the Netherworld Books, especially the Books of the Creation of the Solar Disk,
Tomb of Ramesses VI, Section A, Register 2, Scene 9, which calls Osiris "distinguished
of visible forms").

O Image [Who Manifested] in Me,[45] [...] my solar disk in your grotto.

O Engendering One[46] who manifests through me—behold, I myself am ascending.

O Begetting One who manifests through me—behold, I am crossing over to the place in which you are, so that I might care for you.

O Lord of the *Ba*-Soul upon my own corpse, who illuminates for his corpse in the Hidden Land.

O gods who are in my following, those who manifested through me, who came forth from my limbs. Behold, I am speaking to you, so that I might cause your *ba*-souls to be in my following together with me. O those in my following! Your voice unites with your *ba*-soul, when I illuminate you and discern your needs. I am Re who cares for you, Nehi who exists as your protection together with his brother Isedi.[47] I am indeed your protector. May you breathe, even while I enter among you."

ANNOTATION TO SCENES 22–23

"O, ⌜twelve⌝ gods who are in the following of Osiris, council of Foremost of the Netherworld. O you eight gods, [divine(?)][48] corpses who are in the following of the great gods in the West who are in the Mysterious Place. I cross over your grottos in order to see He Who Is Hidden of Name, in order to traverse the mysterious Netherworld. May your [*ba*-souls go forth]. May your *ba*-souls, whom I have summoned, be strong. You are the gods, the great council who passes judgment, who greet Osiris. You are these who are in my following, mysterious of manifestations. I enter into the earth, from which I have gone forth, that I might go to rest upon my first birth form."

---

45. Tjaihorpata (CG 29306) rationalizes this name as "perfect of manifestations." (Manassa 2007a, 341)

46. Contra Werning 2011a, 95 ("fremd[e Sprachen] Sprechender") and "ꜣ"w," LGG 1:1, since parallelism does not support this interpretation.

47. For the role of Nehi as a solar deity, see p. 100. The deity Isedi appears only here ("*ꜣsdy*," LGG 1:558) and may be related to a term *ꜣsd* "to spit" ("*ꜣsd*," WÄS, 1:134.7–8).

48. Restoration suggested by Werning 2011a, 99.

REGISTER 5 (PLATE 30)

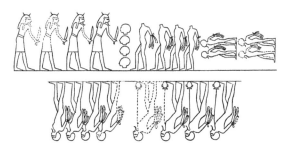

5.25 (top), 5.26 (bottom). Scene 24. Four horned deities brandish knives at depictions of enemies. Immediately in front of the horned deities are four decapitated heads, stacked one above the other. Four decapitated enemies follow, followed by four additional enemies (in two rows) lying prone. Finally, eight enemies are depicted upside down; the last four inverted figures have their hearts ripped out.

> "O decapitated ones, without their heads, foremost of the Place of Destruction.
> O enemies, without their *ba*-souls, foremost of the Place of Destruction.
> O inverted ones, bound ones, foremost of the Place of Destruction.
> O inverted ones, bloody ones whose hearts have been removed, foremost of the Place of Destruction.
> O enemies of the ruler of the Netherworld, Osiris, Foremost of the West.

Behold, I am commanding you to destruction, as I am assigning you to non-existence. The slaughterers who are in the place of punishment of Osiris—they [execute] your massacre according as I have commanded <you> to the slaughter, which has come into existence against you. You are those who have committed offences, who did evil in the West. You are the enemies. You do not exist, and you shall not exist. O, behold, I am entering among you, so that I might assign to you your punishment. I assign you to the Place of Destruction, from which your *ba*-souls may not go forth."

DIVISION 3

INTRODUCTORY TEXT (PLATE 31)

"O Osiris, behold I have traveled the One of the West[49]—for me have your paths been straightened.[50] Behold, my solar disk enters after me, that it might give birth to me, and in turn I give birth to it.[51] Now I am greeting Osiris, ⌈illumining⌉ [those among whom] you are by means of my solar disk, so that they might straighten for me the ways of the Netherworld, causing that I go to rest in their grotto. I shall enter the cavern betwixt the Aker,[52] that I might illumine the great mystery that is beneath him above which is your *ba*-soul, without him being able to ascend to the one who rests [...] the mystery. I strengthen your *ba*-soul upon his corpse. Your *ba*-soul travels the Netherworld, and your grotto in the cavern. Then how content is Osiris, how strong is the *ba*-soul of Foremost of the Netherworld. That I ⌈spread⌉ evil among his enemies [...] them in ⌈the Place of Destruction;⌉ for I am your protector—may you breathe, even while I pass by you.

O Osiris, Ruler of the Netherworld, who is in the Mysterious Place—I am crossing over your grottos, in order to see your corpse and your image, which you have hidden beneath Aker,[53] secret and unknowable, in order to care for the West, in order to traverse the mysterious Netherworld, in order to spread out your *ba*-soul upon your corpse in this cavern of the Mysterious Place, in which is Aker, in order to protect you in your mysterious places, in order to strike impediments into your enemies—Osiris, ruler of the West, lord of mystery in the Mysterious Place. Behold, I am

---

49. Less likely: "I have traveled, (O) One of the West."

50. Compare the name *mꜣꜥ wꜣ.wt* in Book of Adoring Re in the West, Great Litany, Address 48 (p. 93).

51. Compare the statement in the Book of Gates, Hour 2, Register 3, Scene 8: "I am the son who came forth from his father; I am the father who came forth from his son."

52. Literally the back of Aker, as in Division 3, Registers 2–3, Scene 32.

53. Hiding of the corpse under Aker is like the concealment of the corpse within the horizon, as in the concluding scene of the Book of the Hidden Chamber (p. 241) or the giant reclining Osiris in the Book of the Solar-Osirian Unity in the Tomb of Ramesses IX (pp. 569–71). The depiction of Osiris beneath Aker also appears on Third Intermediate period papyri with Netherworldly themes (compare Niwiński 1989a, 196 fig. 69, and pl. 42b, etc.).

entering into the earth, from which I came forth, that I might go to rest upon my first birth form."

REGISTER 1 (PLATE 31)

5.27. Scene 25. A male figure with divine beard rests supine in a horizontal oval; he is labeled "One of the Head-cloth, who is Osiris." Above and below the oval are two serpents—"Poisonous One" and "One Wide of Mouth, Who Spreads (His) Jaws," respectively—each with multiple coils, tail to right, heads raised to left. To the left of the forepart of the upper serpent is a solar disk.

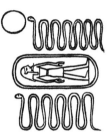

BEHIND THE SCENE

These gods exist in this fashion. Re speaks to them, while he passes by their cavern. They behold the light of his solar disk and rejoice over it when they behold it. Then darkness covers them when he passes by them.

BEFORE THE SCENE

Re says to this cavern: "O One of the Head-cloth, one of rotting, foremost of the sarcophagus, one at the head of his cavern, whom those who came forth from him guard. O, you Poisonous One who is in his cavern, and One Wide of Mouth, Who Spreads His Jaws; behold, I am summoning you. You are the chiefs of your caverns, door-keepers mysterious of arms, watchful because of what they do. O you Osiris, chief of his cavern, in his mysterious <manifestation(?)> of the One of the Head-cloth."

5.28. Scene 26. Seven catfish-headed beings stand, feet to left, arms slightly akimbo, beneath a serpent, the body stretched horizontally above them, tail dropping down to right, the head down to the left. Above the middle of the group is a solar disk. Names

of the catfish-headed beings (left to right): Osiris; Catfish-Like One; Catfish-Like One; Eel-Like One; Fish-Like One; *Seny* (?); Swimming One(?).

These gods exist in this fashion, within the coils of Nehebkau. Re speaks to them, that he might illumine them with the illumination of his solar disk.

———

5.29. Scene 27. Two mounds, side-by-side, a solar disk hovering above each. Within each mound a ram-headed figure, feet together, arms by its side, face down, head to the left. The left ram-headed figure is "Ram-form in which is Re," while the right figure is "Female Sheep in which is Re."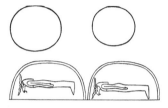

ABOVE THE LEFT RAM-HEADED FIGURE, WITHIN THE HILL

This god is in this fashion, in this his mound, mysterious of nature.[54]

ABOVE THE MOUNDS

These gods exist in this fashion, in their mound in the sole cavern. This great god speaks to them, with the result that they behold the light of his solar disk.[55] That these deities behold the light of the solar disk is when he passes by them. Then darkness covers them.

BEFORE THE SCENE

Re says to this cavern: "O corpses who have manifested from me, my images, my manifestations, whom I have created. Behold, I am reaching your mounds, that I might rest above you, that I might summon you, that I might protect you, with the result that I take care of you. You corpses who manifested from me—my own flesh, my images, my creations—I am causing that your throats breathe, making strong your *ba*-spirits. That they pass is after I pass. O you two mounds. O you who are in them. Behold, I am passing by your mounds, so that you may hear that I am summoning you, that I might light up for you, that I might drive away your darkness."

———

54. For mysterious mounds in the Netherworld Books, see Darnell 2004, 290–93.

55. The interchange of light and speech is common with the corpus of Netherworld Books (see pp. 5–6).

5.30. Scene 28. A solar disk appears above three ovals, each oriented vertically. Within the left and central oval are a single figure, facing right, male to the left, female in the central oval; these deities are named "Silencer of the Gods" (left) and "Silence of the Gods" (center). Within the right oval a male deity facing left, "Great of Rot."

BEFORE THE SCENE

Re says to this cavern: "O you three great gods, who join the earth by means of their corpses, who stand without lying down, according to the words which they say to themselves. You are these deities, because of whose mysteries Anubis has called to Osiris, the one (Anubis) who placed him—Ruler of the West—in his place, without him being able to go forth, the one who caused that he go to rest in the West, setting his corpse in the Mysterious Place, without that which is in his hands having become mysterious.[56] O, behold, me passing by you, so that you might rejoice over me, and that I might honor you, and the one Foremost of the Netherworld."

5.31. Scene 29. A mummiform figure, "Osiris, Foremost of the Westerners," stands facing left, wearing a white crown, atop a *m3ꜥ*-socle, in which is an undulating serpent, head rearing to left. A *per-wer*-like shrine surrounds Osiris, a rearing serpent at each side within the shrine, facing in toward the central figure; within the top of the shrine, swelling to the left, is another undulating serpent, head rearing to left. In front of the shrine are four ovals, vertically ori-

56. Figures in various of the Netherworld Books depict and describe beings whose arms are hidden: "Wrapped Ones of the Earth, those hidden of arm(s)" (Book of Gates, Hour 3, Register 2, Scene 12); deities called "Hidden of Arm" and "Mysterious of Arm" (Books of the Creation of the Solar Disk, Tomb of Ramesses VI, Section B, Register 4, Scene 42); and a god called "Clothed of Arm" (Books of the Solar-Osirian Unity, Second Shrine of Tutankhamun, Side 1, Register 3, Scene 9; Darnell 2004, 90–92). In the Book of Caverns passage, the element in his hands is feminine, suggesting *imy.t-ꜥ* in the sense of "companion" (Hannig 2006a, 189; note also "*imy-ꜥ-Ḥr*" and "*imy-ꜥ-stḫ*," LGG 1:229), probably referring to the central, female figure in the scene. Note also the deities "in the arms of Aker" in the Book of Caverns, Division 3, Registers 2–3, Scene 32.

ented, a standing figure, facing right, in each (from top to bottom they are female, male, jackal-headed male, female), named "She Who Covers the Mystery"; "Powerful of Arms"; "Anubis"; "She Who Guards." Behind the shrine are six such ovals, a figure facing left in each (in the left row are three females and in the right row three males) named "She Who Lets the Throat Breathe"; "She Who Keeps a Vigil over Her Lord"; "She Who Clothes the Mystery"; "One Who Destroys <the Ba-Souls>"; "One Who Extinguishes the Shades"; "One Who Punishes the Enemies."

BEFORE THE SCENE

Re says to this mysterious cavern that hides the gods, as she covers the face(s) of the great ones who are in her, of whose mysterious images, great of manifestations, the one who is in her knows not: "O gods who are in the cavern of Osiris, Foremost of the West, who is ruler of the Netherworld in his chamber of darkness,[57] in the surrounding of whose mysterious shrine these four deities are—I am time,[58] Re who makes you, who creates you, who brings into being you four. You are these gods mysterious of places in the forepart of the Netherworld. O, behold I am passing by you, that I might shed light for you, and that I might drive away your darkness."

REGISTER 2 (PLATE 31)

5.32. Scene 30. A ram-headed deity stands, facing right, one arm down and slightly extended before thigh, palm down, the other arm holding a scepter; a solar disk hovers behind the head of the deity.

BEFORE THE RAM-HEADED DEITY

This god exists in this fashion, entering as an elder, giving his arms to the Westerners, speaking to the ones of the mystery.

57. Compare the ꜥ.t-kky in the Book of Thoth (Jasnow and Zauzich 2005, 36–38).
58. Alternatively "mine is time"; for time in the Book of Adoring Re in the West, compare Great Litany, Addresses 15 and 74 (pp. 81, 101). Note also, the re-creation of time in the Book of Gates (pp. 274, 288).

5.33. Scene 31. Four mummiform deities, dark of color, wearing divine beards, white crowns, and with counter-weights hanging out and down from the backs of the necks, standing, facing left; a solar disk hovers between the heads of the two middle figures.

BEFORE EACH OF THE DEITIES

Osiris, Foremost of the West. This god is in this fashion. This great god speaks to him, with the result that he sees the light of his solar disk.

Clothed One.[59] This god exists in this fashion. This great god speaks to him, with the result that he sees the light of his solar disk.

Adorned One. This god exists in this fashion. This great god speaks to him, with the result that he sees the light of his solar disk.

One of the Mystery. This god exists in this fashion. This great god speaks to him, with the result that he sees the light of his solar disk.

BETWEEN SCENES 30 AND 31

Re says to this cavern: "Ones hidden of place, ones of the clothing(?) [...?] power of Anubis, you are these lords of the Netherworld, who manifested from Foremost of the West. May you open for me your grottos, may you swing open to me your mysteries, so that my solar disk may enter into your caverns. May your arms receive me. Gods, behold, I am entering as the great elder, the solar disk in my following, it expelling your darkness."

---

59. Reading *swt* as <*ḥb*>*swt*, a name that appears elsewhere in the Netherworld Books ("*Ḥbst*," LGG 5:113; particularly relevant is *ḥbst* labeling a male figure in the Books of the Creation of the Solar Disk, Tomb of Ramesses VI, Section A, Register 2, Scene 7). See also "*Swt*," LGG 6:224: "Der Einbalsamierte(?)." Alternatively, but less well suited to the context of the other names, is "one of reeds" (Meeks 1998a, 313) or "one of wheat," a reference to the grain Osiris; the grains are indeed placed in a "Foremost of the Westerners" mold, and can have reeds placed above and below the grain mummy (Centrone 2009, 163). The standing, dark colored, mummiform, White Crown-adorned figures in Book of Caverns, Division 3, Register 2, Scene 31 recall the similar mummiform figures in the Books of the Solar-Osirian Unity, Second Shrine of Tutankhamun, Side 2, Register 2, Scene 15 who have the annotation "These gods are in this fashion: it is the light of Re which clothes their corpses. When he calls their *ba*-souls, they travel behind" (Darnell 2004, 132; see pp. 549–50).

5.34. Scene 32. Central Scene. A complex scene in two registers. Above, a large image of a double sphinx, "Aker," four female deities facing right with arms raised emerging from the right-hand forepaws, three male deities with beards and arms lowered in front, palms down, emerging from left hand forepaws. The female deities are named: "Tefnut who is in the arms of Aker"; "Nut who is in the arms of Aker"; "Isis who is in the arms of Aker"; "Nephthys who is in the arms of Aker." Each male deity is also labeled with a name and short annotation: "One of the Netherworld, as he comes forth from the arms of Aker"; "Atum, as he comes forth from the arms of Aker"; "Turned back one, as he comes forth from the arms of Aker." Above the right shoulder of the Aker is a horizontally oriented oval containing a horizontally oriented scarab, head to right; above the left shoulder is a horizontally oriented figure, feet apart to right, facing down, arms raised and extended in front of the head to left, labeled "Geb who guards Aker."[60] Above these hovers a solar disk. Below, an ithyphallic figure lies on its back, head to left, wearing a beard, feet slightly apart as though in walking pose; a serpent almost entirely surrounds the figure in a box-like fashion. Above the slight gap between the head and tail of the serpent, above the phallus of the supine figure, hovers a solar disk.

ANNOTATION TO THE MALE DEITIES ON THE LEFT

These gods exist in this fashion. Re speaks to them by means of his light. Then darkness covers them, after this great god passes by them.

---

60. For the protective role of Geb in his theology, compare Bedier 1995, 186–91.

These goddesses exist in this fashion, presenting their arms to Osiris, without their coming forth from within the arms of Aker. The solar disk of Re shines for them, their *ba*-souls having passed behind Re. That they behold the light is after he passes by them. Then darkness covers them.

LABEL TO PRONE DEITY ABOVE THE LEFT SHOULDER OF AKER

This god exists in this fashion, as he attaches himself upon the back of Aker, protecting the mystery that is in the Netherworld. This great god speaks to him, with the result that he sees the light of his solar disk.

LABEL TO THE SCARAB ABOVE THE RIGHT SHOULDER OF AKER

This god exists in this fashion, in his oval upon the back of Aker. Khepri who is upon the body of Aker guards the mystery that is in the Netherworld.

LABEL ON THE BODY OF AKER

This god exists in this fashion. Geb and Khepri are guarding the image that is in him. This great god comes to a standstill[61] atop his cavern. Just as he speaks to this great image that carries his body, so he calls out to Foremost of the Netherworld. He illumines those who are in the arms of Aker and causes that the mysterious secret image draws itself together.[62] That the deity sees the light is when Re passes by him.

ANNOTATION WITH AKER

Re says to this cavern, at the same time as he passes by Aker: "O Aker, make a way for me. One mysterious of visible form, bend your arm to me.

---

61. The standstill is a means of confronting opposition—the serpent Apep—in the Netherworld (Barta 1990a, 94; Darnell 2004, 287–88).

62. Literally, "draws together its body"—the idiom is "sich zusammen reissen, sich ermannen," *WÄS*, 4:25.18 (citing the Story of Sinuhe, when the protagonist hears the sound of cattle); similar idioms appear in Kitchen 1979, 371.5; 854.5; Herbin 1994, 185.

Behold, I am summoning you. May those amongst whom you are belong to me, for I have seen your mysteries: (namely,) my solar disk and Geb—these who are upon your back—and Khepri within his sarcophagus. (O) One of the Netherworld, as he comes forth from the arms of Aker; Atum, as he comes forth from the arms of Aker; Turned back one, as he comes forth from the arms of Aker—O give to me your arms; receive me. Behold, I pass by your mysteries, shining for you, driving away your darkness."

ABOVE THE SUPINE FIGURE IN THE LOWER REGISTER

This god is in this fashion, in the cavern which is in the West. The great god speaks to him, as he causes his solar disk to rest in his cavern. The *ba*-soul of this deity in the following of Re is taking care of those who are in the earth. Terrible of Face, foremost of his cavern, pulls together the corpse of this deity.[63]

ANNOTATION TO THE SERPENT

This serpent exists in this fashion, pulling together the corpse of Osiris. In the uniform darkness does this serpent, foremost of his cavern, exist.

BEFORE THE LOWER REGISTER

Re says to this cavern: "O corpse of the one whose *ba*-soul is hidden, Osiris, Ruler of the West; one mysterious of corpse; one hidden of putrefaction; one whom the dead cannot approach; one through the breathing of whose stench of putrefaction those who are in the West live.[64] O, behold, I am passing, Osiris, causing that my solar disk go to rest in your cavern. I am taking care of your *ba*-soul and your shade. I am driving away for you the darkness from you. Terrible of Face who is in the cavern pulls together your corpse. I indeed am passing by your cavern, giving orders to those in your entourage."

63. For the positive role of Terrible of Face (Nehaher), who is elsewhere a hypostasis of Apep, see p. 13.

64. For breathing through putrefaction, compare the mummies who are "living on their putrefaction, breathing from their rot" in the Book of Gates, Hour 4, Register 2, Scene 19 (pp. 273–74).

5.35. Scene 33. On the left a serpent forms a vertical rectangular shape, head (pointing down from above) touching the tail on the left side. Within the serpent-enclosed space, three ovals, one vertical to left—containing a standing figure (facing right) and two smaller ovals, containing a ram head (above) and eye (below). To the right of this group, two rows of two bowing male figures wearing divine beards, facing left, arms out and down before them. Above the upper two bowing figures hovers a solar disk.

LABEL TO THE IMAGES WITHIN THE SERPENT ENCLOSURE

They exist in this fashion. The great one, foremost of his grotto, guards their ovals.

LABELS TO THE BOWING FIGURES, FROM LEFT TO RIGHT

Fighter, who jubilates for Re, when he assumes power over his mystery.
Fighter, who jubilates for Re, when he assumes power over his mystery.
One of the Corpse, who jubilates for Re, when he assumes power over his mystery.
Chief of His Odor, who jubilates for Re, when he assumes power over his mystery.

BEFORE THE SCENE

Re says to this cavern: "O Osiris, mysterious of place, living of *ba*-soul, foremost of his sarcophagus—O my head and my eye—my mysterious forms, my images, my corpses, my manifestations, who exist in the following of Osiris, in the mysterious place in which he has gone to rest, whom the great one, foremost of his cavern, encircles, protecting his mystery. Behold me passing by and taking care of you, with the result that your mystery rests in your place. Indeed you are the sole one, who came forth from myself. I am causing that you see the light of my solar disk."

5.36. Scene 34. Two male figures face left, arms raised before them, the right figure in adoration, called "Praising One,"[65] the left figure, "One Who Leaps Up,"[66] with hands above and below the divine beard of a smaller, rodent-headed figure facing right labeled "Vigorous One." The smaller figure stands atop the body of a serpent, the "Great One," whose body curves around, with tail curling up between the knees of the figure cradling the beard of the smaller figure. The serpent's head rears up in front of the smaller figure, with head facing right. A solar disk hovers above the left male figure.

BEHIND THE TWO FIGURES TO THE RIGHT

These gods are in this fashion, in the cavern of the Vigorous One. They hear the words of Re. His great solar disk shines for them. Then darkness covers them, after this great god passes by them.

ABOVE THE RODENT-HEADED FIGURE

This god exists in this fashion. The great serpent <bears> the corpses of the gods. This great god speaks to this god.

BEFORE THE SCENE

Re says to this cavern: "O Osiris! You Vigorous One, upon his great one, who seizes hold of the sole one who came forth from his body.

The hair of his jaw belongs to the mystery of his divine beard,[67] without that from which he manifested being comprehensible. The Praising

---

65. Following Hornung, who reads "Der Preisende" (see also "*M3ty*," *LGG* 3:239); Werning reads *d'mwti*, one of the djam-scepter (2011a, 140–41). Since the arms are in adoration and there is no scepter visible, Hornung's reading seems more likely. This term may be related to *m3wty* "the two arms" (Wilson 1997, 402).

66. For the term *nhp*, see the commentary at p. 169 n. 70 (label to 288–291).

67. For the significance of the divine beard in the Book of Caverns, see pp. 351–52 and n. 22.

One praises him, and associates his corpse with him. You are these deities who assign the *ba*-souls to the butchery; the ones who fight on behalf of the one from whom they came forth, the great gods in the west. O, behold, I am crossing over you, in order to take care of you, Vigorous One; in order to illumine the darkness for your corpse; in order to strengthen your *ba*-soul, Osiris. You are the sole one, who manifested from the second; you are indeed the second who manifested from Osiris, the one great of corpse in the West."

REGISTER 3 (PLATE 31)

5.37. Scene 35. Eight upside-down fig-ures, facing left, arms raised as though in adoration, four male to the left, four female to the right; the male figures are each labeled "One of Evil," while each female is called "Female enemy." To 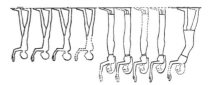 the right of the group is a praising male figure, also upside-down and facing left, called: "Destroyer of the *ba*-soul of the One of Evil, guardian of the enemy of Osiris."

INVERTED TEXT ABOVE THE MALE ENTITIES

They exist in this fashion, unable to see the light of Re, unable to hear his voice. In uniform darkness do they exist, their *ba*-souls unable to go forth from the earth, their shades unable to go to rest upon their corpses. Even after passing them by does Re issue evil against them.

INVERTED TEXT ABOVE THE FEMALE ENTITIES

They exist in this fashion, unable to see the light of Re, unable to hear his voice. In uniform darkness do they exist, unable to see the rays of Re, their *ba*-souls unable to go forth from the earth, their shades unable to go to rest upon their corpses. Even after passing them by does Re issue evil against them.

Re says to this cavern: "O, female enemies, O you males of the enemy,[68] upside-down females, shade-less males. O nonexistent ones, inverted of *ba*-souls, from whose shadows their eye(s) live.[69] You are the female enemies of Osiris, and his male enemies, ones without their *ba*-souls. You are dark, your *ba*-souls having been taken from your corpses. You are those who cannot manifest; you are in the Place of Destruction. One amongst you is your guard, who destroys the *ba*-souls of the ones of evil, the *ba*-souls unable to go forth from beneath his hands. You will not behold light, you will not have power over my rays."

5.38. Scene 36. To left four upside-down male figures, hands crossed at wrists near waists as though bound, schematic blood issuing from upper foreheads, facing left; each is labeled "One of Burning." To right, four upside-down headless male figures, 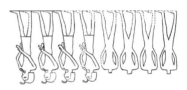 arms as though akimbo, with the annotation "Beheaded One without His Head."

They exist in this fashion, unable to see the light of Re. In uniform darkness do they exist, their *ba*-souls unable to go forth from the earth. Inverted do their corpses exist. Even after he passes by them, this god issues evil against them.

Re says to this cavern: "O ones of burning, deprived of (the use of) arms, unable to make use of their strength, ones who have passed on, great of

---

68. Perhaps a reference to Apep, making these enemies the chaos serpent's confederates.

69. This is an interesting reference to the damned cannibalizing themselves—although cooking shades and other elements appear elsewhere, the self-consumption of their own elements here harks back, in a perverted fashion, to the concept of the king deriving nourishment from the psychic elements of deities in the Cannibal Hymn (Eyre 2002, 120–21, referencing the Book of Caverns [there termed the "Book of Qererets"]).

mourning, whose evil is against them, whose blood is against their flesh, while being massacred. O beheaded ones, without heads, who are not, whose *ba*-souls are ones who have passed on to the earth, whose shades are ones allotted to evil, whose corpses are inverted—the slaughterer cuts off their limbs—You are these who have committed evil, who have done what disturbs the one Foremost of the Netherworld. Osiris, Foremost of the West, commends you to your evil, and assigns you to the Place of Destruction, by means of that which comes forth from my mouth against you. I am Re, who decrees and becomes manifest, unable to go back on what he says."[70]

5.39. Scene 37. To the left right are four upside-down, human-headed *ba*-birds, with divine beards, facing left; an inverted text labels each figure "*Ba*-soul of an enemy." To the right are four upside-down female figures, facing left, schematic blood 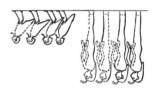 emerging from their upper foreheads, arms down and in front, as though bound near the waist; they are each labeled "She of Slaughter, turned back of arms."

ABOVE THE *BA*-BIRDS

They exist in this fashion, without their corpses, unable to go forth from the earth, unable to see the light of this great god. In the uniform darkness do they exist. After he passes by them, this god sends evil against them.

BEFORE THE SCENE

Re says to this cavern: "O ones against whom slaughter has been committed in the forehall of the Netherworld, blood-spurting ones of the West, turned back of arm beneath their slaughter, clothed by what they have done. You are these slaughtered ones; you are the ones ⌈turned back⌉ of arm, ones of mourning, destroyed of *ba*-soul(s), those who are covered in their blood. O, behold, I am passing by you, with the result that you are commended to the Place of Destruction in your place which is in the Netherworld—that which Osiris said concerning you. The *ba*-souls of the

---

70. For the concept of the solar deity unable to reverse what he has said, compare Coffin Texts Spell 75 (CT 1.385b).

enemies of Osiris are inverted in the Place of Destruction, even without seeing their corpses, being that which I decreed should occur to them, the enemies of Osiris."

INTRODUCTION TO DIVISIONS 4–6

INTRODUCTION (PLATE 32)

5.40. Scenes 38–40. Serpent standing vertically on the tip of its tail, head bent slightly to left, labeled "With the fire of the flame on the tip of his mouth has he filled the cavern." To the left a solar disk in the middle of the space; in the same position to the right a standing male, ram-headed figure, facing right, arms raised in adoring position.

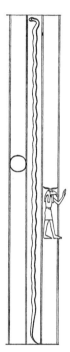

BEFORE THE IMAGE

Re says, at the same time that he reaches the cavern of the great one upon his belly: "O you great one upon his belly, who joins the two Netherworlds;[71] one of the West, whose cavern is filled with fire from that flame which comes forth from his mouth— penetrate into the earth, you of penetrating; cover your head, you wild of face. Behold me, West, as I command the Netherworld, as I cause the gods to become content with my light, as I punish the enemies who are in the flame in the Place of Destruction, as I assign them to the keepers of assignments, from whose guarding there is no escape. Hail, behold me passing by you."

BETWEEN DIVISIONS 3–4

Entering by this great god into the uniform darkness. By the cavern of the great one upon his belly does this great god pass. That his head exists in the uniform darkness, and his rear in darkness, is without gods, *akh*-spirits, or the dead ascending to his cavern, and without them passing by him, except for this great god who is in the sky.

---

71. Probably an allusion to the upper and lower Netherworld (compare Leitz 1989).

The gods who are in the forepart of their caverns, those over their grottos, those who are in their sarcophagi, those who rest upon their corpses—the gods, *akh*-spirits, and the dead say, when they behold Re and when they rejoice, when he passes by: "O come to us, lord of the solar disk, arise and come to us, O one great of light."

LITANIES 1–3 (BETWEEN DIVISIONS 3–4)

All three of the litanies between Divisions 3–4—Litanies 1–3—consist of essentially twelve segments. The pattern of Litany 1 is 2 + 3 + 2 + 3 + 2; that of Litany 2 is 2 + 5 + 1 + 2 + 2 (the final doubling of the jubilation might bring this to fourteen segments); Litany 3 is 1 + 5 (subset of 3 + 2) + 5 (subset of 2 + 3) + 1. The stress on twelve segments probably relates to the hours of the night. The pattern of Litany 1 may evoke endless alternation and the solar perpetuum mobile; the ascending and descending numbers of the internal sections of Litany 3 perhaps serve to associate the beginning and the end of the nocturnal journey, emphasizing the cosmic mystery that the sun sets in order to rise again.

LITANY 1: HOW BEAUTIFUL IS RE WHEN HE PASSES BY THE DARKNESS

This litany consists of twelve segments: two describe the situation: going to rest and traveling the Netherworld; three describe speaking (issuing commands) and causing to speak; two describe actions against enemies (physical and juridical); three describe the interactions of the sun and the West; two conclude the litany. The Tomb of Ramesses VI has insertions following each litany relating the action of Re specifically to the deceased king. For example, following Litany 1 Ramesses VI is said "to be at rest in the entourage of Re."

How beautiful is Re,
  when he passes by the darkness,
  and his great solar disk goes to rest in his following.
How beautiful is Re,
  when he passes by the darkness,
  as he passes the grotto of the one who travels the Netherworld.

How beautiful is Re,
>   when he passes by the darkness,
>   as he issues commands to the Netherworld dwellers.

How beautiful is Re,
>   when he passes by the darkness,
>   as he causes that the *ba*-souls upon their corpses speak.[72]

How beautiful is Re,
>   when he passes by the darkness,
>   as he issues commands to Igeret.

How beautiful is Re,
>   when he passes by the darkness,
>   as he stretches out the arm against the enemies of Osiris.

How beautiful is Re,
>   when he passes by the darkness,
>   as he judges those who are in the earth.

How beautiful is Re,
>   when he passes by the darkness,
>   the honored one going to rest in the Netherworld.

How beautiful is Re,
>   when he passes by the darkness,
>   as he summons the *ba*-souls of the Westerners.

How beautiful is Re,
>   when he passes by the darkness,
>   in order to take care of the Netherworld dwellers.

How beautiful is Re,
>   when he passes by the darkness;
>   the West covers the solar disk.

How beautiful is Re,
>   when he passes by the darkness;
>   when we behold him we draw in breath.

---

72. For speaking *ba*-souls, compare the Book of Adoring Re in the West, Great Litany, Addresses 5, 57, 70, 75.

This litany consists of two initial sentences; the next five lines relate things the deity causes to happen; one describes punishment; two contain epithet-like references to the deity; two more relate to things the deity causes (*di=k*); a final doubling of the jubilation with closing wishes concludes the litany.

> Jubilation belongs to you, Re,
>> with the result that we draw in breath.
>> In the forepart of our cavern do we go to rest.
> Jubilation belongs to you, Re,
>> with the result that we draw in breath.
>> That our shades become strong do you speak to us.

> Jubilation belongs to you, Re,
>> with the result that we draw in breath,
>> you causing that we go to rest in the light of your solar disk.
> Jubilation belongs to you, Re,
>> with the result that we draw in breath,
>> you causing that our *ba*-souls enter our caverns.
> Jubilation belongs to you, Re,
>> with the result that we draw in breath,
>> you causing that the corpses unite with their sarcophagi.
> Jubilation belongs to you, Re,
>> with the result that we draw in breath,
>> you causing that air enter into our nostrils.
> Jubilation belongs to you, Re,
>> with the result that we draw in breath,
>> you setting the *akh*-spirits in their grottos.

> Jubilation belongs to you, Re,
>> with the result that we draw in breath;
>> with the result that you assign the evil to the Place of Destruction do you punish.

> Jubilation belongs to you, Re,
>> with the result that we draw in breath,
>> <with> the one great of plans do we become satisfied.

Jubilation belongs to you, Re,
> with the result that we draw in breath,
> one whom the dead behold with the result that they come to life.

Jubilation belongs to you, Re,
> with the result that we draw in breath;
> may you cause the One Tired of Heart to occupy the shrine.

Jubilation belongs to you, Re,
> with the result that we draw in breath;
> may you cause that the *ba*-souls are entered into the following of the One of the Horizon.

Jubilation belongs to you, Re; jubilation indeed belongs to Re.

May you judge us, powerful one, great of words,
> who came forth from his earth,
> that he might indeed occupy it.
> Call to us, summon our *ba*-souls, one great of council, mighty of *akh*-power.

ADDRESS TO THE ONE TIRED OF HEART

"O, One Tired of Heart, great of weariness, Osiris, Foremost of the Westerners, lord of speech, great one of the Ennead, great chief in his council, to whom those who are in the Netherworld speak, namely the gods foremost of the West, slaughterers of the *ba*-souls of the dead, even while their *ba*-souls are upside down, and their corpses hidden from them. At the same time commands have been given to those who are in Igeret, (namely,) those who are in the Mysterious Place, and evil has been placed in his enemies. Just as they bring into existence the destroyed ones, so they summon the *ba*-soul of Re. Behold him going to rest upon his body, and causing that his corpse receives his light." So they say, the gods of the Netherworld, the *akh*-spirits who are in the West.

Re says to the Netherworld dwellers, as he summons the Westerners: "Behold me passing your cavern. I am crossing over your grotto. O Ennead of Osiris, council of Foremost of the Netherworld. Behold, I am joining your cavern. That I have entered the uniform darkness is in order to protect you in your cavern, in order to judge you, in order to take care of you. Even alone have I acted; on my own have I ordained. As you leap up after me so I leap up after you, in your names of ones of leaping.[73] Ones in the following of the Ruler of the West, content ones, ones foremost of their mounds, honored ones, ones living of *ba*-souls, those having power over their shades—you are these gods great of plans in the Mysterious Place, entourage of Osiris, messengers of Osiris."[74]

LITANY 3: THE POSSESSORS OF PROVISIONS IN THE WEST

This litany consists of twelve segments; one introductory line referencing time; five lines containing gnomic statements (three describing gnomic deeds of Osiris and two describing the actions of other divine beings); five lines containing addresses to beings in the netherworld (two referring to the states of the beings, three referring to those who speak and record); one concluding line describing another gnomic action of Osiris.

> Possessors of provisions in the West,
> > on that night of enquiring about matters,
> > of enacting the judgment of the *akh*-spirits.
>
> Possessors of provisions in the West—
> > Osiris repels his enemies.
> Possessors of provisions in the West—
> > Osiris reckons his body.
> Possessors of provisions in the West—
> > Osiris takes care of those amongst whom he is.
>
> Possessors of provisions in the West—
> > the Ennead of Tatenen rejoices.
> Possessors of provisions in the West—
> > the *benu*-bird passes through the gates of the Netherworld.
>
> Possessors of provisions in the West,
> > (O) gods without sin.
> Possessors of provisions in the West,
> > (O) ones of contentment, lords of Maat.

---

73. Suggesting here that *stp* has the sense of *nhp* (see Darnell 2004, 296–99; note particularly p. 299, citing the Book of Protecting the Divine Bark—*nhp nhp nhpy.w*).

74. For messengers in the Netherworld Books, see p. 112 n. 109, p. 568.

Possessors of provisions in the West,
(O) council of the Hidden Chamber.
Possessors of provisions in the West,
(O) mighty of spell in felling the rebel.
Possessors of provisions in the West,
(O) scribes of Maat in the presence of the sole lord.

Possessors of provisions in the West—
Osiris speaks for himself.

"Gods, you gods who are in the mysterious Netherworld—behold, I am entering the darkness, that I might rise in the uniform darkness. Just as I pass by so I behold, with the result that I behold this one weary of heart in this his rising for the hidden mystery,[75] and I cause that his image sees my solar disk, and I illumine the darkness in his sacred chamber, my light rays glitteringly illumine those amongst whom he is. May you darken your bodies; may you hide your corpses. <With my solar disk> in my following do I pass by,[76] until I travel your mysteries, that I might take care of you, that I might discern your needs—even those who are in the West."

Taking up the good road by this great god; entering into the mysterious caverns of the West.

DIVISION 4

REGISTER 1 (PLATE 32)

5.41. Scene 41. Isis stands to left and Nephthys to right, facing each other, their names atop their heads, arms out and angled down in front of them, palms up. Over the hands, as though supported by them, the oddly curved figure of a deity with divine beard and uraeus, bent at rump, knees bent opposite to the norm, feet to left and head to right; he is labeled "Osiris, foremost of his mystery." He holds his arms for-

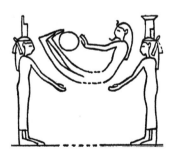

---

75. For this phrase, see Darnell 2004, 289–93.
76. Reading <itn=i> with Werning 2011a, 181; alternatively, the sentence could read "after myself do I pass" as a reference to the unified *ba*-soul and *perpetuum mobile*.

ward (one represented), hands (again, one represented) with palm to a solar disk that hovers over his lower legs.

ABOVE THE BENDING DEITY

This god is in this fashion, foremost of his cavern. The solar disk enters into his cavern.

BEHIND THE IMAGE

Re says to this cavern: "Osiris, in life, Osiris—breath be to you, breathing be to your *ba*-soul. You encircle the Netherworld with your arms; the two goddesses raise up your corpse—Osiris, foremost of his mystery."

5.42. Scene 42. A central figure, "Osiris," wearing a divine beard stands, facing right, between two deities who bend slightly toward him; the deity on the right is falcon-headed—"Horus, heir of his father"—and raises his arms and hands before the face of the central figure, while the deity on the left—"Anubis, son of the god"—is jackal-headed and has his hands lowered before him, palms down (only one arm and hand represented).

ABOVE THE SCENE

These gods are in this fashion in the sole cavern. The solar disk of Re illumines them, and this great god speaks to them. Then they become content, and their *ba*-souls become strong, when this great god passes by them.

BEFORE THE IMAGE

Re says to this cavern: "O you Anubis, son of the god. O you Horus, heir of his father. Stretch out the corpse of your father. Clothe him. Attach for him the heart—you[77] are this one greatest of the Netherworld."

---

77. This statement appears to be addressed to the heart.

5.43. Scene 43. A bull-headed deity stands to right, facing left, slightly bent at the waist, arms in front, bent at elbows, hands raised with palms forward (one arm and hand shown). Before him are two horizontally oriented ovals, one above the other, with a sun disk in between and to the right. In the upper oval is an ichneumon, facing left. In the lower oval is a heart hieroglyph between two solar disk, rays descending from each disk.

LABEL TO THE UPPER OVAL

Horus-Mekhentyenirty. This god is in this fashion in his sarcophagus.

LABEL BETWEEN THE OVALS

These are in this fashion, in the sarcophagus (his sarcophagus) in the sole cavern. This god speaks to his heart.

ABOVE THE SCENE

This god is in this fashion, as guardian of the sarcophagus of Horus. The solar disk of Re illumines for them their darkness, when <this great god passes by them>.

BEFORE THE SCENE

Re says to this cavern: "O Horus-Mekhentyenirty, ichneumon, lord of manifestations in the Netherworld—your eyes belong to you, that you see thereby. Because you are establishing your father, who elevates your corpse—Osiris, Bull of the West[78]—will your heart become content within your body. I illumine your corpse by means of my solar disk, ichneumon foremost of his sarcophagus."

---

78. For the bull concept as "lord," particularly the association of semen and Maat, see Kurth 1984.

BEHIND THE SCENE[79]

Re says, as he passes this grotto: "I speak as I enter into the cavern of Osiris, and cross over the Bull of the West. As for their corpses, I shall illumine them, causing that their *ba*-souls go to rest upon them in the earth, achieving honor for them […] affairs […] their <cor>pses […], and causing that they breathe in the Mysterious Place. You are these great gods, lords of the Netherworld, those of resting upon the West. Your <…> these.

REGISTER 2 (PLATE 32)

5.44. Scene 44. A ram-headed deity, "Re," stands to left, slightly bent at the waist, facing right, one arm forward and down with palm down, the other arm extended forward, bent at elbow, holding a *was*-scepter. In front of him hovers a solar disk, "Solar disk of the great god." To the right of the disk, facing left, are three figures, slightly bent at the waists, wearing divine beards, arms down and forward, palms down, each labeled "The one in whom is Osiris."

ABOVE THE RAM-HEADED DEITY

This god is in this fashion.

ABOVE THE THREE DEITIES TO THE RIGHT[80]

This god is in this fashion. Re speaks to this cavern, after he has given light to their guardians who are in the following. These deities are illumined when this god passes by them, even when <this god> passes <by> them.[81]

---

79. The text of this annotation is perturbated; the following translation follows the text emendations proposed by Werning 2011a, 191.

80. The Tomb of Ramesses IX contains a variant annotation: "The West extends <her> arms, as he speaks to those mysterious of face."

81. The final sentence of the annotation is corrupt.

5.45. Scene 45. A falcon-headed deity, "Horus, Protector of His Father," stands to right, slightly bent at the waist, facing left, arms forward and down, palms down. To the left are two horizontally oriented ovals, one above the other, with a multiply coiled serpent, "Terrible of Face," in between, head raised to left, tail lowered to right. Behind the serpent, in front of the deity to the right, is a solar disk. Within the upper oval a prone, mummiform deity, wearing divine beard, head with  white crown to left, facing downwards, labeled "Osiris, Foremost of the Westerners." In the lower oval is a supine mummiform figure, wearing divine beard, head to left, facing upwards, called "Westerner in whom is Osiris."

ABOVE THE SCENE

They are in this fashion, Horus, Protector of His Father, is Horus as their protector. The solar disk of Re illumines them.

BEFORE THE SCENE

Re says to this cavern: "Behold me entering into the great sand, having divided the uniform darkness. Give to me your arms, and receive me, gods who are with Osiris, that you might become strong, when you see my solar disk. O you Foremost of the West, great god, mighty of white crown. O you official of his sarcophagus, lord of the wig,[82] high of wailing,[83] whose guardian is Horus and whom Terrible of Face separates. O, behold me entering among you, as I illumine you by means of my solar disk."

---

82. A wig appears beneath the "awakening of Osiris" scene, to which this might be a reference (see Roberson 2012, 11–12).

83. Alternatively, Werning 2011a, 197 proposes an otherwise unattested "beard." For the role of hair in mourning, see Manassa 2007a, 30–31. Note as well the chiastic layout of the address to the two deities within their ovals: the upper oval is related to the West, then what is on his head (white crown), the next address to the lower oval begins with what is on his head (a wig) and follows with the relationship to the West (wailing).

5.46. Scene 46. A male figure wearing a divine beard stands with arms akimbo, facing left, labeled "Osiris." To the left stands a male deity with jackal head facing right, labeled "Anubis," slightly bent at waist, arms lowered and in front, palms down. Above the two figures is a solar disk. To the right is a heron, the *benu*-bird, the "*Ba*-Soul of Osiris."[84]

ABOVE THE SCENE

These gods are in this fashion in the sole cavern. Re speaks to them and cares for them. He illumines them by means of his solar disk. That they behold the light is when this great god passes by them.

BEFORE THE SCENE

Re speaks to this cavern: "O Osiris, together with his *ba*-soul, Anubis and his mystery. Behold me crossing your caverns. I transform into your protector, with the result that the *ba*-soul of Osiris rests upon his corpse. Anubis protects the Ruler of the Netherworld, reckoning the mystery of the one whom he assembled, and causing that the corpse occupies its cavern."

REGISTER 3 (PLATE 32)

5.47. Scene 47. A cat-headed male figure stands to the right, facing left, slightly bent at the waist, arms lowered in front, palms down; he is labeled "Cat-Like One." To the left are four upside-down enemies, facing left, wearing divine beards, their arms behind them, elbows bent, fists behind heads, labeled "Ones of Blood"; "Ones of Tears"; "Ones of Swellings"; and "Ones of Cool Water."

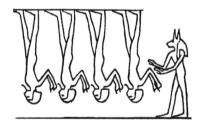

---

84. For the Osirian significance of the *benu*-bird, see p. 123 n. 140.

Re says to this cavern, while he extends his arms against his enemies: "You are the unknowing, the ones of blood, the ones of tears, the ones of swellings, the ones of cool water; you have no head covering among the *akh*-spirits. The Eye of Horus will not draw near to you. You will not behold this (goddess) Tayt. With your bonds already applied have you been given over to the fighter. After I decreed that he guard you have you been assigned to this Cat-Like One, from whose guarding there is no escape. May the bindings bind you."[85]

5.48. Scene 48. Two deities face in toward each other, arms forward and slightly lowered, palms down, hands all but touching; the deity to the left is male with a lion head, "Sakhmet-Like One, Destroyer," while that to the right is female with human head, "Destroyer." Beneath the deities is a male figure lying face-upwards, arms akimbo, feet slightly separated, head to left and overlapping the legs of the left standing deity, legs likewise overlapping those of the standing female figure; he is labeled "One of Destruction, who is protected by those with him."

These are in this fashion, <in> the sole cavern, without seeing Re, without hearing his voice. While he passes their cavern, he inflicts their punishment.

Re says to this cavern: "O Destroyer, she who is foremost of the Place of Destruction; Destroyer, foremost of the Place of Destruction; ones who came forth from the corpse of the destroyed one—you are these of the

---

85. Alternatively: "That you have you been assigned to this Cat-Like One—from whose guarding there is no escape, whom I decreed that he should guard you—is that the bindings might bind you." For the solar deity as "Binder," see the Book of Adoring Re in the West, Great Litany, Address 64 (p. 98).

Place of Destruction, whose darkness exists in blood, who live from the abomination of their hearts. I commend you to this corpse that you come forth from your putrefaction, albeit without you coming forth from the reach of the corpse that you are guarding."

5.49. Scene 49. A male figure wearing a divine beard stands to the right, facing left, slightly bent at the waist, arms lowered in front, palms down; he is labeled "Destructive of Face." To the left are four upside-down enemies, 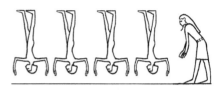 facing left, their arms hanging out and down, each with hands to either side of the head, palms facing outwards; they are called "Ones of Mutilation"; "Ones of Humiliation"; "Ones of Weariness(?)";[86] "Ones of Redness."

ABOVE THE UPSIDE-DOWN ENEMIES

These are in this fashion, without seeing Re, without hearing his words, without glimpsing the rays of his solar disk, without their *ba*-souls going forth. At their corpses does their blood exist. In the uniform darkness do they exist. Just when he passes by them does Re inflict their punishment.

ABOVE THE STANDING DEITY TO THE RIGHT

This god is in this fashion, in the guardianship of the enemies of Re, without seeing him, this god hearing his voice.

BEHIND THE SCENE

Re says to this cavern: "Ones of Mutilation, Ones of Humiliation, Ones of Weariness(?), Ones of Redness—you belong to this one who destroys these my enemies. I am decreeing that you guard that they go upside down. That I examine you is so that he shall do harm to you—the one Destructive of Face—indeed the ones belonging to destruction. The land of your Place of Destruction […]"

---

86. Following Werning 2011a, 205; note also Piankoff 1944, 43, "Enslaved Ones" (perhaps in reference to "*mꜣwd*," *WÄS*, 2:29.1, "gezwungen sein etw. zu tun").

LITANIES 4–6 (BETWEEN DIVISIONS 4–5)

The litanies between Divisions 4–5 do not all lay such exclusive stress on
the twelve hours of the night, although they conclude with a return to that
pattern. Litany 4 consists of seventeen segments describing the entry of the
sun into the Netherworld. Following four segments forming an introduction are three sections of three segments each. The first two groups of three
have an *iw*-clause in the third segment; the third group of three has such
an *iw*-clause in the second and third segments. Ramesses VI reinforces
this 4 + 9 structure by having the first four as ʿ*q.n=f*, the following nine
as ʿ*q=f*. The initial four segments appear to evoke the cardinal points, and
indeed describe the setting of the following. The nine central segments,
three groups of three—literally a plural of plurals—evoke the number of
the Ennead. Four lines describing the interlocking actions of the denizens
of the Netherworld and the solar deity conclude with the sun god's address
to the Netherworld beings.

Litany 5, the Litany of Travel, has twenty-one segments, of the pattern
6 (3 + 3) + 6 (3 + 3) + 3 + 6 (3 + 3). The initial triplet describes past action
by the solar deity for the denizens of the netherworld; the second triplet
describes his passage by his own corpse, each segment concluding with a
purpose clause; together these two triplets set the stage for the remaining,
describing the previous actions of the sun with regard to the denizens of the
Netherworld, and relating the solar element to its own chthonic, corpse-
like counterpart. The third and fourth triplets end with a second *iw sḏm=f*,
and describe the ongoing actions of the solar deity in the netherworld. The
fifth triplet ends with a reiteration of *šꜣs*-crossing with *irf*; both the sixth
and seventh triplets consist of two hortative statements with *m* + adverbial
adjunct, and a third with a prospective *sḏm=f* (the seventh triplet concludes
with two prospectives). The overall pattern is situation (6), ongoing actions
(6), summation of above (3), wishes for what occur (6), thus emphasizing
the number 6, the count of the divisions in the Book of Caverns.

Litany 6 contains twelve segments, of the pattern 3 + 5 + 4. In the first
three, some actor other than the solar deity is the subject of the action following the initial address to "He of the Horizon." In the subsequent group
of five segments, the sun is the actor in what follows the initial address,
and the group of five segments begins and ends with segments incorporating circumstantial *sḏm=f* forms, the central three segments involving
nominal forms. In the final group, the four segments have nonsolar actors
as subjects following the introductory elements.

Taking up the good road by this great god, entering into the mysterious caverns of the West; entering by this great god into the cavern of the Mysterious One. This great god says to those who are in it: "(O) gods, you gods who are within the caverns, who are in the following of Osiris in this his mysterious place. May you hide yourselves away; may you rejoice over me—I am summoning you."

LITANY 4: LITANY OF ENTRANCE

> My solar disk has penetrated the darkness,
>> with the result that the ones of the secret place are in jubilation.
> My solar disk has penetrated the darkness,
>> with the result that those who are within the hidden places are in rejoicing.
> My solar disk has penetrated the darkness,
>> with the result that Osiris gives his arms to me.
> My solar disk has penetrated the darkness,
>> the Ennead of the West being in festival.

> My solar disk penetrates the darkness,
>> so their ba-souls are happy at my approach.
> My solar disk penetrates the darkness,
>> while their corpses are ascending to them.[87]
> My solar disk penetrates the darkness—
>> the two goddesses join their brother.

> My solar disk penetrates the darkness,
>> while Anubis is clothing his mystery.
> My solar disk penetrates the darkness,
>> while Horus gives his eye to his father.
> My solar disk penetrates the darkness—
>> Mekhentyenirty is in his sarcophagus.[88]

---

87. Depictions of "ascending" corpses appear on the Second Shrine of Tutankhamun, Side 2 (Piankoff and Rambova 1955, fig. 41; pp. 545–46); contra the observations of Werning 2011a, 211, n. a.

88. This text also describes the position of the eyeless being on the Corridor G

My solar disk penetrates the darkness,
> his two divine eyes and his heart being in the one who hides them.

My solar disk penetrates the darkness—the Bull of the West <places his> arms upon my *ba*-souls.

My solar disk penetrates the darkness—my solar disk, then has entered the darkness.

The hidden ones, who are in the Netherworld, are joyful over my disk,
> they [making ... for me]; I taking care of them; I placing them in
> their grottos.

I am [passing by them],
> that I might ⌜take care⌝ of their corpses,
>> and cause their *ba*-souls to go to rest upon them.

I [am] passing by their caverns,
> and causing ⌜your⌝ corpses to occupy Igeret, as [I] go to rest.

(O) hidden ones, ones thriving of condition, ⌜your⌝ corpses [...]—
when you come forth from your darkness, your hearts become satisfied, [...],
> pervading your caverns,
>> but without you seeing ⌜the mystery⌝ [...],
>> even after I ⌜have⌝ passed by you.

LITANY 5: TRAVELING OF THE SUN

Your shout of joy for me and my shout of joy for you is that I traveled by you.

I am traveling by you, O Netherworld Dwellers,
> having addressed you.

I am traveling by you, O Netherworld Dwellers,
> having cared for you.

I am traveling by you, O Netherworld Dwellers,
> having shone for you by means of your light.

---

ceiling, near the beginning of the composition, at the place where Re in his solar boat is entering the Netherworld (p. 553). The being is blind and without eyes because it is cut off from the solar and lunar eyes, through the light of which other beings may see (Darnell 2004, 173).

I am traveling by you, O Netherworld Dwellers, and over my corpse,
    that you might receive […].
I am traveling by you, O Netherworld Dwellers,
    and over my corpse in the West
I am traveling by you, O Netherworld Dwellers,
    and over my corpse in the cavern.

I am traveling by you, O Netherworld Dwellers,
    I decreeing for you your festivals.
I am traveling by you, O Netherworld Dwellers;
    you are now foremost of your caverns.
I am traveling by you, O Netherworld Dwellers;
    I am giving to you light.

I am traveling by you, O Netherworld Dwellers,
    I destroying the enemies of your eye.[89]
I am traveling by you, O Netherworld Dwellers,
    I causing the great *ba*-soul to come to rest upon the mysteries.
I am traveling by you, O Netherworld Dwellers;
    my solar disk is giving birth to me.

I am traveling by you, O Netherworld Dwellers;
    Tatenen raises up the one who came forth from him.
I am traveling by you, O Netherworld dwellers;
I am even now traveling by you, O Netherworld Dwellers,
    I causing that you be honored, O mysterious ones.

May you praise me with this my praise;[90]
may you worship my *ba*-soul for me with these my worshipings;
may you adore this mystery.

---

89. Alternatively, "who would harm (lit., do) you." For the transitive use of *iri*, see p. 148 n. 46.

90. The final section of the litany consists of two triplets. The "praise" referred to here may reference a text such as the Book of Adoring Re in the West (see pp. 69–70 for the concept of worshiping by means of an established template or text—here that text is the word of the solar deity himself).

May you praise[91] my corpse with this my [praise];
may your throats breath through my breathing;
may Tatenen give birth to me, that I might come forth rejuvenated.

LITANY 6: THE ONE OF THE HORIZON IS ADORED

The gods, those of the mysterious place, say to Re:

"You are adored, O One of the Horizon;
  we are now raising our arms to you.
You are adored, O One of the Horizon;
  Tatenen is giving birth to you in the Netherworld.
You are adored, O One of the Horizon;
  the ennobled ones[92] having been awakened[93] by your solar disk.

You are adored, O One of the Horizon,
  extending your arms and receiving the morning.
You are adored, O One of the Horizon—
  as one great of visible forms do you manifest.
You are adored, O One of the Horizon—
  as you create the slaughtering of the rebels.
You are adored, O One of the Horizon—
  as you fill the Netherworld with your rays.
You are adored, O One of the Horizon—
  as your solar disk illuminates the Mysterious Place.

You are adored, O One of the Horizon,
  the *ba*-souls having power as they come forth.
You are adored, O One of the Horizon,
  as the haulers are assembling their limbs.
You are adored, O One of the Horizon,
  as Anubis is pulling together his body.

---

91. "*stwt*," *WÄS*, 4:335.12.

92. *sʿḥ* is a state of existence granted by the rays of the sun (see Hornung 1976, 120, n. 189).

93. Reading *srn* as *srs* "to awaken," with Piankoff 1942b, 50; Werning 2011a, 223 (following Hornung) reads *srnp* "to rejuvenate."

You are adored, O One of the Horizon,
  as the Filled One(?) is assembling (his) limbs.

You are adored, O One of the Horizon,
  you are now adored, O One of the Horizon."

We are rejoicing at seeing your solar disk, we are causing your mysterious corpse to become an *akh*-spirit. As Re was born by the earth, so his solar disk was born within the Netherworld. Re is now travelling by your mysterious cavern, hidden of condition. Re is now passing by the grottos of the gods, mysterious of hearts, he imparting to them their breaths. When he passes by them, they live. It is Re who speaks to the gods, and who causes to prosper the one who is in the Netherworld, (specifically) the Mysterious One:

"O gods—mysterious ones!—powerful ones!—majestic ones!—corpse-like ones!—lauded ones![94]—hidden ones!—covered ones!—weary ones![95]—⌜ones of the grotto⌝!—ones of the cavern!—ones of the mound!—ones of visible forms!—ones of manifestations!—ennobled ones!—beatified ones!—heavy-laden ones!—*ba*-like ones!—shades!—ones of the West!—ones of the seat!—ones of the throne!—ones who are gone forth!—ones who go to rest!—strong ones![96]—Osiris![97]

O gods, you gods—behold, I am passing your caverns, and summoning you by your names. I am giving to you your *akh*-power as I pass over the paths[98] of the Mysterious One. I am issuing commands <to> those who are in it, as I exercise power over the divine one who traverses its road. She[99] is now bending her arm to me. She is bending her shoulder to me.

---

94. *qf(ꜣ)y* from *qfꜣ* "fame," which can appear parallel to *sꜣḥ.w* (see Herbin 1994, 119–20).

95. The Osireion version writes *wty.w* "wrapped ones."

96. The Osireion version writes *ḫty.w* "ones of following."

97. The deities are all Osiris—this is Osiris as the Netherworld, equated with the Mysterious One in the following Book of Caverns, Division 5 (Werning 2011a, 229 n. g also suggests a possible equation of the entities and Osiris).

98. Plural *wꜣy.t* for roads—cf. *nṯry.t* for goddesses (see Osing 1976, 223 and CT 5.205i, 6.377f; 7.100h).

99. The goddess "the Mysterious One" (Shetayt).

O One Mysterious of Visible Form, O Mysterious One—you are this one[100] great of darkness. I shall travel by you; I am even now traveling by you, O Mysterious One.

DIVISION 5 (PLATE 33)

5.50. Scene 50. A goddess, who fills the height of all three registers, stands with arms bent, holding a disk in one hand and a ram-headed deity in the other. Standing serpents with human heads rear up to either side of the goddess, their upper bodies crossing in front of her arms. Lines of images pass between the body of the goddess and each of the serpents. In front of the goddess are a series of images facing downwards: immediately beneath her arm is a scarab with sun disk, followed by a ram, solar disk, ram-headed deity (head toward the goddess), another solar disk, a child (head toward the goddess), and finally a pair of arms (depicted as though emerging from the goddess' foot). Behind the goddess are four crocodiles facing upwards; in front of each crocodile is an image, from bottom to top: a ram head, scarab, *udjat*-eye, and solar disk.

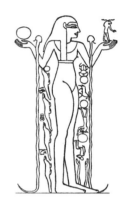

OVER THE STANDING GODDESS

Mysterious One[101]

BEHIND THE GODDESS

It (the image) exists in this fashion, her head in the upper Netherworld, her feet in the lower Netherworld of the gods.[102] On the arms of the Mysterious One does this great god travel through the cavern. When this great god enters into her cavern, then the heads of the gods, *akh*-spirits, dead, those who are in the Netherworld, hide in the darkness, without this great

---

100. For the pattern of independent pronoun plus demonstrative here, see Gilula 1976, 162.

101. On this goddess and her appearance in the Book of Caverns and Books of the Creation of the Solar Disk, see Billing 2006.

102. Compare the text to the right of the goddess, in which the faces of the to be inverted serpents are in the "lower Netherworld of the gods."

god seeing her head. That she extends her arms is in order to conduct the solar disk, while the god is resting upon his heights.

LABEL TO THE LEFT REARING SERPENT BENEATH THE ARM OF THE GODDESS

One of the Umbilical Cord,[103] the enemy of Re. He is like this upon the hand of this one, mysterious of visible forms, one who exists in their darkness as a flame, without the gods and their visible forms approaching.

ON THE GODDESS

The powers who are in[104] the book "Mysterious of Manifestations," the one at the head of the great reckoning.[105]

TO THE RIGHT OF THE GODDESS, IN FRONT OF THE HAND HOLDING THE RAM-HEADED DEITY

As Re comes to rest in the western horizon in order to take care of those who are in the earth, so he shines in the eastern mountain in order to drive out that Wenty-Apep, evil of eye.[106]

ON THE RIGHT REARING SERPENT BENEATH THE ARM OF THE GODDESS

The One of the Navel. He exists in this fashion upon the hands of this one, mysterious of visible forms. In fire does their darkness exist, without the gods approaching their faces. One of the Navel.

---

103. Quack 2006, 2015; Nyord 2009, 388, n. 3887; Werning 2011a, 237. Alternatively (although less likely), for *npꜣy* as "He of the Entrails" or "He of the Bowels," see Manassa 2007a, 408–9; Billing 2006, 62–63.

104. Reading *bꜣ.w imy.w*: three birds for *bꜣ.w*, skin sign for *imy* (Darnell 2004, 64, 68–69); and grasshopper as *w* (Darnell 2004, 108–10).

105. For other possible readings of this enigmatic text, see Darnell 2004, 109 n. 342; Werning 2011b, 236–37.

106. On the concept of the final destruction of the damned in the eastern horizon see Darnell 2004, 319, 348 n. 316, 397.

TO THE RIGHT OF THE GODDESS

This god is in this fashion, after passing this mysterious cavern. It is this great god who placed the manifestations in him, even when this great god passes the mysterious cavern. Then these snakes are upside-down, their faces in the lower Netherworld of the gods. This goddess goes to rest upon her great image, without knowing the *ba*-souls which are in this mysterious place of discovered(?) manifestations.[107]

ABOVE THE HAND OF THE GODDESS HOLDING THE RAM-HEADED DEITY

This god is in this fashion. This deity gives his arms to Osiris, as he illumines his face ... may Osiris be concealed, may the husband be hidden ....

REGISTER 1 (FIRST HALF) (PLATE 33)

5.51. Scene 51. A deity, "Osiris," with arms raised in adoration appears below a disk. Following him are four serpents standing on their tails, with bearded human heads; the serpents are labeled "Human-headed One"; "One of Tears"; "One Come Forth from Re"; "Flesh as Re."

IN FRONT OF THE DEITY

This god is in this fashion, extending his arms toward this great god, when he passes by the mysterious Netherworld.

---

107. The word *gmm* follows the annotation, possibly a reference to the phrase *gm wš* "found missing." Alternatively, as in the translation, this could be "discovered manifestations," a passive participle of *gmi*, referring to the solar forms to either side of the goddess personifying the Netherworld (compare *"gmj,"* WÄS, 5:166.12–13 for divine forms as the object of the verb, and *"gmj,"* WÄS, 5:167.1, for *gmi* referencing earlier texts).

IN FRONT OF THE REARING SERPENTS

These exist in this fashion as this great god passes by them,[108] they standing as Re passes by him, namely, the one of the human head, he passing by them while they are in darkness.

BEHIND THE SCENE

Re says to this cavern: "O Osiris, to me have you extended your arms—behold, I am traveling through the Mysterious One, I am passing by these who are before her, who have come into being from (my) limbs,[109] who were cut out from me.

The evil serpents, whom my flesh drives out, are creating evil. O behold, I am delivering them to darkness, I condemning them to blindness,[110] I passing by them, without them seeing me, that you may guard them, namely these, as they go forth."

5.52. Scene 52. Two gods—"Corpse of Atum, living of word" (to left) and "Corpse of Khepri, living of word" (to right)—bend and extend slightly bent arms, as if in adoration, to either side of a bearded male figure, "Tatenen," standing with face to left, wearing double plumes, a solar disk in front of his feathers.

BEHIND THE SCENE

Re says at this cavern: "O standing ones, who make stand the gods, who have given birth to their birth-forms. O gods, living of corpses. As you speak to me, so do I speak to you, I illuminating you, I driving out your

---

108. In between ḥr=sn and the following sn ʿḥʿ=sn is a misplaced label tpy "Human-Headed One."

109. The book roll following ḥʿ.w=i is probably in error for the š of šʿʿ (Werning 2011a, 242, gives the reading {bookroll} <š>ʿʿ).

110. Ramesses VI provides the variant statement "I condemning them <to> the chastisers (smity.w with eye determinative)." The "chastisers" could themselves be related to the eye as punisher (Darnell 1997; see also "smj.tj.t, WÄS, 4:129.15, "Anklägerin?").

darkness, so that you might appear in glory in your images, and so that you might rejoice in seeing my solar disk. I am this one who causes manifestations to manifest, I seeing the throne of the hidden ones, and causing the Netherworld Dwellers to go to rest."

5.53. Scene 53. Two ovals beneath a central disk appear in the left portion of the scene; two children, one atop the other, in the left oval—the upper child is labeled "Young Form of Re," the lower child is "Child Form of Re." A human headed, mummiform being in the right oval is the "Clothed Visible Form of Osiris." A bending, bearded figure, "Protector," stands to the 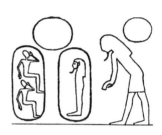 right, beneath a solar disk, facing the ovals, bending forward and extending his arms downwards.

OVER THE TWO OVALS

These gods are in this fashion, in their sarcophagi, as those at the head of the cavern.

REGISTER 2 (FIRST HALF) (PLATE 33)

5.54. Scene 54. Four falcon headed mummies stand facing left, beneath a solar disk (above and between the last two deities), labeled "Horus Who Clothes Re"; "Horus Who Hides Atum"; "Horus Who Forms the Face of Khepri";[111] "Horus Who Comes Forth as Eldest of Osiris." To  the right a jackal-headed deity, "Anubis," bends with arms extended forward and down, facing left. To the far right an oval with disk over *šm*-sign, writing "Power of Re"; the scepter is further labeled: "Scepter which Atum Fashioned."

BEHIND THE JACKAL-HEADED DEITY

This god is in this fashion.

111. For *ṯz-ḥr*, see Fischer-Elfert 1998, 18 n. 43.

These gods are in this fashion, having taken up station in the earth, without wearying.

Re says to this cavern: "O you four great deities who are as corpses. O you foremost of the Netherworld. O you power, great of forms which create the Netherworld and fashion Igeret, whose images are unknown—sole mystery, who makes himself mysterious from those who are in his cavern. O behold, I am passing by you, placing Anubis as your protection, illuminating you, driving off your darkness, giving instructions <to> those who are in your following."

5.55. Scene 55: Four ovals, two to a side, horizontal in orientation, with a disk in the center. A supine female figure lies in each oval, head to the left, arms as though bent akimbo.

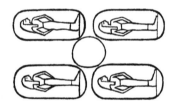

These are in this fashion, in their sarcophagi on both sides. Between them does Re sail. He speaks to them. After this great god passes by them, the darkness conceals them. It is their corpses that speak to the great god, even while their corpses are in this fashion.

Re says to this cavern: "O goddesses, you Netherworldly goddesses who are in their sarcophagi. O behold, I am passing by you. I call to your *ba*-souls, so that you may go to rest in your seats, in which I have decreed that you shall be. I am causing your throats to breathe, and illuminating you with that which is before me. I am that sole one who protects <you>."

REGISTER 3 (FIRST HALF) (PLATE 33)

5.56. Scene 56. A female figure stands facing left, hold-ing arms out and down, each hand supporting a fork-topped post; she is called "Slaughterer." A kneeling prisoner is tied to each post with arms behind back, each prisoner facing away from the standing figure; the prisoners are named (left to right): "Oozing of Face"[112] and "Turned of Face."[113]

ABOVE THE SCENE

This goddess is in this fashion, as the one who watches the enemies of Re, condemned to the two fixed posts, which are in the earth, without loosen-ing that which is given to them. Re stretches out his hand against them, even after he passes by them, without them seeing him.

BEHIND THE SCENE

Re says to this cavern: "O Slaughterer. One who is in the Place of Destruc-tion, who watches my own enemies, whom I have placed in the uniform darkness. O one remaining in this mysterious place, in which I have caused that you remain, without you going forth from this hidden (place), with-out you going forth from the darkness. Raise for yourself your arms, for indeed to you have been assigned the fixed posts of those who are in the earth, <to> which my enemies have been condemned."

112. Reading *sdf* for "*stf*," *WÄS*, 4:342.5–6; also possible is *stf* for *sft* "slaughtered of face."

113. *ʿn-ḥr*, a name appearing as that of one of the human-headed haulers of the solar bark in the concluding scene of the Book of Caverns (Piankoff 1945, 46; p. 441); in the second scene of the Book of Caverns, Division 6, Register 2, Scene 69, a deity *ʿnn-ib* (*ʿnn-ḥr* in Padiamenemope) is one of two beings who charm the *nik*-serpent for Re (Piankoff 1945, 32, pl. 148, no. 21); the name also appears on the Second Shrine of Tutankhamun (p. 538).

5.57. Scene 57. A kneeling uraeus headed human figure—"One of the Uraeus"—faces right, holding a torch[114] to the left of two arms emerging from the ground, holding a curved line that represent a cauldron, in which are four hearts in a row, a bearded human head atop each.

BETWEEN THE ARMS, BENEATH THE CAULDRON

The arms that destroy the *ba*-souls that are in the cauldrons which are in the Netherworld.[115]

ABOVE THE SCENE

This oven is in this fashion—the arms which have emerged from the Place of Destruction lift this one great of flame, to whom are damned the heads of the enemies and the night wanderers. The One of the Uraeus sets fire to this oven.

BEHIND THE SCENE

Re says to this cavern: "O, One of the Uraeus, O One of the Serpent, O One of the Snake, O One of the Arrow,[116] O you god great of manifestations, who lights the fire, who makes the flame leap up in the oven which you watch, into which are allotted the heads and hearts of the enemies who have sinned against me, through the flame which is in it. Light your fire, set your flames in all of my enemies."

---

114. Termed a *tk3* in the portion of the text between Litanies 13–14 (Piankoff 1943, pl. 97, l. 8); see p. 425.

115. Compare Darnell 2004, 94–95.

116. Werning 2011a, 261 n. c cites "Šsry," *LGG* 7:127 for such a suggestion; this would be the arrow-pierced serpent, labeled *sšrw*, "One Who is Shot," in the Book of the Solar-Osirian Unity in the tomb of Ramesses IX (Darnell 2004, 303; p. 565).

5.58. Scene 58. Two arms rise from the ground, supporting another curving line representing a cauldron, within which are four upside-down, headless human figures, arms bound behind each. To either side of the group is a large uraeus serpent, facing in toward the cauldron, spitting fire as a series of dots that fall down to the ground between the arms supporting the cauldron; the uraei are labeled "She of the Fire-Pit" and "She of the Flame."

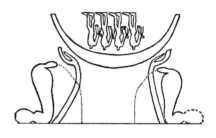

BETWEEN THE ARMS

The arms that combine the *ba*-souls that are in the cauldrons which are in the Netherworld.

ABOVE THE SCENE

These are in this fashion—they are the enemies of Re. These goddesses place fire in the cauldron when this great god passes by them.

5.59 (following page). Scene 59: A serpent rearing on its tail, "One Who Rears up against the Speared One,"[117] stands, head facing left, in front of a standing,

---

117. Werning 2011a, 264–65, reads ʿ*bby*, without translating. However, the assumed equivalence of the arm + two grasshoppers to the ʿ*bby* group is phonetically unlikely and is not in fact paralleled in the orthography of the name of the god Osiris (see the note below). With the Ramesses VI text above ending with *qrr*(.*t*) *štꜣy*(.*t*), the signs for the name of the serpent write *sʿr r* (grasshopper with usual cryptographic value of *r*) ʿ*bby*. Names with *sʿr* are not uncommon (compare "Sʿr," *LGG* 6:190–94), and the verb is particularly suitable for a uraeus serpent (compare "*sjar.t*," *WÄS*, 4:33.20). The term ʿ*bb.t* for spear is prominent in the name of the "spear bearers" in the Book of Gates ("ʿ*bbtyw*," *LGG* 2:90), and appears in the Book of the Hidden Chamber, Hour 10, Register 2, Scene 108 (p. 223, there parallel to arrows). The designation—apparently a *nisbe* from the word ʿ*bb*(.*t*) for spear, unless it is related to the rare harvesting and pottery verb ʿ*bb* (cf. Lichtheim 1988, 113 n. 9; Hannig 2003, 265), a possible allusion to the reaping of the dead (as in the Book of Gates, Hour 1, Register 1, Scene 6)—could provide a reference to Apep as the one harpooned in front of the solar bark.

ithyphallic male figure, "Osiris,"[118] also facing left, arm down by the side, wearing beard, uraeus, arm bands on the upper arm and wrist, and long wig. A dark waterfowl perches atop the head of the large human figure. A solar disk hovers to the left of the middle portion of the rearing serpent.

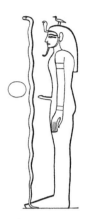

IN FRONT OF THE SERPENT

Entering by this great god into the uniform darkness. Within his mysterious cavern does this god, the lord of the West, pass.

———————————

BETWEEN THE REARING SERPENT AND THE STANDING DEITY

This god is in this fashion within his mysterious cavern, while this great god speaks to him, and spends time in taking care of his condition. After Re does the ba-soul of this god pass. Darkness conceals the corpse after this great god passes by them.

———————————

REGISTER 1 (SECOND HALF) (PLATE 33)

5.60. Scene 60. A human figure stands to left, "Hidden One," and a ram-headed human figure stands to right, "Traveler," facing in toward and supporting an oval, within which is a central ver- tically arranged oval, with two flesh signs to each side, arranged one above the other. Above the large oval is a solar disk.

ABOVE THE OVAL

The ba-souls which are in the place of the members which are in the Neth- erworld.

———————————

—————————

118. Werning 2011a, 264–65.

LABEL TO THE LEFT DEITY

This god is in this fashion, laying his hands upon the hidden image of Osiris, Foremost of the Netherworld. This great god speaks to him, and illumines him with his disk. The darkness envelops him, after this great god passes by his cavern.

LABEL TO THE RIGHT DEITY

This god is in this fashion, laying his hands upon his mysterious sarcophagus, without the <protect>ing deities[119] knowing the mysterious image within it, due to the one who hides what is in it.[120]

BENEATH THE SARCOPHAGUS

This sarcophagus is in this fashion, bearing the great mystery that is in the Netherworld. The solar disk of Re illumines it.

BEHIND THE SCENE

Re says to this cavern: "O two gods, great of sanctity who are the protection of my decomposition. O behold, I am reckoning my hidden elements. My body is going to rest upon me. My limbs are going to rest; my flesh is complete, that which I assemble for myself. Jubilation to you, this my body of which I consist, my limbs, my flesh, my corpse. I am illumining you by means of my shining disk, and driving away from you your darkness."

---

119. Werning 2011a, 266–67.

120. "It" referring to the oval, otherwise referred to as the *ꜣ.t štꜣ.t* at the end of Division 6; for the hiding of the members, and the mound/oval that hides them, see Darnell 2004, 289–93.

Coming forth by this great god from the uniform darkness in the cavern of Osiris. She of the Earth, great of visible form, extends her arms to the one in whom is Osiris.

REGISTER 2 (SECOND HALF) (PLATE 33)

5.61. Scene 61. A ram-headed male figure stands on the left, facing right, in front of a female figure, "She of the Earth"; both deities holds the arms down and out in front, the palms of their hands down. Between them, above their heads, is a solar disk.

IN FRONT OF THE GODDESS

This goddess exists in this fashion, extending her arms toward the great god, whom she guides to the hidden way. This god speaks to her, illumining her by means of his solar disk. Darkness conceals her after [he] passes [over her].

BEHIND THE SCENE

Re says to this cavern: "She of the Earth, please receive me; She of the Earth, you have already extended your arms toward me. Behold, I am passing by, my *ba*-soul in my following, I taking care of the one who came forth from my limbs, issuing for them decrees, reckoning them, establishing their corpses, causing them to go to rest in their caverns, illumining them by means of that which is upon my forehead, (namely,) my great solar disk which is on my head—mine is all entirely."

5.62. Scene 62. Two male figures, the one on the right falcon-headed, stand facing in toward each other, arms raised with hands up and palms facing in toward a solar disk that appears to hover just above their hands; the left deity is labeled "Osiris, foremost of the head of Re," while the left is labeled "Horus, foremost of the head of Re." Between the figures is a large ram's head, "Head of Re," slightly above the ground, facing right.

ABOVE THE SCENE

[These(?) are in] this [fashion ...] their [...]

REGISTER 3 (SECOND HALF) (PLATE 33)

5.63. Scene 63. Two goddesses kneel, arms out and
down in front of them, to either side and facing in
toward two arms that emerge from the ground, a flame
at the inner angle of each arm and the ground; the
goddesses are labeled "Burning One" and "She of the
Flame." The arms support another schematic cauldron,
in which are (in rows of four, listed from bottom to
top) flesh signs, inverted *ba*-birds, and inverted shade-
signs; an unclear and possibly incomplete text (two signs) appears next to the
cauldron in the Osireion version of the scene.[121]

BETWEEN THE ARMS

The arms of the Place of Destruction emerge from the Netherworld, bearing the two cauldrons entirely(?).[122]

BEFORE THE SCENE

The Place of Destruction exists containing the *ba*-souls, corpses, and
shades of the enemies of Re and Osiris. Those to be punished upon their
slaughter—the two goddesses great of burning have become those who set
fire to them.

BEHIND THE SCENE

Re speaks at this cavern: "O you two goddesses, great of flame, powerful
of burning, who fire up their two cauldrons by means of the bones of the
wanderers,[123] who cook the *ba*-souls, corpses, limbs, and shades of my

121. Werning 2011a, 277 n. c, suggests possible reading as *bꜣ.w*.
122. Compare Darnell 2004, 94–95.
123. For bones as fuel compare Eyre 2002, 119–20 and 135; for the *šmꜣ.w* as out-

enemies. Behold, I am passing by you, causing misfortune amongst my enemies. May you remain in front of your caverns, your flames in your cauldrons, even without your *ba*-souls being able to go forth, even without them passing in my following."

LITANIES 7–20 (BETWEEN DIVISIONS 5–6)

The litanies between Divisions 5–6 are more difficult to understand in the sense of the significance of the numbers and interrelationships of segments; each has specific internal structure, however.

Litanies 7–8 appear to be associated through an emphasis on the concept of the sun crossing through the Netherworld. Litany 7 has eight segments, three groups, in the order 3 + 3 + 2. The initial three segments describe the divine headgear; the second group of three addresses the full body of the deity as falcon, mystery, and image (note that this is essentially Ptah-Sokar-Osiris as Sokar, Osiris, Ptah). The concluding group of two segments addresses the god in terms of his face. Litany 8 has five segments, addressing serpent deities. Together Litanies 7–8 contain thirteen groups, the number of groups in the Litany 9 (thirteen was the number of segments in Litany 4, as well, there explicable as the sum of the four cardinal points and the Enneadic 9).

Litany 9 contains thirteen addresses; segments one and thirteen of the group bracket the others with references to divine forms (birth forms in the first, manifestations and visible forms in the thirteenth); the eleven segments in between comprise five dealing with the corpse nature of the deity and six relating the creative aspects of the deity as primeval creator. Litany 15 also contains thirteen segments (pattern 4 + 3 + 3 + 2 + 1): 4 are descriptive of Osiris in the Netherworld; three describe actions of the solar deity; three describe elements of Osiris (*ba*-soul, corpse, *akh*-spirit); two describe Osiris and speech; and one emphasizes his setting again (sarcophagus). Litany 16 as well has thirteen segments, in the pattern 4 + 2 + 3 + 3 + 1, four groups with a concluding line.

Litany 10 contains fourteen segments, although these appear to form six major groups (3 + 3 + 2 + 2 + 2 + 2): three initial segments set the stage for the entrance of light into the West; three concern light specifi-

---

casts, perhaps the "hungry" and neglected damned, see Fischer-Elfert 2005, 19–25 and 31.

cally; two describe the effects of light as breathing and speaking for the dead; two describe actions of the deity; two describe actions of groups of Netherworldly denizens (Ennead of Osiris and council of Tatenen); a final two describe the traveling of the deity. Litany 14 also consists of fourteen segments in five groups, in the pattern 2 + 3 + 3 + 3 + 3. The first segment describes parts of the enemies to be destroyed; the second describes the elements of their destruction (uraeus, the flame, and the cauldron); the third describes the bodies of the damned (corpses, heads, and bindings); the fourth describes the burning of the damned; the fifth and final segment emphasizes destruction.

Litany 20 has fourteen segments as well, in the pattern of 3 + 3 + 4 + 2 + 2, forming five groups; the first two segments have three segments each: the first line of each contains two passive *sḏm=f* form; the second and third lines of the first triplet containing a passive *sḏm=f* with following purpose clause, the second and third lines of the second triplet each having a single passive *sḏm=f* form. The first two groups involve partitioning of body parts, all summarized in the third line of the second stanza ("you are destroyed in the Place of Destruction"). The third stanza consists of four segments referring to the fire of the damned and their paradoxical dwelling in impenetrable darkness. The fourth stanza is almost a parenthetic, a couplet recapitulating the actions of the two staring, fiery uraeus eyes. The conclusion is also a couplet, summarizing the destruction.

In Litany 11 are sixteen "O Anubis" addresses, forming five major groups in the pattern 1 + 3 + 4 + 7 + 1; the first and last are separate addresses, leaving an initial group of three involving references to the corpse body, four making reference to attaching the head, and seven dealing with the environs—sarcophagus to Netherworld—of the body with attached head.

Litany 12 has six addresses, of the pattern 1 + 4 + 1. The group of four addresses four specific goddesses, evoking the quadripartite goddess who is the forerunner of the later Hathor Quadrifrons (Derchain 1972). Similarly, Litany 13, also dealing with goddesses in the Netherworld, consist of twelve addresses forming four major groups, of the pattern 1 + 2, 1 + 2, 1 + 2, 1 + 2; the first segment relates to divine messengers, the second to goddesses as powerful forces in council and speech, the third relates the goddesses to the divinities who personify the Netherworld, and the fourth relates the goddesses to elements of the dead (shades and *ba*-souls). Litany 16 has eleven segments, in the pattern 2 + 2 + 3 + 3 + 1, four groups with a concluding line. Litany 18 also has four sections, in the pattern 3 + 4 + 5 + 2, with the second group (four lines) describing goddesses.

Litany 17 has fifteen segments, in the pattern 4 + 4 + 6 + 1: in the first group (3 + 1), three lines reference the solar-Osirian actors, and a fourth line describes the Netherworld dwellers; in the second group (3 + 1), three lines reference the solar-Osirian actors, and a fourth line describes the Netherworld dwellers; the third group (6) details the actors; and the fourth element, the concluding line, summarizes the litany with a doubling of the initial element.

Litany 19 has eleven segments in three groups, in the order 3 + 2 + 6, with the first group involving the head and light, the second the elements of the divine body, and the third the dwellers in the Netherworld.

INTRODUCTION[124]

Going to rest by this great god in the cavern of the Mysterious One. As this god passes over her arms, so he traverses her cavern.[125] That this Mysterious One exists is with her head in the darkness and her feet in the darkness, those mysterious of face having united with her arms, without gods, *akh*-spirits, or the dead passing by her cavern—except for the great god, his solar disk, and those who are in his following.

LITANY 7: THE SUN CROSSES THROUGH TO ATTEND HIS CORPSE

Re speaks to this goddess—
O West, Mysterious One, warlike of arms for her own protection.
O behold, I am traversing your cavern.
Extend the arms to me, one mysterious of plan.

O One of the Uraeus!
    Behold I am traversing the Mysterious One.
    I am crossing through to take care of my corpse.
O One of the Royal *Khat*-headcloth!
    Behold I am traversing the Mysterious One.

---

124. This text and the following Litany 7 refer to the depiction in Division 5, Registers 1–3, Scene 50.

125. Haplography of *s* for ʿ.*wy=s* and *snn=f*.

I am crossing through to take care of my corpse.
O One of the Royal *Nemes*-headcloth!
    Behold I am traversing the Mysterious One.
    I am crossing through to take care of my corpse.

O Falcon!
    Behold I am traversing the Mysterious One.
    I am crossing through to take care of my corpse.
O Mystery!
    Behold I am traversing the Mysterious One.
    I am crossing through to take care of my corpse.
O Image!
    Behold I am traversing the Mysterious One.
    I am crossing through to take care of my corpse.

O Mysterious of Face!
    Behold I am traversing the Mysterious One.
    I am crossing through to take care of my corpse.
O Hidden of Face!
    Behold I am traversing the Mysterious One.
    I am crossing through to take care of my corpse.

Gods, you gods who are in the cavern of the Mysterious One. Behold, I am passing over you—bend your arms to me, bow to me your shoulders. Please receive my solar disk, Mysterious One. My shining disk is passing after me <in order to?> illumine my corpses and my images in their great caverns, in order to enquire after Osiris, in order to create the requirements of those amongst whom he is."

Then this great god passes by the cavern of the Mysterious One.

LITANY 8: THE SUN CROSSES THROUGH TO ATTEND TO OSIRIS[126]

This god says to the cavern of Sefeg, foremost of his visible forms:

"O Sefeg, one greater before his visible forms than Khepri
for the one foremost of the Netherworld—

---

126. This text refers to the depiction in Division 5, Register 1, Scene 51.

behold I am traversing the Mysterious One.
I am crossing through to take care of Osiris.
O Mysterious of Face (Serpent), lord of the divine beard,
great snake who resides in the cavern—
>   behold I am traversing the Mysterious One.
>   I am crossing through to take care of Osiris.
O Nehebkau, foremost of his cavern attached of head,
great one powerful of face—
>   behold I am traversing the Mysterious One.
>   I am crossing through to take care of Osiris.
O *Nepen*-serpent, foremost of the West,
who commands those who are in his caverns—
>   behold I am traversing the Mysterious One.
>   I am crossing through to take care of Osiris.
O Destroyer, one of the grotto, who destroys those who are in his
    cavern—
>   behold I am traversing the Mysterious One.
>   I am crossing through to take care of Osiris.

Gods, you gods—behold I am entering your darkness. My solar disk is going to rest in your caverns. Bend your arms, bow your shoulders, receive me. Rejoice at my approach. Behold I am illumining your darkness."

Then this great god passes over the cavern of Sefeg, the great one, foremost of his visible forms.

LITANY 9: ADDRESS TO TATENEN[127]

Then the great one reaches the grotto of Tatenen. Re says to the grotto of Tatenen, whom the gods bore after his bearing of them:

"O Tatenen,
>   who has made the birth forms,
>   who begets those who come forth from him, the manifestations.

---

127. This text refers to the depiction in Division 5, Register 1, Scene 52. The following litany combines pre-Ramesside attributes of Tatenen, such as Tatenen as creator deity, with iconography known from the reign of Ramesses II (i.e., the "double plumes"). See Schlögl 1980, 86–88.

O Tatenen,
    powerful of double plumes,
    whose corpse Anubis has made secret.
O Tatenen,
    peaceful of corpse,
    who judges the matter for those amongst whom he is.
O Tatenen,
    who is in his cavern,
    Osiris foremost of his grotto.
O Tatenen,
    hidden of his nature,
    from whom Khepri […], namely, his limbs.
O Tatenen,
    great of corpse,
    whom the *ba*-souls see with the result that they breathe.

O Tatenen,
    who came forth from his primeval form—
        as […] prospers, so […] of the earth prospers therein.
O Tatenen,
    who takes care of the deities who take care of him, having made
    their places.
O Tatenen,
    who created the cavern(s),
    who made the mounds for the gods.
O Tatenen,
    foremost of his darkness,
    who sends forth speech for the mysterious ones.
O Tatenen,
    who made offerings,
    those who are there (the dead) having become content with what
    he has created.
O Tatenen,
    who ejaculates semen,
    whose ejaculate has manifested the manifestations.

O Tatenen,
    great of [manife]stations,
    who made the visible form(s),

who completed the images.

O Tatenen! O behold I am ⌜passing⌝ Tatenen! O Atum who is as (a form of) Tatenen! Khepri foremost of his grotto; two great and grand gods, pacified of *ba*-soul, who have come into being through me—behold I am illumining <your> [corp]ses, your *ba*-souls belonging to me, (namely,) those who are in my following. Receive me. Your arms be toward me. That I tread on you (the earth) is driving away your darkness, your *ba*-souls passing after my *ba*-soul. Behold I am traversing Igeret, causing the corpses to occupy their caverns. Their *ba*-souls become strong because of them, having gone to rest in the bodies, at the same time as I spoke in your grottos. I am passing by you, my solar disk in my following, in order to see my corpse amongst you."

Then this great god passes by the grotto of Tatenen.

LITANY 10: LIGHT IN THE WEST[128]

Then this great god reaches the grotto of the blood red one, great of mystery.[129] Re says to this cavern:

"O blood red one, great of mystery, lord of red (blood), flourishing of slaughtering places. You who are within his sarcophagus, his two children in their sarcophagus; who is satisfied with his two children, the one powerful of visible forms being the one who watches him. O behold I am passing your grotto, one mysterious of visible forms. Give me your hand.

As light appears in the West,
      so the *ba*-soul of the one great of requirements becomes strong.
As light appears in the West,
      the blood red one is occupying his youthful copies.[130]
As light appears in the West,
      [she] (the West) has already extended her arms toward me.

---

128. This text refers to the depiction in Division 5, Register 1, Scene 53.

129. The mention of redness alongside light appearing in the West throughout this litany appears to parallel the redness of dawn (Darnell 2004, 72, 196–97).

130. *swnnw* as specific writing of *snn* of "*snn*," WÄS, 3:460.6–17, with Werning 2011a, 299 n. e, but note the <*m*> he restores, reading "content with," is absent; the text appears to take *swnnw* as the object, meaning "to occupy."

As light appears in the West,
    Osiris is content with my solar disk.
As light appears in the West,
    I cross through the grottos with the result that the darkness is illu-
    minated.
As light appears in the West,
    those in the earth have become content with my light.

As light appears in the West,
    so the throats of the suffocated breathe.
As light appears in the West,
    I am causing that the silent ones themselves speak.

As light appears in the West,
    so I conceal the mystery by means of my rays.[131]
As light appears in the West,
    I am issuing commands to the One Hidden of Name.

As light appears in the West,
    the Ennead of Osiris is rejoicing.
As light appears in the West,
    the council of Tatenen is strong.

As light appears in the West,
    I am passing over the lords of mysteries.
As light appears in the West,
    I am navigating the cavern of the West.

O blood red one! O behold I am passing the blood red one, and traversing those who are in Tatenen, as I pass the mysterious Netherworld in order to see my corpse which is therein, and in order to illumine my visible forms and my images."

Then this great god passes over the grotto of the blood red one.

---

131. This is an important statement regarding the "clothing" properties of light, for which see Darnell 2004, 133–37.

LITANY 11: ADDRESS TO ANUBIS, POWER OF THE WEST[132]

Then this god arrives at the grotto of the visible forms of Osiris. Re says to this grotto:

"O Anubis,
>   who is over his mystery,
>   lord of might,
>   who contents the bandaged ones,
>   who is over the mystery in the West,
>   who creates heads and who binds wrappings.

O Anubis, power of the West,
>   chief of fillets, great of bandaged ones.
O Anubis, power of the West,
>   lord of those of the West, who has made the body mysterious.
O Anubis, power of the West,
>   the corpse from which he came forth is Osiris.

O Anubis, power of the West,
>   who attaches the head of the One Foremost of His Cavern.
O Anubis, power of the West,
>   who attaches the head of the One Hidden of Name.
O Anubis, power of the West,
>   who attaches the head of the One Great of Requirements.
O Anubis, power of the West,
>   who attaches the head of the Ruler of the Netherworld.

O Anubis, power of the West,
>   who sets his power in his sarcophagus.
O Anubis, power of the West,
>   who has buried the great mystery.
O Anubis, power of the West,
>   great one of the West, foremost of Igeret.
O Anubis, power of the West,

---

132. This text refers to the depiction in Division 5, Register 2, Scene 54.

powerful of face, who clothes the Ennead, unique one in the great
Ennead
O Anubis, power of the West,
	lord of the Netherworld, who causes Igeret to breathe.
O Anubis, power of the West,
	who cares for the Lord of the West.
O Anubis, power of the West,
	who calls the lords of requirements,
		so that Osiris ⌜rejoices(?)⌝ in his grotto.

O Anubis! O behold I am passing, Anubis, I am traversing those who are in
Tatenen, I passing the mysterious Netherworld in order to see my corpse
which is therein, in order to illumine my visible form and my images."
	Then this great god passes over the grotto of Anubis.

LITANY 12: ADDRESSES TO HE OF THE NETHERWORLD AND THE FOUR MYSTE-
RIOUS GODDESSES[133]

Then this great god reaches the grotto of the Netherworld Dwellers. Re
says to this grotto:

"O female Netherworld Dwellers who are in the Netherworld, those
of the sarcophagi, foremost of the West! O behold I am passing by you!
May you rejoice over me—ladies of visible forms. May you receive me. No
sooner do your caverns brighten than you see and you breathe.

O Female Falcon,[134] foremost of the West,
	behold I am crossing through the Netherworld,
	I am passing Igeret in order to see my corpse which is in the earth,
		and in order to place my solar disk upon his images.
O Strong One, foremost of the West,
	behold I am crossing through the Netherworld,
	I am passing Igeret in order to see my corpse which is in the earth,
		and in order to place my solar disk upon his images.

---

133. This text refers to the depiction in Division 5, Register 2, Scene 55.
134. *Bik.t* "female falcon" may be related to *Ḥr.t* "female Horus," an epithet used
of Isis in the Greco-Roman Period (see Žabkar 1988, 58, 131, 172 n. 102, 184 n. 8).

O She Who Is Dark of *Ba*-Soul, foremost of the West,
    behold I am crossing through the Netherworld,
        I am passing Igeret in order to see my corpse which is in the earth,
            and in order to place my solar disk upon his images.
O Wenyt, foremost of the west,
    behold I am crossing through the Netherworld,
        I am passing Igeret in order to see my corpse which is in the earth,
            and in order to place my solar disk upon his images.

O you four mysterious goddesses, foremost of the Netherworld, visible forms foremost of the West, may you be covered by means of the sarcophagi, you remaining in your grottos."

LITANY 13: ADDRESS TO THE TWELVE (HOUR) GODDESSES

You are these goddesses with whom Osiris is content.
You are these goddesses, messengers of the One Hidden of Name.
You are these goddesses, the dispatched ones of the female ruler of the
    Netherworld.

You are these goddesses, powerful of *ba*-souls in the land of the West.
You are these goddesses, presenters in the council.
You are these goddesses, possessors of words in the following of the
    Ennead.

You are these goddesses, who hide the body that is among them.
You are these goddesses, the guides of the Mysterious Place.
You are these goddesses, manifested one(s) who are in Tatenen.

You are these goddesses, whose hair locks are mysterious.
You are these goddesses, speakers to their shades.
You are these goddesses, raisers up of the *ba*-souls who attend their
    (your) words.

O goddesses, you goddesses—behold I am passing by—O goddesses—so that I might illumine you by means of the light of my solar disk. I am traveling over those who are in Tatenen, I passing the mysterious Netherworld, in order to see my corpse that is in the earth, and in order to illumine my visible forms and my images.

Then this great god passes over the grotto of the goddesses that is at the front of the Netherworld.

ADDRESS TO THE DESTROYERS AND THE DESTROYED (BETWEEN LITANIES 13–14)[135]

Then this great god arrives at the caverns of the Place of Destruction. Above them the great god crosses through. This great god issues orders above their caverns. Re says to the grotto of the two posts:

> "O One Mysterious of Arm(s),
>> she who in charge of the two posts,
>> she who watches the enemies of Osiris.
>> Bound and tied to the two posts have the enemies of Osiris been assigned to you.
> O One of the Uraeus,
>> who is over his flame,
>> who sets fire in his cook pot,
>>> which holds the heads of the enemies of Osiris and the hearts of the enemies of the Netherworld.
>> Set your torch to your cook pot;
>> cook the enemies of Foremost of the Netherworld.

O you two uraei, Fire and Scalding, ones great of manifestations, possessors of plans in the Place of Destruction—send out your fire. Kindle your firebrands under that cauldron in which are the enemies of Osiris.

O you (enemies) who belong to the posts, whom the posts watch.[136] You are the shouters(?),[137] tied up because of the offences they have committed in the mystery of the great god. Behold, I am giving you to bonds, I am reckoning you <as> those whom the rope lines watch, you having been placed under the hand of Mysteriou<s One>, from whose watch one does not go forth, you having been chopped up <in> the Place of Destruction— may your *ba*-souls and your shades be destroyed."

---

135. This text refers to the depiction in Division 5, Register 3, Scenes 56–58.

136. Note the human heads on the ends of the fork of such a post in a depiction in the Tomb of Mereruka—The Saqqara Expedition 1938, pls. 36–38.

137. Reading *nn* <*n*> *nhmy.w*; alternatively, *nn n ḥmy.w* "burning ones(?)."

"Destroyed be the enemies of Foremost of the Netherworld—
    their heads having fallen in their cook pots.
Destroyed be the enemies of Foremost of the Netherworld—
    their hearts being burnt offerings.

Destroyed be the enemies of Foremost of the Netherworld—
    the one of the uraeus burns them.
Destroyed be the enemies of Foremost of the Netherworld—
    a mighty flame is in the Netherworld.
Destroyed be the enemies of Foremost of the Netherworld—
    the arms of Nun hold their cauldrons.

Destroyed be the enemies of Foremost of the Netherworld—
    the corpses have fallen upside down.
Destroyed be the enemies of Foremost of the Netherworld—
    their very heads having been cut off from them.
Destroyed be the enemies of Foremost of the Netherworld—
    bonds and ropes as their rope lines.

Destroyed be the enemies of Foremost of the Netherworld—
    she who burns sets fire in them.
Destroyed be the enemies of Foremost of the Netherworld—
    the flaming one sets her lasting flame in them.
Destroyed be the enemies of Foremost of the Netherworld—
    their flame has opened the Netherworld.

Destroyed be the enemies of Foremost of the Netherworld—
    the Place of Destruction having been destroyed.

Destroyed be the enemies of Foremost of the Netherworld.
    I am assigning you to your destruction.
Destroyed be the enemies of Foremost of the Netherworld.

Destroyed be the enemies of Foremost of the Netherworld—those of
the darkness, those without illumination; these enemies of Osiris beneath
whom is fire, those burning of corpse—you are the enemies of Osiris, these

who cannot see that I shine, those whom I have placed in the darkness of the Place of Destruction, among whom I have set watchers.

I am proceeding to the grotto of Osiris, causing that his *ba*-soul go to rest upon his corpse."

Then this great god passes by the Place of Destruction, inflicting punishment on those who are therein, as enemies of the ruler of the Netherworld.

ADDRESS TO THE CORPSE OF OSIRIS[138]

Then this great god goes to rest in the grotto of Osiris. Re says to the grotto of the ruler of the Netherworld:

> "O corpse of the Ruler of the Netherworld,
>> great of visible forms, lady[139] of manifestations.
> O you ⌐Foremost of the West, Osiris¬ Foremost of the West—
>> bend your (arm), bow your shoulder.
> Behold I am proceeding to your grotto; my great solar disk goes to rest
>> in my following.
> O Osiris, great god, whose head is in the darkness, whose hinter parts
>> are in darkness;
>> his corpse has traversed the Netherworld,
>> his *ba*-soul having become strong upon his images.
> Bend your arm, bow your shoulder.
> I am causing that you go to rest (by means of) my glowing disk."

LITANY 15: ADDRESS TO OSIRIS, LORD OF THE WEST

> O Osiris, lord of the West,
>> satisfied of *ba*-soul, divine of corpse.
> O Osiris, lord of the West,
>> lord of odor, great of putrefaction.
> O Osiris, lord of the West,
>> his *ba*-soul having gone to rest upon his corpse.

---

138. This text refers to the depiction in Division 5, Registers 1–3, Scene 59.
139. Written *nb.t*, feminine, since it references the corpse.

O Osiris, lord of the West,
  in whose grotto is this Terrible of Face.

O Osiris, lord of the West,
  behold I am passing by your mystery.
O Osiris, lord of the West,
  behold I am crossing through, that I might occupy Igeret.
O Osiris, lord of the West,
  behold I am driving off the darkness,
      that I might illumine you.

O Osiris, lord of the West,
  your *ba*-soul is passing in my following,
  issuing commands to those in your following.
O Osiris, lord of the West,
  whose corpse breathes through my solar disk.
O Osiris, lord of the West,
  powerful of face, living of power.

O Osiris, lord of the West,
  one of the Netherworld, who speaks to his *ba*-soul.[140]
O Osiris, lord of the West,
  great of speech, official <in> his grotto.

O Osiris, lord of the West,
  lord of this One of the Sarcophagus,
  king of the Westerners.

O Osiris! Great god, whose corpse is hidden,
  you with whom is Terrible of Face,
      he causing that he guard the corpse of the One Hidden of
      Name.

---

140. Compare the Book of Adoring Re in the West, Great Litany, Address 57 (pp. 70–71).

LITANY 16: RAISE YOURSELF, ONE HIDDEN OF NAME[141]

"O raise yourself, One Hidden of Name—
    I am illumining the darkness by means of my solar disk.
O raise yourself, One Hidden of Name—
    your *ba*-soul rests atop you.
O raise yourself, One Hidden of Name—
    I am traversing your mysterious grotto.
O raise yourself, One Hidden of Name—
    your *ba*-soul is upon your corpse, I having greeted it.

O raise yourself, One Hidden of Name,
    as I cause that the mysteries of your grotto go to rest.
O raise yourself, One Hidden of Name,
    one who made the Netherworld and who bore Horus.

O raise yourself, One Hidden of Name—
    Anubis is protecting his mystery.
O raise yourself, One Hidden of Name—
    I am traversing those who are in your grotto.
O raise yourself, One Hidden of Name—
    I am passing to the birth of my manifestations.

O raise yourself, One Hidden of Name,
    whom I have made, whose semen I make manifest.
O raise yourself, One Hidden of Name,
    lord of mysteries, great one of those amongst whom he is.
O raise yourself, One Hidden of Name,
    one attached of heart and joined of corpse.

O raise yourself, One Hidden of Name—
    cause yourself to breathe, bend your members.

Breathe, Osiris—Osiris is breathing,
    Osiris is surely breathing, so that his members may bend.

---

141. This text refers to the depiction in Division 5, Register 1, Scene 60.

I am passing by, that I might illumine you by means of my solar disk, <I> placing light in your grotto. That I cross those who are in Tatenen is while I pass the mysterious Netherworld, in order to see my corpse which is in the earth, and in order to illumine <my> visible forms and ⌐my images.¬"

Then this great god passes by the grotto of Osiris. Then this god reaches the grotto of the body. This great god speaks to those who act as its guard. Re speaks to this grotto:

"O Binder(?),[142] chief of his unique body and Osiris, who guards the mysteries. O, behold, I am passing over you, as I protect the body that is within your arms. I illumine you, that which is with you, and your hidden mysteries."

LITANY 17: ADDRESS TO THE BODY OF OSIRIS

"Hidden is the body of Osiris—
    my solar disk will go to rest in his grotto.
Hidden is the body of Osiris—
    his body will have power over its West.
Hidden is the body of Osiris—
    the efflux that is in the Netherworld will be hidden.
Hidden is the body of Osiris—
    those who are in the Netherworld are joining themselves to it (the Netherworld).

Hidden is the body of Osiris—
    the divine *ba*-soul has gone to rest upon his body.
Hidden is the body of Osiris—
    Foremost of the Netherworld has gone to rest in his flesh.
Hidden is the body of Osiris—
    the god is protecting his flesh himself.
Hidden is the body of Osiris—
    (those of) the Netherworld are mourning over him.

Hidden is the body of Osiris—
    my great solar disk is shining upon them.
Hidden is the body of Osiris—

---

142. For doubts regarding this hypothetical reading, see Werning 2011a, 345.

as for the West, her arms are upon that which she hides.
Hidden is the body of Osiris—
   Anubis is hiding that which he prepared.
Hidden is the body of Osiris—
   the falcon-like one is extending (his) arms toward the mysteries.
Hidden is the body of Osiris—
   the lord of wrappings is in his true visible form.
Hidden is the body of Osiris—
   the one complete of *ba*-soul is crossing through before [him].

Hidden is the body of Osiris, ever hidden is the body of Osiris.

His *ba*-soul having been protected does the god go to rest upon his putre-faction, so that his images might manifest. I am even now illuminating the body of Osiris, Foremost of the Westerners, by means of my solar disk, the one great of illumination, so that the body might occupy his grotto, while I am passing by their caverns, traversing those who are in Tatenen, and passing the mysterious Netherworld in order to see my corpse which is therein, and in order to illumine my visible forms and my images."
   Then this great god passes by the grotto of the body of Osiris.
   Then this great god arrives at the grotto of Nephthys, she who is hidden of head. Re says to this grotto:
   "O Nephthys, she who is hidden of head, she who persists behind Osiris (as protection)—give to me your arm, O one hidden of head. Behold I am passing your grotto, my *ba*-soul in my following, that I might illumi-nate the Netherworld."

LITANY 18: ADDRESS TO THE SHE WHO IS HIDDEN OF HEAD[143]

"O She Who Is Hidden of Head, give me your arm—
   the *ba*-soul of Tatenen has been raised up to my solar disk.
O She Who Is Hidden of Head, give me your arm—
   it is your corpse that covers that which is in it.
O She Who Is Hidden of Head, give me your arm—
   may she protect herself by means of her own effective spells.

---

143. This text refers to the depiction in Division 5, Register 2, Scene 61.

O She Who Is Hidden of Head, give me your arm—
  you who are hidden of her corpse as (protection) around her brother.
O She Who Is Hidden of Head, give me your arm—
  you who are great of counsel when passing judgment.
O She Who Is Hidden of Head, give me your arm—
  you who are high of voice in the land of Igeret.
O She Who Is Hidden of Head, give me your arm—
  you whose corpse is more mysterious than (that of) her sister.

O She Who Is Hidden of Head, give me your arm—
  as I cause that your *ba*-soul breathe, so I join together your corpse.
O She Who Is Hidden of Head, give me your arm—
  I cause my solar disk to go to rest in your grotto.
O She Who Is Hidden of Head, give me your arm—
  as I enter so I illumine those who are in the darkness.
O She Who Is Hidden of Head, give me your arm—
  I assign the enemies to the slaughtering places,
    they already having been destroyed.
O She Who Is Hidden of Head, give me your arm—
  I cause that you grow strong as the completed flesh.

O She Who Is Hidden of Head, give me your arm—
  your mystery be to you, O efficacious one.[144]
O She Who Is Hidden of Head, give me your arm—
  may you guide me to the ways of the West.

O Nephthys, you who are hidden of head, whose *ba*-soul breathes by means of the solar disk, whose corpse is (protectively) around Osiris, goddess who hides herself—behold, I am crossing through, my *ba*-soul in my following, that I might illumine the Netherworld and the darkness, and give instructions to those who are in my following, while I pass by this grotto, and they praise and rejoice over me, their *ba*-souls having come to rest upon their corpses. That I traverse those who are in Tatenen while passing through the mysterious Netherworld is in order to see my corpse that is in the earth, and in order to illumine my visible forms and my images."

---

144. For the term *itp.yt*, see Werning 2011a, 480; Hannig 2006a, 439.

Then this great god passes by the grotto of Nephthys. Then this great god crosses through, that he might go to rest in the grotto of his head.[145] Then this great god issues commands to those who are in his grotto.

Re says to this grotto: "O Atum, my own heir, great god, whose *ba*-soul praises Osiris. O corpses of the enemies of Osiris. O Horus, heir of Osiris, whose *ba*-soul attends to the affairs of his putrefaction. Behold I am passing by you, that I might go to rest in the grotto of my images. You are those who came forth from my limbs—give me your arms, rejoice over me. I am Re, whose corpse speaks.[146] The corpse is in its grotto, my *ba*-soul becomes strong because of his putrefaction."

LITANY 19: THE CORPSE AND HEAD IN HER GROTTO[147]

"My corpse and my head are in her grotto—
  I shall receive my mysterious head.
My corpse and my head are in her grotto—
  my illuminating one (disk) endures <upon> my brow.
My corpse and my head are in her grotto—
  the great mystery receives light.

My corpse and my head are in her grotto—
  I shall reckon my body and drive off the enemies.
My corpse and my head are in her grotto—
  my heart is happy and my *ba*-soul is strong.

My corpse and my head are in her grotto—
  to the One Foremost of the Netherworld do I call.
My corpse and my head are in her grotto—
  those who are in the earth rejoice in my following.
My corpse and my head are in her grotto—
  [...] the *ba*-souls of the Netherworld Dwellers, so that they [might speak].

---

145. This passage recalls the different fates of the solar head and Osirian corpse within the Netherworld (Manassa 2007a, 40–41 and references therein).

146. Compare in the Book of Adoring Re in the West, Great Litany, Address 57 (see pp. 70–71).

147. =*s* "her" refers to the goddess in Division 5, Register 2, Scene 61 (Manassa 2007a, 380).

My corpse and my head are in her grotto—
> their [...] shall surely ⌜breathe⌝.

My corpse and my head are in her grotto—
> Osiris reckons those amongst whom he is.

My corpse and my head are in her grotto—
> I inflict punishment among my enemies.

I go to rest upon my corpse and my head; so I go to rest upon my corpse and my head. No sooner do <I> summon those who are in the Netherworld, then they hear. As I summon them, so I traverse those who are in Tatenen, I passing through the mysterious Netherworld, in order to see my corpse, and in order to illumine my visible forms and my images."

Then this great god <pass>es by the grotto of his head. Then this great god arrives above the top of the place of destruction. He issues commands to those who are there, as he passes over them.

Re says to this this cavern:[148] "O *ba*-souls of the enemies of Osiris; O shades of the enemies of Osiris; you against whom the two (uraeus) goddesses are casting fire. You Perceptive One,[149] she who is piercing of flame; you Staring One,[150] powerful of flame—set your fire and your flame amongst the enemies of this One Hidden of Name, and your tapers amongst your cauldrons. Guide their flesh, reckon their limbs. You gods who are in the Netherworld, (namely) the Place of Destruction—I am letting them fall into their traps, they having already been assigned to their cauldrons—they are the enemies of the One Hidden of Name."

LITANY 20: THE ENEMIES OF OSIRIS

"You are the enemies of Osiris—
> your corpses have been cut up and your heads driven off.

You are the enemies of Osiris—
> your *ba*-souls have been driven off so that your blood pours out.

You are the enemies of Osiris—
> your shades have been driven off so that your manifestations come to naught.

---

148. This text and the following Litany 20 refers to the depiction in Division 5, Register 3, Scene 63.

149. See Werning 2011a, 365 n. b.

150. "Gꜣgꜣwt," LGG 7:301.

You are the enemies of Osiris—
>   you have been destroyed and your visible forms have been pun-
>   ished.

You are the enemies of Osiris—
>   your flesh(?) has been cut off from your bones.

You are the enemies of Osiris—
>   you are destroyed in the Place of Destruction.

You are the enemies of Osiris—
>   their fire has been cast, it will not be extinguished.

You are the enemies of Osiris—
>   of whom those who are with me do not speak.

You are the enemies of Osiris—
>   those of darkness, who cannot come forth.

You are the enemies of Osiris—
>   for whom their caverns do not grow bright.

You are the enemies of Osiris—
>   the Perceptive One applies the fiery heat.

You are the enemies of Osiris—
>   the Staring One heats up the cauldron.

You are the enemies of Osiris—
>   those brought to an end, who cannot exist.

You are the enemies of Osiris—
>   to you has evil been applied.

O you enemies of Osiris, who are in the Place of Destruction, whose judgment the great council which is in the Mysterious Place has passed in the presence of Osiris, to whom he assigns their bad places in the forepart of the Place of Destruction, because of these matters which they have committed in the mysterious room of those who are there."

The enemies are in their bad and evil places, without existing, without their own *ba*-souls existing, forever.

Then this great god passes in the upper portion of the Place of Destruction, even while this god is inflicting punishment on the enemies of Osiris.

DIVISION 6

INTRODUCTION

Then this great god reaches his grotto that is in the Netherworld, passing by his mound, as the manifestation goes forth, those who are in the Netherworld presenting their arms.[151]

REGISTER 1 (PLATE 34)

5.64. Scene 64. A jackal headed deity, "Anubis," stands facing left, arms out with hands down over an oval to front and back—a supine figure in each oval, knees drawn up as though kneeling; the figure in the left oval is labeled "Pale One,"[152] while the one in the right oval is labeled "Jubilating One."[153] A bird perches atop each oval, facing in toward the standing deity, above whose forehead hovers a solar disk.

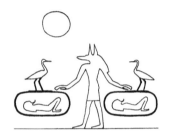

OVER THE SCENE

They are in this fashion, their corpses in their sarcophagi in their cavern, (even) as their corpses pass by. Anubis is the protector. This great god illumines them by means of his great solar disk; it is their *ba*-souls who speak to him. Then darkness covers them, after he passes by them.

BEFORE THE SCENE

Re says to this cavern: "O Anubis, O honored one whose body was made as god, lord in the West—guard the *ba*-souls. Contentment be to the Netherworld because of my plan. Behold, I am passing into the Mysterious Place, I having become manifest, I having been born myself, I having appeared in glory in the cavern of the two hills."

---

151. This text refers to Division 6, Register 2, Scene 68.
152. Werning 2011b, 375, n. b.
153. Werning 2011b suggests *h(ꜣ)y* "Falling one"(?).

Anubis says to Re: "I am this one in the West, hidden of image, who assigns a god to his sarcophagus, who pacifies the corpses of those who are in the earth, who clothes the body, who hides the rot. Illumine us, Re, by means of your light; let the earth become content through seeing your disk."

5.65. Scene 65. A jackal headed deity faces right, slightly bowed with arms down and forward; to the right are two vertically oriented ovals—a standing female figure in each, atop four flesh signs, facing toward the space between them, occupied by a horizontal oval below with solar disk above. The goddesses are labeled (left) "Swallower" and (right) "Breather," while in each case the flesh signs are labeled "Flesh." In the horizontal oval, from right to left, facing right, are a falcon head, a ram, and a solar disk; the falcon head is the "Head of Re," while the ram and disk is the "Ram-form of Re."

ABOVE THE SCENE

These gods are in this fashion, on both sides of this his sarcophagus of Re, whose visible forms are within it, and whose mysteries have transformed for him into his primeval form which already became manifest. This great <god> speaks to them. They speak to him. He illumines them with his shining disk, he making a standstill in the cavern because of what he sees. Even after he passes over them, then darkness covers them.

Re says to this cavern: "O you two great and grand goddesses, guardians of the mysterious sarcophagus—while Anubis is your guardian—which contains my corpse: the head of Re and the mystery of this one, the lord of manifestations. Behold, I am passing your cavern, that I might illumine you, with the result that you drive back your darkness."

The two goddesses say to Re, they speaking to this one who made them manifest: "O one who made us, manifesting of manifestation, who assigns to us the guardianship of his guards, with the result that we guard your mysteries. It is by means of your great solar disk that he illumines the two lands, O lord of manifestations, this one, supplied of birth forms and manifestations, in order to manifest manifestations."

5.66. Scene 66. Two standing goddesses face in from each side of the scene, arms down and out in front; the right goddess is "She of the Netherworld." Between them are two horizontal ovals, one above the other; in the lower, from left to right, are a ram head facing left and a horizontally oriented scarab,  labeled "Head of the Ram-form" and "Scarab"; in the upper is a supine anthropomorphic figure, head to right, "He of the Netherworld." A solar disk is positioned to the left of the upper oval.

ABOVE THE SCENE

They are in this fashion, guarding the images of Re and the corpse of He of the Netherworld. Re speaks to them. They speak to him. This great god sheds light for them by means of his great solar disk, as he enters their cavern. Then the darkness conceals them after he passes by them.

IN FRONT OF THE SCENE

Re says to this cavern: "O you two goddesses, rejoicing ones, you who are my own protection, protecting the One Hidden of Mystery, the great god foremost of the Netherworld. Look at me, I having been born in the Netherworld, I having manifest in the manifestation of Khepri, I having become young in the beautiful West."

BEFORE THE SCENE

The two goddesses say to Re: "O you primeval one, you primeval one, manifest one who manifests himself, who unites himself, who assembles his limbs by means of that which comes forth from his mouth, from whose members the Netherworld has come into being, who shoots forth his semen, who ejaculates his ejaculate.[154] Behold, we are those whom you command, that they cause your solar disk to mount up, O Khepri."

---

154. The various effluvia of the solar deity are mentioned—for the spittle and ejaculate linked, compare the Books of Solar-Osirian Unity, Tomb of Ramesses IX (pp. 532–33).

5.67. Scene 67. A deity, "He of the Netherworld," stands between two mounds, facing right, arms raised as in adoration of the solar disk in front of him. Atop the right mound, facing left, is a falcon, "Horus"; within the right  mound, "Sarcophagus of the Flesh," from left to right, a horizontal oval and four flesh signs. Atop the left mound is a bending deity, "Osiris-Orion," face lowered, facing right, holding a *was*-scepter; within the left mound is a headless human figure, prone, arms tied behind its back, "Enemy."

IN FRONT OF THE SCENE

Re says to this cavern: "O Osiris, Foremost of the Netherworld, sole deity who reaches[155] the West—may you take care of your son; may you make his eye excellent. Make him to be content with his goddess-eye. Take care of this god. Make an end of the robber. The powerful unique one, beneath whose feet is the one whom he punishes, in your visible form of Osiris-Orion. As I illumine you by means of my shining disk, so I care for you by means of that which is upon my brow."

IN FRONT OF THE SCENE

Osiris-Orion says to Re: "Behold us, O Re, doing what you say. The one who manifested as me is taking care of the one who came forth from me,[156] because of this, because of this which you have done for us before making secret our places.[157] May you cover my throne, and let our *ba*-souls speak above us. Illumine us, O Re, great of manifestation."

155. A pun on the name of Orion as *sꜣḥ*.

156. Here Re transforms into Osiris and takes care of the Re who comes forth from him, similar to the paradox expressed in the Book of Gates, Hour 2, Register 3, Scene 8: "I am the son who came forth from his father; I am the father who came forth from his son" (see p. 264).

157. Reading the preposition *n* as negative arms in a *nꞽ sḏmt=f* construction; alternatively (with Baumann 1998, 70) "because of your making our place secret."

These gods are in this fashion, foremost of their cavern. They speak to this great god, with the result that he speaks to them—(namely,) this Netherworldly One, foremost of Igeret, for whom Horus takes care because of his divine eye, the great falcon who rests upon his images—with the result that they behold the light, when this great god passes by them. Then darkness conceals them.

BEHIND THE SCENE

Horus says to Re: "O Re, who bore the one who bore me,[158] you sole one who came into being, the ⌜engenderer⌝. Behold, I am becoming content with this my divine (eye), she who is darkened to me.
      Ascend to me, one great of light—
            you are my <eye>, my divine (eye);
      Ascend to me, one great of solar disk—
            you are my effective eye, my *udjat*-eye;
      Ascend to me, one great of light rays—
            you are the power of the West.
      Jubilation be to you, Re, may you illumine for us,
            O lord of the solar disk, may you dispel our darkness."

REGISTER 2 (PLATE 34)

5.68. Scene 68. Four deities stand on the right, facing left, each slightly bent forward, arms out and down in front; they are named "Standing One"; "Divine One"; "One of the Flood"; "One of the Pouring Out(?)." They face

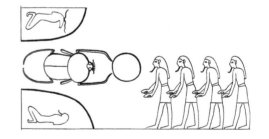

---

158. In the Suty and Hor hymn, the solar deity is (Helck 1958, 5–6) *mss iwty ms.tw=f*, "fashioner unfashioned"; but perhaps the best parallel here is the *ms ms sw*, "who fashions the one who bore him," an epithet of Ramesses II, also appearing elsewhere. See Grimal 1986, 104 n. 268; Spalinger 2009, 17 (*et passim* on the verb *ms*-fashion in the text).

a scarab oriented horizontally toward the right, pushing a solar disk ahead; the scarab emerges from between two hills, each with a kneeling anthropomorphic deity, oriented horizontally, heads to right, facing toward each other. The deity below is human headed, and called "Osiris," while the one above is ram headed and labeled "One of the *Ba*-Soul."

After those who are in the West have been born does this god come forth in this fashion from between the two mysterious caverns of the West.

These gods are in this fashion, they giving their arms to Re—(it is) the birth form of the one who is in the Netherworld, his manifestation of the one who is in the West—while this god has made a pause <at> this cavern. With the result that they behold the light, after this great god passes by them, have the gods who are in it been illumined.

Then the darkness conceals them, after he passes by them.

BEFORE THE FOUR DEITIES

Making the unknown transformation—(it is) this image of the birth form of Re, the powers which are in the birth form of Re, and the two hills which are in the Netherworld.

5.69. Scene 69. A serpent, "Great Serpent," with tail to the upper left, head to upper right, body curving down and around a vertically oriented scarab with solar disk above head, "Great god," occupies the central portion of the scene. The tip of the tail and the head of the serpent curves slightly over a vertical oval at each end. In each oval stands an anthropomorphic figure, facing the center of the scene, the one on the left labeled "The One Who was Brought Away," the one on the right named "The One Turned of Face"; beneath each figure are four horizontally oriented flesh signs, labeled "Flesh."

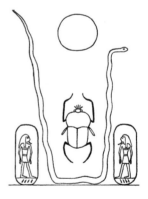

ABOVE THE SCENE

These gods are in this fashion, as they guard the serpent. This great god comes forth and makes a pause in this fashion. As for everything that this god does in this fashion—with their faces in their lands do the gods and the dead do it (also), without seeing the light, (yet) seeing the one who comes.

Re says to this cavern: "Behold me, O gods, as I manifest, I having been born and having taken control of my solar disk. The two great and grand deities, foremost of the Netherworld, unite with me. As for the great serpent surrounding me—they enchant him and cut off the *ba*-soul. Jubilation—I have become manifest four times."

The two great and grand deities say to Re: "O behold, we are enchanting the punished one, we are cutting off the *ba*-soul of the one who is surrounding you, so that you may make manifest what should be manifest. O Re, may you illumine us, so that we become content with the solar disk—surely you are the one who made us, this great sole one, who illumines the darkness."

5.70. Scene 70. In the left half a male deity stands to right, facing left, slightly bowed, arms raised with palms forward in adoration, facing a hemispherical mound; he is labeled "One Who is in the Netherworld." Atop the mound is a ram's head, facing right, surmounted by a solar disk; within the mound is a serpent with head raised and facing to the right, body consisting of three raised coils, with tail down. The label to the left hill (written cryptographically) reads "Great Serpent. The *ba*-souls of the birth form of Re which are in the two mounds." In the right half a male deity stands to right, facing left, slightly bowed, arms raised with palms forward in adoration, facing a tall, round topped mound, within which a male deity, "(Ta)tenen," emerges from the ground (legs hidden below ground line), facing right, arms to sides with elbows slightly bent, wearing twin ostrich feathers atop his head; the adoring figure is labeled "One Who is in the Netherworld."

This god is in this fashion, showing his head and illuminating his cavern by means of his solar disk which is on his brow. One Who is in the Netherworld gives praise to him, as the one who guards his mysterious mound. That this god comes forth entirely is when this god passes through this cavern in which is that one evil of face.

ABOVE THE SCENE TO THE RIGHT

This god is in this fashion, in his memorial place,[159] the sarcophagus of the West. The One of the Horizon(?) is his guardian.[160] When this god comes forth entirely is after this great god passes by his cavern, so that this deity may behold the light. Then darkness conceals him.

BEFORE THE SCENE

Re says to this cavern: "I am appearing in glory so that I might drive off my enemies. The gods punish the one evil of face. Those foremost of the Netherworld join me. I am showing my head in my secret places, while I am causing my place to be hidden. Drive him out from the vicinity of Tatenen."

The gods say to Re: "One complete of visible forms, who has come forth from his mound, lord of the solar disk, great of divine beard—jubilation be to you, who comes forth complete, the one who is in the earth, the one who penetrates into the Netherworld. May you occupy the hill of Tatenen. We are causing that you grow powerful, so that you may appear in glory <in> your lands. May you illumine us, Re, may you illumine us. We are performing adoration for you."

---

159. Note that this is the same term used of the Middle Kingdom Abydene cenotaphs (O'Connor 1985).

160. See Werning 2011a, 207; alternatively, Hornung suggests "Shetay" (for which compare the Book of Adoring Re in the West, Great Litany, Address 52 [p. 94]; Darnell 2004, 59, 289–93).

5.71. Scene 71. A solar disk hovers above and between two vertical ovals. In each oval is a standing, falcon-headed deity, facing right, arms by their sides; the label to each oval reads "Icons[161] of the Gods."

ABOVE THE SCENE

These gods are in this fashion, in their mysterious sarcophagi. This great god speaks to them. They speak to him, when they behold the light of the solar disk, as this god passes by them. Then darkness conceals them.

BEFORE THE SCENE

Re says to this cavern: "O Stomping Ones, ones of the sarcophagus, foremost of the West. O behold I am entering entirely, although[162] I pass through the Netherworld in my manifestation. It is the Horuses who come forth from his limbs. My manifestation is his first birth form. Jubilation be to you. I am illumining you, I am illumining you, O you of the darkness."

The Stomping Ones say to Re: "O, Re, who made the one who made us,[163] who brought into being that from which we became manifest. Speak to us, so that we might pull ourselves together; illumine us, that we might have power over our legs. We are the ones who have become manifest as Horus. Show us your face, O traveler of the Netherworld, so that we grow powerful and behold your rays."

---

161. For the ʿḥm image in the Book of Caverns, see Barta 1990a, 42; the ʿḥm can be a particularly Netherworldly element, which might be singled out as remaining in the Netherworld when Re passes by, as in the tomb chapel of Bakenkhons (TT 35): bꜣ=f r p.t ʿḥm=f r dwꜣ.t "his ba-soul to the sky, his icon to the Netherworld."
162. For the particle swt at the end of the sentence, see Oréal 2011, 414.
163. The succeeding generations of creator deities alluded to here recall the theology of the Ogdoad, created by the generations of Kematef and Iryta (see Klotz 2012a, 135–42).

5.72. Scene 72. Beneath a central solar disk, four vertically oriented ovals in a row, a headless body,[164] arms akimbo, feet pointed to right, in each; the beings in the ovals are labeled labeled (reading right to left): "One of the Head"; "One of Joining"; "One of the Udjat-eye"; "One of the Goddess-(eye)."[165]

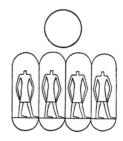

ABOVE THE SCENE

These gods are in this fashion, in their sarcophagi. This great god speaks to them, without them speaking to him. His great solar disk lights up for them. Then darkness conceals them, after he passes by them.

BEFORE THE SCENE

Re says to this cavern: "O you of the pupil-and-iris, headless ones, you inside your sarcophagi, you who stare with their ne<ck>s,[166] without yo[ur …], you who are mysterious of manifestations, you who are in the following of the Netherworldly Horus, whose heads are placed in his eye[167]—O behold, I am passing by you, issuing decrees for you, illumining you in the forepart of the cavern of the mysterious ones. You are the ones mysterious of manifestations, […] of face, who are in (my) following."

REGISTER 3 (PLATE 34)

5.73. Scene 73. Left to right, three divisions of the scene: First section: two headless anthropomorphic figures, arms bound behind, chests and feet pointing up, one horizontally arranged above the other, sev-

---

164. For the significance of headlessness in the Netherworld Books, see the commentary to the Book of Gates, Hour 10, Register 1, Scene 61 (p. 310 and n. 142).

165. A variant writes *itm* (for *itm*), "Atum," or possibly "one who is not."

166. Compare light shining down into the necks of headless mummies in the Book of the Solar-Osirian Unity on the Second Shrine of Tutankhamun (see p. 545).

167. The headless bodies, not inverted and named for the deities, here with their heads off with the sun, are the ambivalent corpses after separation of the solar head— the potentially dangerous aspects of the decoupled aspects of the deity.

ered head facing up and positioned above the legs; they are labeled "Enemies," while below them is written "Apep." A female figure, wearing a long sheath dress, stands to right, facing left, slightly bowed forward and holding a knife before her; she is "Destroyer of the Cut Off Ones."

Second section: two headless anthropomorphic figures, arms bound behind, chests and feet pointing up, one horizontally arranged above the other, severed head facing up and positioned above the legs; they are labeled "Those to Be Punished." A male figure with divine beard, wearing kilt, stands to right, facing left, slightly bowed forward and holding a knife before him; he is called "Destroyer of the cut off ones." Between the upper enemy and the male with the knife is the label "Disturbed One."

Third section: four hearts, one above the other; the hearts are labeled "Hearts of the enemies" and "Hearts of those to be punished." To the right, facing left, stands a female figure, wearing a long sheath dress, slightly bowed forward with her arms outstretched horizontally toward the vertically arranged hearts, her palms facing down; she is called "She of the Place of Destruction."

ABOVE THE SCENE

They are in this fashion, in the Netherworld of the Place of Destruction. These deities are those who guard it. This great god inflicts punishment on them, when he passes by them, with the result that they persist in darkness, without seeing the light. Whenever this great god speaks, they hear, without seeing the light of his solar disk. That these gods who guard them let them breathe is after they hear the speech of this great god, when he passes by them.

BEFORE THE SCENE

Re says to this cavern: "O Igeret of knives, she who is foremost of this Place of Destruction; you who are silent in triumph, and sharp of knives; she who is foremost of the Place of Destruction. O rotting one, great of rot, and your *ba*-soul(s) in the blood of the punished ones—cut off the heads of my enemies, they having been overthrown; destroy their *ba*-souls, that their shades may perish in blood. O behold, I am passing by you, even at the side of those who have done what I have said."

5.74. Scene 74. At each end stands a jackal headed female figure, facing the center of the scene, arms extended forward; the left goddess is named "She of the Bitter Fruit(?)"[168] and the one to the right is called "She of Gall." Between the canid-headed goddesses are four female figures, standing and facing left, arms bound behind their backs; they are named (reading left to right): "One of Blood"; "One of Puss"; "Swallowed One"; "One of Evil."

ABOVE THE SCENE

These are in this fashion. This great god inflicts punishment against them, when he passes by them, without them hearing his words, without them seeing his solar disk. In darkness do they exist, the two goddesses as their guardians. Then this great god passes by them.

BEFORE THE SCENE

Re says to this cavern: "O She of the Bitter Fruit, O She of Gall, O you two great and grand goddesses, foremost of the Place of Destruction, who are the guards of those who are beneath the body, they who seize the images of the lord of the Netherworld. Guard these who seize the bodies, with the result that they are bound and tied in their own limbs, they saying: 'Do not let their *ba*-souls come forth. Do not let <them> have power over their shades. (O) you great one. Act for them in the sacred site, the secret place of Foremost of the Netherworld.' O behold me passing by you, inflicting on you your punishment, I assigning you to the inescapable Place of Destruction."

---

168. "*bꜣj*," *WÄS*, 1:417.9–10; Germer 2008, 55–56, *bꜣy* "a bitter fruit," a material like gall in the following name that would give a bitter taste.

5.75. Scene 75. A male figure stands to left, facing right, while a female figure stands to right, facing left; both are slightly bowed forward and have their arms extended before them, palms down. Between the figures are four kneeling, headless enemies, arms bound behind them, a severed head floating above and slightly forward of each neck.

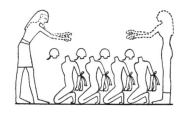

ABOVE THE SCENE

They are in this fashion, without seeing this great god, without glimpsing the rays of his solar disk, without their *ba*-souls going forth from the earth, without hearing the words of this great god, when he passes by their cavern. These gods who guard them hear the words of this god, with the result that their throats breathe, when this great god passes by them.

BEFORE THE SCENE

Re says to this cavern: "O Tousle-haired male, Tousle-haired female,[169] ones who are in the Place of Destruction, under whose guard exist the evil ones, from whose cavern there is no escape. Behold, I am traversing your cavern, passing by the slaughtering place which I have set against you, I assigning you to your evil, I assigning you to the strong ones who are in the Place of Destruction. You are the enemies evil of character, whose *ba*-souls cannot come forth from the earth, they not seeing me."

5.76. Scene 76. At each end of the scene an upside-down male figure, each turned in toward the scene, appears to descend into the earth, the head having apparently already passed out of view; each these figures is labeled "Blood-red One." Between the descending figures is a serpent, "Great Serpent," tail descending from the left, head and upper body rising to the right, the middle part of the body—like the heads of the figures to each side—hidden beneath the ground line. Out of the ground beneath which the ser-

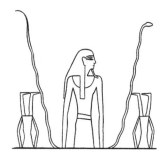

---

169. For these two figures, see Willems 1996, 344–46.

pent's mid-section descends, emerge the hips and upper body of a large male figure, wearing a divine beard and facing to the right.

ABOVE THE SCENE

This god is in this fashion, the heads coming forth from the Place of Destruction.[170] This great god speaks to him. That this god sees the light is when this god passes by him. Then this serpent grows dark, when the serpent passes the gore.

BEFORE THE SCENE

Re says to this cavern: "Osiris, Osiris, whose encirclement is the great serpent, the bloody ones having fallen upside down with face downcast, with face within his cavern. O behold me traversing your cavern, indeed (you are)[171] the one in the coiled one, I giving to you from the light that is in my mouth, so that I might cause you to breathe by means of that which comes forth therefrom.[172] Jubilation be to you, Osiris, so that your *ba*-soul may live, when I illumine your cavern by means of my light, without the one evil of face being able to see them."

END OF REGISTER 3

Re says behind these caverns: "I am passing the cavern of the destroyed ones, assigning them to their evil, even after I have passed Igeret and taken care of <the ones who are in> it. Make for me jubilation, create praise for me, set right for me the roads. Behold I am crossing through, having become manifest upon the road of the one mysterious of visible forms."

---

170. The "heads" refer to the anthropoid and ophidian figures; no need to assume a meaning "upper body" with Werning 2011a, 433.

171. Werning 2011a, 435 n. b.

172. For the interchange of light and breath, see pp. 5–6.

Then this great god comes forth from his two mounds,[173] which are in the Netherworld, this god having transformed into a scarab, by means of the manifestations of Tatenen.[174] This great god says to the gods and to the god who is foremost of his cavern, and those who are in their grottos: "O gods who are in my caverns, foremost of their grottos—behold I am coming forth from my two hills, having been born, having become manifest, so that I might establish my solar disk. These of the council who are in the following of Foremost of the West, they extend their arms toward me, I having become manifest, that my creations be born. May you give praise to me, that I might take care of you, O Netherworld Dwellers, mysterious of visible forms."

LITANY 21: LITANY OF THE MANIFESTATIONS

"O you my corpse of the One Foremost of the Two Hills—
    my body, my image.
O you corpse of Atum—his body,
    his image, his *ba*-soul.
O you *ba*-soul of the One of the Mound—
    his body, his image, his corpse.

O you *ba*-soul of Khepri—
    his body, his image, his corpse.
O you *ba*-soul of Shu—
    his body, his image, his corpse.
O you *ba*-soul of Geb—
    his body, his image, his corpse.
O you *ba*-soul of Osiris—
    his body, his image, his corpse.

O you *ba*-soul of the One Distinguished of Visible Forms—
    his body, his image, his corpse.

---

173. Referencing Concluding Tableau, Scene 78.

174. The opening of the Litany 9 in the Book of Caverns references the manifestations of Tatenen (see pp. 418–19).

O you *ba*-soul of the One Whose Nature Is Hidden—
      his body, his image, his corpse.

O you *ba*-soul of Anubis—
      his body, his image, his corpse.
O you *ba*-soul of Him to Whom Belongs a Ram's-head—
      his body, his image, his corpse.
O you *ba*-soul of the One of the Horizon, head of Horus, who came
forth from Re—
      his body, his image, his corpse.
O you *ba*-soul of She Mysterious of Face—
      her body, her image, her corpse.
O you *ba*-soul of She of the Plan—
      her body, her image, her corpse.
O you *ba*-soul of Anubis—
      his body, his image, his corpse.
O you *ba*-soul of the One Hidden of Seat—
      his body, his image, his corpse.

O you *ba*-soul of Scarab—
      his body, his image, his corpse.
O you *ba*-soul of the head of Re—
      his body, his image, his corpse.

O you *ba*-soul of Isis—
      her body, her image, her corpse.
O you *ba*-soul of Nephthys—
      her body, her image, her corpse.
O you *ba*-soul of Osiris, corpse of Orion carrying the *was*-scepter—
      his body, his visible image, his image.

O you *ba*-soul of the One Who Establishes the Effective Eye—
      his body, his image, his corpse.
O you *ba*-soul of Horus, son of Osiris—
      his body, his image.
O you my own *ba*-soul—
      my manifestations, my visible forms, my images.
O you *ba*-soul of Terrible of Face—
      his body, his image, his corpse.

O you *ba*-soul of the One Who Is in the Earth—
  his body, his image, his corpse.
O you *ba*-soul of the One of the Corpse—
  his body, his image, his corpse.
O you *ba*-soul of this my head which came forth from the mound of
the One Who Is in His Mound—
  his body, his image, his corpse.
O you *ba*-soul of the One Who Is in His Mound—
  his body, his image, his corpse.
O you *ba*-soul of the One of the Mound—
  his body, his image, his corpse.

O you *ba*-soul of Tatenen—
  his body, his image, his corpse.
O you *ba*-soul of the One of the Sarcophagus—
  his body, his image, his corpse.
O you *ba*-soul of the One of Crossing Through—
  his body, his image, his corpse.
O you *ba*-soul of the One of Water—
  his body, his image, his corpse.
O you *ba*-soul of the One Punishing of Face—
  his body, his image, his corpse.

CONCLUDING TABLEAU

5.77. Scene 77. The concluding scene is complex. A central, horizontal division
leads from left to right, ending at a solar disk that is astride the right, vertical division of the scene. At the left end of the scene is the prow of the solar bark, with
the ram-headed deity standing on the deck, facing right, a solar disk on his head,
holding a *was*-scepter; he is labeled "He Who Rightly Guides Those amongst
Whom He Is." In front of him is a vertically oriented scarab, "Khepri," with a bird
perched in front thereof, atop and oval, and named "Osiris." Twelve figures haul
the towrope of the bark toward the right, with (from right to left) four falcon-
headed figures, named "Horus," "One of Hauling," One of Crossing Through,"
and "One Who Holds the Rope"; four ram-headed figures, named "One of the

Ram-head," "Ram-shaped One," "Horned One," and "Great of Horns"; and four human-headed figures, named "[…]," "Beautiful of Face,"[175] "Wakeful One," and "Grasping One."

ABOVE THE HAULING FIGURES

These gods are in this fashion, hauling Re, lord of the horizon, and letting him go to rest in the eastern mountain, they saying to him the words: "The great one is in the Place of Destruction, his place is in the serpent bark."

5.78. Scene 78. The upper and lower divisions are crossed by a diagonal line, focused on the edges of the solar disk in the right end of the middle register, in each register slanting down from a figure at the left end of the upper and lower registers, wearing a divine beard, bending over a dome-like structure, elongated arms stretching down in front of the object; the upper bending deity is named "Hidden of Mystery," while the lower figure is named "Foremost of the Mystery, high of visible form." In the upper register the figure is upside-down. A disk appears in the upper portion of the interior of the object over which they bend.

ABOVE THE UPPER SCENE

This god is in this fashion, bending himself over the mysterious mound, in the forepart of which is the great mystery. This great god speaks before this god, as he positions himself upon the mysterious hill, in which is the great mystery. This great god speaks before this god. This god passes <in> the bark, his corpse, his visible form being content with his throne.

BEFORE THE UPPER SCENE

Osiris says to Re: "O behold me. Re, lord of life. Please call out to my *ba*-soul, cause that (I) run with you.—O Re."

She says to Re: "O Re <in> the upper part; please summon my *ba*-soul. You form the birth brick(s); Nut opens for you her arms."

---

175. Alternatively: "Turned of Face."

ABOVE THE LOWER SCENE

This god is in this fashion, bending himself over the mysterious mound, in the forepart of which is the great mystery. This great god speaks before this god, as he positions himself upon the mysterious hill, in which is the mystery. By him does this great god pass. It is this great god who issues commands to him. The *ba*-soul of this god passes <in> the bark, his corpse, his visible form resting on his throne.

BEFORE THE LOWER SCENE

Re speaks to this cavern, when he issues commands to this divine hill.

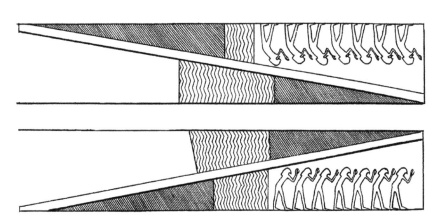

5.79, 5.80. Scene 79. A band of water lines stretches across the upper and lower divisions to the right of the scene. At the right end of the upper and lower divisions, upside-down in the upper division, are seven bowing figures, arms raised up before their faces; those in the upper register have human heads, those in the lower register are falcon-headed. Labels to the human-headed deities in the upper right (right to left) are "Mysterious of Manifestation"; "Mysterious of Visible Form"; "Great of Birth-form"; "One Who Is in the Waterway"; "Foremost of the Waterway"; "Giver (of Light?)"; "Shining One." The falcon-headed gods are named (right to left): "Horus, Great of Rays"; "Horus of Worship"; "Horus, Living of Manifestation"; "Horus of Visible Forms"; "Horus, Great of Glorious Appearances"; "Horus, Great of Nets(?)";[176] "Horus, Foremost of Places."

---

176. Alternatively: "Great of Cauldrons(?)."

BEFORE THE HUMAN-HEADED DEITIES

These gods are in this fashion, giving ovation to Re-Horakhty, when he enters into the belly of Nut.

BEFORE THE FALCON-HEADED DEITIES

These gods are in this fashion, giving praise and <creat>ing protection for Re-Horakhty, when he enters into the belly of Nut.

BETWEEN THE HAULERS AND THE SCARAB

"As we haul Re, so we accompany the sole lord, this one who becomes manifest, one emerging of head. *(to the solar deity)* Praise be to you, one great of *akh*-power. *(to the haulers):* Yours is the *ba*-soul of the one living of manifestations.

May the resting one go to rest within his solar disk—may Re go to rest within his solar disk. May this great god enter into his eastern mountain: (namely) the chief of the gods, who sees the patricians, who brightens the people, who illumines the face(s) of those upon the earth." So they say, the gods of the bank of Re-Horakhty.

5.81. Scene 80. Horizontally oriented at the right end, facing up, as though emerging to the left from the solar disk, are (right to left) the solar disk, a child with hand to mouth, and a ram-headed scarab. The concluding depiction may be read as "The ram-form of the night sun transforms into the flaming child of morning."

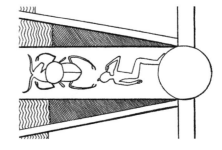

6

THE BOOKS OF THE CREATION OF THE SOLAR DISK

INTRODUCTION

The first study devoted to the Books of the Creation of the Solar Disk is Piankoff (1953), and the standard edition of both New Kingdom and Late period versions is now Joshua Roberson (2012). Commonly also known as the Books of the Earth,[1] the Books of the Creation of the Solar Disk encompass a diverse array of scenes, labels, and annotations that appear never to have coalesced into a single, canonical form. Individual tableaux, such as the image of the solar bark atop the double-headed Aker sphinx, attained a distinctive status and could be employed independently of the remainder of the composition. The predominant visual features of the Books of the Creation of the Solar Disk include scenes of the birth of the solar disk, the double-headed Aker sphinx, and the punishment of enemies. While a few solar barks are present within the tableaux, the solar deity appears chiefly in the form of large disks, as in the Book of Caverns; in several cases, different tableaux within the Books of the Creation of the Solar Disk and the Book of Caverns appear to share a common template (Abitz 1995, 158–64). The annotations within the Books of the Creation of the Solar Disk are often terse descriptions of the interaction of the solar god with specific deities, frequently emphasizing the effects of sunlight on the Netherworldly denizens.

Eight New Kingdom sources preserve major excerpts of scenes and texts from the Books of the Creation of the Solar Disk, including seven royal tombs (ranging in date from Merneptah to Ramesses IX) and the Osireion (Cenotaph of Seti I). In the Valley of the Kings, the Books of

---

1. On the books' chthonic associations and arguments in favor of this title, see Roberson 2012, 5–6.

the Creation of the Solar Disk or scenes pertaining thereto appear only within the sarcophagus chambers of the tombs. During the Third Intermediate period, the book appears in the tomb of Osorkon II, and several Late period Theban tombs also incorporate scenes and texts from the composition (Roberson 2012, 45–55); additional depictions of the double-lion Aker appear on Third Intermediate period "mythological" papyri (Roberson 2012, 295–99).[2]

Within the tomb of Ramesses VI, the composition has traditionally been divided into four sections; in acknowledgment of the book's overall bipartite structure, Roberson's (2012, 11–14) designations A, A2, B, and B2 have been retained in the present work. Due to the fragmentary nature of many of the sources of the Books of the Creation of the Solar Disk, such as the cryptographic texts in the Osireion[3] or the tomb of Ramesses III, not every source of the Books of the Creation of the Solar Disk is included in the present volume. The so-called "Merneptah Template" for the Books of the Creation of the Solar Disk, which also appears in the tomb of Tawosret, does not contain any scenes absent from the tomb of Ramesses VI, with the exception of a concluding representation.[4]

The diverse version of the Books of the Creation of the Solar Disk, like the distinct versions of the Books of the Solar-Osirian Unity, merit their translations as independent compositions in the present work; thus, the four "editions" of the Books of the Creation of the Solar Disk that contain uniquely attested scenes are translated in the present volume: Ramesses VI, Ramesses VII, Ramesses IX, and a textual template appearing on New Kingdom and Late period sarcophagi. The versions are presented in chronological order, and those annotations that are shared between versions cross-reference the appropriate text in an earlier example. The sequence of the four sections from the tomb of Ramesses VI follows that identified by Roberson (2012, 13), and annotations placed in registers

---

2. To these attestations can be added sarcophagi from the Nineteenth Dynasty through the Roman Era with one or more individual scenes of the Books of the Creation of the Solar Disk; as Roberson notes, "the ancient popularity of the Book of the Earth should be acknowledged as comparable to that of compositions like the Book of Caverns and Book of Gates" (2012, 10).

3. Roberson 2007; 2012, 303–7.

4. The concluding representation, which appears above a large ram-headed solar bird (Roberson 2012, 265–66), is a variant to the Concluding Scene of the Book of Caverns (for a comparison of the annotations as well as details within the scenes, see Roberson 2012, 192–95).

below or above their appropriate scenes are translated in the order of the scenes rather than maintaining the perturbated sequence within the tomb.[5] Unlike the other Netherworld Books, the Books of the Creation of the Solar Disk include annotations written in hieroglyphic, and occasionally, hieratic script; even in the hieroglyphic texts, some sign shapes represent adaptations from original hieratic forms (Roberson 2012, 74–79). Furthermore, the Books of the Creation of the Solar Disk evince a number of unusual orthographies (e.g., *nṯr.wt* for *nṯr.w*, *ḥꜣ.wt* for *ḥꜣ.t*), and due to their frequency, such orthographies are neither marked nor commented upon.

Tomb of Ramesses VI

The introduction to the Books of the Creation of the Solar Disk in the tomb of Ramesses VI depicts the king with his arms raised in adoration towards a scene of the king (shown twice), with Isis and Nephthys, holding aloft a winged sun disk above which is a solar bark atop Aker. A goddess called the Mysterious One (Shetayt) embodies the entire Netherworld, and the unified *ba*-soul of Re-Osiris must pass through her; the same goddess appears in Book of Caverns, Division 5 (Scene 50), providing further evidence of a relationship between the two compositions.[6] A large disk embraced by arms and surrounded by smaller disks and stars represents the re-creation of time in the Netherworld, a theme also prominent in the Book of Gates. The final scene of the register shows Osiris within a shrine, his mysterious chest below him, as the corpses and shades of his enemies are cooked in giant cauldrons; the *ba*-soul of the sun alights upon the corpse of Osiris, and he breathes when the sun's rays reach him.

Register 2, which contains two subregisters, opens with a depiction of four ram-headed and flame-headed beings, guardians of the corpse of the West (depicted in the lowest register). The two central scenes within the register depict the lifting up of the *ba*-soul of the unified Re-Osiris and the emergence of Horus from the corpse of his father; solar disks glow in the lower subregister, illumining *ba*-souls and presaging the rising of the sun from the eastern horizon. The Hathor head emerging from disk at the

---

5. For misalignment of annotation and tableaux in the Books of the Creation of the Solar Disk, see also Mauric-Barbério 2010.

6. The template of Shetayt, the Mysterious One, is discussed in Billing 2006.

right end of Register 2 is a particularly powerful evocation of the defeat of Apep and the *perpetuum mobile* of the solar journey.

As in the Book of Caverns, the punishment of the damned dominates the lowest register of Section A. Fiery fates await the corpses of the enemies of the solar god, their heads literally cooked within giant cauldrons at the end of the register. The control of chaotic forces, including the serpent Apep, allows for the regeneration of the solar corpse, here represented as a giant female mummy called "She Who Destroys." The solar god emerges from this corpse as the new-born Khepri, appearing as a winged scarab coming forth from the solar disk and pushing a smaller disk before him.

Associated with the left wall of the sarcophagus chamber (Section A) are scenes on columns at the rear of the chamber (Section A2). In the upper register, the unified *ba*-soul of Re-Osiris emerges from the coils of Apep on his flight through the Netherworld. An anthropomorphic representation of Aker in the middle register interacts with the solar *ba*-soul; to the right, Osirian mummies are bathed in the light of sun disks lifted up from the Place of Destruction, although the putrefaction of the mummies prevents Re himself from visiting this part of the Netherworld. The lower register is again dedicated to the punishment of the "Destroyed Ones," who are bound, and according to the annotation, cut up.

The next part of the Books of the Creation of the Solar Disk consists of Section B and B2, on the right wall and engaged columns of the sarcophagus chamber of the Tomb of Ramesses VI. The top and bottom registers of the four registers of Section B include depictions of Aker (human-headed above, fully leonine below). Section B begins with a depiction of a large mummy called "Gleaming of Head, who guards corpses," and the annotation describes how Re passes by and the mummies breathe by means of his voice. The middle of Register 1 shows Re in his bark atop an Aker sphinx, while below a solar disk illumines the solar corpse; this image summarizes the entire solar cycle as well as portraying the unification of Re and Osiris (Roberson 2012, 136–38). Much of Register 2 focuses upon the re-creation of time, and the unified Re-Osiris appears within a giant funnel-shaped object, probably a clepsydra (Barguet 1978), protected by the Encircling Serpent; the entire scene symbolizes the rebirth of the hours and thus the recreation of time in the Netherworld, a process overseen by the unified Re-Osiris. The lowest register can function as a concluding scene (Roberson 2012, 152–53), an image of the solar god being hauled from the Netherworld, again embodied by Aker.

Tomb of Ramesses VII

The tomb of Ramesses VII (KV 1), possessing one of the simplest plans within the Valley of the Kings, contains excerpts from the Book of Gates and Book of Caverns, as well as the Books of the Creation of the Solar Disk (Hornung 1990b). The axis of the burial chamber of KV 1 is unusual, being parallel, rather than perpendicular, to the main axis of the tomb (Roberson 2012, 42–43). Each long wall of the burial chamber in the tomb of Ramesses VII contains two registers of images with scenes and annotations taken exclusively from the Books of the Creation of the Solar Disk.

On the Left Wall, the composition appears to begin with an image of Osiris, Ruler of the West, and throughout Registers 1–2, various praising and protecting deities interact with representations of the solar corpse. In the second scene, the gods are said to acclaim the "visible forms of Re," which include a jackal-headed staff, the "Neck of Re," and a ram, the "ram of rams." Each register contains a representation of the corpse of Osiris: a striding nude male figure within a sarcophagus (Left Wall, Register 1, Scene 2) or as a series of flesh signs within a mound crowned with a ram (Left Wall, Register 2, Scene 7). Re, as the solar disk, is present throughout the scenes on the Left Wall, most notably within the belly of the crocodile Wenty; as the annotation states, the noxious creature "vomits and ejaculates the eye of Re that is in his belly." The rebirth of the solar disk signals an emergence of the "double *ba*-soul," the unified Re-Osiris.

Register 1 on the Right Wall mirrors that of the Left Wall, being dominated by deities who praise images of the solar deity. The depictions of the corpse of Re-Osiris on the Left Wall are replaced by Re's disk and his flaming eye on the Right Wall; ram-headed figures, the *ba*-soul of Re, appear within disks in Register 1, Scene 10. The register concludes with gods who protect the flaming *akhet*-eye, whose light grants breath to the Netherworld Dwellers. Register 2 includes scenes attested in the burial chamber of the tomb of Ramesses VI and emphasizes Osiris as corpse of the solar deity. In Scene 13, the "Corpse of Khepri" faces the "*Ba*-Soul of Orion," a succinct means of expressing the unity of Re (normally the *ba*-soul) and Osiris (normally the corpse). In the next scene, Osiris emerges from the body of Atum, a process that Horus protects. The last two scenes in Register 2 depict the punishment of solar enemies, including the slicing up of Apep and binding of the damned.

A concluding scene for the composition in the Tomb of Ramesses VII can be found at the beginning of Register 1 on the Right Wall. Despite its restricted size, the rounded, sandy band pierced by a solar disk signals both the departure from the Netherworld and the entry into the eastern horizon. The two horizontally-oriented pairs of arms mimic the arms of Shu in the Book of the Hidden Chamber, Hour 12 and the arms of Nun lifting the solar disk in the Book of Gates, Hour 12. Similar pairs of arms form the concluding scene for the enigmatic composition in the Books of the Solar-Osirian Unity, Second Shrine of Tutankhamun (pp. 551–55).

Tomb of Ramesses IX

The Tomb of Ramesses IX (KV 6) includes excerpts from all of the major compositions of the Netherworld Books.[7] Hastily executed after the death of the pharaoh, the burial chamber is oriented along the main axis of the tomb. The long walls of the burial chamber include scenes from the Book of Caverns as well as the Books of the Creation of the Solar Disk, with a single scene from the Book of the Hidden Chamber. The figures of Osiris and the Mysterious One (Shetayt) from the Book of Caverns, Division 5 flank the doorway into the burial chamber. The short wall opposite the doorway contains the composition the Awakening of Osiris and the Transit of the Solar Barks (Roberson 2013). Originally published by Felix Guilmant (1907, pls. 90–92), the translation of the texts from the Books of the Creation of the Solar Disk presented below employs the collated and improved edition of Roberson (2012, 389–404).

The Left Wall of the burial chamber is divided into three registers that intersperse scenes and annotations from the Books of the Creation of the Solar Disk with depictions from the Book of Caverns. Register 1 focuses upon the corpse of Osiris, variously represented as a mummy or a recumbent, ejaculating figure within a sarcophagus. In the annotation to the fourth scene (Left Wall, Register 1, Scene 4), Osiris is given the epithet "Djeba-demedj," the unified Re-Osiris who appears so prominently in the Book of Adoring Re in the West (p. 63). A more animated corpse, one who has regained his sexual potency, forms of the focus of the next scene (Left Wall, Register 1, Scene 3); this scene—with an often headless figure of Osiris—appears again on a corpus of sarcophagi (see below, p. 521). The register includes a scene from the Book of Caverns that emphasizes the

---

7. Abitz 1990, 10–21; while individual hours of the Book of Gates do not appear within the tomb, doorways reminiscent of the *sbḫ.t*-portals of the composition do appear within the decoration of the tomb (Guilmant 1907).

assembling of the flesh of the solar god within his mysterious sarcophagus, illumined by the rays of the disk (although the annotations to the figures do not appear in the burial chamber of Ramesses IX). Register 2 contains one scene from the Books of the Creation of the Solar Disk—four figures beneath shade-signs that likewise appear within a series of scenes on sarcophagi—and three tableaux from the Book of Caverns. The scarab form of the solar god in the middle of the register, emerging from two mounds, signals the rising of the sun in the eastern horizon. Three partially damaged scenes fill Register 3, with fragmentary annotations; the focus shifts again to the reanimated corpse of the solar god.

The Right Wall of the burial chamber contains two registers—a smaller, upper register and a larger, lower register with a central scene of a deity within a funnel-shaped structure and sub-registers with scenes to either side. Register 1 begins with the birth of the solar disk from the crocodile Wenty, a scene already present in the Tomb of Ramesses VII (Left Wall, Register 2, Scene 8). The remaining scenes in Register 1 lack labels and annotations, but their iconography emphasizes the transformation of Re into Khepri as well as the praising of the solar disk by chthonic, shrew-headed deities.[8] The subdivided Register 2 continues the association with Khepri, depicting a scarab-crowned figure within a multiple-headed serpent, a scene that appears within the Book of the Hidden Chamber, Hour 6, Register 2, Scene 65 and whose annotation labels the figure the "corpse of Khepri" (p. 192). The focal point of the large Register 2 on the Right Wall of the burial chamber in the tomb of Ramesses IX is a large funnel-shaped object containing a large ithyphallic figure and twelve goddesses holding disks; a parallel scene from the Tomb of Ramesses VI was described above (p. 460),[9] and the funnel-shaped object may be identified with a clepsydra. The Tomb of Ramesses IX includes annotations to each of the goddesses, describing their control over light rays. Following this scene is a lengthy speech of Re, describing his journey through the Netherworld and the effects of his presence on those who dwell therein.

---

8. For shrew-headed deities within the Book of Caverns, compare Division 2, Register 1, Scene 16 and Register 2, Scene 18.

9. For other parallels, including a Twenty-Eighth Dynasty cartonnage, see Roberson 2012, 179–88.

Sarcophagi: Ramesside and Late Period

A corpus of Late period sarcophagi (Type I) containing excerpts from the Books of the Creation of the Solar Disk has direct parallels in the New Kingdom (Roberson 2012, 59–63), so while the decorative scheme clearly resonated with Late period theologians, the ensemble of compositions—including the Book of Gates and Books of the Creation of the Solar Disk—dates at least to the Ramesside period.[10] The entirety of the composition on the sarcophagi has been termed the Book of Resurrection through Deconstruction (Manassa 2007a), which along with the Awakening of Osiris and the Transit of the Solar Barques (Roberson 2013) remains one of the shortest Netherworldly compositions. The "book" commences with the Book of Gates, Hour 1, a transitional zone between this world and the next (see pp. 257–59); based on the New Kingdom versions of this text, the "deconstruction" of the solar eye appears as a prerequisite for its resurrection and subsequent creative acts. On the Late period sarcophagi, the sun god's speech, although perturbated, describes the solar deity as a creator deity and "Hidden One."

The next portion of the sarcophagus composition consists of several scenes on the long walls of the sarcophagi; based on the running annotation, the first scene is an image of men kneeling beneath shades who "mourn over the secret corpse of Osiris." The mourning theme is continued with images of Isis and Nephthys who weep for their brother. A scene with an anthropoid Aker and four catfish-headed deities relates strongly to both the Books of the Creation of the Solar Disk and the Book of Caverns; the focus of these figures is a small, egg-shaped object that represents the "secret of the One within the Earth." Ram and jackal-headed staffs labeled the "head" and "neck" of Re respectively and accompanied by a ram-headed god and two rejoicing men complete the first long side.

The second long wall of the sarcophagus presents three scenes, including an ithyphallic (sometimes headless) recumbent figure and ba-birds atop sarcophagi with mummies. These scenes emphasize the fate of the ba-soul, who must alight upon the mummy each night before flying off with the solar deity; although these mummies are rotting they are in the "company of the Great One (Osiris)." The ultimate template of the union

---

10. A parallel for one scene—that on the foot end of the sarcophagi—is first attested in the Books of the Solar-Osirian Unity, Second Shrine of Tutankhamun (see pp. 551–52).

of *ba*-soul and corpse is the ejaculating image of Osiris, whom the solar *ba*-soul visits and vivifies, in some cases dramatically depicting the head itself being carried off with the sun each day.

Re-creation through deconstruction continues in the concluding scene of the book, a tableau that appears within the Book of the Creation of the Solar Disk in the Tomb of Ramesses VI (Section B, Register 2, Scene 31).[11] The sarcophagus annotation, which differs from the Tomb of Ramesses VI version, again describes the unification of the light of Re with the corpse of Osiris. At the appropriate time, this combination of opposite forces initiates a reaction that leads literally to the re-creation of time.

Tomb of Ramesses VI

Section A

Register 1 (Plate 36)

6.1. Scene 1. A depiction in two registers; top: a solar bark containing a ram-headed deity who is flanked by a scarab-headed deity "Khepri" and baboon-headed deity, "Thoth," atop Aker, with a uraeus—human arms raised as though supporting the bark, resting atop the forelegs of Aker, facing in toward the heads of Aker; bottom: Pharaoh Ramesses VI—doubled—lifts up a disk below a winged scarab whose wings are supported by "Isis" and "Nephthys." Scene reproduced from Roberson 2012, fig. 5.1, by permission of the author

The King of Upper and Lower Egypt, Ramesses (VI) lifts up Re.

---

11. Myśliwiec 1981; with corrections in Manassa 2007a, 55–62.

6.2. Scene 2. A standing goddess, "Mysterious One," looks back over her shoulder with her arms bent—the left holds a solar disk while the right holds a ram-headed bird. Two serpents with human torsos rear up to either side of the goddess, while a serpent and crocodile stand on end next to her feet.

ABOVE THE DISK

That which is within them, when those pertaining thereto leap up.[12]

This goddess in this fashion.[13] Over her two hands does this great god pass. He of the Head[14] who is to the west of the Mysterious One acclaims the great god. The head of the Mysterious One is in the Upper Netherworld, her feet in the Lower Netherworld. The Double *Ba*-Soul is passing by her corpse.

The two who go forth are in their place because of the flame and the fire that are in the goddess. The Mysterious One exists with (her) head toward[15] Terrible of Face, the Encircling Serpent who is in the mysterious land, hidden of darkness.

The corpses of those mysterious of face[16] are <in> the places of this goddess. Over the corpse of She of the Earth does this god pass.

He of Terrible of Face is in this fashion, as he leaps up before[17] the feet of the Mysterious One—(it is) Terrible of Face.

---

12. For the verb *nhp*, describing the actions of the snakes crossing the body, see p. 169 n. 70.

13. For the introductory formula *nn n nṯr.w m sḫr pn*, see Roberson 2012, 101–4.

14. This is the name of one of the serpents with human torso.

15. Roberson 2012, 322 proposes reading "upon Nehaher," but since the goddess faces the rearing Nehaher serpent, turning her face over her back, the translation proposed here fits better with the depiction of the goddess in the accompanying scene.

16. Contra Roberson 2012, 323, "the corpses of those who are Mysterious of Places belong to this goddess" (this rendering ignores the *ḥr*-face and takes *n.t* improbably as "belong to"). The mysterious of face who are associated with the Mysterious One appear in the Book of Caverns, in the introduction to Litanies 7–20 (p. 416): "That this Mysterious One exists is with her head in the darkness and her feet in the darkness, those mysterious of face having united with her arms."

17. For *nhp ḥr*, compare the *ʿḥḥ ḥr* "fly up before" of the Book of Gates, Hour 12, Register 2, Scene 89 (Hornung 1979b, 391); text translated on p. 330.

6.3. Scene 3. A large disk—labeled "Solar Disk"—is embraced by two sets of arms emerging from the ground; atop the disk is a mummiform male figure with a large sun disk on his head, "Hidden of Flame." He is flanked by two spitting uraei, whose flames trace the edges of the larger disk; they are labeled "One who goes forth from <the horizon(?)> daily" and "One who goes forth from …." To either side of the 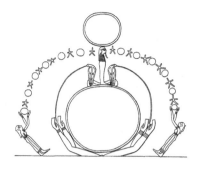 mummiform figure's head is a series of six stars alternating with six disks (total of twelve stars and twelve disks in the entire scene) in an arc extending down to the outstretched arms of two female figures.

Accessing the corpse that is within Nun, after the corpses of the two goddesses, by this great god, while he passes by the corpse of Dark of Heart, who is in the Hidden Chamber.

"O corpse of Nun who is within the earth, who causes the four ba-souls therein to breathe! O corpses of the two goddesses, who guard the corpse of Nun, who receive that which is in his mouth! Cause the ba-souls of the Netherworld dwellers to breathe! O, oh, give to me your arm(s)!—for[18] I am issuing to you your commands! O, oh, give to me your arm(s)!—for I am calling your ba-souls! O, oh, give to me your arm(s)!"

This god exists in this fashion. That he takes up his position atop his horizon is so that he might guard the hours that are in the following of his ba-soul. When he calls to them, they enter after him. When he illumines them, they go forth from the corpse of She Who Is Hidden of Mysteries.[19]

Then this great god passes by after his hours. While making their visible forms do they turn back. After this great god has passed over them, these uraei swallow the flames that are in their mouths, without the gods, the akh-spirits, or the dead entering over the corpse of this great god, because of the flames of his uraei.

---

18. For the use of mk continuing an imperative, see p. 120 n. 129.

19. She Who Is Hidden of Mysteries occurs again below and is the same as the name of the innermost realm of the Netherworld in the Book of Adoring Re in the West, Litany 7 (p. 116): "Indeed, you have caused that I ascend to the chamber, hidden of mysteries, in which Osiris exists." For the phrase "hidden of mysteries," see Darnell 2004, 289–93.

Passing the corpses mysterious of visible forms, who are in the Hidden Chamber, by this great god, while he passes by She Who Is Hidden of Mysteries. "O corpses, mysterious of visible forms, who are within the Hidden Chamber, and you great corpse of Dark of Heart, whose shrine those within the earth guard. O behold, I am crossing over your shrine, setting punishment among your enemies. When you hear my voice, you breathe! That my *ba*-soul comes down[20] is to guard you! When I call the corpses among which you are, their *ba*-souls pass by following me. O, oh, I am traversing your shrine, and my children are coming into being."

The six have passed by after Re. She of the Disk is giving (her) arm to her hidden ones. The six have passed by after Re. She of Hiddenness is giving (her) arm to her hidden ones.

That the flames of this uraeus come forth from the fires of this great horizon is after the two mysterious arms have received him.

That the flames of <this> uraeus come forth from the fires of this great horizon is with the two mysterious arms receiving him.

6.4. Scene 4. This complex scene is focused on a shrine of Osiris, containing in its upper register a figure of the god adored by a male human figure and *ba*-bird emerging from mounds— "Corpse of Geb" (behind) and "*Ba*-Soul of Osiris of the West" (in front)—and in its lower register a chest guarded by a male human figure, "He Who Makes Mysterious," and a jackal-headed male figure, "Anubis"; above these two figures is the label: "These gods in this fashion, their arms above the mysterious chest of Anubis"; labeling the chest: "Mysterious Chest."[21] To either side of the shrine is a male figure holding up a cauldron with pus-

---

20. The term *snk* "go down" ("*snk*," WÄS, 4:175.7) is a pun on *snk* "to be dark" ("*snk*," WÄS, 4:175.11–13), as noted in Roberson 2012, 319 n. 104. The setting of the sun, its darkening, occurs so that the solar deity may protect the blessed denizens of the Netherworld.

21. For the mysterious chest, see Roberson 2012, 283; compare also the scenes in the Book of Caverns, Division 2, Register 3, Scene 21 (pp. 361–62) and the Books of the Solar-Osirian Unity, the Second Shrine of Tutankhamun, Side 1, Register 3, Scene 9 (p. 543).

tule and shade signs to right, pustule signs only to left; flanking each figure are two male mummies. These figures are called (left to right): "He of the Cauldron"; "He Who Swallows *Ba*-Souls"; "He Who Swallows Corpses"; "He Who Swallows Corpses"; "He of the Pit"; and "He Who Swallows Limbs." Three bound, decapitated enemies are placed to either side of the base of the shrine, while above the entire image is an inverted figure holding flames and decapitated enemies, whose blood flows into the cauldrons.

Accessing the corpses, mysterious of visible affairs who are in the Hidden Chamber by this great god, while he enters One Who Hides the Mysteries. "O you corpse, mysterious of visible affairs who is in the Hidden Chamber, this great corpse, Dark of Heart, whose shrine those within the earth guard. O, behold, I am traversing your shrine, setting punishment among your enemies. When you hear my voice, you breathe! That my *ba*-soul comes down[22] is to guard you! When I call the corpses among which you are, their *ba*-souls pass by following me. O, oh, I am traversing your shrine, and my children come into being. O, oh, I am traversing your shrine, and they ..."

These gods in this fashion outside of the Hidden Chamber, in which is the corpse of the god, (and) Osiris Foremost of the West, (and) those who are in the earth.

This god in this fashion, his flame between his two arms, as he chastises the heads, which he burns up.

The shades, corpses, *ba*-souls, and limbs—that amongst which they are: they burn them. This great god is setting their punishments. Afterwards, he passes by them (in) the West.

This god in this fashion, the rays[23] of his mysteries entering into the mysteries that descend from his *ba*-soul, as they enter into the earth that they illuminate.

These enemies are in this fashion, chastised outside of the Hidden Chamber. They are in front of their darkness, without illumination.

These rebels are in this fashion outside of the Hidden Chamber. The great god is setting their punishments (upon) them.

---

22. For the punning of the term *snk*, see above, p. 468 n. 20.

23. For an alternate reading of this as *wȝḏw* "fresh things (=blood?)," see Goebs 2008, 222 (see also p. 223 for an interpretation of this scene in the Books of the Creation of the Solar Disk as "the slow spreading of red light—most likely in the sky or horizon—and this process is symbolically rendered as the blood flowing from beheaded corpses of deceased enemies.")

REGISTER 2 (PLATE 36)

6.5. Scene 5. Four ram-headed deities in a slightly bowed position with their arms placed in front of them alternate with four male figures with flaming tapers in place of their heads.

These gods in this fashion, guarding the interior of the mysterious and hidden sky that is in the Netherworld. The speech of Re over its oval is that which causes the corpses to breathe, as they guard. Re calls these gods, with the result that they guard their *ba*-souls, they passing after him, while their corpses remain in their places. Now, after he passes over them, darkness follows.

What Re says (to) the gods who guard the Fiery Ones: "O eight gods who guard the Fiery Ones, whose *ba*-souls are in the following of the mysterious corpses, who guard for the female one whose head is in the darkness of their feet, who guard and guide (in) the mysterious place which they illuminate with flame. May they guard the West and the two sisters! Oh! I pass by you, Fiery Ones who bear torches."

These gods in this fashion; they guard the Fiery Ones. Re speaks to them, he commending ⌜to them their visible forms⌝. After Re passes by them, they swallow their torches. Their rays follow after the *ba*-souls of these gods who pass by following this god, when he passes by the mysterious place.

What Re says when he passes his mysteries, when he passes the corpses of the West: "O West! O West! She who guards her corpse! (O) West, Maat in the gate that is therein. I pass by you, I traverse you, destroyer of *ba*-souls. Hail to you! Behold, I pass by you. You are indeed the one who hides what is within her, her great mysterious corpse. Hail to you Osiris king, lord of the two lands, Nebmaatre, beloved of Amun, justified. Praise to the son of Re, lord of glorious appearances, Ramesses (VI), divine one, ruler of Heliopolis, justified. Give praise!—for I am passing by you. You are indeed the one whose corpse I illumine."

6.6. Scene 6. A ram-headed deity holding a *was*-scepter with a small disk in
front of him looks to the left over a
scene of a mound and four sarcophagi.
The sarcophagi are arranged vertically in two columns to either side of
the mound; the upper sarcophagi contain male human mummies, while the

lower hold male mummies with *nb*-baskets in place of heads; the uppermost two
sarcophagi have labeled figures: "Thoth" (upper left) and "Clothed One" (upper
right). Within the central mound is a male figure bending over toward the right
with his arms before him, as though in adoration to the ram-headed deity to the
right; his feet and the lower portions of his legs are not visible.

REGISTER 2 (UPPER) (PLATE 36)

6.7. Scene 7. Two male deities—"Honoring One" (left)
and "Protector" (right)—lift
up a *ba*-bird wearing a white
crown, the *ba*-soul of Osiris.
Two mounds, each contain-

ing a supine ram-headed mummy, with head to the left, appear on either side;
inside the left mound is the label "The corpse of the second one, following Re";
within the right mound is "The corpse of He Who Roars, following Re."

These gods in this fashion, they lifting up the *ba*-soul of Osiris for him; they
protect[24] those in the mounds within which are the corpses who follow Re.
This great god speaks to these gods, with the result that he illuminates
for them by means of what is on[25] his head, as he calls to the corpses that
are with him. Their *ba*-souls pass by in his following. Then <darkness>
hides them after he passes by them. The king of Upper and Lower Egypt,
the Osiris king, lord of the two lands, Nebmaatre, beloved of Amun, the

---

24. Roberson 2012, 331 and n. 172, follows Piankoff (1953, 49 n. 7) in reading
ḥknw, suggesting the apparent walking legs may write the *k*. The walking legs probably derive erroneously from the verb *ḥn*, "to hurry" ("*ḥn*," *WÄS*, 3:103.6–21) the signs
writing *ḥn*, the verb "to protect" ("*ḥn*," *WÄS*, 3:101.7–11), the same appearing in the
name of the deity on the right supporting the *ba*-soul of Osiris—"Protector."

25. For *m* as "on," see Darnell 2004, 296; the text appears to make reference to the
White Crown on the head of the *ba*-soul.

son of Re, lord of glorious appearances, lord of Maat, Ramesses (VI), the divine one, ruler of Heliopolis, justified before the lords of Maat. Meanwhile, another is within you, with Isis, your mat among all the great ones.[26]

6.8. Scene 8. A large oval contains a male deity whose recumbent body forms a half circle; he is the "[Corpse] of Osiris." Out of his body comes a praising falcon-headed god, "Corpse of Horus," behind whom is a disk. Two  goddesses, "Corpse of Isis of the Throat"[27] (on the left, at the feet of the deity in the oval) and "Corpse of Nephthys" (on the right, at the head of the deity in the oval), with their arms in a protective gesture appear to either side of the oval.

> What Re says to the goddesses who guard the corpse of the god:[28]
> "O, raise yourself, He Who Belongs to the Netherworld!
> You are casting out the darkness that is within you!
> O, raise yourself, He Who Belongs to the Netherworld!
> Cause your *ba*-soul to go to rest upon your corpse!
> O, raise yourself, He Who Belongs to the Netherworld,
>   as I cause that you unite with those who are in your following!
> O, raise yourself, He Who Belongs to the Netherworld!
> May you go to rest with those who are with my head!
> O, raise yourself, He Who Belongs to the Netherworld—Re!"

This great god is in this fashion in his oval that is in the Netherworld. He of Behdet comes forth from the corpse of his father, acclaiming this one who bore him.[29] His two sisters join together his corpse. This great god speaks to him, when he sees the light of his solar disk.

---

26. Roberson 2012, 331–32 suggests *nb.w* (*m₃ˁ.t*) "possessors (of *maʿat*)."

27. Reading *ḥty.t*; for the throat in this context compare the Book of Adoring Re in the West, Address 35, in which He of the Sarcophagus is said to be "breathing of throat." Note that the first of the twelve goddesses in the Book of the Hidden Chamber, Hour 1, Register 1, Scene 2 is "She of the Throat." For the personified throat, see "Ḥtyt," *LGG* 5:562. Roberson 2012, 172 n. 297, reads the throat sign as *ˁmy.t*, suggesting "that which was swallowed," the phallus of Osiris.

28. Although Re addresses the goddesses, he speaks to the corpse; he perhaps here is speaking on behalf of the goddesses.

29. Horus coming forth from the corpse of his father Osiris is not a normal procreative process, but relates to a series of scenes and texts that suggest the already

What Re says to the gods who raise up the *ba*-soul of Re to the gods: "You gods who raise up the *ba*-soul of Osiris—Behold, I am passing by you, commanding to you your visible forms, so that you might raise up the *ba*-soul of Osiris for him, those within the Netherworld having surely rejoiced for the *ba*-soul of Osiris, even the image of Foremost of the Westerners."

6.9. Scene 9. Seven nude male figures, with frontally depicted faces,[30] striding to the left and facing forward appear within individual mounds, arranged as a group of three over a group of four. To the right is a standing male deity— "Horus of the Two Arms"—facing right, with his arms in a gesture of pro-

tection over a male figure, "He of the West," facing left and emerging from another supine, striding male figure, head to left, facing upward, "Atum."[31] (Note that this text appears to the right of Section A, Register 1, Scene 1.)

Passing the corpses, mysterious of visible forms, by this great god, while he passes by the corpse of Osiris,[32] speaking to those who are in his following.

---

putrid corpse of Osiris engenders Horus; for parallels in other Netherworld Books and the Book of the Dead, see Manassa 2007a, 139–40 (exempting the discussion of the Tomb of Ramesses VI, Section A, Register 2, Scene 9, which depicts the birth of the Osirian corpse, not Horus).

30. The solar significance of frontal depictions in Egyptian art, see Volokhine 2000, 75–76 (with a discussion of these figures from the Books of the Creation of the Solar Disk on p. 79).

31. Atum in not mentioned otherwise in the annotation, so it is important to recognize him as the vessel through which Osiris must be reborn; this process, depicted in the Books of the Creation of the Solar Disk and paralleled in the Book of Caverns (Division 4, Register 1, Scene 41, see pp. 387–88), finds a textual description in Coffin Texts Spell 312 (CT 4.74h–76c): "I am one whom Atum-Re created from his flesh, who came into being from the root of his eye, whom Atum created and he glorified, whose faces he made distinct so that they might exist with him...." (translation and commentary in Dobbin-Bennet 2014, 261–66).

32. The "corpse of Osiris" is the male figure (also labeled "He of the West") emerging from the body of the god Atum; a proper reconstruction of the text indicates that this is not an image of Horus emerging from Osiris as in the Tomb of Ramesses VI, Section A, Register 2, Scene 8, but rather the birth of the Osirian corpse from Atum (Roberson 2012, 170–71; contra Manassa 2007a, 139).

What Re says to Osiris, the corpse of the god that is within the Nether-world: "O, Osiris, mysterious one, distinguished of visible forms, speaking of corpse.[33] O, behold, I am passing by your cavern, unique image who guards the West, to whom those who are there, the Netherworld dwellers, call, whose heart breathes by means of my voice, with the result that the *ba*-souls flourish for me, Protective One."[34]

REGISTER 2 (LOWER) (PLATE 36)

6.10. Scene 10. A central sun disk adored by two human-armed uraei has a winged scarab emerg-ing from it. To the left are three ovals—two on the ground-line, the bottoms of the ovals disap-pearing beneath the ground-line,  with a third, complete oval above the lower left oval—containing bull-headed (upper oval), crocodile-headed (lower left oval), and serpent-headed (lower right oval) mummiform deities, all facing right. The names of the deities are "Bull of the West," "Fierce One," and "He of the Serpent." To the right of the central disk with uraei and winged scarab is an oval containing a vulture-headed mummiform deity, "He of the *Ba*-soul," facing right. To the right of that oval are two praising arms emerging from the earth, palms to the left. At the right end of the scene stands a ram-headed deity, facing left, with *was*-scepter and disk before him.

These gods in this fashion, their corpses and the king of Upper and Lower Egypt, Nebmaatre, beloved of Amun, are in their mounds, while they are to either side of the solar disk—his birth forms and his mysteries.[35] The *ba*-soul of Re speaks over his solar disk, issuing commands to those with him concerning the mysteries of those in heaven, when he goes forth, having come into being as He Who Belongs to His Rays, his two arms having

---

33. Compare the Book of Adoring Re in the West, Litany 6: "O Re, come to me, rightly traveling, with the result that my body speaks as Osiris." Also possible (Rober-son 2012, 328) is a reading "while my corpse speaks."

34. "Protective One" is possibly also the name of one of the bending figures in Books of the Solar-Osirian Unity in the Tomb of Ramesses IX, Enigmatic Wall, Left Section, Register 3 (see p. 567).

35. For birth forms compare the Book of Caverns, Litany 9 and Division 6, Regis-ter 2, Scene 68, where the birth forms are in two mounds (pp. 440–41).

become the two children of Khepri, who is content with his two wings,[36] this great god passing by these gods in this fashion, with the result that they praise his glow. Their *ba*-souls pass by in his following. The great god makes his manifestations, as he calls the *ba*-souls among whom he is. Then the darkness conceals them.

These gods in this fashion, uniting He Who Belongs to the Manifestations, his children that are in the Netherworld. The two uraei receive his wings, the two arms of He of the Earth, with the result that He of the *Ba*-Soul—the *ba*-soul of Re—unites with[37] his officials, the great gods, his manifestations, he going forth (in) his light, when this god passes by in this fashion over the cavern of the mound.

6.11. Scene 11. A Hathoric head, shown en face, emerges from a large disk near the center of this scene. Uraei—"Devourer" to the left and "Flaming One" to the right—flank the disk, facing in toward it, with a serpent in a v-shape atop the disk, tail to left and head to right, with a portion of the serpent body hidden in the area where the head joins the disk; two gods grasp the serpent to either side of the disk, "Atum" to the left and "He Who Seizes" to the right, while a male figure to the far left, "Upper One," raises his arms in adoration. To the right of the group is a ram-headed god, facing left, with *was*-scepter and small disk; at the far-right end of the scene two arms emerge from the ground-line, elbows slightly bent, hands holding up a solar disk; the arms are labeled "Two Arms of Nun."

36. For the appendages of the solar deity as goddesses, compare the texts and depictions in the version of the Books of the Solar-Osirian Unity, Tomb of Ramesses VI (563 and n. 62).

37. Reading *ḫnm n* as *ḫnm m* ("*ḫnm m*," WÄS, 3:380.24).

REGISTER 3 (PLATE 36)

6.12. Scene 12. Two female figures secure a standing prisoner, arms bound behind; they are labeled "She of the Greeting Gesture" (on the left) and "She Who Savors" (to the right). To the right are four alternating figures of goddesses to the left, facing right, and bound male figures, kneeling and facing right, each labeled "Enemy," with fire spouting from their heads; the goddesses are named (left to right): "She Who Burns," "Fire," "She Who Scorches," and "She of the Flame."

These god<dess>es in this fashion, binding the corpses of their enemies, and casting fire among them. This great god is inflicting their punishment even after he passes over them. In the darkness do they exist, without seeing (any) light. What these goddesses hear is the voice of Re, with the result that they breathe from it (the voice of Re), these goddesses placing fire among the enemies of Re, even after he passes by them, and assigns to them their visible forms.

What Re says when he passes over this mysterious cavern, She Who Is Great of Blaze: "O She Who Is Mysterious of Blaze, corpses of Igeret who guard the darkness. O, behold, I pass by you, Mysterious One, I reach She Who Is Great of Fire. O, guide me! O, receive me, one great of mysteries! May you swallow the fire that is within the *ba*-souls who follow those who pass by. Praise to you! I traverse you, those within their rejoicing. I give praise because of the bending (of arms)."[38]

---

38. Roberson 2012, 342 n. 241 reads *qʿḥ* as a term for sunlight, but the actions of the goddesses whom the solar deity addresses involve the twisting back of the arms of the bound enemies. Compare also the use of the term *qʿḥ* for "submit" (Meeks 1998a, 385 [no. 77.4369]), here perhaps with the sense of submission rendered by the prisoners. The term also appears as a verb for bending the arm in the Book of Adoring Re in the West (Hornung 1975, 207; see p. 117).

6.13. Scene 13. Four bearded gods each grasp an inverted, decapitated figure. Beneath each figure is the label "Decapitated," and the figures themselves bear the following four names (left to right): "He Who Belongs to the Decapitated"; "Great of Decapitation"; "He Who Is among the Decapitated"; "He of the Slaughter."

What Re says (to) the gods who guard the fire: "O, gods who guard the fire! O, behold, I am passing over you, while you are called from your cavern, and I commend to you your visible forms, for you are indeed those great of blazing, the conflagration that is among these enemies[39] of Foremost of the West. That the king, the lord of the two lands, Nebmaatre, beloved of Amun, is making this visible form is like Re, who is before him in the Netherworld!"

These gods in this fashion, guarding the corpses that they decapitate, while they invert their bodies. This god inflicts their punishments, without them speaking to him. The *ba*-souls of these their guardians enter after this god. <Then> the darkness conceals them after he <passes> by them, their corpses remaining in their places forever.

---

39. Perhaps a confused writing of "these dead, (namely,) enemies."

6.14. Scene 14. A large multipart scene focused on a large disk from which emerges a winged scarab pushing a disk. To the left are two registers of beings within mounds facing right; the four mummiform beings in the top register are (left to right): a male (sic), "Corpse of Isis"; two females, "Corpse of Nut" and "Corpse of Tefnut"; and a scarab-headed figure, "Corpse of Khepri"; the three mummiform figures in the bottom register are (left to right): a male, "Corpse of Anubis"; an ibis-headed figure, "Corpse of Foremost Horus"; and a hawk-headed figure, "Corpse of Horus of the Netherworld." Right of the sun disk are two sets of four mounds flanking a ram-headed god, facing left, holding a *was*-scepter and an *ankh*-sign. Immediately right of the disk are four male mummiform figures facing left in two registers, labeled (left to right, top to bottom) "Corpse of Geb," "Corpse of Osiris," "Corpse of He of the Sarcophagus," and "Corpse of Shu." Behind the ram-headed god are another four beings in two registers; the upper register has a male and shrew-headed figure facing left, the bottom register a hawk-headed and ichneumon-headed figure facing right. The short annotation to this scene is placed inside the disk.

This god exists in this fashion, his face emerging from the wings of this Khepri, by means of them, he having come forth upon the Mysterious One, from the Hidden One, this Re having manifested as the great Khepri in the West.

REGISTER 4 (PLATE 36)

6.15. Scene 15. This scene focuses on a mummiform figure, "Osiris, Foremost of the West," facing right and wearing a white crown, partially emerging from the ground,  within a mound or sarcophagus. To the left is a bearded god wearing two feathers, "Corpse of Tatenen"; to the right is a bearded god with no crown, "Corpse of Geb." Both of these deities face in toward the Osiride figure and are visible from near the bottoms of their kilts upwards. Over-arching these three figures is a serpent, tail down to the right and head down to the left, with a knife through his neck. Two ram-headed gods facing the central figures grasp the serpent, while a third ram-headed deity appears at the far-right hand side of the scene; the ram-headed entities are labeled (left to right): "He Who Stretches out Apep"; "He Who Destroys His (Apep's) *Ba*-Soul"; and again "He Who Destroys His (Apep's) *Ba*-Soul."

These gods in this fashion, guarding the one belonging to him who is in his earth, the one whom he encircles, the mysterious and hidden gods, and Khepri. Re calls them, issuing commands to their *ba*-souls, while they pass by after him, their corpses hidden in their places, while this great god passes by the cavern of the mysteries for those who are in it, he commanding Maat to the King of Upper and Lower Egypt, Lord of the Two Lands, Nebmaatre, beloved of Amun.

What Re says to the gods of the mounds who guard his solar disk: "May you be at peace, may you be at peace, for the solar disk is in the Netherworld, even while the solar disk goes to rest in the West, the arms of She Who is Mysterious of Face emerging while lifting it up to (me)."

6.16. Scene 16. A large supine goddess within a roughly mummiform shaped sarcophagus dominates this scene; she is called "Corpse of She Who Destroys." From her sarcophagus emerge six smaller sarcophagi (only the upper half visible), each of which contains the upper portion of a praising figure. The three left figures are female and face right; from left to right their names are: "Destroyer of Face(s)";[40] "She of the Body"; and "She of the Mystery"; the three right figures are male and face left; from left to right their names are: "Destroyer of Face(s)"; "He of the Body"; and "He of the Mystery."

What Re says (to) the great image that is beneath the feet of the Mysterious One: "O you image, mysterious of manifestations, that is beneath the feet of the Mysterious One! Bend your arm! Restrain[41] your shoulder! Behold, I am passing over the corpses of the Mysterious Place; my *ba*-soul is tra-

40. Alternatively, "Destroyed of Face."
41. For this gesture, see Dominicus 1993, 86–87; Darnell 1995, 78 n. 163.

versing it over those amongst whom they are. I myself give birth to me,[42] as I pass over you, O great ones. You burn,[43] while you extinguish your fires, so that I might pass by the Mysterious Place, while you are satisfied by means of that which is within my mouth, while I command that you breathe. Jubilate for me! Jubilate for yourselves! You are indeed those who inflict <punishment on your enemies>!"

6.17. Scene 17. A representation of the punishment of the damned, dominated by two cauldrons lifted by human arms; the arms are labeled (left to right): "Two Arms of Fire, Two Arms of

Ejecting (Flame)" and "Two Arms of the Place of Punishment, Two Arms of the Fire Pit." Each cauldron contains two human heads and hearts,[44] while another human head spitting flame, "Shooting of Flame," appears beneath the bowl of the cauldron, between the human arms. A knife-wielding figure guards each cauldron, named (left to right): "He of the Slaughtering Place" and "He of the Knife." In the center of the scene, between the two cauldrons, are two goddesses slightly bending toward each other and holding their hands down and out, palms down over a large heart; they are "She of the Heart" and "She of the Removed (Heart)."

These gods in this fashion, those of the cauldrons placing heads in their cauldrons, flesh and hearts in their ovens,[45] those of the knives receiving their knives, the two goddesses guarding the removed hearts. These four arms of the god raise up their cauldrons, the great god having ignited with his flame, the two goddesses having ignited with their flames, they hiding their corpses, as fire is given to them atop their ovens and the rebels.

---

42. Alternatively, *ms wj ḏ.t=s*, "her body gives birth to me."

43. For this rare example of the use of the proclitic pronoun construction (*ṯn r=ṯn tk3=ṯn*) as an independent sentence, see Roberson 2012, 111; for the grammatical form, see also Roberson 2010.

44. As Roberson 2012, 217 notes, these are not the typical hieroglyph for heart, but rather an elaboration of the standard flesh-sign representing hearts.

45. For *ḥry.t* "oven," see "*ḥrj.t*," *WÄS*, 3:148.15.

SECTION A2

REGISTER 1 (UPPER) (PLATE 37)

6.18. Scene 18. At the right side of the scene, a ram-headed deity holding a *was*-scepter and *ankh*-sign faces to the left with a small sun disk before him. A *ba*-bird, "Power of the West," perched on a stand faces right with its arms raised in adoration. In the middle of the scene is a scarab, "Khepri," above a serpent, "Apep," whose head (to the left) and tail (to the right) are angled upwards sharply; another praising, right-facing *ba*-bird is placed above the beetle. Finally, at the left of the scene are two male figures with their arms held out, palms of the hands down in a protective gesture, bending forward slightly; they are named (from right to left) "Atum" and "Shu."

These gods in this fashion, Re passing over their cavern, as he issues this[46] command to their two *ba*-souls, the mysterious power that is within the Netherworld, while their two arms perform adoration[47] before him. (As for) Apep foremost of his cavern—Khepri emerges from his coils, the *ba*-soul of the two gods going to rest upon them. Atum and Shu join with him, their *ba*-souls having passed behind Re, their corpses remaining in their places. Then the darkness hides them after this god has passed by them. What Re says to this god who presents his arms so that he might receive him: "O that god, lord of the sky!"

---

46. For an interpretation of this passage as an A *pw* sentence, see Baumann 1998, 51.

47. Reading the writing of *ḏwỉ* with adoring man as a mistaken writing of *dwꜣ*.

REGISTER 1 (LOWER) (PLATE 37)

6.19. Scene 19. To the far right, a ram-headed figure holding a *was*-scepter and an *ankh*-sign faces left, while a male figure with his arms raised in adoration faces him. Next, four figures are placed around a disk from which emerges a falcon head: two ram-headed figures to the right and two cobra-headed figures to the left face in toward the disk, holding their arms out, palms down in a protective gesture.

These gods in this fashion, Atum acclaiming Re, as he calls to these among whom he is, with the result that they receive Horus of the Netherworld, as he emerges from his mystery that is in the Netherworld. This great god calls to himself these gods who guard him, and they pass by following him, while their corpses remain in their places. Now after this great god passes by them, then the darkness conceals them.

What Re says to the *ba*-souls of the Watchers who are upon their banks: "O, *ba*-souls of the Watchers."

REGISTER 1 (PLATE 37)

6.20. Scene 20. A male figure, facing left and bending deeply forward at the waist, leans heavily upon a *was*-scepter; in the annotation in the tomb of Ramesses VI, this figure is called the "Corpse of Aker" who holds a "*djam*-scepter." Facing him is a human-headed *ba*-bird with his arms raised in  adoration. A mound appears on either side of this central group, each containing a sun disk with a single shaft of light descending from it; a female figure, with her arms raised in adoration towards the central figure, emerges from each mound and faces toward the central scene; the lower legs and feet of both figures are not present, as though hidden within the mounds.

[These gods] in [this] fashion, the corpse of Aker grasping the *djam*-scepter, the two goddesses having come forth from their mounds, the great mysteries, this one going forth from their Aker, having passed ahead of the two goddesses. The *ba*-soul of great Aker acclaims him, so that the god might see what is within them, the arms of the Netherworld upon the mysteries, his hidden eye, and his flesh, as he goes forth therefrom.

6.21. Scene 21. Four standing male figures, bearded and wearing white crowns, are surrounded by light emitted by disks held aloft by pairs of hands.[48] At the left side of the scene, the head, shoulders, and arms of the figure lifting up the disk are all visible.

According to the annotation, all of the arms emerge from the "Place of Destruction," depicted in more detail in Register 2, which shows the punishment of enemies; the description of *ba*-souls redolent of putrefaction within the annotation refers to those same enemies.

[...] their two arms that raise up what is with them (from) the Place of Destruction, without seeing (it); they raising up the mysteries that the gods see by means of their arms [...] They [...] from their [...], without this great god passing into their cavern, because of the putrefaction, stench, and rot of their *ba*-souls.[49]

REGISTER 2 (PLATE 37)

6.22. Scene 22. A male and a female figure face right with their arms in a gesture of praise. Following them are four male figures, each facing right and grasping a human-headed stake.[50]

These gods in this fashion, their corpses that guard their stakes. This great god speaks to them, without them speaking to him, he calling to the mysterious personified stakes who guard the *ba*-souls of the dead. Their *ba*-

48. In the Tomb of Ramesses VI, the first figure to the right is damaged, but it is restored in fig. 6.21.

49. Contra Roberson 2012, 350: "at their cavern on behalf of its {?}, which {?} their *bas*."

50. The human head on the stake before the first figure has been restored.

souls pass after him, while their corpses remain in their places. Then the darkness conceals them.

What Re says to the gods who are in the following of Osiris-Orion: "O raise yourself, Aker! Great are your *ba*-soul and your corpse that I have protected."

6.23. Scene 23. Three male, bearded figures each guard a kneeling male enemy whose arms are tied behind his back; each of the male figures is called "Chief of the Bindings," while the enemies are labeled "Destroyed Ones."[51]

These gods in this fashion, guarding their destroyed ones. It is the great god who inflicts their punishment, even after he has passed over them. These destroyed ones shall be nullified,[52] when they (the guardians) carry out the dismemberment of their non-existent ones, without this god passing into this cavern, and without him speaking to them. In the darkness do they exist.

What [Re] says [...] [... *4 destroyed columns* ...] you pass by [...]

6.24. Scene 24. Although the scene is partly damaged in the tomb of Ramesses VI, it once contained three iterations of a goddess guarding an oval atop which is an awakening male mummy (prone

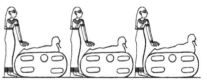

with his head raised); inside each oval are four smaller ovals, horizontally oriented, two to each side, with a disk in between, near the upper line of the large oval.

[...] you pass [over ...yo]ur, while they pass by afterwards, your corpses remaining in your places.

---

51. The last human figure bending over the captive is damaged from the waist up and has been restored on the basis of the other two figures. The Tomb of Ramesses VII replaces one male figure and captive with a ram-headed figure labeled "Atum, lord of *Maat*" (Roberson 2012, 218).

52. For the apt translation "shall be nullified," see Roberson 2012, 351, correctly identifying the form as a *sḏmm=f* passive (for this form in the Netherworld Books, see also Baumann 1998, 370–81).

These gods in this fashion, spending the night upon their faces (in) their proper places, their flesh and their bodies beneath them. It is those mysterious of arm who guard <them>. This great god calls to them, summoning their *ba*-souls, while they pass by, following him, their corpses remaining in their places. Now after the great god passes over them, then the darkness hides them.

SECTION B

REGISTER 1 (PLATE 38)

6.25. Scene 25. A large central mummiform deity (facing right) with a disk floating over his head forms the focus of this scene; he is called "Gleaming of Head, who guards corpses." A large rectangular mound with rounded edges encloses the lower half of the mummiform god and contains six additional figures: four female mummies on the left, facing right, and two male mummies on the right, facing left. Each goddess has the label: "This goddess in this fashion in this, the dark mound."[53] The male mummies have a short annotation: "This god in this fashion in this, the  hidden and dark mound. This god in this fashion in this, the dark mound. This god in this fashion, being the protected corpse of those who are with him."

These gods in this fashion in the mound of the unique one, He Who Guards the Corpses having set his head toward the solar disk, presenting his corpse. This god illumines those with him by means of the rays of the side of his flesh. This great god calls these gods, but without them seeing him. At the hearing of his voice do they breathe; as they protect him do they light up, except (for) these gods in darkness. Just as Re passes in the West, so does the corpse of the god navigate in order to illumine those with him. The *ba*-souls of the weary ones pass in his following, their corpses foremost of their mound.

---

53. The version in the tomb of Osorkon II adds "She of the mouth, who proceeds behind Gleaming of Head" (Roberson 2012, 242).

The *ba*-souls of the weary ones have passed the banks. The *ba*-soul of the king, lord of the Two Lands Nebmaatre, beloved of Amun, passes over this great bank above this cavern. Then the darkness of his light conceals it. Now afterwards, the god passes by, the divine *ba*-soul having gone to rest atop his mound, the god receiving the two mysterious eyes.

Passing by the corpses of those Warlike of Face by this great god, while he passes by the corpses of those who manifest. "O corpses of those War-like of Face, ones great of provisions in the West! O corpses of those War-like of Face, without *akh*-spirits over them. O corpses of those Warlike of Face, who acclaim me. Hail to you, those Warlike of Face who pass by as visible manifestations after them. O corpses of those Warlike of Face whose eyes are flaming, whose corpses are a devouring flame. May they ignite the *ba*-souls!"

6.26. Scene 26. One of the most iconic images from the Books of the Creation of the Solar Disk, this scene depicts the solar bark atop a double-headed Aker sphinx.[54] Above the prow is the label "Going forth from Aker," while over the stern is "He Who Is in the <Two Caverns.>"[55] To the left of Aker is a male deity, "Atum," to the right a scarab-headed god, "Khepri," both with arms raised in adoration. The solar bark has papyrus buds at the prow and stern, and a uraeus rides atop the prow. The bark contains five gods: a male figure at the prow, "He Who Guides," a male figure praising the solar deity, the ram-headed god crowned with disk and holding a *was*-scepter, a scarab-headed god praising the solar deity, and a hawk-headed god—named "Horus"—tending the steering oars.

This god in this fashion on the back of the mysterious Aker, having gone to rest in his bark. He within His Netherworld calls the mysterious corpse, the great mystery beneath Aker at the hour She Passes by the Darkness,

---

54. For a collection of parallels to the example in the Tomb of Ramesses VI, see Roberson 2012, 135.

55. In the tomb of Tauseret the labels above the left and right paws of the Aker sphinx are: "This One Who Enters" and "One Who Goes Forth"; in the Tomb of Ramesses IV, the labels are "Perfect Entrance" and "Perfect Emergence" (Roberson 2012, 135).

as he places light in the corpse of He of the Horizon, and as he enters into the solar disk, so that he might light up the mysterious corpse of the two mighty and great gods who are in the mysterious Aker, they being in their transits of the bark, as they traverse atop the land of He of the Horizon. Just as their feet exist on the earth, so do they watch over the *ba*-soul of He of the Horizon. The guide who calls the gods guides Re upon the mysterious roads—it is the hours of Re who guide them.[56]

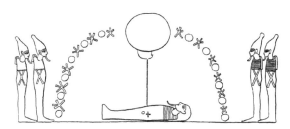

6.27. Scene 27. Located directly beneath Scene 26, a supine mummy below a large shining sun disk from which emerges a falcon head; this mummy is "The great god who is in his cavern; [the corpse] in which is Re."[57] Arranged in a semi-circle around the mummy, centered on the disk, are twelve stars and twelve small disks. On each side of the central group are two standing, mummiform figures, each wearing a white crown, with counterweight depending over the shoulder and crossed bands over the middle of the body, facing in toward the scene; the mummies are labeled (left to right): "He Who Hurries"; "He of the Hour"; "Mysterious of Heart"; "He Who Is Wrapped(?)."[58]

These gods in this fashion, they guarding the corpse of this god. Re calls to them, with the result that their *ba*-souls pass by, in his following.

These gods in this fashion, they guarding the corpse of this god. Re calls to them, with the result that their *ba*-souls pass by, in his following.

This god in this fashion, He of the hour of the mysterious hours, as the light enters his corpse by means of the speech[59] that has come forth from the solar disk at the hour She Enters the Darkness. That the *ba*-souls shall pass

---

56. Compare Roberson 2012, 355: "and the Hours of Re, they (also) lead."

57. For the reverse *nisbe*, see Roberson 2012, 270 n. 904. The first statement is in Merneptah, Tausret, and Ramesses III.

58. Following Piankoff and Rambova 1954, 331, n. 3; see "*Sty*," *LGG* 6:688. An alternate reading might be "He of the Stench."

59. This is one of the many examples in which the light of the solar deity is equated with speech (Darnell 2004, 106, 364–65, *et passim*).

by is when He of the Horizon speaks: "Six be to his head; six be to his feet—
Let one summon the image of the one who passes by." So says this great god.

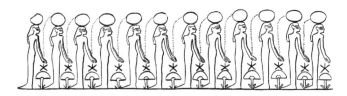

6.28. Scene 28. Twelve goddesses crowned with disks stand in a line; each is labeled
"Hour." The upper bodies of the goddesses face to the right, while below the waist
their bodies are turned to the left; their hands are placed over images of a shade
with a star atop. The disk of each goddess projects light back over her shoulder
onto the tops of the down-turned hands of the goddess behind her.

These hours in this fashion, their visible forms at their fingertips, their
shades beneath their zenith,[60] as they guide this great god in the mysterious West, the visible forms of Re being at their hours, they doing their
tasks.[61] As one passes, so one enters into the earth at the cavern of He Who
Conceals His Hours, while their shades are beneath their rays, their rays
being in the flesh of the one whom they conceal. In the following of the
ba-souls does this god pass by the banks, those who guide their corpses
having entered their darkness.

What Re says to the Westerner, as he passes by those who guard the
corpses, mysterious of arm, the chief of his mysteries, mysterious Aker:
"Hail, you are the Westerner, who engenders (his own) corpse, living of
visible forms, peaceful of corpse in the West, who guards for the one who
engenders those great of manifestations!

> How peaceful is the corpse of the Westerner,
>   they becoming mysterious, having entered into his corpse!
> How peaceful is the corpse of this Westerner,
>   this one of the serpent Nehayu beneath his two soles!
> How peaceful is the corpse of the Westerner,
>   as he guards those among whom is the Westerner!

---

60. "wp.t," WÄS, 1:297.21; in the depiction, the shades are beneath the stars,
which themselves represent the zenith of the goddesses' activities.

61. Alternatively, "they assuming their visible forms."

How peaceful is the corpse of the Westerner,
>the mysterious ones presenting their heads!
O, hail to this one, the Westerner, foremost of his cavern within the
>Netherworld.
O, hail to this one, Westerner!

That I call the corpses that are with him, is while they pass by, in my following, as they become mysterious by means of their arms, as they guide me upon their roads, as they carry out this which I have commanded. More than those with him have I protected this one, the Westerner. I have protected the bodily son of Re, Ramesses (VI), the divine one, ruler of Heliopolis, justified, while I call to the corpses that are with him, without these gods seeing the light of Re, as they guard in his darkness. It is when they hear his voice that they breathe. In his following do their *ba*-souls pass."

This god in this fashion, beginning to travel in the Netherworld, while those who are with him haul those who are in his following, having gone to rest in his light. This great god makes a pause[62] in the cavern that hides his hour, while he issues commands to those with him. The voice of the god is what they hear, without him seeing them, since what is with them is mysterious.

REGISTER 2 (PLATE 38)

6.29. Scene 29: Three mummiform deities, with solar disks in their torsos, form the focus of this complex scene. The central mummy, crowned with ram horns and two plumes, faces right, while the two other, slightly smaller mummiform gods face in toward him. Text flanking the large, central mummy reads "This god in this fashion, He Who Guards the Corpse being upon the West. These mysterious ones, their *ba*-souls pass by in their following." The mummy to the right has a large disk above his head and below his feet, each containing three

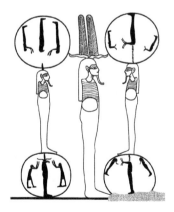

---

62. Roberson 2012, 360 suggests the possible "spend a lifetime"; based on other parallels, the text more likely refers to a solar apogee (compare Darnell 2004, 126–27 and 287–88).

deities. The upper disk has three, inverted, shrew-headed mummiform deities (the central one being larger); the central shrew-headed figure (facing left) is labeled "This god in this fashion, the Shrew," while the flanking gods (facing in toward the central figure within the disk) are each labeled "Inverted One." The bottom disk has a shrew-headed deity (facing left), "Terrifying of *Ba*-Soul," with two bearded human-headed mummies to either side (facing in toward the central figure within the disk), each labeled "Chief of the *Ba*-Soul." A retrograde text next to this right mummiform figure reads "This god in this fashion, his head <in the upper region>, his feet in the lower region, as the great one enters."

The mummy to the left has the same configuration of disks but different figures within them: above, a hawk-headed mummy (facing right) praised by two goddesses (facing in toward the central figure within the disk), all inverted; the hawk-headed figure has the annotation "This disk is what is above. This god in this fashion, his corpse is Re," while the goddesses are labeled "She Who Is Following" and "She Who Worships." The disk below contains a ram-headed mummy (facing right), "He of the Two Horns; [it is] his corpse, he adoring Re," praised by two gods (facing in toward the central figure within the disk), "He Adoring of Face" and "He of the Oval." Within each disk are captions, with the text inverted in the upper disks to match the orientation of the figures. An annotation to the left mummiform figure reads "This god in this fashion, his head[63] in the upper region, his feet in the lower (region), when the light enters the natures[64] of these, namely, *ba*-souls and corpses."

A variant to this scene with an almost entirely destroyed annotation appears in the tomb of Mutirdis (Roberson 2012, 252, 431).

6.30. Scene 30. A central mummiform figure with a long wig and divine beard, wearing a broad collar and two long streamers, stands facing to the right, with a large disk hovering above him. Four mummiform figures flank the central figure, two to each side: to the right, a female, "Tefnut," and a male mummy, "Shu"; to the left, a scarab-headed mummy, "Khepri," and a male mummy, "Nun." All four flanking figures wear broad collars, but only the outer two figures wear two long streamers, after the fashion of the larger, central mummiform being. Columns flanking the five mummiform figures read "This god in this fashion in the

---

63. The word *tp* "head" is written with a disk, and a reading of "solar disk" is also possible here.

64. The word *rḫ.w* here for *rḫ.t*, which itself can interchange with *ḥr.t* "form, nature" (Meeks 1998a, 220 [no. 77.2415], citing Hornung 1975, 95).

land of the *ba*-soul"; followed by a sentence repeated three times: "This god in this fashion, the corpses in the land of the *ba*-soul, as he passes by the darkness."

These gods in this fashion. Re passes by their corpses, while he calls to them <commands>. The light of this great god enters into the limbs.

He (Re) calls <commands> to your corpses, namely Tefnut who is within Atum. He (Re) calls commands to the corpse of <Nun> who is within Atum. He (Re) calls commands ...

6.31. Scene 31. A large figure dominates this scene, but all that is visible is the male's head and two large arms extending upward, labeled (right to left) "West" and "East." At the right arm is the text "Seeing this god entirely, the two arms having gone forth." A goddess, "She Who Destroys," her arms raised and palms upward, stands atop the figure's head, with a sun disk floating above her. She is labeled "The goddess in this fashion, as she emerges from the darkness." The upturned palms of the raised hands of the central figure hold two small praising male figures, each 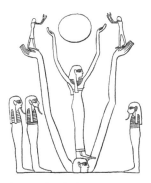 facing in toward the goddess. Three male mummiform figures flank the scene, one to the right and two to the left, all facing in toward the center of the scene; the two mummies to the left are labeled "Manifesting One," while the right one is "One Who United the Corpse." Text associated with the two mummies on the left reads "The goddess in <this> fashion, as the corpse guards the darkness"; at the mummiform figure on the right is "This god in this fashion, as <he> guards the darkness."

REGISTER 2 (UPPER)

6.32. Scene 32. A lengthy scene. At the far right is a depiction of the solar bark with a lotus blossom prow and stern, labeled "One that Moors." The ram-headed solar deity, "the Great God," stands in the middle with a *ba*-bird before him, "The *Ba*-Soul of Re," and a scarab-headed figure, "Khepri," praising him. A male figure works the steering oars, "Horus, the *Ba*-Soul of Horus," while a uraeus, "She Who Guides," appears at the prow. A male figure to the left of the bark appears to be pushing against the prow; a *ba*-bird with his arms raised stands to the left of this figure. The next element of the scene to the left consists of fourteen ram-headed gods facing left, with their heads turned back over their shoulders looking towards the solar bark; small *ba*-birds with their arms raised in praise occur to the left next to the forward shin of each deity. At the far left end of the scene is a large solar disk.

This god in this fashion, having begun to travel in the Netherworld. Meanwhile, those who are with him are hidden by means of those who are in his following, after having come to rest in his light. This great god has made his pause in the cavern that hides his hours, having commanded his visible forms among whom he is. The voice of the god is what they have heard, without him seeing them, since what is with them is mysterious.[65]

These gods in this fashion, they receiving the light of Re. Meanwhile, the secret ones cross over the great one who is with them. The *ba*-souls of these have gone forth from their darkness, as they receive the light of the one who is with them. The *ba*-souls of these mysterious ones haul him.

These gods in this fashion, as they acclaim the great god, while he passes by [the darkness(?)] in which they are, with the result that they receive the solar disk.

REGISTER 2 (LOWER)

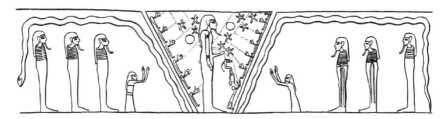

6.33. Scene 33. A large, ithyphallic mummiform figure stands in the middle of a funnel-shaped vessel that has been identified as a clepsydra (see above, p. 460). A child, "Flame," is placed immediately below the erect phallus of the central figure, while a male figure, "He of Blood" stands below the child. The interior of the funnel has images of six goddesses on each slanting side, their backs to the sides; dotted lines connect the disks that the goddesses hold to a series of disks and stars arranged around the ithyphallic deity—three stars (two over one) above a disk to the left of the deity, a disk above three stars (one above two) to the right. At the bottom of the interior right side is a single male deity, body facing the inner side of the "clepsydra," arms forward, light emerging from between his

---

65. This text is parallel to Tomb of Ramesses VI, Section B, Register 1, Scene 28. Alternatively, "until those amongst whom they are become secret."

hands. The entire funnel-shaped space is enclosed by a serpent—head to left, tail to right, mid portion disappearing as though beneath the funnel—whom the captions identify as the Encircling Serpent. Three mummiform gods and two praising figures (as though emerging from the ground line, below which their lower legs are hidden) appear to either side of the funnel; the mummies to the left, beneath the head end of the serpent, are each labeled "This god is in this fashion, the great Encircling Serpent," while at the far left is "This god in this fashion, the Encircling Serpent over him." The mummies to the right are called (left to right): "Distant of Face," "Manifesting of Face," and "Elderly of Face." Next to the right praising figure is a short annotation: "One among the earth. This god in this fashion, with the Encircling Serpent over him. This god in this fashion, the great serpent, the Encircling Serpent, over him. This god in this fashion, while he praises those with him."

Those who do not see these lights of Re, as they guard in his darkness. That they breathe is when they hear his voice, as their *ba*-souls pass in his following.

REGISTERS 2–4 (PLATE 38)

6.34. Scene 34. Spread over three registers, this scene contains a total of seven semi-circular mounds each holding a supine female figure (not mummiform) within an oval sarcophagus; two of these are placed in the lower half of Register 2, three in Register 3 (with a solar disk at the far left of the scene), and two in the lowest register, Register 4. Three of the female figures are labeled as "Noble One who is within the mound," "Noble One of the 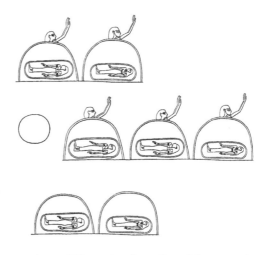 mound," and "Noble One of the sarcophagus." Emerging from five of the mounds are praising figures whose heads and arms are visible; the lowest two mounds do not contain praising figures. Each praising figure has the annotation: "The one who is in his mound springs forth."

These gods in this fashion, they acclaiming the great god, as he passes by those who are with them, with the result that they receive his solar , great of shadow,[66] and with the result that they receive their corpses, the goddesses being hidden.

These gods in this fashion in their mounds, as they place their heads at the front of their mysterious places, so that they might receive the light of Re, breathing by means of his rays in their mounds (namely,) by means of the words of Re <against> his evil ones.

It is every mound of those who come forth after he passes by the mysteries at the front of their sarcophagi. This great god calls.

REGISTER 3 (PLATE 38)

6.35. Scene 35. Two large, bearded mummiform figures, facing right, appear in this scene. A praising goddess emerges from the head of the left mummiform being, facing right, her arms held up and forward in a gesture of praise; the large, male figure is labeled "He of the Oval." The rightmost mummiform being is crowned with a large disk from which emerges the upper portion of a scarab with human arms, lifted in praise to the left; the mummiform figure is labeled "He of the Birth." Within the annotation, these two large mummies are called the "Corpse of Tatenen" and the "Corpse of Nun." Three small disks are placed between the praising goddess and the praising scarab. A caption to the right of the scene states: "This god in this fashion, as he raises up He of the Birth."

Passing the corpse of Tatenen by this great god, as he crosses over the corpse of Nun.

"You are indeed the corpse in whom he is!
O corpse in which I manifested,
    whom I bore as the one who bore himself for me afterwards.[67]
O corpse in which I manifested,
    this one who is at peace with what he creates.

---

66. The epithet "great of shadow," a seemingly paradoxical description of the solar god, relates to the clothing properties of light (Darnell 2004, 134–38).

67. This passage of eternal re-creation resembles a statement of Atum in the Book of Gates, Hour 2, Register 3, Scene 8: "I am the son who came forth from his father; I am the father who came forth from his son" (see p. 264).

O corpse in which I manifested,
> unique one whose own places I created.

O corpse in which I manifested!"

6.36. Scene 36. One of the most commonly attested scenes within the Books of the Creation of the Solar Disk, this tableau enjoyed a post-New Kingdom existence on the head end of a corpus of Late period sarcophagi (see p. 522). A central mummiform figure with solar disk is flanked by two uraei (facing inward toward the mummy), called "Powerful of Visible Forms" and "Assembled of Visible Forms." Next are two large arms, each emerging from a human head; the left arm is named "She

Who Hides the Head" and the right arm is named "He Who Destroys the Hours." Atop the arms are male figures holding disks, facing outwards; the left figure is called "Formed One," while the right is "He Who Travels." Two mummies, each labeled "Aggressive of Face" and crowned with disks, appear on the ground line next to each arm. Atop the entire scene is another large solar disk, above which is the text: "The hours that pass by the darkness beneath the soles."

Passing the corpses Warlike of Face by this great god, as he passes by the corpse of Khepri. "O corpses of those Warlike of Face, great of provisions in the West!"

These gods in this fashion, guarding the destroying arms, foremost of the Place of Destruction. It is they who shall raise up their solar disk. Their arms raise up Re. Their arms unite the corpses of the Netherworld dwellers at the (appropriate) hour—they guard the hour of the *ba*-soul for the *ba*-soul of Re.

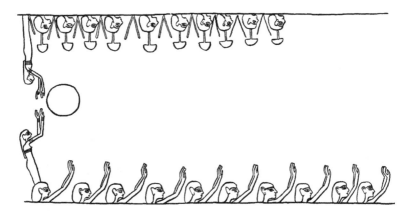

6.37. Scene 37: The middle portion of the scene is empty, as if leaving space for the sun disk to travel. The disk, called "Great of Shadow,"[68] indeed appears at the far left of the scene, between two goddesses, one of whom is inverted, facing right and with their arms raised in praise. The inverted goddess is called "She Who Is in Shadow" (with the shadow sign itself inverted), while the goddess who comes forth from the praising head below is named "She Who Is in the Following (of the Great God)." Emerging from the ceiling are ten heads crowned with shades and v-shaped sticks between them; in front of the inverted heads, facing right, is the caption "He of Shadow" referring collectively to the figures.[69] From the floor come forth ten human heads and arms lifted in praise, also facing right; above nine of the figures is the expression "in the following" referring to the gods being in the entourage of the solar deity.

These gods in this fashion, acclaiming the great god, as he passes by towards those who are with them, with the result that they receive his solar disk, great of shadow, and with the result that they receive their corpses. The goddesses, hidden of corpse, they acclaim, as they present their heads. She Who Elevates the Ground,[70] who protects the gods, gives her arm to the solar disk of He of the Horizon. The *ba*-souls pass in his following while their corpses remain in their places.

---

68. See 494 and n. 66.
69. For an alternate translation "Place of shadow," see Roberson 2012, 226.
70. Reading *tn* for *tni* "to elevate" and *st* as *sꜣtw* "ground, foundation."

REGISTER 4 (PLATE 38)

6.38. Scene 38. Part of a larger tableaux known as the "Book of Aker," this scene depicts the solar bark hauled by seven *ba*-birds, bodies facing left, heads turned to the right looking over their backs. The crew of the bark consists of six different deities: two goddesses at the far left, called "She Who Judges" and "Opet"; a scarab beetle named "Khepri"; the unnamed, ram-headed solar deity; a goddess with her arms in a position of respect, called "She Who Adores"; and finally, the oarsman "Horus." Each one of the *ba*-birds towing the bark is aptly named "One Who Tows."

Taking the good road by this great god. Those between whom he is rest in the bark, the *Ba*-Souls of the Banks of Re. Passing the banks by this great god in the bark, as he crosses the caverns of Nun.

6.39. Scene 39. This scene contains a number of different figures. The rightmost set of images cluster around a mound with a mummy, called "Body," resting atop it. Two arms,[71] the "Arms of Geb," appear to either side of the mound and inside the mound are a weeping eye and four flesh signs. Two praising figures—one male "He Who Grieves" (to the left) and one female, "She Who Grieves" (to the right)—face right towards the mummy and the mound. The next group consists of three figures, two women facing in towards a crouching male figure with divine beard, facing left, all of whom have their arms raised in praise; the goddesses are called "She Who Jubilates" and "Secret of Flame," while the male is called "Begsy."[72] To the far left is another scene with a right facing crouched, praising figure, also male and wearing a divine beard, "He Who Worships," flanked by two uraei "She Who Scalds" and "Flaming One"; a bearded mummiform figure called "He of the Embers" appears at the leftmost portion of the scene.

71. Most of the right arm has been restored in fig. 6.39.
72. Name of uncertain derivation (see Roberson 2012, 142 n. 104).

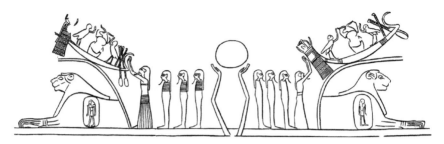

6.40. Scene 40. A double lion Aker, labeled "Aker," appears to either side of this tableau; inside the shoulder of each Aker is a male figure wearing a kilt inside a vertically oriented oval (sarcophagus), called "the corpses of Shu" within the annotation. An arching pathway that divides Register 4 into two halves descends midway into the body of the Aker lion, and on this pathway sails the solar bark. Each solar bark, the prow of which is decorated with an elaborate "solar mat," contains a ram-headed scarab praised by two *ba*-birds; in each bark these are called the "Ba-soul of Khepri" and the "Ba-soul of Atum." The solar bark on the right is depicted as though descending into the body of the Aker lion, while that on the left appears to be emerging from the body of the left Aker lion; each bark is supported by a male figure who is shown emerging from the earth—to the left is "Nun," while at the right is "Tatenen." The central portion of the scene contains two arms, "the Two Arms of Nun," lifting a solar disk, and flanked by six mummiform figures, three facing right on the right, and three facing left on the left, each called "those of the water of Nun"; above the solar disk is the caption: "Your corpses remain in your places." The entire scene depicts the duality of the day and the night barks, whose journey is fueled by the creation of the solar disk, lifted by the arms of the chaotic waters; as Roberson (2012, 148) notes, one can read the front of each lion literally as *ḥꜣ.t* "beginning," as if the solar god travels from one beginning to another without ever reaching the "end." This scene also appears on several Third Intermediate period papyri, which preserve alternate captions to some of the figures (Roberson 2012, 146–47).

What Re says at the Place of Destruction, as he goes forth and passes by those who guard the West: "O Nun and those who are therein!" (he says), as he passes by Tatenen.

Aker in this fashion, the corpses of Shu in his breast. What Re says to the mysterious goddesses who are in the West.

6.41. Scene 41. Fourteen uraei with female heads and arms face to the right, arms raised and grasping a rope that ends in a great coil to the left; they are hauling the day bark as it sails out from the body of Aker (see previous scene). The seven uraei to the left are called "She of the Bank," while the seven to the right are named "She Who Guides."

Hauling this great god by the goddesses who guide, those within the waterway, in order to shine in the eastern mountain. What is said by the goddesses, those within the waterway, to Re-Horakhty: "Behold, Re! Haul for him! How beautiful it is, as he passes by the cavern of Nun." This god passes by in this fashion after he arrives.

6.42. Scene 42. A human-headed mummy facing left, "*Ba*-Soul of the Hidden Land" stands to the right of two sarcoph-agi, each containing a male figure with head to

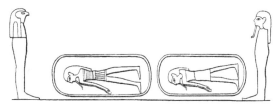

the left, facing towards the ground. The right figure is called "Hidden of Arm," while the left is "Mysterious of Arm." A falcon-headed god, "Horus of the Nether-world," stands at the left of the scene, facing right.

These gods in this fashion in their sarcophagi, their mysteries at their fin-gertips, and their faces in the earth, those mysterious of that which is in their arms.

What Re says, as he passes by the bank: "O, Mystery! O …!"

SECTION B2 (PLATE 39)

Unlike the other sections of the Books of the Creation of the Solar Disk from the Tomb of Ramesses VI, Section B2 does not divide entirely into registers. Instead, the central, mummiform figure fills both registers, dividing the section roughly in half. Consequently, the following scenes are ordered from right to left, but top to bottom within each section.

6.43. Scene 43. Four bearded, mummiform gods appear within vertically oriented sarcophagi. A large serpent (whose head is damaged) is placed above these four sarcophagi and is not mentioned in the annotation. A caption to each sarcophagus reads: "Praising One, who stands. This god in this fashion in his mound as one who stands."

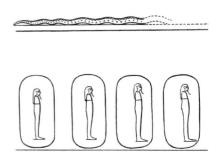

These gods in [this] fashion, [their corpses on the mound], they [placing their head at the forefront] of their mysteries, so that they might receive the light of Re, with the result that they breathe from his rays. It is by means of the voice of Re that their mound becomes bright, when he calls to them. Now afterwards he passes by them. Then they hide themselves in their mound there.

These gods in this fashion, their corpses standing, while they see (Re).

[These] gods in [this] fashion in their mound, [standing at the forefront of their] sarcophagi, they putrefying in their rottenness. This great god calls to their *ba*-souls, without him seeing them, because of their stench and their rot.[73]

6.44. Scene 44. Four vertically oriented "awakening" mummies are each placed within a mound. A caption to each mound reads: "This god in this fashion, guardian of the one with him. Awakening One, who stands."

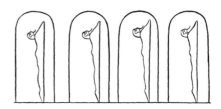

73. For the impact of smell upon the solar god, compare the Books of the Creation of the Solar Disk, Tomb of Ramesses VI, Section A2, Register 1, Scene 21 (p. 483) and the Book of Gates, Hour 10, Register 1, Scene 62 (p. 311).

6.45. Scene 45. A large bearded, mummiform figure dominates this scene; he faces right, wears no crown, and has a sun disk placed within his torso.[74] Before him is a large, rearing serpent, facing left, who emerges between two arms that come out of the ground, hands extended palms upwards. The right hand holds a praising female, the left hand supports a human-bodied serpent—"He of the Head"—the tip of whose tail touches the feet of the large mummiform being; above the human-bodied serpent with praising arms is the caption: "One who is within the bank throughout the West, He of the Head." Behind the mummiform figure are two arms, bent at the elbows, "Arms of Darkness:" the right hand holds a ram-
headed scepter, "Head of Re," the left holds a jackal-headed staff, "Neck of Atum." A vertically oriented crocodile, Penwenty, his snout pointing into the air, back to the left, appears immediately behind the mummiform figure and above the bent elbows of the left pair of arms emerging from the ground line.

The serpent in this fashion, their guardian of the corpse of the god, who comes forth upright opposite the corpse. He of the Head! He of the Head! He of the Head! They raise up for themselves, so they might acclaim. This god in this fashion, he guarding the West and the two sisters. Penwenty in this fashion, as your guardian of the corpse of the god, as he comes forth from the arms of darkness, and the corpse is hidden. The Head of Re, the Neck of Atum, and the Arms of Darkness—they raise up Penwenty.

6.46. Scene 46. A vertically oriented scene contains four supine mummies in sarcophagi; the top two contain male figures, while the bottom two contain female figures, named "Double *Ba*-soul" and "He of the Corpse" (the fourth has a vulture[?] head), named "Tefnut" and "Nut." Between the two pairs of sarcophagi is the label "Their mound." The first and third sarcophagi each have two praising *ba*-birds atop them; those above the third sarcophagus have shades emerging from their heads. The Tomb of Ramesses VI labels the two bottom sarcophagi with the caption: "These goddesses in this fashion."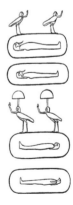

---

74. Compare the giant Re-Osiris in the Books of the Solar-Osirian Unity, Second Shrine of Tutankhamun (pp. 525–26, 541).

6.47. Scene 47. Two barks are arranged one above the other with the caption "The bark in this fashion." The upper bark contains a supine mummiform figure, labeled "Osiris," guarded by "Isis"; the lower bark contains a supine, hawk-headed mummiform figure, "Horus [of the Netherworld]," watched over by "Nephthys." Two heads, facing one another, emerge from the line above each bark; small strokes emerge from the heads above the top bark. Sun disks are placed above the stern of each bark, with a disk at the prow of the lower bark as well.

6.48. Scene 48. A large mound contains a solar disk in its upper curved portion and a male figure with arms raised in praise below. Above the mound, emerging from the ceiling of the scene, are two human heads, facing in towards one another.

[Seeing the light. This great god cal]ls them, with the result that [his voi]ce causes that they breathe, while their protector gives praise. Then <darkness> conceals them. This god in this fashion.

6.49. Scene 49. A central sarcophagus contains two male figures facing in towards one another, standing on a ground line below which are six "flesh" signs; the two gods are labeled "Hidden One above the Limbs" and "Hidden of Limbs." Above the sarcophagus hovers a solar disk. To either side is a praising goddess ("She Who Praises the One within the Earth"), in front of whom and closest to the central oval is another praising figure whose head and arms are the only parts visible.

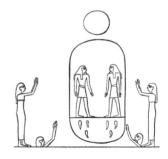

These gods in this fashion in their sarcophagus, with their flesh[75] beneath them. The eye of Re goes forth from them, when they turn back the flame

---

75. The *sp*-sign is a writing of *iwf* "flesh," through confusion of the hieratic similarities of the two signs (contra Roberson 2012, 381, who reads *sp snw*).

that is in the healthy eye of Re. The two goddesses acclaim [for them], the goddesses being their guardians.

6.50. Scene 50. A disk hovers above the scene, which contains four male figures with their arms lifted, palms upwards, as if supporting the disk. Three male figures appear to the left of the disk and are named (left to right), "Praising of Arm," "Powerful of Arm," and "Luminous of Arm." A short text between the

two gods immediately below the disk reads "The two who raise up for it." In front of each male figure is a *ba*-bird (with human head) and shade.

This great god passes by in his solar disk, after he arrives at the mysterious waterways. Those who are within the waterways raise up this great god upon their two arms. The day bark and the night bark pass by Nut after him, when the god goes forth from the *ba*-soul and the shade. The *ba*-soul and the shade receive him into heaven, so that they might raise up the Netherworld, the two great goddesses and the great ones.

Tomb of Ramesses VII

LEFT WALL

REGISTER 1 (PLATE 40)

6.51. Scene 1. Four praising gods face left towards a large disk. The disk contains a ram-headed figure whose arms reach out and grasp the forearms of the first praising deity; behind the ram-headed solar deity stands a possibly baboon-headed deity. No captions or annotations accompany this scene.

6.52. Scene 2. Four male figures, with their arms held down at an angle and their palms facing downwards, appear around a sarcophagus, two to each side, all facing the central oval. The sarcophagus contains the Corpse of Osiris (as stated in the annotation)—a supine,  striding figure facing upwards, with his upper arm held over his face; the preserved example in the Tomb of Ramesses IX indicates that the figure within the sarcophagus was ithyphallic (see below, Scene 10, p. 512).

These gods in this fashion, their arms (upon) the mysterious sarcophagus in which is the corpse of Osiris. The great god speaks concerning the cavern, he calls those who are in his following: "The corpses of the necropolis are in your vicinity above it, while I proclaim them."

6.53. Scene 3. Two praising male deities face outwards, their backs to a central solar disk; the left figure is named "One Who Offers (to) Re." To the right is a praising ram, "Corpse of Re," depicted as though emerging from the ground line, below which the lower rear legs are still hidden; on the far left is a praising jackal-headed staff, "Neck of Re." Both the ram and jackal-headed staff face in towards the center of the scene.

These gods in this fashion, they acclaiming the visible forms of Re, the great corpse who is within the horizon, the divine and mysterious corpse, they giving their arms to the ram of rams.[76] Re calls to them, with the result that they go forth from the two caverns.

---

76. Alternatively: *ba*-soul of *ba*-souls; compare P. Salt 825, IX, 5 (Derchain 1965, 12*); Assmann 1969, 78–81; Klotz 2006, 37.

6.54. Scene 4. A central Osiride figure, mummiform, wearing a white crown, and facing left, is labeled "Ruler of the West." To either side of him are four mounds, filled with sand. A praising figure emerges from each mound, facing the central being—to the left two female figures, to the right two male figures.

REGISTER 2 (PLATE 40)

6.55. Scene 5. Four kneeling deities, facing left, are beneath shades that arch over the figures; the two middle deities are named (right to left): "He Who Illumines the Great God" and "He Who Engenders

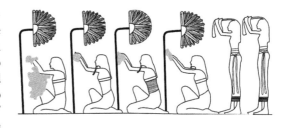

the Great God." The shades are called "shades of the lords of Maat" (see also pp. 519–20). Two goddesses (left to right), "Isis the Great" and "Nephthys, possessor of Maat," stand at the right end of the scene, facing left and pulling strands of their hair, a mourning gesture.

These gods in this fashion, their arms in the vicinity of their faces. Their shades al[ighting] upon them, because they mourn over the mysterious corpse of Osiris, foremost of the Netherworld. It is the two goddesses who seize their tresses, the water within the eyes of these goddesses descending, being their tears, being the blood of the Netherworld (Dwellers).

6.56. Scene 6. A male figure, arms raised in praise, faces left, towards a disk that contains two damaged deities, facing right.

6.57. Scene 7. Four ram-headed deities—two to the left and two to the right—face inwards towards a mound; they are named, right to left: "Mysterious One"; "Horned One"; "He of the Horns"; "Ram-like One." The mound contains three flesh signs above four pellets. A ram with his front legs raised in praise ("Corpse of Re") emerges from the mound, his hind legs still hidden within the mound.

These gods in this fashion, the great god having power over his solar disk, Thoth at rest within it.[77] Those who are with Re, they acclaim his *ba*-soul. His mysterious corpse emerges at its mound, and his body. They see the two gods foremost of the mound, mysterious of nature, without those in his following perceiving the mysterious image. Those who are in his mound, they see the light of Re, with the result that they become pacified through the rays of his solar disk. Then the darkness conceals them.

6.58. Scene 8. A vertically oriented crocodile, called Wenty in the annotation, appears at the center of the scene, back to the left; a solar disk is placed within his belly, and a ram head "[Head] of Re," facing the ground line, emerges from the right side of the disk. To the right are three goddesses facing left, their arms hanging at their sides, named (right to left): "She Who Looks"; "She Who Bears (Children)"; "Great Nut." To the left are three praising deities facing right, named (right to left): "Atum, Lord of the Two Lands"; "He of the Vulture"; and "He of the Heron."

These gods in this fashion in the cavern of Penwenty, foremost of the Place of Destruction. The solar disk of this great god opens the Netherworld of Wenty. The god goes forth from his mysterious place. Wenty vomits and ejaculates the eye of Re that is in his belly,[78] and its pupil, as it enters into its glorious appearances. Atum gives his arms to Re; Nut protects. The two gods acclaim the double *ba*-soul.

---

77. The contrasting actions of the great god and Thoth "probably relates to their roles as sun and moon" (Roberson 2012, 385 n. 497).

78. For the (Pen)wenty crocodile who gives birth to the sun, see Darnell 2004, 320–21; Roberson 2012, 211–12.

RIGHT WALL

REGISTER 1 (PLATE 41)

6.59. Scene 9. A complex scene dominated by the sandy curve of the eastern horizon on the right, in which a solar disk is rising. A pair of arms, horizontally oriented, hold the disk as it interrupts the sandy line of the end of the 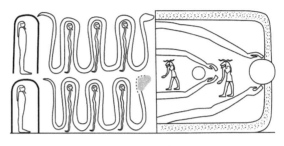 Netherworld; between the arms is another pair of arms with disk and two ram-headed figures, one between the inner pair of arms to the left of a small solar disk, the other larger and to the right of the hands of the inner arms. To the left of the pairs of arms are two large serpents, facing right, head and tail raised, each with three human-headed rearing serpents beneath their three arching coils. Behind each serpent is a mummy standing within a mound and facing right.

6.60. Scene 10. A god to the right and a goddess to the left each bend over a large sun disk containing a ram-headed, kneeling figure, facing right.

These gods in this fashion, joining with the solar disk of Re. The *ba*-soul of the god is manifested as this, without this god entering into the Netherworld as a *ba*-soul, great of mourning, as he speaks by means of his light, which is in him, with the result that they breathe by means of his voice. Now afterwards, this god enters.

6.61. Scene 11. Four deities cluster around a large solar disk that contains a ram-headed deity, two to each side of the disk. On each side nearer the disk is a male with his arms raised in prayer; behind the praising male entity is a female deity with her arms down; the male on the right is named "He Who Honors," while the deities on the left are called "He Who Mourns and Adores" and "She Who Mourns and Adores."

These gods in this fashion. The two goddesses call the *ba*-soul of Re in his solar disk, as the *ba*-soul hears the words that are in it, and the god reckons his limbs, even while the one there calls their *ba*-souls, while their corpses remain in their places. Now, afterwards, this great god passes by them. Then [the darkness] in which they are conceals them. After the birth form of this great god do their birth forms manifest, in order to place his rays in the following of the gods who are with him, every day.

These gods in this fashion. The two goddesses call the *ba*-soul of Re in his [solar disk], with the result that the *ba*-soul hears the words that are therein.

6.62. Scene 12. Four gods, two to each side, bend over a sarcophagus containing a sun disk, from which emerges a flame; the flaming disk and oval receive the label "*Akhet*-eye." The flame spews two thin lines of fire that cross the hands of the gods and descend to the forward foot of the rear deity on each side. The gods are each labeled (right to left): "Flame"; "Extended [of Arm]"; "Divine One"; "Blazing One."

These gods in this fashion, their arms over the eye of Re and the mysterious sarcophagus that contains the *akhet*-eye. The flame comes up from the sarcophagus, so that those with it may breathe. Indeed, Re adores his eye, as he summons its guardians.

REGISTER 2 (PLATE 41)

6.63. Scene 13 (= Tomb of Ramesses VI, Section A2, Register 1, Scene 20). In the Tomb of Ramesses VII, additional captions are preserved. The right female figure emerging from the mound is "She of Adoration," while the goddess on the left is "Corpse of Selket." The bending male figure is named "Corpse of Khepri," and the praising *ba*-bird is "Ba-Soul of Orion, lord of Maat."

6.64. Scene 14. Two deities stand facing one another: to the left, "Horus of the Two Arms," reaches out and grasps the arm of "He of the West." The figure "He of the West" stands over a supine figure labeled "Atum." The same group of figures appears in the Tomb of Ramesses VI, Section A, Register 2 (Upper), Scene 9.

6.65. Scene 15 (= Tomb of Ramesses VI Section A, Register 4, Scene 15). The captions in the Tomb of Ramesses VII are slight variations of those found in the Tomb of Ramesses VI.

6.66. Scene 16 (= Tomb of Ramesses VI, Section A2, Register 2, Scene 23). The captions in the Tomb of Ramesses VII are parallel to those in the Tomb of Ramesses VI, with the label to the ram-headed deity as noted above, p. 484 and n. 51.

Tomb of Ramesses IX

LEFT WALL

REGISTER 1 (PLATE 42)

6.67 (left). Scene 1 = Book of Caverns, Division 5, Register 1, Scene 60 (p. 410).
6.68 (right). Scene 2 = Tomb of Ramesses VII, Left Wall, Register 1, Scene 3

6.69. Scene 3. An ithyphallic supine figure within a cauldron (placed within a mound), head to the right, ejaculates into the hands of two praising figures who flank the central mound. Within the mound are two female figures with their arms raised in adoration, labeled "Adorer" 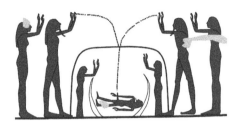 and "Praiser," facing the central figure; the mound is flanked by two pairs of male and female praising figures, facing the mound. To the left is "She Who Supports" and "He Who Supports," while to the right is "He Who Receives" and "She Who Receives." Although the Ramesses IX version of this scene does not provide an annotation, a text accompanies the images on a corpus of sarcophagi (see p. 521).

6.70. Scene 4. A central sarcophagus contains a supine mummy, head to the right, with sun disk above. Two female figures, slightly bending forward and pulling on hair locks, appear on each side of the sarcophagus, all facing toward the central sarcophagus.

These goddesses in this fashion, mourning over the mysterious mound of Osiris, *Djeba-demedj*.[79] They themselves cry out atop the mound, mysterious of visible forms. Re calls them and commands them that they mourn. Re adores the *ba*-soul of this god (Osiris), as he illumines the darkness that is in his mound. Their *ba*-souls pass in his following.

(Re says) "Your entourage is in their following, and also my corpse, which is in their protection.[80] Their mysteries are at their fingertips, as they praise me."

---

79. For this form of the unified Re-Osiris who appears frequently in the Book of Adoring Re in the West, see pp. 63–65.

80. Literally, "in their arms."

REGISTER 2 (PLATE 42)

6.71 (left). Scene 5 = Book of Caverns, Division 5, Register 2, Scene 61 (p. 412).
6.72 (right). Scene 6 = Book of Caverns, Division 5, Register 2, Scene 62 (p. 412)

6.73. Scene 7 = Book of Caverns, Division 5, Register 2, Scene 68 (pp. 440–41)

6.74. Scene 8. Four kneeling figures with their arms raised in adoration appear beneath bent shades. No captions to the figures appear in the Tomb of Ramesses IX, but they appear with this group in the Tomb of Ramesses VII, Left Wall, Register 2, Scene 5 (p. 505) and on a corpus of sarcophagi (p. 519). The annotation parallels that of the Tomb of Ramesses VII but provides several additional passages.

These gods in this fashion, their arms in the vicinity of their faces. Their shades alight upon them, while they mourn over the mysterious corpse of Osiris, foremost of the Netherworld. It is the two goddesses who seize their tresses, while the water within the eyes of these goddesses descends, being their tears, being the blood of the Netherworld Dwellers, who breathe by means of them.

This great god speaks to them, and their *ba*-souls pass by in his following, (likewise) the Osiris king, Lord of the Two Lands, Neferkare, chosen of Re, justified.

REGISTER 3 (PLATE 42)

6.75. Scene 9: A mostly damaged scene consists of two prone male deities in sarcophagi, facing downwards with their heads to the right. Between the ovals is a standing goddess, facing left and holding human-headed serpents in each hand. Another, larger serpent coils atop the sarcophagi and below the goddess.

This goddess in [this] fashion [...] two gods and two goddesses [...] as guardian, they [...]

6.76. Scene 10 = Tomb of Ramesses VII, Left Wall, Register 1, Scene 2 (p. 504)

6.77. Scene 11. Partially damaged, this scene shows five deities facing left, their arms held out and down, the palms of their hands down in a position of protection. The first three from the left are ram-headed, while the following two are female figures. At the left side of the scene is a ram-headed figure facing right, arms held out and down, followed by a disk with a damaged figure within it.

These gods in this fashion, their arms worshipping this great god. He speaks to them; (then) the darkness conceals <them.> These gods in this fashion, remaining [...] over the mystery of [this] great god. [...] rot, as he calls, its mystery goes forth [...]. Its rays [extend] to the arms of these [gods ...]. Those of blood, their throats breathe by means of their mysteries. Afterwards, this great god passes by over them. Then one hides these [gods].

RIGHT WALL

REGISTER 1 (PLATE 43)

6.78. Scene 12 = Tomb of Ramesses VII, Left Wall, Register 2, Scene 8; in the Tomb of Ramesses IX version, the left-most female figure is mummiform.

These gods in this fashion in the cavern of Penwenty, foremost of the Place of Destruction.[81] The solar disk of this great god opens the Netherworld of Wenty. The god goes forth from his mysteries. Wenty vomits and ejaculates the eye of Re that is in his belly; its pupil enters into its appearances. Atum gives his arms to Re; Nut protects that between which she is.[82] The two gods acclaim the double *ba*-soul. The two goddesses, their corpses breathe by means of the birth-forms of the great god. May they cause that the Osiris king, lord of the Two Lands, Neferkare, whom Re chose, living, prosperous, healthy, justified, exist with you, so that he might acclaim you in your mysteries. Without you seeing him, he lights up. May you guide him along your paths, so that he might become effective like your *akh*-spirits because he is one among you.

---

81. Note the parallel annotation in the Tomb of Ramesses VII (p. 506).
82. For the spelling *cf.* "*imj-wtj*," *WÄS*, 1:76.6 (*r imi-wtj-nj*).

6.79. Scene 13. Three standing mum-  mies (two male, flanking a single female) stand on the right side of the scene, facing right. Behind them is a male figure (facing left) who bows over another male figure whose torso (facing right) emerges from the ground, his arms raised in adoration. Above the adoring figure is an oval containing two shining sun disks flanking a central heart. No labels or annotations accompany this scene.

6.80. Scene 14. A large scarab below  a solar disk forms the focus of this scene. To either side are bowing deities: scarab-headed to the right, ram-headed to the left; both figures hold their arms out slightly and down before them, palms down in a gesture of protection. Immediately behind the ram-headed deity is a large solar disk containing a *ba*-bird in front of (to the right of) a right facing, baboon-headed deity with arms raised in adoration, the wrists and hands extending beyond the limb of the solar disk. No labels or annotations accompany this scene.

6.81. Scene 15. Seven shrew-headed gods on the right side of the scene, facing left, have their arms raised in adoration before a ram-headed god holding a *was*-scepter. Behind him is a baboon-headed god and disk followed by two gods with both arms raised, facing right. No labels or annotations accompany this scene.

REGISTER 2 (UPPER) (PLATE 43)

6.82. Scene 16. This scene is identical to the Book of the Hidden Chamber, Hour 6, Register 2, Scene 65 (p. 192). The serpent "He of Many Faces" is labeled twice.

This god exists in this fashion, the two mysterious ones having [gone to rest?]. He shall endure, and his corpse, which [... gods?], the daughter(?) as guardian [...]

REGISTER 2 (LOWER) (PLATE 43)

6.83. Scene 17. Two male deities—both labeled "Mysterious Putrefaction"—place their arms protectively over an oval that contains a smaller, vertically oriented oval and four flesh signs, two to either side of the small oval; a solar disk with rays radiating from the bottom shines above the oval. This scene is similar to the right portion of the Book of Caverns, Division 1, Register 4, Scene 12.

The gods exist in this fashion [...] upon this putrefaction. The gods exist with their arms over this putrefaction.

REGISTER 2 (PLATE 43)

6.84. Scene 18 (= Tomb of Ramesses VI, Section B, Register 2 [Lower], Scene 33). The tomb of Ramesses IX also includes captions to the figures in the scene that augment those of the Tomb of Ramesses VI. The three mummiform figures to the left are labeled "This god in this fashion [...]. He of the Mystery. This god in [this fas]hion"; the three mummiform figures to

the right are named "Elderly [of Face ...] this god [...] Manifesting [of Face ...]

hidden [...]." The large ithyphallic deity in the center of the funnel-shaped object (probably a clepsydra—see p. 460) is labeled "He Who Hides the Hours," while the child in front of his phallus is the "Flame."[83] Within the funnel, the goddesses holding disks are given their own annotations; on the left from top to bottom: "She who is chief of the light rays in He of the Mystery, she who guides, as she illumines the Hidden Ones"; "She who is chief of the light rays in He of the Mystery, she who guides, as she illumines the Hidden Ones"; "She who is chief of the light rays in He of the Mystery, as she illumines the darkness that is in her arms, as she opens the utter darkness of the two roads"; "She who is chief of the light rays in He of the Mystery, she who acclaims, as she protects the visible forms, she who acclaims joins together her *ba*-soul." On the right side of the funnel, the goddess holding the disks are labeled "She who is chief of her light rays (in) He of the Mystery, in the corpses of those who hide the hours"; "She who is chief of her light rays in He of the Mystery, who gives birth to his mysterious corpses"; "She who is chief of her light rays in He of the Mystery, the one whom he engendered descends into the Bloody One, as he receives them"; "She who is chief of her light rays in He of the Mystery, who gives birth to the mysteries, with the result that they manifest as children."

These gods who do not see the light of Re.[84] It is in the darkness that they guard. When they hear his voice, they breathe. In his following do their *ba*-souls pass. May they cause the Osiris King Neferkare, whom Re chose, son of Re, Ramesses (IX), living, prosperous, healthy, to enter upon the mysterious paths which are in the West. He has illuminated the utter darkness, as he sees He Who Hides the Hours.

These gods who do not see the light of Re. It is in the darkness that they guard. When they hear his voice, they breathe. In his following do their *ba*-souls pass. May they cause the Osiris King Neferkare, whom Re chose, son of Re, Ramesses (IX), living, prosperous, healthy, go forth and enter in the West. They shall not impede his *ba*-soul. May his visible forms shine together with the Mysterious one who guides him, namely the One within His Hours.

This god in this fashion, as he engenders flame[85] [...] the Bloody One, as he receives. Then this god enters, so that he might place his fire in the Place of Destruction.

---

83. For the flaming child, compare the Book of Adoring Re in the West, Address 61 (p. 97) and the child forms of the sun in Books of the Solar-Osirian Unity, The tomb of Ramesses IX, Enigmatic Wall, Left Section, Register 3 (p. 567).

84. Following Roberson 2012, 396.

85. A reference to the child before the phallus of the deity, who is called "Flame" (Roberson 2012, 185).

REGISTER 2 (UPPER) (PLATE 43)

6.85. Scene 19 = Tomb of Ramesses VI, Section B, Registers 2–4, Scene 34

REGISTER 2 (LOWER) (PLATE 43)

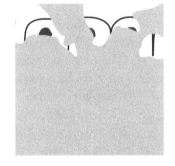

6.86. Scene 20 = Tomb of Ramesses VI, Section B2, Scene 43 (the version in the Tomb of Ramesses IX is mostly damaged). In place of the annotations that accompany this scene in the Tomb of Ramesses VI, the Tomb of Ramesses IX includes a lengthy speech of Re.

What Re says when he enters the corpse of the Westerner, foremost of the West:

> "O, hail, that I have passed by the Netherworld,
>> is traversing that which is in the earth.
> O, hail, that I have passed by the corpses,
>> is having illumined the darkness by means of my solar disk.
> O, hail, that I have passed by the Netherworld,
>> is giving(?) [...] their bodies.
> O, hail, that I have passed by the Netherworld,
>> is having traversed the mystery of Igeret.
> O, hail, that I have passed by the Netherworld,
>> is inflicting punishment on my enemies.
> O, hail, that I have passed by the Netherworld,
>> is destroying the enemies of Osiris.
> O, hail, that I have passed by the Netherworld,
>> is while those that are in them praise me.
> O, hail, that I have passed by the Netherworld,
>> is with the *ba*-souls passing in my following.
> O, hail, that I have passed by the Netherworld,
>> is passing by the corpses of the Waking Ones.

O, hail, that I have passed by the Netherworld,
    is illumining their corpses and praising their *ba*-souls.
O, hail, that I have passed by the Netherworld,
    is issuing commands to those who are foremost of the banks.
O, hail, that I have passed by the Netherworld,
    is traversing the mysterious sarcophagi.
O, hail, that I have passed by the Netherworld,
    is while my children fashion my birth-form.
O, hail, that I have passed by the Netherworld,
    is honoring the *ba*-souls of the Resting Ones.
O, hail, that I have passed by the Netherworld,
    is with those who manifest from me guiding me.
O, hail, that I have passed by the Netherworld,
    is causing the rotting ones and their corpses to breathe.
O, hail, that I have passed by the Netherworld,
    is issuing commands to the goddesses.
O, hail, that I have passed by the Netherworld,
    is traversing the caverns of the West.
O, hail, that I have passed by the Netherworld,
    is while resting in the great bark.
O, hail, that I have passed by the Netherworld,
    is having been born, so that I might go to rest in Nut.
O, hail, that I have passed by the Netherworld,
    is entering into you, I having caused that the corpses breathe.
O, hail, I have passed by the Netherworld. O, hail, I have passed by
    you.
O, hail, O, hail, that I have passed by the Netherworld,
    is with the result that those who are in my following go to rest in
    my following.
O, hail, that I have passed by the Netherworld,
    is causing the Osiris King Neferkare, whom Re chose,
    to pass by that which is therein."

These [gods in] this [fash]ion, [their] corpses [standing in their sarcophagi, they seeing the light][86] of Re. Their [*ba*-souls] pass by in his following,

---

86. Restoration after Roberson 2012, 403.

although the gods exist in their utter darkness. Their *ba*-souls open their darkness afterward. Re passes by [... ...]. [These] gods in this fashion in their sarcophagi, standing in front of their sarcophagi, while they putrefy in their rot.

SARCOPHAGI: RAMESSIDE AND LATE PERIOD

FOOT END

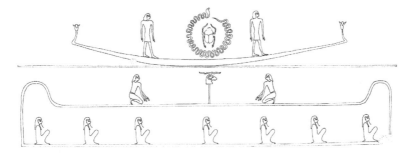

6.87. Foot End. A version of the introduction to the book is equivalent to the Book of Gates, Hour 1 (see pp. 257–59).

LONG WALL 1 (PLATE 44)

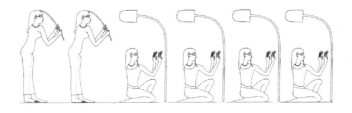

6.88. Scene 1. Four figures with their arms raised in adoration kneel beneath shades, alternatively represented as pouring vessels; they are named (right to left) "He of the Shade"; "He Who Mourns"; "He Who Begets"; "He Who Illumines." These gods are followed by two goddesses—Isis and Nephthys—who pull at a hair-lock flipped over their heads.

These gods in this fashion, with their arms near their heads, the shade(s) before them alighting upon them, when they mourn over the mysterious corpse of Osiris, foremost of the Netherworld. It is the two goddesses who pull their tresses, while water that is within the eyes of these two goddesses descends, as tears and blood. It is the Netherworldly beings who breathe by means of them. This great god speaks to them and their *ba*-souls, so that they follow him and their *ba*-souls pass by.[87]

6.89. Scene 2. Four catfish-headed gods, distributed in two pairs facing in towards one another, pull at a rope; the catfish are named (left to right): "He of the Nar-catfish"; "He of the Khessy-Catfish"; "He of (Fish) Form"; "He Relating to Slaughter."[88] In the center of the tableaux stands a god, "Aker," bending slightly forward and facing left, holding an egg-like object.

What <Re>[89] says to the catfish, when they receive the mystery of the One within the Earth. "O, these catfish who receive the mysteries of the One within the Earth. I cause your *ba*-souls to breathe! It is so that I might make his *ba*-soul breathe that Osiris N enters!"

6.90. Scene 3. Two gods stand with both arms raised in a gesture of acclamation; behind them is a ram-headed figure slightly bent over a disk. Some versions include a jackal-headed staff and ram-headed staff labeled "Neck of Re" and "Head of Re," respectively.

These gods in this fashion, transfiguring the supporters of Re. As for those who adore his head and mysterious neck, they praise the *ba*-soul of Re, and the *ba*-soul of Re praises them (in return). This great god calls to them, with the result that their *ba*-souls traverse behind him, <their corpses> enduring in their places.

87. The last sentence of this annotation may refer to Long Wall 2, Scene 5.
88. An alternate version writes "Wakeful One."
89. Following Roberson 2012, 450 and n. 835.

LONG WALL 2 (PLATE 45)

6.91. Scene 4. For a description of this scene, see Tomb of Ramesses IX, Left Wall, Register 1, Scene 3 (p. 510).

What <Re> says in order to clothe their image upon the divine mound whose appearance is hidden: "O you two gods and two goddesses who are in the following of your secret mound. Behold, Osiris N passes over you. Your *ba*-souls praise, so they might breathe when he enters them, but without them seeing him."

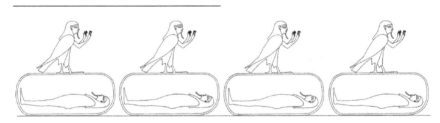

6.92. Scene 5. Four sarcophagi containing male mummies are placed in a row; above each sarcophagus is a large *ba*-bird. The mummies are labeled (left to right): "Formed One"; "He Who Wanders"; "He Who Escapes"; "He Who Awakens." This scene is similar to the Tomb of Ramesses VI, Section B2, Scene 46 (p. 501).

What Re says to the putrefying ones in the company of the Great One, (to) the rotting ones who are in the company of the Great One. "O rotting ones who are surrounded with their mysteries, whose corpses having expelled that which is in them.[90] Hail to you and those with you! O hail to you, Osiris N!"

90. Following Roberson 2012, 452; contra Manassa 2007a, 51.

6.93. Scene 6. Two male deities face right with their arms raised in a gesture of acclamation; they are named "Pacifier" and "He Belonging to the Great One." A ram-headed god holding a *was*-scepter faces left; he is not labeled.

HEAD END (PLATE 46)

6.94. Head End. For a description of this scene, see Tomb of Ramesses VI, Section B, Register 3, Scene 36 (p. 495).

These gods in <th>is fashion, the ones who fill[91] the shrine of Osiris, the Hidden Cham-

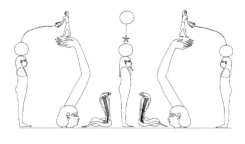

ber, secret of condition, the name of that which is within does not exist. This god in this fashion, the light of Re having entered into his corpse, illumining the darkness under his soles and the mysterious image beneath his legs. His *ba*-soul follows Re. This god is in this fashion at the (appropriate) hour, Re having entered into his own corpse, he protecting the hours that have entered the darkness beneath his two soles. His two uraei protecting him forever and ever (namely,) Osiris N.

---

91. Roberson 2012, 448.

7

BOOKS OF THE SOLAR-OSIRIAN UNITY

INTRODUCTION

Already during the mid-nineteenth century Théodule Devéria (1897) began the study of the cryptographic texts of the Books of the Solar-Osirian Unity, which encompass three separate compositions that all share similar themes and are written almost entirely in cryptographic script. The original publication of the Second Shrine of Tutankhamun is Piankoff (1952, pl. II, IV) with improved copies in Piankoff and Rambova (1955, pls. 47–53); translations of the shrine text were attempted by Drioton (1949) and Hornung (1983a). The Corridor G Ceiling in the Tomb of Ramesses VI is published in Piankoff and Rambova (1954, pl. 179–82), with an initial attempt to translate the Protective Image (Schutzbild) in Hornung (1988). The enigmatic composition of the third corridor in the Tomb of Ramesses IX, Right Wall is published in Guilmant (1907, pls. 63, 76–81) with discussions in Hornung (1987a) and Abitz (1990, 25–28). Updated translations and collated text copies of all three of the compositions are published in Darnell (2004).

The three compositions grouped under the heading "Books of the Solar-Osirian Unity" are not versions of a single work, but rather represent three variant constructions based on a common conceptual template, focusing on an image of the unified Re-Osiris, and incorporating labels and annotations primarily composed in cryptography. In the Tombs of Ramesses VI and Ramesses IX, the compositions lack titles, while the Second Shrine of Tutankhamun, Side 1 explicity designates the text an *imy-dwꜣ.t* "What is in the Netherworld," an "Amduat."[1] The solar-Osirian treatises emphasize a syncopation of the Netherworld, in which the time

---

1. Darnell 2004, 38; see p. 537.

of cosmic crisis in the midst of the night and the moment of solar victory at dawn draw together both graphically and textually. In the composition in the Tomb of Ramesses IX, Enigmatic Wall, the solar eye aground on the back of Apep shoots fiery arrows at serpent foes who stretch in line almost to the edge of the image of the union of Re and Osiris to the right. On the Second Shrine of Tutankhamun, the unfied Re-Osiris dominates the middle of Side 1 of the shrine, a short distance from the posts that mark the entrance to the Netherworld; on Side 2 of the same shrine, the concluding scene itself represents the upper and lower, eastern and western nodes of the solar cycle—the totality of the chthonic and diurnal journeys of the sun. Even the Tomb of Ramesses VI, Corridor G Ceiling reveals but little separation between the entry of the sun into the Netherworld and the appearance of the giant anguipede who embodies the concept of the solar-Osirian unity.

The Second Shrine of Tutankhamun

The first exemplar of the enigmatic Books of the Solar-Osirian Unity appears on one of the gilded shrines that surrounded Tutankhamun's sarcophagus, the second in number, counting from the outer-most shrine. The two long walls of the gilded shrine are each decorated with three registers of scenes and cryptographic annotations; the three-register structure is interrupted on Side 1 by a large image of Re-Osiris, whose head and feet are surrounded by uroboroi. Since the Second Shrine of Tutankhamun is the only attestation of this particular Netherworldly composition, its completeness is unknowable; the use of only Hours 2 and 6 of the Book of the Hidden Chamber on the Third Shrine may hint at a use of select elements from a larger, unpreserved treatise. The rich iconography of the scenes on the Second Shrine of Tutankhamun appear to compensate for the terseness of the enigmatic annotations, providing visual expression for concepts that otherwise appear only in textual descriptions within other Netherworld Books.

Each side consists of nine scenes, with the introductory images (Scenes 1–2) at the right side of Side 1 and the concluding image (Scene 18) at the left end of Side 2. The jackal-headed and ram-headed staffs in the introductory scene of the Second Shrine of Tutankhamun find parallels in the Book of Gates, Hour 1, although the former eliminates the image of the solar bark and replaces the scarab with a ram-headed bird. The concluding image, enclosed by pairs of arms, mirrors several scenes within the different templates of the Books of the Creation of Solar Disk,[2] in which the solar god illumines his corpse and re-creates time itself. The "Destroying Arms" and bull-heads of the concluding image also find parallels in the introductory scene in the Corridor G Ceiling composition of the Tomb of Ramesses VI, suggesting that the final scene on the Second Shrine of Tutankhamun is also to some extent another opening scene, allowing the treatise to read—in a manifestation of *perpetuum mobile*—in from each end, toward the great mystery of the solar-Osiris who dominates the first side of the shrine.

As in other Netherworld Books, the enigmatic treatise on the Second Shrine of Tutankhamun depicts varied denizens of the nightly journey of the solar deity, who himself appears as the large mummiform figure in the middle of Side 1; the solar bark of the earlier attested compositions—the Book of the Hidden Chamber and the Book of Gates—is absent, while the solar disk of the compositions first attested during the Ramesside Period— the Book of Caverns and Books of the Solar-Osirian Unity—is prominent. Four larger disks in both halves of the composition contain images of the ram-headed *ba*-soul (Side 1, Scenes 1–2, 6; Side 2, Scene 18), while smaller disks accompany almost every scene on Side 2; the annotations on Side 2 also emphasize the "light of Re." Overall, Side 1 may be characterized as a place of caverns and darkness, with several deities still within their sar-cophagi, while Side 2 is epitomized by light that shines upon the heads of Netherworldly gods and goddesses, and even billows from out the mouths of some of those entities.

Side 1 is divided into two halves by the giant mummiform image of Re-Osiris. The deities in Register 1 of the right side are in the Upper Region, while those in Register 3 are within the Place of Destruction; this geographical division suggests that the central, mummiform Re-Osiris occupies the entire Netherworld, his rays penetrating the uniform dark-ness of this portion of the nightly realm. Behind the mummiform figure are three registers, beginning at the top with seven goddesses within sar-cophagi. The names of the first four goddesses relate them to the regions of the Netherworld, in terms both macrocosmic—the upper region, the Mysterious Place—and microcosmic—a cavern, a sarcophagus; the names of the final three goddesses are elemental—fire, water, and earth. Praising

---

2. Tomb of Ramesses VI, Section B, Register 3, Scene 31 (p. 491); Sarcophagi, Head End (p. 522).

gods, who simultaneously mimic the illuminating power of the sun, grasp a rope in Register 2 behind the mummiform figure; although the solar bark remains unseen on the Second Shrine of Tutankhamun, the rope signals the path of the sun, the tow-rope hauled by so many Netherworld dwellers in the Book of the Hidden Chamber and Book of Gates. In the final scene of Side 1, a human-headed serpent protects the Osirian corpse, which is juxtaposed with the "mysterious chest" that also appears in the Book of Caverns and Books of the Creation of the Solar Disk.[3]

Side 2 of the treatise focuses not on a central image, as does Side 1, but rather has the appearance of three horizontal registers of images and primarily cryptographic annotations, the majority of the figures facing toward the left end. Not only do the annotations on Side 2 describe the action of the light of the sun as it illuminates the corpses of the Netherworldly deities, this side of the Second Shrine of Tutankhamun provides one of the most graphic depictions of light within the corpus of Netherworld Books. Rather than a sun disk simply hovering above a mummy to indicate illumination, rays of light here connect the disk and the mummies—be it with their heads (Scenes 1, 3) or with headless corpses (Scene 2). In Registers 1–3, large uraei and felines—a cat and a lion—oversee the illumination of the corpses, an action that both resurrects them and frees their *ba*-souls (depicted as independent elements in Scene 1). In Registers 2–3, deities literally inhale the divine light, a striking equation of light, breath, and speech often attested textually in other Netherworldly compositions.[4] The lion-headed deities who inhale the light in Register 2 have their arms hidden beneath their cloaks; they are bearers of the "mysteries," like the gods in the Book of Gates, Hour 6, Register 2, Scene 38 (p. 28). In Register 3, light billows around a series of Osiride figures; disks in front of the mummiform figures are crowned with uraei and lion heads who appear to suck in and spit out the light that clothes the Osirian manifestations.[5] In Scene 6, sails occupy the position of lines of light descending from the *ba*-souls in the first group of the top register (Scene 1), the jux-

---

3. See the Book of Caverns, Division 2, Register 3, Scene 21 (pp. 361–63) and the Books of the Creation of the Solar Disk, Tomb of Ramesses VI, Section A, Register 1, Scene 4 (pp. 468–69).

4. Particularly the Books of the Creation of the Solar Disk (see pp. 5–6).

5. For the clothing properties of light and the many parallel texts (and post-New Kingdom material) that can be brought to bear on this scene, see Darnell 2004, 133–38.

taposition suggesting the concept of the light of the sun dispensing breath in the Netherworld.[6] The central scene of Side 2, Register 3 shows a lion presiding over the illumination of ram-headed mummiform deities, who are "distinguished" by means of the solar light that shines down in front of them. In the final scene, female beings whose names allude to fiery punishment in the eastern horizon both suck in light from disks and dispense light atop the heads of serpents labeled "Evil of Face." The names of the goddesses and the nature of the serpents suggest that the light that flows from the hands of the goddesses is a fiery punishment of the hypostases of Apep (Gaber 2015).[7]

Corridor G in the Tomb of Ramesses VI

The two additional exemplars of the Books of the Solar-Osirian unity do not appear until the Twentieth Dynasty, in the Tombs of Ramesses VI and Ramesses IX. The construction of the Tomb of Ramesses VI (KV 9) began during the reign of his predecessor, Ramesses V, and during the course of the completion of the tomb, a miscalculation resulted in collision with another tomb, KV 12 (Abitz 1989, 28–31). At the point where the fifth corridor in the Tomb of Ramesses VI (Corridor G[8]) broke into the earlier tomb KV 12, the architects of KV 9 were forced abruptly to lower the height of the rear portion of the ceiling in that corridor. Those in charge of the decoration of the tomb were left to deal with an architecturally peculiar ceiling that also contained an opening potentially both physically and psychically noxious to the future incumbent of the as of yet unfinished sepulchre. The resulting decoration of the Corridor G Ceiling, including the main portion of the ceiling, a dropped element, and a high lintel above the doorway into Hall H, was a unique combination of scenes and enigmatic annotations; the treatise is a version of the Books of the

---

6. For the call of the eye bringing light and breath, compare the Book of Caverns, Division 6, Register 3, Scene 76 (pp. 448–49) and the Book of Adoring Re in the West, Address 7 (p. 78); see also Darnell 2004, 100–3, 109–10, 113–14, 248, and 364–65.

7. The upward-facing palms of the goddesses are reminiscent of the *nyny*-gesture (Westendorf 1991), the greeting of the celestial mother to the returning son; pouring water also appears in representations of the defeat of Apep, such as variants of the Book of the Hidden Chamber, Hour 7 in Late period sources (Régen 2015, 254–55).

8. Retaining the designation of the corridor in Piankoff and Rambova 1954; the plan published by the Theban Mapping Project labels the corridor as "H" (http://tinyurl.com/SBL1547b).

Solar-Osirian Unity, so peculiarly appropriate to the changed architecture of Corridor G that it may have been composed specifically for the Tomb of Ramesses VI.

The left portion of the treatise, on the longer, high part of the Corridor G Ceiling, has three horizontal registers. The upper and lower registers each contain three scenes based on a similar template: an introductory image with punishing goddesses and four bull's heads; three double-domed structures; and seated solar gods/goddesses. The middle register consists of four scenes: a large solar-disk paralleling the introductory scenes above and below; an unusual ophidian solar bark; disk-headed praising entities; and a scene of stellar resurrection. The treatise begins on the left end, and the introductory scenes mingle the western horizon, the entrance to the Netherworld (marked by both the bull's heads in the upper and lower register and a stela in the middle register), with the punishment of the damned that takes place within the Netherworld itself (featured most prominently in the cauldrons atop the goddesses' heads in the upper and lower registers). The following groups of three twin-domed structures contain unusual depictions of Netherworldly denizens, including blind deities (Scene 2) and hands (atop mummiform bodies) that dispense light (Scene 9); based on the accompanying annotations, the doubled, domed structures are *nm.t*-slaughtering places, apparently revealing the association of sarcophagus oval, mound of sand, and slaughtering place occurring in several of the Netherworld Books.

The beginning portion of the middle register emphasizes the nocturnal, ram-headed solar deity, who appears thrice in the first two scenes: as a ram-headed bird praising a large disk, a ram head emerging from the disk itself, and a ram-headed figure standing in an unusal bark. A short hieroglyphic inscription within a stela[9] at the beginning of the middle register and a scarab emerging from the large solar disk together describe the actions of Khepri. The hull of the solar bark in the middle register is a giant serpent, a transformation that also appears in the Book of the Hidden Chamber, Hours 4–5; here the assistance of the serpent Life of the Gods in the end of the Book of the Hidden Chamber finds concrete expression as the boat that is upon—and in essence embodying—the aspects of decay that presage the regeneration of the sun. The Corridor G

---

9. The round-topped monument parallels the human-headed stelae in the Book of the Hidden Chamber, Hours 1–2 (see pp. 141–42, 149).

Ceiling in the Tomb of Ramesses VI adds an additional detail: the ship's deck is anthropomorphic, formed of the bodies of Isis and Nephthys; a fully anthropomorphic bark appears in the dropped portion of the Corridor G Ceiling.

Following the solar bark in the middle register are seven disk-headed gods, their arms raised in adoration (Scene 6); the names of the entities form four groups—a single name with three pairs of names following. The first name, "He of the Disk," relates directly to the solar orb, whose journey is described. The following, first group of two names describes the place of the nocturnal sojourn of the sun. The second pair of names, "Red One" and "Mysterious (Corpse)," refer to the corpse of Osiris at the root of the eastern horizon. The third and final pair of names references the actions of the Netherworld dwellers under the influence of the sun. At the end of the middle register is a scene with two pairs of gods "protecting" a goddess, the embodiment of the "secret Netherworld"; the goddess appears inverted in both scenes, but her head is turned upwards in the second image, another representation of the "turning over" (*pn‛*) necessary for the continued existence of the blessed dead within the Netherworld (Darnell 2004, 426–48). The annotation that fills the middle register describes the sun travelling through the Mysterious Place and the Place of Destruction, inspiring movement in the *ba*-souls of the Netherworldly denizens, while their corpses remain ensconced in the darkness.

The concluding portion of the upper and lower registers is filled with seated deities: disk-headed gods above and goddesses associated with disks in the lower register.[10] In addition to names primarily (and predictably) related to luminosity, lengthy annotations detail the actions of the sun's light within the Place of Destruction; the upper register also mentions the toponym Imhet, otherwise only attested within the Book of the Hidden Chamber, Hours 4–5 (Barta 1990a, 47), which also share an ophidian solar bark in the middle register of the composition. The annotations in the Corridor G Ceiling also emphasize the re-creation of time and actions of the hours, a theme also present in the Book of Gates (see pp. 274, 288).

The rear portion of the Corridor G Ceiling in the Tomb of Ramesses VI is lower than the main ceiling and is decorated with two short registers. The upper register of the dropped portion is dominated by a large solar

---

10. The male disk-headed deities appear to be the equivalent of the female beings with disks as attributes; if the goddesses' heads were replaced with disks, their feminine quality would be obfuscated.

disk atop a lunar crescent, and the combination of solar and lunar elements is yet another allusion to the *perpetuum mobile* of the solar cycle (Abitz 1989, 154). The ram-headed solar deity in the lower half of the scene has goddesses as his two arms; in the protective image on the lintel at the end of Corridor G, the arms of the solar god are identified as the "Two Sisters," indicating that the goddess arms are Isis and Nephthys, the two goddesses identified as the deck of the solar bark in the main portion of the ceiling. The annotation mentions the "spells" of the deities "coming forth" for the solar god, a succinct allusion to the defeat of the chaos serpent Apep through the magic of Isis in the Book of the Hidden Chamber, Hour 7 (pp. 196, 199). Overall, the decoration of the dropped portion of the ceiling parallels scenes in the middle register of the longer, high part of the ceiling as well as the protective image on the adjoining high lintel of the doorway in Hall H, interrelationships suggesting that all three portions of the ceiling decoration were indeed composed as a unity.

On the vertical face of the dropped portion of the Corridor G Ceiling, the high lintel of the doorway in Hall H, is a depiction of the disk-headed, serpent-legged solar deity;[11] to the right, four serpents emerge from a central disk, an enemy opposite each serpent head. Another anguipedal deity appears to have occupied the now all but destroyed left portion of the scene. The surviving texts—only that accompanying the right serpent legged solar god is intact—emphasize the ability of the deity to penetrate into the innermost regions of the Netherworld, as he does here, seeming to move out from the then covered and now exposed break into the older tomb (KV 12). This unique scene was termed a "Schutzbild," protective image, in earlier descriptions of the tomb (Hornung 1988; Abitz 1989); the apotropaic qualities of the Schutzbild are embodied within the anguipedal Re-Osiris who punishes the damned.[12] As mentioned above, elements within the text also refer to the lower part of the dropped portion of the ceiling, showing that the protective image of the sun on the vertical surface is fully integrated within the decorative and textual program of Corridor G.

---

11. As in the catalogue of the king's members in the Book of Adoring Re in the West ("My toes are uraei") the toes of the solar god are also uraeus serpents (p. 118).

12. The snake-legged deity within the Tomb of Ramesses VI also provides an earlier Egyptian origin for the entity Abrasax on Graeco-Roman magical gems (Darnell 2004, 387–90).

The Enigmatic Wall in the Tomb of Ramesses IX

The third and final extant template for the Books of the Solar-Osirian Unity appears within the Tomb of Ramesses IX (KV 6), on the right wall (facing into the tomb) of the third corridor. A band of hieroglyphs crowns the tri-partite scenes on the "Enigmatic Wall"; written primarily in normal hiero-glyphic orthographies, the line describes the deceased pharaoh Ramesses IX as the four-faced supreme deity, like the four-headed solar deity who appears in the entrance corridor decoration first in the Tomb of Ramesses IX (Lüscher 2000, 54–55). As this powerful deity, Ramesses IX repels Apep by means of his efficacious spells, and indeed, Register 2 of the treatise on the Enigmatic Wall incorporates the defeat of the nefarious serpent.

The left portion of the Engimatic Wall is divided into three registers, with the solar bark present in Register 2. Register 1 lacks any annotations, although the upside-down figures within disks may be read as "Lords of the Netherworld."[13] In Register 2, the ophidian solar bark contains a scarab beetle pushing a disk flanked by two *udjat*-eyes. The replacement of the bark by a giant serpent finds important parallels in the Book of the Hidden Chamber, Hours 4–5, as well as the barks in the Book of the Solar-Osirian Unity on the Corridor G Ceiling in the Tomb of Ramesses VI. Unlike all other depictions in the Netherworld Books corpus, however, the solar bark in the Tomb of Ramesses IX appears atop the chaos serpent Apep, and the destruction of that creature and his compatriots, those "ter-rible of face," form the focus of the register. The left-most *udjat*-eye within the bark dispenses a fiery arrow[14] and additional fiery arrows pierce or shoot flame at rearing serpents in front of the solar bark, while guard-ians[15] atop mounds oversee the destruction of yet more serpents shot with

---

13. The figures evoke the ideographic sign of a figure swimming in an oval of dots as writing of the verb *nbi*, "to swim"; they also give the appearance of stars in circles as orthographies of *dwȝ.t*, albeit inverted. The images are thus cryptographic writings of the *nb.w-dwȝ.t*, "lords of the Netherworld," as well as representations of tumbling celestial light sources. The darkness of the figures evokes the dead as those who are "dark in Nun" in the Book of the Hidden Chamber, Hour 10. They are probably iden-tical to the inverted *sḥd.w*-stars of Book of the Dead chapter 99 and link the Datian Netherworld to the astronomical realm (Kákosy 1982, 182–84).

14. For the solar eye who "shoots" flame and arrows, see Darnell 2004, 305–8.

15. The long hair of the figures suggest that they are female, but the fourth figure from the left wears a curved beard; one may compare the bearded depictions of the

arrows. The guardians "leap up" for Re (Darnell 2004, 296–99), celebrating his victory over Apep, whose very annihilation they guarantee.

A line of normal hieroglyphic text above Register 3 makes a comparison, through a string of divine syncretisms, between Atum, the Great Flood (Mehetweret) cosmic goddess, the *udjat*-eye, the goddess Great of Magic, and finally Ptah as Pedjaha. Essentially, the text claims that Ramesses IX deserves salvation from evil sendings because he is a physical manifestation (Ptah) of the most transcendent deity (Atum), the two linked by magic and the solar goddess—physical manipulation and appeasement of physical forces. The scenes of Register 3 consist of two quartets of deities followed by two mummiform figures and a solar disk transected by a goddess and from which two scarabs emerge. The enigmatic annotation at the left end of the Register 3 refers to all of the deities being located in the Place of Destruction, a cavern that is simultaneously the place of the birth of the solar disk. The first four goddesses dominate serpents; the labels to the snakes indicate that they are manifestations of Apep, the same inimical force repeatedly shot in Register 2.

The following four androgynous figures have long flowing hair and erect phalli, these latter appendages now damaged; the images that surround these beings—the child, scarab, disks, and flame—are in keeping with a representation of the eastern horizon, where the sun is reborn, and the damned receive their ultimate fiery punishment. The term *ḥnsk.tyw*, "lock-wearers," describing the personification of the winds, and dangling locks of the figures bending backwards, may associate the four Ramesses IX deities with the cardinal points and the four winds.[16] These winds spit in assisting the *ḫprw*-manifestation of the sun, and the winds themselves may be said to have been spat out.[17] The dots of effluvia emerging from the figures pun on the verbs *nḥ* and *nḥḥ*, "spit" and "ejaculate,"[18] the spitting and ejaculation of creation (Allen 1988, 30) and find a textual parallel in P. Bremner-Rhind, in which the creator deity describes the engendering of Shu and Tefnut: "I made masturbation with my hand, I poured out from

---

goddesses Isis and Nephthys on the Corridor G Ceiling in the Tomb of Ramesses VI (p. 556).

16. See Hornung 1963b, 44 n. 15. The association of the four winds with tumbling dancers is attested (Kurth 1994), and it is to this association that the Tomb of Ramesses IX, Enigmatic Wall, refers.

17. See Parker, Leclant, and Goyon 1979, 71 n. 27.

18. Compare Derchain 1969, 34 and n. 4.

my mouth, I spat out Shu, I expectorated Tefnut."[19] They also recall the crocodile Wenty in the Books of the Creation of the Solar Disk: "Wenty vomits and ejaculates the eye of Re that is in his body" (Tomb of Ramesses VII, Left Wall, Register 2, Scene 8; Tomb of Ramesses IX, Right Wall, Register 1, Scene 12, pp. 506, 513). In the scenes in the lower register of the main portion of the Tomb of Ramesses IX, Enigmatic Wall, the *ḫprw*-manifestation of the sun is spat out, and the *mswt*-birth form is ejaculated.

The Tomb of Ramesses IX, Enigmatic Wall, Right Section consists of two scenes: a reclining image of Re-Osiris and the king offering Maat to Ptah. In Scene 1, the mummiform, ithyphallic Re-Osiris raises his arm—according to the cryptographic annotation, the arm lays within the "upper region," while the figure's feet are in the "Place of Destruction"; the slanting figure rests on a serpent, called the *Nehep*-serpent in the annotation. In the Tomb of Ramesses IX, Enigmatic Wall, Left Section, Register 2, serpents receive the solar wrath, while another in the Right Section protects the Osirian corpse. The emphasis on ophidian elements is consistent with the stress on the syncopation of time concomitant with the union of solar and Osirian elements. In chapter 175 of the Book of Going Forth by Day, Atum—the aged sun—proclaims that he will survive a return of creation into the chaotic abyss by assuming a chaotic, ophidian form (Klotz 2012a, 199).

The cryptographic annotation accompanying the Enigmatic Wall, Right Section, Scene 1 refers both to Osiris (this god), and to Re (the "great god").[20] In the scene, the solar-Osirian figure evokes the location of the mummiform figure at the end of the Book of the Hidden Chamber, Hour 12, the corpse of Osiris being atop and literally becoming the hill of the eastern horizon, both corpse and hill the feminine elements with which the solar disk is uniting as it passes through the liminal space separating the lower and upper worlds. In the concluding scene (Scene 2), the image of Ptah stands back to back with the depiction of the reclining Re-Osiris—Ptah graphically represents the cult image of Re on earth (Assmann 1969, 173), counterpart to the image of the mystic union of the corporeal mystery and solar disk to the left.[21] The image of the king offering Maat to Ptah

---

19. Zandee 1992, 171, citing Faulkner 1933, 60, ll. 11–13 (P. Bremner-Rhind 26, 24–27, 1).

20. For the birth of "this great god" compare the of the "Short" Book of the Hidden Chamber, Hour 12 (p. 248).

21. Ptah himself, as creator, may be a giant like the unified Re-Osiris, filling heaven and earth (Erman 1901, pl. 39, l. 4).

in the company of Maat both ensures the rising of the sun and creates a representation of unity with the victorious sun parallel to that of the image of the reclining, ithyphallic Osiris.[22]

The Unified Solar *Ba*-Soul

In the giant deity on the Second Shrine of Tutankhamun, the anguipedal solar deity on the dropped portion of the Tomb of Ramesses VI, Corridor G Ceiling, and the reclining Osiride giant on the eastern horizon in the tomb of Ramesses IX, Enigmatic Wall, the cryptographic treatises focus on the "unified *ba*-soul" that represents the solar-Osirian unity. Appearing already in the Book of Adoring Re in the West (pp. 63, 75), the deity appears as a cosmic giant, filling all of the time and space at the moment of (re)-creation, the body of the giant deity both inhabits and becomes the space-time extent of the Netherworld (Darnell 2004, 374–424). The manifestations of the deity, even the very anthropomorphic limbs thereof—as in the goddess-armed deity in the Tomb of Ramesses VI—are the gods and goddesses through which the creator manifests its ever renewing and dividing self within the imminent world (Stadler 2010).

In the Book of Caverns, Division 5, the solar *ba*-soul perches atop the giant Osiris (Scene 59, pp. 409–10); in the Second Shrine of Tutankhamun depiction, the ram-headed soul bird is within a solar disk. This latter is a depiction of the "corpse in which is Re" of the Books of the Creation of the Solar Disk, a corpse associated there with the eastern horizon, as in the Tomb of Ramesses IX, Enigmatic Wall.[23] The ram-headed *ba*-bird within the disk-womb within the giant figure on the Second Shrine of Tutankhamun represents the "august *ba*-soul who is in his solar disk" (Assmann 1983a, 340–41). As Shetayt (Štȝy.t), the Mysterious One, the goddess in the

---

22. Maat is a symbol of "Gemeinschaft mit dem Sonnengott" (Assmann 1969, 162–63; 2001c, 174–195). The king holding Maat, with Maat as a representation of the semen of the god (Kurth 1984), parallels the sexual imagery of the ithyphallic Osiris. Maat is a symbol of passage through a liminal phase (Assmann 2001c, 174) here corresponding to the union of Re and Osiris, and the sun's passage from the Netherworld into the upper sky.

23. P. 487; see Piankoff 1953, 9; note also the Books of the Creation of the Solar Disk, Tomb of Ramesses VI, Section B, Register 1, Scene 25, annotation: "as he places light in the corpse of He of the Horizon, and as he enters into the disk, so that he might light up the mysterious corpse …" (pp. 486–87)

Books of the Creation of the Solar Disk, Section A,[24] is a representation of the corpse of Osiris, the "mysterious corpse" (ḥꜣ.t štꜣ.t), a goddess as personification of the feminine element of the unified Re-Osiris.[25] Just as the solar child may inhabit the womb of the pregnant celestial goddess, so the ram-headed sun may occupy the belly of the Osirian half of the unified deity.[26] This is the solar-Osirian creator deity "who binds his seed with his body in order to create his seed within his mysterious corpse."[27]

Within the mortuary contexts in which the Books of the Solar-Osirian Unity have survived, the focus of the treatises on the unified Re-Osiris is ultimately a focus on the ruler whose mummy was originally the corporeal Osirian element within the tomb. The hieratic annotation accompanying the penultimate scene in the Tomb of Ramesses IX, Enigmatic Wall (Right Section, Scene 1)—the reclining Osiride figure at the moment of union with the solar disk—makes explicit the identity of the royal person—soul and corpse—with the cosmic elements of Re and Osiris. Four lines of hieratic text appear beneath the hieroglyphic annotation in the upper left. The text refers to the deceased king and alludes to chapter 17 of the Book of Going Forth by Day:[28]

The Osiris king Neferkare-Setepenre, living, prosperous, healthy, is come before you, great god. From the reapers of Babai has he been protected.[29] May you set the son of Re Ramesses (IX), beloved of Amun, in your *sanctum*.[30] May you hide his forms. He is the efflux of your limbs, your

---

24. Tomb of Ramesses VI, Register 4, Scene 16 (p. 479).

25. Westendorf 1974; Assmann 1969, 325–26.

26. Piankoff 1934; Piankoff and Rambova 1954, pls. 149 and 187; see also Barta 1990a, 63.

27. P.Leiden 1.350, II 27 (see Gardiner 1905, 25).

28. Copy in Guilmant 1907, 77; Kitchen 1983, 460, l. 15; p. 461, l. 2, published a transcription into hieroglyphic script; improved transcription, based on collation in the tomb, in Darnell 2004, pl. 37

29. The deity Babai appears here, as patron of reaping beings, "those of the sickle," counterparts to the sickle-wielding demons in the Book of Gates, Hour 7, Register 3, Scene 47 (p. 296) A graphic depiction of the association appears in the thirteenth vignette in the mythological papyrus of Djedkhonsefankh II—behind a woman reaping wheat with a sickle stands a feline-headed female holding a severed human head (Piankoff and Rambova 1957, pl. 22). On the deity Babai, see also Leitz 1994.

30. Caminos 1974, 97 n. 4.

august ram-form.[31] For those in heaven and for those in the earth has he been born, for he is yesterday, while he knows tomorrow.

The deceased king as the unified deity belongs to both the celestial and chthonic realms. He is the sun of the upper and nether skies;[32] in the Tomb of Prince Amunherkhopeshef, the deity Qebehsenewef leads Ramesses III by the hand, saying (Hassanein and Nelson 1976, 102 [text C 11]): "As I bring to you those in heaven, so I bring to you those in the earth." Even the living king may manifest himself with the powers of the nocturnal solar deity—so the vizier Khaemtore (usurped by Pareemhab) may address the living ruler Amenmesse (usurped by Seti II) with the line (Habachi 1978, pl. 11a): "You are like Re, when he sets in the Netherworld, having filled the Two Lands with his rays, (O) king of Upper and Lower Egypt Userkheperure [...]." As a likeness of Shu—whom the giant figure in the Tomb of Ramesses IX evokes with his raised arm—the Egyptian ruler occupies the space between the solar and chthonic realms of the cosmos (Westendorf 1984). The hieratic text labeling of the Tomb of Ramesses IX, Enigmatic Wall, Right Section, Scene 1 concludes with a paraphrase of a portion of chapter 17 of the Book of Going Forth by Day. This expression of the moment of unification of the two elements of the unified Re-Osiris at the instant of corporeal resurrection and solar regeneration as a combining of opposites is in keeping with the Egyptian concept of creation as division into balanced pairs of opposite—if not opposing—elements and forces.

THE ENIGMATIC TREATISE ON THE SECOND SHRINE OF TUTANKHAMUN

SIDE 1

LABEL TO THE COMPOSITION: A HORIZONTAL TEXT ABOVE THE RIGHT PORTION OF SIDE 1, BETWEEN THE RAM-HEADED POST TO THE RIGHT AND THE HEAD OF THE LARGE MUMMIFORM FIGURE TO THE LEFT

The good god, lord of the Two Lands, Nebkheperure, the beloved, bodily son of Re, the lord of appearing in glory, Tutankhamun, ruler

---

31. The ram-form of the sun is that appearing within the belly of the giant unfied Re-Osiris on the Second Shrine of Tutankhamun (p. 541).

32. For Osiris as sun of the nethersky, see Derchain 1965, 35–37.

of Upper Egyptian Heliopolis, beloved of the great Ennead which is in the Netherworld:

It is what he has made as his monument for his father Re-Horakhty, the making for him of a (book of) "What is in the Netherworld": the birth of Re, and the tracks[33] of the god in Igeret.

REGISTERS 1–3 (RIGHT) (PLATE 47)

7.1, 7.2. Scenes 1–2. The right end of Side 1 depicts a disk containing a ram-headed bird, with human arms raised in adoration (directed toward the mummiform image to the left), a sky sign atop the disk, between two staffs praised by goddesses, light shining from the disk onto the head of the lower staff. The upper scene (1) depicts two goddesses, "Isis" to the right and "Nephthys" to the left, praising a ram-headed staff labeled "Head of Re." The lower scene (2) shows two goddesses—"Netherworld" (right) and "Mysterious One"[34] (left)—praising a jackal-headed staff labeled "Neck of Re."

---

33. For an alternative, although less likely reading, assuming an omitted ꜥḥꜥ-sign, see Quack 2005, 25.

34. Alternatively, "Desert"; the reading "Desert" (Darnell 2004, 52–54) better parallels the similar scene of two gods praising the jackal-headed staff in the Book of Gates, Hour 1, Register 2, Scene 2 (p. 257).

TEXT ACCOMPANYING SCENE 1

These are in this fashion, the head lighting up, they being around him (as protection).

TEXT ACCOMPANYING SCENE 2

May you live like Re every day. Around you (as protection) do they exist.

REGISTER 1 (RIGHT) (PLATE 47)

7.3. Scene 3. Eight mummiform beings stand facing right; each has a different head, a cryptographic annotation appearing in front of each figure. From right to left, the deities appear with the following names and attributes.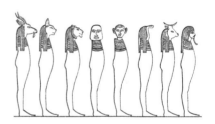

HUMAN HEAD WITH DIVINE BEARD: Mysterious One
BULL HEAD: He of the West
URAEUS HEAD: He of the Uraeus
HUMAN FACE EN FACE: Turned of Face
LARGE, JOWLY HUMAN HEAD EN FACE: Provided with a Face
LION HEAD: Wild One
CAT HEAD: Cat-Like One
CAPRID HEAD: Ascending One

ANNOTATION ABOVE THE FIGURES

These gods are in this fashion in their caverns which are in the Upper Region: It is in the darkness that their corpses(?) exist.

To the left of Scene 3, in twelve vertical columns ending in front of the upper body of the giant deity to left, is a version of the a portion of the opening of chapter 17 of the Book of Going Forth by Day. This section describes "Re in his glorious appearances when he began to rule what he had made," with elaborations and definitions of the primordial solar deity.

REGISTER 2 (RIGHT) (PLATE 47)

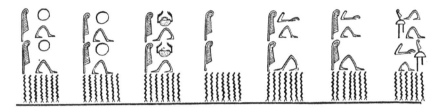

7.4. Scene 4. To the left of the central ram-headed bird within the disk (Scenes 1–2) is a register of cryptographic groups to the right, with normal hieroglyphic text to the left. The cryptographic groups to the right appear to reiterate the perpetual motion of the light of the sun; they consist of seven pairs of signs, vertically grouped, vertical water signs as light raining down from the lower group of each pair. Taking the central pair as referencing the period of the "standstill" of the sun in the middle of the day and night—no walking legs accompany the single šw-sign in both the upper and lower text—the six pairs to the right and six to the left evoke the hours of the day and the night.

CRYPTOGRAPHIC GROUPS, READ AS PAIRS (UPPER AND LOWER), RIGHT TO LEFT

Entering and exiting the West; entering the West.
The light enters; the light travels.
The light enters; the light travels.
The light; the light.
The light of Khepri goes forth; the light of Khepri goes forth.
The light of Re goes forth; the light of Re goes forth.
The light of Re goes forth; the light of Re goes forth.

To the left of Scene 4 (Side 1, Register 2) is a version of chapter 27 of the Book of Going Forth by Day, in three horizontal lines. The text seeks to ensure that no outside powers are able either to seize or damage the heart of Tutankhamun.

REGISTER 3 (RIGHT) (PLATE 47)

7.5. Scene 5. As in Scene 3, an enigmatic annotation runs above the heads of eight standing deities, facing right. The first four deities have the upper bodies of scarabs in place of the shoulders of an anthropomorphic body, with a different head atop each; the enigmatic annotations to each of these forms are as follows.

HUMAN HEAD ON SCARAB-TO-HUMAN BODY: Khepri
RAM HEAD ON SCARAB-TO-HUMAN BODY: Destroying Ram-form
FALCON HEAD ON SCARAB-TO-HUMAN BODY: Horus Living of Manifestations
JACKAL HEAD ON SCARAB-TO-HUMAN BODY: Manifesting One(?)[35]

The four beings to the left have mummiform bodies, facing right, with a different head atop each:

HUMAN-HEADED FIGURE WITH DIVINE BEARD: *Ba*-Soul of Tatenen
RAM-HEADED FIGURE: Red of Face
FALCON-HEADED FIGURE: Falcon
JACKAL-HEADED FIGURE: Anubis

ANNOTATION ABOVE THE FIGURES

These gods are in this fashion in their caverns that are in the Place of Destruction. It is in the uniform darkness that their corpses exist. When Re <pa>sses by, their *ba*-souls follow after his disk, his rays having entered into their caverns.

To the left Scene 5 is a version of a portion of chapter 1 of the Book of Going Forth by Day, in ten columns of hieroglyphic text in front of the lower legs of the mummiform deity who occupies the middle portion of the Second Shrine of

---

35. Alternatively, Ika(?), for which see Darnell 2004, 71. Possibly related to the name Ikeky in the Book of Gates, Hour 8, Register 1, Scene 49 (p. 299).

Tutankhamun, Side 1. The text contains an address of the king to Thoth as Bull of the West and a reply by the latter, who assures the king of his justification against his enemies in the *ḥw.t-sr* of Heliopolis.

REGISTERS 1–3 (CENTER) (PLATE 47)

7.6. Scene 6. The dominant image on Side 1 is that of a large, mummiform deity, facing right, head and feet encircled by uroboroi, mirrored cryptographic annotations to either side of the head, and another pair to either side of the lower legs. Within the middle body of the giant deity is a disk, within which stands a ram-headed bird, facing left, with human arms raised as in adoration. A line emerges from the upper left of the disk, exits the body of the standing deity, and passes above the heads of the seven standing beings (Scene 8) in the middle register to the left of the mummiform deity.

LABEL TO THE UPPER UROBOROS

Encircling Serpent

ANNOTATION (TWICE) TO EITHER SIDE OF THE HEAD OF THE GIANT DEITY, CONTINUED IN THE TEXT TO EITHER SIDE OF THE LOWER LEGS OF THE SAME

Adoration of the circling one; the circling one is Re.

REGISTER 1 (LEFT) (PLATE 47)

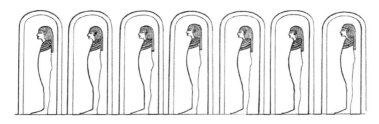

7.7. Scene 7. To the left of the head of the giant, mummiform deity are seven mummiform female figures, facing left, each enclosed within a double line taking the form of a round-topped shrine, apparently depicting the sarcophagi to which the annotation refers. In front of the scene is a hieroglyphic text in four columns. The names of the goddesses (left to right) are: "Upper Region"; "Mysterious Place";

"Cavern Dweller"; "Sarcophagus Dweller"; "She Relating to Fire"; "She Relating to Water"; "She Relating to Earth."

ANNOTATION ABOVE THE MUMMIFORM FEMALE DEITIES

These goddesses are in this fashion in their sarcophagi, they behold-ing the light of his solar disk. Their *ba*-souls enter after him, <their> corp<s>es <remaining in their places.>

The text in normal hieroglyphic script to the left of Scene 7 does not appear to make specific reference to the female mummiform deities immediately to the right and reads rather like the opening of a more extensive text that is not present.

Words spoken by the greater Ennead and the lesser Ennead, who exist as protection under the supervision of the king, the lord of the Two Lands, Nebkheperure, the son of Re Tutankhamun, ruler of Southern Heliopolis, who lives forever like his father Re in his manifestations.

REGISTER 2 (LEFT) (PLATE 47)

7.8. Scene 8. The line emerging from the disk within the solar plexus of the giant, mummiform deity in the center of Side 1 stretches above the heads of the seven male figures within the left central register, suggesting they are to be read following contemplation of the dominant central image. Each figure strides to the right, arms raised as though in adoration, facing the disk-enclosed, ram-headed *ba*-soul whose gesture they appear to return. The first six deities are given names in enigmatic labels that refer to adoration and luminosity: "Adoring One"; "Receiving of Arm"; "Shining of Arm"; "Shining One"; "One of the Beaming"; "Shining of Arm."

ANNOTATION ABOVE THE FIGURES

These gods are in this fashion, receiving the light of his luminous eye when he illumines the bodies of the Netherworld dwellers. When he passes, they turn back <af>ter the *ba*-souls enter.

To the left of Scene 8 is a hieroglyphic text of ten columns, in normal hieroglyphic orthography, a version of chapter 29 of the Book of Going Forth by Day. The text seeks to ward off presumably dangerous divine messengers, probably the sort referenced as "the messengers of Babai-Min" in the Tomb of Ramesses IX, Enigmatic Wall (p. 568).

REGISTER 3 (LEFT) (PLATE 47)

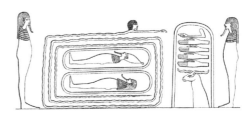

7.9. Scene 9. The most complex imagery within the major divisions of the horizontal registers on Side 1 of the shrine appears in the left side of Register 3. Two mummiform male deities frame the images toward which they face, "Clothed of Arm" (left) and "Destroyed of Arm" (right). On the left, a human headed serpent, "Human-Headed One," human arms outstretched before him, encircles in a rectangular manner two horizontal ovals, one positioned above the other. Within the upper oval is a supine mummiform figure, wearing the white crown, labeled "He of the Sarcophagus"; in the lower oval another supine mummiform figure, wearing a long wig. To the right is a round-topped, double-lined structure, similar to the sarcophagi in Scene 7, containing an enigmatic annotation above the head of a ram emerging from the ground line. The round-topped structure is called "(Mysterious) Chest."[36]

ANNOTATION ABOVE THE SCENE

These gods are in this fashion, in the cavern that is in the Place of Destruction. The *ba*-soul of Re calls his corpses therein, when he enters into this cavern, the light of the Human-headed One being therein. It is by his voice that Re illumines those who are in it. It is after being called that they breathe.

To the right of Scene 9 is a text in normal hieroglyphic orthography, occupying nine columns, containing a version of Chapter 26 of the Book of Going Forth by

---

36. The chest is likely an allusion to the canopic chest of Osiris (Heerma van Voss 1969), an object having a solar counterpart in the chest of Re that serves as a sarcophagus for the Osirian aspect of the nocturnal solar deity (Borghouts 1973–1974); see also pp. 361–62, 468–69. The image of the solar ram emerging from the ground also appears in the Tombs of Ramesses VII and Ramesses IX (Roberson 2012, 260–61, Scene 61).

Day. The text ensures that the deceased ruler has his heart, and that he has use of his mouth and limbs in the Netherworld.

SIDE 2

REGISTER 1 (PLATE 48)

7.10. Scene 10. A large uraeus serpent, "Uraeus," body coiled beneath its spread hood, faces right at the left end of the group. Lines representing light emerge from its mouth and spread slightly before they fall on the forehead of the first of six standing, mummiform, human-headed figures, each wearing a divine beard and facing left; the mummiform figures are labeled from left to right: "One of the Netherworld(?)"; "One of the Star(?)"; "Clothed One"; "One of the Mummy Wrappings"; "Incomplete One"; "Bound One." In front of each figure is a human-headed *ba*-bird, each labeled "Traveler," facing the figure in front of it, with four lines stretching down from just beneath the feet of the soul-bird to just above the ground line. Over each of the heads of the first five figures from the left is a five-pointed star. From each of the lower right "arms" of the stars above the heads of the first two figures from the left emerge three lines of light that fall on the forehead of the mummiform figure behind that above which the star hovers (those being the second and third figures from the left). The stars above the final four figures to the right are connected by three lines of light stretching between the lower arms of each star.

ANNOTATION ABOVE THE GROUP

These g<ods> are in this fashion, the light of Re having entered their corpses. When he calls their *ba*-souls, they set out after the (other?) *ba*-souls.

7.11. Scene 11. The ground line of the deities in Scene 11 rests atop the undulating back of a great serpent, head to left. At the left end of the scene, a cat, labeled "Cat,"[37] emerges from the ground, hind quarters invisible beneath the groundline, facing right, toward the group of six headless, mummiform figures, turned to the left.

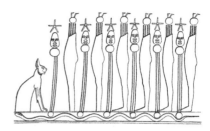

The feet of the first two mummiform bodies from the left disappear beneath the groundline, while the remaining four figures stand atop the line. The heads are labeled left to right: "Head of Horus"; "Face of Horus"; "Throat of Horus"; "Body of Horus"; "Unknown One"; "Unknown One." Above each body hovers a solar disk, from the top of which emerge two human legs with feet facing to the right. Four vertical lines of light stretch from beneath each disk to the neck area of each mummiform figure. In front of the chest of each mummy hovers a bread-loaf-shaped head, viewed en face, each atop a solar disk, from each of which stretch three lines of light down to the ground. Beneath each group of these lines, below the ground line, atop the coils of the serpent, is a small solar disk.

ANNOTATION TO THE GROUP (ABOVE THE FELINE AT THE LEFT END)

These gods are in this fashion, and their heads.[38]

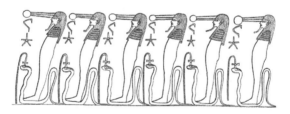

7.12. Scene 12. Six mummiform, human-headed deities, wearing divine beards, face left, standing with a distinct slant back, as though they are just rising to a vertical position. Each stands atop a serpent, individually labeled as "Encircling Serpent," the head of which rears up in front, the body rising in a coil behind each mummiform figure, the tail then falling to the ground. A hieroglyphic taper

---

37. Alternatively, "Cat-Shaped One"; for feline deities within the Book of Adoring Re in the West, see pp. 72–73.

38. Alternatively, "it is their heads." For the significance of headlessness in the Netherworld Books, see the commentary to the Book of Gates, Hour 10, Register 1, Scene 61 (pp. 310–11).

appears atop each serpent head, with the long tongue of flame falling before each serpent. In front of the head of each mummiform figure hovers a solar disk, with three rays of light extending from each disk to the forehead of the figure to the right. Below each disk is the hieroglyph of the walking legs, pointing toward the ground, feet to the right; below each of the walking legs is a star.[39] From left to right, the mummiform figures are labeled as: "One of the Encircling Serpent"; "(Re)born of Corpse"; "(Re)born of Members"; "Begotten One"; "One Relating to Movement"; "Leaping of Corpse." The figures appear to rise upon and out of the coils of the encircling serpents, and the name of the last figure to the right references their rising postures. All of the images in the third group rest atop the upper groundline of Register 2, which extends unbroken to the right; the space between the upper and lower lines in Scene 12 is entirely empty.

ANNOTATION TO THE SCENE

> These gods are in this fashion: It is their encircling serpents that guard their corpses, the *Hereret*-snakes of Atum.[40] When he calls to their *ba*-souls, they rise up.

CONCLUDING TEXT TO REGISTER 1

Two columns of text in normal hieroglyphic signs conclude Register 1 of Side 2, addressing the deceased ruler directly.

> That you exist among the Ennead is without your being distinguished from one among them, (O) Osiris king Nebkheperure, vindicated.

REGISTER 2 (PLATE 48)

7.13. Scene 13. A prone, mummiform figure extends its hands, palm upwards, beneath the solar disk (containing a ram-headed bird) that rests between the two

---

39. The group may be read as R^c $^c q$ m $dw_3.t$, "Re enters into the Netherworld."
40. Alternatively, "Re-Atum."

pairs of arms that form the right boundary of Scene 18, the concluding scene, thereby providing the clearest link between the three registers to the right and the concluding portion of the treatise. Above the arms of the figure is a group of nine signs (identical to the group that appears above the feet of another prone deity in Scene 14), apparently a graphic textual depiction of the solar cycle. From the foot of the prone deity rises a serpent, facing right, within a group of slanting lines that appear to represent light streaming from the walking legs—facing right—beneath a sun disk, hovering above the head of the serpent.

From the sun disk emerge three lines of light that converge in the mouth of four lion-headed deities, facing left, wearing knee length garments that cover their arms, their elbows out and bent to their sides, hands hidden but seemingly meeting at their chests. From the back of the head of each of the first three lion-headed beings emerge light lines, converging in the mouth of the creature behind.

ANNOTATION TO THE GROUPS (EXTENDING OVER THE PRONE FIGURE AND THE LION-HEADED BEINGS)

These gods are in this fashion, the light of Re having entered into their corpses. When they see his *ba*-soul they rejoice, he calling to their *ba*-souls, they being in his following, they guiding him in the Myster[ious Place].

LABEL TO EACH OF THE LION-HEADED FIGURES

It is the (solar) bark that travels the earth.

Group of signs above the raised hand of the prone figure: An ꜥḥꜥ-sign in the middle, with two columns of text to each side, a sun disk at the top and bottom of each column. In the middle are two walking legs to each side, the first from the top in each column right-side up and facing in toward the central ꜥḥꜥ-sign, the next upside-down and both facing to left. The four disks appear to represent the eastern and western ends of the diurnal and nocturnal solar journey, the inverted legs indicating the voyage from west to east, and the legs facing in toward the ꜥḥꜥ-sign referring to "entering into and going out from heaven."[41] The central ꜥḥꜥ-sign represents the apogees of the solar cycle, the whole perhaps reading: "The solar disk entering into and going out from heaven, and traversing the Netherworld, pausing at the solar apogees of midday and midnight."

---

41. For ꜥq and *pr* as summaries of the solar cycle, note the annotations to the solar bark in Hornung 1990b, pls. 1b and 84. For ꜥḥꜥ and the solar apogees, see Darnell 2004, 287–88.

7.14. Scene 14. A prone, mummiform figure extends its hands, palm upwards, beneath a group of signs (from top to bottom a solar disk, inverted walking legs with feet to right, and land sign); beneath the uplifted palm of the deity is an ꜥḥꜥ-sign. Light lines emerge from the right side of the solar disk above the hand, and converge at the mouth of the prone figure. The same group of signs that appear above the raised hand of the prone figure in Scene 13 are placed above the feet of the prone figure in Scene 14. Following the prone deity in Scene 14 is a light-framed serpent as in Scene 13, with walking legs and sun disk above, from which emerge three light lines that converge in the mouth of a lion-headed deity. Behind the first lion-headed deity are five more identical figures (totaling six, rather than four in Scene 13), each facing left, wearing knee length garments that cover their arms, their elbows out and bent to their sides, hands hidden but seemingly meeting at their chests. From the back of the head of each of the lion-headed beings emerge light lines, converging in the mouth of the creature behind.

GROUP OF SIGNS NEAR THE HAND OF THE PRONE FIGURE

UPPER GROUP: The solar disk enters into the earth.

HAND AND LOWER SIGN: Assigning the position (to the disk).[42]

ANNOTATION TO THE SCENE

These gods are in this fashion, the light of Re having entered into their corpses. When they see his *ba*-soul, they rejoice, they hauling him in the <Mysteriou>s Place, their arms bearing their mysteries, the secret images which are in the Netherworld. The *ba*-soul of Re calls to them, when their *ba*-souls have passed by.

---

42. For the concept of entering the earth, compare Darnell 2004, 129; Klotz 2011, 485–86. In the Book of the Hidden Chamber, Hour 11, Horus Who Is upon His Stairs sets the stations of hours within the Netherworld.

LABEL TO EACH OF THE LION-HEADED FIGURES

It is the (solar) bark that travels the earth.

CONCLUDING TEXT TO REGISTER 2

Six columns of text in normal hieroglyphic signs conclude Register 2.

The king, lord of the Two Lands Nebkheperure continues to appear in glory like his father Re, in heaven and in earth, in his manifestations of rising and setting; the bodily, beloved son of Re, lord of glorious appearances, Tutankhamun, ruler of Upper Egyptian Heliopolis, in his manifestations of earthly existence. He will live like Re forever, the king of Upper and Lower Egypt Nebkheperure, who lives forever and ever.

REGISTER 3 (PLATE 48)

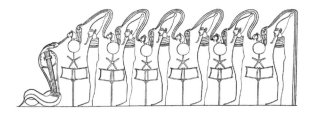

7.15. Scene 15. The group is dominated by six standing, mummiform figures, facing left, wearing divine beards and white crowns, labeled left to right: "One of the Hidden Chamber"; "Bent of Arm"; "Stirring of Arm"; "Brightening of Arm"; "Hidden of Arm"; "Covered of Arm." In front of each figure is a large hieroglyph of a sail, atop which rests a star, itself topped by a solar disk from which emerge two heads—a feline head on the left, facing left, and a uraeus head with hood emerging from the right upper shoulder of the disk, facing right.

A large uraeus serpent, "Uraeus," faces right at the left end of the group, seeming to exchange three lines of light between its mouth and the mouth of the feline head atop the disk in front of the first figure. Within the groups of figures, the uraeus atop the disk hovering in front of each mummiform figure spews three light lines from its mouth; these lines billow up and over the crowns of the figures, and enter the mouth of the feline head atop the solar disk behind. The light lines emerging from the uraeus atop the disk in front of the last figure to the right flow over the crown of the final figure, and then descend vertically down to the ground line.

> These gods are in this fashion: it is the light of Re, which clothes their corpses. When he calls their *ba*-souls, they travel behind.

7.16. Scene 16. Parallel to Register 1, Scene 11, six mummiform figures— here with ram heads, facing left— stand atop an upper ground line, beneath which is a large serpent. As in the top register, six small disks rest atop the coils of the serpent; however, rather than being distributed beneath  the upper disks as in Register 1, here they are somewhat bunched together beneath the forepart of the lion and the first three mummiform figures to the left. In front of each mummiform figure hovers a solar disk, above the level of the head; beneath each disk is a small square, down from which descend three lines of light. Above the head of each ram-headed figure is a large sign of the walking legs, facing right; above this group are the labels to the ram-headed mummiform deities (left to right): "Distinguished of Head"; "Distinguished of Face"; "Distinguished of Form"; "Distinguished of Manifestations"; "Distinguished of Corpse"; "Distinguished of Body." In front of the group, at the left end, is a rearing forepart of a lion, "Cat-Shaped One," parallel to the cat in Register 1, Scene 11.

> These gods are in this fashion, seeking the great mysteries, and seeing the King of Upper and Lower Egypt, Nebkheperure, given life like Re forever.

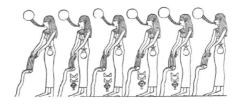

7.17. Scene 17. Similar to Register 1, Scene 12, six female figures face to the left, their arms lowered and slightly extended, palms facing upwards; a serpent, depicted as if rising from the ground, appears in front of each goddess. Each of the rising serpents is labeled "Evil of Face," while the goddesses' labels are (left to right): "She of the (Eastern) Portal"; "She of the Fire"; "She of Cooking"; "She of Burning"; "She of the Morning Glow"; "She of Destruction."[43] From the goddesses' hands descend lines[44] that reach the top of the head of a serpent that emerges from the ground, slanting up slightly to the right, facing the figure. In front of the head of each female figure hovers a solar disk, with light lines emerging from the lower right of the disk, converging at the mouth of the female figure. Within the abdomen of each goddess is a solar disk topped by a star, appearing to label each female figure as "Hour." A hieroglyphic group in front of each goddess writes "Traveler."

ANNOTATION TO THE SCENE

> These goddesses are in this fashion, their hours having entered into their corpses. The *ba*-soul of Re calls to them, and they see the light of his disk. Their *ba*-souls travel after him above, remaining in their place of the *ba*-soul.[45]

REGISTERS 1–3 (PLATE 48)

7.18. Scene 18. The overall shape of the scene is that of a mandorla, flattened at the top and bottom. At the middle of the curving left and right sides—formed by doubled curving lines—is a solar disk to each side; within each disk is a ram-headed *ba*-bird, arms raised in adoration and facing to the right, positioned so that the raised hands touch and slightly emerge beyond the upper right limb of each disk. Just inside the doubled outer line, emerging from each side of the upper and lower ground lines, are pairs of arms, palms turned out towards the outside of the scene, as though cradling the sun disks; in the lower scene, each pair of arms is labeled "Destroying Arms." Between the pairs of arms and also

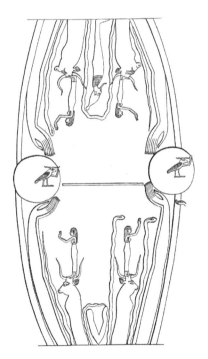

---

43. Alternatively, "Place of Destruction."

44. For their gesture, the *nyny*, and the identity of the lines emerging from their hands, see p. 527 and n. 7 above.

45. Alternatively, "*akh*-spirit."

emerging from both the upper and lower ground lines are two forparts of bulls, oddly elongated, each facing out from the middle of the scene; in the lower scene, the bull heads are labeled "Longhorn." On top of the head of each bull, between the horns, stands a goddess, facing out from the middle of the scene, arms raised in front of her, palms forward.

In the lower scene, a serpent's tail appears in the upper left, the body—between the lower left pair of arms and the lower left bull—descending and disappearing below the ground line, emerging to the right between the lower right bull and the lower right pair of arms, with the head just below the hands of the arms. Between the two bulls, another snake appears, head and forebody emerging from the groundline to the right, tail emerging from the groundline to the left, partly curled around the central group of a large, bent human arm, with a hieroglyphic annotation above: "Arm of Re." In the upper scene, the tail of a large serpent appears between the upper right arms and the upper right bull, disappearing below the groundline, with the forebody and head emerging from the groundline to the left, between the upper left arms and the upper left bull. The midsection of the serpent emerges again to the left of the upper right bull, ultimately descending to the right of the upper left bull and forming a shrine-like shape enclosing a standing mummiform figure, wearing a divine beard and white crown, facing right.

ANNOTATION WITHIN THE UPPER (INVERTED) PORTION OF THE SCENE, IN NORMAL HIEROGLYPHS

The Osirs, the king, lord of the Two Lands, Nebkheperure, exists in justification together with the great Ennead.

CRYPTOGRAPHIC ANNOTATION RUNNING BETWEEN THE TWO SOLAR DISKS WITH RAM-HEADED BA-BIRDS IN THE MIDDLE OF THE SCENE

Adoration of the one who enters, carrying light.

CRYPTOGRAPHIC ANNOTATION WITH THE LOWER PORTION OF THE SCENE

Those who are in this manner in the presence of the one who conceals them—they are unable to see his light, the goddesses being protection.

The Enigmatic Treatise on the Corridor G Ceiling in the Tomb of Ramesses VI

REGISTER 1 (PLATE 49)

7.19. Scene 1. Four bovid heads—with solar disks between the horns—emerge from each corner of the scene; beginning in the upper left and moving clockwise, the names of the bovid heads are: "Young Bull," "Bull," "Ramming of Horns," and "Far One." Among the bovid heads stand two female deities, back to back, each wearing a cauldron on her head; the left goddess is called "Frightener," while her companion to the right is named "Enchantress." The cauldrons contain (from left to right) disks and stars. Facing the left goddess is the head of an antelope, labeled "Horned Animal."[46]

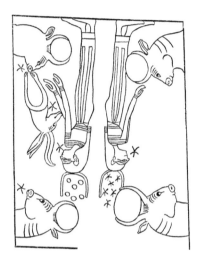

7.20. Scene 2. Three nested, dome-like structures, called *nm.t*, "slaughtering place," in the annotation, contain mummiform figures: a janus-faced deity occupies the left and right domes, feet facing in toward the middle dome; the deity in the leftmost dome is called "Blind in Both Eyes,"[47] while the deity in the third dome is not labeled. Within the middle dome is a small, standing, mummiform figure, facing left, labeled "Corpse." Above the mummiform figure and enclosing it are

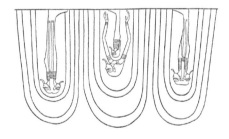

46. Compare the four antelope heads in the Book of Gates, Scene 33 (pp. 284–85).

47. The eyeless deity recalls "those who exist as Mekhentyenirty" in the Book of Caverns, Division 2, Register 4, Scene 12. The closest parallel is the eyeless deity within a sarcophagus enclosure in the litanies between the Book of Caverns, Divisions 4–5 (p. 396): "My solar disk penetrates the darkness—Mekhentyenirty is in his sarcophagus." The term for blindness in the Corridor G Ceiling text (*k[ȝ]mn*) may refer to removal of the eyes, which in the case of Mekhentyenirty may be the sun and moon (Junker 1947; Manniche 1978, 15; Darnell 2004, 172 n. 36). The reading *mtn-ḥr.wy* "mit leitenden Gesichtern" (Quack 2005, 29) is untenable.

extended arms dropping down from a head wearing a divine beard and facing left named "Corpse of (Re)birth."

TEXT TO THE LEFT AND RIGHT DOMES

This god is in this fashion. When Re calls out to them, the flame which is in his mouth comes forth, his corpse lighting up by means of that which is in him.

TEXT TO THE MIDDLE DOME

This god in this fashion in the slaughtering place, he lighting up by means of that which is in his mouth when Re calls out to him.

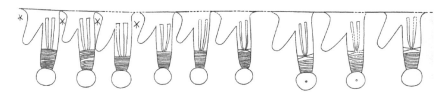

7.21. Scene 3. In the upper register are nine squatting figures, each with a disk instead of a head, facing left and oriented as though upside-down relative to the rest of the section. The text comprises fifty columns of varying length, written above and between the seated figures; at the bottom of five of the lines are the following names: "Shining One"; "One of the Forehall"; "Proper One"; "One of the Nethersky"; "One of the Morning Glow."

ANNOTATION TO THE SCENE

These gods in this fashion, within the Place of Destruction, protecting the hours. Re calls to their corpses, with the result that their heads remain upon them therein,[48] after this great god passes by them. When Re calls out, the corpses grow dark, and their flesh becomes hidden.[49] Then this great god summons these gods in the nethersky.

---

48. Quack 2005, 29 attempts to emend the text to "their heads remain in their pl<aces>," although a perturbation is required to reach this reading.

49. The text indicates that the heads remain, rather than accompanying the sun on its journey, a concept also expressed in the text accompanying Register 2. That the

The god casts light before its denizens, while the cavern-dwellers give praise. These gods exist in darkness. When this great god casts light, Imhet brightens, that which this great god travels, while illumining the uniform darkness that hides the corpses. When the hours pass, a solar disk ascends in the following of an hour. When they speak in the following of Re, they descend by means of his manifestation. When the solar disk travels She Who Destroys Throats, the corpses enter into <their> darkness. Passing by this great god, in the place of the denizens of the uniform darkness; [...] When the hours pass, a solar disk ascends in the following of an hour. When they speak in the following of Re, they descend by means of his manifestation. When the solar disk travels She Who Destroys Throats, the corpses enter into their darkness, and they do what they have to do, their [...], their *ba*-souls having entered after Re, they guiding him in the Mysterious Place.

REGISTER 2 (PLATE 49)

7.22. Scene 4. A ram-headed bird perches atop a stela. On each side of the stela is a human-headed, mummiform deity, standing with back to the stela; within the stela is the short label "Khepri, who travels inverted, who gives birth to the five (epagomenal) days(?)." To the right is a large solar disk, the forepart of a scarab emerging from the bottom of the disk, a ram head emerging from the top. The ram head is designated "Clothed One."

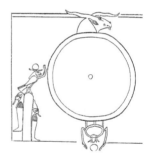

RIGHT OF THE STELA

Re entering within the West
Re, (solar) star who goes around the Netherworld

ANNOTATION TO THE LEFT OF THE STELA

The (solar) star who enters and goes forth from the Netherworld

call of Re does not illumine their bodies recalls the Books of the Creation of the Solar Disk, Tomb of Ramesses VI, Section B, Register 1, Scene 25: "except (for) these gods in darkness" (p. 485 = Piankoff 1953, pl. 1, l. 4; Roberson 2012, R6.B.1.51.47–49).

ANNOTATION TO THE LOWER LEFT OF THE LARGE DISK

Re who enters and goes forth from the Netherworld

ANNOTATION TO THE RIGHT OF THE FOREPART OF THE SCARAB:

The king, lord of the Two Lands, lord of heaven, Nebmaatre, beloved of Amun, is in heaven, driving away the darkness.

ANNOTATION BELOW THE FOREPART OF THE SCARAB, CONTINUING INTO THE UPPER MIDDLE OF THE INTRODUCTORY SCENE TO THE LOWER REGISTER

The king of Upper and Lower Egypt, the lord of the Two Lands, Nebmaatre, beloved of Amun, who enters among those who are in the Place of Destruction, he uncovering the Netherworld.

7.23. Scene 5. The scene consists of a depiction of the solar bark sailing to the right, the keelson of the boat formed of a serpent, the deck ending in the heads and arms of two deities wearing divine beards, but given female names: "Isis" (left) and "Nephthys." In the central deck stands a ram-headed anthropomorphic deity facing right. In front, facing the standing god, is a ram-headed bird. To the right of the bird is a bending goddess, facing right, labeled "West," her hands out with palms over the head of the personified prow. To the left of the standing deity is a mummiform god lying prone on the deck, head raised to left and facing left; he is labeled "He Who Draws Near."[50]

7.24. Scene 6. Seven disk-headed deities stand with their arms raised in adoration. Labels to the entities facing and adoring the solar bark (left to right) are "He of the

---

50. Compare the Book of Gates, Doorway 4 (p. 277).

Solar Disk"; "He of the Netherworld"; "He of the West"; "Red One"; "Mysterious (Corpse)"; "One Who Lights Up"; "Luminous One."

7.25. Scene 7. Two pairs of deities face each other, arms out and fingertips touching. Above the hands of each pair, facing right, is a disk topped by a human head; below each disk is an inverted star. Beneath the first pair (to the left) is a goddess, face down, feet to left; beneath the second pair (to right) is another goddess, face up, feet to left.

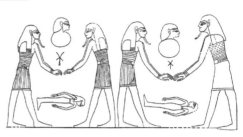

LABEL TO SCENES 5–7

The main text comprises eighty-three columns of text, of varying and often extremely short length. The first portion (ll. 1–59) describes the approach of the bark and its encounter with the Netherworld. The remaining portion (ll. 60–83) is in retrograde orthography, and describes Scene 7, the two pairs of deities at the right end of the register.

> The shining one comes. These gods are in this fashion, the light of Re having entered into their corpses. Their *ba*-souls travel after him, and conduct him in the Mysterious Place; the *ba*-souls travelling, the (solar) *ba*-soul shedding light in the Mysterious Place. These goddesses[51] are in this fashion, praising those who are travelling in the Place of Destruction, their *ba*-souls being after him. It is the darkness that hides them in the Mysterious Place, they having passed by the light. These gods are in this fashion, they praising this god, and adoring the great one in the West. When the great god passes by them in the Mysterious Place, casting light in their following, the heads (of) these gods remain therein, they turning back after this great god calls to them. Now when this great god calls to them, now when this great god calls to them, and when he passes by them, they hide the corpses.[52]

---

51. Apparently Isis and Nephthys—these particular lines are placed above West and Nephthys.

52. For the concept of *ba*-souls following the deity while the corpses are hidden, compare the Books of the Creation of the Solar Disk, Tomb of Ramesses VI, Section B, Register 2, Scene 24 (p. 485).

These gods are in this fashion, protecting the secret Netherworld. When this great god passes by these hours, the star emerges from the Netherworld(?). The corpses are in <th>is burial pit, [...] their corpses, they [...] heaven, those who are on their corpses(?), manifestations manifesting in [...] upon their faces.

REGISTER 3 (PLATE 49)

7.26. Scene 8. Four bovid heads—with solar disks between the horns—emerge from the corners of the scene, each one labeled "Shade of Re." Two goddesses, each wearing a cauldron, stand in the middle of the scene; the goddesses are not named, and their cauldrons contain (from right to left) shades and birds, the latter a generic hieroglyph substituting for the *ba*-bird, designating the souls of the damned. Facing the left goddess is an antelope head atop human arms labeled "Horned Animal."

7.27. Scene 9. Three structures, each a set of two nested domes, each contain a divine image. A standing, mummiform deity occupies the left and right domes, chest facing in to the central domes. Instead of a head, the mummy in the left pair of domes has a hand, slanting up to right, palm up, with dots falling from the middle of the hand to the ground; the deity is labeled "Giver (of Light?)."[53] A similar object with dots falling appears instead of the head on the mummiform figure in the right dome, who also has the name "Giver (of Light?)." Within the central dome is a head with arms depending from it and dots descending from the mouth to the ground line; the upper dome contains the name "Burning of Breath." A solar disk rests above the ground line, between the hands descending from the upper head, and a falcon head facing left emerges from the top of the solar disk; the name in the lower part of the dome is "Corpse of Atum."[54]

---

53. The name recalls the *wdy*, "giver (of light?)," who appears with a being *psdy*, "Shining One," in the concluding scene of the Sixth Division of the Book of Caverns in the tomb of Padiamenemope (Piankoff 1945, 45; p. 454).

54. The Corpse of Atum here and "Corpse of (Re)birth" (Register 1, Scene 2), in

TEXT TO THE LEFT DOME

This god is in this fashion. When Re calls to him, there comes forth the flame that is in his mouth. It is by means of that which is therein that the corpse lights up.

TEXT TO THE MIDDLE DOME

This god is in this fashion in the slaughtering place, he lighting up by means of that which is in his mouth when Re calls out to him therein.

TEXT TO THE RIGHT DOME

This god is in this fashion. When Re calls out to him, there comes forth the flame that is in his mouth, he lighting up by means of that which is in his mouth.

7.28. Scene 10. Eight seated goddesses are crowned with a star, with a line of dots as light dropping from each star to the top of the head of each goddess. A disk sits on the ground line in front of each goddess. The first four goddesses are labeled "She Relating to the Beaming"; "She Relating to the Gleaming"; "She Relating to the Light"; "Female Disk."[55]

These goddesses in this fashion within the Place of Destruction. <This?> great god casts his light in the corpses of these goddesses. When the mysterious god calls, and light enters into the goddess, then

---

the upper and lower registers respectively, recall the corpse of Atum and the corpse of Re to which the solar deity calls in the Book of Caverns, Litany 21 (p. 450) and depicted within the Concluding Scene, apparently hidden within the domed mounds with disks inside appearing in the left portion of the scene, each mound protected by a bending figure and labeled "mysterious mound."

55. For the female disk, compare p. 362 and n. 39.

the ones belonging to the Place of Destruction call out.[56] When the hour(s) travel into the darkness, they hear the voice of Re, with the result that they breathe, and they have their light. When he passes by their land, then their *ba*-souls call out before his light. These goddesses are in the light of the solar disks that appertain to them. When the god passes, the great solar disk comes forth <from> the darkness. The hours become satisfied with their light, when this great god passes by them, they calling to this god. This god calls to them. When he passes by them, their darkness covers them. The darkness covers them, the hours withdrawing to the corpses, their face(s) being therein, these goddesses lighting up by means of the light of the disks that belong to them. When the deity travels, the great solar disk goes forth in the darkness. After this great god passes by them, they come to rest in their light, and they call out to this god; it is this god who calls them. Now when he passes by them, their darkness covers them. When Re rests therein at his (appointed) place, the hours withdraw to the corpses at their mysterious [...], their *bas* having entered <into> the P[lace of Destruction(?)], they protecting [...], he listening to them [...]. These goddesses are in this fashion in the nethersky(?).

DROPPED PORTION OF THE CORRIDOR G CEILING (PLATE 50)

7.29. Scene 1. The dropped portion contains two registers, the upper larger than the lower. Scene 1, which encompasses the entire upper register, is a large solar disk atop a lunar crescent, with two deities standing to each side, facing the central disk, arms out and down in front, palms over what appear to be hybrid signs of a heart with *djed*-pillar emerging from the top.

56. The concept of the breath-giving call of the solar deity finds numerous parallels in the Book of Caverns, and even more in the Books of the Creation of the Solar Disk.

7.30. Scene 2. A central bark dominates Scene 2, which fills the entire lower register of the dropped portion of the ceiling. The prow and stern of the bark terminate in the upper bodies of deities, facing down, arms out behind them stretching toward the figure standing in the middle of the vessel. The prone figure to the right of the standing deity in the bark is labeled "He Who Draws Near."[57] The anthropomorphic, ram-headed deity stands in the middle of the bark, arms out and down, each forearm terminating in the forepart of a goddess, each of whom reaches out toward the arms of the stems of the bark. A falcon head comes out of each side of the deity, and he stands on two prone, mummiform beings, heads raised and facing away from the standing deity. The hands of the goddesses and personified prow and stern hold disks; two disembodied heads appear to the side of the central deity. To the right of the bark is a group of two deities bending forward and placing their hands above a prone female figure, with disk and head above their hands.

LABEL TO SCENES 1–2

The surviving portions of the annotations to the upper and lower registers appear to be parallel; together they may be read as:

> These deities exist in this fashion, they guarding throats. That which is in the mouths comes forth before them against these shades, in order to destroy them, the deities being surrounded by <their(?)> manifestations.[58] It is while going about in peace that the deity breathes. This

---

57. The being Tekemy—"He Who Draws Near"—appears in the prow of the solar bark in the middle register of the main portion of the ceiling, and jackal-headed—as in the enigmatic orthography of the name on the dropped portion of the ceiling—he appears in the Book of Gates, Doorway 4 (p. 277) An excellent description of the twin Tekemy-beings on the dropped portion of the ceiling is chapter 404 of the Coffin Texts (CT 5.197c–f): "He Who Draws Near is his name; he opens the western horizon and knows the eastern horizon; He Who Draws Near is his name."

58. A parallel for Netherworld entities who both let throats breathe, and function at the same time as punishing demons, appears in the label to Apep in the Book of the Hidden Chamber, Hour 7, Register 2, Scene 75 (p. 200): "Then She Who Makes Throats Breathe throws the lasso on (his) head, while Chief of His Knives places the punishing knife into his legs."

deity knows that he shines. If their spells come forth to him, they will breathe.

PROTECTIVE IMAGE ON LINTEL BETWEEN CORRIDOR G AND HALL H (PLATE 51)

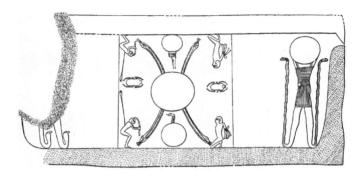

7.31. Protective Image. The frame of the protective image is a sandy hill, forming an elongated *ḏw*-mountain, whose hills are the right and left boundaries of the scene; the edges of a sky-sign touch the tops of the hills (the left side is destroyed). At the right of the scene is a single, large figure with a human torso wearing a corselet, but whose shoulders and head are replaced by a disk. The lower portion of the figure wears a kilt and has human legs that end in rearing serpents, rather than feet. A block of enigmatic text separates the righthand anguipede from a central scene with a large disk in the middle from which emerge four serpents; smaller disks appear above and below: a crocodile head emerges from the upper disk, while a serpent head emerges from the disk below. Two scarabs appear to the left and the right, and in the corners of the scene are depictions of the damned— two bound figures on the right and two shot figures, blood pouring from their heads, to the left. Another block of enigmatic text is placed between the central image and another large figure to the left, mostly destroyed, with the exception of the legs, which end in uraei.

ANNOTATION TO THE RIGHTHAND ANGUIPEDE

> This god exists in this fashion, his two (visible) limbs being two snakes, his two arms remaining in the solar disk.[59] It is after entering into this cavern that the manifestation of the horizon dweller manifests.[60] As

---

59. The alternate reading in Quack 2005, 31 assumes several omitted words, rendering it a less likely possibility to the translation presented here.

60. The realization of the forms or manifestations of the deity is part of the solar preparation for battle with the chaotic forces of Apep, such as in the Book of Gates,

for this god in this fashion, it is against one who is evil (Apep)[61] that he shoots (light/flame). It is the Two Sisters[62] whom this god determines to be his two arms,[63] in order that the visible forms of those who are there (the dead) may shine.[64] It is the deity who will call, in order that they might come forth from their cavern, in order to perform protection.[65] It is this god who has made the burial pits.[66] When he calls, the Damager of the Earth is held back, they coming forth. Those who are in the earth rest, as this god travels about, traveling rightly through the Mysterious Place, this god slithering about therein.

Hour 5, Register 2, Scene 27 (p. 280): "As you guard that my manifestations manifest, so you bind that my glorifications come about."

61. Compare P.Bremner Rhind 32, 15 (Faulkner 1933, 89, l. 3).

62. The two sisters—Isis and Nephthys—may assume the outward appearance of two uraei (Hornung 1975, 153, 209; 1976, 80 [n. 359] and 87 [n. 471]), and uraei depending from a solar disk may be labeled as Isis and Nephthys (Ockinga and al-Masri 1990, 21). Elsewhere associated with the legs, the two sisters here are the arms of the deity; though hidden within the disk in the depiction on the vertical portion of the ceiling, the goddesses form the forearms of the solar god on the dropped portion of the ceiling. In the Book of Adoring Re in the West (p. 110) and the Books of the Creation of the Solar Disk (p. 472), the two sisters unite with the reborn *ba*-soul of the solar deity. The apparent contrast between the power of the sisters as visible forms assisting in the mafestation of the sun recalls a wordplay on the terms "visible form" and "manifestation" in the Book of Adoring Re in the West, Address 4. The deity composed of other beings is the creator god (DuQuesne 2002b).

63. The arms as goddesses also appear textually in the Books of the Creation of the Solar Disk, Tomb of Ramesses VI, Section A, Register 2, Scene 10 with: "his two arms having become the two children of Khepri, who is content with his two wings" (pp. 474–75).

64. The alternate reading in Quack 2005, 32 finds no parallels in the corpus of Netherworld Books.

65. The *sḥnw*-protection is a protective embrace, that of the Encircling Serpent for the solar deity whom the ophidian power encircles (see the "Short" Book of the Hidden Chamber, Hour 8, p. 246). The deities 795 (Hour 11) and 901 (Hour 12) in the same composition are also named *sḥn*, perhaps referring to an extended meaning of "embrace" in protection as a web of protective magic. Such magical protection is appropriate for the solar deity at the time his encounter with Apep—a combination of physical and magical attack against chaos appears in the Book of Gates, Hour 3, Register 3, Scene 13 (pp. 268–69).

66. The deity in the protective image is said to have made the burial pits, echoing the description in the Book of Adoring Re in the West, Address 51, in which the solar deity is "Who makes caverns, who creates corpses by means of what he himself has commanded" (p. 94).

ANNOTATION TO THE LEFTHAND ANGUIPEDE

[…] Khepri is the one whose manifestation has manifest […] ⌜against⌝ the one who is evil (Apep), he hiding the mysteries […] ⌜the West⌝. This great god calls out, he being endowed […] the West, this flame therein. As for the seven punishing deities,[67] th[ey] shoot […] breath, their corpses traveling around therein, their […] therin in the desert.

THE ENIGMATIC WALL IN THE TOMB OF RAMESSES IX

HORIZONTAL TEXT ABOVE THE TREATISE; the hieroglyphic text, written right to left, contains scattered elements of cryptography (cf. *nb tȝ.wy* with two herons writing *tȝ.wy*)

Live the good god, the divine falcon, arisen in Thebes, the son of Osiris, who performs benefactions for the lords of the sacred land, who awakens the Netherworld dwellers as is his custom; this singular one, together with Magic who defeats the One Evil of Character (Apep) with his effective spells, Thoth—the third face—and Khepri, totaling four; the Osiris, lord of the Two Lands, Ramesses IX, justified, beloved of Ptah-Sokar, foremost of the Netherworld, the great.[68]

LEFT SECTION

REGISTER 1 (PLATE 52)

7.32. In the upper register, a mummiform figure stands to the left, facing right, toward eight large disks, four yellow to the left (top figure) and four red to the right

---

67. The seven deities are apparently punishers of Apep, one for each of the seven neck vertebrae of the chaos serpent. So on the Enigmatic Wall in the Tomb of Ramesses IX, seven beings atop sandy *nm.t*-slaughtering places assist the passage of the bark of the sun over the back of Apep. See also Rochholz 2002.

68. In the text, Ramesses IX as the son of the solar-Osirian deity—the solar Osiris who awakens the Netherworld dwellers—is: (1) the singular one, *deus unus,* designation of the creator Re-Atum (compare Iversen 1984, 48); (2) Heka who employs *ȝḫ.w*-incantations (effective spells) to fell Apep (see Ritner 1993, 30–35; the king does the same in Epigraphic Survey, 1963, pl. 422 A, l. 1; see also Piankoff 1942b, 10); (3) Thoth (as the third face, perhaps an early allusion to Thoth's epithet "Trismegistos"); and (4) Khepri.

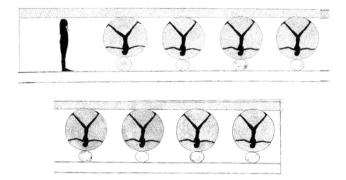

(bottom figure). Within each large disk, as though swimming in concentric circles of dots, is an inverted anthropomorphic figure, arms and legs spread. Each large disk sits atop a smaller, red solar disk, as though the disk were atop the head of the inverted figure. No annotations appear within this register, although the human figures within disks may be read collectively as: "Lords of the Netherworld."[69]

REGISTER 2 (PLATE 52)

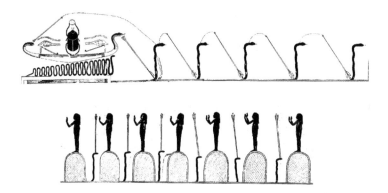

7.33. The register begins with a scene (top figure) of the solar serpent bark atop a multicoiled serpent, "Terrible of Face," whose rearing head is depicted higher than his tail. Within the bark is a vertically oriented scarab supporting a disk, an *udjat*-eye to each side. The eye to the left shoots arrows at five serpents rising from the ground; each of these serpents is labeled "One Who Is Shot." To the right (bottom figure) are seven round-topped mounds, in front of each of which rears a serpent; each serpent to the right of the first mound has an arrow protruding from

---

69. For these figures, see above, p. 531.

its head. Atop each mound stands an anthropomorphic, apparently female figure, facing left, arms raised as in adoration; a label in front of these figures labels them as "One Who Lays Low."[70]

HORIZONTAL TEXT

The hieroglyphic text is composed in cryptography. Roughly above the space between the first and left standing deities (numbering from the left) is a spatium, separating the text describing the standing deities (to the right) from that describing the journey of the solar bark (to the left).

RIGHT PORTION OF THE TEXT

They exist in this fashion, the snakes Terrible of Face that Re slaughtered, when he pauses at their slaughtering pit of sand; He Who Hides the Mystery, who praises the limbs that are in it (the mystery).[71]

LEFT PORTION OF THE TEXT

This god travels in this fashion in his boat, navigating upon the back of Apep. As soon as he passes by, they loose their arrows. While they cast this fire, those on their mounds leap up for him. Those armed with their arrows burn up the enemies of Re, even when he passes by them.

REGISTER 3 (PLATE 52)

7.34. The left portion of the register (top figure) contains two groups of four deities. The first group are four goddesses standing atop serpents, tails rearing up behind them, heads rising before them, all facing right; the goddesses stand in an unusual manner, knees slightly bent and arms hanging down with each hand making a fist. Each figure and serpent is labeled in cryptographic orthographies (left to right):

---

70. For the combination of concepts, compare PT § 1545 (= Utterance 580): "The one who has stretched you out (*pd*) is stretched out, the one who shot (*śśr*) you is shot."
71. The final name and epithet may refer to the figures standing atop the mounds (Darnell 2004, 289–93).

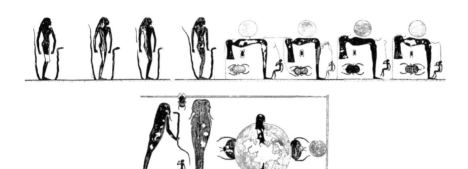

FIGURE: Mother(?)	SERPENT: He within the Earth
FIGURE: She of the Sarcophagus(?)	SERPENT: Terrible of Face
FIGURE: She of the Shrine(?)	SERPENT: Evil of Face
FIGURE: Milk(?)	SERPENT: Apep

The next four deities are shown bending back, long hair down to left, a large disk hovering over the belly, a scarab beneath them, a small hieroglyphic child in front of the lower legs of each. Dots connect the beetles to the figures' mouths, and the children to their phalli (these last damaged).

CRYPTOGRAPHIC LABELS PROVIDE THE NAME OF EACH FIGURE AND THE ACCOMPANYING CHILD (LEFT TO RIGHT)

FIGURE: Protective One(?)	CHILD: He of the Flame[72]
FIGURE: no name given	CHILD: He of the Flame
FIGURE: Naked One	CHILD: He of the Flame
FIGURE: Pleased One	CHILD: He of the Flame

To the right (bottom figure) is a deity whose body bends forward to the right, holding a rearing serpent facing left, a small hieroglyphic child depiction below

---

72. "He of the Flame" is the youthful rising sun (Jansen-Winkeln 1990, 218–19, n. 3; Hornung 1976, 117 [n. 170] and 120 [n. 195]; see p. 97). Child and scarab together recall Book of Going Forth by Day, chapter 15B, in which the $p^c.t$ and $rḥy.t$ worship the rising sun "in his visible form of the youth, Re, the child come forth as Khepri" (Parker, Leclant, and Goyon 1979, 38–40). The groups also recall the tableau in the Books of the Creation of the Solar Disk, Tomb of Ramesses VI, Section B, Register 2, Scene 33 (p. 492).

the serpent; the serpent being grasped by the slanting figure is called a "*Nau*-serpent."[73] A janus-faced mummiform deity follows, each face wearing a divine beard.[74] At the right end of the register, a female deity stands within a large disk, head emerging above the upper curve, facing right. From each side of the disk emerges the forepart of a scarab, that to the right pushing a smaller solar disk.

HORIZONTAL TEXT

Although occasional unusual orthographis appear (cf. Osiris), the text is essentially a normal hieroglyphic composition.

> Osiris, Lord of the Two Lands, Neferkare, whom Re chose, justified, says: "O you gods who exist as the protection of my father Osiris— Come to me, that you may do for me what you have done for Osiris. You should save me from the messengers of Babai-Min, because I am Atum as he comes forth alone from Nun, I being the child of the Great Flood; because as for the Great Flood, (she is) the *udjat*-eye of the god great of magic; because as for the god great of magic, he is Pedjaha, when he shines in the morning."

VERTICAL COLUMNS OF TEXT IN THE UPPER PORTION OF REGISTER 3

The forty-nine short columns of text contain two divisions, lines 1–24 (numbering from the left) written in cryptography, oriented and reading left to right, while lines 25–49 are in—for the most part—normal hieroglyphic orthography, and read retrograde left to right, the signs facing to the right. Although both texts read from left to right, the retrograde orientation of the right half causes the lines visually to converge on lines 25–26, the epithets and name of Ramesses IX (the opening of the second section).

---

73. In the Book of the Hidden Chamber, Hour 12, Register 2, Scene 126 the serpent through the tail of which the bark of the night sun is being pulled is also referred to as *nʿw* (p. 238).

74. Two-headed beings appear in the Book of the Hidden Chamber, Hour 2—in Register 1 is He of the Two Faces (138) and in Register 3 is His Two Faces and His Two Arms (180). The Janus-faced being is probably a depiction of the *bꜣ-dmḏy*, the "unified *ba*," the combined Re-Osiris at the time of solar regeneration, a small version of the much larger image in the right portion of the treatise, to which this smaller figure is linked by the scarabs emerging from either side of the disk to his right.

LEFT PORTION OF THE TEXT

They exist in this fashion in the Place of Destruction. This god calls out to them, that they should be high for him. It is the numerous manifestations which they assume for him, they being endowed with their manifestations. When this god goes to rest, his solar disk is in this cavern, and his birth forms manifest therein. After this great god passes by these goddesses, they stand up. Then the uniform darkness covers them.

RIGHT PORTION OF THE TEXT (BEGINNING WITH A VERSION OF THE BOOK OF GOING FORTH BY DAY, CHAPTER 106)

Osiris king, Lord of the Two Lands, Lord of Maat, Neferkare, whom Re chose, justified, says: "O great bread who is in heaven, O provision who is in the earth—may you give bread and beer to Ptah, that he may dine on the two shanks; may bread and beer belong to the Son of Re Ramesses (IX), who has appeared in Thebes, beloved of Amun, that he may dine on the two shanks together with Ptah. O these you four gods who are over these two sides of the sky, who it is that fixed the earth upon its beams, and the nethersky upon its four supports, and who it is that cause that Re travels in a fair wind, he having traversed heaven in peace—may you place Osiris king, Lord of the Two Lands, Lord of Maat, Neferkare, whom Re chose, <in> heaven together with the one who made it."

REGISTERS 1–3

RIGHT SECTION

7.35. Scene 1. The penultimate scene of the treatise, and the left scene in the pair of scenes that make up the right portion of the Enigmatic Wall depicts the Osiride king, one arm raised above his head, the other (not clearly depicted) grasping his erect phallus, atop a sandy slope. A large serpent, tail curving up beneath the feet and toes of the giant deity, forms the lower right corner of the scene, its head facing the back of the king's head. A solar disk hovers above the chest area of the king, at the level of the wrist of the raised hand; between the disk and wrist, its hind legs touching the disk, is a scarab.

LABEL TO THE OSIRIDE FIGURE

Two columns of text appear beneath the scarab, containing the names of Ramesses IX, as a label to the Osirian figure beneath.

> The lord of the Two Lands Neferkare, whom Re chose, the lord of glorious appearances, Ramesses (IX), who has appeared in Thebes, beloved of Amun.

CRYPTOGRAPHIC ANNOTATION

Five columns of text occupy the upper left corner of the scene; four and a half of the columns are in cryptography.

> This god is in this fashion, his arm in the Upper Region, his feet in the Place of Destruction. It is at the cavern of this god that the birth of this great god occurs. He calls to Osiris; and Osiris calls to him. It is in the uniform darkness that this god, foremost of the Netherworld, exists. The Leaping-serpent is his protection. He shines at the birth of Re. <Re>, may you place Horus, who has appeared in Thebes, together with you, that he may greet you.[75]

7.36. Scene 2. In the final image of the Enigmatic Wall the king offers Maat to Ptah, with whom stands the image of Maat.

---

75. The disk greets the corpse, as in Book of the Hidden Chamber, Hour 1, Concluding Text, in which the the solar god states (p. 146): "That I have come here is to greet myself and give breath to my limbs, so that they (the limbs) might arise for him (Osiris)." The greeting of Osiris by Re also occurs in the Book of Caverns, Litany 16 (p. 429): "O raise yourself, One Hidden of Name—your *ba*-soul is upon your corpse, I having greeted it."

LABEL TO THE KING

The lord of the Two Lands, Neferkare; whom Re chose, the lord of glorious appearances, Ramesses (IX), who has appeared in Thebes, beloved of Amun.

LABEL TO PTAH

Words spoken by Ptah, lord of Maat, king of the Two Lands, Perfect of face, who created crafts, one presiding over the great place at rest.

PLATE 1

573

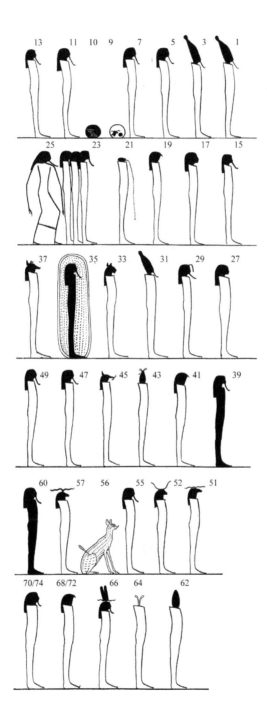

PLATE 3   575

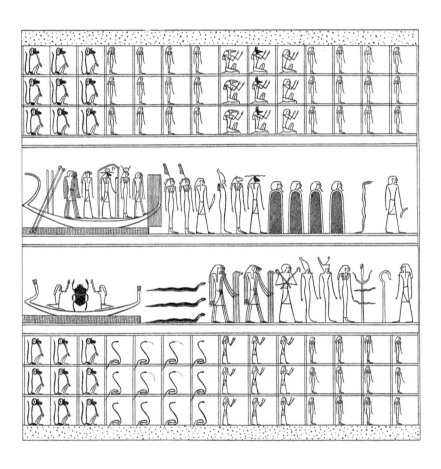

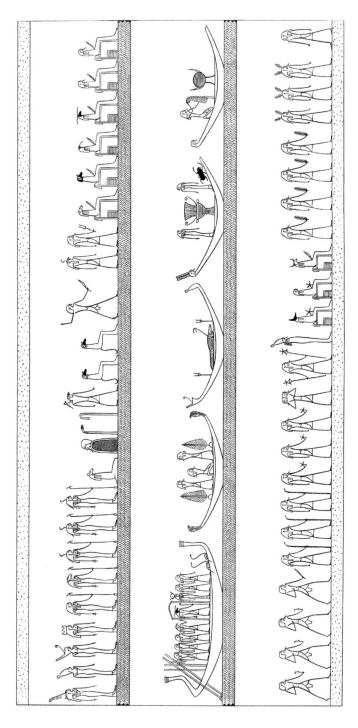

PLATE 5 577

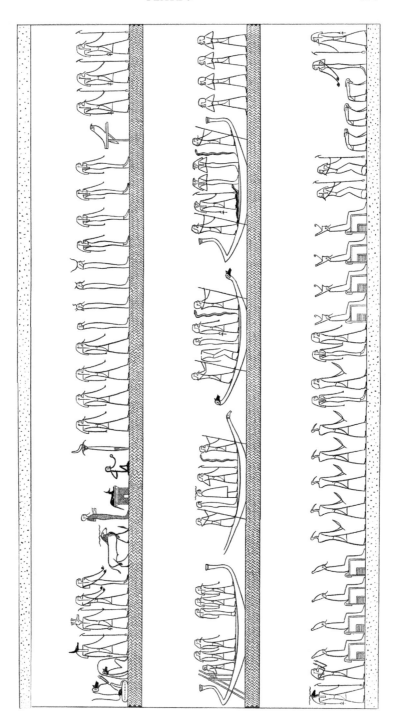

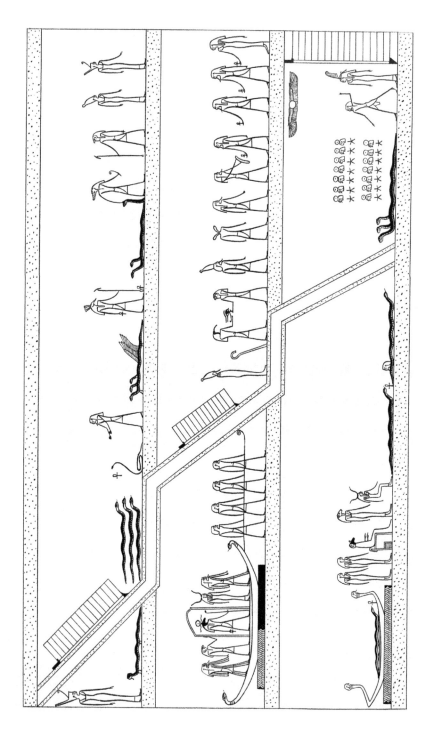

PLATE 7   579

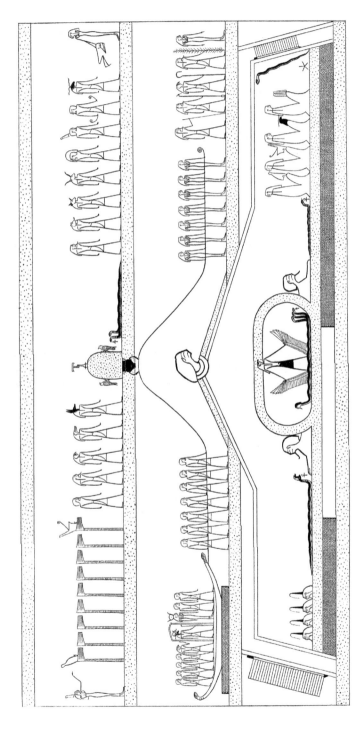

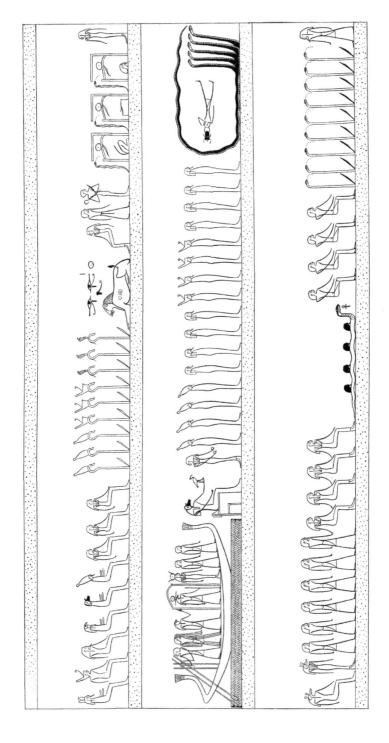

PLATE 9   581

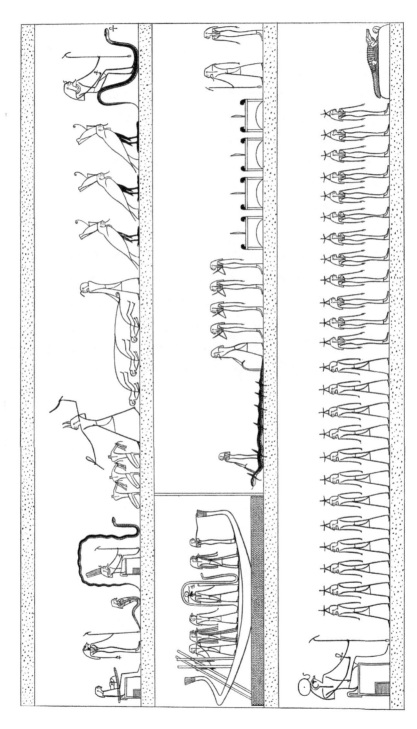

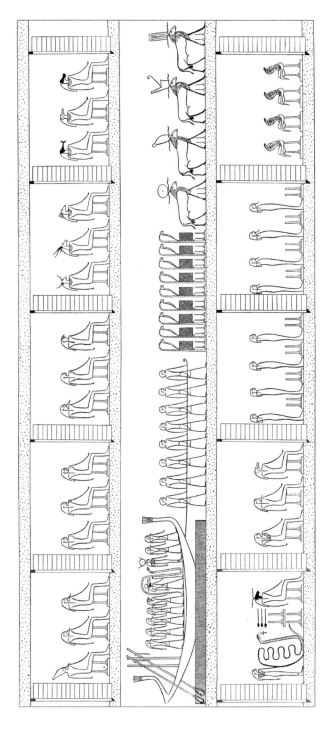

PLATE 11   583

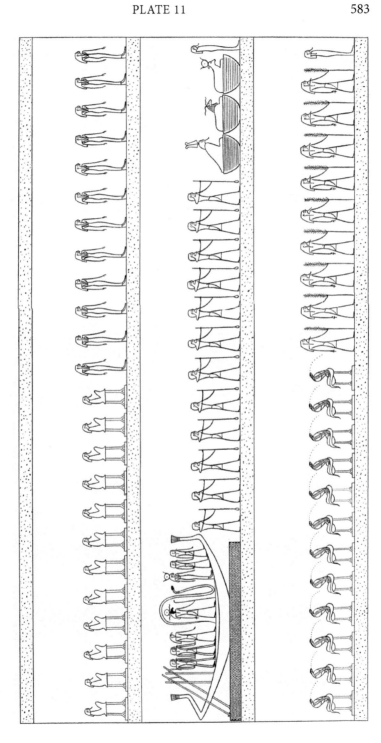

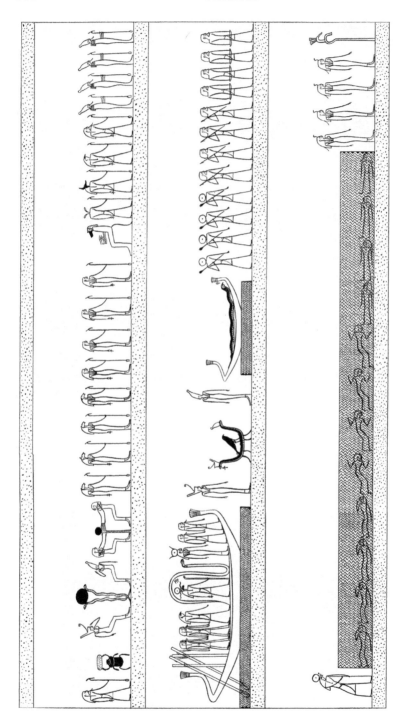

PLATE 13   585

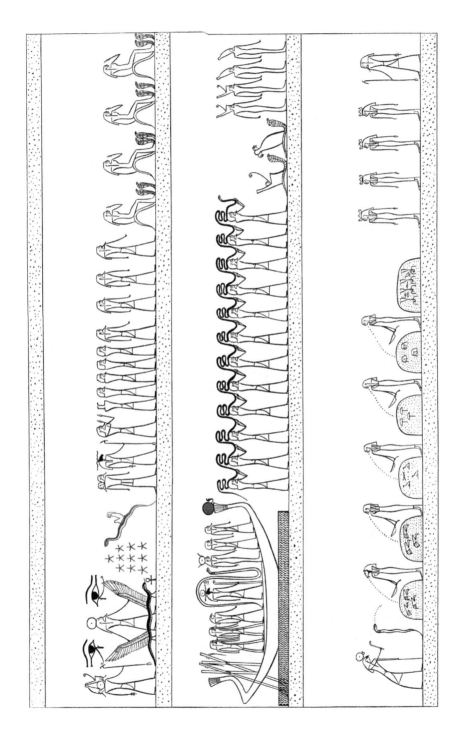

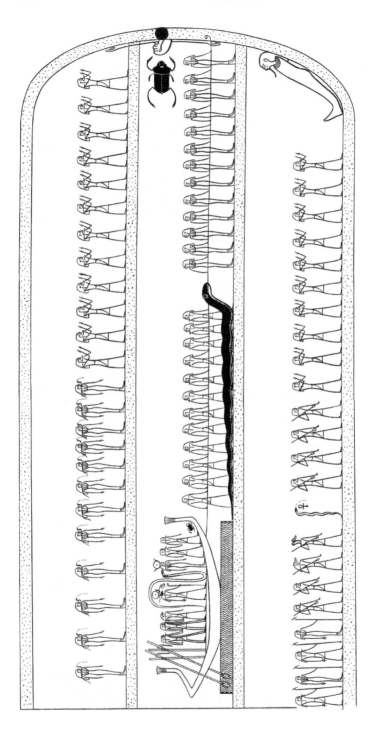

PLATE 15   587

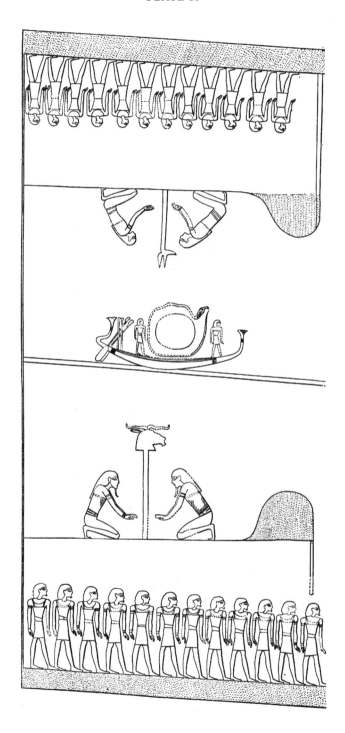

PLATE 17   589

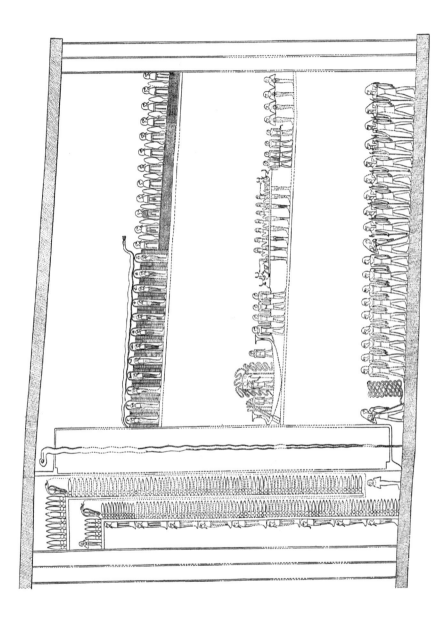

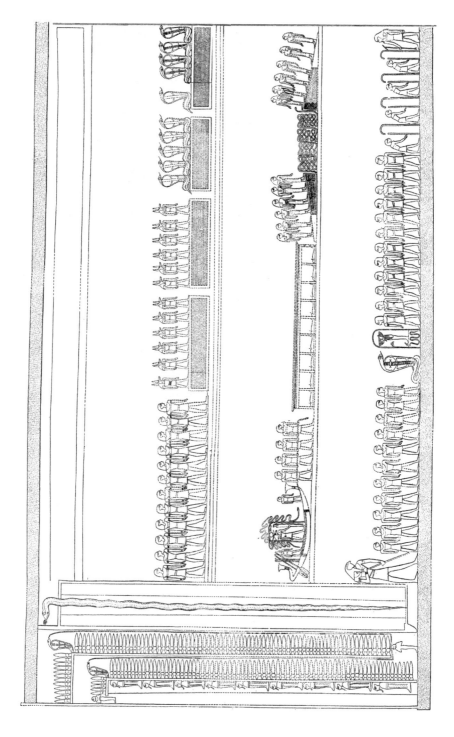

PLATE 19   591

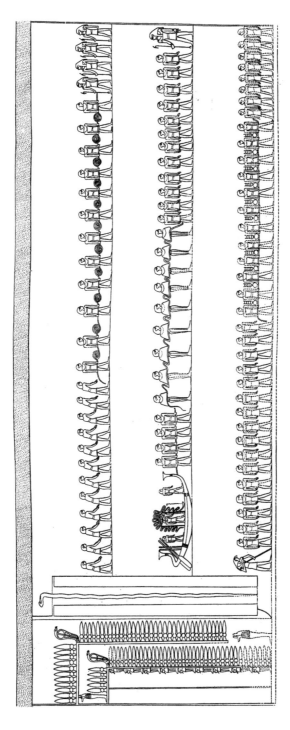

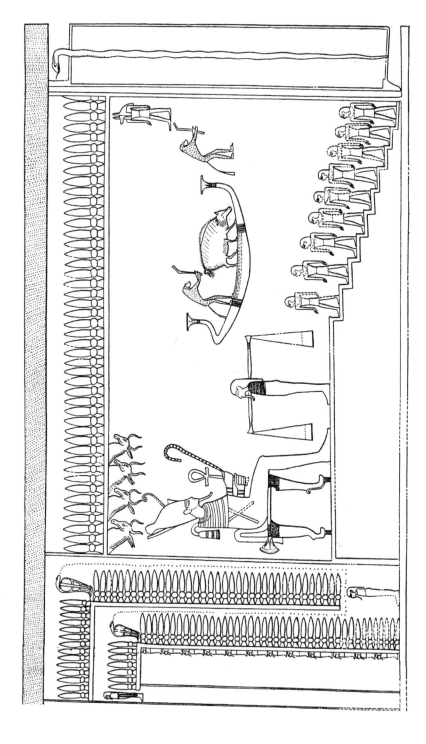

PLATE 21   593

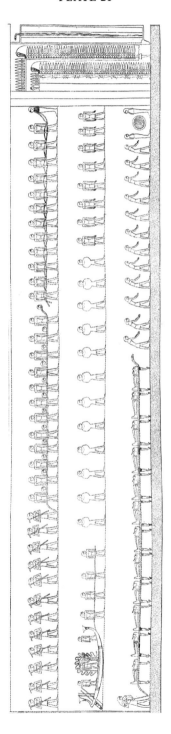

PLATE 22

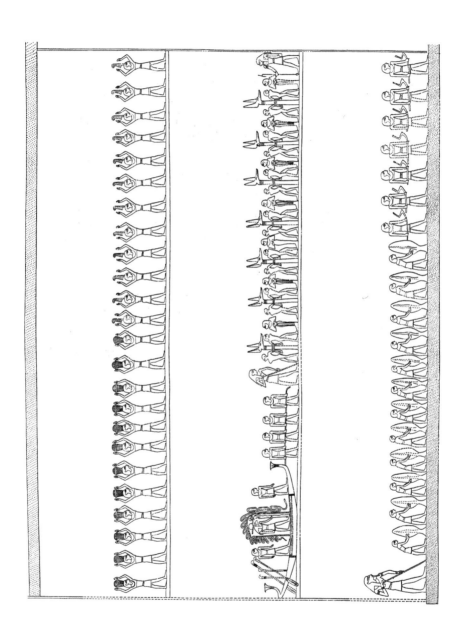

PLATE 23   595

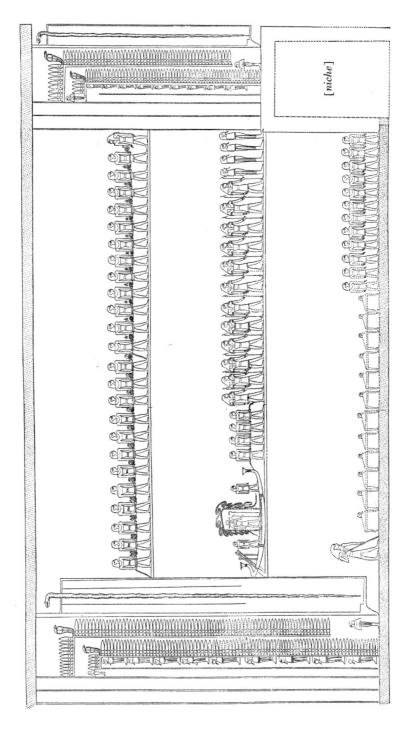

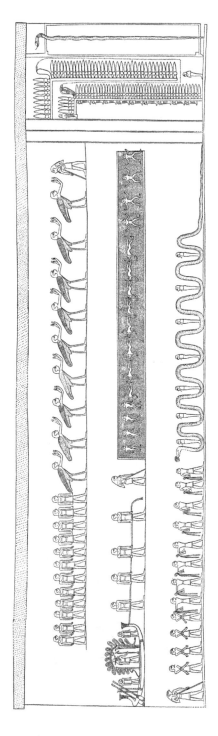

PLATE 25 597

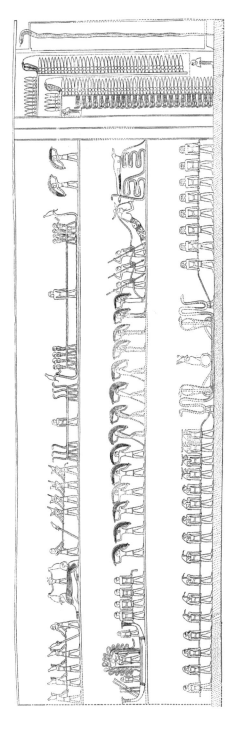

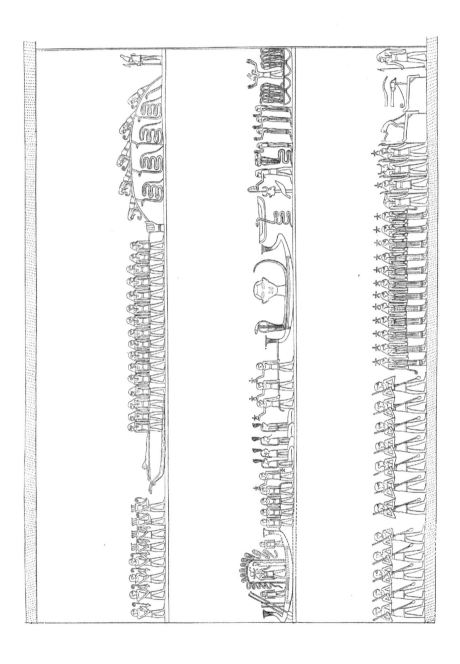

PLATE 27   599

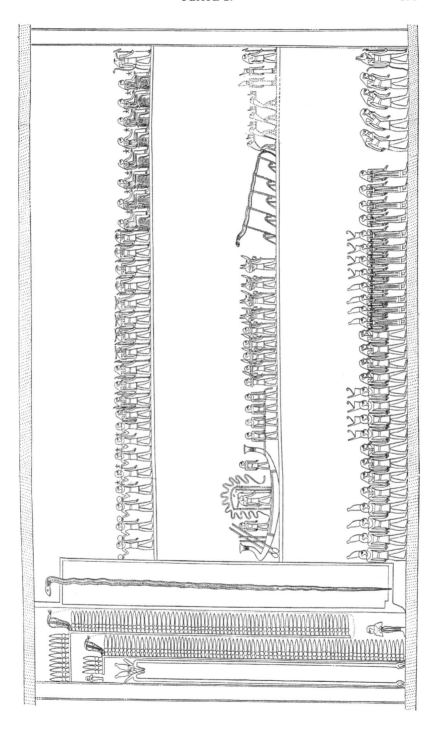

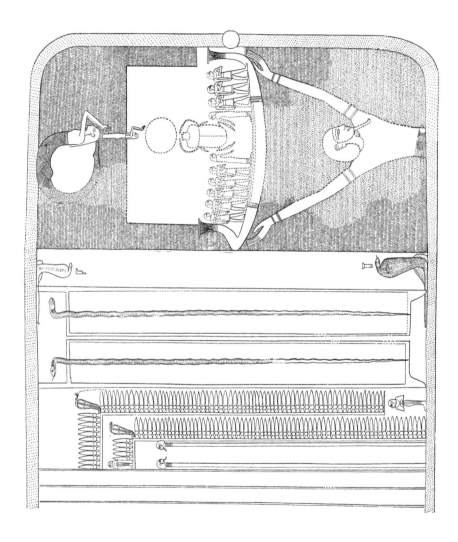

PLATE 29 601

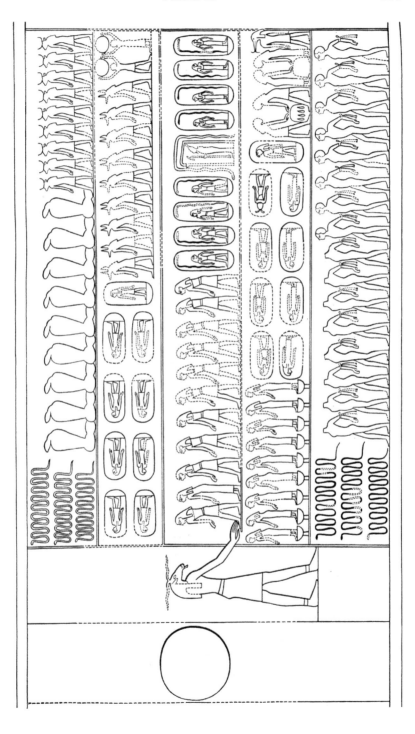

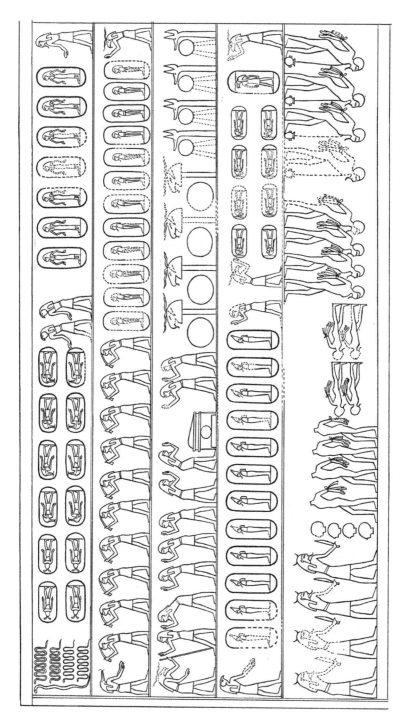

PLATE 31   603

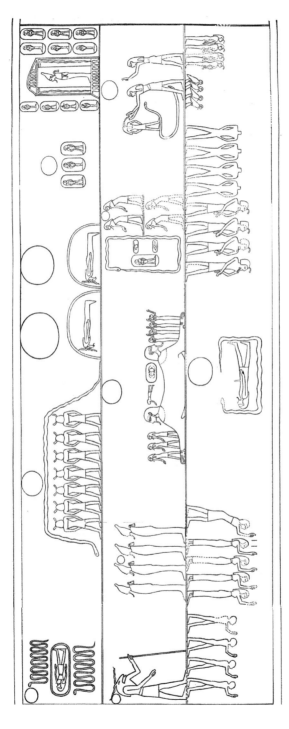

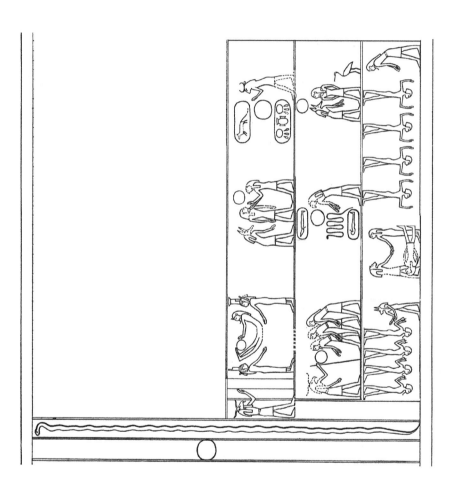

PLATE 33 605

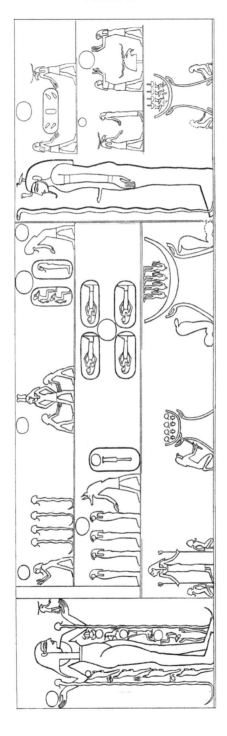

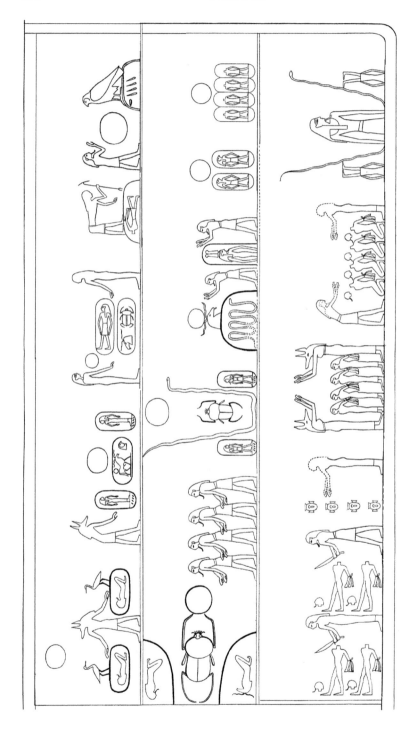

PLATE 35   607

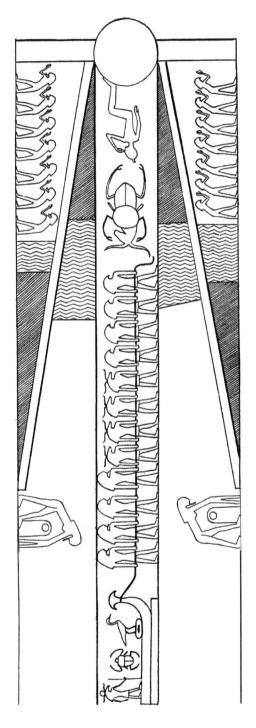

PLATE 36

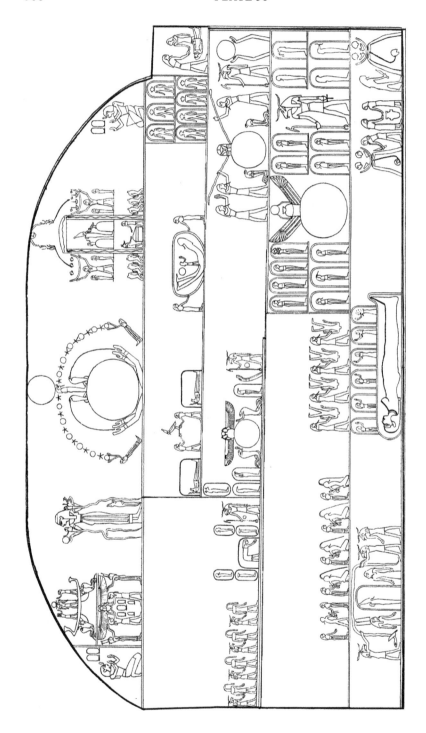

PLATE 37 609

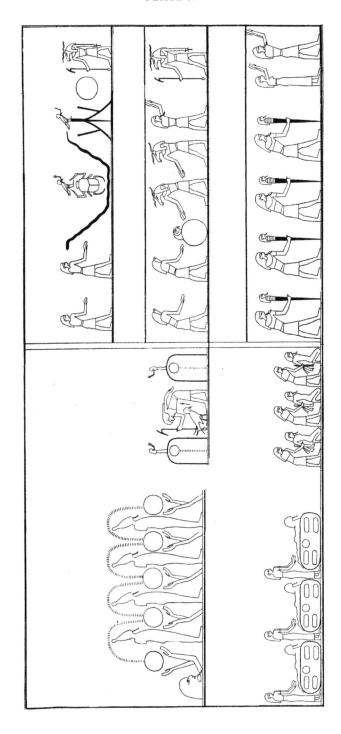

PLATE 38

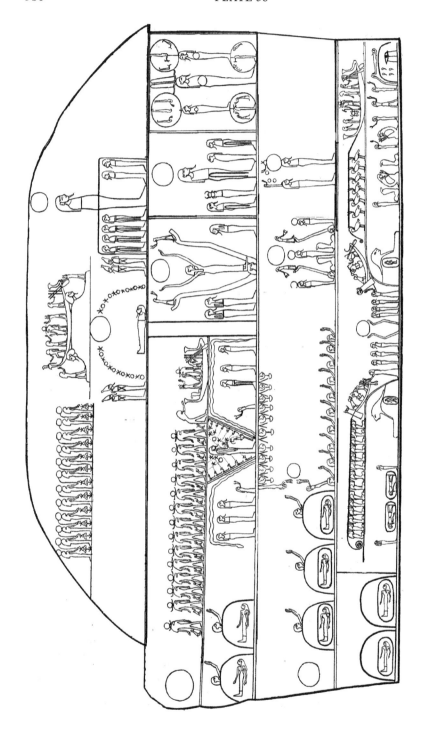

PLATE 39

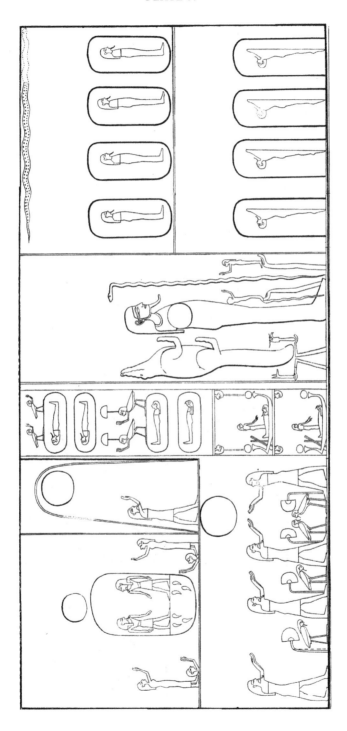

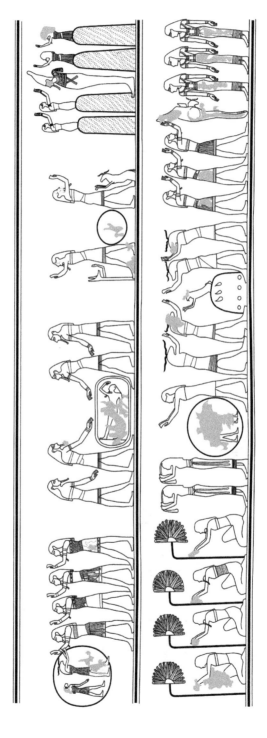

PLATE 41

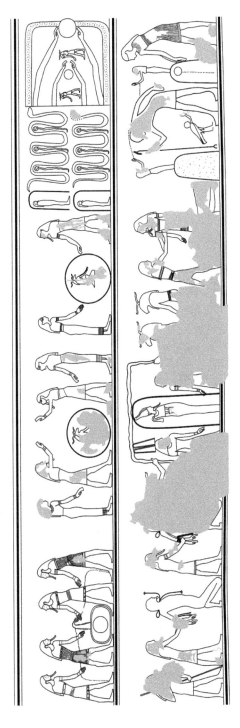

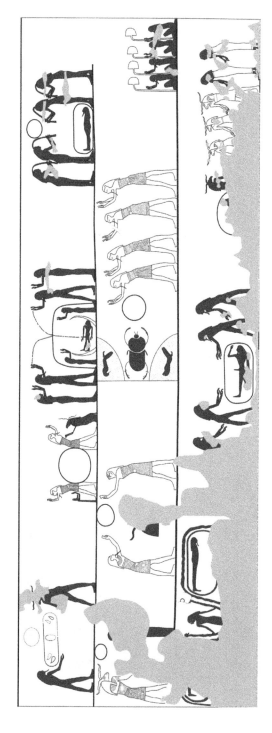

PLATE 43   615

PLATE 44

PLATE 45

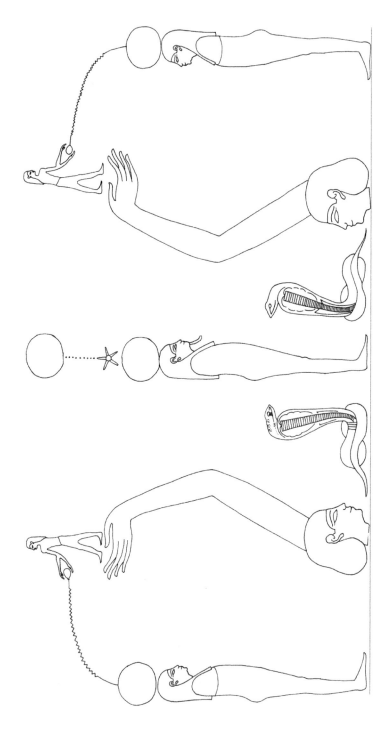

PLATE 47

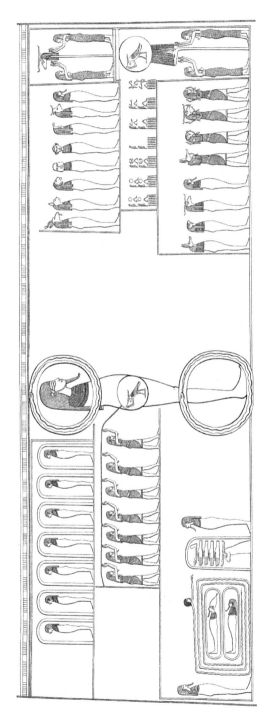

PLATE 48

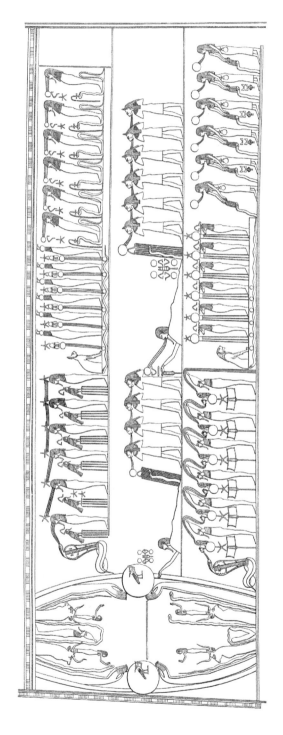

PLATE 49 621

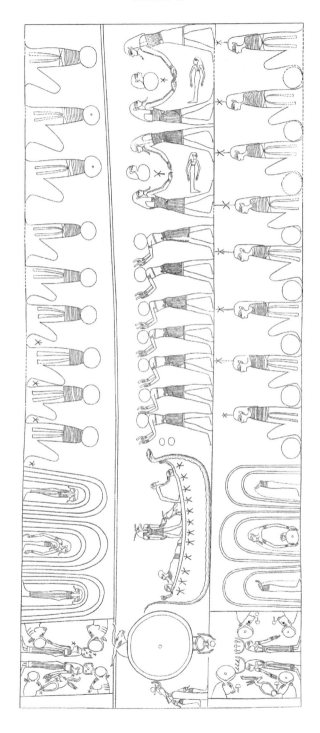

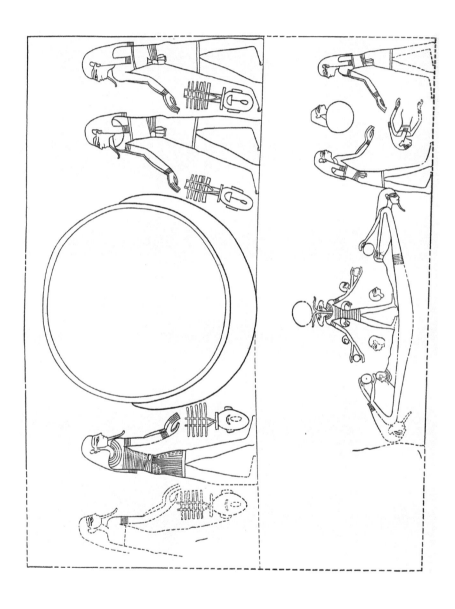

PLATE 51   623

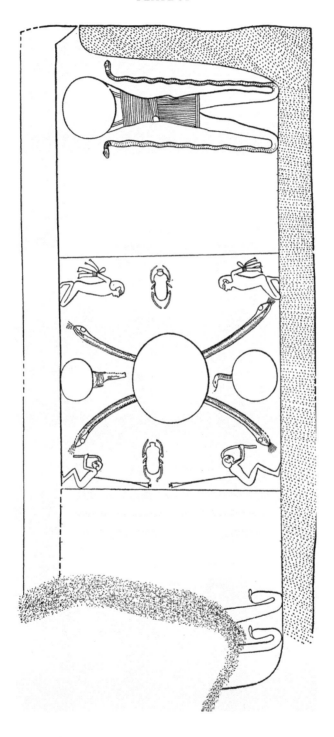

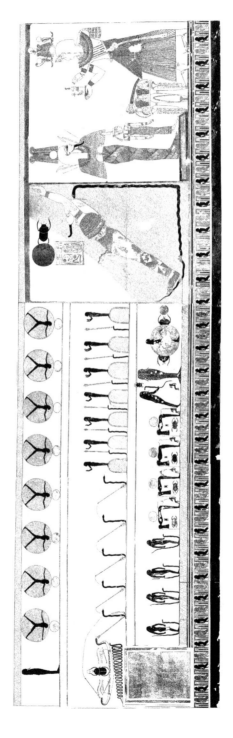

CONCORDANCE OF TEXTS

The concordance of texts lists the page numbers of the hieroglyphic edition most conveniently consulted for each translated passage.

CHAPTER 2: BOOK OF ADORING RE IN THE WEST

Title: Hornung 1975, 1–3
Address 1: Hornung 1975, 4–5
Address 2: Hornung 1975, 5–6
Address 3: Hornung 1975, 7–8
Address 4: Hornung 1975, 8–9
Address 5: Hornung 1975, 10
Address 6: Hornung 1975, 11
Address 7: Hornung 1975, 12
Address 8: Hornung 1975, 13
Address 9: Hornung 1975, 14
Address 10: Hornung 1975, 15
Address 11: Hornung 1975, 16
Address 12: Hornung 1975, 17
Address 13: Hornung 1975, 18
Address 14: Hornung 1975, 19
Address 15: Hornung 1975, 20
Address 16: Hornung 1975, 21
Address 17: Hornung 1975, 22
Address 18: Hornung 1975, 23
Address 19: Hornung 1975, 24
Address 20: Hornung 1975, 25
Address 21: Hornung 1975, 26
Address 22: Hornung 1975, 27
Address 23: Hornung 1975, 28
Address 24: Hornung 1975, 29
Address 24 (Late period variant): Manassa 2007b, pl. 156
Address 25: Hornung 1975, 30

Address 26: Hornung 1975, 31
Address to Foremost of the West: Manassa 2007b, pl. 156
Address 27: Hornung 1975, 32
Address 28: Hornung 1975, 33
Address 29: Hornung 1975, 34
Address 30: Hornung 1975, 35
Address 30 (Late period variant): Manassa 2007b, pl. 156
Address 31: Hornung 1975, 36
Address 32: Hornung 1975, 37
Address 33: Hornung 1975, 38
Address 34: Hornung 1975, 39
Address 35: Hornung 1975, 40
Address 36: Hornung 1975, 41–42
Address 37: Hornung 1975, 42–43
Address 38: Hornung 1975, 44
Address 39: Hornung 1975, 45
Address 40: Hornung 1975, 46–47
Address 41: Hornung 1975, 47–48
Address 42: Hornung 1975, 49
Address 43: Hornung 1975, 50
Address 44: Hornung 1975, 51
Address 45: Hornung 1975, 52
Address 46: Hornung 1975, 53
Address 47: Hornung 1975, 54
Address 48: Hornung 1975, 55
Address 49: Hornung 1975, 56
Address 50: Hornung 1975, 57
Address 51: Hornung 1975, 58–59
Address 52: Hornung 1975, 59–60
Address 53: Hornung 1975, 61
Address 54: Hornung 1975, 62
Address 55: Hornung 1975, 63
Address 56: Hornung 1975, 64–65
Address 57: Hornung 1975, 65–66
Address 58: Hornung 1975, 67
Address 59: Hornung 1975, 68
Address 60: Hornung 1975, 69
Address 61: Hornung 1975, 70
Address 62: Hornung 1975, 71
Address 63: Hornung 1975, 72
Address 64: Hornung 1975, 73
Address 65: Hornung 1975, 74
Address 66: Hornung 1975, 75

Address 67: Hornung 1975, 76
Address 68: Hornung 1975, 77
Address 69: Hornung 1975, 78
Address 70: Hornung 1975, 79
Address 71: Hornung 1975, 80
Address 72: Hornung 1975, 81
Address 73: Hornung 1975, 82
Address 74: Hornung 1975, 83
Address 75: Hornung 1975, 84
Litany 1: Hornung 1975, 85–94
Litany 2: Hornung 1975, 94–97
Litany 3: Hornung 1975, 97–126
Litany 4: Hornung 1975, 126–36
Litany 5: Hornung 1975, 136–57
Litany 6: Hornung 1975, 158–203
Litany 7: Hornung 1975, 203–38
Litany 8: Hornung 1975, 238–59
Litany 9: Hornung 1975, 259–65

Chapter 3: Book of the Hidden Chamber

"Long" Book of the Hidden Chamber

Title: Hornung 1987b, 100–109
Hour 1, Introductory Text: Hornung 1987b, 110–13
Hour 1, Register 1, Scene 1: Hornung 1987b, 114–16
Hour 1, Register 1, Scene 2: Hornung 1987b, 116–20
Hour 1, Register 1, Scene 3: Hornung 1987b, 120–22
Hour 1, Register 1, Scene 4: Hornung 1987b, 122–26
Hour 1, Register 2, Annotation: Hornung 1987b, 126–29
Hour 1, Register 2, Scene 5: Hornung 1987b, 129–30
Hour 1, Register 2, Scene 6: Hornung 1987b, 131–33
Hour 1, Register 2, Continuation of Annotation: Hornung 1987b, 133–36
Hour 1, Register 2, Scene 7: Hornung 1987b, 136–37
Hour 1, Register 2, Scene 8: Hornung 1987b, 137–39
Hour 1, Register 3, Scene 9: Hornung 1987b, 140–42
Hour 1, Register 3, Scene 10: Hornung 1987b, 142–45
Hour 1, Register 3, Scene 11: Hornung 1987b, 146–47
Hour 1, Register 3, Scene 12: Hornung 1987b, 148–50
Hour 1, Concluding Text: Hornung 1987b, 150–73
Hour 2, Introductory Text: Hornung 1987b, 174–82
Hour 2, Register 1, Annotation to the Entire Register: Hornung 1987b, 182–89

Hour 2, Register 1, Scene 13: Hornung 1987b, 189–92
Hour 2, Register 1, Scene 14: Hornung 1987b, 192–94
Hour 2, Register 1, Scene 15: Hornung 1987b, 195–97
Hour 2, Register 2, Annotation to the Entire Register: Hornung 1987b, 197–200
Hour 2, Register 2, Scene 16: Hornung 1987b, 201–2
Hour 2, Register 2, Scene 17: Hornung 1987b, 202–3
Hour 2, Register 2, Scene 18: Hornung 1987b, 203
Hour 2, Register 2, Scene 19: Hornung 1987b, 204
Hour 2, Register 3, Annotation to the Entire Register: Hornung 1987b, 205–11
Hour 2, Register 3, Scene 20: Hornung 1987b, 212
Hour 2, Register 3, Scene 21: Hornung 1987b, 213–14
Hour 2, Register 3, Scene 22: Hornung 1987b, 214–15
Hour 2, Register 3, Scene 23: Hornung 1987b, 215–16
Hour 2, Register 3, Scene 24: Hornung 1987a, 216–17
Hour 2, Concluding Text: Hornung 1987b, 218–69
Hour 3, Introductory Text: Hornung 1987b, 270–77
Hour 3, Register 1, Annotation to the Entire Register: Hornung 1987b, 278–83
Hour 3, Register 1, Scene 25: Hornung 1987b, 283–85
Hour 3, Register 1, Scene 26: Hornung 1987b, 285–87
Hour 3, Register 1, Scene 27: Hornung 1987b, 287–88
Hour 3, Register 1, Scene 28: Hornung 1987b, 288–90
Hour 3, Register 2, Annotation to the Entire Register: Hornung 1987b, 291–95
Hour 3, Register 2, Scene 29: Hornung 1987b, 296–97
Hour 3, Register 2, Scene 30: Hornung 1987b, 297–98
Hour 3, Register 2, Scene 31: Hornung 1987b, 298–99
Hour 3, Register 2, Scene 32: Hornung 1987b, 300
Hour 3, Register 2, Scene 33: Hornung 1987b, 301
Hour 3, Register 3, Annotation to the Entire Register: Hornung 1987b, 302–7
Hour 3, Register 3, Scene 34: Hornung 1987b, 307
Hour 3, Register 3, Scene 35: Hornung 1987b, 308–10
Hour 3, Register 3, Scene 36: Hornung 1987b, 310–12
Hour 3, Concluding Text: Hornung 1987b, 312–41
Hour 4, Introductory Text: Hornung 1992, 343–49
Hour 4, Texts within the Descending Path That Zig–Zags across Hour 4: Hornung 1992, 349–53
Hour 4, Register 1, Scene 37: Hornung 1992, 354–56
Hour 4, Register 1, Scene 38: Hornung 1992, 356–59
Hour 4, Register 1, Scene 39: Hornung 1992, 359–63
Hour 4, Register 2, Scene 40: Hornung 1992, 363–71
Hour 4, Register 2, Scene 41: Hornung 1992, 371–73
Hour 4, Register 2, Scene 42: Hornung 1992, 373
Hour 4, Register 3, Scene 43: Hornung 1992, 374–75
Hour 4, Register 3, Scene 44: Hornung 1992, 376–78

Hour 12, Introductory Text: Hornung 1994c, 793–800
Hour 12, Register 1, Scene 122: Hornung 1994c, 800–808
Hour 12, Register 1, Scene 123: Hornung 1994c, 809–16
Hour 12, Register 2, Scene 124: Hornung 1994c, 816–20
Hour 12, Register 2, Scene 125: Hornung 1994c, 821–26
Hour 12, Register 2, Scene 126: Hornung 1994c, 826–29
Hour 12, Register 2, Scene 127: Hornung 1994c, 829–34
Hour 12, Register 3, Scene 128: Hornung 1994c, 834–36
Hour 12, Register 3, Scene 129: Hornung 1994c, 837–41
Hour 12, Register 3, Scene 130: Hornung 1994c, 841–48
Hour 12, Register 3, Scene 131: Hornung 1994c, 848–49

"Short" Book of the Hidden Chamber

Title: Hornung 1987b, 1–2
Hour 1: Hornung 1987b, 2–8
Hour 2: Hornung 1987b, 8–19
Hour 3: Hornung 1987b, 19–30
Hour 4: Hornung 1987b, 31–38
Hour 5: Hornung 1987b, 38–49
Hour 6: Hornung 1987b, 49–62
Hour 7: Hornung 1987b, 63–73
Hour 8: Hornung 1987b, 74–77
Hour 9: Hornung 1987b,78–82
Hour 10: Hornung 1987b, 83–86
Hour 11: Hornung 1987b, 87–90
Hour 12: Hornung 1987b, 91–94
Concluding Title: Hornung 1987b, 94–97

CHAPTER 4: BOOK OF GATES

Hour 1, Register 1, Scene 1: Hornung 1979b, 1–3
Hour 1, Register 2, Scene 2: Hornung 1979b, 3–6
Hour 1, Register 2, Scene 3: Hornung 1979b, 6–11
Hour 1, Register 3, Scene 4: Hornung 1979b, 11
Doorway 1: Hornung 1979b, 12–14
Hour 2, Register 1, Scene 5: Hornung 1979b, 15–19
Hour 2, Register 1, Scene 6: Hornung 1979b, 19–24
Hour 2, Register 2, Scene 7: Hornung 1979b, 24–33
Hour 2, Register 3, Scene 8: Hornung 1979b, 33–42
Doorway 2: Hornung 1979b, 42–49
Hour 3, Register 1, Scene 9: Hornung 1979b, 50–56

Hour 3, Register 1, Scene 10: Hornung 1979b, 56–62
Hour 3, Register 2, Scene 11: Hornung 1979b, 63–70
Hour 3, Register 2, Scene 12: Hornung 1979b, 70–73
Hour 3, Register 3, Scene 13: Hornung 1979b, 74–79
Hour 3, Register 3, Scene 14: Hornung 1979b, 79–85
Doorway 3: Hornung 1979b, 85–91
Hour 4, Register 1, Scene 15: Hornung 1979b, 92–97
Hour 4, Register 1, Scene 16: Hornung 1979b, 97–103
Hour 4, Register 1, Scene 17: Hornung 1979b, 103–7
Hour 4, Register 2, Scene 18: Hornung 1979b, 108–12
Hour 4, Register 2, Scene 19: Hornung 1979b, 112–17
Hour 4, Register 2, Scene 20: Hornung 1979b, 118–23
Hour 4, Register 3, Scene 21: Hornung 1979b, 124–36
Hour 4, Register 3, Scene 22: Hornung 1979b, 136–40
Doorway 4: Hornung 1979b, 140–46
Hour 5, Register 1, Scene 23: Hornung 1979b, 147–52
Hour 5, Register 1, Scene 24: Hornung 1979b, 152–58
Hour 5, Register 1, Scene 25: Hornung 1979b, 159–61
Hour 5, Register 2, Scene 26: Hornung 1979b, 162–65
Hour 5, Register 2, Scene 27: Hornung 1979b, 165–69
Hour 5, Register 2, Scene 28: Hornung 1979b, 169–73
Hour 5, Register 2, Scene 29: Hornung 1979b, 174–75
Hour 5, Register 3, Scene 30: Hornung 1979b, 176–81
Hour 5, Register 3, Scene 31: Hornung 1979b, 181–86
Hour 5, Register 3, Scene 32: Hornung 1979b, 185–89
Doorway 5: Hornung 1979b, 190–91
Judgment Hall of Osiris, Scene 33: Hornung 1979b, 192–203
Hour 6, Register 1, Scene 34: Hornung 1979b, 204–9
Hour 6, Register 1, Scene 35: Hornung 1979b, 209–15
Hour 6, Register 1, Scene 36: Hornung 1979b, 215–20
Hour 6, Register 2, Scene 37: Hornung 1979b, 220–23
Hour 6, Register 2, Scene 38: Hornung 1979b, 224–29
Hour 6, Register 2, Scene 39: Hornung 1979b, 230–34
Hour 6, Register 3, Scene 40: Hornung 1979b, 234–43
Hour 6, Register 3, Scene 41: Hornung 1979b, 243–48
Doorway 6: Hornung 1979b, 249–51
Hour 7, Register 1, Scene 42: Hornung 1979b, 252–54
Hour 7, Register 1, Scene 43: Hornung 1979b, 254–57
Hour 7, Register 2, Scene 44: Hornung 1979b, 257–59
Hour 7, Register 2, Scene 45: Hornung 1979b, 259–64
Hour 7, Register 3, Scene 46: Hornung 1979b, 264–68
Hour 7, Register 3, Scene 47: Hornung 1979b, 268–71
Doorway 7: Hornung 1979b, 271–74

Hour 8, Register 1, Scene 48: Hornung 1979b, 275–77
Hour 8, Register 1, Scene 49: Hornung 1979b, 277–80
Hour 8, Register 2, Scene 50: Hornung 1979b, 280–83
Hour 8, Register 2, Scene 51: Hornung 1979b, 283–86
Hour 8, Register 2, Scene 52: Hornung 1979b, 286–87
Hour 8, Register 3, Scene 53: Hornung 1979b, 288–92
Hour 8, Register 3, Scene 54: Hornung 1979b, 292–95
Doorway 8: Hornung 1979b, 295–98
Hour 9, Register 1, Scene 55: Hornung 1979b, 299–304
Hour 9, Register 1, Scene 56: Hornung 1979b, 305–8
Hour 9, Register 2, Scene 57: Hornung 1979b, 308–12
Hour 9, Register 2, Scene 58: Hornung 1979b, 312–17
Hour 9, Register 3, Scene 59: Hornung 1979b, 318–23
Hour 9, Register 3, Scene 60: Hornung 1979b, 323–26
Doorway 9: Hornung 1979b, 326–30
Hour 10, Register 1, Scene 61: Hornung 1979b, 331–36
Hour 10, Register 1, Scene 62: Hornung 1979b, 336–38
Hour 10, Register 1, Scene 63: Hornung 1979b, 338–41
Hour 10, Register 1, Scene 64: Hornung 1979b, 341–43
Hour 10, Register 2, Scene 65: Hornung 1979b, 343–44
Hour 10, Register 2, Scene 66: Hornung 1979b, 344–46
Hour 10, Register 2, Scene 67: Hornung 1979b, 346–47
Hour 10, Register 3, Scene 68: Hornung 1979b, 347–53
Doorway 10: Hornung 1979b, 354–55
Hour 11, Register 1, Scene 69: Hornung 1979b, 356–60
Hour 11, Register 2, Scene 70: Hornung 1979b, 360–62
Hour 11, Register 2, Scene 71: Hornung 1979b, 362
Hour 11, Register 2, Scene 72: Hornung 1979b, 362–63
Hour 11, Register 2, Scene 73: Hornung 1979b, 363–64
Hour 11, Register 2, Scene 74: Hornung 1979b, 364–65
Hour 11, Register 2, Scene 75: Hornung 1979b, 365
Hour 11, Register 2, Scene 76: Hornung 1979b, 365–66
Hour 11, Register 2, Scene 77: Hornung 1979b, 366–67
Hour 11, Register 2, Scene 78: Hornung 1979b, 367
Hour 11, Register 3, Scene 79: Hornung 1979b, 368–69
Hour 11, Register 3, Scene 80: Hornung 1979b, 369–71
Hour 11, Register 3, Scene 81: Hornung 1979b, 371–72
Doorway 11: Hornung 1979b, 373–76
Hour 12, Register 1, Scene 82: Hornung 1979b, 377–79
Hour 12, Register 1, Scene 83: Hornung 1979b, 379–80
Hour 12, Register 1, Scene 84: Hornung 1979b, 381
Hour 12, Register 1, Scene 85: Hornung 1979b, 381–82
Hour 12, Register 1, Scene 86: Hornung 1979b, 382–83

Hour 12, Register 1, Scene 87: Hornung 1979b, 384–86
Hour 12, Register 2, Scene 88: Hornung 1979b, 386–89
Hour 12, Register 2, Scene 89: Hornung 1979b, 389–92
Hour 12, Register 2, Scene 90: Hornung 1979b, 393–94
Hour 12, Register 2, Scene 91: Hornung 1979b, 394–95
Hour 12, Register 3, Scene 92: Hornung 1979b, 395–96
Hour 12, Register 3, Scene 93: Hornung 1979b, 396–97
Hour 12, Register 3, Scene 94: Hornung 1979b, 397
Hour 12, Register 3, Scene 95: Hornung 1979b, 397–98
Hour 12, Register 3, Scene 96: Hornung 1979b, 398–99
Hour 12, Register 3, Scene 97: Hornung 1979b, 399–400
Hour 12, Register 3, Scene 98: Hornung 1979b, 400–401
Hour 12, Register 3, Scene 99: Hornung 1979b, 401–2
Hour 12, Register 3, Scene 100: Hornung 1979b, 402
Doorway 12: Hornung 1979b, 403–9
Concluding Scene: Hornung 1979b, 410

Chapter 5: Book of Caverns

Division 1, Scenes 1–2: Piankoff 1942a, pl. III
Division 1, Register 1, Scene 3: Piankoff 1942a, pl. III
Division 1, Register 1, Scene 4: Piankoff 1942a, pl. IV
Division 1, Register 1, Scene 5: Piankoff 1942a, pl. IV
Division 1, Register 1, Annotation to Scenes 3–5: Piankoff 1942a, pl. IV–V
Division 1, Register 2, Scene 6: Piankoff 1942a, pl. V
Division 1, Register 2, Scene 7: Piankoff 1942a, pl. V
Division 1, Register 2, Scene 8: Piankoff 1942a, pl. V
Division 1, Register 2, Annotation to Scenes 6–8: Piankoff 1942a, pls. V–VI
Division 1, Register 3, Scene 9: Piankoff 1942a, pls. VI–VII
Division 1, Register 4, Scene 10: Piankoff 1942a, pl. VII
Division 1, Register 4, Scene 11: Piankoff 1942a, pl. VII
Division 1, Register 4, Scene 12: Piankoff 1942a, pl. VII
Division 1, Register 4, Annotation to Scenes 10–12: Piankoff 1942a, pls. VII–VIII
Division 1, Register 5, Scene 13: Piankoff 1942a, pl. VIII
Division 1, Register 5, Scene 14: Piankoff 1942a, pl. VIII
Division 1, Register 5, Annotation to Scenes 13–14: Piankoff 1942a, pls. VIII–IX
Division 2, Register 1, Scene 15: Piankoff 1944, pls. XI–XII
Division 2, Register 1, Scene 16: Piankoff 1944, pls. XII–XIII
Division 2, Register 1, Scene 17: Piankoff 1944, pls. XIII–XV
Division 2, Register 2, Scene 18: Piankoff 1944, pls. XV–XVII
Division 2, Register 2, Scene 19: Piankoff 1944, pls. XVII–XIX

Division 2, Register 3, Scene 20: Piankoff 1944, pl. XIX

Division 2, Register 3, Scene 21: Piankoff 1944, pls. XX–XXI

Division 2, Register 4, Scene 22: Piankoff 1944, pls. XXI–XXIII

Division 2, Register 4, Scene 23: Piankoff 1944, pl. XXIII

Division 2, Register 4, Annotation to Scenes 22–23: Piankoff 1944, pls. XXIII–XXIV

Division 2, Register 5, Scene 24: Piankoff 1944, pls. XXIV–XXV

Division 3, Introductory Text: Piankoff 1944, pls. XXV–XXVI

Division 3, Register 1, Scene 25: Piankoff 1944, pls. XXVI–XXVIIII

Division 3, Register 1, Scene 26: Piankoff 1944, pl. XXVIIII

Division 3, Register 1, Scene 27: Piankoff 1944, pl. XXIX

Division 3, Register 1, Scene 28: Piankoff 1944, pl. XXIX

Division 3, Register 1, Scene 29: Piankoff 1944, pls. XXIX–XXX

Division 3, Register 2, Scene 30: Piankoff 1944, XXX

Division 3, Register 2, Scene 31: Piankoff 1944, XXX

Division 3, Registers 2–3, Scene 32: Piankoff 1944, pls. XXXI, XXXV

Division 3, Register 2, Scene 33: Piankoff 1944, pl. XXXII

Division 3, Register 2, Scene 34: Piankoff 1944, pl. XXXIII

Division 3, Register 3, Scene 35: Piankoff 1944, pls. XXXIII–XXXIV

Division 3, Register 3, Scene 36: Piankoff 1944, pls. XXXV–XXXVI

Division 3, Register 3, Scene 37: Piankoff 1944, pls. XXXVI–XXXVII

Introduction to Divisions 4–6, Scenes 38–40: Piankoff 1944, pls. XXXVII, XXXIX

Litany 1: Piankoff 1944, pls. XXXIX–XL

Litany 2: Piankoff 1944, pls. XL–XLII

Address to the One Tired of Heart: Piankoff 1944, pls. XLII–XLIII

Litany 3: Piankoff 1944, pls. XLIII–XLV

Division 4, Register 1, Scene 41: Piankoff 1944, pl. XLV

Division 4, Register 1, Scene 42: Piankoff 1944, pls. XLV–XLVI

Division 4, Register 1, Scene 43: Piankoff 1944, pls. XLVI–XLVII

Division 4, Register 2, Scene 44: Piankoff 1944, pl. XLVII

Division 4, Register 2, Scene 45: Piankoff 1944, pl. XLVII

Division 4, Register 2, Scene 46: Piankoff 1944, pls. XLVII–XLVIII

Division 4, Register 3, Scene 47: Piankoff 1944, pl. XLVIII

Division 4, Register 3, Scene 48: Piankoff 1944, pls. XLVIII–XLIX

Division 4, Register 3, Scene 49: Piankoff 1944, pls. XLIX–L

Litany 4: Piankoff 1944, pls. L, LII–LIII

Litany 5: Piankoff 1944, pls. LIV–LV

Litany 6: Piankoff 1944, pls. LV–LVIII

Division 5, Scene 50: Piankoff 1944, pls. LXXVI, LVIII–LXIII

Division 5, Register 1 (First Half), Scene 51: Piankoff 1944, pls. LXXVI, LXIII–LXIV

Division 5, Register 1 (First Half), Scene 52: Piankoff 1944, pls. LXXVI, LXIV

Division 6, Register 2, Scene 70: Piankoff 1945, pls. CXXIX–CXXX, CXLVIII–CXLIX
Division 6, Register 2, Scene 71: Piankoff 1945, pls. CXXX–CXXXI, XCLIX
Division 6, Register 2, Scene 72: Piankoff 1945, pls. CXXXII, CXLIX
Division 6, Register 3, Scene 73: Piankoff 1945, pls. CXXXII, CL–CLI
Division 6, Register 3, Scene 74: Piankoff 1945, pls. CXXXIII–CXXXIV, CLI
Division 6, Register 3, Scene 75: Piankoff 1945, pls. CXXXIV–CXXXV
Division 6, Register 3, Scene 76: Piankoff 1945, pls. CXXXV–CXXXVI, CLI
End of Register 3: Piankoff 1945, pl. CXXXVI
Litany Following Division 6: Piankoff 1945, pls. CXXXVI–CXXXVII
Litany 21: Piankoff 1945, pls. CXXXVII–CXLIII
Concluding Tableau, Scene 77: Piankoff 1945, 45–46
Concluding Tableau, Scene 78: Piankoff 1945, pls. CXLIII–CXLV
Concluding Tableau, Scene 79: Piankoff 1945, pls. CXLIV–CXLV
Concluding Tableau, Scene 80: Piankoff 1945, pl. CXXI

Chapter 6: Books of the Creation of the Solar Disk

Tomb of Ramesses VI

Section A, Register 1, Scene 1: Roberson 2012, 133 (Scene 1)
Section A, Register 1, Scene 2: Roberson 2012, 253 (Scene 56), 321–23 (R6.A.1.56.8–11)
Section A, Register 1, Scene 3: Roberson 2012, 198 (Scene 25), 317–21 (R6.A.1.25.2–7)
Section A, Register 1, Scene 4: Roberson 2012, 279–82 (Scene 74), 324–27 (R6.A.1.74.12–18)
Section A, Register 2, Scene 5: Roberson 2012, 221 (Scene 35), 335 (R6.A.3.35.26)
Section A, Register 2, Scene 6: Roberson 2012, 237 (Scene 48)
Section A, Register 2 (Upper), Scene 7: Roberson 2012, 267 (Scene 66), 331 (R6.A.2.66.23)
Section A, Register 2 (Upper), Scene 8: Roberson 2012, 172 (Scene 14), 329–31 (R6.A.2.14.20–22)
Section A, Register 2 (Upper), Scene 9: Roberson 2012, 162–63 (Scene 13), 328 (R6.A.2.13.19)
Section A, Register 2 (Lower), Scene 10: Roberson 2012, 174–75 (Scene 16), 332, 334 (R6.A.3.16.24–25)
Section A, Register 2 (Lower), Scene 11: Roberson 2012, 268 (Scene 67)
Section A, Register 3, Scene 12: Roberson 2012, 214–15 (Scene 31), 341 (R6.A.4.31.30)

Section A, Register 3, Scene 13: Roberson 2012, 212–13 (Scene 30), 339–40
(R6.A.4.30.28–29)
Section A, Register 3, Scene 14: Roberson 2012, 176 (Scene 17), 339
(R6.A.4.17.27)
Section A, Register 4, Scene 15: Roberson 2012, 286–87 (Scene 76), 345–46
(R6.A.5.76.33–34)
Section A, Register 4, Scene 16: Roberson 2012, 277–78 (Scene 72), 343
(R6.A.4.72.31)
Section A, Register 4, Scene 17: Roberson 2012, 216–17 (Scene 32), 344
(R6.A.5.32.32)
Section A2, Register 1 (Upper), Scene 18: Roberson 2012, 178–79 (Scene 18),
348 (R6.A2.2.18.36)
Section A2, Register 1 (Lower), Scene 19: Roberson 2012, 347 (R6.A2.2.15.35)
Section A2, Register 1, Scene 20: Roberson 2012, 238–39 (Scene 49), 349 (R6.
A2.2.49.37)
Section A2, Register 1, Scene 21: Roberson 2012, 350 (R6.A2.2.58.38)
Section A2, Register 2, Scene 22: Roberson 2012, 352 (R6.A2.3.43.41)
Section A2, Register 2, Scene 23: Roberson 2012, 218–19 (Scene 33), 351–52
(R6.A2.3.33.39–40)
Section A2, Register 2, Scene 24: Roberson 2012, 262 (Scene 63), 353 (R6.
A2.3.63.42)
Section B, Register 1, Scene 25: Roberson 2012, 241–43 (Scene 51), 361–63
(R6.B.1.51.47–49)
Section B, Register 1, Scene 26: Roberson 2012, 135–36 (Scene 2), 354
(R6.B.1.2.43)
Section B, Register 1, Scene 27: Roberson 2012, 270 (Scene 68), 364–65
(R6.B.1.68.50–52)
Section B, Register 1, Scene 28: Roberson 2012, 224 (Scene 38), 356–60
(R6.B.1.38.44–46)
Section B, Register 2, Scene 29: Roberson 2012, 248–51 (Scene 55)
Section B, Register 2, Scene 30: Roberson 2012, 274–75 (Scene 70), 369
(R6.B.2.70.57–58)
Section B, Register 2, Scene 31: Roberson 2012, 205–6 (Scene 27)
Section B, Register 2 (Upper), Scene 32: Roberson 2012, 188–90 (Scene 20),
366–68 (R6.B.2.20.54–56)
Section B, Register 2 (Lower), Scene 33: Roberson 2012, 180–82 (Scene 19), 366
(R6.B.2.19.53)
Section B, Registers 2–4, Scene 34: Roberson 2012, 235–36 (Scene 47), 373
(R6.B.3.47.63–64), 377 (R6.B.4.47.73)
Section B, Register 3, Scene 35: Roberson 2012, 197 (Scene 24), 370
(R6.B.3.24.59)
Section B, Register 3, Scene 36: Roberson 2012, 201–2 (Scene 26), 371
(R6.B.3.26.60–61)

Section B, Register 3, Scene 37: Roberson 2012, 226 (Scene 40), 372
 (R6.B.3.40.62)
Section B, Register 4, Scene 38: Roberson 2012, 139–40 (Scene 3), 374
 (R6.B.4.3.65)
Section B, Register 4, Scene 39: Roberson 2012, 142–43 (Scene 4)
Section B, Register 4, Scene 40: Roberson 2012, 145–46 (Scene 5), 374–75
 (R6.B.4.5.66–68)
Section B, Register 4, Scene 41: Roberson 2012, 156 (Scene 6), 375–76
 (R6.B.4.6.69–70)
Section B, Register 4, Scene 42: Roberson 2012, 157 (Scene 7), 376–77
 (R6.B.4.7.71–72)
Section B2, Scene 43: Roberson 2012, 285 (Scene 75), 379–80 (R6.B2.1.75.75–77)
Section B2, Scene 44: Roberson 2012, 264 (Scene 64)
Section B2, Scene 45: Roberson 2012, 207–8 (Scene 28), 381 (R6.B2.1–2.28.79)
Section B2, Scene 46: Roberson 2012, 159–60 (Scene 8)
Section B2, Scene 47: Roberson 2012, 162 (Scene 9)
Section B2, Scene 48: Roberson 2012, 378 (R6.B2.1.53.74)
Section B2, Scene 49: Roberson 2012, 289 (Scene 77), 380 (R6.B2.1.77.78)
Section B2, Scene 50: Roberson 2012, 164 (Scene 10), 382 (R6.B2.2.10.80)

Tomb of Ramesses VII

Left Wall, Register 1, Scene 2: Roberson 2012, 384 (R7.A.1.37.2)
Left Wall, Register 1, Scene 3: Roberson 2012, 261 (Scene 61), 385 (R7.A.1.61.3)
Left Wall, Register 1, Scene 4: Roberson 2012, 240 (Scene 50)
Left Wall, Register 2, Scene 5: Roberson 2012, 167–68 (Scene 12), 386
 (R7.A.2.12.5)
Left Wall, Register 2, Scene 6: Roberson 2012, 292 (Scene 80)
Left Wall, Register 2, Scene 7: Roberson 2012, 261 (Scene 62), 385 (R7.A.1.62.4)
Left Wall, Register 2, Scene 8: Roberson 2012, 209–10 (Scene 29), 383
 (R7.A.1.29.1)
Right Wall, Register 1, Scene 9: Roberson 2012, 196 (Scene 23)
Right Wall, Register 1, Scene 10: Roberson 2012, 387 (R7.B.1.11.6)
Right Wall, Register 1, Scene 11: Roberson 2012, 260 (Scene 59), 388
 (R7.B.1.59.8–9)
Right Wall, Register 1, Scene 12: Roberson 2012, 220 (Scene 34), 387
 (R7.B.1.34.7)
Right Wall, Register 2, Scene 13: Roberson 2012, 238–39 (Scene 49)
Right Wall, Register 2, Scene 14: Roberson 2012, 191 (Scene 21)
Right Wall, Register 2, Scene 15: Roberson 2012, 287 (Scene 76)
Right Wall, Register 2, Scene 16: Roberson 2012, 218–19 (Scene 33)

Tomb of Ramesses IX

Left Wall, Register 1, Scene 1: Guilmant 1907, pl. XC
Left Wall, Register 1, Scene 2: Roberson 2012, 261 (Scene 61)
Left Wall, Register 1, Scene 3: Roberson 2012, 244–45 (Scene 52)
Left Wall, Register 1, Scene 4: Roberson 2012, 389 (R9.A.1.54.1)
Left Wall, Register 2, Scene 5: Guilmant 1907, pl. XC
Left Wall, Register 2, Scene 6: Guilmant 1907, pl. XC
Left Wall, Register 2, Scene 7: Guilmant 1907, pl. XCI
Left Wall, Register 2, Scene 8: Roberson 2012, 390 (R9.A.2.12.2)
Left Wall, Register 3, Scene 9: Roberson 2012, 393 (R9.A.3.71.5)
Left Wall, Register 3, Scene 10: Guilmant 1907, pl. XC
Left Wall, Register 3, Scene 11: Roberson 2012, 392 (R9.A.3.60.4)
Right Wall, Register 1, Scene 12: Roberson 2012, 210 (Scene 29), 394
    (R9.B.1.29.6)
Right Wall, Register 1, Scene 13: Roberson 2012, 229 (Scene 42)
Right Wall, Register 1, Scene 14: Roberson 2012, 235 (Scene 46)
Right Wall, Register 1, Scene 15: Roberson 2012, 278 (Scene 73)
Right Wall, Register 2 (Upper), Scene 16: Roberson 2012, 221 (Scene 36), 399
    (R9.B.2.36.10)
Right Wall, Register 2 (Lower), Scene 17: Roberson 2012, 225 (Scene 39), 399
    (R9.B2.39.11)
Right Wall, Register 2, Scene 18: Roberson 2012, 182–84 (Scene 19), 396–98
    (R9.B.2.19.7–9)
Right Wall, Register 2 (Upper), Scene 19: Guilmant 1907, pl. XCII
Right Wall, Register 2 (Lower), Scene 20: Roberson 2012, 400–403
    (R9.B.2.75.12–13)

Sarcophagi: Ramesside and Late Period

Foot End: Manassa 2007b, pl. 5
Long Wall 1, Scene 1: Manassa 2007b, pls. 13, 20–23; Roberson 2012, 449 (Sar-
    cophagus Text 2)
Long Wall 1, Scene 2: Manassa 2007b, pls. 13, 25–27; Roberson 2012, 256 (Scene
    57), 168 (Scene 12), 451–52 (Sarcophagus Text 3)
Long Wall 1, Scene 3: Manassa 2007b, pls. 13, 29–31; Roberson 2012, 228 (Scene
    41), 451 (Sarcophagus Text 3)
Long Wall 2, Scene 4: Manassa 2007b, pls. 19, 23–25; Roberson 2012, 244–45
    (Scene 52), 449 (Sarcophagus Text 2)
Long Wall 2, Scene 5: Manassa 2007b, pls. 19, 27–29; Roberson 2012, 160 (Scene
    8), 451 (Sarcophagus Text 3)
Long Wall 2, Scene 6: Manassa 2007b, pls. 19, 29–31; Roberson 2012

Head End: Manassa 2007b, pls. 36–40; Roberson 2012, 447 (Sarcophagus Text 1)

CHAPTER 7: BOOKS OF THE SOLAR-OSIRIAN UNITY

Second Shrine of Tutankhamun

Side 1: Piankoff and Rambova 1955, fig. 41
Side 2: Piankoff and Rambova 1955, fig. 42

The Enigmatic Treatise on the Corridor G Ceiling in the Tomb of Ramesses VI

Corridor G Ceiling, Registers 1–3, Scenes 1–10: Piankoff and Rambova 1954, pls. 179–180; Darnell 2004, pls. 17–25
Corridor G Ceiling, Dropped Portion, Scenes 1–2: Piankoff and Rambova 1954, pl. 181; Darnell 2004, pl. 28
Corridor G Ceiling, Protective Image: Piankoff and Rambova 1954, pl. 182; Darnell 2004, pl. 30

The Enigmatic Wall in the Tomb of Ramesses XI

Horizontal Text above the Treatise: Guilmant 1907, pls. LXVIII–LXXIX; Darnell 2004, pl. 33
Enigmatic Wall, Left Section, Register 1: Guilmant 1907, pl. LXXIX
Enigmatic Wall, Left Section, Register 2 and Horizontal Text: Guilmant 1907, pls. LXXX–LXXXI
Enigmatic Wall, Left Section, Register 3 and Horizontal Text: Guilmant 1907, pls. LXXX–LXXXI
Enigmatic Wall, Left Section, Register 3, Vertical Columns of Text: Guilmant 1907, pls. LXXX–LXXXI; Darnell 2004, pl. 34
Enigmatic Wall, Right Section, Scene 1: Guilmant 1907, pl. LXXVII; Darnell 2004, pl. 37
Enigmatic Wall, Right Section, Scene 2: Guilmant 1907, pl. LXXVI

GLOSSARY

This glossary includes the most significant divine names, epithets, top-onyms, and objects within the Netherworld Books. Unique occurrences of divine names, epithets, or toponyms for which notes appear in the main translation chapters are not generally included here. The definitions focus on each name and concept as it relates to the corpus of Netherworld Books and other religious texts, predominately of New Kingdom date.

Aker (*ꜣkr*): A double sphinx or lion symbolizing the earth and its two hori-zons and personifying the Netherworldly realm, with particular reference to its entrance and exit; Aker can protect the corpse of Osiris during the unification with Re.

akh-spirit (*ꜣḫ*): An element of the personality related to the soul, deriv-ing from the root meaning "luminosity, efficaciousness," embodying a transfigured state. During the New Kingdom, the concept of the "excellent *akh*-spirit of Re" appears to represent a magically potent, ancestral spirit. The *akh* aspect of the personality relates to texts termed *sꜣḫw*, "glorifica-tion spells," that aid in the transformation of the soul during the passage between the immanent and transcendental worlds.

akh-uraei (*ꜣḫ.t*): A rare term for cobra that creates a word play on the effective eye (*ꜣḫ.t*) of Re, part of the constellation of uraeus-eye, goddess, and crown in ancient Egyptian theology.

ankh (*ꜥnḫ*): The sign phonetically writing the root for "life, to live," appar-ently derived from a belt with depending penis sheath and ties. The *ankh*-sign can appear in the hands of deities and may itself assume a personified form.

Anubis (*Inpw*): A deity, depicted as a jackal or jackal-headed figure, who embalms Osiris, described variously as "hiding" the corpse or "protecting" the Ruler of the Netherworld; he can be associated with a chest, which conceals the mystery (a further reference to the corpse of Osiris).

Apep (ʿ₃pp): An ophidian manifestation of primal chaos and chief enemy of the solar god; the neck vertebrae of Apep are compared to the sandbanks on which the solar bark is in danger of running aground. The destruction of Apep appears repeatedly throughout the Netherworld Books.

Aqen (ʿqn): A deity who participates in the renewal of time within the Book of Gates.

Atum (ʾItm): Creator deity at the head of the Heliopolitan ennead, who can represent a Netherworldly form of the sun god; he participates in the destruction of the chaos serpent Apep (especially in the Book of Gates) and his arms and corpse aid in the re-creation of the solar deity.

ba-soul (b₃): An element of the personality associated with the concept of the soul as mobile power, generally depicted as a human-headed bird; the term is related to the plural term (b₃w) as manifestation of power. In the Netherworld Books, the *ba*-soul can be a solar element that unites with the Osirian corpse.

Babai (B₃b₃y): Also called Bebon, originally a baboon deity characterized by his sexual power, resulting in specific associations with Seth and Thoth in magical and mortuary literature; he also appears as a divine messenger and overseer of other inimical powers, such as the reapers.

Behdet (Bḥd.t): Toponym (used primarily in religious contexts) referring to the city of Edfu.

Benben sanctuary (Bnbn): A portion of the solar cult center in Heliopolis, focused on a sacred stone named after the pyramidal mound representing the first land that emerged from Nun; the term shares the same root—referencing a pointed shape—as the *benu*-bird.

benu-bird (bnw): The ancient Egyptian prototype of the later phoenix, taking the form of the heron; the *benu* is a solar bird symbolizing resurrection that can also be associated with the god Osiris within the Netherworld Books.

Bull of Maat (K₃ M₃ʿ.t): A member of the crew of the solar bark in the Book of the Hidden Chamber, depicted as an anthropomorphic deity; the element k₃ in his name may also mean "lord."

Bull of the West (K₃ ʾImn.t): An epithet of Osiris, also meaning "Lord of the West."

Children of Weakness (ms.w bdš.t): Ophidian minions of the chaos serpent Apep.

Cryptographic writing: A system of writing employing signs with abnormal values to create a difficult composition, typically describing an important aspect of the solar journey.

Director of the Bark (*Ḫrp wἰȝ*): Divine helmsman within the solar bark in the Book of the Hidden Chamber.

Divine Perception (*Sἰȝ*): A hypostasis of the creative power of the solar deity as one who perceives the actions necessary to achieve Maat; often paired with Divine Utterance, Divine Perception is a member of the crew of the solar bark in the Book of the Hidden Chamber and the Book of Gates (in the latter paired with Magic).

Divine Utterance (*Ḥw*): A hypostasis of the creative power of the solar deity as expressed in the spoken word; often paired with Divine Perception, Divine Utterance is a member of the crew of the solar bark in the Book of the Hidden Chamber (and apparently replaced by Magic in the Book of Gates).

djam-**scepter** (*ḏ ʿm*): A scepter that can appear in the hands of deities whose basic form is that of the *was*-scepter (and with which the *djam*-scepter can be substituted in depictions), but with a spiral or undulating shaft. See *was*-scepter.

Djeba-demedj: A name (translation uncertain) of the unified Re-Osiris that appears frequently in the Book of Adoring Re in the West. Possible translations include "United Enclosed One" and "United Clothed One." See also United One.

djeseret-**drink** (*ḏsr.t*): A type of beer that appears within statements of offering in the Book of Gates.

doorway (*sbḫ.t*): An elaborate portal that marks the point at which two hours meet in the Book of Gates.

Duamutef (*Dwȝ-mw.t=f*): One of the four sons of Horus. See Sons of Horus.

Effective Eye (*ȝḫ.t*): A description of the solar eye as an object both luminous and magically efficacious.

Elder Magician (*Ḥkȝ smsw*): An hypostasis of the deity Heka, personification of magical power, as eldest son of the solar deity; he plays an important role in the defeat of Apep during the seventh hour of the night as described in the Book of the Hidden Chamber.

Encircling Serpent (*Mḥn*): A protective serpent who can surround the shrine of the solar deity, protecting the sun against noxious forces, especially the chaos serpent Apep; Encircling Serpent also appears as a twin uroboros around the feet and head of the giant solar deity in the Book of the Solar-Osirian Unity on the Second Shrine of Tutankhamun.

Ennead (*psḏ.t*): A group of nine deities, originally apparently the members of the Heliopolitan creation account, and ultimately a way of designating the totality of deities of an area or temple (plural of plurals). The "two enneads" (*psḏ.ty*) comprise the "great ennead" (*psḏ.t ꜥ₃.t* or *wr.t*) and "lesser ennead" (*psḏ.t nḏs.t*), designating the deities of Lower and Upper Egypt, respectively.

Field of Reeds (*sḫ.t i₃rw*): A portion of the Netherworld symbolizing the fertile, cultivated land that provisions the deceased in the afterlife.

fillet (*sšd*): A textile band representative of royal authority; in the Netherworld Books, the fillet symbolizes the triumph of Osiris over his enemies.

Flesh (*'Iwf*): A common name of the solar deity within the Book of the Hidden Chamber and the Book of Gates (in the latter with the added designation "Flesh of Re [*'Iwf Rꜥ*]"), referencing the corpse of the solar deity that must be resurrected in the Netherworld.

Foremost of the West(erners) (*Ḫnty-imn.t[yw]*): Early, a deity associated with Abydos, ultimately identified so closely with Osiris that the name becomes an epithet of Osiris as ruler of the denizens of the Netherworld (the West).

Geb (*Gb*): A member of the Heliopolitan ennead as son of Shu and Tefnut; personification of the earth, especially paired with his sister-wife Nut who embodies the sky.

Great Flood (*Mḥ.t-wr.t*): A female personification of the primordial flood, iconographically she usually has a bovid or hybrid bovid-human shape, and can be associated with the goddess Hathor.

Great God (*nṯr ꜥ₃*): A common epithet of the solar god Re.

Hapi (*Ḥpy*): One of the four sons of Horus. See Sons of Horus.

Hathor (*Ḥw.t-Ḥr*): An important goddess who can personify the sky as well as the eye of the solar god. Hathor has associations with the mortuary cult, in particular at Thebes, where her shrine at Deir el-Bahari is the goal of the "Beautiful Festival of the Valley." Hathor can be an element in a four-part divine unity of goddesses, and by later phases of Egyptian religion she is a universal goddess in her form of the four-faced goddess.

He of the Horizon (*₃ḫ.ty*): An epithet of the solar god, often occurring in the syncretized form Horakhty (Horus-He of the Horizon) or Re-Horakhty (Re-Horus-He of the Horizon).

Heh (*Ḥḥ*): Divinity whose name means "millions," in reference to the endlessness of the cosmos; as a member of the Hermopolitan Ogdoad, he has a female counterpart Hehet.

Hehet (*Ḥḥ.t*): Goddess whose name means "millions," in reference to the endlessness of the cosmos; as a member of the Hermopolitan Ogdoad, she has a male counterpart Heh.

Heliopolis (*'Iwnw*): A city near modern-day Cairo that was a chief center of solar worship; edifices within the city included the Benben sanctuary.

Hidden Chamber (*'.t imn.t*): A description of the Netherworld, which appears most frequently in the instructions of the Book of the Hidden Chamber, where the term refers to the physical space bearing the text and scenes of the twelve hours of the night.

Horakhty (*Ḥr-ȝḫ.ty*): Horus of the Horizon, often syncretized as an epithet of the solar deity, Re, denoting his status as the ruler of the liminal area of the sunrise. See also He of the Horizon.

Horus (*Ḥr*): Divine falcon or falcon-headed figure who, as the son of Osiris and Isis, assumes the mantle of kingship; within the Netherworld Books, his main functions include protecting his father Osiris, presiding over various Netherworldly denizens (e.g. the stars, the entourage of Osiris, and the blessed dead [Egyptians and foreigners]), and punishing enemies; in addition to a specifically Netherworldly form (*Ḥr Dwȝ.ty*), Horus can be related to Sokar and Mekhentyenirty.

Horus Who Praises (*Ḥr ḥknw*): A member of the crew of the solar bark in the Book of the Hidden Chamber; he can appear as fully anthropomorphic or hieracocephalic.

hour (*wnw.t*): A division of time; the nocturnal journey of Re consists of twelve hours, providing an organizational principle for the Book of the Hidden Chamber and the Book of Gates.

Igeret (*'Igr.t*): The Netherworld as the land of the dead, literally, the "realm of silence."

Imhet (*'Imḥ.t*): The deepest portion of the Netherworld, used in particular to describe Hours 4 and 5 of the night in the Book of the Hidden Chamber.

Imsety (*'Imst*): One of the four sons of Horus. See Sons of Horus.

Isis (*'Is.t*): Sister-wife of Osiris, mother of Horus, and member of the Heliopolitan ennead; she possesses multiple protective roles in the Netherworld Books, including the embodiment of chthonic space in Hour 5 of the Book of the Hidden Chamber, and the role of the magician (along with the Elder Magician) who repels Apep in Hour 7 of the same composition.

Island of Fire (*iw nsrsr*): Portion of the Netherworld in Hour 9 of the Book of Gates where the souls of the blessed dead are provisioned; in other religious texts, the Island of Fire can be associated with the tomb chapel or even the land of the living.

iteru (*itrw*): A measurement of length, corresponding to 20,000 cubits (approximately 10.5 km).

ka-spirit (*k3*): An element of the personality relating to an animating spirit that represents the social, inherited aspect of the soul, linking the individual to his/her predecessors and descendants.

Kenset (*Kns.t*): A region to the far south-east of Egypt whose theological significance lies in its solar associations.

khat-headcloth (*ḫ3.t*): A royal headcloth with a bag-like back, ending in a gathered, hanging portion, but lacking the lappets of the *nemes*-headcloth.

Kheraha (*Ḫr-ʿḥ3*): A toponym located near ancient Heliopolis; as early as the Pyramid Texts Kheraha is a location of the battle between Horus and Seth.

Khepri (*Ḫpri*): Personification of the rejuvenating power of the solar deity as a scarab, relating to the verb *ḫpri* "to manifest, transform;" the scarab beetle is particularly associated with the morning and day form of the solar deity, but his corpse is present within the Netherworld.

Khnum (*Ḫnm*): A creator deity associated with the forming of humans and their *ka*-spirits on a potter's wheel. At home in Aswan, he is frequently in the company of the goddesses Satet and Anukis.

Lake of Fire (*š ḥb.t*): Netherwordly toponym, whose waters provide refreshment to the blessed dead, but whose fire devours the damned.

Life of the Gods (*ʿnḫ nṯr.w*): Giant serpent through whose body the solar god travels in Hour 12 of the Book of the Hidden Chamber; by entering the tail and emerging from the mouth, Re is rejuvenated.

Maat (*M3ʿ.t*): The female personification of ultimate cosmic order, established by the solar deity of whom she may be termed the daughter; Maat also represents proper ethical behavior by which people are judged in the afterlife. The proper ruler maintains Maat and thereby presents her to her father. The judgment hall within the Netherworld can be called the "Hall of Two Maats."

Magic (*Ḥk3*): A hypostasis of the creative, magical power of the solar deity; a member of the crew of the solar bark in the Book of Gates (paired with Divine Perception and apparently replacing Divine Utterrance). See also Elder Magician (*Ḥk3 smsw*).

Mekhentyenirty (*Mḫnty-n-ir.ty*): A deity, sometimes described in ancient Egyptian texts as "blind," who is associated with Horus; in the Netherworld Books, Mekhentyenirty can appear as an ichneumon-headed figure.

migratory one (*gšy*): An epithet of Re in the Book of Adoring Re in the West, comparing the solar deity—in his ability to cross liminal boundaries—to a migratory bird.

Mistress of the Bark (*Nb.t wỉꜣ*): Hypostasis of Hathor and member of the crew of the solar bark in the Book of the Hidden Chamber. She wears cow horns and sun disk, the standard headdress of the goddess Hathor.

Mysterious One (*Štꜣy.t*): Embodiment of the realm of the Netherworld and feminine counterpart to the corpse of Osiris; as a giant goddess in the Book of Caverns and Book of the Creation of the Solar Disk (in the tomb of Ramesses VI), she fills and personifies the entire Netherworld, with manifestations of the solar god traveling over her body.

Mysterious Place (*Štꜣy.t*): Description of the Netherworld as a realm that hides the mysteries of the solar cycle; often personified as the goddess Mysterious One.

Nehebkau (*Nḥb-kꜣ.w*): A primordial serpent deity with primarily beneficent funerary functions who is associated with the provisioning of the blessed dead. His cult center at Heliopolis relates him to Re and Atum.

Neith (*N.t*): A goddess whose cult center was in Sais in Lower Egypt; associated with warfare through her sign of shield and crossed arrows, Neith may function as a protector of the king.

Nemes-**headcloth** (*nms*): A royal headcloth appearing by the time of the Third Dynasty, having a bag-like back ending in a tail-like appendage, with two lappets in front, leaving the ears exposed and flaring to just above the shoulder, with a narrowing bottom falling on the chest to each side.

Nephthys (*Nb.t-ḥw.t*): Sister of Isis, who often appears alongside her as mourner or figure supporting the solar disk; in a rare independent role she is assigned a grotto in the Book of Caverns.

Nepri (*Npri*): A grain god who also appears in the guide of Nepri-Hety.

nethersky (*nn.t*): Description of the Netherworldly realm as a heavenly space.

Netherworld (*Dwꜣ.t*): A realm of both space and time through which the sun god travels during the night between the western and eastern horizons of the sky; the Netherworld can be envisaged as existing beneath the earth or in the sky and can be divided into "upper" and "lower" regions, the latter often called the "Place of Destruction (*Ḥtmy.t*)."

Netherworld Dwellers (*Dwꜣ.tyw*): A general term for the inhabitants of the Netherworld whom Re visits during the twelve hours of the night.

Nun (*Nwn*): A personification of the creative, undifferentiated waters that surround the ordered world; the Nun-waters within the Netherworld provide re-creative energy for the solar deity (at times represented as the arms of Nun lifting the disk) and the drowned, blessed dead float within Nun; as a member of the Hermopolitan Ogdoad, Nun possesses a feminine counterpart Nunet.

Nut (*Nw.t*): A member of the Heliopolitan ennead, daughter of Shu and Tefnut; personification of the sky, especially paired with her brother-husband Geb, who embodies the earth; as heavenly goddess, Nut swallows the sun god at night and gives birth to him in the morning, her body doubling as the location of the Netherworld (*Dwꜣ.t*).

Ogdoad (*ḥmnw*): A group of eight deities, specifically the four male-female pairs representing divine personifications of the first developments of cosmic creation deriving from the primordial Nun. Their original cult center appears to have been Hermopolis.

One Evil of Character (*Ḏw-qd*): An epithet of the chaos serpent Apep.

Opener of Paths (*Wp-wꜣ.wt*): Member of the crew of the solar bark who stands at the prow, protecting and guiding Re along the paths of the Netherworld; he appears as an anthropomorphic deity within the Book of the Hidden Chamber, and in other religious contexts he appears most often as a jackal or jackal-headed deity. As a jackal atop a standard, Opener of Paths was a lead element in royal and divine processions.

Opet (*ꜣp.t*): An apotropaic mother goddess, most often appearing as a hippopotamus.

Orion (*Sꜣḥ*): The constellation associated with the deity Osiris.

Osiris (*Wsir*): A member of the Heliopolitan ennead (son of Geb and Nut), husband-brother of Isis, father of Horus, whose most important role in the Netherworld Books is ruler of the Netherworld and "foremost of the Westerners"; he appears most often as a mummified human figure, wearing a white crown, indicating his royal status; in the depths of the Netherworld, Re (the *ba*-soul) unifies with Osiris (the corpse), fueling the solar cycle.

Pakhet (*Pꜣḫ.t*): A lioness goddess whose main cult center was near Beni Hasan in the sixteenth Upper Egyptian nome.

Penwenty (*Pn-wnty*): See Wenty.

Place of Destruction (*Ḥtmy.t*): A description of the Netherworld as the place of "deconstruction"—the atomizing and reconstruction of the gods and blessed dead as well as the place of the punishment of the damned (particularly through eternal repetition of the process of destruction through deconstruction).

Place of Hauling (*Rꜣ-sṯꜣw*): Early, a designation for the necropolis of Giza; in the Netherworld Books the Place of Hauling is particularly associated with roads and desert landscape of the realm of Sokar in Hour 4 and Hour 5 of the Book of the Hidden Chamber.

Ptah (*Ptḥ*): The god of the Memphite creation account who brings the cosmos into existence through his pronouncements, Ptah is particularly associated with crafts; in his appearance Ptah can be conceived as a personification of the outward appearance of a deity as cult image.

Qebehsenuef (*Qbḥ-sn.w=f*): One of the four sons of Horus. See Sons of Horus.

Re (*Rʿ*): The solar deity who travels through the twelve hours or different divisions of the night within the Netherworld Books; he appears most often in the form of a ram-headed male deity within a bark or as a large solar disk, and one of the chief goals of the Netherworldly journey is his union with the god Osiris.

Re-Horakhty (*Rʿ-Ḥr-ꜣḫ.ty*): A syncretized solar deity, combining Re and Horus as He of the Horizon.

Roasting Flame (*Wꜣmmty*): Hypostasis of the chaos serpent Apep; the name may refer to the serpent's fiery breath (sharing the root *wꜣm* "to scorch").

Ruler of the West (*Ḥqꜣ-imn.t*): An epithet of Osiris. See "Foremost of the West(erners)."

Sais (*Sꜣw*): Important cult center in the Delta, particularly associated with the goddess Neith.

Sakhmet (*Sḫm.t*): A goddess whose name means "Powerful One," associated with the fiery power of the sun and the potential for weal and woe inherent in the New Year; she often has a leonine or mixed leonine-human form and can appear in a quartet of goddesses, with Hathor, as an element of a universal goddess. Sakhmet is the angry eye of the sun in the winter in the concept of the wandering eye of the sun, and can turn her violent tendencies against the enemies of Egypt. Her emissaries may travel as fast as an arrow, and bring disease and malevolent influence.

sarcophagus (*ḏbꜣ.t*): Oval enclosure (sometimes appearing partially hidden in the ground) that can surround deities in the Netherworld Books; the term is also used in New Kingdom documentary texts for a sarcophagus as an outermost element in which coffins are placed.

scarab (*ḫprr*): The scarab is associated with the transformative and manifesting aspects of the solar cycle, particular in the form of Khepri.

Selket (*Srq.t*): A goddess associated with scorpions who—along with Isis, Nephthys, and Neith—protects the organs of the deceased; in the Netherworld Books she can assist the sun god in his combat with Apep.

Seth (*Stḫ*): The god of chaotic behavior and violent cosmic potential, associated with foreign lands, storms, and war; closely associated with the goddess Nephthys, he is a counterpart and even opponent of Horus, nevertheless appearing with the latter in scenes of the unification of Egypt. Seth can be seen as the murderer of Osiris and ultimately vanquished foe of Isis and Horus, yet Re can appoint Seth to the prow of the solar bark to combat Apep.

Shu (*Šw*): A member of the Heliopolitan ennead, son of Atum and brother of Tefnut (with whom he is a member of the first divine male-female pair), Shu embodies the luminous space between heaven and earth (his children Nut and Geb); he can assist with the rising of the sun in the eastern horizon.

Sokar (*Skr*): A chthonic deity who symbolizes the re-creative potential of the funereal soil; he can be syncretized with Ptah and Osiris, and the netherworldly region of Hour 5 of the Book of the Hidden Chamber is particularly identified as his "land." He has falcon associations in iconography.

Sons of Horus: The four sons of the deity Horus—Hapy, Imsety, Duamutef, and Qebehsenuef—who assist Horus in punishing enemies in the Netherworld, including the chaos serpent Apep. They are associated with the canopic jars that hold the embalmed viscera of the dead.

Sopdu (*Spdw*): A deity associated with foreign regions, especially the east. He appears frequently in falcon form, and can be closely associated with Horus. His name "Sharp One," appears to reference his talons as falcon deity, although in the Pyramid Texts he also takes a crocodilian form.

Tayt (*T3y.t*): The goddess of weaving, closely associated with the mummification process.

Tatenen (*T3-ṯnn*): A god of the earth and personification of the first mound of creation, the "risen land"; he can also embody the entire Netherworldly realm, and along with other chthonic creator deities (like Nun) can assist the solar deity's rise in the eastern horizon.

Tebiu-bark (*T3wb*): An apparent designation of the solar bark, probably related to the solar deity as Tebi (*Tbi*), who appears in the Pyramid Texts.

Tefnut (*Tfn.t*): A member of the Heliopolitan ennead, daughter of Re-Atum and sister of Shu (with whom she is a member of the first divine male-female pair); she can appear as one of the goddesses of the eye of the sun, often in association with Hathor.

Temple of the Benben (*Ḥw.t-bnbn*): See Benben sanctuary.

Terrible of Face (*Nḥ3-ḥr*): A name used most commonly in the Netherworld Books as an epithet of Apep or his minions; in the Book of Caverns, Terrible of Face can also be a protective serpent who pulls together the corpse of Osiris.

Thoth (*Ḏḥwty*): A deity with lunar associations, Thoth functions as god of writing and recording, a divine sage, messenger, and mediator.

Tired of Heart (*Wrḏ-ib*): An epithet of the god Osiris, referencing the ancient Egyptian concept of the "weariness" of death.

United One (*Dmd*): A name that references the union of Re and Osiris in the Netherworld.

udjat-eye (*wḏꜣ.t*): Apotropaic symbol of a divine eye (belonging typically to Horus or Re, but also Atum), having the form of a hieroglyphically depicted human eye with stylized elements of a falcon's eye added to the bottom thereof; as the eye of Horus, the *udjat*-eye embodies the restoration of damage, which texts outside the corpus of the Netherworld Books indicate was specifically wrought by the deity Seth.

uraeus (*iꜥrr.t*): A rearing cobra; fire-spitting uraei can be associated with the goddesses Isis and Nephthys and act as defenders of the solar deity and punishers of the damned.

uroboros: A serpent biting its own tail; the Encircling Serpent (*Mḥn*) appears as a uroboros in the Book of the Solar-Osirian Unity on the Second Shrine of Tutankhamun.

Wakeful One (*Nhs*): Hypostasis of solar wakefulness and member of the crew of the solar bark in the Book of the Hidden Chamber; he may be related to the god Seth, since a scepter with Seth-animal head labeled *Nhs* appears in Hour 10 of the Book of the Hidden Chamber and the same term can refer to Seth as hippopotamus, and in Graeco-Roman texts *Nhs* is a name for the Seth-animal.

Warlike of Face (*ꜥḥꜣ-ḥr*): Mummiform figures who appear in the Book of Gates and Books of the Creation of the Solar Disk as guardians of sun god and his re-creation in the Netherworld.

was-scepter (*wꜣs*): A scepter having the form of a curving animal's head with long snout and ears/protuberances at the top, with a forked bottom, apparently ultimately equated with—if not even deriving from—the earlier icon of the giraffe as solar symbol. The sign hieroglyphically writes "dominion," and the scepter is frequently held by gods, and by the goddess Maat. Two *was*-scepters flanking an *ankh*-sign can symbolize the deities Shu and Tefnut as a graphic depiction of the ordered cosmos.

Wennefer (*Wnn-nfr*): An epithet of the god Osiris that refers to his perfection/completion (*nfr*).

Wenty (*Wnty*): A deity who takes the form of the crocodile (also called Penwenty), who can both swallow and ejaculate the eye of Re; the destructive aspects of the crocodile can lead to his syncretism with Apep.

Wernes (*Wrns*): A well-watered region of the Netherworld encompassing Hour 1 and Hour 2 of the Book of the Hidden Chamber.

West (*Imn.t*): A toponym, also personified as a goddess, often used interchangeably with the Netherworld as the place of the setting sun and the nightly solar journey; "Westerners" is a term used for the denizens of the Netherworld, over whom Osiris rules.

Westerner (*Imn.ty*): An epithet of Osiris. See Foremost of the West(erners).

wsr-post (*wsr*): A jackal-headed staff that is identified in the Netherworld Books as the "neck of Re"; in the Book of Gates, the *wsr*-post serves as pillory for the damned.

Bibliography

Abbas, Eltayeb Sayed. 2010. *The Lake of Knives and the Lake of Fire: Studies in the Topography of Passage in Ancient Egyptian Religious Literature.* BARIS 2144. Oxford: Archaeopress.

Abitz, Friedrich. 1974. *Die religiöse Bedeutung der sogenannten Grabräuberschächte in den ägyptischen Königsgräbern der 18. bis 20. Dynastie.* ÄA 26. Wiesbaden: Harrassowitz.

———. 1984. *König und Gott: Die Götterszenen in den ägyptischen Königsgräbern von Thutmosis IV. bis Ramses III.* ÄA 40. Wiesbaden: Harrassowitz.

———. 1989. *Baugeschichte und Dekoration des Grabes Ramses' VI.* OBO 89. Freiburg: Universitätsverlag; Göttingen: Vandenhoeck & Ruprecht.

———. 1990. "Bauablauf und Dekoration des Grabes Ramses' IX." *SAK* 17:1–40.

———. 1992. "The Structure of the Decoration in the Tomb of Ramesses IX." Pages 165–85 in *After Tut'ankhamun: Research and Excavation in the Royal Necropolis at Thebes.* Edited by Nicholas Reeves. London: Kegan Paul International.

———. 1995. *Pharao als Gott in den Unterweltsbüchern des Neuen Reiches.* OBO 146. Freiburg: Universitätsverlag; Göttingen: Vandenhoeck & Ruprecht.

Abt, Theodor, and Erik Hornung. 2003. *Knowledge for the Afterlife: The Egyptian Amduat—A Quest for Immortality.* Zurich: Living Human Heritage.

Allen, James P. 1988. *Genesis in Egypt: The Philosophy of Ancient Egyptian Creation Accounts.* YEgS 2. New Haven: Yale Egyptological Seminar.

———. 1989. "The Cosmology of the Pyramid Texts." Pages 1–28 in *Religion and Philosophy in Ancient Egypt.* Edited by William K. Simpson. YEgS 3. New Haven: Yale Egyptological Seminar.

———. 1994. "Reading a Pyramid." Pages 5–28 in Vol. 1 of *Hommages à Jean Leclant*. Edited by Cathérine Berger, Gisèle Clerc, and Nicolas-Christophe Grimal. BiÉtud 106. Cairo: Institut Français d'Archéologie Orientale.

———. 2002. *The Heqanakht Papyri*. New York: Metropolitan Museum of Art.

———. 2005. *The Ancient Egyptian Pyramid Texts*. Edited by Peter der Manuelian. WAW 23. Atlanta: Society of Biblical Literature.

Altenmüller, Hartwig. 1967–1968. "Zur Überlieferung des Amduat." *JEOL* 20:27–42.

Assmann, Jan. 1969. *Liturgische Lieder an den Sonnengott*. UAH 1; MÄSt 19. Berlin: Hessling.

———. 1970. *Der König als Sonnenpriester: Ein kosmographischer Begleittext zur kultischen Sonnenhymnik in thebanischen Tempeln und Gräbern*. ADAIK 7. Glückstadt: Augustin.

———. 1972. "Die Inschrift auf dem äußeren Sarkophagdeckel des Merenptah." *MDAIK* 28:47–73.

———. 1977a. *Das Grab der Mutirdis*. Vol. 6 of *Grabung im Asasif 1963–1970*. AV 13. Mainz am Rhein: von Zabern.

———. 1977b. "Die Verborgenheit des Mythos in Ägypten" *GöMisz* 25:7–43.

———. 1983a. *Sonnenhymnen in thebanischen Gräbern*. Theben 1. Mainz am Rhein: von Zabern.

———. 1983b. "Das Dekorationsprogramm der königlichen Sonnenheiligtümer des Neuen Reiches nach einer Fassung der Spätzeit." *ZÄS* 110:91–98.

———. 1989. "Death and Initiation in the Funerary Religion of Ancient Egypt." Pages 135–59 in *Religion and Philosophy in Ancient Egypt*. Edited by William K. Simpson. YEgS 3. New Haven: Yale Egyptological Seminar.

———. 1995. *Egyptian Solar Religion in the New Kingdom: Re, Amun and the Crisis of Polytheism*. Translated by Anthony Alcock. London: Kegan Paul International.

———. 2001a. *The Search for God in Ancient Egypt*. Translated by David Lorton. Ithaca: Cornell University.

———. 2001b. *Tod und Jenseits im Alten Ägypten*. Munich: Beck.

———. 2001c. *Maʿat: Gerechtigkeit und Unsterblichkeit im alten Ägypten*. Munich: Beck.

———. 2003. "Das Leichensekret des Osiris: Zur kultischen Bedeutung des Wassers im alten Ägypten." Pages 5–16 in *Hommages à Fayza Haikal*. Edited by Nicholas Grimal, Amr Kamel, and Cynthia May Sheikholeslami. BiÉtud 138. Cairo: Institut Français d'Archéologie Orientale.

———. 2005. *Death and Salvation in Ancient Egypt*. Ithaca: Cornell University Press.

Aufrère, Sydney H. 1991. *L'univers minéral dans la pensée égyptienne*. Vol. 2. BiÉtud 55. Cairo: Institut Français d'Archéologie Orientale.

———. 1999. "Les végétaux sacrés de l'Égypte ancienne, d'après les listes géographiques d'Edfou et du Papyrus géographique de Tanis et les autres monographies sacrées." Pages 121–207 in *Encyclopédie religieuse de l'Univers végétal: Croyances phytoreligieuses de l'Égypte ancienne*. Edited by Syndney Aufrère. Vol. 1. OrMonsp 10. Montpellier: Université Paul Valéry-Montpellier III.

———. 2001. "À propos de 'Ceux qui font les arbes' (jrw nhwt) de la IXe section du Livre de l'Amdouat." Pages 163–69 in *Encyclopédie religieuse de l'univers vegetal: Croyances phytoreligeuses de l'Égypte ancienne*. Edited by Syndney Aufrère. Vol. 2. OrMonsp 15. Montpellier: Université Paul Valéry-Montpellier III.

Backes, Burkhard. 2005. *Das altägyptische "Zweiwegebuch": Studien zu den Sargtext-Sprüchen 1029–1130*. ÄA 69. Wiesbaden: Harrassowitz.

———. 2014. "Auf der Suche nach kartographischen Darstellungen des altägyptischen Jenseits—Oder: Wie viel Karte braucht der (tote) Mensch?" Pages 63–98 in *Raumkonzeptionen in antiken Religionen, Beiträge des internationalen Symposiums in Göttingen, 28. und 29. Juni 2012*. Edited by Kianoosh Rezania. Wiesbaden: Harrassowitz.

Baines, John. 1990a. "Restricted Knowledge, Hierarchy, and Decorum: Modern Perceptions and Ancient Institutions." *JARCE* 27:1–23.

———. 1990b. "Interpreting the Story of the Shipwrecked Sailor." *JEA* 76:55–72.

Barguet, Paul. 1975. "Le Livre des Portes et la transmission du pouvoir royal." *REg* 27:30–36.

———. 1976. "Le Livre des Cavernes et la reconstitution du corps divin." *REg* 28:25–37.

———. 1978. "Remarques sur quelques scènes de la salle du sarcophage de Ramsès VI." *REg* 30:51–56.

Barré, Jean-Yves. 2003. *Pour la survie de Pharaon: Le texte funéraire de l'Amdouat dans la tombe de Thoutmosis III*. Paris: Errance.

Barta, Winfried. 1969–1970. "Zur Verteilung der 12 Nachtstunden des Amduat im Grabe Tuthmosis' III." *JEOL* 21:164–68.

———. 1974. "Zur Stundenanordnung des Amduat in den ramessidischen Königsgräbern." *BiOr* 31:197–201.

———. 1984. "Die Anbringung der Sonnenlitanei in den Königsgräbern der Ramessidenzeit." *GöMisz* 71:7–10.

———. 1985. *Die Bedeutung der Jenseitsbücher für den verstorbenen König.* MÄSt 42. Munich: Deutscher Kunstverlag.

———. 1986. "Bemerkungen zur 'großen Litanei' im Buch der Anbetung des Re im Westen." *ZÄS* 113:83–88.

———. 1985–1986. "Osiris als Mutterleib des unterweltlichen Sonnengottes in den Jenseitsbüchern des Neuen Reiches." *JEOL* 29:98–105.

———. 1987. "Der Weg des Sonnengottes durch die Unterwelt in Amduat und Höhlenbuch." *GöMisz* 100:7–14.

———. 1990a. *Komparative Untersuchungen zu vier Unterweltsbüchern.* MÄU 1. Frankfurt am Main: Lang.

———. 1990b. "Zum Wesen des Gottes Osiris nach Zeugnissen der älteren Totenliteratur." *ZÄS* 117:89–93.

Baum, Nathalie. 1988. *Arbres et arbustes de l'Égypte ancienne: La liste de la tombe thébaine d'Ineni (no. 81).* OLA 31. Leuven: Departement Oriëntalistiek.

Baumann, Andrew. 1998. *The Suffix Conjugation of Early Egyptian as Evidenced in the Underworld Books.* PhD diss., Department of Near Eastern Languages and Civilizations, University of Chicago.

Beaux, Nathalie. 1991. "Ennemis étrangers et malfaiteurs égyptiens: La signification du châtiment au pilori." *BIFAO* 91:33–54.

———. 1994. "La *douat* dans les Textes des Pyramides: Espace et temps de gestation." *BIFAO* 94:1–6.

———. 2004. "La pintade, le soleil et l'éternité: À propos du signe (G 21)." *BIFAO* 104:21–38.

Bedier, Shafia. 1995. *Die Rolle des Gottes Geb in den ägyptischen Tempelinschriften der griechisch-römischen Zeit.* HÄB 41. Hildesheim: Gerstenberg Verlag.

Beinlich-Seeber, Christine. 1976. *Untersuchungen zur Darstellung des Totengerichts im Alten Ägypten.* MÄSt 35. Munich: Deutscher Kunstverlag.

———. 1998. "Ein römerzeitliches Sargfragment in Marseille." Pages 9–40 in *Ein ägyptisches Glasperlenspiel: Ägyptologische Beiträge für Erik*

Hornung aus seinem Schülerkreis. Edited by Andreas Brodbeck. Berlin: Gebrüder Mann.

Bell, Lanny. 1976. *Interpreters and Egyptianized Nubians in Ancient Egyptian Foreign Policy: Aspects of the History of Egypt and Nubia.* PhD diss. University of Pennsylvania.

Belzoni, Giovanni Battista. 1820. *Plates Illustrative of the Researches and Operations of G. Belzoni in Egypt and Nubia.* London: Murray.

Betrò, Maria Carmela. 1985. *I Testi solari del portale di Pascerientaisu (BN 2).* Saqqara 3. Pisa: Giardini editori e stampatori.

Bickel, Susanne. 1998. "Die Jenseitsfahrt des Re nach Zeugnissen der Sargtexte." Pages 41–56 in *Ein ägyptisches Glasperlenspiel: Ägyptologische Beiträge für Erik Hornung aus seinem Schülerkreis.* Edited by Andreas Brodbeck. Berlin: Gebrüder Mann.

———. 2002. "Aspects et fonctions de la déification d'Amenhotep III." *BIFAO* 102:63–90.

Bidoli, Dino. 1976. *Die Sprüche der Fangnetze in den altägyptischen Sargtexten.* ADAIK 9. Glückstadt: Augustin.

Billing, Nils. 2002. *Nut, The Goddess of Life: In Text and Iconography.* Uppsala: Department of Archaeology and Ancient History, Uppsala University.

———. 2006. "The Secret One: An Analysis of a Core Motif in the Books of the Netherworld." *SAK* 34:51–71.

Binder, Susanne 2006. "The Twelfth Hour of the *Amduat.*" Pages 45–55 in *Egyptian Art in the Nicholson Museum, Sydney.* Edited by Karin N Sowada and Boyo G. Ockinga. Sydney: Meditarch Publishing.

Bommas, Martin. 2005. "Situlae and the Offering of Water in the Divine Funerary Cult: A New Approach to the Ritual of Djeme." Pages 257–72 in *L'acqua nell'antico Egitto: Vita, rigenerazione, incantesimo, medicamento.* Edited by Alessia Amenta, Maria Michela Luiselli, and Maria Novella Sordi. Rome: L'Erma di Bretschneider.

———. 2015. "New Thoughts on the Late Transmission History of the Book of Amduat (Including the Unpublished Papyrus Eton College Windson, ECM 1573)." Pages 49–56 in *Joyful in Thebes: Egyptological Studies in Honor of Betsy M. Bryan.* Edited by Richard Jasnow and Kathlyn M. Cooney. London: Lockwood.

Bónannó, Marianó. 2015. *La duat como espacio de una dialéctica de la regeneración: In-habitación y resignificación del espacio funerario en los Textos del Amduat.* BARIS 2738. Oxford: Archaeopress.

Bonomi, Joseph, and Samuel Sharpe. 1864. *The Alabaster Sarcophagus of Oimeneptah I., King of Egypt: Now in Sir John Soane's Museum, Lincoln's Inn Fields*. London: Longman, Green, Longman, Roberts, and Green.

Borghouts, Joris F. 1973–1974. "The Enigmatic Chests." *JEOL* 23:358–64.

———. 1978. *Ancient Egyptian Magical Texts*. Leiden: Brill.

———. 2007. *Book of the Dead (39): From Shouting to Structure*. SAT 10. Wiesbaden: Harrassowitz.

Brand, Peter. 2000. *The Monuments of Sety I: Epigraphic, Historical and Art Historical Analysis*. PAe 7. Leiden: Brill.

Broek, Roel van den. 1972. *The Myth of the Phoenix: According to Classical and Early Christian Traditions*. Leiden: Brill.

Broze, Michèle. 1991. "'Entretemps, ce vaincu du nom de Teti-an était arrivé…': À propos de la forme ʿḥʿ.n.f + pseudoparticipe dans une narration." Pages 65–77 in *Religion und Philosophie im alten Ägypten: Festgabe für Philippe Derchain zu seinem 65. Geburtstag am 24. Juli 1991*. Edited by Ursula Verhoeven and Erhart Graefe. OLA 39. Leuven: Peeters.

———. 1996. *Les Aventures d'Horus et Seth dans le Papyrus Chester Beatty I: Mythe et roman en Egypte ancienne*. OLA 76. Leuven: Peeters.

Brunner, Hellmut. 1973. "Änigmatische Schrift (Kryptographie)." Pages 51–58 in *Ägyptische Schrift und Sprache*. HdO 1.1.1. Leiden: Brill.

———. 1977. *Die südlichen Räume des Tempels von Luxor*. Mainz am Rhein: von Zabern.

———. 1980. "Vom Sinn der Unterweltsbücher." *SAK* 8:79–84.

Brunner-Traut, Emma. 1965. *Spitzmaus und Ichneumon als Tiere des Sonnengottes*. NAWGPH 7. Gottingen: Vandenhoeck & Ruprecht.

Bucher, Paul. 1932. *Les textes des tombes de Thoutmosis III et Aménophis II*. MIFAO 60. Cairo: Institut Français d'Archéologie Orientale.

Budge, E. A. W. 1899. *Facsimiles of the Papyri of Hunefer, Anhai, Karasher and Netchemet*. London: British Museum.

———. 1925. *The Egyptian Heaven and Hell*. London: Hopkinson.

Caminos, Ricardo A. 1974. *The New-Kingdom Temples of Buhen 2*. ASE 34. London: Egypt Exploration Society.

Capart, Jean, Alan H. Gardiner, and B van der Walle. 1936. "New Light on the Ramesside Tomb-Robberies." *JEA* 22:169–93.

Carrier, Claude. 2009. *Grands livres funéraires de l'Égypte pharaonique*. Paris: Cybele.

Centrone, Maria Costanze. 2009. *Egyptian Corn-Mummies: A Class of Religious Artefacts Catalogued and Systematically Analysed*. Saarbrücken: Müller.

Champollion, Jean-François. 2009. *The Code-Breaker's Secret Diaries: The Perilous Expedition through Plague-Ridden Egypt to Uncover the Ancient Mysteries of the Hieroglyphs*. Preface by Joyce Tyldesley. London: Gibson Square.

Clère, Jacques Jean. 1958. "Fragments d'une nouvelle représentation égyptienne du monde." *MDAIK* 16:30–46.

———. 1979. "Recherches sur le mot ⸢𓎃𓏤⸣ des textes gréco-romains et sur d'autres mots apparentés." *BIFAO* 79:285–310.

Clère, Jacques Jean, and Jacques Vandier. 1948. *Textes de la Première Période Intermédiaire et de la XIème dynastie*. BAeg 10. Brussels: Fondation Égyptologique Reine Élisabeth.

Cooney, Kathyln M. 2000. "The Edifice of Taharqa by the Sacred Lake: Ritual Function and the Rule of the King." *JARCE* 37:15–47.

Corteggiani, Jean-Pierre. 1995. "La 'butte de la Décollation,' à Héliopolis." *BIFAO* 95:141–51.

Darnell, John Coleman. 1995. "Hathor Returns to Medamud." *SAK* 22:47–94.

———. 1997. "The Apotropaic Goddess in the Eye." *SAK* 24:35–48.

———. 2004. *The The Enigmatic Netherworld Books of the Solar-Osirian Unity: Cryptographic Compositions in the Tombs of Tutankhamun, Ramesses VI and Ramesses IX*. OBO 198. Fribourg: Universitätsverlag; Göttingen: Vandenhoeck & Ruprecht.

———. 2006. *The Inscription of Queen Katimala at Semna: Textual Evidence for the Origins of the Napatan State*. YEgS 7. New Haven: Yale Egyptological Seminar.

———. 2008. "The Eleventh Dynasty Royal Inscription from Deir el-Ballas." *REg* 59:81–110.

———. 2009. "Iconographic Attraction, Iconographic Syntax, and Tableaux of Royal Ritual Power in the Pre- and Proto-Dynastic Rock Inscriptions of the Theban Western Desert." *Archéo-Nil* 19:83–107.

———. 2013. *The Rock Shrine of Pahu, Gebel Akhenaton, and Other Rock Inscriptions from the Western Hinterland of Naqada*. Vol. 2 of *Theban Desert Road Survey*. YEgS 1. New Haven: Yale Egyptological Seminar.

Davis, Theodore M. 2001. *The Tombs of Harmhabi and Touatânkhamanou*. London: Duckworth.

Delia, Diana. 1992. "The Refreshing Water of Osiris." *JARCE* 29:181–90.

Derchain, Philippe. 1962. "L'adoration du Soleil levant dans le temple de Psammétique Ier à El Kab." *CdÉ* 37.74:257–71.

———. 1965. *Le papyrus Salt 825 (B.M. 10051), rituel pour la conservation de la vie en Égypte.* Vol. 2. Brussels: Palais des Académies.

———. 1969. "Le démiurge et la balance." Pages 31–34 in *Religions en Égypte hellénistique et romaine.* Edited by Philippe Derchain. Paris: Presses Universitaires de France.

———. 1972. *Hathor Quadrifrons, recherches sur la syntaxe d'un mythe égyptien.* Istanbul: Nederlands Historisch-Archaeologisch Instituut in het Nabije Oosten.

———. 1975–1976. "Perpetuum mobile." *OLP* 6–7:153–61.

Devéria, Théodule. 1897. "L'écriture secrète dans les textes hiéroglyphiques des anciens Égyptiens, premier essai." Pages 49–80 in *Bibliothèque Égyptologique.* Edited by Gaston Maspero. Vol. 5. Paris: Ernest Leroux.

Dobbin-Bennett, Tasha L. 2014. "Rotting in Hell: Ancient Egyptian Conceptions of Decomposition." PhD Diss. Department of Near Eastern Languages and Civilizations, Yale University.

Dodson, Aidan. 2016. "Earlier Royal Tombs, the Royal Cemeteries of Thebes, and the Beginnings of the Valley of the Kings." Pages 54–72 in *The Oxford Handbook of the Valley of the Kings.* Edited by Richard H. Wilkinson and Kent R. Weeks. Oxford: Oxford University Press.

Dominicus, Brigitte. 1993. *Gesten und Gebärden in Darstellungen des Alten und Mittleren Reiches.* SAGA 10. Heidelberg: Heidelberger.

Dorman, Peter F. 1999. "Creation on the Potter's Wheel at the Eastern Horizon of Heaven." Pages 83–99 in *Gold of Praise: Studies on Ancient Egypt in Honor of Edward F. Wente.* Edited by Emily Teeter and John A. Larson. SAOC 58. Chicago: The Oriental Institute of the University of Chicago.

Drioton, Étienne. 1936. "Les protocoles ornementaux d'Abydos." *REg* 2:1–20.

———. 1944. "La cryptographie par perturbation." *ASAE* 44:17–33.

———. 1949. "La cryptographie de la chapelle de Toutânkhamoun." *JEA* 35:117–22.

———. 1953a. "Les principes de la cryptographie égyptienne." *CRAI* 97.3:355–64.

———. 1953b. "Les origines pharaoniques du nilomètre de Rodah." *BIE* 34:291–316.

DuQuesne, Terence. 2002a. "'Effective in Heaven and on Earth': Interpreting Egyptian Religious Practice for Both Worlds." Pages 37–46 in

Ägyptische Mysterien? Edited by Jan Assmann and Martin Bommas. Munich: Fink.

————. 2002b. "La déification des parties du corps: Correspondences magiques et identification avec les dieux dans l'Égypte ancienne." Pages 237–71 in *La magie en Égypte: À la recherche d'une définition.* Edited by Yvan Koenig. Paris: La Documentation Française.

Edel, Elmar. 1955. *Altägyptische Grammatik.* Vol. 1. AnOr 34. Rome: Pontifical Biblical Institute.

————. 1959. "Die Herkunft des neuägyptisch-koptisch Personalsuffixes der 3. Person Plural–w." *ZÄS* 84:17–38.

El-Sayed, Ramadan. 1981. "Nehaher." Pages 119–40 in *Bulletin du Centenaire.* BIFAOSup 81. Cairo: Institut Français d'Archéologie Orientale.

El-Sawi, Ahmed, and Farouk Gomaa. 1993. *Das Grab des Panehsi, Gottesvaters von Heliopolis in Matariya.* ÄAT 23. Wiesbaden: Harrassowitz.

Epigraphic Survey. 1934. *The Calendar, the "Slaughterhouse," and Minor Records of Ramses III.* Vol. 3 of *Medinet Habu.* OIP 23. Chicago: University of Chicago Press.

————. 1963. *The Re Chapel, The Royal Mortuary Complex, and Adjacent Rooms, with Miscellaneous Material from the Pylons, the Forecourts, and the First Hypostyle Hall.* Part 2 of *The Temple Proper.* Vol. 6 of *Medinet Habu.* OIP 84. Chicago: University of Chicago Press.

————. 1994. *The Festival Procession of Opet in the Colonnade Hall, Translation and Commentary.* Vol. 1 of *Reliefs and Inscriptions at Luxor Temple.* OIP 112. Chicago: Oriental Institute of the University of Chicago.

Erman, Adolf. 1901. *Rituale für den Kultus des Amon und für den Kultus der Mut.* Vol. 1 of *Hieratische Papyrus aus den königlichen Museen zu Berlin.* Leipzig: Hinrichs.

Eschweiler, Peter. 1994. *Bildzauber im alten Ägypten: Die Verwendung von Bildern und Gegenständen in magischen Handlungen nach den Texten des Mittleren und Neuen Reiches.* OBO 137. Freiburg: Universitätsverlag; Göttingen: Vandenhoeck & Ruprecht.

Espinel, Andrés. 2014. "Play and Display in Egyptian High Culture: The Cryptographic Texts of Djehuty (TT11) and Their Sociocultural Contexts." Pages 297–336 in *Creativity and Innovation in the Reign of Hatshepsut.* Edited by José Galan, Betsy Bryan, and Peter Dorman. SAOC 69. Chicago: The Oriental Institute of the University of Chicago.

Eyre, Christopher. 2002. *The Cannibal Hymn: A Cultural and Literary Study.* Liverpool: Liverpool University Press.

Fairman, H. W. 1943. "Notes on the Alphabetic Signs Employed in the Hieroglyphic Inscriptions of the Temple of Edfu." *ASAE* 43:193–318.

———. 1945. "An Introduction to the Study of Ptolemaic Signs and Their Values." *BIFAO* 43: 51–138.

Faulkner, Raymond O. 1933. *The Papyrus Bremner-Rhind (British Museum No. 10188).* BAeg 3. Brussels: Fondation Égyptologique Reine Élisabeth.

Fischer-Elfert, Hans-Werner. 1998. *Die Vision von der Statue im Stein: Studien zum altägyptischen Mundöffnungsritual.* SPHKHAW 5. Heidelberg: Universitätsverlag C. Winter.

———. 2005. *Abseits von Ma'at: Fallstudien zu Außenseitern im Alten Ägypten.* WSA 1. Würzburg: Ergon.

Frankfort, Henri. 1933a. *Text.* Vol. 1 of *The Cenotaph of Seti I at Abydos.* EES Memoir 39. London: Egypt Exploration Society.

———. 1933b. *The Cenotaph of Seti I at Abydos, Volume 2: Plates.* EES Memoir 39. London: Egypt Exploration Society.

Gaber, Hanane. 2015. "Asperger ou brûler le serpent 'au mauvais visage (ḏwy-ḥr)'? L'interprétation d'une scène de la deuxième chapelle de Toutânkhamon." *ENiM* 8:67–71.

Gabolde, Marc. 1998a. *D'Akhenaton à Toutânkhamon.* Lyon: Université Lumière-Lyon 2.

———. 1998b. *Le "grand château d'Amon" de Sésostris 1er à Karnak: La décoration du temple d'Amon-Ré au Moyen Empire.* Paris: Diffusion de Boccard.

———. 2006. "Une interpretation alternative de la 'pesée du coeur' du Livres des Morts." *EAO* 43:11–22.

Gabolde, Luc, with Marc Gabolde. 1989. "Les temples 'mémoriaux' de Thoutmosis II et Toutânkhamoun (un rituel destiné à des statues sur barques)." *BIFAO* 89:127–78.

Galan, José M., Betsy M. Bryan, and Peter Dorman, eds. 2014. *Creativity and Innovation in the Reign of Hatshepsut.* SAOC 69. Chicago: The Oriental Institute of the University of Chicago.

Gardiner, Alan H. 1905. "Hymns to Amon from a Leiden Papyrus." *ZÄS* 42:12–42.

Geisen, Christina. 2004. *Die Totentexte des verschollenen Sarges der Königin Mentuhotep aus der 13. Dynastie: Ein Textzeuge aus der Übergangszeit von den Sargtexten zum Totenbuch.* Wiesbaden: Harrassowitz.

George, Beate. 1970. *Zu den altägyptischen Vorstellungen vom Schatten als Seele.* Habelts Dissertationsdrucke, Reihe klassische Philologie 7. Bonn: Habelt.

Germer, Renate. 2008. *Handbuch der altägyptischen Heilpflanzen.* Philippika 21. Wiesbaden: Harrassowitz.

Gessler-Löhr, Beatrix. 1983. *Die heiligen Seen ägyptischer Tempel: Ein Beitrag zur Deutung sakraler Baukunst im alten Ägypten.* HÄB 21. Hildesheim: Gerstenberg Verlag.

Gestermann, Louise. 1999. "Königliche Vorstellungen zu Grab und Jenseits im Mittleren Reich, Teil II: Osirisgräber des Mittleren Reiches in königlichem Kontext: Amduat 6. Stunde." Pages 97–110 in *Das frühe ägyptische Königtum, Akten des 2. Symposiums zur ägyptischen Königsideologie in Wien.* Edited by Rolf Gundlach and Wilfried Seipel. ÄAT 36.2. Wiesbaden: Harrassowitz.

Gilula, Mordechai. 1976. "An Unusual Nominal Pattern in Middle Egyptian." *JEA* 62:160–75.

Goebs, Katja. 1998. "Expressing Luminosity in Iconography: Features of the Solar Bark in the Tomb of Ramesses VI." *GöMisz* 165:57–67

———. 2008. *Crowns in Egyptian Funerary Literature, Royalty, Rebirth, and Destruction.* Oxford: Griffith Institute.

Gordon, Sophie. *Cairo to Constantinople: Francis Bedford's Photographs of the Middle East.* London: Royal Collections.

Goyon, Jean-Claude. 1984. "Une identification possible de la plante *hdn* des anciens Égyptiens." Pages 241–50 in *Sprache.* Vol. 1 of *Studien zu Sprache und Religion Ägyptens: Zu Ehren von Wolfhart Westendorf.* Göttingen: Hubert.

Gozzoli, R. B. 2010. "Old Formats, New Experiments and Royal Ideology in the Early Nubian Period (ca. 721–664 BCE)." Pages 183–207 in *Egypt in Transition: Social and Religious Development of Egypt in the First Millennium BCE.* Edited by Ladislav Bares, Filip Coppens, and Květa Smoláriková. Prague: Czech Institute of Egyptology, Faculty of Arts, Charles University.

Graindorge, Catherine. 1992. "Les oignons de Sokar." *REg* 43:87–105.

———. 1999. "L'oignon, la magie et les dieux." Pages 317–34 in *Encyclopédie religieuse de l'Univers végétal: Croyances phytoreligieuses de l'Égypte ancienne.* Vol. 1. Edited by Syndney Aufrère. OrMonsp 10. Montpellier: Université Paul Valéry-Montpellier III.

Griffiths, J. Gwyn. 1992. "Some Egyptian Conceptual Triads." Pages 223–28 in *The Intellectual Heritage of Egypt, Studies Presented to László Kákosy by Friends and Colleagues on the Occasion of His Sixtieth Birthday.* Edited by Ulrich Luft. StAegSM 14. Budapest: La Chair d'Égyptologie de l'Université Eötvös Loránd de Budapest.

Grimal, Nicholas-Christophe. 1986. *Les termes de la propagande royale égyptienne de la XIXe dynastie à la conquête d'Alexandre.* Paris: Imprimerie Nationale.

Guilmant, Felix. 1907. *Le tombeau de Ramsès IX.* MIFAO 15. Cairo: Institut Français d'Archéologie Orientale.

Gunn, Battiscombe. 1933. "The Graffiti and Ostraka." Pages 87–96 in *Text.* Vol. 1 of *The Cenotaph of Seti I at Abydos,* by Henri Frankfort. EES Memoir 39. London: Egypt Exploration Society.

Habachi, Labib. 1969. *Features of the Deification of Ramesses II.* Glückstadt: Augustin.

———. 1978. "King Amenmesse and Viziers Amenmose and Kha'emtore: Their Monuments and Place in History." *MDAIK* 34:57–67.

Hannig, Ranier. 1990. "Die Schwangerschaft der Isis." Pages 91–95 in *Festschrift Jürgen von Beckerath zum 70. Geburtstag am 19. Februar 1990.* Edited by Bettina Schmitz and Arne Eggebrecht. Hildesheim: Gerstenberg.

———. 2003. *Altes Reich und Erste Zwischenzeit.* Vol. 1 of *Ägyptisches Wörterbuch.* Mainz am Rhein: von Zabern.

———. 2006a. *Mittleres Reich und Zweite Zwischenzeit.* Vol. 2.1 of *Ägyptisches Wörterbuch.* Mainz am Rhein: von Zabern.

———. 2006b. *Mittleres Reich und Zweite* Zwischenzeit. Vol. 2.2 of *Ägyptisches Wörterbuch.* Mainz am Rhein: von Zabern.

Hassanein, Fathy, and Monique Nelson. 1976. *La tombe du Prince Amon-(Her)-Khepchef.* Cairo: Centre d'études et de documentation sur l'ancienne Égypte.

Hays, Harold. 2009. "Unreading the Pyramids." *BIFAO* 109:195–220.

———. 2012. *The Organization of the Pyramid Texts: Typology and Disposition.* PAe 31. Leiden: Brill.

Heerma van Voss, Matthieu S. H. G. 1969. *Een Mysteriekist Ontsluierd.* Leiden: Brill.

———. 1998. "Späte Texte aus dem Pfortenbuch." Pages 1001–10 in *Egyptian Religion: The Last Thousand Years: Studies Dedicated to the Memory of Jan Quaegebeur.* Vol. 2. Edited by Willy Clarysse, Antoon Schoors, and Harco Willems. OLA 85. Leuven: Peeters.

Hegenbarth[-Reichardt], Ina. 2002. "'O seht, ich gehe hinter meinem ꜣḫ.t-Auge.': Einige Überlegungen zu den Barken des mittleren Registers der zweiten Stunde des Amduat." *SAK* 30:169–85.

———. 2006. *Der Raum der Zeit: Eine Untersuchung zu den altägyptischen Vorstellungen und Konzeptionen von Zeit und Raum anhand des Unterweltbuches Amduat.* ÄAT 64. Wiesbaden: Harrassowitz.

Helck, Wolfgang. 1958. *Inschriften von Zeitgenossen Amenophis' III.* Vol. 4.21 of *Urkunden der 18. Dynastie.* Berlin: Akademie.

Herbin, François René. 1994. *Le livre de parcourir l'éternité.* OLA 58. Leuven: Peeters.

Hermsen, Edmund. 1991. *Die zwei Wege des Jenseits: Das altägyptische Zweiwegebuch und seine Topographie.* OBO 112. Freiburg: Universitätsverlag; Göttingen: Vandenhoeck & Ruprecht.

Hornung, Erik. 1963a. *Text.* Vol. 1 of *Das Amduat: Die Schrift des verborgenen Raumes.* ÄA 7. Wiesbaden: Harrassowitz.

———. 1963b. *Übersetzung und Kommentar.* Vol. 2 of *Das Amduat: Die Schrift des verborgenen Raumes.* ÄA 13. Wiesbaden: Harrassowitz.

———. 1967. "Der Mensch als 'Bild Gottes' in Ägypten." Pages 123–56 in *Die Gottebenbildlichkeit des Menschen.* Edited by Oswald Loretz. Munich: Kösel.

———. 1968. *Altägyptische Höllenvorstellungen.* Berlin: Akademie-Verlag.

———. 1975. *Text.* Vol. 1 of *Das Buch der Anbetung des Re im Westen (Sonnenlitanei): Nach den Versionen des Neuen Reiches.* AH 2. Geneva: Editions de Belles-Lettres.

———. 1976. *Übersetzung und Kommentar.* Vol. 2 of *Das Buch der Anbetung des Re im Westen (Sonnenlitanei): Nach den Versionen des Neuen Reiches.* AH 3. Geneva: Editions de Belles-Lettres.

———. 1979a. "Lehren über das Jenseits." Pages 217–24 in *Studien zur altägyptischen Lebenslehren.* Edited by Erik Hornung and Othmar Keel. OBO 28. Freiburg: Universitätsverlag; Göttingen: Vandenhoeck & Ruprecht.

———. 1979b. *Text.* Vol. 1 of *Das Buch von den Pforten des Jenseits.* AH 7. Geneva: Editions de Belles-Lettres.

———. 1980. *Übersetzung und Kommentar.* Vol. 2 of *Das Buch von den Pforten des Jenseits.* AH 8. Geneva: Editions de Belles-Lettres.

———. 1981a. "Auf den Spuren der Sonne: Gang durch ein ägyptisches Königsgrab." *ErJb* 50:431–75.

———. 1981b. "Zu den Schlußzenen der Unterweltsbücher." *MDAIK* 37:217–26.

————. 1983a. "Ein aenigmatisches Unterweltsbuch." *JSSEA* 13:29–34.

————. 1983b. "Vom Sinn der Mumifizierung." *WO* 14:167–75.

————. 1986. "Ein königliches Fragment von Totenbuch 180." Pages 427–28 in *Hommages à François Daumas.* Vol. 2. Montpellier: Université de Montpellier.

————. 1987a. "Eine aenigmatische Wand im Ramses' IX." Pages 226–37 in *Form und Mass: Beiträge zur Literatur, Sprache und Kunst des alten Ägypten; Festschrift für Gerhard Fecht.* Edited by Jürgen Osing and Gunter Dreyer. AÄT 12. Wiesbaden: Harrassowitz.

————. 1987b. *Kurzfassung und Langfassung, 1. bis 3. Stunde.* Vol. 1 of *Texte zum Amduat.* AH 13. Geneva: Editions de Belles-Lettres.

————. 1988. "Zum Schutzbild im Grabe Ramses' VI." Pages 45–51 in *Funerary Symbols and Religion.* Edited by J. H. Kamstra, H. Milde, and K. Wagtendonk. Kampen: Kok.

————. 1990a. *The Valley of the Kings: Horizon of Eternity.* Translated by David Warburton. New York: Timken.

————. 1990b. *Zwei ramessidische Königsgräber: Ramses IV. und Ramses VII.* Theben 11. Mainz: von Zabern.

————. 1991. *Der ägyptische Mythos von der Himmelskuh: Eine Ätiologie des Unvollkommenen.* 2nd ed. OBO 46. Freiburg: Universitätsverlag; Göttingen: Vandenhoeck & Ruprecht.

————. 1992. *Langfassung, 4. bis 8. Stunde.* Vol. 2 of *Texte zum Amduat.* AH 14. Geneva: Editions de Belles-Lettres.

————. 1994a. "Black Holes Viewed from Within: Hell in Ancient Egyptian Thought." *Diogenes* 42:133–56.

————. 1994b. "Die 'königliche' Dekoration der Sargkammer." Pages 42–47 in *Die Gräber des Vezirs User-Amun: Theben Nr. 61 and 131.* Eberhard Dziobek. AV 84. Mainz: von Zabern.

————. 1994c. *Langfassung, 9. bis 12. Stunde.* Vol. 3 of *Texte zum Amduat.* AH 15. Geneva: Editions de Belles-Lettres.

————. 1996. *Conceptions of God in Ancient Egypt: The One and the Many.* Translated by John Baines. Ithaca: Cornell University Press.

————. 1998. *Das Totenbuch der Ägypter.* Düsseldorf: Artemis & Winkler.

————. 1999. *The Ancient Egyptian Books of the Afterlife.* Translated by David Lorton. Ithaca: Cornell University Press.

————. 2002. *Die Unterweltsbücher der Ägypter.* Düsseldorf: Patmos.

Hornung, Erik, and Harry Burton. 1991. *The Tomb of Pharaoh Seti I/Das Grab Sethos' I.* Zürich: Artemis.

Hornung, Erik, and Theodor Abt. 2014. *The Egyptian Book of Gates.* Zurich: Living Human Heritage.

Huyge, Dirk. 2002. "Cosmology, Ideology and Personal Religious Practice in Ancient Egyptian Rock Art." Pages 192–206 in *Egypt and Nubia: Gifts of the Desert.* Edited by Renée Friedman. London: British Museum Press.

Iversen, Erik. 1984. *Egyptian and Hermetic Doctrine.* Copenhagen: Museum Tusculanum Press.

Jansen-Winkeln, Karl. 1990. "Die Stele London BM 1224." *SAK* 17:215–19.

———. 1998. "Zur Charakterisierung der Nachbarvölker der Ägypter im 'Pfortenbuch.'" *AoF* 25:374–79.

———. 2004. "Sprachliche Bemerkungen zu den 'Unterweltsbüchern.'" *SAK* 32:205–32.

Jasnow, Richard, and Karl-Theodor Zauzich. 2005. *The Ancient Egyptian Book of Thoth: A Demotic Discourse on Knowledge and Pendant to the Classical Hermetica.* Wiesbaden: Harrassowitz.

Jéquier, Gustave. 1894. *Le Livre de ce qu'il y a dans l'Hadès.* Abridged version. Paris: Bouillon.

———. 1935. *La pyramide d'Aba.* Fouilles à Saqqara. Cairo: Institut Français d'Archéologie Orientale.

Jenni, Hanna. 1986. *Das Dekorationsprogramm des Sarkophages Nektanebos' II.* AH 12. Geneva: Editions de Belles-Lettres.

———. 2011. "Die Sonnenlitanei." *TUAT* NS 6.5:236–72.

Jürgens, Peter. 1999. "Das Stemma des *Amduat* nach den Textzeugen des Neuen Reiches." *SAK* 27:141–71.

Junker, Hermann. 1947. *Der sehende und blinde Gott (Mḫntj-irtj und Mḫntj-n-irtj).* SBAWPH 7. Munich: Bayerische Akademie der Wissenschaften.

Kákosy, László. 1982. "Decans in Late-Egyptian Religion." *Oikumene* 3:163–91.

Kitchen, Kenneth. 1976. *Ramesside Inscriptions: Historical and Biographical.* Vol. 1. Oxford: Blackwell.

———. 1979. *Ramesside Inscriptions: Historical and Biographical.* Vol. 2. Oxford: Blackwell.

———. 1983. *Ramesside Inscriptions: Historical and Biographical.* Vol. 6. Oxford: Blackwell.

Klotz, David. 2006. *Adoration of the Ram: Five Hymns to Amun-Re from Hibis Temple.* YEgS 6. New Haven, CT: Yale Egyptological Seminar.

———. 2008. "Domitian at the Contra-Temple of Karnak." *ZÄS* 135:63–77.

———. 2011. "A New Edition of the 'Book of Nut.'" *BiOr* 68.5–6:476–91.

———. 2012a. *Caesar in the City of Amun: Egyptian Temple Construction and Theology in Roman Thebes.* MRÉ 15. Turnhout: Brepols.

———. 2012b. "Once Again, Min (𓂝𓅓): Acrophoany or Phonetic Change?" *GöMisz* 233:21–29.

Koemoth, Pierre. 1994. *Osiris et les arbres: Contribution à l'étude des arbres sacrés de l'Égypte ancienne.* AegLeo 3. Liège: C. I. P. L.

Koenig, Yvan. 1994. *Magie et magiciens dans l'Égypte ancienne.* Paris: Pygmalion.

Konrad, Kirsten. 2006. *Architektur und Theologie: Pharaonische Tempelterminologie unter Berücksichtigung königsideologischer Aspekte.* KSG 5. Wiesbaden: Harrassowitz.

Krauss, Rolf. 1997. *Astronomische Konzepte und Jenseitsvorstellungen in den Pyramidentexten.* ÄA 59. Wiesbaden: Harrassowitz.

Kruchten, Jean-Marie. 1982. *Études de syntaxe néo-égyptienne: Les verbes ʿḥ, ḥmsi et sḏr en néo-égyptien; Emploi et significations.* AIHPhSup 1. Brussels: Editions de l'Université de Bruxelles.

———. 1989. *Les annales des prêtres de Karnak (XXI–XXIIImes dynasties) et autres textes contemporains relatifs à l'initiation des prêtres d'Amon.* OLA 32. Leuven: Peeters.

Kuhlmann, Klaus P., and Wolfgang Schenkel. 1983. *Das Grab des Ibi, Obergutsverwalters der Gottesgemahlin des Amun (thebanisches Grab Nr. 36).* AV 15. Mainz am Rhein: von Zabern.

Kurth, Dieter. 1984. "'Same des Stieres' und 'Same': Zwei Bezeichnungen der Maat." Pages 273–81 in *Sprache.* Vol. 1 of *Studien zu Sprache und Religion Ägyptens zu Ehren von Wolfhart Westendorf.* Göttingen: Hubert.

———. 1988. "Zum Pfortenbuch, 12. Stunde, 90. Szene." *GöMisz* 105:49–54.

———. 1994. "Das Lied von den vier Winden und seine angebliche pantomimische Darstellung." Pages 135–46 in *Essays in Egyptology in Honor of Hans Goedicke.* Edited by Betsy Bryan and David Lorton. San Antonio: Van Siclen Books.

Labrique, Françoise. 2013. "Le regard d'Hérodote sur le phénix (II, 73)." Pages 119–43 in *Hérodote et l'Egypte: Regards croisés sur le livre II de l'enquête d'Hérodote; Actes de la journée d'étude organisée à la Maison de l'Orient de la Méditerranée, Lyon, le 10 mai 2010.* Edited by Laurent Coulon, Pascale Giovannell-Jouanna, and Flore Kimmel-Clauzet. Lyons: Maison de l'Orient et de la Méditerranée.

Lapp, Günter. 2002. *The Papyrus of Nebseni (BM EA 9900): The Texts of Chapter 180 with the New Kingdom Parallels.* London: British Museum.

Lefébure, Eugène. 1878. "The Book of Hades." Pages 79–134 in *Records of the Past: Being English Translations of the Assyrian and Egyptian Monuments.* Vol. 10. London: Bagster.

———. 1881. "The Book of Hades." Pages 1–35 in *Records of the Past: Being English translations of the Assyrian and Egyptian monuments.* Vol. 12. London: Bagster.

Leitz, Christian. 1989. "Die obere und die untere Dat." *ZÄS* 116:41–57.

———. 1994. "Auseinandersetzungen zwischen Baba und Thot." Pages 103–17 in *Quaerentes scientiam: Festgabe für Wolfhart Westendorf zu seinem 70. Geburtstag.* Edited by Heike Behlmer. Göttingen: Seminar für Ägyptologie und Koptologie.

———. 2009. "Das Ichneumonweibchen von Herakleopolis—Eine Manifestation der Bastet." *SAK* 38:161–71.

Lichtheim, Miriam. 1988. *Ancient Egyptian Autobiographies Chiefly of the Middle Kingdom: A Study and an Anthology.* OBO 84. Freiburg: Universitätsverlag; Göttingen: Vandenhoeck & Ruprecht.

Lieven, Alexandra von. 2001. "Scheiben am Himmel—Zur Bedeutung von *itn* und *itn.t*." *SAK* 29:277–82.

———. 2002. "Mysterien des Kosmos: Kosmographie und Priesterwissenschaft." Pages 47–58 in *Ägyptische Mysterien?* Edited by Jan Assmann and Martin Bommas. Munich: Fink.

———. 2007a. "Bemerkungen zum Dekorationsprogramm des Osireion in Abydos." Pages 167–86 in *6. Ägyptologische Tempeltagung, Funktion und Gebrauch altägyptischer Tempelräume.* Edited by Ben Haring and Andrea Klug. Wiesbaden: Harrassowitz.

———. 2007b. *Tafeln.* Vol. 2 of *Grundriss des Laufes der Sterne: Das sogenannte Nutbuch.* The Carlsberg Papyri 8. CNI Publications 31. Copenhagen: Museum Tusculanum Press.

———. 2007c. *Text.* Vol. 1 of *Grundriss des Laufes der Sterne: Das sogenannte Nutbuch.* The Carlsberg Papyri 8. CNI Publications 31. Copenhagen: Museum Tusculanum Press.

Liptay, Éva. 2006a. "Between Heaven and Earth II: The Iconography of a Funerary Papyrus from the Twenty-First Dynasty; Part I." *BMusHongr* 104:35–61.

———. 2006b. "Between Heaven and Earth II: The Iconography of a Funerary Papyrus from the Twenty-First Dynasty. Part II." *BMusHongr* 105:11–40.

———. 2011. "From Middle Kingdom Apotropaia to Netherworld Books." Pages 149–55 in *From Illahun to Djeme: Papers Presented in Honour of Ulrich Luft*. Edited by Eszter Bechtold, András Gulyás, and Andrea Hasznos. BARIS 2311. Oxford: Archaeopress.

Loprieno, Antonio. 2003. "Drei Leben nach dem Tod, Wieviele Seelen hatten die alten Ägypter?" Pages 200–25 in *Grab und Totenkult im alten Ägypten*. Edited by Heike Guksch, Eva Hofmann, and Martin Bommas. Munich: Beck.

Lorand, David. 2009. *Le papyrus dramatique du Ramesseum: Étude des structures de la composition*. Lettres Orientales 13. Leuven: Peeters.

Lüscher, Barbara. 2000. "Dekoration." Pages 35–62 in *Das Grab Ramses' X. (KV 18)*. Edited by Hanna Jenni. AH 16. Basel: Schwabe & Co.

Lull, José. 2002. *Las tumbas reales egipcias del Tercer Período Intermedio (dinastías XXI–XXV): Tradicion y cambios*. BARIS 1045. Oxford: Archaeopress.

Malaise, Michel. 1990. "Bès et les croyances solaires." Pages 680–729 in *Studies in Egyptology Presented to Miriam Lichtheim*. Edited by Sarah Israelit-Groll. Vol. 2. Jerusalem: Magnes Press, Hebrew University.

Manassa, Colleen. 2006. "The Judgment Hall of Osiris in the Book of Gates." *REg* 57:109–42.

———. 2007a. *The Late Egyptian Underworld: Sarcophagi and Related Texts from the Nectanebid Period*. Vol. 1. ÄAT 72. Wiesbaden: Harrassowitz.

———. 2007b. *The Late Egyptian Underworld: Sarcophagi and Related Texts from the Nectanebid Period*. Vol. 2. ÄAT 72. Wiesbaden: Harrassowitz.

———. 2008. "Sounds of the Netherworld." Pages 109–35 in *Mythos and Ritual: Festschrift für Jan Assmann zum 70. Geburtstag*. Edited by Benedikt Rothöhler and Alexander Manisali. Berlin: LIT.

———. 2013. "Divine Taxonomy in the Underworld Books." *AR* 14:47–68.

Manniche, Lise. 1978. "Symbolic Blindness." *CdÉ* 53:13–21.

Mariette, Auguste. 1880. *Abydos: Description des fouilles exécutées sur l'emplacement de cette ville*. Vol. 2. Paris: Imprimerie nationale.

Martin, Geoffrey Thorndike. 1974. *The Royal Tomb at El-'Amarna*. London: Egypt Exploration Society.

Maruéjol, Florence. 2007. *Thoutmosis III et la corégence avec Hatchepsout*. Paris: Pygmalion.

Maspero, Gaston. 1888. Review of *Le Tombeau de Séti Ier*. Part 1 of *Les Hypogées royaux de Thèbes*, by Eugene Léfebure et al. *RHR* 17:251–310.

———. 1893. *Études de mythologie et d'archéologie égyptiennes*. Vol. 2. Paris: Leroux.

Mauric-Barbério, Florence. 2001. "Le premier exemplaire du *Livre de l'Amdouat.*" *BIFAO* 101:315–50.

———. 2003. "Copie de textes à l'envers dans les tombes royales." Pages 175–93 in *Deir el-Médineh et la Vallée des Rois.* Edited by Guillemette Andreu. Paris: Éditions Khéops.

———. 2010. "Nouvelles considérations sur le *Livre de la Terre* dans la tombe de Ramsès VI." *BIFAO* 110:175–220.

Maystre, Charles, and Alexandre Piankoff. 1939. *Le Livre des Portes I.* MIFAO 74. Cairo: Institut Français d'Archéologie Orientale.

———. 1961. *Le Livre des Portes II.* MIFAO 75. Cairo: Institut Français d'Archéologie Orientale.

Meeks, Dimitri. 1998a. *Année lexicographique: Égypte ancienne.* Vol. 1. 2nd ed. Paris: Cybele.

———. 1998b. *Année lexicographique: Égypte ancienne.* Vol. 2. 2nd ed. Paris: Cybele

———. 1998c. *Année lexicographique: Égypte ancienne.* Vol. 3. 2nd ed. Paris: Cybele.

Meeks, Dimitri, and Christine Favard-Meeks. 1996. *Daily Life of the Egyptian Gods.* Translated by G. M. Gosharian. Ithaca: Cornell University Press.

Méndez Rodríguez, Daniel M. 2015. "pBarcelona E-615: Unveiling a New Source of the Book of the Twelve Caverns." *Trabajos de Egipología* 6:71–106.

Menu, Bernadette. 1998. "Le serment dans les actes juridiques de l'ancienne égypte." Pages 27–42 in *Recherches sur l'histoire, juridique, économique et sociale de l'ancienne Égypte II.* Cairo: Institut Français d'Archéologie Orientale.

Minas-Nerpel, Martina. 2006. *Der Gott Chepri: Untersuchungen zu Schriftzeugnissen und ikonographischen Quellen vom Alten Reich bis in griechisch-römische Zeit.* OLA 154. Leuven: Peeters.

Miniaci, Gianluca. 2011. *Rishi Coffins and the Funerary Culture of Second Intermediate Period Egypt.* GHP Egyptology 17. London: Golden House.

Miosi, Frank T. 1982. "The *wsrt* of Geb." *JSSEA* 12:77–80.

Morenz, Ludwig. 1997. "(Magische) Sprache der 'geheimen Kunst.'" *SAK* 24:191–201.

———. 2004. "Apophis: On the Origin, Name, and Nature of an Ancient Egyptian Anti-God." *JNES* 63:201–5.

——. 2005. "Akrophonisches oder konsonantisches Prinzip—Eine angemessene Alternative für Visuelle Poesie?" *DE* 61:101–13.

——. 2008. *Sinn und Spiel der Zeichen: Visuelle Poesie im Alten Ägypten.* Cologne: Böhlau.

Morschauser, Scott. 1988. "The End of the *sdfȝ tryt* 'Oath.'" *JARCE* 25:95–116.

——. 1991. *Threat-Formulae in Ancient Egypt: A Study of the History, Structure and Use of Threats and Curses in Ancient Egypt.* Baltimore: Halgo.

Müller-Roth, Marcus. 2008. *Das Buch vom Tage.* OBO 236. Freiburg: Universitätsverlag; Göttingen: Vandenhoeck & Ruprecht.

Myśliwiec, Karol. 1981. "La renaissance solaire du mort." Pages 91–106 in *Bulletin du Centenaire.* BIFAOSup 81. Cairo: Institut Français d'Archéologie Orientale.

Naville, Édouard. 1875. *La litanie du soleil, inscriptions recueillies dans les tombeaux des rois à Thèbes.* Leipzig: Engelmann.

——. 1886. *Das aegyptische Todtenbuch der XVIII. bis XX. Dynastie.* Berlin: Asher.

Neugebauer, Otto, and Richard Parker. 1969. *Decans, Planets, Constellations and Zodiacs.* Vol. 3 of *Egyptian Astronomical Texts.* Providence: Humphries.

Niwiński, Andrzej. 1987–1988. "The Solar-Osirian Unity as Principle of the Theology of the 'State of Amun' in Thebes in the Twenty-First Dynasty." *JEOL* 30:89–106.

——. 1989a. *Studies on the Illustrated Theban Funerary Papyri of the Eleventh and Tenth Centuries B.C.* OBO 86. Freiburg: Universitätsverlag; Göttingen: Vandenhoeck & Ruprecht.

——. 1989b. "The Twenty-First Dynasty Religious Iconography Project, Exemplified by the Scene with Three Deities Standing on a Serpent." Pages 305–14 in *Akten des Vierten Internationalen Ägyptologen Kongresses München 1985.* Edited by Sylvia Schoske. Vol. 3. SAKB 3. Hamburg: Helmut Buske.

——. 2000. "Iconography of the Twenty-First Dynasty: Its Main Features, Levels of Attestation, the Media and Their Diffusion." Pages 21–43 in *Images as Media: Sources for the Cultural History of the Near East and the Eastern Mediterranean (First Millennium BCE).* Edited by Christoph Uehlinger. OBO 175. Freiburg: Universitätsverlag; Göttingen: Vandenhoeck & Ruprecht.

Nordh, Katarina. 1996. *Aspects of Ancient Egyptian Curses and Blessings: Conceptual Background and Transmission.* Boreas 26. Uppsala: Universitet.

Nyord, Rune. 2009. *Breathing Flesh: Conceptions of the Body in the Ancient Egyptian Coffin Texts.* CNI Publications 37. Copenhagen: The Carsten Niebuhr Institute of Near Eastern Studies.

Ockinga, Boyo. 1984. *Die Gottebenbildlichkeit im alten Ägypten und im Alten Testament.* Wiesbaden: Harrassowitz.

Ockinga, Boyo, and Yahya al-Masri. 1990. *The Tomb of Anhurmose: The Inner Room, and The Tomb of Imiseba.* Vol. 2 of *Two Ramesside Tombs at El Mashayikh.* Sydney: Ancient History Documentary Research Centre, Macquarie University.

O'Connor, David. 1985. "The 'Cenotaphs' of the Middle Kingdom at Abydos." Pages 161–77 in *Mélanges Gamal Eddin Mokhtar.* Vol. 2. Cairo: Institut Français d'Archéologie Orientale.

Ogdon, Jorge R. 1986. "Some Notes on the Name and the Iconography of the God ꜣkr." *VA* 2:127–35.

Onstine, Suzanne. 1998. "The Relationship between Osiris and Re in the Book of Caverns." *JSSEA* 25:66–77.

Oréal, Elsa. 2011. *Les particules en Égyptien ancien: De l'Ancien Égyptien à l'Égyptien Classique.* BiÉtud 152. Cairo: Institut Français d'Archéologie Orientale.

Osing, Jürgen. 1976. *Die Nominalbildung des Ägyptischen.* Vol. 2. Mainz am Rhein: von Zabern.

———. 1986. "Zur Disposition der Pyramidentexte des Unas." *MDAIK* 42:131–44.

Otto, Eberhard. 1951. "Das Pelikan-motiv in der altaegyptischen Literature." Pages 215–22 in *Studies Presented to David Moore Robinson on His Seventieth Birthday.* Saint Louis: Washington University.

Parker, Richard, Jean Leclant, and Jean-Claude Goyon. 1979. *The Edifice of Taharqa by the Sacred Lake of Karnak.* BES 8. Providence: Brown University Press.

Parkinson, Richard. 1991. *Voices from Ancient Egypt: An Anthology of Middle Kingdom Writings.* London: British Museum Press.

———. 2002. *Poetry and Culture in Middle Kingdom Egypt: A Dark Side to Perfection.* London: Continuum.

Petschel, Susanne, and Martin von Falck, eds. 2004. *Pharao siegt immer: Krieg und Frieden im alten Ägypten.* Bonn: Kettler.

Piankoff, Alexandre. 1934. "La déesse Chenit." *EgRel* 2:100–5.

———. 1942a. "Le livre des Quererts, 1er tableau." *BIFAO* 41:1–11.

———. 1942b. *Le Livre du jour et de la nuit*. BiÉtud 13. Cairo: Institut Français d'Archéologie Orientale.

———. 1944. "Le livre des Quererts, seconde division, troisième division, quatrième division, cinquième division." *BIFAO* 42:1–62.

———. 1945. "Le livre des Quererts, sixième division." *BIFAO* 43:1–50.

———. 1946. *Le Livre de Quererts*. Cairo: Institut Français d'Archéologie Orientale.

———. 1947a. "Le livre des Quererts (fin)." *BIFAO* 45:1–42.

———. 1947b. "Les grandes compositions religieuses dans la tombe de Pédéménope." *BIFAO* 46:73–92.

———. 1952. *Les chapelles de Tout-Ankh-Amon*. MIFAO 72. Cairo: Institut Français d'Archéologie Orientale.

———. 1953. *La création du disque solaire*. BiÉtud 19. Cairo: Institut Français d'Archéologie Orientale.

———. 1955. "Le Livre de l'Am-Duat et les variantes tardives." Pages 244–47 in *Ägyptologische Studien, Hermann Grapow zum 70. Geburtstag gewidmet*. Edited by Otto Firchow. Berlin: Akademie.

———. 1958. "Vallée des rois à Thèbes-Ouest, la tombe No 1 (Ramsès VII)." *ASAE* 55:145–56

———. 1964a. *The Litany of Re*. ERTR 4. New York: Pantheon.

———. 1964b. "Quel est le 'livre' appelé 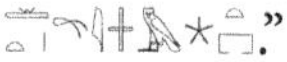." *BIFAO* 62:147–49.

———. 1964c. "Les grandes compositions religieuses du Nouvel Empire et la réforme d'Amarna." *BIFAO* 62:207–18.

Piankoff, Alexandre, and Helen Jacquet-Gordon. 1974. *The Wandering of the Soul*. ERTR 6. New York: Bollingen Foundation.

Piankoff, Alexandre, and Natacha Rambova. 1954. *The Tomb of Ramesses VI*. ERTR 1. New York: Bollingen Foundation.

———. 1955. *The Shrines of Tut-Ankh-Amon*. ERTR 2. New York: Bollingen Foundation.

———. 1957. *Mythological Papyri*. ERTR 3. New York: Bollingen Foundation.

Piccione, Peter. 1990. "Mehen, Mysteries, and Resurrection from the Coiled Serpent." *JARCE* 27:43–52.

Pococke, Richard. 1743. *Observations on Egypt*. Vol. 1 of *A Description of the East, and Some Other Countries*. London: Bowyer.

Polz, Daniel. 2007. *Der Beginn des Neuen Reiches: Zur Vorgeschichte einer Zeitenwende*. Berlin: de Gruyter.

———. 2008. "Mentuhotep, Hatschepsut und das Tal der Könige—Eine Skizze." Pages 525–33 in *Zeichen aus dem Sand: Streiflichter aus Ägyptens Geschichte zu Ehren von Günter Dreyer*. Edited by Eva-Maria Engel, Vera Müller, and Ulrich Hartung. Menes 5. Wiesbaden: Harrassowitz.

Pommerening, Tanja. 2005. *Die altägyptischen Hohlmasse*. BSAK 10. Hamburg: Buske.

Quack, Joachim F. 1997. Review of *Le Livre de la Nuit*, by Gilles Roulin. *WO* 28:177–81.

———. 1999. "Frühe ägyptische Vorläufer der Paranatellonta?" *Sudhoffs Archiv* 83:212–23.

———. 2000. Review of *Pfortenbuchstudien*, by Jürgen Zeidler. *BiOr* 57:541–59.

———. 2005. "Ein Unterweltsbuch der solar-osirianischen Einheit?" *WO* 35:22–47.

———. 2006. "Apopis, Nabelschnur des Re." *SAK* 34:377–79.

Quirke, Stephen. 2003. "Measuring the Underworld." Pages 161–81 in *Mysterious Lands*. Edited by David O'Connor and Stephen Quirke. London: UCL Press.

———. 2005. Review of *Die Totentexte des verschollenen Sarges der Königin Mentuhotep aus der 13. Dynastie: Ein Textzeuge aus der Übergangszeit von den Sargtexten zum Totenbuch*, by Christina Geisen. *Journal of Ancient Near Eastern Religions* 5:228–37.

Rashed, Mohamed Gamal. 2015. "The Hieroglyph 𓎬 and Its Assimilation with the Iconography of the Sun God." *ENiM* 8:11–31.

Redford, Donald B. 1986. *Pharaonic King-Lists, Annals and Day-Books: A Contribution to the Study of the Egyptian Sense of History*. SSEA Publication 4. Mississauga: Benben Publications.

Reeves, Nicholas, and Richard H. Wilkinson. 1996. *The Complete Valley of the Kings*. London: Thames & Hudson.

Refai, Hosam. 1996. *Die Göttin des Westens in den thebanischen Gräbern des neuen Reiches: Darstellung, Bedeutung und Funktion*. Berlin: Achet Verlag.

Régen, Isabelle. 2006. "Recherches sur les versions tardives du Livre de l'Amdouat et du Livre des Portes (époques saïte-ptolémaïque): Présentation du projet." Pages 1587–97 in *Actes du IXe Congrès International des Égyptologues, Grenoble, septembre 2004*. Edited by Jean-Claude Goyon and Chr. Cardin. OLA 150. Louvain: Peeters.

————. 2014. "The Amduat and the Book of the Gates in the Tomb of Padi-amenope (TT 33): A Work in Progress." Pages 307–20 in *Thebes in the First Millennium BC*. Edited by Elena Pischikova, Julia Budka, and Kenneth Griffin. Newcastle: Cambridge Scholars Publishing.

————. 2015. "Quand Isis met à mort Apophis: Variantes tardives de la 7e heure de l'Amdouat." Pages 247–71 in *Documents de théologie thébaine tardive 3 (D3T3)*. Edited by Christophe Thiers. CENIM 13. Montpel-lier: Université Paul Valéry (Montpellier III).

Richter, Barbara. 2008. "The Amduat and Its Relationship to the Archi-tecture of Early Eighteenth Dynasty Royal Burial Chambers." *JARCE* 44:73–104.

Ritner, Robert. 1984. "A Uterine Amulet in the Oriental Institute Collec-tion." *JNES* 43:209–21.

————. 1989. "Horus on the Crocodiles: A Juncture of Religion and Magic in Late Dynastic Egypt." Pages 103–16 in *Religion and Philosophy in Ancient Egypt*. Edited by William K. Simpson. YEgS 3. New Haven: Yale Egyptological Seminar.

————. 1993. *The Mechanics of Ancient Egyptian Magical Practice*. SAOC 54. Chicago: The Oriental Institute of the University of Chicago.

Roberson, Joshua. 2007. "An Enigmatic Wall from the Cenotaph of Seit I at Abydos." *JARCE* 43:93–112.

————. 2009. "The Early History of 'New Kingdom' Netherworld Iconogra-phy: A Late Middle Kingdom Apotropaic Wand Reconsidered." Pages 427–45 in *Archaism and Innovation: Studies in the Culture of Middle Kingdom Egypt*. Edited by David P. Silverman, William K. Simpson, and Josef Wegner. New Haven, CT: Yale Egyptological Seminar.

————. 2010. "Observations on the so-called '*sw sḏm.f*,' or Middle Egyptian Proclitic Pronoun Construction." Pages 185–205 in *Millions of Jubi-lees: Studies in Honor of David P. Silverman*. Edited by Zahi Hawass and Jennifer Wegner. Vol. 2. Cairo: Supreme Council of Antiquities.

————. 2012. *The Ancient Egyptian Books of the Earth*. Wilbour Studies in Egypt and Ancient Western Asia 1. Atlanta: Lockwood Press.

————. 2013. *The Awakening of Osiris and the Transit of the Solar Barques: Royal Apotheosis in a Most Concise Book of the Underworld and Sky*. OBO 262. Freiburg: Universitätsverlag; Göttingen: Vandenhoeck & Ruprecht.

————. 2016. "The Royal Funerary Books, The Subject Matter of Scenes and Texts." Pages 316–32 in *The Oxford Handbook of the Valley of the*

Kings. Edited by Richard H. Wilkinson and Kent R. Weeks. Oxford: Oxford University Press.

Robinson, Peter. 2003. "Crossing the Night: The Depiction of Mythological Landscapes in the Am Duat of the New Kingdom Royal Necropolis." Pages 51–61 in *Current Research in Egyptology 3*. Edited by Rachel Ives et al. BARIS 1192. Oxford: Oxbow.

Rochholz, Matthias. 2002. *Schöpfung, Feindvernichtung, Regeneration: Untersuchungen zum Symbolgehalt der machtgeladenen Zahl 7 im alten Ägypten*. ÄAT 56. Wiesbaden: Harrassowitz.

Roehrig, Catherine, ed. 2005. *Hatshepsut, from Queen to Pharaoh*. New York: Metropolitan Museum of Art.

———. 2006. "The Building Activities of Thutmose III in the Valley of the Kings." Pages 238–59 in *Thutmose III: A New Biography*. Edited by Eric H. Cline and David O'Connor. Ann Arbor, MI: University of Michigan Press.

Roque, Fr. W. Bisson de la. 1931. "Notes sur Aker." *BIFAO* 30:575–80.

Romer, John. 1981. *The Valley of the Kings*. New York: Morrow.

Ronsecco, Paolo. 1996. *Due Libri dei morti del Principio del Nuovo Regno, il lenzuolo funerrio della principessa Ahmosi e le tele del sa-nesu Ahmosi*. Catalogo del Museo Egizio di Torino 7. Turin: Ministero per i Beni Culturali e Ambientali and Soprintendenza al Museo delle Antichità Egizie.

Rössler-Köhler, Ursula. 1984–1985. "Zum Problem der Spatien in altägyptischen Texten: Versuch einer Systematik von Spatientypen." *ASAE* 70:383–408.

———. 1999. "Königliche Vorstellungen zu Grab und Jenseits im Mittleren Reich, Teil I: Ein 'Gottesbegräbnis' des Mittleren Reiches in königlichem Kontext: Amduat 4. und 5. Stunde." Pages 73–96 in *Das frühe ägyptische Königtum*. Edited by Rolf Gundlach and Wilfried Seipel. ÄAT 36.2. Wiesbaden: Harrassowitz.

Roulin, Giles. 1996a. *Copie synoptique*. Vol. 2 of *Le Livre de la Nuit: Une composition égyptienne de l'au-dela*. OBO 147. Freiburg: Universitätsverlag; Göttingen: Vandenhoeck & Ruprecht.

———. 1996b. *Traduction et commentaire*. Vol. 1 of *Le Livre de la Nuit: Une composition égyptienne de l'au-dela*. OBO 147. Freiburg: Universitätsverlag; Göttingen: Vandenhoeck & Ruprecht.

———. 1998b. "Les tombes royales de Tanis: Analyse du programme decorative." Pages 193–276 in *Tanis: Travaux recents sur le tell San el Hagar*. Edited by Philippe Brissaud and Christiane Zivie-Coche. Paris: Noêsis.

Sadek, Abdel-Aziz Fahmy. 1985. *Contribution à l'étude de l'Amdouat*. OBO 65. Freiburg: Universitätsverlag; Göttingen: Vandenhoeck & Ruprecht.

The Saqqara Expedition. 1938. *The Mastaba of Mereruka 1*. OIP 31. Chicago: University of Chicago Press.

Sauneron, Serge. 1958. "L'abaton de la campagne d'Esna (note préliminaire)." *MDAIK* 16:271–79.

Schenkel, Wolfgang. 1978. *Das Stemma der altägyptischen Sonnenlitanei: Grundlegung der Textgeschichte nach der Methode der Textkritik*. Wiesbaden: Harrassowitz.

———. 1980. "Weiteres zum Stemma der Sonnenlitanei." *GöMisz* 37:37–9.

Schillinger, William F. 2017. "Winter Pea: Promising New Crop for Washington's Dryland Wheat-Fallow Region." *Frontiers in Ecology and Evolution* 10. https://doi.org/10.3389/fevo.2017.00043.

Schlögl, Hermann Alexander. 1980. *Der Gott Tatenen, Nach Texten und Bildern des Neuen Reiches*. OBO 29. Freiburg: Universitätsverlag; Göttingen: Vandenhoeck & Ruprecht.

Schmidt, Heike C. 1995. "Szenarium der Transfiguration—Kulisse des Mythos: Das Grab der Nefertari." *SAK* 22:237–70.

Schneider, Thomas. 2010. "The West Beyond the West: The Mysterious 'Wernes' of the Egyptian Underworld and the Chad Palaeolake." *JAEI* 2.4:1–14.

Schott, Sigfried. 1958. *Die Schrift der verborgenen Kammer in Königsgräbern der 18. Dynastie*. NAWGPH 1.4. Göttingen: Vandenhoeck & Ruprecht.

———. 1964. *Der Denkstein Sethos' I. für die Kapelle Rameses' I. in Abydos*. NAWGHPH 1964.1. Göttingen: Vandenhoeck & Ruprecht.

———. 1990. *Bücher und Bibliotheken im alten Ägypten*. Wiesbaden: Otto Harrassowitz.

Schweizer, Andreas. 2010. *The Sungod's Journey through the Netherworld: Reading the Ancient Egyptian Amduat*. Cornell: Cornell University Press.

Seele, Keith. 1959. *The Tomb of Tjanefer at Thebes*. OIP 36. Chicago: University of Chicago Press.

Servajean, Frédéric. 2003. *Les formules des transformations du Livre des morts: À la lumière d'une théorie de la performativité, XVIIIe–XXe dynasties*. Cairo: Institut Français d'Archéologie Orientale.

Sethe, Kurth. 1932. *Urkunden des Alten Reiches*. 2nd ed. Leipzig: Hinrichs.

Shaw, Ian, ed. 2000. *The Oxford History of Ancient Egypt*. Oxford: Oxford University Press.

Smith, Mark. 2006. "The Great Decree Issued to the Nome of the Silent Land." *REg* 57: 217–32.

———. 2009. *Traversing Eternity: Texts for the Afterlife from Ptolemaic and Roman Egypt*. Oxford: Oxford University Press.

Sourdive, Claude. 1984. *La main dans l'Égypte pharaonique: Recherches de morphologie structural sur les objects égyptiens comportant une main*. Bern: Lang.

Spalinger, Anthony. 2009. *The Great Dedicatory Inscription of Ramesses II: A Solar-Osirian Tractate at Abydos*. Leiden: Brill.

Stadler, Martin Andreas. 2010. "Metatranszendenztheologie im Alten Ägypten. Pyramidentextspruch 215 und der ramessidische Weltgott." Pages 3–31 in *Kulte, Priester, Rituale: Beiträge zu Kult und Kultkritik im Alten Testament und Alten Orient; Festschrift für Theodor Seidl zum 65. Geburtstag*. Edited by Stephanie Ernst and Maria Häusl. Erzabtei St. Ottilien: EOS.

———. 2014. "Elysische Gefilde und Orte der Schrecknisse: Die Fahrt des Sonnengottes durch die Unterwelt nach den altägyptischen Unterweltsbüchern." Pages 6–28 in *Unterwelten: Modelle und Transformationen*. Edited by Joachim Hamm and Jörg Robert. Würzburg: Königshausen u. Neumann.

Stauder, Andréas. 2014. *The Earlier Egyptian Passive: Voice and Perspective*. LingAeg-StudMon 14. Hamburg: Widmaier.

Tacke, Nikolaus. 2013. *Das Opferritual des ägyptischen Neuen Reiches*. Vol. 2. OLA 222. Leuven: Peeters.

Taylor, John H. 2010a. "Changes in the Afterlife." Pages 220–40 in *Egyptian Archaeology*. Edited by Willeke Wendrich. Malden, MA: Wiley-Blackwell.

———, ed. 2010b. *Journey through the Afterlife: Ancient Egyptian Book of the Dead*. Cambridge: Harvard University Press.

———. 2016. "The Amduat Papyrus of Panebmontu." *BMSAES* 23:135–51.

Te Velde, Herman. 1969–1970. "The God Heka in Egyptian Theology." *JEOL* 21:175–86.

———. 1988. "Some Remarks on the Mysterious Language of the Baboons." Pages 129–37 in *Funerary Symbols and Religion*. Edited by J. H. Kamstra, H. Milde, and K. Wagtendonk. Kampen: Kok.

Teeter, Emily. 1997. *The Presentation of Maat. Ritual and Legitimacy in Ancient Egypt*. SAOC 57. Chicago: The Oriental Institute of the University of Chicago.

Thomas, Elizabeth. 1956. "Solar Barks Prow to Prow." *JEA* 42:65–79.

Traunecker, Claude. 2014. "The 'Funeral Palace' of Padiamenope (TT 33): Tomb, Place of Pilgrimage, and Library." Pages 205–34 in *Thebes in the First Millennium BC*. Edited by Elena Pischikova, Julia Budka, and Kenneth Griffin. Newcastle: Cambridge Scholars.

Traunecker, Claude, Francois Le Saout, and Olivier Masson. 1981. *Texte*. Vol. 2 of *La chapelle d'Achoris à Karnak*. Paris: Editions A.D.P.F.

Troy, Lana. 1986. *Patterns of Queenship in Ancient Egyptian Myth and History*. Uppsala: Universitetet.

Tylor, J. J., and F. Ll. Griffith. 1894. *The Tomb of Paheri at El Kab*. EEF Memoir 11. London: Egypt Exploration Fund.

Valloggia, Michel. 1986. *Balat I: Le mastaba de Medou-Nefer*. FIFAO 31. Cairo: Institut Français d'Archéologie Orientale.

Vercoutter, Jean. 1947. "Les Haou-Nebout (𓏏𓈖)." *BIFAO* 46:125–58.

Verhoeven, Ursula. 2007. "Das Kind im Gehörn der Himmelskuh und vergleichbare Rindermotive." Pages 1899–1910 in *Proceedings of the Ninth International Congress of Egyptologists*. Edited by Jean-Claude Goyon and Christine Cardin. OLA 150. Leuven: Peeters.

Vernus, Pascal. 1975. "Inscriptions de la troisième période intermédiaire (II)." *BIFAO* 75:67–72.

Volokhine, Youri. 2000. *La frontalité dans l'iconographie de l'Égypte ancienne*. CSÉG 6. Geneva: Société d'Égyptologie.

———. 2014. *Le porc en Égypte ancienne*. Liège: Presses Universitaires de Liège.

Voß, Susanne. 1996. "Ein liturgisch-kosmographischer Zyklus im Re-Bezirk des Totentempels Ramses' III. in Medinet Habu." *SAK* 23:377–96.

Warburton, David. 2007. *The Egyptian Amduat: Book of the Hidden Chamber*. Revised and edited by Erik Hornung and Theodor Abt. Zurich: Living Human Heritage Publications.

Weeks, Kent R. 2000. *Atlas of the Valley of the Kings*. Cairo: American University in Cairo Press.

———, ed. 2006. *A Preliminary Report on the Excavation of the Tomb of the Sons of Rameses II in the Valley of the Kings*. Cairo: American University in Cairo Press.

———. 2016. "The Component Parts of KV Royal Tombs." Pages 98–116 in *The Oxford Handbook of the Valley of the Kings*. Edited by Richard H. Wilkinson and Kent R. Weeks. Oxford: Oxford University Press.

Wegner, Josef. 2009. "The Tomb of Senwosret III at Abydos and Considerations on the Development of the Royal Amduat-Tomb." Pages 103–69 in *Archaism and Innovation: Studies in the Culture of Middle Kingdom Egypt*. Edited by David P. Silverman, William K. Simpson, and Josef Wegner. New Haven: Yale Egyptological Seminar.

Wente, Edward F. 1982. "Mysticism in Pharaonic Egypt?" *JNES* 41:161–79.

Werning, Daniel A. 2007. "An Interpretation of the Stemmata of the Books of the Netherworld." Pages 1935–49 in *Proceedings of the Ninth International Congress of Egyptologists*. Edited by Jean-Claude Goyon and Christine Cardin. OLA 150. Leuven: Peeters.

———. 2008. "Aenigmatische Schreibungen in Unterweltsbüchern des Neuen Reiches: gesicherte Entsprechungen und Ersetzungsprinzipien." Pages 124–52 in *Miscellanea in honorem Wolfhart Westendorf*. Edited by Carsten Peust. Göttingen: Seminar für Ägyptologie und Koptologie.

———. 2011a. *Textkritische Edition und Übersetzung*. Vol. 2 of *Das Höhlenbuch, Textkritische Edition und Textgrammatik*. GOF 4.48. Wiesbaden: Harrassowitz.

———. 2011b. *Überlieferungsgeschichte und Textgrammatik*. Vol. 1 of *Das Höhlenbuch, Textkritische Edition und Textgrammatik*. GOF 4.48. Wiesbaden: Harrassowitz.

———. 2013. "Linguistic Dating of the Netherworld Books Attested in the New Kingdom: A Critical Review." Pages 237–81 in *Dating Egyptian Literary Texts*. Edited by Gerald Moers et al. LingAeg-StudMon 11. Göttingen: Widmaier.

———. 2017. "Inner-Egyptian Receptions of a Theological Book between Reproduction, Update, and Creativity: The Book of Caverns from the Thirteenth to the Fourth Century BCE." Pages 41–67 in *Proceedings of the Conference "(Re)productive Traditions in Ancient Egypt"*. Edited by Jean Winand, Stéphane Polis and Todd Gillen. Liège: Presses universitaires de Liège.

Westendorf, Wolfhart. 1974. "Horizont und Sonnenscheibe." *StAeg* 1:389–98.

———. 1984. "Der Eine im Himmel, der Andere in der Erde." Pages 239–44 in *Mélanges Adolphe Gutbub*. Montpellier: Publications de la Recherche, Université de Montpellier.

———. 1991. "Die Nini-Begrüßung." Pages 351–62 in *Religion und Philosophie in Alten Ägypten*. Edited by Ursula Verhoeven and Erhart Graefe. OLA 39. Leuven: Peeters.

———. 2003. "Verborgene Gottheiten in den Unterweltsbüchern: Eine Göttinnen-Gruppe im Amduat." Pages 471–76 in *Es werde niedergelegt als Schriftstück: Festschrift für Hartwig Altenmüller zum 65. Geburtstag*. Edited by Nicole Kloth, Karl Martin, and Eva Pardey. SAKB 9. Hamburg: Buske.

———. 2004. "Drei Gräber einer dreigeteilten Gottheit im Amduat." *GöMisz* 200:97–104.

Wiebach-Koepke, Silvia. 2000. "Die Verwandlung des Sonnengottes und seine Widdergestalt im mittleren Register der 1. Nachtstunde des Amduat." *GöMisz* 177:71–82.

———. 2003a. *Annotierte Transkription und Übersetzung*. Vol. 2 of *Phänomenologie der Bewegungsabläufe im Jenseitskonzept der Unterweltbücher Amduat und Pfortenbuch und der liturgischen "Sonnenlitanei."* ÄAT 55. Wiesbaden: Harrassowitz.

———. 2003b. *Untersuchungen*. Vol. 1 of *Phänomenologie der Bewegungsabläufe im Jenseitskonzept der Unterweltbücher Amduat und Pfortenbuch und der liturgischen "Sonnenlitanei."* ÄAT 55. Wiesbaden: Harrassowitz.

———. 2007. *Sonnenlauf und kosmische Regeneration: Zur Systematik der Lebensprozesse in den Unterweltsbüchern*. ÄAT 71. Wiesbaden: Harrassowitz.

Wilkinson, Richard H. 1994. "Symbolic Location and Alignment in New Kingdom Royal Tombs and Their Decoration." *JARCE* 31:79–86.

Wilkinson, Richard H., and Kent R. Weeks, eds. 2016. *The Oxford Handbook of the Valley of the Kings*. Oxford: Oxford University Press.

Willems, Harco. 1988. *Chests of Life: A Study of the Typology and Conceptual Development of Middle Kingdom Standard Class Coffins*. MEOL 25. Leiden: Ex Oriente Lux.

———. 1996. *The Coffin of Heqata (Cairo JdE 36418): A Case Study of Egyptian Funerary Culture of the Early Middle Kingdom*. OLA 70. Leuven: Peeters.

———. 2001. "The Social and Ritual Context of a Mortuary Liturgy of the Middle Kingdom (*CT* Spells 30–41)." Pages 253–372 in *Social Aspects of Funerary Culture in the Egyptian Old and Middle Kingdoms*. Edited by Harco Willems. OLA 103. Peeters: Leuven.

Wilson, Penelope. 1997. *A Ptolemaic Lexikon: A Lexicographical Study of the Texts in the Temple of Edfu.* OLA 78. Leuven: Peeters.

Winkler, Andreas. 2006. "The Efflux that Issued from Osiris." *GöMisz* 211:125–39.

Xekelaki, Georgia, and Reem El-Khodary. 2011. "Aspects of the Cultic Role of Queen Nefertari and the Royal Children during the Reign of Ramesses II." Pages 561–71 in *Ramesside Studies in Honour of K. A. Kitchen.* Edited by Mark Collier and Steven Snape. Bolton: Rutherford Press.

Yoyotte, Jean. 2003. "À propos de quelques idées reçues: Méresger, la Butte et les cobras." Pages 281–308 in *Deir el-Médineh et la Vallée des Rois: La vie en Égypte au temps des pharaons du Nouvel Empire.* Edited by Guillemette Andreu. Paris: Khéops.

Žabkar, Louis V. 1988. *Hymns to Isis in Her Temple at Philae.* Hanover: Brandeis University Press.

Zago, Silvia. 2018. "Classifying the Duat: Tracing the Conceptualization of the Afterlife between Pyramid Texts and Coffin Texts." *ZÄS* 145, forthcoming.

Zandee, Jan. 1960. *Death as an Enemy according to Ancient Egyptian Conceptions.* Leiden: Brill.

———. 1969. "The Book of Gates." Pages 282–324 in *Liber Amicorum: Studies in Honour of Professor Dr. C. J. Bleeker.* Leiden: Brill.

———. 1992. *Der Amunhymnus des Papyrus Leiden I 344, Verso.* Vol. 1. Louvain: Orientaliste.

Zeidler, Jürgen. 1999a. *Kritische Edition des Pfortenbuches nach den Versionen des Neuen Reiches.* Vol. 2 of *Pfortenbuchstudien.* GOF 4.36. Wiesbaden: Harrassowitz.

———. 1999b. *Textkritik und Textgeschichte des Pfortenbuches.* Vol. 1 of *Pfortenbuchstudien.* GOF 4.36. Wiesbaden: Harrassowitz.

Zivie, Alain. 1979. *La tombe de Pached à Deir El-Medineh [No 3].* MIFAO 99. Cairo: Institut Français d'Archéologie Orientale.

CPSIA information can be obtained
at www.ICGtesting.com
Printed in the USA
FFHW02n0114131018
48804706-52950FF